A N O V E L

MARGARET RITTER

IN THE WIND

SIMON AND SCHUSTER   New York

This novel is a work of fiction. Names, characters, places and incidents are either the product of the author's imagination or are used fictitiously. Any resemblance to actual events or locales or persons, living or dead, is entirely coincidental.

COPYRIGHT © 1985 BY THE RITTERHILL CORPORATION
ALL RIGHTS RESERVED
INCLUDING THE RIGHT OF REPRODUCTION
IN WHOLE OR IN PART IN ANY FORM
PUBLISHED BY SIMON AND SCHUSTER
A DIVISION OF SIMON & SCHUSTER, INC.
SIMON & SCHUSTER BUILDING
ROCKEFELLER CENTER
1230 AVENUE OF THE AMERICAS
NEW YORK, NEW YORK 10020
SIMON AND SCHUSTER AND COLOPHON ARE REGISTERED TRADEMARKS OF
SIMON & SCHUSTER, INC.
DESIGNED BY KAROLINA HARRIS
MANUFACTURED IN THE UNITED STATES OF AMERICA
10 9 8 7 6 5 4 3 2 1

LIBRARY OF CONGRESS CATALOGING IN PUBLICATION DATA

Ritter, Margaret.
    Women in the wind.
    I. Title.
PS3568.1827w6 1985   813'.54   85-2331
ISBN: 0-671-54327-X

DEDICATED TO MY MOTHER AND TO THE MANY PEOPLE
WHO HELPED TO MAKE THIS BOOK POSSIBLE,
WITH SPECIAL THANKS TO PAT AND TONY MYRER,
TED RITTER, AND HERMAN GOLLOB.

O N a blustery February evening in 1905, Reanna Lovell stood before a pier glass in the guest room of her cousin Lucy Marr's house in Washington, D.C., waiting impatiently for her mother to finish adjusting the skirt of her new green, watered-silk gown.

As she studied her reflection she found it unfamiliar and very unsettling. Her long, red-gold hair, which she usually wore loose or in a thick braid down her back, had been piled up on her head in an elaborate, formal style. She'd been corseted and laced until she could scarcely breathe. Her already fine complexion had been dusted with rice powder, and she'd been liberally sprinkled with eau de violet.

At last her mother stood back and surveyed her daughter with satisfaction. "You look lovely, Reanna."

"I feel like Florinda."

Mrs. Lovell looked bewildered. "Florinda was a horse."

"A filly, Mama—my filly. And when we couldn't afford to keep her, you bought her a lot of expensive new tack, show-groomed her and sent her to the fair to be auctioned off to the highest bidder."

Mrs. Lovell shook her head sadly. "I don't understand you, Reanna. I never have."

Reanna's eyes blazed with anger. "That's really why we're here in Washington, isn't it? To get me a husband."

"Reanna, I never said that."

"No, you told me you and Papa and I were coming to visit Cousin Lucy because she was lonesome for the sight of Virginia homefolks."

"Cousin Lucy and Mr. Marr are tickled pink to see us."

"You said you were getting me all these new dresses because you didn't want me to feel like a country cousin come to town."

"Your papa and I spent far more than we could afford because we wanted you to have pretty things. Most girls would be grateful for new dresses."

"I'm not most girls, Mama, I'm me. And the plain truth is you got me tricked out and brought me up here in hopes that, now Cousin Lucy had her own lumpy daughters married off, she'd help you trap a husband for me."

"That's so unkind." Her mother's lower lip trembled and she put one hand to her heart. "I only want what's best for you."

"Best for me, Mama, or for you?"

"You must marry sometime!"

"Why?"

"What else could you do?"

"I could earn my own keep."

"How? Be an old maid schoolteacher or a librarian? Be sensible; every girl wants a husband."

"I don't." She lifted her chin in a gesture of defiance.

"You wouldn't have any of the boys at home. You made fun of them; you laughed at them and drove them away."

"I laughed at them because they were silly and stupid."

"Well, this is different. Mr. Marr is very high up in the Department of the Interior. He's asked a lot of eligible men here tonight. You'll have the opportunity to meet men of substance and position—men who can give you all the things you should have."

"What is it, Mama, that you're so determined that I have?"

"A husband who will give you a home, children and security." She dabbed at her eyes with a lace-trimmed handkerchief. "Security is important for a woman. I know. Your papa is a fine man but he's a dreamer. He's never been practical. He's never been able to provide for his family as he would like to have."

"Papa's a gambler."

Mrs. Lovell gasped. "Reanna, I forbid you to talk like that about your papa."

"It's true, Mama, and you know it. I love Papa with all my heart. He's the most charming, adorable man in the Old Dominion, but he'd put his last dollar on the turn of a card. He mortgaged the farm to buy gold mine stock because some sly trickster told him it would make his fortune, and then he had to sell off land to pay up his debts. The farm gets smaller every year. I have eyes in my head, Mama. I know we're nearly broke."

Mrs. Lovell was silent, her eyes wide with shock. When she could collect herself she said, "You can be very hard, Reanna."

"I'm only telling the truth. And the truth is I don't want to get married."

Mrs. Lovell sighed. She felt as she often had before, that she'd been outwitted by her stubborn, willful, difficult daughter. "Then tell me, if you don't want to marry, what do you want?"

"I want—" Reanna began earnestly, "I want something *more*. I don't want to be some man's property. I want to live my own life, not just barter it away for security and let it slip by, little by little, so that one day when I'm old I'll wake up and find my chances to have my hopes and dreams are all gone." She stopped, hoping that her mother would understand at least a part of what she was saying, but she saw that she might as well be talking to the wind.

From below stairs there came the faint sound of musicians tuning up their instruments. Cousin Lucy's musical evening with supper afterwards was about to begin.

"It's time we went down." Mrs. Lovell pressed her lips together in a thin line and sighed. "Please, Reanna, be sensible. You won't have a chance like this again to meet suitable men. For my sake, make an effort to be agreeable to them." Tears glistened in her eyes.

Reanna bowed her head and sighed. "All right, Mama, for your sake I'll try."

"And remember to stand up straight, and for heaven's sake, smile."

As they descended the stairs Reanna wanted to scream, not smile. There must be some way to have control of her own life. She was filled with a passion to live, to find adventure, to meet some great, unknown challenge. She could not, would not, willingly exchange those longings for the promise of security, a fine house and a husband who would keep her in a golden cage. She couldn't face the prospect of sitting silent in some proper parlor window watching life passing her by.

She knew how it must please her mother to see the admiring look on men's faces as they came into the drawing room. Even her father beamed and nodded his satisfaction that it was his daughter who was the center of attention, but his pride did nothing to comfort Reanna.

She grudgingly allowed her mother to parade her around the circle of eligible men. She was presented to a young lawyer with damp hands. She smiled. She was introduced to a sallow doctor already going bald. She smiled. She smiled when she was thrust toward a rich old widower whose belly was so large she thought he must have to order extra links for his watch chain. She smiled until she thought she would choke on her smiles. And then, like a bounty from providence, a man walked into the room who was utterly different from all the others.

It was more than the clothes he was wearing that made him stand out, although they were singular enough. He had on a money-weight Stetson, pointed-toed boots and a whipcord suit that had not been tailored in the East. Instead of a cravat he wore a string tie caught in a silver clasp set with coral. He was a striking man: tall, spare, flagrantly masculine compared to the tame men in this room. He had a full, sandy mustache that drooped at the ends, and when he reluctantly handed his hat to Cousin Lucy's maid, Reanna saw his hair was even more fair than his mustache. But it was his eyes that were truly startling. They were a pale turquoise that seemed to have faded to that particular shade from squinting into a bright sun. The lines around his eyes betrayed his life in the out-of-doors. She felt sure he could see everything, even from great distances. His gaze swept the room and fixed on her with a look that was frank in its approval. She felt flattered and it occurred to her, as she watched Cousin Lucy sweeping down on him, that she was drawn to him not only because he was different but because for some reason of his own he disliked being in that room as much as she did.

Andrew MacClaren was not pleased to be there. He felt as out of place as a bull in a sheep pasture. He had been in Washington before on Chickasaw tribal business, but this was the first time anyone in the Department of the Interior had ever asked him home to meet his wife and friends. Why now? It didn't sit right, but then nothing about this trip had gone to suit him.

He'd been in Washington for over a week, trying to get an appointment. He'd been given the runaround, shunted from office to office, and when he finally had gotten an appointment it was for tomorrow morning at eleven with a man he'd never heard of. Just one hour before noon to conduct his business—that was cutting it mighty fine. Then, by chance, he'd run into Marr by the Capitol and Marr had asked him to dinner. Why? What was his angle? Andrew couldn't figure it, and that made him even more wary and suspicious than he usually was.

Andrew had always been a cautious man by nature. He hadn't survived in this world by being open and trusting. He certainly didn't trust any of these Washington boys; smooth, educated bastards, they knew every twist and turn of the law and they had used them all since the country began to get control of Indian land.

The law that had brought Andrew to Washington now was one that forbade the Chickasaw to lease out their tribal land for grazing without the permission of the Department of the Interior. Permission to lease out his pasture land was something Andrew had to have. His and his family's livelihood depended upon it.

So he'd gone to Washington, hat in hand, wasting precious time when he should have been on the spring cattle drive. It galled him to have to come begging for what should have been his by tribal right. No amount of fine victuals or polite conversation at Marr's was going to satisfy him. He'd only accepted the invitation hoping to get a line on what kind of man he was going to be up against tomorrow.

And as he stood there in the doorway looking at all the fine people, he had the uneasy feeling that by asking him into the parlor these Washington boys were somehow setting him up for the kill. His hostess, Mrs. Marr, was already smiling at him and sweet-talking him into the room like a steer into the slaughter chute.

"Come, Mr. MacClaren, there are some people I want you to meet," Mrs. Marr said.

Andrew seriously doubted any of the people in the room wanted to know him. To them he was a country hick with manure on his boots. Some day that would be different. Some day he would come to this town to call the tune and watch them dance. At last Andrew and Mrs. Marr were coming toward the girl he'd seen from the doorway. She was all in green with a lot of red-gold hair piled on top of her head. She was easily the most beautiful girl he had ever seen. She was certainly the highest bred. Standing next to her was a woman obviously her mother. It never failed to amaze Andrew that an ordinary-grade cow could produce an outstanding calf. It must mean that the bull had some mighty fine bloodlines.

"Minnie," Mrs. Marr was saying, "may I present Mr. Andrew

MacClaren. Mr. MacClaren, my cousin Mrs. Lovell and her daughter, Reanna. Mr. MacClaren is here in Washington from way out in the Indian Territory and we must do all we can to make him feel at home."

While her Cousin Lucy was talking, Reanna couldn't help noticing that Mr. MacClaren kept looking at her. His frank stare made her flush. She didn't know exactly where the Indian Territory was. For all she knew of geography he could have come from the moon, but her mother, who liked to keep up with current events and belonged to the Salmagundi Club, brightened at once.

"Oh yes," she said, "our club just had a paper read to us on the Indian Territory. Very exciting; one day there was nothing out there but a lot of Indians"—she waved dramatically toward the conservatory as if it were the frontier—"and the next day you settlers lined up, a gun went off and you all rushed to get your homesteads. It must have been a truly stirring event." Mrs. Lovell was almost breathless when she had finished and she looked quite pleased with herself at having been so knowledgeable. Mr. MacClaren did not laugh out loud but Reanna saw that his eyes were a mighty bright blue and the corners of his mustache twitched. When he spoke his voice had a decided western drawl.

"I'm afraid that was the Oklahoma Territory you ladies heard about, Mrs. Lovell. I'm from the Indian Territory, south of the Canadian River."

Mrs. Lovell looked bemused, as she always did when contradicted. "But aren't they the same," she challenged him, "the Oklahoma and the Indian Territory?"

"No, ma'am." He answered respectfully, but her mother was still not satisfied.

Undaunted, Mrs. Lovell tried another attack. "But you *are* a settler out West?"

"No, ma'am, I'm a rancher and a mercantile man, but I've talked to men who made the run and they say there was nothing like it, not since God created the world. That took the Almighty seven days, while out there men made the cities in one."

This was too much for Mrs. Lovell. She wasn't sure if Mr. MacClaren had blasphemed when he had invoked the deity or if he was making fun of her or possibly both. When she looked to her cousin Lucy for help, Mr. MacClaren once more turned his gaze on Reanna. Reanna wished her mother would disappear, and she blushed scarlet, for she felt sure that he could in some way read her thoughts.

Fortunately Cousin Lucy came to the rescue. "Mr. Marr says it is only a matter of time now until the Oklahoma Territory and the Indian Territory join and ask for statehood."

"The Five Indian Nations have not agreed to it." Mr. MacClaren grew serious with no hint of his former good-humored indulgence. His eyes had gone cold as glass.

"But surely they will." Cousin Lucy seemed quite determined on the issue. "The Indians should be all in favor of statehood. It is, after all, to their advantage."

Mr. MacClaren looked thoughtfully at his boots. "That's a matter of opinion, Mrs. Marr. The Five Civilized Tribes each have tribal governments that must vote on the matter." And Cousin Lucy, sensing that things were not going to improve, took Mrs. Lovell away on the pretext of overseeing the punch bowl and left Reanna with Andrew MacClaren.

They stood in total silence for what seemed to her an eternity. She had never been at a loss for conversation before but now she could think of nothing to say. He was no help. She soon realized that if they were to talk at all she must begin.

At last she said, "It must be very different out there in the Indian Territory." And after a considerable silence in which he seemed to weigh and compare every factor he said,

"Very different."

She waited to see if he was going to offer any further comment. When it became apparent that that was his total contribution, she began again.

"I'd like to see the West some day."

"Most women find the life too hard." He regarded her as if he were measuring her against all the other women he had ever known.

"Does your wife like it?" she asked, avoiding his gaze.

"I don't have a wife," he said, "if that answers your question."

This time her blush rivaled the red in her hair. She hadn't been very subtle and her penance was another silence between them. It made her angry to be so transparent, to be rebuffed at every attempt to make conversation. Most men talked of nothing but themselves. He seemed to be a monument to silence, hewn out of granite. In a last effort to draw him out she asked, "Why do most women find the life so hard?"

"There aren't many comforts for the ladies," he said, "and few of the necessities. They don't like being isolated out there with nothing but the wind for company. Things are better now than they used to be. We have neighbors and a trading town within a day's ride, but that's still not what you might call close. The climate is the worst. You can't count on it two days hand running. We have a saying out there, 'If you don't like the weather, wait a little minute.' Mostly it's the wind the women don't like."

She was stunned by the length of his reply. At last she had found a topic he could speak on. "I like the wind," she said, and for some reason her heart beat a little faster, as if she stood on the threshold of the unknown.

"It's easy to say you like the wind when you're safe indoors." His eyes narrowed as he stared her up and down. "You don't look like you could stand up in a strong gale."

She lifted her head in defiance. "I'm very strong, Mr. MacClaren. I daresay I'd survive."

"You'd never last a week out in the rough."

"I'm not some fragile city girl," she snapped. "I grew up on a farm."

Suddenly, without warning, he took her hand and turned it palm up as if to read her fortune. "You've never done a day's work in your life."

"I haven't worked in the fields, if that's what you mean. But I could if I had to."

He smiled and let go her hand. She couldn't tell if he was amused or if he was mocking her. "A girl like you will always have servants to wait on her. You wouldn't find that kind of easy life in the Territory."

"There would be other things to make up for the hardship," she said stiffly.

"What, for instance?" It was a direct challenge.

"Freedom, adventure. Being a part of a new world." She was pleased with her answer, but he only smiled that maddeningly superior smile.

"You think you want adventure, but that's only a young girl's romantic dream. Grown men and women have gone out there with nothing but their dreams, and they didn't last long."

"I would last." She spoke too loudly and heads turned. She was surprised by the force of her reply.

"You don't have any idea of what you would be up against." His smile vanished. "I've seen women driven mad by the wind. Their faces blank, their minds wiped clean." Something in the tone of his voice made her realize that if she pursued the matter she would be walking on forbidden, dangerous ground.

"If it's so hard, then why do you like it, Mr. MacClaren?"

The tenseness and anger in him subsided as he answered. "It's my land, my home. I like the open range and the wide sky. I don't want neighbors breathing down my neck. I like to be free to do as I please." To Reanna the idea of being free to do as she pleased was irresistible. When he found his tongue Mr. MacClaren could paint a picture in words. It was obvious that he had a passion for his country.

"You must be anxious to go back." She needed no reply from him to tell her that there was nothing in this room or in this city that could compare to that country far beyond her sight or imagining. She'd been drawn to him at first because he was different. She'd spoken the truth when she had said she would like to go out to the West. Now she found she not only wanted to see the land, she wanted to see it through his eyes. She had heard what he had said about the hardships, but she had not listened or believed him. All she had really heard was the excitement and the challenge.

"Yes," he was saying, "I'm anxious to go home. I'm only here in Washington on business."

"What kind of business?" She saw his jaw tighten. She had provoked him. "I know," she said, "I ask too many questions. My mother is always telling me I do, but if I don't ask, how will I learn anything?"

He looked at her carefully. It was hard to remember that she was one of this Washington crowd. He suddenly found he wanted to be open and free with her. It was a new sensation for him, one he hadn't experienced in a woman's company before.

"I'm here because I have to get permission from the Department of the Interior to lease out our family grazing land."

"If it's your land why do you have to ask permission?"

"That's a question you should ask the Department of the Interior." He shrugged. "But I doubt you'd be interested in the answer."

"I might be if you explained it to me."

"It's not an easy thing to explain." He shifted uneasily, wishing he'd never started on this in the first place. "It's all tied up in a two-hundred-year tangle of federal laws and Indian land. I wouldn't know where to begin."

"Please try."

He hesitated and then decided on a tack she might be able to follow. "You said you lived on a farm, right?"

"Yes, in Virginia."

"Your family has a clear title to that land, right?"

She nodded, wondering if she should mention the mortgage.

"Well, that makes it yours under the law. It means you own it. But Indians have always had a different idea about their land. My family lives in the Chickasaw Nation. Our land belongs to the whole tribe. Anyone in the tribe has a right to take as much tribal land as he needs for his own use."

"Are you an Indian, Mr. MacClaren?"

"Yes."

"You don't look like an Indian."

"What does an Indian look like?"

"Well . . ." She hesitated. "Someone with dark hair and red skin, not someone with fair hair and blue eyes."

He grinned. "The Chickasaw have been intermarrying with whites for over a hundred years. The full bloods and half bloods show the Indian, but a lot of Chickasaw are fair, with blue eyes."

"Mr. MacClaren, you're the first Indian I ever met."

He grinned again. "I'm not an Indian by blood, Miss Lovell. I was adopted by an Indian family. That makes me a full member of the tribe and a citizen of the Chickasaw Nation, not a citizen of the United States."

"How curious." She found him fascinating.

"I'm in Washington because the federal government has passed a law, the Dawes Act, to take all Indian land and allot it out to the individual members of the tribe in little homestead parcels. Until they enroll us, give us all a number and make us our allotments, the law says I have to get permission from the Department of the Interior to lease out my grazing land. See, we lease our grazing land to a Texas rancher, Colonel Cecil Goodwell. We drive up a big herd of his every year to fatten on our grass before he ships them to fat market in Kansas City." Suddenly Andrew stopped short, self-conscious at having talked so much. He'd never talked so straight to a woman before. He didn't know why he had now, except she had seemed interested in getting it out of him. "So that's it, that's why I had to come to Washington."

"But surely," she burst out indignantly, "they can't deny you permission to lease out your own land. That's not fair."

He gave a short, dry laugh. "Tell that to the Department of the Interior or to Mr. Marr; he's got friends in high places." Andrew felt his face go red. He'd said far more than he'd meant to. "I've talked too much," he said curtly. "Leases and land aren't topics to interest a lady."

"This is the most interesting conversation I've had since I came to Washington, believe me." She smiled. She'd heard enough to know she felt a great sympathy for him and for his cause.

Once again he found her smile disturbing. He was not used to being so open with any woman, especially one as highbred as this. "Please, Miss Lovell, don't think you have to be polite and stand here talking to me."

"I'm not being polite. I'd rather talk to you than any man in this room."

He found that difficult to believe. He looked across the room at Mrs. Lovell, standing by the punch bowl glaring at them. "I believe your mother thinks I've taken too much of your time. She's over there trying to catch your eye."

There was only a moment's hesitation and then Reanna grinned at him, a wide smile of pure mischief. "Mr. MacClaren, if we go through those doors into the conservatory, my mother won't be able to see either of us anymore." She put her arm through his and turned him smartly and firmly toward the one place she knew where they might be alone. It was a bold move, she knew, but now she had met him she wanted to know more about him. The wild thought came into her mind that if she must marry, then she'd like to marry someone like this—a man who led a life completely different from any she had ever known.

THE conservatory was warm and moist, filled with the fragrance of freesias and early lilies. The green of the ferns and palms was soothing and restful to the eye. The shadows were larger than nature, reflected against the gleaming glass. There was an almost cloying sweetness that overlay the pungent richness of the potted soil.

"I've never been in a place like this," Andrew said, as they walked around the glass room, pausing first at one display and then another.

"It always seems sad to me," Reanna said, "to see things forced to bloom before their season." She was conscious of her hand on his arm. She knew he too was aware of how close they were. "Do you have flowers in the Indian Territory?"

"Yes." Her questions took him by surprise. She asked the damnedest things. "In the spring the place is full of wildflowers. They'll be in bloom in a few weeks."

She wished that she could see them, that in the spring she would be there, not here or back at home living under her mother's disapproving eyes. She wanted to be free, far away in a country different from any she had experienced. She felt sad, not for the forced flowers but for herself. She felt as if she had lost something of great value. She looked at a rosebush with its buds closed tight, a rose that would never feel the rain.

"Here," she said, as she broke a bud from the stem and turned to put it in his lapel. She stood very close to him. She touched him. She found herself being attracted to this very masculine man. She was bothered by his presence as she had never been before by any of the boys she had known.

"Here is something to remember Washington by—and me." She glanced up at him and then away again. "A token so you will not forget us."

"I'm not likely to forget either Washington or you." His voice had deepened and he spoke the words roughly, as if he were unwilling to say them at all. It was a long time since he had felt these stirrings within him. This girl disturbed him. He had never met anyone like her. She was a highbred, an unknown, a threat to him. He was pulled toward her, magnetized by her. As always when he felt himself threatened, he lashed out to strike away the danger.

"Do girls like you do this often in Washington?"

"Do what?"

"Flirt with strangers."

His words cut her. She heard herself gasp. With quiet deliberation she stared at him, holding his blue eyes in the grip of hers.

"I never flirt, Mr. MacClaren. I don't flirt and I never lie."

He saw his image reflected in the depths of her brown eyes. She was more dangerous than he had thought. He couldn't break away from her. He found himself wanting to take her in his arms and hold her. She said she never lied. He wondered: if he asked her what he most wanted to know, would she answer him?

"If one of those men in that room brought you here, one of your Washington beaux, would you have given him a flower?" She kept looking at him. Her gaze did not waver but there was a curl to her lips.

"I wouldn't have been here with one of them."

"But if you were, what would he do?"

"He'd try to kiss me."

"Would you let him?"

She shook her head. "No."

Reluctantly he pulled himself away from her. She was a tease after all, either that or he had misread what he'd seen in her eyes. In a strange way he was relieved. He felt he had just been reprieved. Then, as he was congratulating himself on his escape, her hand reached out to him.

"I said I would say no to them, but I didn't say I wouldn't want you to kiss me."

Feeling lighthearted but lost forever, he took her in his arms. At first her lips were closed but as they opened to him and unfolded he was shocked at the sensation of desire they aroused within him. These were feelings of need, of longing he had thought belonged to his past. He felt the blood run warm in his veins; he could not suppress his feelings. His desire was revealed rising hard against her and he stepped back, angry at his lack of control.

She stood, eyes wide. She'd never expected to want to have a man kiss her, let alone a stranger. She certainly hadn't anticipated the effect it would have on them both. It seemed astonishing that one kiss could alter her heartbeat and provoke a sensation of warmth in her limbs and along her thighs. She didn't want him to pull away from her, as she had before when others had tried to kiss her. She wanted him to hold her close, to continue to touch, to hold, to explore. But for some reason she couldn't fathom he seemed angry, as if this were a mistake that should not have occurred.

"Well," he said wryly, "now you'll have an amusing story to tell tomorrow. You and your friends can have a good laugh at my expense, and you'll have another scalp to hang on your belt."

"I won't laugh at you, Mr. MacClaren." She couldn't imagine what had provoked this outburst. "I like you better than any man I ever met and I'd like to see you again."

Her straight gaze and even tone threw him off balance even more than the kiss. She had a way of doing and saying things that put him at a disadvantage.

Reanna didn't understand him but now that she'd met him she didn't want to let him go. She knew she had to see him again. "What time is your appointment tomorrow?"

"It's in the morning, at eleven," he answered, not sure why she wanted to know.

"In the afternoon Mama and Cousin Lucy and I are going to an exhibit at the Smithsonian. If you came too I could see you there. You could tell me what happened." She felt vulnerable to disappointment but it was a chance she had to take.

"Why should you care?" He was abrupt with her because he felt events crowding in on him. It made him wary and uncomfortable.

"I care about everything that happens to you."

She was a siren, singing a song. He felt hypnotized, dizzy, out of focus. He wondered if they were growing here in this greenhouse some kind of intoxicating locoweed that had twisted his brain.

"Will you come?" she asked again, pressing him for an answer.

"I don't know." He had to think. He was getting in deep here, too deep for comfort. The bottom was going out from under his feet. Once he'd nearly drowned in the river and this felt much the same.

"Please say you'll try. You do want to see me again, don't you?" She wouldn't let it alone. She was like a puppy worrying at his heel.

"Yes," he said, "I'll try." He didn't know what to make of her; he had never run into any situation like this. In his mind there were two kinds of women and she didn't seem to fit into either category. He felt overpowered by this girl he had just met and whom he had kissed almost as if she had willed him to. He was afraid of what she would will him to do next. He didn't like the sensation. Then, to his great relief, he was saved by the appearance of Mr. Marr in the doorway to the conservatory. Mr. Marr seemed in no doubt that he would find them there, together and alone. As for Andrew, he felt as if Taffy Owen, his ranch foreman, and some of the boys had just come riding to his rescue.

"Ah, MacClaren, there you are. Reanna showing you the house? I thought we might have a cigar in the library while the ladies go to their music. Reanna, I believe your mother is wanting to see you."

Mr. Marr paused, waiting for Reanna to leave them. She felt dismissed like a naughty child. She wished she could stay with them instead of being sent away and forced to listen to some dull, dreadful woman sing.

SHE found a chair at the back of the music room, as far from her mother as possible. She'd seen the look on Mrs. Lovell's face, the deep lines of disapproval formed like parentheses about her mouth. All during the music, Reanna sat thinking of Andrew and that kiss, plotting how she might sit with him at supper. She was determined to take every opportunity to be with him, but her mother prevented that by having Cousin Lucy pair her off with the damp-handed lawyer.

As he held out her chair for her to be seated at the dinner table, he said, "Miss Lovell, I trust you remember my name?"

"No," she said, "I'm sorry, I don't." He seemed to think she was being coy and that no girl could forget him.

"It's Stoner, Marshall Stoner." He started to spell it out for her and she foresaw it was going to be a very dull dinner indeed. She was wedged between a pompous lawyer and the formidable widower, Mr. Mount.

Mr. Stoner began giving her a seemingly endless account of some of his more famous clients while Mr. Mount made jovial remarks about the weather. Reanna looked hopefully across the table at Andrew but he did not return her glance.

He had the dreadful singer, Mrs. Hess, as his partner. Andrew was manfully trying to engage Mrs. Hess in polite dinner-table small talk, but he had to compete for Mrs. Hess's attention with the food she was shoveling down at an alarming rate. On Andrew's other side, Dr. Croydon's wide, bare forehead gleamed in the candlelight, as he carefully dissected his fish, removing the bones with a surgeon's skill. None of these so-called eligible men her mother was so anxious for her to marry could offer her the kind of life Mr. Mac-Claren lived. They were all as stiff and correct as Cousin Lucy and Mr. Marr, who sat sedately at the head and foot of the table with her mother and father as their guests of honor.

Reanna had a sense of pride in noting that her parents were the best-looking people there. Her father was a distinguished-looking man. His red hair was streaked with gray and tipped with silver at the temples. He was witty, charming and seldom out of temper. Her mother, taller by a head than her father, was dark, with classically sharp features and an air of perpetual anxiety.

From her father's end of the table, Reanna could hear the laughter that followed one of his stories. She glanced at her mother in time to see Mrs. Lovell frown. Her mother had never understood the point of any of her father's jokes. Both her father and mother were from old Virginia county families: Byrds, Randolphs and Cabells. When her father had inherited the farm from a bachelor uncle and had asked her mother to marry him, no one was surprised. They said Tom had always been sweet on Minnie. What had come as a surprise to Minnie was her husband's inability to pass up a wager on a horse or a card. Their domestic life had been feast or famine, depending on his run of luck. The one thing she had always been able to count on was that her husband adored her.

Once, when she was younger, Reanna had been looking out her window at the farm and had seen her mother and father walking in the moonlight. She had seen her father stop, take the pins from her mother's hair and caress it as it fell about her shoulders. Then she had seen her father kiss her mother—three children and he still kissed her in the moonlight.

Reanna had been lost in her own thoughts when she suddenly realized that Cousin Lucy had turned the table; she was supposed to be talking to Mr. Mount on her right. Even an old widower would make a welcome change from Mr. Stoner, going on and on about himself.

Then, from the subdued murmur of dinner-table voices, Dr. Croydon's bass boomed out at Andrew. "I understand, Mr. MacClaren, that you're a cattleman from out West." The conversation subsided, everyone waiting for Andrew's answer.

"That's right," Andrew mumbled uncomfortably. He disliked being made the center of attention like some Wild West exhibit.

"How many cows do you have?" Dr. Croydon continued.

"We keep two or three hundred head of our own on the home place." Andrew felt his voice was thin and unnatural. They kept staring at him as if they expected him to spear his peas with his knife.

"Mr. MacClaren," Reanna spoke up, eager to come to Andrew's rescue, "leases out his grazing land to a Texas rancher with a big herd of cows."

"Is that right?" Dr. Croydon peered at Andrew.

"Yes," Reanna said. "Mr. MacClaren drives a big herd up from Texas every year." Andrew looked at her and grinned. She had spunk, he'd give her that.

"How many head of cattle do you drive up from Texas?" Mr. Stoner demanded.

"We drive a different number every year."

"How many head did you drive last year?" Mr. Stoner would not let it alone.

"About two thousand." The answer seemed to surprise Stoner.

"You must have a lot of land to feed that many cows. Just how many acres do you have?" Stoner challenged Andrew as if he were interrogating a witness in court.

"We graze on about seventy sections." Andrew felt his jaw go tight. That was going to be his last word on the subject.

"How many sections?" Mrs. Lovell asked.

Andrew saw Reanna was laughing. He sure as hell hadn't meant to say anything funny.

"That would be about forty-five thousand acres." Reanna's eyes crinkled up at the edges. "So you see, Mama, Mr. MacClaren is hardly a small homesteader."

"Forty-five thousand acres?" Mr. Stoner repeated.

"Give a little, take a little," Andrew said. "We've grazed on more than that if we've needed to." How in thunder did the girl know all that about land? She was brighter than he'd thought. He had begun to feel better, seeing the new look on their faces as they studied him. They might be men of consequence up here, but they none of them had that kind of land beneath their feet.

"Of course," Stoner put in, "if it's Indian land, Mr. MacClaren doesn't own the land. Nobody owns the land. Indians don't have our sense of property."

"Are you an Indian, Mr. MacClaren?" Mrs. Lovell asked, eyeing him closely, as if to be an Indian might be a crime.

"Mr. MacClaren's not an Indian by blood, Mama, he's an adopted member of the tribe."

"Reanna." Her father tapped his water glass. "Let Mr. MacClaren answer his own questions." Her father seldom reprimanded her, but when he did she obeyed him.

There was a silence all around the table. Then Mrs. Marr chimed in brightly, "Well, and what do you all think about Mr. Roosevelt's new visiting hours at the White House?" and Andrew was relieved that the attention was turned away from him at last. He gave Reanna an appreciative nod.

The rest of the supper went better for him. They all talked Washington politics and left him alone. Then the ladies excused themselves and left the gentlemen to drink brandy and smoke their cigars. The smoke drifted up around their heads like smoke signals from a hostile tribe. Andrew was more than ever aware that the only way he could fit in with these men was to own them. They'd never accept him as an equal. He thought they were going to leave him out of the conversation entirely, but Mr. Stoner, the lawyer, started in on him again.

"What brings you to Washington, Mr. MacClaren? If you don't mind my asking?" Stoner was an unctuous toad.

"I have to get permission from the Department of the Interior to lease out my tribal grazing land." He'd disliked Stoner's remark at dinner about Indian land. Stoner seemed to want to provoke him.

"I understand it will only remain tribal land until the Dawes Commission has finished allotting the land to the tribes in severalty."

Dr. Croydon made a face as he blew out a pillar of smoke. "What does all that mean, Stoner? Your legal mumbo jumbo is worse than my doctor's Latin."

"It means," Stoner said smugly, avoiding Andrew's gaze, "that the government is going to allot each Indian a homestead and open up the Five Nations for white settlement."

"What are these Five Nations?" Mr. Mount seemed genuinely interested.

"Chickasaw, Choctaw, Cherokee, Creek and Seminole," Andrew said. "They're all sovereign nations within the United States, with their own citizens, legislatures and right to make laws."

"And are these Indians willing to give up their tribal land for government allotments?" Mr. Mount asked.

"They're not willing, Mr. Mount; it is United States law that says we must."

"Damn funny law to let us take other nations' land." Mount shook his head in wonder.

"The Dawes Act," said Mr. Stoner, as if delivering himself of a legal opinion, "was passed because so many people, Indian and white, found the situation in the Indian Territory untenable."

"What situation was that?" Dr. Croydon asked.

"White people living there had no recourse to any but Indian law."

"I thought we had treaties with the Indians. Don't we have treaties?" Mr. Mount seemed confused.

"Treaties," Andrew said, "never stopped the government from taking the Indians' old nations on the eastern seaboard. Treaties never stopped the government from moving the Indians over the Trail of Tears to the Indian Territory. After the Civil War, the government declared all Chickasaw treaties worthless."

"Why after the Civil War?" asked Mr. Lovell politely.

"The Chickasaw sided with the Confederacy. We paid for being on the losing side by losing our treaty rights."

"Ah." Mr. Lovell nodded. "We Virginians know about being on the losing side of the war."

"After the war," Andrew went on, "the government let the railroads come in, and the whites. There was nothing we could do to stop them."

"You seem to think of the federal government as a bunch of carpetbaggers," Mr. Stoner half sneered. There was silence at the table. Sympathy for the Confederacy was still strong in those who, like Mr. Lovell, had belonged to a lost cause.

"Who are you seeing at Interior?" Mr. Marr asked, as he refilled Andrew's glass.

"A Mr. Almer Williams. Do you know him?" Andrew hoped to get some notion of what the man was like.

"Oh yes," Mr. Marr replied. "I know him, though not well. I hear he's an excellent man, excellent. He is considered to be fair. I'm sure he'll do his best to help you."

"Williams is a stickler for regulations." Stoner had to put in his two cents' worth. "Or so I hear."

It was not a recommendation that filled Andrew with optimism. "Thanks," he said dryly and stood up with the rest of the gentlemen as they prepared to join the ladies.

Mr. Lovell cleared his throat. "I wish you luck tomorrow, Mr. MacClaren."

"Thank you, sir." In Andrew's opinion, Mr. Lovell was the best of this sorry lot.

As Andrew came into the parlor, he saw Reanna's eyes light on him and follow him, pulling him toward her like quicksand. But he was determined not to be caught. He wanted to get away from her and from these people. At the first opportunity he said, "If you will excuse me, Mrs. Marr, I have an important meeting tomorrow morning. I want to thank you for your hospitality. I must say good night." He turned to Mrs. Lovell. "And good night to you, Mrs. Lovell, and to your daughter."

"Goodbye," Mrs. Lovell said firmly.

"Good night," Reanna said, smiling up at him, "but I hope it will not be goodbye." As he nodded to Miss Lovell, Andrew heard Mrs. Lovell gasp and it gave him some brief satisfaction. Everything about the old cow rubbed him the wrong way, especially the idea she seemed to have that he had broken into the herd just to steal their prize heifer. He could not deny that he had been attracted to her, but it had been a chance encounter. He congratulated himself on being well out of it. Tomorrow he would know one way or another about his lease, and then he could leave this damn town.

Reanna couldn't wait for the evening to end so she could hide away in her room. Mr. MacClaren was gone. She would probably never see him again. It seemed cruel that she should have met him at all if nothing was to come of it. Her mother said nothing to her as she brushed Reanna's hair. That silence was more terrible than if she had scolded. Reanna felt sure her mother only held her tongue because she thought Andrew MacClaren was gone out of their lives forever.

That night Reanna dreamed of open, rolling prairies and a wide, blue sky that stretched out cloudlessly to the vanishing horizon. She couldn't see Andrew in her dream, but she knew he was somewhere just out of sight. When she woke, she had dark circles under her eyes.

At breakfast, Reanna turned abruptly to Mr. Marr. "Mr. Marr, please tell me all you know about the Indian Territory."

His spoon stopped, suspended over his oatmeal. "I've never been there," he said, "but I hear it's going to be a state soon. Everyone says there's great opportunity for growth. A man could do well out there. What put that into your head?" he asked out of frank curiosity.

Reanna saw her mother frown. She knew well enough her mother was not pleased with her. "Mr. MacClaren." Reanna tried to sound casual. "He was talking about the Territory last night. Do you know him well?"

"Not well," Mr. Marr said. "He's come to Washington several times on tribal business."

"Will he get permission to lease out his land?" Reanna asked.

"I really can't say." Mr. Marr looked uncomfortable. "It's not up to me."

"Why did you ask him here if you weren't going to help him?" Reanna's eyes flashed with righteous anger.

"Mr. MacClaren is a stranger in town." Mr. Marr looked decidedly uncomfortable. "I asked him here as a courtesy, nothing more."

Mrs. Lovell bristled. "Why should you care about that, Reanna? What happens to Mr. MacClaren is no business of yours."

Mr. Lovell looked up from his sausages. It was not his way to interrupt women or to take sides. He only liked to speak if he was sure of saying something popular, but this line of conversation, if not checked, might detain him from getting out of the house and into the clubs where he could meet and drink with men of his own mind who were not averse to taking or giving a little wager or sitting down to a game of cards. "Change the subject, Reanna."

"Yes, Papa." She said no more but that did not mean she didn't *think* about Mr. MacClaren. She thought about him all the time.

That morning some flowers came from the florists for Cousin Lucy from Andrew. There was a card thanking Mrs. Marr for her gracious hospitality. He must have made a special point of ordering them before he went to his important meeting.

"How thoughtful," Mrs. Marr said. "What nice manners."

"To make up for his being so rude at supper, I suppose," Mrs. Lovell said.

Reanna said nothing, but she wished with all her heart that he had sent the flowers to her. It might have been a sign she would see him again.

Reanna and her mother and Cousin Lucy had luncheon at the Capitol with a congressman from home. Mrs. Lovell was cross because Reanna was quiet and didn't shine. As they drove toward the Smithsonian, Mrs. Lovell remarked that she hoped Reanna's mood would improve because this whole day had been arranged as a special treat for her. It seemed a sort of punishment, the way she said it.

At the Smithsonian, Reanna was sure the exhibit was interesting and uplifting, but she couldn't focus on anything she saw. It was all a blur. As the minutes went by and he didn't come, she was afraid they would soon run out of pictures to see. At last, as they turned the corner into the final gallery, Reanna glanced back and there, at the end of the corridor they had just left, she saw Andrew coming toward them. His head was lowered and the heels of his boots echoed against the marble floors. His approach was as devastating to her as Sherman's march through Georgia.

Making sure her mother's and Cousin Lucy's attentions were directed toward the next gallery, Reanna turned back to meet Andrew. Perhaps she could have at least a few minutes alone with him before they missed her. She went toward him quickly, her heart light with joy. Then she saw his face. It was set and hard.

As Andrew strode toward Reanna, the angry memory of his meeting with Williams twisted a knot in his stomach. That morning he'd shaved close, shined up his boots and arrived for his appointment five minutes early so as to be in good time. Then a snippety secretary had kept him cooling his heels for a quarter of an hour while he silently cursed Washington and everyone in it.

When he'd finally been ushered into Williams' office, Andrew had found a small, pasty-faced man with a pince-nez pinching the bridge of his nose. He was sitting behind a big desk covered with papers that he kept shuffling from one pile to another. Without looking up at Andrew he said, "Sit down, sit down, Mr., ah . . . ?"

"MacClaren, Andrew MacClaren." And he'd sat down on a hard, straight-backed chair with no place to put his hat but his lap.

"I'm sorry to have kept you waiting, Mr. MacClaren." Williams glanced up briefly and then looked down again at the papers. "We're very busy, I'm afraid, and badly understaffed." He gave a dry cough as he at last found the folder he'd been looking for. "Now then, Mr. MacClaren, you're from the . . . ?"

"The Chickasaw Nation, Indian Territory."

Mr. Williams looked pained, as if his glasses pinched too tightly. "Ah, yes, well—you've had a long journey from the Indian Territory to Washington."

"Yes."

"How was your trip?"

"Tolerable." Andrew shifted uncomfortably, wanting to get on to the business at hand.

"Personally, I find travel tiring." Williams gave a thin, apologetic smile, leaned back and put the palms of his two hands together as if he were about to pray. "Now, what can I do for you, Mr. MacClaren?"

Andrew's throat felt tight. His resentment at having to be here in this room with this man nearly choked him. "I need permission to lease out some tribal land."

"You wish to lease the land for yourself?"

"No." Andrew felt the blood pound in his temple. "I want to lease our tribal grazing land to a Texas rancher, Colonel Cecil Goodwell." Andrew paused, waiting for some response from Mr. Williams; when there was none he went on. "Colonel Goodwell is willing to contract us his cattle for summer and fall grazing, as he always does."

"And this land you want to lease him is Chickasaw tribal land?"

"Yes."

Williams studied him for a moment. "Ah yes, I see." Williams drew the words out to a great length, and then his hands flew apart as if they were about to take wing and fly away. "It's unfortunate, Mr. MacClaren, that you've been put to the trouble and expense of coming to Washington. You could have seen our agent in Muskogee. He could have explained our policy on the matter of tribal leases."

"He told me that I needed permission from the Department of the Interior, and that's why I'm here in Washington, to get that permission."

Williams frowned. "At present the Department is reluctant to grant any more leases on Chickasaw tribal land."

"So your agent said." Andrew tried to keep his tone even. "But you can still grant that permission. Isn't that so?"

"We feel that to grant any leases during this period of land allotment might put all parties concerned in a difficult situation."

"My situation is this." Andrew sat forward in his chair. "My family's livelihood depends on leasing out our grazing land. Not to have your permission means a loss of income, and that means hardship for us."

"The Department regrets that during this period of tribal enrollment and land survey there should be any unnecessary hardship to the Chickasaw."

"It will be another year at least before the enrollment is completed and all the allotments are taken. Surely you can see your way clear to let us lease out our land for one more year." Andrew was begging and it shamed him, but he felt he had no other choice.

Williams sighed. "Believe me, I appreciate your predicament but I hope in turn you can see the Department's view. In the future, when the enrollment is completed, perhaps we will take a different stand."

"The time to grant me permission is now." Andrew's hands gripped the rim of his hat. "When the enrollment and survey are completed, the land will be allotted and the cattle trail across the Chickasaw Nation will be closed."

Williams took off his pince-nez and wiped it carefully with his pocket handkerchief. "I believe I have stated our Department policy."

"And that's to be it, then?" Andrew could almost taste his disappointment and it was bitter as herbs.

"For the time being, yes."

"Tell me something, Mr. Williams." Andrew eyed him coldly. "There's nothing in the law that says you can't grant me the lease, is that right?"

"No, but it's my job to uphold the spirit as well as the letter of the law. The law was, after all, passed to protect the Chickasaw."

"No law ever passed in Washington was for the benefit of the Chickasaw."

Williams flushed. "Come now, Mr. MacClaren." Williams replaced his glasses. "That's most unfair. This law was passed to keep unscrupulous men, both white and Indian, from taking advantage of this period of transition from tribal to state government."

"Then it's not the law but you, Mr. Williams, who keep me from leasing out my land."

"I am sorry you choose to make this a personal issue."

"It's personal to me. I can't see how the law benefits me or my family. If we can't lease out our land, how can we make a living? What does the law do for me?"

"There is nothing in the law," Williams said with exaggerated patience, "that says a Chickasaw family can't drive and graze their own cattle."

"Are you saying that if we drive our own herd up from Texas we don't need the Department's permission?"

"Not as long as the trail fees are paid to the Chickasaw Council and the rules concerning time allowed on the trail are observed."

Andrew let Williams' words sink in and take hold. "We've always run a few hundred head of our own," he said quietly. "But we've made our real money leasing out the grazing land."

Williams shrugged. "What you choose to do is, of course, your own business."

(32)

Andrew stood up, turning his hat in his hands. "You're right, Mr. Williams, it is our business." As he spoke an idea began to take shape in his head. "I'm sorry if I took up your valuable time."

"Not at all." Williams was overly cordial. "It's what I'm here for. I'm only sorry to send you away empty-handed."

"Oh." A mirthless grin cracked the corner of Andrew's mouth. "I'm not going home empty-handed. I've just had a fine sample of Washington hospitality. Good day, Mr. Williams."

"Good day, Mr. MacClaren."

As Andrew walked out of the building and toward the Smithsonian, his anger and chagrin gnawed at his gut. He felt sure that Marr and his cronies had known last night that Williams was going to turn him down and they hadn't had the decency to tell him so. They had let him swing in the wind. For his part he'd let the girl sidetrack him or he'd have seen it for himself.

Then he saw Reanna at the end of the corridor. He walked smartly toward her, took her arm in his hand and ringed it as tightly as if his fingers were made of steel.

"Williams turned me down," he said roughly. "The pennyweight paper-pushers won't let me lease out my land."

Reanna's heart skipped a beat. She was sorry for his disappointment, but it was of less significance to her than the fact that Andrew would be going away.

"That means you'll be leaving Washington?"

"Yes." He carried her along beside him, away from her mother and Cousin Lucy. "I can't wait to get out of this damn town. I'll never come here again until I have enough money to put in the right hands. It's the only language these tinhorns understand. Those railroad boys know a thing or two; if you want to do business in Washington you buy you a senator—and make sure you buy the best."

She'd known men who were given to anger, but Andrew's rage possessed him so completely she wasn't sure if he even knew it was her arm he held. "What will you do now?" she asked.

"I'll do what I've always done. I'll graze Texas cattle."

Reanna had meant, what would he do within the next hour; he was thinking of the weeks and months to come, time he would spend without her. "But how can you graze cattle if it's against the law?"

"The law be damned." He stopped and wheeled on her as if she were the enemy. "That bastard has shown me how to use the law to my advantage. If I drive my own cattle the law can't touch me." As he spoke, for the first time he seemed to notice her and where they were. "I'm sorry," he said, "I shouldn't use language like that in front of a lady."

She smiled. Nothing mattered now that he was here. "I'm glad you came," she said.

"Are you?" One eyebrow rose like a question mark. "Why?"

"I was afraid I wouldn't ever see you again."

"Well, after tomorrow you'll be rid of me. I'll be long gone for home. The agent in Muskogee led me to believe if I came up here I'd get permission. But Williams was never going to let me lease my land. I came up here to Washington on a fool's errand. The agent in Muskogee knew it, your friends all knew it, everybody but me knew it. I made a fool of myself last night. They must all have had a good laugh at me."

Before she could reply, they were cut off at the far end of the corridor by the appearance of Reanna's mother and Cousin Lucy. The ladies had completed their tour and had unluckily come out at the crossroads of the corridors. Mrs. Lovell's displeasure was evident. Hoping her mother wouldn't say anything which would further fuel Andrew's anger, Reanna said,

"Mr. MacClaren has just come from the Department of the Interior."

"Oh?" Mrs. Lovell's voice rose ominously. "What a coincidence that he should find us here." She turned the full force of her next remark on Andrew. "I can't imagine your being even vaguely interested in art." Reanna saw his color rise. It seemed his anger had only been diverted from the Department of the Interior to her mother.

"Then you would be wrong, Mrs. Lovell. We have quite a few civilized folks out in the Territory. In fact, I'd say that a lot of them are a piece more civilized than some I've met here in Washington."

"Would you indeed, Mr. MacClaren?" Mrs. Lovell digested this and found it unpalatable. "Well, we won't interrupt your appreciation of art any longer. We must be going. It's getting late." She drew Reanna from his side and placed her between Cousin Lucy and herself.

"So soon, Mama? But why?"

"We're dining early this evening."

"Are we?" Cousin Lucy let the words slip before she saw her cousin Minnie's awful glare. "Oh, yes," she stammered, "I remember now." It was such a bald lie that Reanna made one more desperate move of her own just to gain a little more time.

"I know how tired you are, Mama and Cousin Lucy. I'm sure Mr. MacClaren would gladly give us tea at his hotel. You would, wouldn't you, Mr. MacClaren?" She appealed to him. For a second she thought he might refuse, but then he caught on to her joke at their expense. He smiled and made a small mock bow.

"I would be happy to give you ladies tea at the Willard. I understand it's quite a respectable hotel. Being seen there even with me would not harm your reputations. Besides, I would like to do something to repay your Washington hospitality." There was a hard edge of irony in his words.

Mrs. Lovell had begun her reply before he had finished. "No, thank you, Mr. MacClaren. We wouldn't want to trouble you. I know I speak for Mrs. Marr and my daughter as well."

"Perhaps another time?" Reanna begged. Andrew shrugged and looked at Reanna with what she hoped was regret.

"When did you say you were leaving Washington?" she asked, feeling her mother's hold on her tighten.

"Day after tomorrow."

"Will we see you again before you go?" She could hope for that at least.

"No, that's out of the question," Mrs. Lovell broke in. "We're going to be far too busy, I'm afraid." And she turned Reanna and Cousin Lucy in the direction of the exit.

Reanna had time only to call back, "I hope you have a safe journey home," and he was out of her sight.

ALL the way home Reanna sat in cold silence between her mother and Cousin Lucy. At first Mrs. Marr tried to make a few bright, cheerful remarks to fill the void, but she soon gave it up as a lost cause.

Once inside the house, Reanna went straight through the hall and up to her room, followed by her mother. The last word had not yet been said by either of them. Reanna heard the door shut behind her and turned to face her mother.

"Why, why couldn't we at least have had tea with Mr. Mac-Claren? What could have been the harm in that?" Her eyes were blazing but her mother was not in the mood to be intimidated by Reanna's temper.

"He's not suitable, Reanna. He's not a gentleman."

"I like him." Reanna's chin went up in defiance. "He's different."

"Isn't he? I won't let you throw yourself away, Reanna."

"I'm not throwing myself away. I doubt if he would even have me after the way you've all treated him. But let me tell you this, Mama, you don't own me. You can't transfer title to me like a piece of property. If I'm going to be disposed of, I prefer to dispose of myself!"

"Reanna!" Mrs. Lovell was shocked at the force of the outburst. "You don't know this man. You don't know anything about him."

"I know I like him better than any man I've ever met."

"But he's a nobody! He can't *compare* with the sort of men you met last night."

"No, thank God, Andrew's not at all like them. He has courage and spirit. He'll always find a way to survive and come out on top of the pile."

Reanna was sorry to have lost her temper and hurt her mother's feelings, but not half as sorry as she was not to have spent the afternoon with Andrew. Each word Mrs. Lovell said against him made Reanna like him more. Her mother was right. She didn't know Andrew—but she knew he led the sort of life she wanted. He lived in an exciting, far country where each day made a new beginning.

"The man is rough and crude." Mrs. Lovell was shocked by Reanna's behavior. "How could you allow a man like that to touch your arm?"

"I thought he was very gallant." There was something in Reanna's tone and eyes that filled Mrs. Lovell with a sense of dismay. "But you don't have to worry, Mama. I'm probably never going to see him again. You've made sure of that. Are you proud of yourself, Mama?"

All evening Reanna thought of Andrew. She wondered where he was and with whom. When she said her prayers she prayed she would hear from him, but as the next morning passed and there was no knock at the door, she knew it had been a vain hope. Andrew was not coming.

Even the weather was against her. It was chilly, heavy and damp. Washington was a terribly swampy, inclement city. She wished she were home again, where she could ride out in the fields and be alone.

(36)

After luncheon her mother, who had promised to go shopping with Cousin Lucy, was forced to lie down with a sick headache. "It's the weather," Mrs. Lovell said. "It's stirred up my sinus. I know that Cousin Lucy has her heart set on going shopping. There's a sale at Dixon's, one of her favorite shops." Mrs. Lovell put a handkerchief to her throbbing brow. "But I simply can't move. I wonder if you'd be a good girl and go with her? I think perhaps if I just lie down for an hour or so I'll feel better."

To Reanna, even if there had been diamonds for sale, the afternoon wouldn't have been worth it. The weather grew even more close. The shops were crowded and the customers cross and snappish.

Cousin Lucy on impulse bought six pairs of kid gloves that didn't match her costume at all, though she insisted they did. At last, too chilled and tired to care what bargains were to be had, they called it a day and set out for home.

When they came out of the shop, the sky had begun to darken and it looked as if it might rain at any moment. With luck Reanna managed to hail a passing hackney. As she was helping Cousin Lucy into the cab, the sky off to the west cleared—a sweeping expanse of gold and azure hues—and Reanna gazed at it ardently. She was suddenly overpowered by the conviction that she had to see Andrew MacClaren again. This was her chance to change her destiny, control her own life; she mustn't let it go. Quickly she put her umbrella behind her back and, bold as brass, she who prided herself on telling the truth told a shameless lie.

"Cousin Lucy," she said in a rush, "you go on. I've left my umbrella in the shop. I must go back and get it."

Cousin Lucy nobly offered to go with her, but Reanna wouldn't hear of it. Telling the address to the driver, she closed the door of the cab and turned back into the crowd. She walked swiftly, her heart pounding, waiting for a thunderbolt to strike her because she had told such a terrible lie. She felt quite ill with fright and excitement. It made her ashamed of herself. She'd always despised cowards, and here she was with her knees shaking.

It had all been so sudden, she had no idea of what she intended to do. She only knew she must see Andrew. She had no idea of where to find him except at the Willard Hotel. She dared not think what her mama would say if she knew she was going to a man's hotel alone.

At first she sat in the lobby for a while, and then it occurred to her she might be too late, he might already have left Washington.

She asked the desk clerk if Mr. MacClaren was still registered. To her relief the clerk said that he was but that there was no answer to the bell in his room. He offered to have him paged if she liked, but she refused. That was too bold even for her. She sat in the lobby again, willing him to appear. And then, as if it were a miracle, there he was in the doorway, coming into the hotel. He was almost past her before he saw her.

She'd taken him by surprise, to say the least of it, but he recovered himself and came toward her. "Miss Lovell?" He glanced about for her mother or her cousin Lucy. She knew it was improper for her to be there unchaperoned. She began to stammer out some lame excuse.

"I was supposed to have met my cousin Lucy here, but I seem to have missed her. Perhaps it's the weather that has delayed her." Then her excuses seemed all too apparent and trivial. The situation was much too serious for that kind of subterfuge. This was a matter that would influence the rest of her life.

"None of that's true," she said, rising to face him. She'd always been self-conscious about being so tall, but now it didn't matter. It put them nearly eye to eye, on a kind of equal footing. "I haven't been waiting for Cousin Lucy. I've already lied once today and I don't want to do it again. I came because I wanted to see you."

"I'm glad you did." He found it was true. When he'd seen her sitting there alone, a little forlorn, his heart had taken a tumble. Now he felt ridiculously happy, as if everything had suddenly gone right with the world. He reached out and tucked a wisp of her hair beneath her bonnet. It was a naked, intimate gesture and revealed more of the soft side of his nature than he ever cared to expose to public view.

"Have you had your tea?" he asked roughly.

"No."

"Well, then, I owe you that from yesterday." He took command of the situation. He ordered tea, a plate of sandwiches and some cake as if he did it every day of his life, and sat watching her as she tried to appear natural.

After yesterday, he'd made up his mind not to see her again. She was so young, so vulnerable and lovely that even when he'd been preoccupied with his business he'd found he still wanted to see her, to hold her. It was a kind of perverse madness she seemed to provoke in him.

"Are the sandwiches all right? If you don't like them I can order something else." She shook her head, dumb with nerves and misery.

"What would you like?" he asked.

"Could we go for a walk?"

"It's going to rain."

"I don't care." They abandoned the tea and walked out into the dusky drizzle. She still couldn't throw all her pride away. She made a dozen false starts in her mind as they walked on toward the Potomac. Then at last she found her voice.

"I was afraid you'd be gone."

"Were you?"

She stopped and turned toward him. They stood close together, not touching, but the fine line between them was like a wall. "Yes," she said. "How could you go without saying goodbye?"

He hesitated. "I thought it best."

"Best for whom?"

"For both of us."

"I'm miserable, is that what you want?"

"You can't always have what you want. No one can."

"If you go tomorrow you might never see me again for the rest of your life. Have you considered that?" She was angry now. Anger was better to clear the mind than a flood of tears.

"Yes," he said, "I thought about it." He was so calm and so unemotional that it made her want to shake him.

"Wouldn't that matter to you at all?" He was silent, as the traffic and night sounds flowed about them. It seemed she must always be the one to make the first move. "It would matter to me," she said, "and I think it would matter to you." He shifted uneasily. "It would matter, wouldn't it?"

"Yes." He gave the word grudgingly.

"You haven't asked me what I want. Well then, I'll tell you. Andrew, I want you to marry me." He couldn't have been more surprised if she had asked him to jump in the river.

"You don't know what you're saying."

"Oh yes I do." She wasn't going to let him off the hook. This was her one chance and she meant to take it.

"You don't know anything about me," he said.

"I know all I need to know. The moment you walked into Cousin Lucy's drawing room, I knew we had something in common."

"What?"

"Neither of us wanted to be there."

"What else do you think you know?"

"I know you lead the kind of life I'd like to live. I think we'd suit each other. Many people have started with less."

"You don't have any idea of what my life is. You're a schoolgirl with a head full of romantic notions about the wild and woolly West."

"I can't help being young." She was on the defensive but she quickly changed her tack. "I'm quick and strong. I can ride, and I can learn to do all the rest. You can teach me. I'll last in the wind, you'll see. I won't blow away or go mad." Still he was silent, but she thought she'd scored at least a point with him.

At last he said, "I was married before."

"Oh." That was something she hadn't known. He'd said he didn't have a wife. Somehow she hadn't imagined that he'd been married in the past.

"She died. If there had been a proper doctor she might have lived. We had only been married a little over a year."

"I'm sorry," she said.

"My mother died out there when I was a boy. The climate and the hard life killed her. And I have a daughter."

She hadn't expected that he was a widower or that she'd have a child to raise, but these did nothing to make her want him less. She'd formed an idea of him and of their life together. She wouldn't give it up simply because the realities failed to match her dream.

"Her name is Snow."

She smiled. "Then I'll start married life with a ready-made family."

"I don't think you've heard a thing I've said to you. I haven't asked you to marry me. That was your idea, not mine. I didn't come to Washington looking for a wife." He felt she was driving him, goading him; he wanted to break away and yet he couldn't leave her. She had him between a rock and a hard place and there was nowhere to go.

"I thought you wanted me," she said. "I think so now. I don't know why you won't ask for me. If you want me, please say so." She was there before him ready for the taking. She held out a promise and she made the invitation tempting, but still he hung back.

It had been his first lesson in life—never to say what he wanted because it would be taken from him. His father had taught him that in a hard school. Andrew had learned to keep his feelings, his desires, to himself. It had made him a good poker player but he'd been lonely, a solitary man. Even to himself he did not often admit what he most would like to have. He did want this girl. He couldn't deny that. He wanted her and he could think of no good reason why he shouldn't have her. He'd always done what other people wanted; didn't he deserve something for himself? This had begun with a single kiss, a kiss he hadn't intended to happen, one he certainly had not expected would lead anywhere, and now he felt trapped. If he married her it would be against his better judgment, but want her he did. And in some dark, perverse way he despised himself for wanting and needing her. He felt that desire was a flaw in his character, an unpardonable sin.

"I think you want me, but if you do, you will have to say so." Once again he felt he was in deep water, going down for a third time.

"I'm afraid for you, Reanna. You're a highbred girl. You won't fit in out there. I wouldn't want anything to happen to you."

She looked at him and considered his evasions. "Shall I tell you what I think you are really afraid of? I think you're afraid to tell my parents and Cousin Lucy and Mr. Marr that you want to marry me." He was still silent but now he looked at her in a different way. "You're afraid that if they wouldn't let you have a lease, they won't let you have me."

If she'd thought for a hundred years she couldn't have found a more powerful argument. Her words were her weapons and they cut to the bone. It was true what she said. They wouldn't think he was good enough for her. It was like a dare he couldn't resist.

"No, I'm not afraid to ask them." They might not want him to marry her but, by God, one day he'd come back here and nobody in this town would refuse him anything!

"Then ask them, Andrew. I'll marry you no matter what they say. Would you like to kiss me just once more to make sure?"

Even as he embraced her the idea stayed in his mind that in marrying Reanna he would be taking away their golden girl. He could almost see the look of shocked surprise on their faces when they heard the news.

He wasn't disappointed. When he took Reanna home, they were all in the parlor waiting. They sat in a tight circle, Mr. and Mrs. Marr and Mr. and Mrs. Lovell. They looked as if they'd circled the wagons to repel an Indian attack. Mrs. Lovell was near tears.

"Where have you been, Reanna? We've been so worried, wondering what had happened to you."

"You shouldn't have worried, Mama," Reanna said calmly. "Mr. MacClaren and I have been getting ourselves engaged. We're going to be married."

"*Impossible!*" Mrs. Lovell's eyes were round with shock and two pink circles began to glow in her cheeks.

"I should think you'd be pleased, Mama. It's what you want for me, isn't it? To be married? Well, I'm going to marry Mr. Mac-Claren and go to live with him in the Indian Territory."

Her mother made a face that looked as if she were laughing at some preposterous joke. "But we don't know anything about him." Mrs. Lovell spoke as if he were not in the room.

"Mr. Marr can vouch for my financial situation."

"And we know nothing whatever about his family," she said stiffly, as if that might settle the whole unhappy affair.

"My mother and father were missionaries to the Indians. When they died of a fever Miss Jane Beauvaise, a very fine Indian lady, took me in and raised me like her own."

This was all far worse than Mrs. Lovell had feared. He meant to marry her daughter and she could think of no way she could prevent it. "Reanna, you can't give up security and comfort to go to the end of the earth with a man you've just met."

"The Territory is not at the end of the country, ma'am. It's right in the middle. I may be a stranger here, but it's Reanna who will be the stranger out there."

"It's not civilized out there. Where would you live?"

"She wouldn't have to live in a wigwam or a log cabin, if that's what's worrying you. I've tried to be fair and tell her what the climate is like and that it won't be an easy life, but she won't listen."

Reanna went to her father then and knelt at his knee. "I know the life will suit me; no two days will be the same and there will be the chance to make a future for our children and our children's children." All the time she was talking she could hear her mother stifling sobs. Cousin Lucy and Mr. Marr sat dumbfounded, while Andrew turned his wide-brimmed hat this way and that.

"Are you sure, Ree?" her father asked. There had always been a special bond between them. She understood better than anyone his love of gambling, taking a chance. She was his daughter more than her mother's, even though she had a more practical head than he for facts.

(42)

"Yes, Papa, very sure."

He touched her cheek with his hand, a gesture of love. "Then, Minnie, I'd say it was already out of our hands."

Her mother wouldn't give up so easily. "Very well, then, if after a year's engagement you still feel the same, I won't stand in your way."

Reanna rose to face them all. "We're going to be married at once."

"But you can't. You have no trousseau."

"I won't need a wedding dress, Mama, or a trousseau. You and Papa have already bought me a trunk full of new clothes. I want to be married at once here in Cousin Lucy's parlor, if she will agree, and I think being married in a traveling costume would be most suitable, don't you?"

Mrs. Lovell reached for her heart, a gesture she often made when things were going out of control. "No trousseau, no real wedding."

"Just a simple wedding, Mama, just the family. You see, Mr. MacClaren has to get home so he can round up some cows." Reanna was afraid Andrew might laugh at her, but he kept his face straight. She was determined to be married and as soon as possible, so that neither her mother nor Andrew could change her plans.

"We'll need at least a week," her mother said finally in a faint voice. "We must send for Patrick and Thomas to come up from Virginia. You can't mean to be married without your brothers being here. And you haven't asked Cousin Lucy if she will agree to let you be married here."

Mrs. Marr beamed. It was a chance to shine again in her own house. "We'll start the wedding cake in the morning," she said.

"Well then," Reanna said happily, "it's all settled, isn't it?" She'd triumphed. She was going to marry Andrew MacClaren.

"This calls for a drink." Mr. Marr rose. "Would you gentlemen care to join me in the library?"

Andrew MacClaren followed, feeling as if he'd been roped, tied, branded and shipped to market.

*T*HE week was not long enough for all Mrs. Lovell considered the bare essentials of a proper wedding. There were lists to be made, shopping to be done and trunks to be packed. Reanna felt she lived in a constant cloud of tissue paper.

Her mother kept giving her housekeeping instructions: the family recipe for chowchow, a sure way to remove rust stains from lace, the care of tarnished silver. It didn't give Reanna much time to be with Andrew. Mr. Marr and her father had to be depended upon to keep him diverted.

The day before the wedding the boys arrived from Virginia, bursting into the Marrs' house like they'd been shot from a cannon. They were scrubbed, combed and dressed in their Sunday suits. Patrick, thirteen, was the elder; dark and serious, he was painfully eager always to say and do the correct thing. He felt it his duty to subdue his brother Thomas's high spirits.

Thomas, ten, was redheaded, irrepressible and unaware that there was anyone in the world but him. He was an open-natured child who'd always come to Reanna for help when he got into scrapes.

"We came all the way on the train!" Thomas shouted in glee.

"Don't shout, Thomas," Patrick corrected him, holding Thomas back from rushing at Reanna.

"How was your trip?" she asked.

"Very nice, thank you," Patrick answered. "At Lynchburg we got to go up into the cab of the engine and talk to the driver. It was very interesting."

"And I ate three ice creams," Thomas announced.

"Thomas was sick," Patrick said, frowning and looking very like his mother.

"Was not," Thomas argued.

"Was so," Patrick countered.

Thomas grinned. "Well, not very sick." He broke away from Patrick and came running to Reanna. "Where is he?" he asked.

"Where is who?"

"This man you're going to marry. Patrick says he's a cowboy. I say he's an Indian."

"He is an Indian."

"There," Thomas crowed. "I told you so, Patrick. Now pay up. We had a bet."

"He's an Indian and a cowboy, so you're both right," Reanna said.

"How can that be possible?" Patrick began to ponder the question.

THAT evening when Reanna introduced the boys to Andrew they bowed, then stood, trying not to stare.

"Do you have a gun?" Thomas asked.

"Of course he has a gun," Patrick stated. "He'd have to."

"But not with me," Andrew assured him.

"But you do have a gun, and a horse?"

Andrew nodded. "Yes, and a horse."

"When you were our age," Thomas said, standing on one foot and then the other, "how could you play cowboys and Indians if you were both?"

Andrew roared with laughter. "I never thought about that." Dinner went off well, the boys sitting close to Andrew, asking questions about the Indian Territory.

When Reanna went up to her room to get ready for bed, her mother came in looking uncomfortable and strained. "Reanna, I must have a talk with you. Oh dear, it's so difficult to know how to begin."

Reanna knew her mother had been trying all week to find a way to tell her about what Queen Victoria called "the dark side of marriage." Mrs. Lovell sat, twisting her handkerchief, then blurted out, "You remember poor Aunt Ida."

"Yes, I remember Aunt Ida." It was common family gossip that poor Aunt Ida had been so shocked by the unhappy carnal events of her wedding night that she had gone mad. It was Reanna's opinion that Aunt Ida had always been a little peculiar. Besides, Reanna already knew most of the facts of life. Growing up on a farm had been a great advantage.

"Well, no matter what you may have heard, Aunt Ida was highstrung. I mean to say, whatever happens, it is all just a part of being married." Mrs. Lovell sighed and her eyes darted away. "Oh, it's so difficult. I hope you understand what I'm saying, Reanna."

"Yes, Mama, thank you. You've done your best. Goodnight, Mama."

Her mother kissed Reanna on the forehead and tiptoed quietly out of the room.

On the wedding day Reanna was more curious than frightened. She wanted very much to be a married lady and go to the Indian Territory; she took it for granted that she wanted Andrew as well. But if, on the day she married him, Andrew had told her that he was going to stay in Washington and work in an office, she couldn't swear that she would have gone through with the ceremony.

Andrew and Reanna were married as planned in Cousin Lucy's parlor with just the family. Patrick and Thomas were her pages, wearing new velvet britches and high, starched collars. His collar made Thomas squirm. Cousin Lucy was her matron of honor.

Her mother cried and her father blew his nose repeatedly. Andrew put a wide gold band on her finger and kissed her for the third time. His lips, beneath that astonishing mustache, were warm and reassuring. They signed the parson's register, which stated that Reanna Alice Lovell was now the wife of Andrew Robert MacClaren.

She was going to eat and sleep with him. She was going to have children by him in some as yet unexplored manner. She was going, God willing, to grow old with him and be his until death did them part. And in return for swearing to obey him, she would now be able to go on a journey with him into an unknown country where she would be free to do as she pleased.

They drank champagne and ate a wedding breakfast of creamed chicken and mushrooms on toast points. There was asparagus and fresh hothouse fruit. There were hot, tiny, flaky rolls and a cake made with a dozen eggs and an icing of spun sugar with candied violets for decoration.

Suddenly, from the corner of her eye, Reanna saw Thomas carefully picking off every other candied violet from the wedding cake and popping them into his mouth. She tiptoed up behind him. "I see you, Thomas," she said.

He jumped and turned, looking frightened.

"Thomas, did you think if you took every other violet that no one would notice?"

Thomas grinned and swallowed. "You won't tell on me, will you, Ree?"

"No, I won't tell."

"Promise?"

"Promise." She bent down to hug him. "Oh Thomas, what am I going to do without you and Patrick? I'll hate leaving you."

Thomas's face puckered. "Leaving? Where are you going, Ree?"

"I married Mr. MacClaren. I'm going with him to the Indian Territory. You knew I was getting married."

"I knew that." His tears began coming fast. "But I didn't know you were going away."

"Oh Thomas, I love you." She wiped at his tears. "Wives have to live with their husbands. You and Patrick can come and visit me, and I'll write you both letters. And you can write to me. Now come on, Thomas, we're going to have our pictures taken."

Andrew wouldn't have his photograph taken. He was determined, no matter how much Cousin Lucy coaxed him, so Reanna had hers taken alone. She was wearing a traveling costume of snuff-brown twill which her mother had said would not show the dust. Her hat was happily more frivolous. It was an Italian straw trimmed with ribbon rosettes in a variety of bright colors. She stood straight and stiff, holding her bridal bouquet of lily of the valley close to her bosom, hoping her hands would not shake and spoil the picture.

When the photographer had finished, it was time to go. Reanna kissed her mother, who was still weeping, and hugged the boys. Then she kissed her father, who held her close and whispered so that only she could hear, "Be happy, Ree. And remember, it's not so bad to take a flyer on a long shot now and again."

Then Andrew came toward her, watch in hand, saying that if they didn't hurry they would miss their train. He was impatient, anxious to be off. He'd spent a whole week out of his life getting married, a thing he hadn't intended to happen.

ANDREW might not be generous with his time, but he made up for it by being lavish with his money. He'd taken a double compartment for their journey west. It made Reanna feel very rich and grand. Yet he seemed to feel it wasn't enough.

"Some day," he said, "we'll travel in our own private car." It surprised her that he should have such ambitions. She was also surprised by his taste for the exotic. There were bottles of French champagne and a hamper full of expensive food. There were even fresh flowers in the window vases.

"How thoughtful of you, Andrew, to think of all this."

"I didn't think of it." He looked sheepish. "I left the ordering to the manager of the hotel." Then he turned defensive. "That's what you pay them for, to know about such things. You can buy anything if you have the money."

They had their dinner in the dining car. She noticed that Andrew left the ordering to the waiter and, although he seemed pleased to be buying the most expensive dishes, he didn't eat them. She was more adventuresome and sampled a bit of everything from the oysters to the bombe meringue.

She would have enjoyed the feast more if her anxieties about the wedding night had already been resolved. Yet she managed the meal somehow, and when they could put it off no longer they walked back down the long corridor to their compartments. Andrew left her at the door, saying he thought he would go to the smoking car for a cigar while she prepared for bed.

It was an adventure in itself, unpacking and changing in that small space. As she got into the made-up berth, surely not wide enough for two, she heard Andrew let himself into the adjoining compartment. After what seemed a very long time, the door opened and she caught a glimpse of Andrew in a dressing gown just as he turned down the gas lamps. She wondered if the hotel manager had chosen the dressing gown as well as the food and the drink. It didn't seem in character that he would own such a garment.

Then he came toward the bunk, threw the dressing gown to one side and slipped in beside her. First there was some shifting to accommodate both of them in the narrow space. Next there was a kiss, which she didn't dislike. Andrew smelt of cigars and bay rum, a very manly combination. He had a hint of peppermint about his breath.

His hands explored her shoulders, breasts and back, and that too seemed pleasant enough, although she had expected him to remove her nightdress, as he was naked. As Andrew continued to caress her, she found herself responding to his touch. She felt a compelling warmth, a quickening of her senses. She drew closer to him and began to touch his body as he had hers. She was glad that his experience in these matters made up for her lack of it, but as she became more confident suddenly he stopped, almost as if her willingness had in some way displeased him. Abruptly, he lay over her, parted her legs with his hand and entered her.

She wished that he might have prepared her, given her some warning of his intentions. She would have been less tense. At first there was sharp discomfort, but that soon passed, and with a spasm and a great sigh Andrew lay still like a great, dead weight on top of her.

She didn't know what to do. She didn't want him to stay there all night. She tried but she couldn't budge him. She was afraid that if she pushed too hard it would wake him, and she didn't want that other business to begin all over again. Suddenly, in that narrow bunk, on a train moving west, with a sleeping bridegroom on top of her, she began to laugh. All she was able to think of was Aunt Ida. She knew she'd been right all along. Nothing had happened on Aunt Ida's wedding night that was so shocking it would drive any sane person mad. In fact, in time, this might become agreeable. She had liked the kissing and the fondling. If Andrew were patient she might like the rest, now that she knew what to expect.

Andrew, who must have heard her laughing, stirred himself and moved away from her. There was nowhere very much for him to go, so they lay like two spoons in a small drawer. Reanna lay awake a long time, listening to the click-clack of the wheels on the track, thinking of the future.

IN the morning when she awoke, she was surprised to see that Andrew was already up and dressed. He'd ordered some coffee; as she sipped it she asked, "Andrew?"
"Yes?"

(49)

"About last night."

He flushed, the stain spreading from his neck to his forehead, deeper than the windburn.

"I won't make too many demands on you," he said gruffly. "I won't trouble you often, and you needn't worry about having a child. I'll see to that."

She was amazed. Her mother's friends had whispered that having children was a woman's only joy in marriage, yet Andrew had found a way to prevent motherhood. She hadn't known there was any choice in the matter. Could she too prevent children, or only Andrew?

"But how," she asked, "can you prevent a baby?" Again he flushed, this time an even darker red.

"It's not a thing to talk about."

"It's something you do," she said, "but it's not something we talk about. Like what we did last night."

"Yes." He nodded. "Now get dressed."

But she had another question. "And these demands"—she used his words—"how will I know when you are going to make a demand upon me?"

For some reason her question made him angry. She saw him harden his jaw and clench his teeth to keep from giving her a sudden, overly sharp answer.

"I said that's enough, Reanna. Stop asking questions and get your clothes on." But no matter how it might provoke him, there was one more question she felt she had to ask.

"Andrew, do you love me?"

He seemed startled and offended that she would ask. "Why would you ask that? You're my wife." In his mind the matter seemed settled, but as she dressed Reanna considered the fact that he hadn't ever said he loved her.

They'd only been married a day, but already she'd learned that there were topics of conversation that Andrew put out of bounds. If she asked a question and he wanted to answer, he would; if not, she would only get a thundering silence. If she pressed him too hard, she could make him very angry. Andrew wasn't a man for having things brought out in the open.

It was not that they didn't talk on the journey, but it seemed to her that she did most of it. She told Andrew about the farm in Virginia where she had grown up and about all the games she and Patrick and Thomas had played and their secret hiding places.

(50)

"I hope you won't be homesick," he said, frowning.

"I won't," she promised. "But I've talked enough about me. Now it's your turn to tell me more about you and your folks." She felt him stiffen as his whole attitude changed.

"I told you about them in Washington. There's nothing more to tell. When they died, Miss Jane Beauvaise took me in and raised me. She's a fine lady. You'll like her."

"Will she like me?" Reanna asked.

"Of course." But he seemed awfully uneasy about it. Reanna wished he were more optimistic. She waited for him to say something more. In the end she had to entice him into revealing any more about himself.

Andrew had stopped thinking of his childhood and the past long ago. He had forgotten it, as one forgets pain. Now it seemed to him that he was held captive on this long journey west. Reanna would keep at him all the way until he told her more. He shrugged and sighed in resignation. He supposed there were some things about him that she ought to know before they got home. He began to talk—slowly, haltingly, his drawl more pronounced with every mile they rode toward the West.

"I didn't like my father. He was a man who used religion to make people obey him. He gave others to understand that God Almighty spoke only to him. He alone had the true vision. He made my mother's life a living hell. He preached at her day and night. His text was that she never did anything right. He was a jealous, vengeful man. He begrudged any time she spent away from him. He was even jealous of me."

"Did you love your mother?" Reanna asked. This was a view of Andrew she hadn't expected. She couldn't from her own experience imagine such a childhood.

"Oh yes." Andrew's face softened. "And she loved me. Sometimes in the spring, when he was away, we took a picnic up onto the Beauvaise Ridge. She drew the wildflowers and painted them in watercolors. But even then on those fine days without a cloud in the sky, she was nervous, fearful always, watching for a storm to come. When the wind rose I could see her begin to tremble. The wind was a torment to her, a demon. She lived in terror of a twister."

"Twister?"

"Cyclone. We get them sometimes. They're bad medicine." Reanna could begin to see why he had been so afraid for her. She wanted to reassure him but she was too engrossed in his story to want him to stop. She had never expected him to be capable of talking at such length.

"But if she was so afraid," Reanna couldn't help asking, "and if the life was so hard for your mother, why didn't she leave?"

Andrew looked at Reanna with disbelief. It amazed him that she could find life's problems so simple to solve. She'd had life too easy, that was what it was. "Where would she have gone? My father wouldn't willingly let her leave the house, let alone the countryside. He said she must learn to control her fear, that for her soul's sake she must endure the terror. I think he got his pleasure out of watching her suffer. I think he liked to see her in pain. She had only to tell him what she wanted for him to deny it to her. It was the same for me. I learned early on never to tell him what I had my heart set on."

Andrew paused, his hands smoothing at his trousers as if he could erase the memory of the past like an inconvenient crease. "Once, for my birthday, he took me to town, to the store. He asked me to choose a present. He knew before we went what it was that I wanted. It was a pocketknife. It was there in the case just behind the glass. It had a bone handle and two blades and an awl. He said all I had to do was tell him what I wanted and he would give it to me. 'The knife,' I said, and I reached out my hand for it. But then I saw him smile. It was a smile of pure, mean pleasure.

" 'You expect me to give you the knife?' he asked me.

" 'Yes,' I said. He stood there shaking his head and smiling.

" 'I would if you'd been a good boy, if you'd obeyed me. But when you're willful and disobedient I won't give you presents.' I wasn't wise then. I hadn't learned my lesson. I was angry and I shouted at him. I said he'd promised and then broken his word. It was then that he thrashed me. I could see it was what he'd meant to do all along. I never made the mistake of telling him anything again."

"But that was cruel." Reanna still had difficulty believing in such a father. Her own had always been so loving and kind. "It was cruel of him to ask and then deny you what he'd promised."

"He was a cruel man," Andrew said quietly.

"Did you ever get the knife?" Reanna asked. In her experience there always had to be a happy ending.

"No." Andrew's smile was grim. "Not that knife. Later I got another one twice as good." He took a knife from his pocket and held it out for her to see. Its handle was dark as ebony, worn smooth with use. "I got it on a trade."

"How old were you when your parents died?" Reanna asked. She wanted to know his whole life, good and bad.

He shifted uneasily. "Eleven. They both came down with summer fever. My mother had been so hard worked that she had no resistance or will to fight it. He was too mean with his money to send for the doctor. When a neighbor finally did, the doctor arrived too late to do any good. When she was gone I walked her to the graveyard and cried my heart out. I didn't care who saw me. It was the last time I cried over anything. When my father took the fever he cursed her because she'd got away from him and gone to heaven to tell her side of the story first. When I walked him to the graveyard I never shed a tear."

"What happened then? Who took care of you?"

"I had no relatives that wanted me, so out of charity the church had to keep me. They were going to send me to an orphanage. I was all packed and ready to go when Miss Jane Beauvaise came to get me and took me home to live with her at Lochleven."

"I can't understand how they just gave you to an Indian woman."

"They were happy to see me go. Miss Jane is somebody come out there. She's of the royal clan, a princess of the Chickasaw Nation. She had a big say in the running of the school. Besides, she didn't just come and take me, she asked me if I wanted to go with her, if I would consent to be her son. She gave me the choice. It was a big opportunity."

"But why did she come for you?" Reanna was sure Andrew had been a winning little boy, but there must have been more to it than that. "Had you known her before?"

"No. Oh, I knew who she was, everybody did. Miss Jane said she came for me because my mother had been kind to her. Miss Jane is a woman who never forgets a kindness. Indians are particular that way. They never forget a kindness or a wrong. Anyway, that was how I came to live with Miss Jane. We drove up to her house on Beauvaise Ridge. It's a place called Lochleven. She let me hold the reins all the way. I was proud to go with her. I liked it when all the school watched me drive away. I know she took me because she liked my mother, but I also figured she took me because she wanted a son who could talk both white and Indian and was quick at sums. Even these days a lot of Indians would rather get someone white to transact their business for them than do it themselves."

"Did she live alone? Were there just the two of you?"

"No." Andrew looked surprised at Reanna's question. It had seemed perfectly reasonable to her. "Her husband had been killed and she worked the place with Cima, a freed nigger woman, and a few old hands. She already had two children, both younger than me. There was a boy named Pride, after her husband, and Letty, her daughter. Because I was the oldest she trusted me and gave me responsibility. She told me what to do and I went right ahead and did it. Together we built up the place. It had gotten pretty run down after her husband died. She made me her man of business and when I was sixteen she sent me off to Texas to get some cattle and make a deal with Colonel Goodwell, who wanted to lease grazing land from us."

"What about her children? How did you get on with them?"

"Pride, he's like my little blood brother. He's partial to me, always used to follow me everywhere. He's a good-looking boy, I'll say that for him. Now he's grown up he's smarter than me in some ways." His lips curled in a wry, humorless grin. "It seems like everything comes easy to him. Things I had to learn the hard way he was born knowing. Everybody likes Pride, seems like. He can whittle and make anything you name him out of wood or deer bone.

"He's better at tracking and hunting than any man I ever met. He can follow the trail of anything on four feet or two and he knows all there is to know about pasture grass. He's fair to middlin' at horsebreaking, too." Andrew's eyes glinted like gemstones. "But I can still take him in a fight, and I can trade him out of anything he's got. That knife I showed you—it was the first thing we ever dickered for, and I got it."

"What about Miss Jane's daughter?" Reanna asked. "How old is she?"

Andrew turned toward Reanna and looked at her sharply, as if she had deliberately set out to provoke him. It was as if she had suddenly trespassed on private, forbidden ground.

"She's dead. It was Letty I married. Letty was the mother of my little girl, Snow." Reanna felt as though the wind had been knocked out of her. Once she'd fallen from her horse and it had been like this. She hadn't known that his wife had been Miss Jane's daughter, but if she'd been quicker or more clever she might have guessed.

"I thought I told you that," Andrew said in an accusing tone.

"No, you didn't." Reanna's lips felt stiff and her words sounded unnatural. "What was she like? Was she pretty?" It was not what she'd meant to say.

"Pretty enough, I guess." Andrew looked away. "I'd grown up with her. Letty had always been there."

"And then you fell in love with her?" That was not what Reanna had meant to say either. She felt clumsy and stupid.

"I'm not going to talk about Letty," he said sharply, his voice high and hard. "She's dead and that's an end to it. Indians don't believe in talking about the dead. They think it keeps them from their journey west, to the place under the sky."

Reanna felt a door had been slammed shut in her face. She said quietly, "How will Miss Jane feel about your bringing back another wife?"

He looked very uncomfortable. "It may take her time to get used to the idea, but whatever I do has always suited her. It will be all right when we get home, you'll see."

"You mean we're going to live at Lochleven?" Reanna had not considered that possibility.

"Yes. It's a big house, Reanna. There's plenty of room."

"But—I thought we'd have our own home." She tried to hide her disappointment.

"Lochleven *is* my home. We all live there, all the family. Miss Jane, Pride, Snow, Cima and now you."

"But later we'll have a house of our own?"

"You're my wife, Reanna." His eyes narrowed again. "You'll live where I do." It was a closed subject. Any more questions might make matters worse. But it was something for her to think about. She looked out the window at the changes in the countryside as they went from east to west.

Already they had passed through several different regions. Never in her wildest imagination had she been able to foresee how big this country was or how far away from home she was going. Crossing Tennessee alone was a journey in itself, and as they went on across the Mississippi suddenly there was a dramatic difference. Before there had been nothing but dense, rolling hills; now the land, though still hilly, was abruptly diminished. The grass was of a different variety and every crag and rock seemed somehow misshapen.

"Is this the way it will look in the Territory?" she asked. "How far is it now? When will we get there?"

"That's a hundred questions you've asked today, Reanna," Andrew said. "It's worse than traveling with a child. No, it's nothing like the Territory. The Indian Territory is not something you can rightly describe. It's a dream as much as it is a place."

"I don't understand."

"It's hard to put into words. It's a last chance for settlers to get cheap land. It's a last dancing for the Indians. The Indians know it's all over but they don't want to face up to it. There will be statehood soon."

"But won't statehood benefit the Indians?"

Andrew gave a hard, short laugh. "Nothing the white man ever did was for the benefit of the Indians."

"But what will happen to you, to us? You aren't a settler, and you aren't really an Indian."

"I'll make out." He patted her hand. "Someday I'll swim in cream."

SHE didn't ask him any more, but at Fort Smith, as they crossed the Arkansas, she kept her eyes open. After a few hours she was rewarded with the sight of her first Indians. Some were on painted ponies and others were walking. They almost seemed caught in the middle of nowhere on an invisible road toward the horizon.

"Where are they going?"

"To town."

"But there isn't one."

"Maitland, over the next rise. You'll see it soon. They're Choctaw going in for a little tobacco and some whiskey if they can find it. We're going to Maitland, too. It's where our part of the railroad ends."

"How can you tell one Indian tribe from another?"

"Clothes, language, customs; there are about forty tribes in this part of the world, all of them as different as night and day."

As soon as the train pulled into the station, Andrew could not wait to get off and head for home. He had telegraphed the livery stable for a wagon to be waiting to haul their goods but there wasn't any wagon. The station was deserted save for the telegrapher.

Reanna hurried after him as he strode through empty back streets toward the livery stable. A dog, bony and half-starved, slunk across their path, tail between his legs.

There was no one in the livery stable except for a man who had gone to sleep in the hay. He was, by the look of him, at least part

Indian. Andrew pulled him up and shook him until he opened his eyes and then, as he recognized Andrew, he smiled a foolish, drunken smile.

"Mornin', Mr. MacClaren." The greeting had used up all his conscious energies and he closed his eyes again. The man stank of liquor; it was an old, stale, sour smell, as if he hadn't bothered to bathe or change clothes in a long winter past.

"Where is everybody?" Andrew shook him again. "Where's the wagon I ordered, Mitcher? Speak up, or I'll cut your gizzard out!"

Once more the man's eyes opened, fear concentrating the sodden mind. "All gone to the hangin'." He sank back to the hay.

Andrew, angry and disgusted, took Reanna by the elbow and began marching her quickly back down the streets toward the center of town. She could hear a faint singing, and the hum and buzz of a crowd. When they turned onto the end of the main street there was a single tree. Over a branch was a rope and a young man scarcely more than a boy astride a pony with his hands tied behind his back. The boy's head was being put into a thickly knotted noose. Reanna heard herself gasp.

"What are they doing?" She knew without asking, but she hoped there was some other possible explanation.

"They're going to hang him."

"Why?"

Andrew spoke to a man standing next to him. The man answered him in Indian.

"The boy's brother was killed in a fight and he killed his brother's murderer. It's the Indian way. They'll walk a thousand miles to even a score."

"An eye for an eye, a tooth for a tooth," Reanna said.

"That's one way of looking at it. He thinks he'd lose his honor if he didn't revenge his brother's death."

"But where does it all end, this killing and hanging?"

"It doesn't end until the score is even. Sometimes there's no one left alive in a family."

The crowd grew silent; a dead hush fell as the boy's executioner stepped forward.

"I don't want to stay here," Reanna whispered. She felt faint, so weak she was not sure her legs would hold her.

"We can't go until the hanging's over. The man in charge there is Wood Penny. He's also the owner of the livery stable."

Reanna glanced up at Andrew. What he'd said was doubtless

true, but it was only an excuse. His eyes hadn't left the boy on the pony. He wanted to stay to see the hanging, that was his real reason. Wasn't it? She felt a wave of disgust. She turned to walk away, but he caught her arm and held her.

"Don't make a fuss, Reanna. It will be over soon." His eyes had that hard, bright glint again. "You don't want to miss your first sight of the Wild West, do you? This is what you came to see. Take a good look and tell me if it's romantic enough for you."

Angry, she forced herself to look, to see the horse whipped from under the boy. She heard the thin, small sound his neck made as it broke, saw the stain on his trousers as he lost life and control of himself. She felt sick, ashamed of herself and of Andrew.

"Well," Andrew said, as the crowd broke into talk and flowed about them, "now the show's over we can all go home."

"Is your town like Maitland?"

"MacClaren City?" Andrew laughed. "No, this place is all romp and stomp. MacClaren City is as peaceful as a tub of angels." But Reanna was not reassured about what the future might hold.

She was even less reassured when she saw Andrew buckle on his gun belt before he helped her up into the loaded wagon that they would drive to MacClaren City. Nor did it comfort her to see his Winchester in its sheath lying just beneath the wagon seat. "I didn't expect you'd wear a gun every day."

He glanced at her in surprise. "Well, you never know when you'll need it, that's the thing. Don't take it so hard, Reanna," he added, not unkindly, as they drove up the dusty street. "It's always good to leave Maitland."

"He was only a boy." Reanna kept seeing that slender, graceful body hanging limp and lifeless, swaying and turning.

"Well," Andrew said, "look at it this way. It didn't hurt the tree none." Reanna was shocked. She turned to him to give him a sharp answer but he broke in on her. "It's a joke, Reanna. For God's sake, can't you take a joke?"

She said nothing.

"Open your parasol," he said gruffly. He must have seen how angry and bewildered she was. "This wind can burn and blister you before you know it."

They rode awhile in silence. Her eyes were not big enough for all she had to see. She wanted to take in every twig and blade of grass. There was no road but a double wagon-wheel track that led out into open, rolling prairie. There had been no rain for some time and the ruts were hard and almost axle deep. She was not prepared for the jerking and rolling of the wagon. Sometimes she had to hang on to the seat with both hands. Andrew didn't slow the pace because of it. He was eager to get to MacClaren City by nightfall.

"There's nothing better than a pair of mules," he said, "not for making time. They can set out smart and go this pace all day." The pair of mouse-gray mules kept their even step.

"You need rain," Reanna said, to keep the conversation going.

"We've needed it for a couple of years." Andrew's eyes began to scan the sky as if he hoped to see rain clouds suddenly appear. She couldn't imagine what it must be like when the rains did come. The earth showed red beneath the patches of grass. This whole plateau could turn into a lake of tomato puree–colored mud.

"How far now to MacClaren City?" She had waited as long as she could to ask. Andrew smiled indulgently, happier with her and himself now he was closer to home.

"We've come more than halfway," he said. "We'll be there before dark."

"You must be honored to have a town named after you."

Andrew laughed. "It was no honor," he said, "it just happened. Besides, it's hardly a metropolis."

JUST before dusk they came over a rise and there before them was the tiny town. She saw why he'd laughed. MacClaren City was one street and a few small buildings crudely put together out of raw lumber. There were some stores, a smithy and not much else. What there was had Andrew's name on it: MacClaren Hardware, MacClaren and Levy Dry Goods, The MacClaren Livery and Blacksmithing. There was no school and no church, but one was being built. Its steeple was a small box made of pine clapboard.

"It's just a trading town," Andrew said. He'd read her thoughts. "Miss Jane and I agreed we needed one here so we wouldn't have to travel two days just to get a sack of beans. But soon the railroad will come, and then you'll see some real growth."

"I like it now," Reanna said. Andrew looked at her closely.

"I wonder what you'll say a year from now?"

"I'll still like it," she protested, but Andrew had already turned his attention from her to his business.

"I've got a lot to attend to," Andrew said. "I want to find out what's been going on. I'll start with Jack Levy. I guess you'll have to come with me. I don't know what else to do with you." It wasn't a very warm or enthusiastic invitation.

As Reanna trotted along behind Andrew, trying to keep up, she said, "Is Mr. Levy a Jew?" She wanted to know as much as possible about Andrew's friends and his business.

"I don't know. I never asked him." Andrew stopped abruptly and turned on her. "Look here, Reanna, when you're out here it's best not to go around asking a lot of questions. Everyone here came from somewhere but most of them had damn good reasons for leaving where they'd been. It's not polite or wise to inquire into what those reasons might be. Especially don't go asking a lot of damn fool questions about family and kinfolk. I know that where you were brought up it's topic A, but here it's safer to stick to the weather." She felt hurt and harshly used. She had only meant to try to fit in, to be a part of his world.

Seeing he'd perhaps gone too far and been too rough on her, Andrew said, "If you want to know something, wait until we're alone and ask me, all right?"

She'd thought they were alone. She wished they were already at Lochleven. She'd come so far and now she must be patient a little longer.

Mr. Levy was delighted to see her—Andrew had wired ahead from Washington with their good news. He was young and slightly built, with large, brown eyes. There was a soft shyness in his manner but a twinkle in his eye.

"You're without any doubt the best thing Andrew ever brought back from Washington. Would you like some tea?" He brought it in a glass. It had been made in a large samovar. She had never seen one before and it enchanted her.

While the men talked business in the back of the store where Mr. Levy lived, Reanna was free to wander among the merchandise. Once more she was irritated at always being excluded from men's conversations, but at least this time she was able to overhear what they were saying.

It seemed that the weather was not a very safe topic of conversation after all. Jack Levy said there had been no rain to speak of since Andrew left. The dry grass put the whole prairie in danger of fire. To the north, in the Oklahoma Territory, the homesteaders had plowed under the grassland to plant wheat, and now for the second year in a row there was no crop. The soil, without the grass to act as anchor, had begun to blow and shift.

(60)

The government still hadn't paid the annual annuity money owed the Chickasaw for their land in Mississippi that they'd sold to the government before the remove. Everyone was hard up for cash. Their oldest customers were asking for extension of credit, and now the wholesalers were wanting their money. The country was heading into another panic and there seemed no way to stop the stampede.

Reanna watched the two men. They were easy together, obviously old friends and partners. She hoped that sometime in the future Andrew would have confidence enough to confide his business to her. She wanted to be his wife and his partner in whatever he did.

She liked the store. It was small and stocked with yards of dress stuff in sprigged calico. There were stout, sturdy shoes for men, women and children. They looked as if none would really make a comfortable fit. There was a variety of sewing supplies—needles, thread in all colors, scissors and packets of pins. There were buttons, ribbons, elastic and ladies' stays.

Reanna smiled. She'd always hated lacing. The first day on the train, her first act as a free, married woman had been to throw her corset out of the train window. She hadn't told Andrew—somehow she didn't think he would approve—but she would never be trussed up and breathless again.

"Here, what are we thinking of, Andrew?" Mr. Levy rose, one of his cats falling from his comfortable lap with a cry of outrage. "Doc and Amoretta Hersey are expecting us for dinner. They're planning to put you up for the night. She'll skin me alive; I was supposed to bring you over the minute you got here. She can't wait to get a look at the bride."

Reanna looked questioningly at Andrew. She'd do whatever he said they must, but she didn't like to stay with people she'd never met.

"Won't it be an imposition?" she asked. "We could stay at a rooming house or eat at a cafe." Both men laughed as if she had just made a huge joke.

"MacClaren City has a lot of things to offer," Andrew said, "but a cafe and a rooming house are not among them. No, Jack's right, we ought to get over there. Amoretta is the first lady of MacClaren City, or was till you came. Your arrival is the social event of the year. If I know Amoretta she's been cooking for a week."

They closed the store, and as they walked down the dirt street the wind blew the dust about in tiny, playful storms and spirals. Even before they got to the Herseys', Reanna could smell the fragrance of baking meats and pies. It was a tidy, two-room frame house with an ample shed and outbuildings. In MacClaren City, Reanna thought, it must be considered a residential showplace.

"Have you warned Reanna about the Doc?" Jack Levy asked, grinning.

"First of all"—Andrew made a face—"he's from Massachusetts."

"I guess you heard the expression, 'A Yankee is a northerner who comes out here. A damn Yankee is a northerner who stays.' Doc went to Harvard College." Jack drew out the word Harvard so that it seemed to have more letters than were necessary.

"Why did he come here?" Reanna asked.

"There she goes again, asking questions." Andrew spoke to the air. "You'll find out, Jack, she can ask more questions than a hen's got feathers." It was said as another joke, but Reanna promised herself not to give him a chance to hold her up to ridicule again before his friends.

"Doc came because he wanted to and because we needed a doctor," Andrew said. "You can judge Amoretta for yourself."

Andrew was impatient, but Jack Levy was more considerate of her feelings. "Doc claims he came out here for his health. He says he had T.B., but I expect he's made that up just to copycat Doc Holliday. Doc Hersey is plum crazy about anything he thinks is real old Wild West. Anyway, he's healthy as a horse, and I expect he'll outlive all of us if he doesn't drink himself to death. He's always telling tales. He claims Amoretta was a tent girl working the railroad when everyone knows she and her sister were telegraphers. He only says it because he knows he can get a rise out of her every time."

Reanna would have liked to ask what a tent girl was, but she was afraid she knew the answer and that it would draw another reprimand from Andrew. With a cry of excitement, Amoretta Hersey came out on the porch to meet them. She was as round and short as the doctor was tall and lean. She had two apple cheeks that glowed with the warmth of the cookstove and the anticipation of another woman's company. When she drew back to look at Reanna there were tears welling up in her eyes.

"I'm sorry, honey, but it's so grand to see Andrew's new bride and know you're going to be a neighbor." She shook her head. "My, my, aren't you a pretty thing. And what red hair." She turned and pointed out her husband, as if without the gesture he might be invisible.

"This here's Doc, my husband." She was proud of him, Reanna could see that, but he seemed to take all his wife's adulation as if it were his due and Amoretta had come with the house merely for his convenience.

"Mrs. MacClaren." He made a low, courtly bow. She saw Jack Levy had been accurate. The doctor was not entirely sober. "*Enchanté*, and welcome to my humble abode. Please do sit down. You gentlemen will doubtless join me in a dram?"

Inside the crowded kitchen, the table, set for five, was laid with an odd assortment of glass, cutlery and china. The table almost filled the room. On the far wall was a large, iron, woodburning stove covered with bubbling pots. Set out on a makeshift counter beside it was a display of baked goods.

Amoretta rubbed her hard-worked red hands on her apron and said, "Well, if I know *them*," pointing at the men, "they're going to drink a spell, so we might as well go into the polite part of the house."

Reanna followed her out onto the porch and to the other outside door, which Amoretta held open for her. As Reanna entered the second room Amoretta raised up her lamp as if to reveal a great work of art.

In the center was a double brass bedstead piled high with feather mattresses and covered with a snow white, handwoven coverlet. Against the walls were a sofa and two matching chairs covered in red velvet. On the floor was a rag carpet and on every wall there were shelves filled with bric-a-brac, gilt jars stuffed with gilded cattails, pretty speckled stones and brightly colored bottles. For wallpaper Amoretta had chosen illustrations cut from ladies' magazines. Some she had hand colored. The room was clearly set aside for special occasions. Reanna knew she must say something appropriate.

"I've never seen anything like it," she ventured.

"I have to dust every day," Amoretta said proudly, as a mother might speak of some small failing in an otherwise perfect child. "You'll find you have to dust a lot out here. The wind."

"It's very kind of you to take us in like this," Reanna said, "but I don't like to think we're putting you and the doctor out."

"Oh, we don't sleep here!" Amoretta said, horrified. "We sleep in the shed, always have done. The Doc won't sleep in the warm. Says it's bad for his lungs."

"Don't you get cold?" Reanna could not help asking.

"You bet I do, but the Doc got me an old buffalo robe last winter and that helps. He's real thoughtful, lets me have anything I want." She glanced lovingly at the room. "So I humor him other ways." She went crimson. "But you're a married lady and you understand," she whispered. "You'll take it kindly, I hope, but if you have a good man you want to humor him. Andrew is one of the best. We wouldn't be here if it weren't for him. Before Andrew got those two into this town, Doc was drunk more often than not and Jack Levy was just a peddler going up and down with some cut-rate stock in a broken-down wagon. I guess everybody in the place could tell you a story like that about Andrew. He got us a post office. Jack Levy is postmaster. The mail wagon comes right to the store. You'll see, pretty soon he'll get the railroad here and then, look out. Mac-Claren City will *really* be on the map! I truly believe Andrew MacClaren could be President of the United States if he put his mind to it."

"I hope Andrew won't aim as high as Washington," Reanna said.

"Well then, mayor for sure—and governor if he takes a fancy to the job." Amoretta grinned. "I guess you can see how we admire Andrew."

"It's nice of you to say," Reanna answered.

Perhaps Amoretta Hersey was not the woman her mother would have chosen to be her first new friend, but no one could have been more warm and welcoming. When everything in the astonishing room had been looked at, admired and returned to its place, they went back into the steaming kitchen. The gentlemen had by then had their dram and several more besides.

"Your bride is very peaked," Doc said after giving Reanna a considered appraisal. "But fear not, Amoretta will put some meat on her bones."

Reanna started to say that Amoretta hadn't had much luck in fattening *him* up, but she held her tongue. It was not so much that she took offense at the doctor's remark but that he had spoken as if she were one of Amoretta's objects, inanimate and incapable of speech. It was the first time she'd been spoken about, not spoken *to*. It seemed that out here men considered women were to be seen and not heard.

After a short grace given by Doctor Hersey, standing unsteadily at the head of the table, Amoretta began to serve up from the stove. Reanna had never seen so much food, not even when there had been threshers to dinner on the farm. There were chicken and dumplings, beans and ham, two kinds of potatoes and poke salad—the first of the year, Amoretta said. There were biscuits and corn bread and, to ease any possible pangs of hunger, there were mounds of fresh-churned butter and jellies and jams. When all that was cleared away and they sat stuffed, unable to eat any more, an apple cobbler appeared with a pitcher of thick cream to pour over it and a pot of hot, steaming coffee.

"It was a delicious dinner," Reanna said, and Andrew grunted in agreement.

"Amoretta is the premiere chef in the Territory," the Doctor declared, and his wife blushed as little rivulets of perspiration streaked the rouge on her cheeks.

"When there's company I do tend to overdo."

"Let me help you with the dishes," Reanna offered.

"I wouldn't hear of it. You've come a long way today and you must be tired. There's a washstand on the porch. I'll get you a kettle of hot water. The privy's out back where it belongs. Now you act like company and go on off to bed."

Reanna said goodnight to them all gratefully and gave an especially warm word to Jack Levy. He hadn't said much at dinner, but she knew she could count on him, as she was sure of Amoretta as a loyal friend.

She was so tired that when Andrew finally came to bed she only vaguely remembered holding him as they sank into the center of the mattress and stayed there till morning in a valley of feathers.

JUST as they finished breakfast, Doc came in looking gray and drawn. It had been one of his usual night calls—a knife wound to be sewn up, a bullet to be removed, a baby who had decided to be born before it was due. He sat silent and bleary-eyed. He held one trembling hand out before him and regarded it distantly. "I'm infinitely steadier when I drink," he observed. "They say whiskey and medicine don't mix, but I haven't killed any of my patients yet." He grinned. "At least none that I know of."

Standing on the porch waiting for Jack and Andrew to hitch up the buggy, Reanna and Amoretta embraced each other. "Remember," Amoretta said, "if you need a white woman to talk to I'm always here." Reanna drew back and looked at Amoretta sharply.

"Oh, don't misunderstand me," Amoretta hastened to say, "Miss

Jane is a fine woman, none better, but it's not the same for them. They don't feel the heat and the wind—not like we do."

Andrew, impatient to be off, helped Reanna up into the buggy. A wagon with their trunks and supplies would be sent out after them.

As they left the town's one street, the road was no more than a narrow track hidden in the high grass; like the sea it opened before them and closed in their wake. The grass made a soft, stirring sound, whispering secrets to the earth below. Reanna felt a sense of exhilaration. This was what she'd come for. This was what she'd wanted, this wide open place where they were alone beneath the sky. "How far is it now, Andrew?"

"We're better than halfway there." They drove in a steady, gentle climb up the eastern slope of Beauvaise Ridge. When they came to the high ground at the top Andrew pulled up so Reanna could see the view.

"This is the eastern end of Beauvaise Ridge. Behind us to the southeast is MacClaren City and to the northwest across our western range our nearest neighbor is another ten miles away. We run cattle on all the grass you can see."

As her eyes scanned the whole long ridge and the plains on either side, she felt suffused with a wild joy. It was far more beautiful than she'd dreamed it would be. Everything she saw delighted her heart and pleased her eye.

From where she sat she could see the untamed, untouched prairie rolling out to the far rim of the horizon. Here and there a line of trees—elm, sycamore, scrub oak and cottonwood—marked the course of clear, running creeks. Everywhere there were unexpected thickets of Chickasaw plum and tangles of wild grapevines. The bois d'arc trees with their strange, inedible fruit went uncut, for there was no need of fencing to mark the boundaries. Far off in the hidden folds of the rich land, half masked by the tall bluestem grass, cattle grazed and fattened.

"Are those your cattle?" she asked.

"Yes. That's just a few hundred head of home stock. Soon the grass will be high. I'll have to hurry to get the Texas herd up and onto it. When the Texas herd gets here, you'll know it."

She turned back to look at the display of bright, vivid flashes of color as the waving grass revealed the red of Indian paintbrush, the pastel pink and white of mallow, the delicate purple vetch and the yellow sage. Overhead in the wide sky, a single hawk with fringed

(66)

wings circled in solitary splendor, overlord of all creation. This was their private, impregnable universe, Andrew's and hers; nothing could ever happen to alter their happiness or harm them here.

Suddenly, as if to foreshadow its true power, a gust of wind blew the hat from Reanna's head and sent it skimming like a straw pebble over the sea of grass. Andrew jumped down from the buggy and ran after it as if it were a golden prize.

Reanna laughed as she watched Andrew doing the wind's bidding. She laughed out loud, loosed her hair from its pins and let it blow in the wind.

When Andrew came back with her hat in his hand he was frowning, his jaw clenched tight. He was angrier than she'd ever seen him.

"What's the matter, dearest?"

"Nothing. Take your hat and hold on to it."

She didn't know why he was so displeased. Andrew often bewildered her with his change of moods. Perhaps he felt he had lost dignity running after a lady's hat; or had he felt she'd been laughing at him? As they drove away he flicked his whip sharply against the mules' rumps.

Reanna sat, not looking at him, but straight ahead so he couldn't see the tears start up in her eyes. It would be easier to possess the wind than Andrew. Sometimes Andrew could be a very hard man.

MISS Jane Beauvaise stood on the wide verandah of Lochleven waiting for Andrew and the strange woman to arrive. One hand shielded her eyes, scanning the Ridge for a glimpse of them.

She was an imposing figure, not tall but arrow straight; she was dressed in a long, loose, calico gown with a ruffled yoke. Her hair, once black as the raven's wing, was touched with gray and coiled like a crown on top of her head in a braided coronet twined with bright ribbons. When she was young she had been a great beauty. Now that she was old, that beauty remained in the grace of her walk, the set of her head and the music of her voice.

Her house, Lochleven, set inside a fenced, mowed field, was a two-storied, double-galleried, white clapboard. The verandahs ran on three sides of the house, with the right wing curved like the bow of a river steamer. Upstairs was a cupola room; from its projecting bay windows she could command a clear view of the grass ranges east and west of the Ridge. This was her castle, her fortress. She ruled here with a soft hand and an iron will.

Below her on the steps, Cima stood like a tall black sentinel, ready to ward off any danger. Cima had been with Miss Jane since they were both children. Cima had been the daughter of a slave, but Miss Jane had given Cima her freedom before it became the law of the tribe or the government in Washington. Cima was Miss Jane's friend, her companion, her right hand and now her eyes. It had been Cima who had seen Andrew at the far end of the plateau and had ridden back with the news.

"You're sure you saw them?" Miss Jane asked.

"Yes, Andrew was running in the grass and she was sitting there in the buggy laughing."

"Laughing?"

"Yes. Her hair was blowing wild in the wind."

"But they didn't see you?"

Cima smiled, a smile of grim satisfaction. Her face was a darker, weathered mirror of her mistress's. "Nobody sees me if I don't want them to."

"Andrew sees more than you think he does."

"Andrew sees what he wants to see."

Miss Jane stood immovable. She betrayed no trace of her emotions. In recent years, since her eyesight had begun to fail her, she had developed a new awareness of the world around her, but she needed no second sight to tell her that the woman Andrew was bringing home was his wife. Andrew was young; it was natural he would marry again. She must accept the change and the fact that a man could love more than once.

It had not been so for her. She had loved only her cousin Pride Beauvaise, the legend, the glory, the leader of his people. Even before she had seen him, Pride Beauvaise had been as much a part of her heart and spirit as the stories of the tribe her grandmother, Sara, had told her when she was a child.

Miss Jane had been born in Mississippi near Ponti-atoc, the place of the waving cattails, twenty years after the great remove of the Chickasaw from their old Nation to the new one in the west. She had lived at the old Lochleven with her grandmother, Sara, the daughter of the great warrior, Duncan. Miss Jane's father was dead, her mother gone off with a white man who did not want the child of another man. She had been left in her grandmother's care, but she had never felt unloved or unwanted. She had had Cima's mother, Kera, for a body slave and Cima for her playmate.

Jane and Kera and Cima lived apart from the rest of the household. She seldom saw her grandmother Sara's second husband, old man Lytton, or his two grown white sons, Robert and Harry. She could not remember how old she had been when she realized that Lochleven was no longer her grandmother's house.

Before the tribe had gone west, they had been declared noncitizens in their own Nation and forced to sell all their land to the government and to white settlers. To stay on in Mississippi when the others left, grandmother Sara had married old man Lytton and deeded him her house and a thousand acres. He had promised her protection under the law and the right to live under her own roof for her lifetime, but when he died the property would go to his sons, Harry and Robert, with no portion for any of Sara's blood.

It was strange to live as they did, divided from each other, but Miss Jane had accepted the fact, as a child will. For her, Lochleven was the only home she had ever known. From her nursery she could hear old man Lytton roaring out his orders and from her window she could see his sons, Robert and Harry, riding out to oversee their cotton plantation.

And on long afternoons when Cima and Kera were resting and thought her asleep, Miss Jane would steal away to find her grandmother Sara sitting in her cupola room in an old cane-bottomed rocking chair, staring out over the long, rolling ridge that had once been an open sea of waving grasses, a plateau over which Chickasaw warriors had had time to see their enemies approaching and prepare for battle. Quietly, like a shadow, Miss Jane would slip along the halls, tiptoe up to that room and climb up into her grandmother's lap to lean her head against the old woman's bosom. She could feel her grandmother's arms hold her close and Jane would say, "Tell me the story of our people. Tell it all from the beginning."

"From the beginning?" Sara would pretend surprise. "You can't want to hear it all, for it is a long story."

But Jane knew it was only her grandmother's way of teasing. "Yes, Grandmother, please. From the beginning and don't leave anything out."

"Well then," and her grandmother would begin to set the old rocker in motion, lulling Jane, transporting her to a place far away and a time long past. "Well then, in the beginning our people came from far far in the west. They came from under the sky, across a bridge of land that spanned the ocean. And when they had come they settled in the west in a land of their own choosing. It was a fine, rich place and they lived there many years until they were set upon by powerful enemies. Then the two chiefs of the people, Chikasah and Chahtah, sat with the council and decided it was time for the people to move on. The two wise chiefs were brothers—Chikasah the taller, fairer brother and Chahtah the shorter, darker brother.

"On the appointed day all the people came to the meeting place with their families and their belongings. They were told that, though they must leave their land, they must not be afraid, for they had the Fa-bus-sah, the sacred pole, to guide them and Panti, the fierce war dog, to defend them. And in the morning the two chiefs agreed that the Fa-bus-sah was leaning toward the east, so they set out toward the rising sun.

"As they moved, each night when they made camp they set the Fa-bus-sah in the center of the camp and in the morning they moved in the direction it was leaning—always toward the east. And no enemy touched them, for Panti, the fierce war dog, saw to that.

"For a long time they wandered out of the west toward the east until they came to the Mis-cha Sip-ok-a-ni, the great river. And although on their journey they had crossed many wide rivers and climbed many high mountains, no one had ever seen anything like this river. It was the father of waters.

"It was difficult and dangerous, but they crossed the river on rafts and all were safe except for Panti, who fell in the water and was never seen again.

"And?" her grandmother said, and waited for Jane to finish the story. "And?"

"And forever after the warriors defended their own people. But before a battle the young braves would go down to the river to make an offering to Panti, so he would be with them in war. And because he was invisible to their enemies, he could run among them, knocking them down and making them take to their heels and run away." Jane liked to tell this part of the story, for the idea of Panti, the invisible guardian, a protector against all harm, made her feel safe and secure.

"But now," her grandmother chided, "be patient, our story has just begun and there is much more to tell."

"When Chikasah and Chahtah were safe on the east side of the river, they made camp. But in the morning when they woke they had a bitter quarrel, Chahtah saying that the Fa-bus-sah stood straight and that they had reached the promised land, and Chikasah saying that the pole leaned toward the east and that they had not yet come to the place they sought. After many bitter words, Chikasah stood and cried out, 'All that are of Chikasah follow me!' He took his people and his warriors and left the camp. The angry warriors of Chahtah made ready to follow him but Chahtah said, 'Hamonockma, iskia ahmishke, chiksash!' (Halt, follow them not, they are rebels.)

"And so it was that the two brothers broke into two tribes, the Chickasaw and the Choctaw, and the old, wise ones wept and said that when the two brothers joined again it would be the end of the people forever."

The rocking stopped and Sara said, "But surely you have heard enough of our people for today."

"No, don't stop!" Jane protested. "Not now, for you have not told me of the time when Chikasah came here to the old fields or to the place of the waving cattails, the Ponti-atoc, the heart of the Nation."

"No." Sara hesitated. "I have not told you of that time but then, as you know the story already, you must tell this part yourself."

And Jane would sit up proud and straight and begin to recite what she had learned by heart.

"It was then at Ponti-atoc that we built our towns. We lived here many years and fought many wars to defend our land but we were never defeated. We were always a small tribe but our warriors were as cunning and brave as our women were beautiful.

"In our towns we had many different houses. Our people never lived in tepees like the savage, wild tribes. We had round houses to protect us from the winter cold and summer houses divided into two convenient rooms to keep us cool in the hot weather. And in every town there was a longhouse where the town chief and his council met to see to tribal business.

"Each town was built on an open square, where the young braves played stickball and where the ritual campfires were laid. On one side of the fire sat the clans of the koi, the warriors, and on the other sat the clans of the ishpanee, the chiefs, and above them all sat our clan, the minco, from which came the king, the wise istehotopah, and his beautiful queen, the picaunli. By the king sat the tisu-minco, the kings-waiter from the clan of the koi, who advised the king in time of war.

"Our tribe was lucky in their kings and chiefs and in the wise men who kept our history both in memory and in the shells sewn on long strips of deerskin, called wampum.

"In our land all the people of every clan and house were well provided with every good thing. There were fish in our streams and rivers and game for our hunters to kill with their bows and arrows. In our forests there were possum and quail and deer and wild turkey, and in those days bear and cougar could be trapped in pits as easily as rabbits could be snared in the fields.

"Our hunters knew every secret, even how to kill the wolf by putting a sharp stick in frozen bear fat so that when the wolf came to lick the fat he cut his tongue and at the scent of blood the wolves in the pack fell on him, tearing him and themselves to pieces.

"We were a small tribe with many enemies who wanted our rich land, but we won against all by our cunning. We traveled far to trade. We went to the sea in the east and from the bluffs at Memphis down to Natchez we traveled free on land and river with no man brave enough to stop us. Everywhere all people spoke our tongue, for we had power to command in both trade and war.

"But trade and war and hunting were for men and boys. The women had other work to do. We cured the hides and dried the meat the hunters brought in from the kill. And women, as was their right, planted the corn. It was a sacred duty—for without corn there could be no *pishofa* and without *pishofa* there could be no ritual feastings to cure the sick or to mark the seasons.

"First the corn was planted row on row, and when it was green we sometimes danced with our neighbors, the Creek, in celebrations. Then came the harvest and the year's first *pishofa*. To make it in the old, right way the women put the shelled corn in the stump of a tree that had been hollowed out with fire. Then boiling water was added and the lye from the wood ash peeled away the outer skin of the corn and left the white heart of the kernel. Then the corn was rinsed with clear water and cooked slowly in a great, iron pot over an open fire to be eaten fresh as hominy. But the corn to be used for the whole year was dried, parched or ground for meal.

"But our most sacred feast was in celebration of the New Year, when every fire was put out and new ones lit. At this feast we danced and sang for four days and nights and gave thanks to the One Above as we kept a circle of love and drank of the cup that held the *hahtok*, the red drink made from the red willow root. Even after a night of dancing it made the dancer feel strong and full of health.

"Besides the corn the women gathered in yams and wild peas, strawberries, crabapples, mulberries, parsley and onions, spinach and Chickasaw plums and wild hanging grapes. They made feasts of mussels from the river, and they knew the proper way to render bear fat to store in earthen jars for flavoring the cooking and the way to keep honey for sweetening corn cakes.

"In the autumn the women made a party to gather in nuts—pecans, walnuts, hazelnuts, acorns and, best of all, the hickory nuts from which they made a rich, pure milk."

Jane stopped and looked shyly at her grandmother.

"Go on," her grandmother said, "and what did the women do with this hickory milk?"

"Many things, *iposi*." Jane used the Chickasaw name for grandmother. "But they always used it to moisten persimmon bread." Jane waited, holding her breath as her grandmother reached into the crockery jar on the table beside her and broke off a morsel of delicious persimmon bread to give Jane as a reward. The bread was sweet, but not so sweet to Jane as her grandmother's praise.

"You have remembered well, my Jane, and now will you also tell the part of the story that comes next?"

Jane swallowed quickly and she felt her heart begin to thump in her chest. She turned her face away and hid it in the old woman's shoulder, shutting her eyes tight so the dark might keep her safe. "No, Grandmother, please, you tell that story. You know it better than I."

"But you know what is going to happen?" her grandmother asked softly.

"Yes, *iposi*, I know." Jane took comfort from her grandmother's steady voice. "It is now that the cruel Spanish come to our land."

"Yes." Her grandmother's breath brushed against Jane's cheek and made her shiver. "It was then that the cruel Spanish came. Our warriors saw them from a long way off, hundreds of them marching towards us. These Spanish were like no men we had ever seen. They were wearing suits of bright armor that shone in the sun. They carried firesticks and some were riding on big beasts that frightened our braves, who had never seen a horse before."

Her grandmother held her close and went on with the story. "And they had with them men in black skirts, the black kings they called priests. And at the end of the procession, to carry their burdens and herd the squealing pigs of which we had none, was a band of slaves, made up of men and women from all the other tribes the Spanish had visited before they came to us.

"Our braves would have fought with them, for they had come upon us uninvited and unannounced, but the Spanish told us that they came in peace, and so we let them stay as our guests." Her grandmother cleared her throat. The sound was sharp and made Jane tremble, for even now all this time later she was afraid of the cruelty of the Spanish barbarians.

"The Spanish stayed through the winter," her grandmother continued, "and we fed them from our stores. We gave them our houses, our food—the best of all we had, as one does to an honored guest. We even gave them our food when we went without. And when they did us wrong and some of their soldiers killed our braves in a quarrel, we let it go without taking revenge and waited patiently for them to leave in the spring, as they had promised.

"But in the spring, when it was nearing the appointed time for the Spanish to go, they demanded some of our young men and women to go with them as slaves to carry the many fine things they had taken from us.

"The other wrongs we had accepted as the price of peace, but it was unthinkable that we let our young men and women go as slaves. No Chickasaw brave had ever been a slave; none of our women had lived without honor. But the Spanish were many and we were few; they had horses and armor and their firesticks, which none of our warriors had used in battle.

"We let them think we would obey and we waited, knowing that if we were to win over them it must be done not by strength but by our bravery and our cunning. And on the morning the Spanish were to leave us, when they were not expecting it, we rose up against them and drove them out of our land. And in their flight they left behind some of their horses and pigs, so we had the best of the Spanish after all, for now, ever after, we ride horses to our feasts and we have the pig to season our *pishofa*."

Her grandmother smiled. "And so that was the end of the Spanish and the end of our stories. And you, my *picaunli*, should be resting. A small girl must take a nap if she is to grow up beautiful and strong."

Jane was pleased her grandmother had called her *picaunli*; it meant blossom as well as princess. Jane knew she was a princess—for she came, like her grandmother and her mother, from the *minco* clan—but the term blossom was a mark of special favor. Still, she could not let the stories end, not before her grandmother told her of James Beauvaise.

"Please don't stop now," Jane pleaded. "Not before you tell me of the English and the day the first Beauvaise came to us."

"Well then," her grandmother began again, "after the Spanish were driven out of our land we lived in peace for a long time until the English came. Like the Spanish they spoke a strange tongue, and they too carried firesticks. But they were mannerly and brought gifts, and so we agreed to trade with them. But we did not trade with the French as our brothers the Choctaw did, for the French had with them the black kings. We remembered what those devils had done to our captured warriors, when they made a cross of wood and tied them hand and foot and burnt them in the fire. Our warriors did not cry out, but we knew what they had suffered and we did not forget.

"But the English sat with us at the fire, eager to trade. They called us brothers and sometimes together we made war against the French. And it was from the English ships that the Scotsman came to us."

"And his name was James Beauvaise," Jane cried out. She knew her grandmother had paused so that she might name him herself.

"Yes, James Beauvaise."

"And what did he look like, this James Beauvaise?" Jane asked, although she knew the answer.

"Oh," Sara laughed, her head thrown back, "he was handsome. He had red hair and a red beard and sky blue eyes. He wore trousers of many colors, and as he came walking into the old town all alone, with his gun slung over his shoulder, he was whistling a tune."

"And what did he do?"

"He went up to my grandmother, the *picaunli*, went right up to where she was sitting in a circle of women shelling corn. He knelt down before her on one knee." Sara paused, as if lost in the past.

"And what did he say?"

"He said, 'I'm James Beauvaise. I've come a long way and I'm weary. Will you give me my wee supper and a place to rest my head?'"

"And she gave him his supper?" Jane asked.

"Yes."

"And then?"

"And then he sat by her at the fire and opened a leather pouch he had tied to his belt. And he took out a silver cup and handed it to my grandmother."

"And he said?" Jane's eyes were shining.

"He said, 'This cup was given to the Beauvaises by Mary, a Queen

(76)

of Scotland, and I give it to you, a Queen of the Chickasaw!' "

"And was she a queen, your *iposi?*"

"No, but she was a princess of the *minco,* and if she had wished she could have married the king and become the queen."

"But she did not marry the king?"

Sara smiled. "No, she did not. She took the silver cup and she took the redheaded James Beauvaise and they broke the ear of corn together." Jane clapped her hands in delight. No matter how often she heard the story, it still gave her pleasure.

"And," Sara said proudly, "she gave him houses and lands and many rich goods, and the right to sit with the *minco* at the fire, a right her children would have forever. For one has one's rights from the mother. And in return he gave her five sons; the first of them was my father, the great Duncan.

"And James Beauvaise became a chief in war and trade, a man who brought change to our people. And like the other English and Scotsmen who married our women, he built bridges and roads and mills."

"And then you were born, Grandmother?" Jane asked.

"Yes, then I was born. I came too late to the world to see the redheaded James or his *picaunli,* but my father, the great Duncan, told me stories of them. How he loved to tell stories, especially of witches and spells and of the little folk who live in the forest and do mischief to bad children. I was so frightened I dared not go alone in the night, and my mother scolded him for it, but he did not listen. He was a rogue, a rascal, my father, but he never spoke sharply to me. If I had done something wrong he would send me to the Dog King, an uncle of the tribe who was there to punish all naughty children so their parents would not have the sorrow of it. And if I had been very naughty, then the Dog King might give me a scratch on the arm with a sharp stick."

Sara smiled to herself. "Sometimes my father would take me in his lap, as I have you now, and tell me stories of the wars the redheaded James had fought with the English against the French and of the wars he himself had fought for General Washington. And he would tell how he had met with General Washington, the first great father, and how General Washington had given him a plow and told him to go home and farm. My father said it was a strange present for one warrior to give to another, but then the times of war were changing to times of peace.

"Washington promised the great Duncan friendship with the Chickasaw forever. And he said a prayer to his God so that there might never be anything but peace between them.

"When my father returned to our people, because he believed Washington had a powerful God for war and peace, he gave land for the first mission church to be built here near Ponti-atoc. And that was how the Reverend Frazier came to our people and later the Reverend Wyatt, who baptized you and who is our present friend.

"Even before the church was finished, Reverend Frazier asked that we all become Christians and worship his and Washington's God. And my father agreed, for if he had said no it would have disappointed Reverend Frazier and General Washington. To have said yes did us no harm, for our One Great Spirit above keeps us all, and in the end Breathholder waits to take us all under the sky."

Then her grandmother laughed and rocked more quickly. "To tell the truth, my father gave the little mission church and the land because he thought it would be a fitting place for the bones of James Beauvaise. My father had kept them wrapped in a white deerskin under this fine house that James Beauvaise had built and called Lochleven, but Reverend Frazier told my father how in Scotland they buried men in a box in a churchyard. Wanting to do his father every honor, Duncan took his bones to the little churchyard and let the Reverend Frazier say a prayer over them, but, just to be sure, he also did James Beauvaise honor in the Chickasaw way. My father built a little house over the grave. For in those days it still seemed possible for all men to live together in both the Chickasaw and the white man's ways.

"My father sent my mother Molly and all her children to church, and his two wives that came after my mother and all their children. Soon there were so many Beauvaises of my father's line and that of his four brothers, and so many of mixed blood from other marriages between white men and Indian women, that the full bloods began to grumble and say that we should be a clan of our own and sit apart at the council fire, for we were no longer of the Chickasaw way.

"It made my father so angry to hear these words that he came to the church drunk and fell down in the aisle and had to be carried home. The Reverend Frazier forbade him to come again unless he repented before the congregation." Her grandmother's eyes clouded. "So my father, the great Duncan, the mighty warrior, came and humbled himself before the church as he had never been humbled in war. He came, he said, because he could not forsake the bones of his father. Then he went out of the church and spoke before the full bloods, and he said that the many changes that had come into the Nation with the white men were for the good of all, that as times had changed the people must change too, that now there was no use for warriors in a land where there were no more wars.

"But the full bloods and the old ones turned their faces from him, and it broke his heart. He lived to see more and more white men come into our land, down the roads and over the bridges that the Beauvaises had built, and he watched as the settlers plowed the land, made their farms, and circled them with fences to keep our people out. He watched and drank himself blind, so he could not see white men making their fences around all our land and our people."

Her grandmother's voice dropped so low Jane could barely hear her. "My father said that no matter what the Beauvaises had done or not done, the white men would have come anyway, that nothing would have stopped them coming, for we had made them welcome and asked only that they obey our laws. But that the white men would not do. They wanted to own our land, and worst of all they wanted us to forsake our old ways and our laws and obey theirs.

"It was shameful to think of Chickasaw obeying laws other than our own. My father drank then, so he could not see the faces or hear the voices of the white men crying for the land or the full bloods blaming him for what would soon be the end of our Nation in the east.

"We knew the end of us had come when President Andrew Jackson sent for our chiefs to come to Washington City. My father was too old and too sick at heart to go with them, but Jackson told our chiefs either our people must now live by white men's laws or move to the west where other Indian tribes had gone before us.

"He promised that, if we would go west, we might have the new land for as long as the grass grows and the waters run. Those were his words, but by the time he came to write them down in treaties, he had already forgotten his promise.

"When the chiefs came home again, all agreed we must go. None of us, mixed blood or full blood, wanted to live without our way or our laws. Still, we did not know where we would go. We had sent out scouting parties to seek this new Nation, but no land we had seen was as sweet or as good as the old, beloved Nation.

"At last, when we saw we would be forced by the government in

Washington to leave if we did nothing, we settled on buying a one-third interest in the new Nation of our brother the Choctaw, who had already moved west.

"It was then the old ones began to weep and say it had been told that when the two brothers came together again as one, it would be the end of the Chickasaw. But no one listened, for now the government sent soldiers to hound us, and the settlers began to make every day a torment.

"We knew we must make ready to go, but we held fast to the condition of our going. We would remove ourselves. It must not be for us as it had been for the Cherokee, who had been taken in the night, rounded up like cattle, put into pens and then driven down the Trail of Tears to the west, while all along the way the young and old had sickened and died, and no man had lifted his hand to help them. Nor would we go like the Choctaw, taken by the army like prisoners.

"We were determined to go in our own companies with our own leaders. The soldiers traveling west with us would be there only to see to supplies and to protect us from hostile whites. We would go with the dignity a great and rich people deserved."

Suddenly her grandmother stopped rocking. The chair was still, and in the silence Jane could hear the beat of her grandmother's heart.

"And so then it began, the selling of our land to the government and of our homes to the greedy settlers. It was up to us to get the most we could for our family property. Those of us who had much to sell had much to lose. Many of the mixed bloods like the Beauvaises had land they had farmed, houses they had built and slaves they had bought to work their fields."

Jane felt uneasy. She did not like to think of anyone being a slave. She had already promised Cima her freedom. It was better to have a friend than a slave. She said, "And it was then that my cousin, Pride Beauvaise, came to help his people."

Her grandmother nodded. "Yes, it was then Pride Beauvaise came, when he was needed. He was only a boy, but he had learned to read and write at Reverend Frazier's mission school. Pride spoke many tongues—English, French and the speech of all the neighbor tribes of the Chickasaw. Pride came to us from his schoolroom and sat day after day with the council, reading each treaty, bargaining over each deed and sale of land."

"And Pride Beauvaise was your father's brother's grandchild?"

Jane asked. She had taken pains to work out the exact relationship.

"Yes," her grandmother answered, "he was my father's grand-nephew."

"And so that is how Pride Beauvaise is my cousin?"

Her grandmother nodded. "It is so, he is your cousin, your *itiba-pishi pila*. And while your cousin Pride sat with the men, his mother Mary Letty, who was of the *ishpanee*, and the other women who were to travel in Pride's company made ready for the great remove. Everything must be taken that would be needed for their new homes in the western wilderness. It was no easy thing to decide what must be carried in the wagons and what must be left behind." Her grandmother stopped again and then in a low voice said, "I myself could not consent to go to the west. I could not."

Her grandmother stood up abruptly, pushing Jane away from her as she walked toward the window of the cupola room. "I could not leave the great Duncan. He was too old, too sick to travel. Besides, I had your mother, my own Rose. She was only a little girl then and I thought that, if I stayed here at Lochleven at Ponti-atoc in the old fields and kept this house and the Beauvaise cup, one day the people might return again."

She looked out the window, staring out over the trees. "And more than all the rest, my true heart was here lying in the mission churchyard. I would not leave my first husband, Flying Moon. I could not go and leave his bones behind.

"So Pride Beauvaise found a way for me to stay. He sold Loch-leven to old man Lytton and I gave Lytton a deed, a piece of paper, to say that he owned it forever. And to make sure my father and I would not be turned from our own door, I married Lytton at the mission, but we did not break the ear of corn.

"And here from this window I watched them go, my king the *isteho-topah*, and the queen and the *tisu-minco*. I saw them pass by, my king, my *iksa*—those related to me by clan, all my people but the few who had run away to hide in the hills like criminals in their own land. And on the morning Pride and Mary Letty and their company of wagons left, I saw Pride, a boy on horseback, turn and hold up his hand in farewell.

"For Pride's company the journey was not a trail of tears. They had soldiers to protect them, and gold, and slaves to build their campfires. They had food and medicine and warm blankets, but still the way was hard, and many were not so lucky.

"On the great remove of the Chickasaw to the west many died

of fevers and of smallpox. The weather was cruel and struck down the weary and the sick at heart. On the way west the last great war chief, Tishomingo, died. And here in the year after the remove my father, the great Duncan, died at Lochleven and was buried beside his father, the redheaded James. And in time your mother Rose went away and was lost to me, and then my heart cracked. There is nothing left for me forever but bitter tears."

Jane looked up and saw the tears that ran down in the deep lines on the old woman's face like drops of rain into a dry creek bed.

"They are gone now, all of them, and I am alone, *aii, aii*."

It hurt Jane to see her grandmother cry. She had not meant to make her grandmother sad with the telling of the old stories.

"Don't cry, Grandmother." Jane tugged at her grandmother's skirt. "You are not alone. You have me. I am here."

The old woman wiped at her wrinkled cheeks with her hand. "It was wrong of me to name the dead. Naming them has brought back their spirits and made them uneasy. We must speak of them no more."

"I will not leave you, Grandmother. I promise. I will stay with you forever."

"I know you will stay with me, Jane. You are a good girl, a fine girl. But I am tired now. Let me rest. We have had enough stories for today."

And seeing that her grandmother had closed her eyes and shut Jane out from her thoughts, Jane had gone away, wandering along the corridor to the stairs, where she sat on the landing looking down into the shuttered, dark hall below. In the shadows she could see the outline of the fireplace and the pale gleam of the silver Beau-vaise cup on the mantelpiece. She often sat here looking at the cup, dreaming of the boy, Pride Beauvaise, a clever, handsome boy on horseback who one day would come for her and take her far away to the new Nation in the west.

The thought of him made her sigh with longing. She had woven a web of magic around Pride Beauvaise, but as she dreamed of him she could not have guessed that when he did come it would be death and war that brought him back to rescue her.

WITHIN a year, war between the states was declared. All the talk of secession of South from North had meant little to Jane. She might as well have been hearing of a storm far away that could not touch her, but then the cruel reality of the war came home to Loch-leven.

Harry and Robert Lytton went to fight for the gray. Old man Lytton tried to keep the plantation going without them, but there was no market for cotton. Soldiers, both blue and gray, came to take what they wanted from the place.

Sara and Kera hid what they could and put the Beauvaise cup, wrapped up in a shawl, beneath the floorboards in the cupola room. The soldiers found the horses and cows and grain and hams and corn and hay. Lochleven was stripped bare, but the Beauvaise cup was safe.

There was little left to feed any of them. The slaves ran away and then came back again, for there had been no place to go that was better. And in the winter that followed, a fever took Jane's grand-mother Sara. When Kera nursed the old woman, she came down with it too.

Suddenly Jane and Cima were orphans with no one to comfort them but Reverend Wyatt, as old man Lytton roamed the house like a *haksi*, a crazy man, talking wildly. He shouted and cursed and then shot at the soldiers in blue who came again. This time they took old man Lytton away with them.

Cima and Jane hid in a cupboard beneath the stairs until the soldiers had gone. And then, with the Beauvaise cup and what little they could take in a carpetbag, the two girls had gone hand in hand in the night down the dark road to the mission.

The church and churchyard were overflowing with homeless peo-ple, both whites and the Indians who had come out of hiding and had nowhere else to go. The Reverend Wyatt was trying to feed and shelter them all, but there was little enough he could do. Out of pity and remembrance of how the mission had been built on the great Duncan's land, he took Jane and Cima into his own house, into his own family. Jane and Cima slept clasped in each other's arms on a narrow trundle bed barely big enough for one, the Beau-vaise cup safe beneath their pillow.

The Reverend Wyatt was a kind man but Jane knew he could not keep them forever. He said he had written to Pride Beauvaise to tell him what had happened at Lochleven and of the Chickasaw left behind in Mississippi, but he had had no reply from him. Wyatt tried to put a good face on their situation but Jane could not find much to hope for. Still, each night she said a prayer for Pride to come for her and for Cima.

Then, one night late, she woke to the sound of voices. The door from the bedroom to the parlor was ajar and she could hear the Reverend Wyatt talking to a stranger. She climbed out of bed without waking Cima, tiptoed to the door and peeped through the crack. It was then she saw Pride Beauvaise for the first time. She stared, unable to believe it was really he. She had been told by her grandmother that Pride was a boy, and she had imagined him still as a boy about her own age. But this Pride Beauvaise was a man.

Her wish had come true, but not in the way she had expected. She was torn between her disappointment and her joy that he had come at last.

She stood, her bare feet on the cold puncheon floor, not making a sound, staring at this handsome man as he told Reverend Wyatt of the years between his leaving Lochleven and of his coming back again. His voice was soft and low, but it had an authority that made her listen as if caught in a spell.

"When the Chickasaw came to the new Nation there was nothing there but a few Choctaw settlements in the eastern half of the land. At first we stayed, afraid to move too far west for fear of attack by the Comanche. The government had promised troops to protect us, but there were not enough of them, and when we moved west the Comanche burned our houses and took our children.

"The life in the new land was harder by far than the journey west. We had to begin again—to build everything from nothing—but we worked hard. We built houses, schools and towns. We began to prosper but, though we tried, it was not easy to live with our brother Choctaw. We were too used to going our own way and not walking to another's command. So we divided from the Choctaw and bought the western third of the Nation outright. By treaty and by deed it was to be ours forever.

"Again we began to make schools and towns and churches. We laid out roads and traded to the north, and south into Texas. We wrote a constitution because we needed a new set of laws and plan of government for a new Nation. The old clans and house groups had vanished in the past and died out on the great remove. We had no king now, but a governor elected by the people. In our capital, Tishomingo, we had a legislature instead of *koi* and *ishpanee*.

"For ten years we worked and built and made some creditable progress, even though it meant always having to go to Washington to ask for money owed us or to argue that the treaties be honored.

(84)

We only had ten years of building and progress before the war came. It stopped us when there was still so much to be done."

Pride stared into the fire. The light caught his face and cast shadows around his deep-set eyes and his wide, generous mouth. He was not a boy but, all the same, to Jane he was beautiful.

"Within a week after war was declared," Pride said, "the federal government began to pull out all their troops. We watched as the cavalry rode north. They left the forts undefended and us unprotected. Without so much as a goodbye, they had broken their agreement to protect us. We had been abandoned by Washington.

"Then Jefferson Davis and the Confederates sent a delegate, Albert Pike, to the Five Civilized Tribes. He held a big meeting, and we listened as he told us that Jefferson Davis wanted us to fight for the South. I was against going to war for North or South, but other voices were louder and stronger than mine. Jefferson Davis promised the Five Nations that we could keep our slaves. He promised to send money and supplies if we raised troops, and he reminded us that, as we came from the South, it was to our interest to fight for the Southern cause.

"The Five Tribes agreed. To them the wrongs of the world were all the fault of the government in Washington. To them the Confederates were already their allies against that government.

"Companies of soldiers, both foot and horse, were raised. The old war dances and songs were recalled, and at the crossroads of Choctaw and Chickasaw our soldier boys danced with paint on their faces, yelled war whoops and threw their tomahawks at the red war pole to declare they were ready for battle.

"It was all bluster and swagger. We could barely raise up a few companies. Little money and few supplies came from Davis, just promises and more talk. I came east now to see him, only to get nothing but more promises."

Reverend Wyatt rose and stirred at the fire. "Davis is an honorable man, Pride. He may want to send money and supplies, but he doesn't have them to send. The Indian Nations are a long way off, and he has more pressing problems closer to home. The real war is being fought here, not in the west."

"Then you think he will still try to help us?" Pride asked.

"Yes."

There was quiet in the room save for the snap and fall of a log on the fire. Then Pride said, "I think the South will lose the war."

"It is possible." Wyatt avoided looking at Pride.

"If the South loses the war, we will lose as well." Pride waited, hoping for some protest from Wyatt, and when it did not come he said, "I must go home again as soon as I can and prepare the council for the worst. And somehow I must take these people here with me, though I have nothing to feed them with and no way to defend them."

"They have no place else to go, Pride. You know what will happen if they stay here. You must take them with you." Then Wyatt turned his head and caught sight of Jane. He called to her, "Jane, you're awake. Come in here. There's someone to see you, all the way from the west." She hung back. "Come on, Jane. Don't be shy, not of Pride."

Pride held out his hand to her. "I'm your cousin, Jane, your cousin Pride Beauvaise. I've come to take you home."

Still she hung back, shy and unhappy. He had come as she had dreamed he would, but he had not come back just for her; he had come for all of them.

WITH what provisions Pride could find, some half-lame horses and a broken-down wagon, he set off for the west with his ragged band. He put Jane and Cima up on the wagon seat. There were not enough horses for all to ride, and to keep pace with the people walking made the going slow. They traveled at night and slept in the day to avoid soldiers. It seemed to Jane that they were always listening or hiding in the woods like wild, hunted things.

They soon ran perilously short of food. Pride left them camped by a stream, took the girls and went into town. His Confederate scrip was refused. They were turned away at shops, pushed and jostled on the streets. No one showed them any kindness or courtesy. The war had divided families and made everyone suspicious of strangers. At last Pride found a merchant who, for a price, grudgingly sold him flour filled with weevils and some coffee made of parched, ground acorns. There was no sugar to be had, not even for gold.

Jane was proud of Pride as she saw how he dealt with the people in the town and how he looked after those in his charge. He somehow managed to give them all confidence and hope. On the journey, her child's dream of loving him had turned into a reality. Day after day, as her love for him grew, his thoughts were not of her but of survival.

(86)

By the time they came to the Arkansas River, they were all so tired and starved they hadn't the strength to go on. They camped, huddled down by the river's edge, a weak and wretched band.

Pride said he would go back to the last farm they had passed and try to buy some milk and eggs. The children at least must be fed. Jane would not be left behind and tagged along beside him. At the farm an old man with a shotgun met them on the porch, shouting at them to go away. Jane began to cry, afraid for Pride. Then suddenly a woman appeared in the doorway of the farmhouse. She must have seen the fear and the hunger in their faces.

"Put the gun down, Tate," she said to the old man, who, muttering, did as he was told. "We're alone here, just my hired man and me. We've learned to be careful." Then, having looked them over, she let them draw water from her well and listened to Pride's story. Then, without being asked, she made up a huge kettle of nourishing soup and baked a basketful of bread.

That would have been enough to earn Jane's gratitude, but the woman did more. She came to their camp and spoke kindly to the old ones and helped nurse the sick. For as long as Jane lived, she would remember that woman with red hair like a halo and fire blue eyes.

As a parting gift she gave Jane and Cima each a corn dolly, their faces made from painted pecan shells. Cima kept hers until the dry husks crumbled into dust, but Jane gave hers to one of the younger children. Loving Pride made her feel too old to play with dolls.

When they came at last into the Chickasaw Nation, Jane had expected that everything would be easier. All along the hard way she had looked forward to good food, clean beds and freshly ironed clothes, but when she came to Pride's house on Beauvaise Ridge, she discovered it was only a big, double log cabin. All around it were people more ragged and hungry than she, living in tents or any kind of makeshift shelter they could find. They were the homeless, the dispossessed, all fleeing from the war, driven from the northern Nations across the South Canadian. They had come here hoping for safety. Jane knew she and Cima were lucky to be taken in by Pride's mother, Mary Letty, but—Beauvaise or not—they were expected to work as they had never worked back home at Lochleven.

The nearest Protestant mission school had been turned into a hospital. There was not a proper doctor and the old way of the medicine men was not enough to care for the terrible wounds of this war. Jane saw men with no legs, others with festering, gaping wounds that would never heal, but the most terrible of all to her were the men who had lost their hands. In the battle to the north at Pearidge, some tribes had gone back to savage ways; when they took a prisoner they cut off his hands to make sure he never fought again.

It seemed the horror of the war would never end. But when the end came, the defeat was doubly bitter, for the Chickasaw had not been beaten in any way. This defeat was theirs only for having chosen a losing ally. They had lost no battles, only the war.

To punish them for their stand with the Confederacy, the government in Washington broke their treaties. Their Nation no longer had the power to make war or to declare peace. They were subjects, to be ruled by Washington. This land that they had bought and paid for with tribal monies was now the government's, to lease out to railroads or to annex and give to other western blanket tribes. Not even Pride's great power to plead their tribal cause in Washington could lift the restrictions placed upon them.

When Pride came home from Washington, he brought with him a portrait of himself. Painted in oils by a Washington artist, it showed him as a handsome man in a severe, black broadcloth suit and white, starched shirt. His soft, brown eyes were searching, yet saddened by what they had seen of mankind and human nature. His wide mouth was held firm to keep back the words of outrage at the neglect and abuse of his people. When she was alone, Jane stood before the portrait and wanted to weep for all his hurts and disappointments.

Yet, with his old courage and persuasion, Pride rallied the people to begin building again. He ran and was elected to the legislature, which meant that more often than not he was away from the Ridge, traveling to every part of both the Chickasaw and Choctaw Nations, where many of the old families still lived.

His message was always the same. The Chickasaw must build schools for their children, and they must put aside old differences. There must be no more bickering between progressive and conservative, no more division between full blood and mixed blood. Only a strong tribal government could withstand the great changes that were surely coming. He spoke and he was listened to, but his words were not always heeded.

As Jane grew up, she measured out the years in waiting for Pride to come home again. She stood at the edge of the Ridge watching for him, a lovesick girl, hoping that when at last he did come, one day he might notice her.

She did all she knew how to attract Pride's attention. She made herself a skirt of many colors. She braided her shining black hair with ribbons and she learned from Mary Letty to cook all his favorite dishes. Yet when he did come home she was too shy to speak. She blushed even when she spoke his name. Cima said she acted like a fool, and the other women looked at her with pity, but she could not help it if she wore her heart on her sleeve.

When Pride was home they walked out together in the evening and he told her of where he had been and of how tangled tribal politics had become. He sometimes brought her a book or a token of his travels, but he never spoke of love or of marrying. More than anything in life, she wished to marry him.

Pride had never married. He could have had his pick of girls, all of them, Jane felt, prettier, wittier and more graceful than she, but he said he had no time for a wife. He was married to the tribe. It was true that they needed him, but Jane was sure that, if only he would look at her, he must see that she needed him too and that no one he might meet would ever love him more than she did.

When Pride was at home, he was busy with the ranch or trying to settle an ongoing quarrel with a family named Starrett who claimed that they had settled on the land before the Beauvaises. It was not so. When they had first arrived, Pride had done nothing to prevent the Starretts from taking any part of the Nation they wanted for their own use. That right was theirs by Chickasaw law. The truth was that the Starretts were a lazy, shiftless lot who had rather steal Pride's cattle and cause trouble than work. There seemed no way to talk reason to any of them. Pride had called in the Chickasaw Light Horse Police to drive them off, but just when he thought he had the matter settled, they would return. The quarrel would erupt again in angry words and threats.

To keep the situation in hand, Pride began to spend more time on the Ridge. He expanded his ranching interests, tried a little cotton farming, and when he prospered he began to talk of building a house. He asked Jane to draw up a likeness of Lochleven.

It had been years since she had thought of Lochleven. Her memory was clouded. When she had first come out here she had been homesick; now the Ridge was the only home she could imagine. But because Pride asked it, she and Cima sat at the kitchen table and put their heads together, trying to remember every detail of the old house. It brought back a lifetime of memories. Jane and Cima had shared every hardship and joy. Jane had other friends, but none as close as Cima.

When Pride's new house was finished, much of the old Loch-leven was in it, the cupola room and the entrance hall and stairs. Pride had added the wide verandah that ran on three sides of the house and an upper gallery. Mary Letty furnished it with the fine pieces she had brought from Mississippi and with goods hauled up from Texas.

It was that spring, just before the new year, that Mary Letty came to Jane with a shawl full of gifts and laid them at her feet. From the bundle fell printed calico and ivory combs and a lace fan. There was a necklace made of coral and a golden locket. Jane looked at Mary Letty, bewildered.

Mary Letty smiled at Jane's confusion. "You know," she said, "that Pride has never married."

Jane nodded dumbly.

"It is time that he took a wife." At the doorway Jane could see a cluster of women and Cima among them, grinning as though it were Christmas morning.

Jane felt as if her heart had turned over.

"So in the old way I have come from Pride to you with this bundle of gifts from him. If you accept them, then it means you will consent to marry him."

At first Jane was unable to speak. She could not believe that after all these years Pride was asking for her. She wanted to answer but she could not.

"What is your answer?" Mary Letty asked.

"Say yes," Cima called out to her.

"Yes, yes! I say yes!" Jane took the gifts, and at the feast for the new year, with half the Nation present, she broke the ear of corn with Pride.

SHE had dreamed of him before she had ever seen him. She had loved him always, and still each day that he was her husband she was astonished by the happiness she found with him and by the tranquillity of her life in that fine house.

To others he was a legend; to her he was a lover, a friend and her heart. Their first child, a girl, they named Mary Letty for his mother. Then, in a time of sorrow, his mother died and they lost

they came because they believed she had inherited, like a legacy from Pride, both his wisdom and his compassion.

They told her freely all their hopes and their fears. Once again they were being threatened by white settlers. More new settlers came to trespass every day. They came by rail, by horse, by wagon and on foot. By legal tricks they had settled towns and made farms. It was worse now than it had been in the old Nation before the great remove, when the white men had first wanted their land. Now if the land was taken from them, where was there for the Chickasaw to go? How were they to live as a people?

Miss Jane tried to comfort them but she was tired, a sickness of the spirit weighed her down. She longed for the time when Breath-holder would call to her and she could go under the sky where her Pride would be waiting. She yearned for his arms to be around her. But the time was not yet come. Today her place was still here at Lochleven, waiting patiently for Andrew to come back again from Washington, bringing with him the strange woman.

*T*HE buggy came into Miss Jane's view. Cima started forward, but Miss Jane motioned her to be still, as Andrew helped the woman down and led her toward the house. The woman was only a girl with red-gold hair and fine, white skin. She was very beautiful. Miss Jane could see why Andrew would want to possess her. And there could be no comparisons made, for she was nothing like Letty. Andrew stood waiting obediently for her greeting.

"*Icla tco.*" You are come, she said in Chickasaw. It was the traditional greeting when a member of the clan returned home.

"*Alali-o.*" I am come, he answered as he had been taught. "Miss Jane, I've brought back my wife, Reanna." He waited for Miss Jane to make a sign that they were welcome, and then Miss Jane held out her hands and he led Reanna up onto the porch.

"Miss Jane, this is Reanna." Andrew waited for Miss Jane to speak. When she did not, he said, "We were married in Washington."

"Why not let us know?" Cima snapped. "Have all the telegraph lines between here and Washington blown down?" Andrew glared at Cima and his cheeks reddened.

Miss Jane, afraid that Andrew might lose his temper before the girl, said to her, "This is Cima. She saw you when you first came onto the Ridge."

Andrew didn't relax, but the color left his cheeks. "Cima," he said, "is better than a watchdog."

"I'm sorry Andrew did not let us know you were coming," Miss Jane went on, ignoring the feeling between Andrew and Cima. It was not the first time she had had to make peace for him. "We would have had a fitting welcome for you."

"It doesn't matter," Reanna said, glancing quickly at Andrew.

"Ah, but it does matter," Miss Jane said. "There is a traditional tribal welcome for a new bride. We Chickasaw are jealous guardians of our traditions. We feel we must keep them or we will lose ourselves."

Miss Jane studied the girl. She was more than pretty. She had an air about her that bespoke her breeding. This girl would never be ashamed to let the world hear of her wedding. The true reason that Andrew had not let her know he had taken a new wife before he came home to Lochleven was simple: he had been afraid she would not accept the girl. Now that they were here, Andrew was confident she would not turn her away. She could see by the girl's face that he had not told her as much as he should, for clearly the girl did not expect the house or the greeting.

"Will you come inside?" Miss Jane motioned Reanna to enter.

In the center of the large entry hall was a table long enough to seat a meeting of the tribal council. There were three sets of double doors that led out onto the verandahs and a wide fireplace over which hung the portrait of a young Pride Beauvaise, painted in Washington on one of his visits there on tribal business. He was wearing a black broadcloth suit and a white shirt with a high, starched collar. Centered on the mantel beneath the portrait was a chased silver cup, like a religious chalice.

"This is a beautiful house," Reanna said.

"It is a pleasant house. But not so fine as the one we left in the old Nation."

Reanna's eyes darted to Andrew. She didn't want to ask questions—that displeased him—but everything she saw was new and strange.

"I'm sorry you had to leave your home," Reanna said. Perhaps it wasn't what Andrew would have liked her to say, but it was what she felt. He should have prepared her for this house and this woman. The woman was an Indian, but she was no simple, savage child of the forest. She was a force, a presence. She spoke soft, unaccented English, but it seemed as if it were a careful translation of her native tongue. The two women looked at each other more closely.

Miss Jane liked the girl. Andrew must have counted on that. Though she was not Indian, she had a depth and a kindness about her, and perhaps in time she would find her way in this strange, hard country.

"It has been a long journey for you," Miss Jane said. She felt Andrew's uneasiness. If he had not told her he was bringing home a bride, what else was he keeping to himself?

He had been secretive even as a child. He told the truth, but not all of it, and he withheld more than he gave, both in facts and of himself. She had tried to make him feel he could say anything without fear and that she would not disapprove or deny him what he wanted. She had tried to keep him from being jealous of Pride. She had set herself to be evenhanded to both of them, but there was always something that kept Andrew apart. What, she did not know. Perhaps it was his father's mean blood that haunted him. She had hoped to love Andrew enough to make up for the loss of his parents. She had loved all three of her children; and Pride and Andrew were so different.

"I'm happy to be here," Reanna was saying. "It's far better than anything I imagined. The house, the land—I like it all. And I hope you will like me."

"This house is always open to anyone who has need to come here." She was touched by the girl's openness and warmth, but she could not embrace her as a daughter, not just yet. Perhaps with time. Right now the memory of Letty still stood like a cloud between them.

"Everyone in the tribe is free to come here," Andrew said proudly. "The people all look to Miss Jane for advice. She's their wise woman."

"No, it was my husband, Pride Beauvaise, who was the wise one. He was a great leader of his people. That is his portrait hanging over the fireplace." Miss Jane looked up at it, as she did whenever she came into the room. The mouth was sensual and firm; the deep, searching eyes were shadowed with sorrow and compassion. The artist had caught his spirit well.

"He looks—he must have been a very good man," Reanna said. "Strong and yet understanding."

"Yes." Miss Jane nodded. "My son Pride looks like him a little."

(96)

"And your daughter Letty, did she look like you or your husband?" Reanna had spoken without thinking. She had named the dead, which Andrew said was not done, but it had been an honest mistake.

Miss Jane waited for Andrew to answer and when he said nothing she spoke for him. "Letty looked like both of us, I think." She was vexed with Andrew. This girl would not be so curious if Andrew had told her what she wanted to know about the past. Andrew frowned as if to rebuke Reanna and then dropped his eyes. Andrew was certainly the harder of her sons to understand.

"What an unusual cup." Reanna pointed toward the mantel. "I have never seen one like it. Is it family silver?"

"Yes." Miss Jane smiled. "It is the Beauvaise cup. I brought it with me from Mississippi. The first white man who came to the Chickasaw was a Scotsman named Beauvaise. He married my great-great-grandmother, the *picaunli*. They say that she was beautiful and that he was a fine, tall man with red-gold hair like yours, and that he laughed a lot. His people had come to Scotland from France with Mary, Queen of Scots. You have heard of her?"

"Yes," Reanna said.

"When James Beauvaise came to the New World, this cup was all he brought with him. He gave it to my great-great-grandmother on their wedding day and made her promise to keep it forever. We Beauvaises believe that as long as we have this cup we will survive." Miss Jane stopped, suddenly self-conscious. "I must ask you to forgive me." She looked again at Pride Beauvaise's portrait. "I am telling stories of the past and you have been very patient to listen."

"It has been wonderful." Reanna flushed. "Andrew is always scolding me because I ask too many questions, but I would like to know everything about him and his family."

Miss Jane stood straight for a moment. She had forgotten all she had meant to say to Andrew when he came home.

"We will talk another time, then," she said to Reanna, "when Andrew cannot hear or scold. I like telling stories, and you cannot ask too many questions for me. Now I know you must be tired and will want to go up and rest for a while."

"Oh, I'm not tired." Reanna meant to reassure Miss Jane, but she saw at once that she had spoken out of turn. Miss Jane had given a command, and though it was put as a soft and gentle request, it was meant to be obeyed.

"While you rest and have a chance to wash the dust away, I will talk with Andrew. There is much to be said between us. Cima will take you up and show you to your room."

"Where is she to go?" Cima asked. Her voice was flat, her eyes avoiding Reanna.

"To my room, of course," Andrew answered sharply. "We're married; Reanna is my wife."

"She can't go there." Cima glared at Andrew. "That was Letty's room."

"And now it is Andrew's and his wife's. *You will make her welcome.*" Miss Jane's voice was suddenly filled with force. Cima hesitated, but Reanna was sure she would not disobey her mistress, even if Cima considered herself to be something more than a servant. Miss Jane's word was law in this house. Miss Jane continued as if nothing had happened to mar the moment.

"The east room is large. I hope you will be comfortable there. We will open up the little room next door so that you can have a sitting room. You will want some privacy. It is only right that you should have it." Cima still hesitated. Miss Jane spoke again and this time her voice had the ring of fine steel.

"Cima, when you take Andrew's wife upstairs, perhaps she would like to see some of the rest of the house. Down here is this hall and to the east the dining room and to the west the sitting rooms. Andrew and I will talk in the little parlor. I know you will excuse us. We have a lot of business to discuss. I thought he would be back before this. The grass is already high and we have many decisions to make."

Reanna followed Cima up the stairs. She had been sent from the room again like a child, but here at Lochleven she had been sent by a woman, not a man. Miss Jane, not Andrew, was the power at Lochleven. He might insist Reanna obey him, but he did as he was told. Reanna wondered if he secretly resented it.

Cima, too, had been given her orders, and she carried them out to the letter if not in the spirit. She didn't like this woman being here. She had come here like some fine lady putting on airs. She was the unknown, the unexpected, a threat to Miss Jane and to Snow. As they reached the top of the stairs, she said, "This is Miss Jane's room."

Through the open door Reanna could see a large room with a fireplace that matched the one in the hall below. It was a combination bedroom, sitting room and office. There were large, worn leather chairs, a long oak table desk and a canopied bed covered in a delicate, hand-worked coverlet. Like the rest of the house, this room seemed both a part of the Southern plantation life Miss Jane's people had left behind and of the new, raw country in which they had found themselves. From the cupola windows in a bay at the far end of the room, there was a commanding view of the prairie both to the east and to the west.

"Miss Jane always sat in those cupola windows and waited for her Pride to come home." Cima spoke as if she could see Miss Jane there in the room. "She often sits there now, watching and waiting."

"Waiting for what?" Reanna asked.

Cima shrugged. How could you tell this girl that Miss Jane waited, living for the day when she could be free to join her Pride. She couldn't go until she had set the house in order. When Letty had married Andrew MacClaren, Miss Jane had thought her work was nearly finished. Now all that had changed. Cima turned abruptly and left the room, preceding Reanna down the hall. She indicated the first room on the left.

"This first room is Snow's room. She's Mr. MacClaren's daughter, Miss Jane's granddaughter." She made each word sound like an indictment of Reanna's presence.

"Where's Snow now?" Reanna asked.

"She's not here. She's out with her uncle Pride and Taffy Owen. He's the foreman. They take Snow out when she asks them pretty. You're sure going to be a surprise to all of them. The young, they can stand a shock and it don't hurt them, but not Miss Jane. Andrew should have told her. She's an old woman."

Reanna did not know how to answer Cima. She felt she must say something in reply, but before she could think of anything suitable Cima went on. "My room is next to Snow's." There was something perverse in Cima that made her add, "I've always lived right here in the house. My mother was Miss Jane's body slave. We've been together most all my life."

Reanne felt bewildered. She hadn't questioned Cima's place in this house. Not by word or deed had she shown that she wanted to take anything from her. Yet Cima's resentment was open and naked.

"That's Pride's room across from Snow's. Then Letty's sitting room and bedroom. They were hers till Mr. MacClaren married her. Now they're yours, I guess." Cima spoke in a flat, even tone, but her meaning was unmistakable.

"Thank you for showing me the house," Reanna said, as she turned into a large, pleasant room, which like the rest of the house was furnished in a mixed style of East and West.

"Miss Jane told me to." Cima stood impassive, a woman made of black stone.

"I thank you all the same."

"I'll have some hot water sent up for you," Cima said, ringing a bell rope by the door.

"I can go down for it."

"One of the girls, Annoyi or Rose Dawn, will bring it up to you. They know you're here and they'll want to have a look at you. Your trunks will be coming out by wagon?"

"Yes."

"I guess you'll want them unpacked for you."

"No, I'll do that." Reanna wasn't sure if Andrew would approve, but she must have this out now with Cima. "I'm not used to being waited on hand and foot. I think we ought to get things straight between us, Cima. I'm not helpless. I expect to do my share in this house."

Cima said nothing, but Reanna thought she saw some change in her eyes, as if she'd been taken by surprise. To cover the silence, Reanna turned away toward the double window that led out onto the upper verandah. She was amazed at her own spunk. But here she was and here she intended to stay. It was best to get things clear from the start. In a gesture of independence she opened a window, but it was a mistake. The wind whipped into the room, blowing a gale of dust.

"Shut that window!" Cima commanded. "You have a lot to learn about living in the Territory before you can be of much help here. Nobody but a stranger would open a window out *here* when the wind was blowing." Then, as if she felt she'd gone too far, Cima asked, "Is there anything else I can get you for now? Miss Jane will want you to be waited on."

"No, thank you," Reanna said stiffly, "just some hot water." She felt as if she were a child at home, being spoken to sharply by her mother. She hadn't married Andrew and come more than a thousand miles to be a child again. She meant to live here and to belong here. She looked about the room that was to be hers. On the writing desk she saw a picture of a girl set in a gilt, oval frame. She picked it up and studied the face. The picture was not well made, but you could see the gentleness in the large eyes.

"Is this Letty?" Reanna asked.

Cima stepped forward to take the photograph from Reanna's hand, then stopped herself just in time. "Yes," she said, her mouth a straight, grim line.

Reanna looked at the photograph again. It was the likeness of a girl who seemed imaginary, as if she had never been flesh and blood with dreams and hopes and sorrows. It seemed impossible that this girl could ever have been Andrew's wife and borne him a child. It seemed like a story, not a reality, that she had lived and loved Andrew and then died.

Reanna turned and looked out through the closed windows toward the eastern end of Beauvaise Ridge. She suddenly felt alien, isolated and cut off from everything she'd ever known. She'd wanted to marry, to come here and find adventure and a new way of life. Now that she was here, there was something wrong with the dream. It was as if the most important element were missing. In her heart she knew that she felt so alone because somehow, in a way she couldn't define, something had already gone wrong in her marriage to Andrew. She loved him—she must have or she wouldn't have married him—but she wasn't sure if he loved her. He seemed to resent her; he found fault with everything she did or said. At first she'd thought it was because he was comparing her with Letty, but now she didn't think that was so. It was something between just the two of them—a flaw, a crack, one she couldn't see or define. But she knew it was there.

Cima opened the door and two young Indian girls came in carrying a large copper vessel of steaming water. The girls stared and giggled. They set down the can of hot water and stood staring at Reanna, round-eyed.

"Which of you is Annoyi and which is Rose Dawn?"

They hesitated for a moment and then pointed at each other and ran away giggling. She wasn't sure if they spoke English or if they had understood a word she'd said. Cima looked annoyed.

"They're willing but useless, those girls. If you want anything done, tell me and I'll see to it." Without another word, Cima left the room and closed the door firmly behind her.

Reanna poured out some hot water into a basin and washed her face and combed her hair. She wished Andrew had let Miss Jane know they were coming; she'd assumed he had when he wired Jack Levy. She wanted so badly to be a part of the house and his life; to be an unexpected guest it made it all the more difficult.

When she thought enough time had passed, she went downstairs. At the foot of the stairs she heard the sound of voices coming from the front parlor, and she realized Miss Jane and Andrew were talking about her. She didn't know whether to run or to stay. Miss Jane's voice was low and insistent.

"You have put us in a very awkward position, and the girl as well. And for no good reason. Surely you see that. How are we to invite the people?"

"I tell you, it happened so *fast*—I didn't half know it had happened myself! There wasn't any time."

"Not even time for a simple telegraph message?"

"I've *told* you I'm sorry."

"*Sorry* is the coyote's answer to the prairie hen. You know, you are at times very selfish in your secretiveness. You put a burden on those who love you and rely on you."

Reanna walked as far away from the parlor door as she could, so as not to hear any more, and stood at the mantel looking up at the portrait of Pride Beauvaise. She had the feeling that he understood what she felt, that he would always be there to look after her and make things right. No, it was foolish to indulge in such a fantasy. What happened would be up to her, not up to some portrait of a man long dead.

She took the silver cup from the mantel and held it in her two hands. The story Miss Jane had told her was just as romantic as the feeling the portrait gave her. There was no telling how that first Scotsman had come by the cup. Mary, Queen of Scots, indeed! For all anyone knew, he could have stolen the cup and made up a story to go with it. And as for saying that as long as the cup stayed in the family they would survive, that was as much wishful thinking as her own need to feel secure, to feel protected and cared for, when in reality Andrew had put her in this awkward, humiliating position.

Someone else was in the room. She turned to see a man standing, looking at her, a man who might have been an imperfect copy of the man in the portrait. He was watching her with an open, easy gaze.

He was the most beautiful man she'd ever seen. His mixed blood gave him a dark cast, as if he'd spent his life in the warm sun. He wore blue work denims, a blue shirt and a leather vest. Around his neck was a faded red bandana. In his hand was a worn cowman's hat. His fine, handmade boots were high-heeled to fit the stirrups.

Everything about him pleased and delighted her much as the

country had done. Like the land, he was what she'd hoped for. For a moment they stood smiling at each other, liking what they saw. There was no constraint; they were old friends from some other life.

At last he said, "You have found the Beauvaise cup."

"Yes." She set it back on the mantel and turned again to face him. "And you are Pride Beauvaise."

"You know me, but we've never met. I wouldn't have forgotten." His voice was low-placed; it sounded like water under the wind.

"No, we haven't met. I'm Andrew's wife, Reanna."

Pride didn't show any surprise, but she sensed his disappointment. At last he asked, "Does Miss Jane know?" It seemed strange to her to hear him call his mother *Miss Jane*, but it was said to show respect.

"Yes, she's talking to Andrew now."

"That's all right, then. Welcome to Lochleven. May I kiss the bride?" Without waiting for an answer, he came across the hall to kiss her on the cheek. As his lips touched her face, the door of the front parlor opened and Miss Jane and Andrew appeared. There was a short, tense silence, and though Andrew was grinning, Reanna could feel his displeasure.

"I see, little brother, that you've already met my wife. I hoped you'd be friends. Now I see I have no worries on that score."

"My congratulations, Andrew," Pride said.

Andrew crossed the hall and stood by Reanna, his arm around her shoulders.

"She's a beauty, isn't she, Pride?" It was asked with no more consideration than if she had been a new head of livestock he had brought home with him. She found this gesture of ownership repellent. "I must warn you," Andrew continued, squeezing her shoulder, "Pride thinks he's old enough to court the ladies now." And Andrew laughed out loud.

Pride looked away and said nothing.

The atmosphere in the hall was strained. Miss Jane had hoped that in time the rivalry between Pride and Andrew would diminish, but if anything it had grown over the years. It was not so naked as it had once been; their feelings were smoothed by good humor, but the jokes had an edge. She had tried to be evenhanded to the son she had borne and the son she had taken in and to love them both equally. If she sometimes seemed to favor Andrew, it was because he was the elder and she had given him responsibility before Pride.

Pride had not resented it. Andrew had taken the place of the father he did not remember. He had tried to copy Andrew in everything, but they were opposites; they walked with a different gait. Pride always seemed easy with life, while Andrew always needed to prove himself. Andrew was at odds with the world.

Miss Jane heard the sound of Snow's voice calling out Andrew's name as she ran from the kitchen down the hall.

"Papa, you're home!" She ran to Andrew and flew into his arms.

"There's my girl, my princess." He held her high, turning her around and around.

When they were children, Letty had always sided with Andrew. Andrew, right or wrong, was always perfect in her eyes. If Letty could not have married Andrew, Miss Jane did not think Letty would have married anyone; every other man in the world was a poor second to Andrew. Andrew had married Letty, but Miss Jane had never believed that his affection was completely held by anyone until Snow was born.

Reanna caught a glimpse of Andrew's face as he turned past her; it was one of pure, unalloyed pleasure. Reanna hoped that one day Andrew would look at her like that, lovingly, without reserve.

When he set Snow down she seemed only a child again, a less formidable rival. She was about six, Reanna guessed, a small, delicate girl with fair hair. Her Indian blood had been dominated by Andrew's blond hair and blue eyes. Snow was a mirror in which he could see and love himself. Was that true?

"Did you bring me a present?" Snow asked, as if she already knew the answer; whatever Snow asked of Andrew, she seemed sure of getting it.

"I have a surprise for you."

"Where is it?" Her face was full of anticipation. Snow ran about looking for her surprise as if it were Christmas in the spring. "Where is it?"

"Here." Andrew pointed to Reanna. "I've brought you a new mother."

Snow's smile vanished. She stood looking at her father in disbelief. Her head began to shake from side to side. "No. My mama is dead. I don't want a new mother."

"We're married, honey. Reanna is my wife now."

"*No!*" Snow screamed. "I don't *want* another mother; you promised me a present!" She ran to Miss Jane and buried her face in her skirt, sobbing as if her heart were past mending. Miss Jane put her arms around Snow, who looked up at her, tears streaming down her cheeks. The child was making her appeal to Miss Jane as if she were the judge and the jury.

Andrew went quickly to his valise in the hall and took out a box wrapped in silver paper.

"Look'ee here, princess, look what I got for you." He went to Snow, who was still holding fast to Miss Jane. Snow watched as he knelt down like a suitor before her and took the top from the box to reveal a beautiful and expensive china doll. The doll had a wig of golden hair and she was dressed in the latest fashion, with a real fur muff to match her hat.

"Look, Snow. See, she can open and close her eyes." Snow watched as Andrew bent the doll back and forth and the cold, expressionless, blue glass eyes opened and closed.

"Do you like her?" Andrew asked. Snow nodded. "Do you want her?" Andrew asked, and again Snow nodded. The present was more than she had hoped for. "Then she's yours, honey. As soon as you say hello to Reanna." Snow glared at Reanna, her eyes bright with resentment. Her mouth drooped into a grim, determined pout.

"Say hello to Reanna," Andrew repeated in warning.

"No. I won't." Snow had a will to match Andrew's. She turned her face away from the doll and hid again in Miss Jane's skirts. Reanna could bear the scene no longer.

"Don't, Andrew," Reanna said in a low voice, "don't force her to do something she's not ready for. Remember, she's had no warning. Give her time. Let us get to know each other first."

"Reanna is right, Andrew," Miss Jane concurred. "In time everything will be all right."

Andrew hesitated, then held out the doll to Snow. She wouldn't look at him or the prize he offered, until he coaxed and petted her. Only then would she allow him to give her the thing she wanted most.

Miss Jane said sadly, "Since Snow's mother died, the child has depended on Cima and me for affection. She is like a stray calf."

"Snow's spoiled," Pride said. "It's time she learned how to live in the world with others." He spoke gently, but Andrew gave him a sharp, resentful glance. No one would put a curb on Snow, not if *he* knew of it.

"I hope that when she gets to know me she'll like me." Reanna found the words hard to say; the possibility of their coming true seemed remote.

"Snow is willful and spoiled, but she has lost a great deal," Miss Jane said. "She has no mother and Andrew is gone a lot. Perhaps you will not let her go uncorrected."

"I'm not the one to discipline her," Reanna said in alarm. "I don't want her to think of me as a—as a cruel, unfeeling stepmother."

"In the old days," Miss Jane said, "any child in the tribe who had to be punished was sent to the Dog King. He had a long stick, and if you were bad he scratched your arm for a first offense and if you were bad again you would feel his stick on your hand or your back. Nowadays there is no Dog King; the parents must say harsh words and give punishment."

"My princess isn't spoiled, is she?" Andrew was saying to Snow, ignoring them all. "She's a good girl, and a happy one."

"Thank you, Papa. Thank you for the lovely doll. You're the best papa in the world." Snow held the doll with one arm and put the other around Andrew's neck. She leaned over to kiss his cheek, and as she did she looked slyly out of her long lashes at Reanna.

"I don't *need* a mama," she said, "when I have you."

"Well, you've got me and she's here." Andrew pushed Snow away from him abruptly. "So you might as well make up your mind to it."

"Are you staying too, Papa?" Snow's face clouded.

"I'll have to go to Texas to get some cattle, honey."

"When?"

"Soon as I can," Andrew answered. "I've put it off too long as it is." Snow's eyes began to fill with tears. There might have been another scene, but a bell sounded, deep and loud as a doomsday call. Reanna jumped at the sound.

"I hope now you're here," Pride told her, "you'll get us another dinner bell. That one's a holdover from the days when we used it to call the hands. Now Lochleven's too spread out for that. The men mostly stay out on the line."

They walked into the dining room behind Miss Jane and Andrew, who was carrying Snow. The table could seat a dozen easily and, with extra leaves, twice that number. None of the chairs matched the table or the sideboard; all the furnishings had come to this house piecemeal, and yet they fit the house and the people who lived in it.

"Where's Taffy?" Andrew asked. "Why isn't he here?"

"And why," Miss Jane asked Cima, who was setting down a steaming dish of greens, "isn't there a place set for either you or Taffy?" Cima smiled a grin of pure mischief.

"We going to eat our supper in the kitchen tonight, so jes' the immediate family will set in the dining room. When you folks finish, *then* the help will make an entrance." And with an arrogant toss of her head she went into the kitchen.

Miss Jane sat at the head of the table, Andrew on her right hand and Pride on her left. As Reanna started to take the chair by Andrew, Snow stepped before Reanna and began to beg.

"Please let me sit by you, Papa. Please say yes. You've been gone so long."

"Of course, princess, you can sit by your papa." Andrew held the chair for Snow and left Pride to seat Reanna by him.

"Taffy Owen is our foreman," Pride explained. "No matter what Cima says, the truth is Taffy's shy of strangers—and ladies in particular. Taffy prefers to be out on the range. It's a compliment to you that he's even willing to come in after dinner." Reanna thought it kind of Pride to try to excuse Cima's rudeness and Taffy's absence.

"You could be a Washington diplomat," Reanna said to Pride, "if you care to give up ranching."

"I've always wanted to go to Washington." Pride grinned. "Was Washington your home?"

"No," Reanna said, "Virginia."

"They say it's gentle country," Miss Jane added, "both Virginia and Washington."

"To tell the truth," Pride said, "I've never seen so few at this table. At Lochleven you never know who will show up for meals. People traveling by come and go through here as though it were their own house. You'll be meeting a lot of different people."

"Miss Jane feeds half the Nation," Andrew broke in wryly. "They act like she runs a hotel where they can come and go at any time."

Miss Jane frowned at him. "When Pride's father was alive, he always took care of our people. We cannot refuse them a meal or a bed for the night if they need it. What kind of hospitality would that be?"

"They'll eat you out of house and home."

"That's quite possible," Pride said with a smile. "The whole tribe will probably show up tomorrow."

"Tomorrow?" Andrew looked at him in amazement.

"We are having a bride feast for Reanna," Miss Jane said, "as you should have known we would. I have sent out the sticks."

"In the old days, when there was a feast and a dancing or a tribal meeting," Pride explained to her, "a bundle of sticks was sent out to every household. They subtracted one stick from the bundle each day, and when there was none left, they knew it was the right day to attend."

"But you didn't know we were coming!" Andrew broke in. "How could you have sent out invitations?"

"When Cima saw you, I sent the first messengers," Miss Jane said, looking Andrew straight in the eye.

Cima, who had been standing by the sideboard with a stack of dishes, gave a short, harsh laugh. She knew that Andrew was angry but didn't dare to show it before Miss Jane. "And we're cuttin' this so fine, we only had to send out one twig to everybody."

"That is enough, Cima," Miss Jane said. "Although you are already married, Andrew, we must have a bride's dancing for your wife."

"There's no need for that." Andrew was trying to keep the anger from his voice.

"There is every need." Miss Jane was firm. "You have brought a wife into this family and now respect must be shown her. I don't want our people to think this is a *toopsa tawah*, a makeshift marriage. Or worse. She must take her place with honor."

"She doesn't expect a big powwow."

"No, but our friends do. *Every* bride in this house will have a proper bride's welcome."

"They can't come on such short notice," Andrew said crossly.

"They will come," Miss Jane said. "I have sent the invitations. If they have to travel all day and all night, they will come. This is a gathering of our clan. It is not every day we Beauvaises have a bride feast."

"But Andrew is not a Beauvaise . . ." Reanna began and stopped.

"Andrew is not my blood son, but he is my son. He is also an intermarried citizen. He bears all rights. They will come because you are Andrew's wife and because you are a Beauvaise bride."

"Well, it will make us even, Reanna." Andrew smiled his wry, mirthless smile and then turned to Miss Jane. "When I was in Washington, I met all her friends. This will show her how we do things out here in her new home." Sometimes even when Andrew was smiling he was not happy. Reanna had observed that sometimes that smile meant he was bent on getting even with those he felt had done him wrong.

"By the way, little brother," Andrew went on in the same tone, "what have you been doing with yourself while I've been away in Washington? Watching the grass grow and whittling the days away?"

"A little of both," Pride answered evenly, but Reanna knew that Andrew was taking a gibe at Pride.

"Only trouble with whittling," Andrew said, "it's got nothing to do with real work."

"And you, big brother," Pride asked finally, "besides finding a lovely bride, what real work did *you* do in Washington?"

"If we are going to talk business," Miss Jane interrupted, "Taffy should be here. Cima, will you bring Taffy in?"

Cima came back with Taffy Owen, who was following her as reluctantly as if she were leading him on a rope. He was a short, square man with bandy legs that had curved like barrel staves from living on a horse. He had a great wad of tobacco stuck unshifting in his lower lip. He was so shy that when he was introduced to Reanna he could not look directly at her. Little beads of water glistened on his slicked-down hair. Taffy had washed and shined himself up as best he could to meet Andrew's bride. Once he caught a glimpse of her, his eyes darted away as if she were the noonday sun. Reanna thought she had never met a more bashful man.

"Sit down, Taffy," Miss Jane said. "And you too, Cima."

When they were all served dessert, Miss Jane said, "All right, Andrew, you must tell us now what happened in Washington."

Andrew was silent for a long moment, like an orator who wants to make sure he has an audience's attention. Then he said, "The Department of the Interior turned us down. They won't let us lease out the land to Colonel Goodwell."

"Why not?" Pride asked, bewildered. He'd been sure that somehow Andrew would talk them around.

"They said it was their new policy." Andrew spoke dispassionately, betraying nothing of what he might be feeling.

"Well, that's it then, isn't it?" Pride looked downcast, as did Cima and Taffy.

"No, by God, that's not it!" Andrew raised his voice and his surface calm vanished. "We're not going to just *leave* it there!"

"What choice do we have?" Pride was puzzled by Andrew's change of manner.

"They won't let us lease out our land, but there's nothing they can do to keep us from buying the cattle, driving our own big herd up from Texas and grazing it on our own grass. That way we'll fatten the herd and send them to market, and we'll make the killing this time, not Goodwell." Pride stared at Andrew, saying nothing. "What's the matter with you, Pride? Cat got your tongue? I thought you'd be all in favor of it. You've always wanted us to graze more of our own cattle."

"A few hundred head, not a big herd." As they stared at each other, Pride realized that for some reason Andrew was trying to pick an argument with him. Andrew must feel ashamed, coming from Washington with nothing to show for it.

"You got a better solution, Pride?" Andrew demanded. "If so, let's hear it."

"We can wait until next year and maybe the law will change."

"Next year will be too late. You all know the situation as well as I do." He included them all in a cold, sweeping glance, but he let his eyes stay the longest on Miss Jane. "Washington has already taken the tribal census; they're making up the tribal rolls, and by next year they'll be giving out our allotments."

"Surely not as soon as next year." Miss Jane suddenly looked older than her years and as fragile as glass.

"Miss Jane, I know you don't want to face up to it, but it's going to happen. The surveyors have already laid out townships and run section lines on our pasture. Believe me, we'll never have the chance to use this much land again. We don't know how many acres we'll be able to keep when we get our allotments." Miss Jane said nothing. "Add it up, Miss Jane. You and Pride and Snow and I will get our homestead allotments and a little surplus land. Cima as a freedwoman will get forty acres and that's it." He finished speaking and waited for someone else to say something in reply.

It was Pride who broke the silence. "How big a herd are you talking about, Andrew?"

Andrew's turquoise eyes narrowed; he pulled at the edge of his mustache. "Three thousand head, maybe more."

"Jesus, Mary and Joseph!" Taffy exploded and then hung his head, his face a fiery red.

Cima stared open-mouthed before she said, "You done gone crazy, *haksi* crazy. Washington done affected your brain."

"You want us to buy three thousand head?" Miss Jane repeated the figure. She had not guessed that Andrew had that large a herd in mind.

"Yes, ma'am, more if we can swing it."

"And how do you mean to pay for them?" She forced her voice to remain steady.

"With cash."

"We haven't got that kind of money and you know it," Pride said flatly.

"We can borrow it, little brother, that's what the big boys do. Think big, get big. Think small, stay small."

"We've never borrowed and we won't start now." Miss Jane was adamant.

"Where will you get this three thousand head?" Taffy asked. He couldn't figure Andrew. Three thousand head was a lot of cows.

"From Colonel Goodwell. It's to his benefit to sell to us. He's short on pasture and the market's not been that good this year. We ought to be able to pick them up cheap."

"If the market's not good for him, it's not good for us." Pride scored his point.

"And I'm saying the market will go up by fall. If we take the chance and buy Goodwell's cattle, we'll be in the big money. Think big, get big. Think small, stay small."

"You *sure* Goodwell will sell to you?" Cima didn't like the sound of anything Andrew had said so far tonight.

"He'd sell to the devil himself if the price was right. Without pasture he's between a rock and a hard place."

Cima shook her head in wonder. "You sharp, Mr. Andrew, you real sharp. One day you'll hone so sharp you'll cut your own self." She saw that she had got under Andrew's skin; it pleased her to goad him. He was getting entirely too big for his britches.

"Listen." Andrew was angry now and his voice rose. "Time is running short. I want to buy a herd, drive them up from Texas over the Red River Crossing, and bring them on home along the old Chisholm Trail. As long as we pay the trail fees and keep them moving, there oughtn't to be any problem."

"There's a problem all right," Pride cut in.

"And what might that be, little brother?" Andrew spoke with heavy sarcasm.

"Grass." Pride's eyes flashed with restrained anger. "There's not enough grass for us to graze three thousand head—not this dry year, not even if we get rain. If you bring in three thousand head, you'll overgraze the pasture down to the nub. It could take years for the grass to come back." Andrew usually managed to buffalo him, but Pride meant to stand his ground on this.

Andrew would not give way. "I say this is the year to go flat out. Fish or cut bait."

The two men stared at each other, neither willing to be the first to look away. There was a silence in the room. This was the time for a decision that would affect them all for years to come. The light from the overhead kerosene lamp cast an eerie shadow on their faces.

"I want to hear from each of you," Miss Jane said, turning to Andrew. "Well, Andrew?"

"I say we buy up everything in Texas with four feet."

Miss Jane nodded, then looked at Pride. "Pride?"

"I say there is not enough grass. There would barely have been for Goodwell's two thousand; three thousand is impossible."

Now Miss Jane turned to Taffy, who was looking as uncomfortable as if he were sitting in nettles. "You've been a trail boss a long time, Taffy," Miss Jane said. "What do you think?"

He cleared his throat. "If you're planning to drive a mixed herd up from Texas this year, you'll want to get started. If we drive them more than ten days in this hot, dry weather, they'll lose weight. If they get poor and start looking for grass and water, we could have the biggest stampede since Noah's Ark." He hastily lowered his eyes and began to wish for a spittoon.

"What do you say, Cima?" Cima had ridden range in her younger days and had always given good advice in the past.

"I'll go along with you, Miss Jane. Whatever you decide."

"Reanna?" Reanna looked up startled; she had been listening intently, but she hadn't been prepared to speak.

"No need to ask her," Andrew answered sharply. "Reanna doesn't know horn from hoof."

"She is part of our family now," Miss Jane declared. "What we do will affect her."

"Then I'll speak for her." Andrew was clearly angry. "We go to Texas and get all the cattle we can."

Reanna was relieved that she didn't have to speak. At the same time she was grateful to Miss Jane for including her in the council.

"Well," Andrew said in that aggressive, almost defiant way of his, "now it's up to you, Miss Jane."

"I'll have to see how much money I can raise." She had not yet made up her mind. She'd learned long ago that a hasty decision was rarely a wise one. She would have to go to Tishomingo and see the Indian Agent before she would know how much she could count on. But it felt wrong. Andrew was pulling them along in his voracious hunger for security. If the grass was destroyed, though, there would be no security for any of them ever.

"I don't like it," she said aloud. "It seems like a very great risk."

"You've got to take risks in this world, Miss Jane. Or you go under, one way or another."

"If we're going to buy cattle from the Colonel," Taffy put in, "we don't want any of his swamp angels."

"Or," Andrew added, "any of his new fancy breeds, either." This last was another cut at Pride, who was experimenting with different strains, arguing that a mixed breed might make more of a weight gain than the old longhorn.

"When do we go to Texas?" Pride asked.

"You'll stay here. We need you to stay on the ground."

Snow stirred and rubbed her eyes. She'd slept through most of the grown-ups' talk, but she'd come awake with the word *Texas*. "You all talked and talked," she complained, "but nobody asked me what *I* wanted."

"What do you want, princess?"

"It's past her bedtime," Cima muttered.

"I want you to stay home with me," Snow said.

"I can't, sweetheart, Papa has to go to Texas."

"Then will you take me up and tell me a bedtime story?"

"Not tonight, honey. We have to talk some more."

"I'll take you up and put you to bed," Reanna volunteered.

"No." Snow pouted at her. "I don't want you."

"Cima, take Snow," Andrew ordered.

"I don't *want* Cima, I want you!"

"What you want, princess, and what you git are two different things. And old Cima is what you got." Cima swung Snow onto her hip and carried her up the stairs.

They sat late that night around the dining table at Lochleven, discussing the cattle, the grass, the money, and Miss Jane watched and listened. Andrew, obeying his impulsive gambler's nature, argued vehemently for the great herd, convinced it was the last chance they would ever have for a big killing; Pride, conservative and prudent, fought him, equally certain it would destroy the grazing land; Taffy, excited by the grand challenge of it, swayed toward Andrew's position, as he always did; Cima, bred to penury and small ventures, increasingly sided with Pride. Yes, this might be the last year they could act before the land was divided—unthinkable as that event was—but if the pasturage was denuded, if the vast, rolling, rippling sea of grass was destroyed, what *then* could be salvaged? It wouldn't matter how ruthlessly the land was divided, for everyone alike would starve. It would be the Trail of Tears all over again.

"No," Miss Jane said quietly into a silence. "I am opposed to your plan, Andrew." Amazed, he started to protest still again, and she held up one hand. "These are dry years. Government policy toward us is tighter. If the grassland is destroyed, *we* are destroyed." She heard Pride sigh in relief, saw Andrew's eyes glitter at his brother once. "Too much is at stake here. You may drive a thousand head, no more. As it is, you must wait until I can see how much cash money I can raise. A great sum is owed me on my annuity, but I don't know how much of it I can collect from the Indian Agent."

Andrew shoved back his chair abruptly and rose; a muscle in his cheek flexed once. "That's it then," he said. "I'm going up to bed."

Pride and Reanna exchanged a swift, naked glance—Miss Jane saw it—then Reanna looked down at her hands. Andrew was making a great mistake to treat his new wife this way. Miss Jane hoped he was doing it to give the impression he didn't mean to set Reanna in Letty's place. But this girl was not remotely like Letty; she had brains as well as beauty. And beyond that, she had a mind of her own, a very definite sense of herself. Was Andrew afraid that if he answered Reanna's questions, the pupil would one day outstrip the teacher? If he continued to ignore the girl, to turn his back on her this way, he would have only himself to blame.

But the consequences would fall upon them all.

"Andrew," Miss Jane called softly. He turned at the doorway, his cheek flexing. She hadn't realized how much he'd set his heart on the big herd. "Andrew, it is not always the brave thing to dare *too* much."

His eyes fixed on her, pale as sea jade; then he nodded once and left the room. Pride was watching Reanna again, with that steady, shy intensity. The moment made Miss Jane uneasy. Looking at the two of them, hearing Andrew's boot heels sharp on the stairs, she sensed danger and she was afraid.

IN the morning, when Reanna awoke in the unfamiliar room, she found Andrew had already left. She dressed hurriedly and went downstairs. Everyone else was already at the breakfast table; their upturned faces and the silence that greeted her told her she was still the outsider.

"Why didn't you wake me?" she whispered to Andrew.

"I thought you needed your beauty sleep," he answered loud enough for them all to hear.

"She looks fine to me," Pride said gallantly.

The coffee was strong, black and hot. The heaping plate of gravy, biscuits and steak helped to revive her spirits. Andrew and Pride were going to break horses that morning. The sun coming in at the windows was magnified by the glass and warmed her back. Surely everything would be right in her world in a day or two.

"You ride a horse?" Cima asked her. The question was almost insolent in its challenge.

"Yes, I ride," Reanna answered evenly. "I am sure I'm not up to your standard, but I ride."

"Sidesaddle, I suppose, like a fine lady?"

"Yes, but I'm willing to learn to ride a western saddle."

"Reanna may ride any way she likes." Miss Jane gave Cima a long, meaningful glance. "I rode sidesaddle when I was young, and you never reproached me for it." Miss Jane rose, said a brisk good morning and headed for her study.

"May I come too, Papa?" Snow was saying. "Please, may I?"

"Sure, princess, come and see if your uncle Pride can keep up with your papa." Nothing Andrew did seemed to provoke Pride, neither the challenge nor the manner in which it was given.

"Where are they going to break the horses?" Reanna asked Cima.

"In the corral, silly," Snow answered, "where do you think?"

"I think *you'd* best mind your manners, missy." Cima gave Snow a look of stern rebuke. Miss Jane had apparently changed Cima's attitude toward Reanna, and now Cima passed the lesson on.

They went out the back door, past the kitchen garden and the chicken house, toward the barn and corral. Above, the sky was bright blue and the wind ran strong from the south. Both Pride and Andrew were in Levis, boots and faded blue work shirts. Each added worn chaps, gauntlet gloves and a bright bandana to his outfit. Their hats, drawn down low on their foreheads, made Reanna think of knights making ready for a jousting tournament.

The two wild horses were stalled in separate chutes, pawing at the earth and whinnying in protest at their confinement. Taffy, who was their guardian and the marshal of the joust, waved his hat at Reanna.

Reanna smiled and waved back. Then she, Cima and Snow perched in a row on the rail fencing of the corral. Cima shook her head as if this was an event of which she did not altogether approve.

"They've been at this kind of foolishness ever since I can remember. Each one's dead set on outdoing the other, proving he's champion. Andrew started it, and now it seems like he just can't let it alone."

"My papa's the best horsebreaker in the world," Snow called proudly to the wind.

"So far, the count's about even," Cima said. She pointed at the chutes. "You see those two cow ponies there? Each man gets a horse by the draw, and then they compete to see who can get his critter saddle-broke first. The horses were range wild and Taffy has already worked them in, but neither has been saddle-broke or rode yet. You need a lot of Quarter horses and cutting horses in an outfit this size."

"What's the difference?" Reanna was eager to learn.

"A cutting horse will know by instinct how to cut out a cow from the herd and keep it separate. A Quarter horse is bred to run fast for a quarter mile so a cowboy can catch and rope a calf. And he'll obey a command to pull rope while the cowboy dismounts and ties the calf for branding. Quarter horses are the smartest horses I know of. They've got to be strong so they can last on a long trail and not tire. They're as smart as they are wild, these ponies. It takes a good hand to break them to be a part of a remuda."

The two horses, one a paint pony, the other a dappled gray, seemed aware that something of importance was about to occur. They reared and slammed against their prison. Taffy tossed a coin; Reanna saw it flash silver in the sun and bounce in the dust below. When Taffy retrieved it, Andrew had drawn the first ride on the paint pony.

Andrew pounded two stakes in the hard ground, setting them securely. Then he laid out coils of rope and signaled Taffy to lead the horse from the chute. The bronco came fighting, screaming, unwilling into the ring. His hind legs were hobbled, but his fore-feet were dangerous weapons. He couldn't use them as he would have liked; if he did, he would throw himself off balance and fall. Still, he managed to paw the ground into dust.

Reanna saw the concentration on Andrew's face, the determina-tion; beads of perspiration mingled with the dust and dark, damp patches showed at the back of his shirt and beneath his armpits.

Pride watched Andrew move in toward the horse. There had been a time when Pride had wanted Andrew's approval so much that he would have let him win just to please him, but those days were past. He no longer saw Andrew as a god. Andrew could make mistakes. Sometimes his opinion was not only wrong but actually dangerous. This determination to buy and drive every head of cattle he could muster had the seeds of destruction in it; the move wasn't sound or well thought out. It was a plan born of desperation. An-drew was trying to prove something, to himself and to Miss Jane. This morning's horsebreaking was only the beginning of some-thing; he knew Andrew meant to win today, no matter what.

"Watch Papa!" Snow said, her eyes shining. "You'll see, he'll win."

"How do you know that?" Reanna asked teasingly.

"Because he wants to show off for me, that's why."

Reanna thought that was only a part of the truth. It was more likely that Andrew wanted to win today because he liked to have his own way in everything. Last night Pride had opposed Andrew and Miss Jane had sided with Pride. In Washington the government had refused to let him lease grassland. The government and Miss Jane might thwart him, but Andrew didn't mean to let a mere horse get the better of him.

The horse was tethered, hobbled and unable to move. His eyes rolled in his head with fear as Andrew moved hand over hand up the ketch rope to the horse's shoulder and forced his mouth open to receive the bit. Reanna had seen the bridle and bit in Andrew's hand. The bit was grooved and sharp. She knew enough of horses to know it was an instrument of torture.

The horse struggled against the violation, but the bridle went over his ears and the bit into his mouth. He chewed, jerked and fought, but the bit went deeper and deeper into his tongue and mouth. He screamed with pain and outrage and then was suddenly quiet.

"Stand still, you bugger." Reanna heard Andrew issue the command as if it would be instantly understood and obeyed. All the horse knew was that it must avoid further pain at the cost of freedom of movement. Yet the sound of Andrew's harsh voice caused him to jerk his head in time to see the man approaching with blanket and saddle. First the blanket came down on his back. That could be borne, but the saddle and the grip of the cinch being drawn tighter and tighter was a second torture. Andrew had drawn the cinch twice as tight as he would ordinarily have done, so that the horse could not blow out his lungs and chest and then, when Andrew was in the saddle, exhale, causing the saddle to slip. Andrew knew almost every turn of a horse's mind. Taffy had taught him well.

When the saddle was securely in place, Andrew mounted quickly, and sat the horse like a conqueror. At the feel of the alien weight, the horse arched his back, grinding savagely at the bit until foam flecked with blood slobbered from his mouth.

"Let him loose," Andrew called out to Taffy, who slipped the ropes front and back. The horse stood still for one brief second—and then flung himself upward, arching and bucking in a fury to be rid of his unwanted burden. Andrew held the reins with one hand, swept his hat in the other through the dusty air. He snapped back and forth in taut, ugly jerks and spasms, turning out the toes of his boots and digging his spurs into the sides of the horse until Reanna could see dark, ugly weals on his flanks. Around and around the horse went, plunging and fishtailing; then, in a desperate attempt to dislodge his tormentor, he ran close to the fence, while the man riding him yelled above the wind, "Settle, damn you, settle down!"

Reanna couldn't imagine how Andrew managed to stay on the horse. Snow shouted until she was hoarse. Cima's face was grim and disapproving; the lines around her mouth were etched into marks of scorn. "You can learn a lot about a man by the way he breaks a horse," she said.

"Pick up!" Reanna heard Andrew shout. She didn't know what he meant until she saw Taffy, mounted on a second horse, chase after Andrew. When Taffy was alongside, Andrew jumped from the paint pony onto Taffy's horse. Taffy slowed to let Andrew slide to the ground. It took Andrew a few moments to find his walking feet; he leaned against the fence, panting, his shirt dark with sweat.

The paint, thinking the torment was over and that he'd triumphed, stood still. Andrew took a coiled rope from a fence post and expertly lassoed the pony. Pulling it to him again, he swung into the saddle, this time keeping the rein even shorter than the first time.

Again the horse bucked and reared, wheeling right and left, but this time without the fire of their first encounter. Again Andrew called to Taffy to be pick-up man.

The third time Andrew mounted, he signaled Taffy to open the gate of the corral. Holding the horse's head upward, he walked him through the gate and then let him run, still holding his head unnaturally high, so that if the paint tried to twist or throw him, in one motion Andrew could snap the rein and break the horse's neck. As Andrew rode away, he whipped the horse with lariat and spurs; the animal, lunging toward the open land, had terror in his eyes as well as pain.

When Andrew had run the horse toward the eastern end of the Ridge and back again, he tied him at a hitching post by the barn. Both horse and rider showed signs of fatigue, but the horse was now marked for life. He was broken, willing to run and to stop when the man told him to. He'd learned to obey.

Andrew left the horse—still saddled, blowing and trembling—and walked toward the women, mopping at his face and neck with a red cotton handkerchief. He was grinning happily, his teeth white under his mustache.

"You did it, Papa, you broke him!" Snow cried.

"He should take the saddle off and walk that pony to cool him out," Cima muttered. "The cayuse will get a muscle cramp and be too sore tomorrow to ride anywhere."

"I know what I'm doing," Andrew said. He'd heard what Cima said, because she'd meant him to, though she'd spoken to Reanna. "I broke that horse *my* way. When I give that horse an order now, he'll obey."

"Yes sir, Mr. Bossman." Cima's distaste was clear. "He'll obey you only because he's scared not do. You rode him all right, cowboy, but you rode the heart clean out of him."

"What's my time?" Andrew called out to Taffy, turning away.

"The horse looks thirsty," Reanna said softly, and Cima laughed once.

"Looks a good deal more than that."

"A horse has got to learn to obey, not to be a pet." Andrew turned to one of the ranch hands who had drifted up to watch. "When he cools down take the saddle off him, but *don't* give him any water or mash. If he has water too soon, he'll end up being a blower, with his lungs all shot." Then, without any word to Reanna, Andrew pulled himself up on the corral fence, whistling between his teeth.

"When a horse is that hard broke, there's no reward in it for the rider or the animal." Cima wouldn't let him alone. "There'll come a day, Andrew, when you ask that horse to go an extra mile with you. And he won't have the heart for it."

Reanna shivered in the warm spring breeze and looked across the yard at the horse. When the saddle was removed, there was a dark stain where his coat had been rubbed to the raw. As the ranch hand led him into the barn he was limping, and on his flank she saw the cuts of the spur. She kept her eyes away from Andrew and fastened on the corral.

Now it was Pride's turn. Taffy pulled the stakes from the ground and set one single one in the center. Then he led out the gray, who came nervous, unsure, defiant in these new surroundings. Taffy chewed at his wad and spit into the wind to find which way it blew, then fastened the horse by a rope to the stake and nodded to Pride to signal his time had begun to run.

Pride walked slowly upwind of the tethered horse. When he began his approach the horse drew back, straining against the rope. Pride caught at the ketch rope. The horse's nostrils flared as he caught the near scent of the man. His ears went back and he shied away, but the man was sure and confident; every movement signaled a command.

As Pride moved up the rope, drawing closer, hand over hand, the horse's eyes rolled in terror. Then, the man spoke to him, a word Reanna didn't understand. Pride said it over and over—*hahpohnshe, hahpohnshe.* The word itself was soft and compelling; it had the sound of the wind in it.

"What is he saying?" Reanna asked Cima.

"He's saying easy, easy." Cima smiled. She kept her eyes on Pride. "It isn't so much the word as the sound of Pride's voice. And the way he's let the horse catch his scent."

The animal trembled as the man gently put his hand on his nose; he whinnied, pawed at the ground, yanking away from the unfamiliar touch, but the man went on stroking, talking, whispering in the horse's ear. The horse, now afraid of losing his freedom, began to fight against the man and the rope, but Pride held him fast, soothing, calming, insisting that the horse listen to the secret he was telling him.

"Watch," Cima said. "Pride is telling the horse his secret."

"What secret?"

"Every Chickasaw horsebreaker knows. Though each may use different words. Pride is telling him that today, together, the two of them will fly together in the wind." Cima smiled again, her gaunt black face wrinkled with pleasure. "Sometimes I think Pride is part horse."

As Pride whispered he slowly took the bridle from around his waist, where he had tied it with a bit of rope, and slipped it gently over the horse's head. The bit slid into his mouth; the animal strained up against the strange, foreign object. Then, as Pride continued to talk, the gray stood still, more uncertain than frightened now of what would happen next. All the horse was sure of now was the sound of Pride's voice. It soothed him into standing when the blanket was put on his back and the saddle was cinched into place.

Then the man betrayed the beast. He vaulted into the saddle on his back and the horse went wild with outrage. Plunging, whirling, jolting, the creature dashed headlong around the enclosure; but the man stayed on him. One hand was in the air gauging the next swing of the horse, and the man was saying over and over, singing it into the air, "Be quiet, be still." Where Andrew's movements had been jerky and fierce, Pride was all fluidity and grace. Even in the head-snapping, arm-flailing fury of the ride, he seemed loose, easy, one with the animal.

At last, when the horse stood tired, quivering with rage and bewilderment, the man dismounted, still holding on to the bridle, and spoke again into the horse's ear.

"Now then, now then, that wasn't so bad, was it? You'll get used to the weight. Don't be afraid, you know me. You're not afraid of me, are you? It's only the weight on your back that you don't know."

Pride walked the horse to where Taffy was waiting with a sack of grain in his arms. The two men hoisted up the sack and fastened it in the saddle. The horse, unable to guess the cause of the weight when he could see the man, allowed himself to be led round and round the circle of the corral. He went unwillingly, pulling and kicking, but going on as Pride kept telling him that he had nothing to fear, that he was a fine horse and that today, together, they would ride.

At last, when Pride considered it was time, Taffy took the sack from the saddle. When Pride remounted, Taffy ran to open the gate to the corral. Rearing, screaming, with an awesome burst of strength, the horse made for the open. Reanna could hear Pride as he cried out, "Now we go. Together, we go like the wind!"

The horse galloped in wild, uneven patterns, kicking and skidding, trying every way he knew to throw the man from him. But the rider remained, and together they raced toward the far end of the Ridge. By the time they came back toward the corral, the horse's gait was more even and Pride was in control. He rode the horse up to the hitching post, dismounted and secured the reins. The animal was lathered and winded, but he seemed willing to accept his fate. He stood patiently as the man took off his saddle and began to rub him down with hands full of hay. At first the horse trembled, unused to the man's hands on his back and flanks, but soon the trembling stopped. The horse stood, resigned to the pleasure of the sensation. When Pride had finished grooming he gave the horse some water and fed him from his hand, and then he said, loud enough so that Reanna could catch the words, "I told you we would ride today. Tomorrow we will ride again, and for many days after." The horse's head came up from his oats, but the sound the man made was something he was growing used to. Whatever the man said to him, he knew it would do him no good to refuse. The horse bowed his head again and ate.

"Tomorrow I'll put shoes on this one," Pride called.

"Time, Taffy!" Andrew shouted. "Call time and tell us who won." There was a silence around the ring. Reanna felt troubled and uneasy; she had the vague sense that she was threatened somehow by what she'd seen.

"You won, Andrew," Taffy said, peering at the big gold watch. "By a good half hour."

"Papa won—I knew he'd win!" Snow turned to Reanna; she even had a smile for her now. "He's the fastest breaker in the world."

"Both them horses will obey," Cima said, climbing down from the top rail. "But for Pride that gray horse will be willing to pour out his very heart."

THE first guests began to come in about sundown. They came on horses, in buggies and wagons, and on foot. They were young and old, Indian and white. There were single travelers and large families. Some rode on the finest of saddles, some bareback. They all spoke in different and strange languages and they all spoke at once.

Reanna stood on the steps with Andrew on one side and Miss Jane on the other. Miss Jane was dressed in white buckskin. The dress had been embroidered in colored beads. Cima and Pride stood beside Miss Jane and Snow by her father, holding his hand. Taffy tried to appear invisible. They were a royal family and Miss Jane's courtiers streamed up Beauvaise Ridge from all directions. Soon the yard was filled with people eating, talking, laughing, but first they all filed past Miss Jane to give greetings and look at Reanna.

"If they're disappointed in me," Reanna said to Andrew, "at least they'll have plenty to eat!" But Andrew didn't laugh.

"Of course they'll like you. You're my wife."

Reanna wanted to say that in that case she did not even have to appear, but she was learning to hold her tongue. Great preparations had been made by Miss Jane and Cima to feed the multitude. There were pots of bubbling *pishofa*, a hominy and pork dish without which no Indian tribal meeting would be complete. There were whole beeves turning on spits. There were barbecued pigs, and although it was too early for the summer corn, last year's crop had been ground and made into a dough to be fried in pots of boiling oil; the traditional Indian fry bread was considered a great delicacy.

Most of all there were the people, unlike any she had ever met before. When they spoke in Chickasaw Miss Jane would translate for her.

"This one says you have the sun in your hair." Miss Jane smiled. "She also says your husband must be a happy man to lie in your bed." Reanna blushed. She wondered if Andrew would agree.

"Thank her for me and please tell me her name."

"There are too many names for that," Miss Jane assured her, but she was pleased the girl had asked. She was holding herself with dignity; she had courage and grace. If she could learn to control her emotions, to discipline herself, she might survive in this harsh place. She might some day be of use to the people.

"I want to know everyone as soon as I can," Reanna said, "and their names."

"Very well, you can try. This is T Cali and his children." There were at least a dozen children crowding around a large man who was naked to the waist, wearing only breeches and a few feathers in his plaited hair. On his back was a quiver of arrows and in his hand a bow. He might have stepped from the past. He didn't belong in the world of trains and telegraph.

"Where is his wife?" Reanna asked, thinking that the mother of all these children must be a remarkable woman.

"He has three wives," Miss Jane replied with a hint of a smile.

"With all those children, I suppose he wore them out," Reanna said.

"No, they are all still very much alive. They are there walking behind him, to show their respect for him as the head of the house. Also because if they walk together, it is a sign that one is not more favored by him than another."

Reanna tried not to stare at the three wives, but she was fascinated. They were all young and they had on as many clothes and beads and ribbons as T Cali was bare. It was clear that she had a lot to learn about the people and their customs.

"Do most men have three wives?" she asked.

"No," Miss Jane said, "it is not lawful to have more than one these days, but these three are so happy that the law looks the other way. To keep the church happy, he says he married only one at a time. But I don't think anyone believes him."

If Reanna was curious about the guests, they were even more so about her. They tried not to stare, but like children told not to do a thing, they couldn't help themselves. She allowed herself to be circled, inspected and touched; she was criticized by one woman for being too thin and by another for being too tall. They seemed to think she was deaf, or that she didn't understand English any better than Chickasaw.

"Many are of my clan," Miss Jane said. "All are of my tribe. Because I am descended from the *picaunli*, and because I am Pride Beauvaise's widow, they think I am responsible for them. They come to me with their worries and their fears. These days times are hard and they need more than advice; they need food, clothes and medicines, and most of all they need to learn how to live in a world they did not make and do not understand. Andrew says I do too much for them, but who else is there to do it? My husband took care of them and now I must." She looked at Reanna. "Do you understand?"

"Yes," Reanna said. "I think so. If you'll let me, I'll help you all I can. I know I can learn if you will teach me."

Miss Jane felt strangely moved by the sincerity of the offer. It was more generous than she had hoped. For a moment she felt lighter and less tired.

"I will depend on you as a daughter. You are an ornament to this house."

Snow couldn't bear to see Reanna getting all of the attention. She pulled at Andrew, begging him to take her away to see the cookfires and the people. To Snow, this evening was as good as a fair. Andrew, who couldn't say no to his princess and who was bored standing still for so long, took Snow up on his shoulder and carried her around the porch toward the barbecue.

Miss Jane and Cima had been called away to settle some crisis in the kitchen, and Pride and Reanna stood alone on the steps. As one of the newcomers knelt and stroked the skirt of Reanna's dress, she turned to Pride and said, "I feel I am a waxwork doll Andrew brought home with him and put on exhibition. I'm not sure they think I'm real."

"You're real." Pride's eyes were merry and bright. "They all came to see you, and they like what they see."

"Do you really think so?"

"I know so. They all think Andrew is a lucky man. And so do I."

She didn't know how to answer him. He gave her such a sense of courage and confidence. She was amazed that to be near Pride seemed the most easy and natural place in the world to her. He alone made her feel at home, as if she belonged. The uneasy constraint, the sense of resentment she'd felt from the beginning with

Andrew was nonexistent when she was with Pride. She felt she belonged to him, not as his property but making up two halves of the same circle.

A short, fat woman wrapped in a scarlet blanket came up the steps to them. She spoke rapidly to Pride, who kept trying to interrupt her, but to no avail.

To Reanna's surprise the woman spoke again, this time in English. "They told me Miss Jane's son had brought home a wife. Pride is her only son, so I thought you must be his woman."

"I am her son as well." Andrew had come around the corner of the porch in time to hear the woman's words. He still carried Snow on his shoulders. He reached up and set Snow down as if suddenly she'd become too heavy for him. It was a remark he knew was made often but never to his face. To the full bloods he would always be a squaw man and nothing more.

"You are called Miss Jane's son, but only Pride is of her blood," the woman said. She turned and left them standing in strained silence.

Before Reanna could think of anything to say, there was a great commotion in the yard. Up from the west slope of the Ridge, a man in a red coat came riding one horse and stringing another behind him. He was followed by a pack of baying hounds. In one hand he was brandishing a bottle. He rode right up to the steps of Lochleven through the crowd and, dismounting, flung himself down on one knee before Reanna and shouted, "To the bride! By God, she's even better-looking than they said." He rose and kissed her soundly on both cheeks.

"This buffoon," said Pride, laughing, "is Simon Frampton, our neighbor to the north. He has the best horses, dogs and brandy in the Oklahoma Territory."

"And," Andrew added, shaking Frampton's hand, "the worst cattle."

"Now that sort of talk won't do." Frampton stood back, eyeing Reanna with obvious satisfaction. He was young and rather handsome, with blue eyes and a ruddy, round face. "I can't very well tell you what I think of *you* Andrew—not in front of this lady of yours." He took Reanna's hand and led her down the steps. "My dear, I have a bridal gift for you." He put the reins of the stringer in her hands. "This filly is a highbred sorrel. Her name is Molly May and she is yours."

Reanna was filled with delight. She could see from Andrew's

frown that he disapproved of the gift. She didn't know why and she didn't care. The horse danced nervously, skittish because of the crowd.

"She's lovely! I know I shouldn't take her. She's far too valuable."

"Nonsense," Frampton said. "If you don't take her, I'll set her loose and the mustangers will steal her." He reached for the reins but Reanna held them away from him.

"I thought you didn't want her," Frampton bellowed joyfully.

"Oh, but I do! I want her with all my heart. Please Andrew, may I keep her?"

"Yes," he said grudgingly, "why not? If you don't, this English renegade would probably turn her loose. You never know what he'll do, or why."

Frampton held up one hand to silence them all. "There's one condition." He bowed again before Reanna. "That you will save the first dance for me. Remember I got here first, before Father Soule. That old scallywag in priest's clothing is coming right behind me."

"I'll gladly give you your dance," Reanna said, stroking the velvet nose of the horse. This beauty was her passport to freedom, she knew; on Molly May she could ride anywhere she pleased.

"Tallyho!" Frampton roared. Turning, he caught sight of Cima. Flinging aside the empty bottle and kicking the dogs out of his path, he embraced the tall black woman and lifted her up into the air. "Ah, my black beauty! How I've missed you and your wicked, wicked tongue!" He carried her off toward the tables while she protested and struggled in amusement.

"Don't pay him any mind," Andrew said with a disdainful smile. "Frampton is outrageous. No wonder his family pay him to stay out of England."

"Is that true?"

"Nobody knows for sure," Pride answered evenly. "And it doesn't matter. Frampton's been a good friend and a good neighbor."

Before Reanna could ask any more, she saw a priest riding a mule approach the house. He was an elderly man and was perspiring freely. A swarm of Indian children ran to greet him and to help him dismount. He seemed to know each one by name. He had a pat on the head and a kind word for each of them save one, to whom he gave a smart cuff. Instead of resenting the blow, the child seemed to feel it was well deserved.

"Father Soule," Pride said, "won't ride a horse. He prefers that old mule. We used to think it was because he wished to appear more like one of the prophets in the Bible but it turns out it is all because of his wine."

"His wine?"

"Yes, he's proud of his vineyard. He carries his wine in a basket, a *panier* he calls it, on the back of the mule. He says wine travels best by mule."

"I thought there was supposed to be no whiskey or spirits in Indian Territory," Reanna said. Andrew gave a harsh laugh.

"That's the law," Pride said. "Besides, he lives across the river in Oklahoma Territory."

"It's a stupid law," Andrew scoffed. "All anyone has to do is ride across the river into Oklahoma Territory and you can get all the rotgut you want at the Triangle Saloon."

Father Soule mounted the steps with difficulty; in an old-world flourish he took Reanna's hand and bent down to kiss it.

"*Enchanté,*" he said.

He was an old man, very slight and frail-looking, which belied the work he had done and the strength which still remained in his soul. His eyes were as bright and alive as a young man's. He spoke with a pronounced French accent. His greatest conceit outside of his wine was his firm belief that he spoke with no trace of his old tongue. He was so well loved that when members of his flock could not understand his words they had been known to pretend they were deaf rather than deflate his vanity.

"I am very sorry," Father Soule said, "that I could not perform your wedding ceremony myself. *Ma chérie,* I have brought you some of last year's wine. No, please"—he held up his hand—"do not thank me. It is a trifle. The grapes were not so good last year, but I hope it will bring a blessing to your house."

As if Father Soule's arrival had been a signal that the real festivities could begin, boys with flaming torches touched them to a dozen pipes jutting out of the ground and a burst of light suddenly illuminated the Ridge, the house and the yard. It was brighter than a dozen bonfires. Reanna had never seen anything like it. The flames made the night about the house almost as bright as day. As the flares were ignited, the people all gave a great gasp and cry of delight.

"It never fails to please them," Andrew said.

"But what is it?" Reanna asked.

"It's gas from the ground," Pride said. "There are some cracks in the Ridge. All you have to do is run a pipe in and ignite the escaping gas and you have light. Don't you have gas like this in the East?"

"But why doesn't the Ridge explode?"

Pride laughed. "There's only a little gas escaping. It's nothing to worry about." And Reanna saw Doc Hersey, Amoretta and Jack Levy driving past one of the flares in a smart buckboard as little concerned as if it were something that they did every day of the week.

Reanna could not imagine what her mother would say to any of these people. A mad Englishman, a French priest, Indians naked to the waist, not to mention a Jewish merchant, a bibulous Yankee doctor and his wife, an ex-telegrapher who painted her face—and no matter how she tried, she could never have explained to her mother, or to anyone else for that matter, why this night was the happiest of her whole life.

Under the splendor of the gas flares, the campfires added their warm glow. From one fireside and then another, Reanna heard the sound of drums and the whistle of a flute. In a different rhythm, a fiddler on the porch struck up a country tune. The singing and dancing had begun. Reanna was held by the sound of a deer-bone flute; it seemed to pierce her heart.

"What a sweet sound," she murmured. "I've never heard anything like it."

"Thank you." Pride looked pleased. "I carve the flutes, when Andrew thinks I should be out on the range. Perhaps you'll let me give you a flute for a bride gift." He smiled and moved away in the crowd.

"Enjoying yourself?" Andrew asked her.

"Oh, very much."

"It must hit you as plain crazy, all this." He gestured toward the leaping campfires, the surging, shouting figures.

"Crazy? No. I'm so happy to be here, Andrew."

"I was afraid you'd hate it."

"Why?"

"It's not your wild, wild West." But he wasn't mocking her now; his eyes were different, uncertain. He seemed genuinely troubled about her, and it moved her deeply. She took his hand. Maybe things would turn out well between them after all. She wanted it with all her heart.

"I love you, Andrew," she said softly. "I want to be . . ." She broke off.

Taffy was running toward them. "Andrew, you better come quick. We got trouble."

"What is it?"

"Some of the Ponca have come in from the north. They're down by the corral."

"How the hell did they get this far south?"

"Beats me. Probably just passing through and heard there was a powwow. Anyway, they're out there now, raising Cain, and I'm worried about what they may do next."

"Have they been at the firewater?"

"I'd say yes and then some." Taffy rolled his eyes.

"OK, get a beef and put it in the corral. I'll take care of it."

Reanna watched him walk off toward the barn, his head down, purposeful and intent. His world was the world of action, not thought; reactions, not emotion. Was that true? Did this land do that to people? No, there was Pride . . .

Snow ran up to her, looking tense and excited. "Come on, let's go see the Ponca. They're wild. Not like our people."

"Do you think your father would want us to?"

"Papa won't mind." Snow paused. "Unless, of course, you're afraid. But I'll be with you."

It was the first time Snow had asked her to do anything. Reanna wanted them to be friends.

"All right then," Reanna agreed, "I'll come with you."

She followed Snow around the house, past the kitchen garden to the corral. Snow wouldn't let go of her hand; Reanna felt like a captive. As they drew close to the corral, she could see a crowd beginning to gather; they were packed around the railing so that Snow had to push them aside to make room at the front. Snow was determined to get them a good view.

There in the corral where Reanna had watched Andrew and Pride breaking horses was a small band of Ponca Indians. They were in a circle, standing mute, looking down at a beef that had been staked out in the center of the ground. Andrew stood over the creature with his hand raised above its head. In his hand was a knife. The cold, honed steel glittered, and then in a flash the knife came down into the animal's throat. The animal bellowed as an artery spouted blood. Then, as the beef thrashed dumbly against the ropes that held it, Andrew withdrew the knife and in a second motion cut along the abdomen, opened the belly and cut out a big chunk of meat.

"That's the liver," Snow whispered. Reanna could hear the excitement in her voice. "They like it raw; they think it's a treat."

Reanna could not take her eyes from the steaming piece of bloody meat while the Ponca tore it from Andrew's hand and, crouching down in the dirt, began to hack off pieces and season it with warm gall. As they ate, the warm blood streamed down their chins, staining their cheeks and hands. Always in the center of this hideous picture was the image of Andrew and his bloody hand holding the killing weapon. That hand that held the knife had touched and caressed her body.

"Would you like to try some?" Snow asked. "It's best when the blood is still warm. You may not like the gall. It's very bitter." Reanna slowly turned to look at Snow. Her face was open and innocent, but her eyes were as wise and calculating as a witch's. Reanna felt her own blood running hot in her veins; she heard a ringing in her ears and then she fell to the ground.

"Look, look!" Snow was saying. "Look everyone, the strange woman has fallen down."

REANNA'S first sight as she opened her eyes was Andrew washing his hands in the basin; blood was streaming down his arms. She saw that she had blood on her dress and thought she might faint again. She felt that somehow she was a sacrifice, like the animal in the corral.

"Oh my God," she whispered.

Andrew turned to her, angry and puzzled.

"What happened to you? What made you do a damn fool thing like that?" Why he should be so angry with her she did not know.

"I saw you," she said through stiff lips. She felt frozen with a sickening revulsion. "I saw you open the poor animal, cut it when it was still alive. And then those Indians took the meat and . . ."

"That's their way," he said curtly. "It's their greatest delicacy. I was only showing hospitality to our guests."

"They're savages, bloodthirsty savages." Her stomach turned. She thought she was going to be sick and disgrace herself even further.

"I told you you wouldn't fit in out here. This is not some polite Washington party. This is my house and these are my people. Now get up and change your dress and come down—if you think you can do that without fainting. I don't want to have to make any more excuses for you."

Reanna shifted to the edge of the bed. She felt weak and fearful, but she wouldn't let him know that, not if it killed her.

"I'll change my dress and come down. I won't be long. I won't give you any further cause to be ashamed of me," she said.

"Good." He finished drying his hands and walked to the door.

"Andrew," she called after him, and he stopped. "Andrew, I promise you this; no matter what happens, I won't ever faint again." He turned, sensing some new strength in her voice. He looked at her for a long time and then without a word he went out the door and down the hall.

She stood up and tore off her dress and let it slide to the floor. She stepped out of it and kicked it into a corner. She would never wear that dress again. She looked in the clothes press for a suitable gown. She found one she'd worn for Sundays back on the farm in Virginia. It was a pretty yellow sprigged muslin. She washed her hands and face from water in the pitcher. She couldn't look at the basin Andrew had used. Then she put some cologne behind her ears and unpinned her hair, letting it fall like a sheet of red-gold flame. She stood up very straight, her shoulders back, and then with her head high she went back down to the party.

Miss Jane and Cima were waiting for her at the bottom of the steps. They'd been worried that she might be ill. Behind them in the shadows Reanna saw Snow hiding behind a chair.

"Are you all right?" Miss Jane asked. "Are you sure you feel well enough to come down again?"

"I'm fine," Reanna said. "It must have been the excitement, nothing more. I'm sorry to give you any trouble." Miss Jane was relieved and so was Snow. Snow had been sure Reanna would tell on her. She knew Reanna had every right to be angry.

"And now, if it's all right with you, I'm going to dance," Reanna said. Miss Jane nodded.

"Of course my dear, the evening is for you."

Reanna swept across the hall and onto the porch. She saw Pride standing there. He held out his arms to her and she started to move into his embrace, where she knew she'd feel safe, when the voice of Simon Frampton stopped her.

"No you don't, Pride Beauvaise!" Frampton bellowed. "I've already claimed the first dance for me." Without waiting for a reply, he spun Reanna away around and around the porch in a spiraling circle. There were other couples dancing to the scrape of the fiddle, but none made a greater show of it. Frampton set her off in style.

No matter what talk or gossip there had been when Andrew had carried her away unconscious, her reappearance and her smile reassured them all. She waved to Amoretta and Doc. She smiled at Jack Levy.

Miss Jane, watching from the hall, saw Reanna's effort to make everyone think she was well and happy. Once again, Miss Jane was afraid for Reanna and Andrew. He could wound without meaning to. He was often hard when a little kindness would have made all the difference. She had done what she could to help him, but somewhere within him was a strain of cold suspicion, a green shoot of jealousy that she could never uproot. If Andrew was to change, it would have to be Reanna who would change him.

On the porch, Reanna and Simon Frampton had not gone for a second turn on the floor before Father Soule came to claim her. As Frampton handed her over he said, "I didn't know you could dance, Father."

Father Soule pretended outrage. "Dance! My dear Frampton, I may never go to heaven for my prayers or my wine, but I will surely be welcome for my dancing."

Yet Father Soule only took a step or two with Reanna before he stopped. "I am too proud," he said, "to let that young reprobate see I cannot dance any more. I am too old, too short of breath, but I wished to pretend I was young again, such is my vanity. And now I will give you to Pride."

And Pride was waiting for her. "Will you dance with me?"

"Yes," she said, unsure why she should feel so tremulous. It was only a dance.

Pride took her hand and led her down the steps out toward the wide, clean-swept yard.

"Where are we going?" she asked.

"We are going to dance the Indian way."

"But I don't know the steps."

"Then Miss Jane and I will teach you. They're not hard to learn."

He held her hand in a firm clasp that reassured her and gave her confidence. It was all so new and so different. Behind her, on the porch, the fiddlers still played, beating time with their feet, and the people were dancing waltzes and polkas, just like any country gathering back home.

(133)

But before her she saw Indians of the Chickasaw and Choctaw tribes in colorful costumes that she could not begin to identify, mingled together with white people, all forming into a long chain and beginning to move in a circle. The circle changed shape, lengthening with each added dancer, the tempo kept even by the beat of an Indian drum.

Reanna had never seen such a mingling of different people, and it was that very variety that she found most compelling. What a wonderful place this Nation was in which a diverse people could live and dance together. She marveled at the harmony she felt all around her.

All seemed able to do as they pleased. The children played and laughed in separate groups. The men were wagering on a throw of the bones or telling stories, and the women sat and gossiped. There seemed to be no formal rules to follow, yet there was an order in the freedom that made her feel a oneness with the universe.

Miss Jane came across the yard to Reanna, and the three of them joined in the moving circle of the snake dance. The gas flares cast an eerie light on their movements. The changing shadows made it seem an enchanted place on which the ancient gods must look down and smile. Reanna was surprised at the ease with which she kept time to the drum and the flute. She saw Miss Jane's pleasure and she felt that for the first time she was doing something as right as it was good.

"You are one of us now," Miss Jane said. To Reanna it was more than a compliment, it was a coronation.

"How long does the dancing go on?" Reanna asked Pride.

"Sometimes all night, sometimes for days. It depends on the occasion. People come and go as they please. Are you tired?" he asked.

"No, I've never had a better time in my life."

They danced in a snake pattern, coiling around the house and back again into the wide yard before the steps. In the snake dance each went single file, but in the next dance, the corn dance, there were two lines, one of men and the other of women. For this dance there were new steps, but Miss Jane kept Reanna beside her.

Miss Jane, in the center of the moving line, looked like a queen in her white buckskin worked with bright beads. On her ankles there were terrapin rattles bound with leather thongs. The beat of the drum was amplified by the rattles as the women kept repeating the ancient steps. The line swayed forward, then back, inviting the men to follow, until each woman was captured by the man of her choice.

There was something intoxicating in the repeated rhythms, in the flickering of the fires and the throbbing beat of the drum. Pride's eyes, as he drew close and then withdrew, held a message that mesmerized Reanna; he and this dance held her in a magic spell. She felt herself swaying toward him helplessly, like a willow in the wind, bound in wonder, nameless yearning, overborne.

The rifle shot snapped her alert. There was another, then a ragged fusillade followed by war whoops that shattered the night air. The dancers were stopped in their tracks; the drums had fallen silent. The jarring of a log in one of the fires sounded like the fall of a great tree deep in a forest.

Beyond the ring of gas flares Reanna saw three riders wheeling and capering, brandishing rifles. The lead man swept up to the nearest flare—a face wolfish and wild under his battered Stetson.

"Come out, Beauvaise! Come out and fight!" He swept the rifle barrel through the plume of flame, snarling in laughter. "Or are you still afraid? Still hiding behind your mama's skirts?"

Reanna saw Pride start forward and stop abruptly; Miss Jane's hand had gripped his arm.

"No," she said flatly. "No, Pride."

"Come on out, yellow-livered Beauvaise coyote! Come out and fight with us!"

Miss Jane walked toward the whirling, capering figures, as stately and solemn as though she were mounting a ceremonial altar. "You are not welcome here, Grady Starrett," she said.

The interloper reared his horse high above her and cursed. "Now listen, old woman—"

"*Silence!*" Miss Jane had not flinched; only her arm rose deliberately and pointed at his throat, unwavering. "I do not fear you, nor does my son. Go off, and drink and brawl in the saloons across the river, and pretend you are men! You are not welcome here at Lochleven. Now go—before you make great trouble for yourselves."

Grady Starrett glared at her, his mouth working. Reanna saw that several men in the crowd were holding rifles now, waiting, their women ranged behind them. She noticed with surprise that Pride had placed his body between her and the riders. Somewhere a rifle went on cock, the sound flat as a trap sprung. Starrett lowered the Winchester, staring down at the celebrants; Reanna fancied his eyes caught hers for an instant, savage and glittering. Then, he spun the hammerheaded palomino around, shouted something incoherent to the others, and they galloped off into the shadows. And the yard eased into talk and movement again.

"Who are they? What do they want?" Reanna asked.

"They are Jasper Starrett's boys," Pride answered.

"What do they want?"

"They are our sworn enemies." Pride was stiff with leashed anger.

"They have never been welcome at Lochleven," Miss Jane said severely, coming back to them. Reanna saw her fists were clenched.

"Riffraff," Andrew said, "prairie scum."

"They want more than a fight," Pride said. "They say I must kill them."

"I don't understand." Reanna felt out of her depth again.

"It's an old quarrel," Pride tried to explain. "Their father killed my father." Reanna suddenly had the image of the boy she had seen hanging in the town square the first day she had come into the Territory.

"Is it a blood feud?"

"It is. Jasper Starrett and my father first quarreled over Lochleven. He claimed he had spoken for the land before the Beauvaises. When the Civil War came there was another division between them. Jasper wanted to go to war. My father did not."

"What will you do?" Reanna asked Pride.

"Nothing," he said. "Why should I? I was a baby when my father was killed by Jasper Starrett. By the time I was grown, Jasper Starrett was already dead. He died peacefully in his bed. His sons think I must one day come to avenge my father's death. They live in the hopes of seeing my blood or theirs."

"But you will not take an eye for an eye?" Reanna asked, looking at Pride in a new and different way.

"No." Pride shook his head. "I will not."

Reanna glanced at Andrew, who was watching his brother with a curious half smile; it struck her that he hadn't once moved during the entire incident.

"Even if it's the Indian way?" she asked Pride.

"Who told you that?"

"Andrew. He says that an Indian must take revenge or lose his honor."

Pride shook his head sadly. "An eye for an eye only makes two men blind, instead of one. As for my honor, believe me, my honor does not depend on murder."

"But what will they do?"

"They will shout and fire off guns and curse me from a distance, but they will do nothing more. They will not try to kill me because they wish to live as much as I do."

"One day they may do more than talk. Then what will you do?" Miss Jane asked it as if she spoke to the wind.

"I will not know until that day comes." Pride touched his mother gently on the shoulder. "Do not worry. I will do what I have to do."

"Killing them will not bring back your father."

"No." Pride's eyes were warm with love for his mother. Reanna had never seen such devotion of a son for a mother. She hoped that one day she might have such a tie to bind her to a son.

"Some say I am a coward because I will not kill them." Pride glanced at Andrew, then ran his eyes over the yard. The dancing and feasting had started up again. He turned to Reanna. "What do you think?"

"I don't know how to answer you," Reanna said. "This country and its customs are new to me. But I know this, Pride: you are no coward."

"Let's go on with the dancing," Pride said, and he took Reanna's hand. This time he led her out in the "old" dance, a traditional dance of joy and celebration. They danced until nearly dawn, when Andrew came to get her, insisting that she must go inside.

"You've danced enough," he said gruffly. "You'll wear yourself out. It's time for you to come in now."

Reanna wanted to protest, to say she wasn't tired, that she'd never felt more alive, more full of life, but she was afraid she'd anger him again, that he'd say something in front of all these people that he'd be sorry for later.

"You cannot go in, Andrew," Miss Jane said, "until you have broken the ear of corn."

"There's no need for us to do that." Andrew flushed, the stain darkening his cheeks.

"But," Miss Jane protested, "everyone is expecting it. It is our custom." She turned to Reanna. "When a man and a woman marry, they break an ear of corn before their relations. It shows that they promise to divide all life's joys and sorrows."

"Reanna isn't an Indian," Andrew said gruffly.

"I will do it gladly," Reanna said, wanting to please Miss Jane, wanting to be a part of these people.

"Well, I won't," Andrew said. "I did it with Letty to please them, but there's no need to repeat it."

"They won't believe you are married." Miss Jane was shocked at Andrew's attitude, though she tried not to show it. "Not properly married."

"They'll think it's a sign of bad luck." Pride spoke softly. "You know how superstitious the Chickasaw are."

"That's their lookout," Andrew said. "As for my not being married, they can think what they please." He took Reanna by the arm and before the silent, watchful company, he led her into the house.

IN the bedroom, she was grateful to see that someone had cleared away the bloody basin and that the dress too had vanished. What had happened tonight was past and she wouldn't dwell on it, but neither would she forget. Reanna watched as Andrew took off his boots and spurs and unstrapped his gun belt. When she'd met him, she'd been fascinated and drawn by the difference between him and the other men she'd known, but now the very things that had enchanted her repelled her strongly. They seemed to threaten her in some unspoken, unexplained way. Even so, she would try to please him. He was her husband and it was her duty.

"I hope I made you proud of me." Reanna sat on the edge of the bed, unwilling to undress or lie beside him just yet.

Andrew glanced at her. She sat so still. He never knew what thoughts ran in her head to make her ask such damn fool questions. He didn't know what made her laugh and what made her cry. He was sure that she was upset with him now because he'd made her stop dancing and because he wouldn't break that silly ear of corn with her. He couldn't say exactly why he'd refused. He should have done it just to keep Miss Jane happy, but sometimes he got tired of playing Indian. The world had gone on and left the Indians behind. They were getting farther behind every day. Why did they keep up these old customs? They only held the people back. He'd married once in the Indian way. He wouldn't do it again.

"Pride seemed pleased enough with you," he answered. It wasn't what he'd intended to say.

"Miss Jane was pleased with me. She said as much." Reanna looked up at Andrew through lowered lashes. What was it that made Andrew twist what she said and turn her words against her?

"You were pleased with him, too—by the look of the two of you." Once he had begun, Andrew couldn't stop himself. He was like a man caught in the rapids.

"Pride has been very kind."

"You like him, don't you?"

"Yes. He's a gentle man."

"And I'm not?"

"I didn't say that."

"But you think it."

"Well, he's easy to be with. He's made me feel welcome." If Andrew was going to question her, she wouldn't lie. She had no reason to. If he was jealous, it was a beast from his own mind.

"Pride can afford to be gentle." Andrew's voice was rough. "I've had to work for what he was born to. He must hate my guts sometimes."

"Why would he hate you? You are his brother and he loves you."

"You think so?" Andrew's smile was full of bitterness. "When Miss Jane took me in and made me her son, Pride had to share his mother and his sister in this house with me. If the shoe had been on the other foot, I wouldn't have liked it."

"Has Pride ever said anything to you that makes you think he resents you?"

"No," Andrew admitted grudgingly.

"Then maybe you're wrong. Maybe Pride doesn't feel that way at all."

Andrew gave her a scathing look. "You don't know anything about human nature. It's only natural he would envy me. I know I envy him sometimes."

"What for?" She found it hard to believe that Andrew could envy anyone.

"Pride can carve anything out of wood," Andrew said. "He can make anything, while I only get a pile of shavings. When he was just a kid, I made a bet with him I knew he'd lose, and I got him to put up his knife as the prize. I won the knife and I thought, now I can carve as well as Pride. But it wasn't so. I kept the knife as a reminder."

Reanna looked down. Pride had promised her a deer-bone flute that made sweet music; Andrew gave her nothing but his scorn. She could do nothing to please Andrew.

THE bride's dancing and the festivities went on for four days. When they were over, when the people had all gone home and the pots and fires were cleared away, Reanna felt as lost as if she were in a void. While the company had been there, she didn't have to think about the future; she'd been too distracted meeting new people and learning the ways of the tribe. Miss Jane had insisted Reanna sit with her while she held court.

"Anyone who needs help feels he can come to the Beauvaises," Miss Jane had said. "Now that times are bad, they depend on us more than ever."

Reanna marveled at the patience with which Miss Jane listened to every complaint, heard every story, and answered every need within her power. Sometimes it was only a request for a blanket or food. Other times it was a dispute over a field or a family quarrel that had to be put right.

Now those full days were over and there was nothing for Reanna to do with herself. Pride and Taffy and Andrew were out on the range studying the grass, and Miss Jane had gone to Tishomingo to see the Indian Agent about raising cash money to buy cattle. It must be humiliating for Miss Jane to have to ask and beg for the annuity money that was hers. Reanna felt a burning anger at the injustice; she could not imagine what it must be like to live in your own nation as a second-class citizen and still pay such a price for the honor.

Cima wouldn't accept any help from Reanna in running the

house. Reanna was waited on hand and foot by Annoyi and Rose Dawn. She'd tried to make some conversation with them at breakfast, but they'd giggled and fled from the dining room.

Reanna felt abandoned and useless. It was a fine day and she had nothing to do. Andrew had said she could not go out riding alone. He was right, of course; she didn't know where to go or how to get back again. Still, she would have liked to take Molly May for a run.

Before they left, Doc and Amoretta had asked her to visit them in town and Simon Frampton and Father Soule had both made her promise to come and see them. But they had only just departed, and she had no excuse for returning calls so soon.

She decided to use the time to write her first letter home. She had promised her mother that she would write often. She found pen and paper in the table drawer and then sat, undecided how much to tell and how much to leave out. She chewed thoughtfully at the pen and began.

Dear Mama and Papa,

I sent you all two picture postcards, one from Memphis and the other from Fort Smith. I hope you received them both. The journey was very comfortable and easy. We arrived in Maitland on Monday. The train was on time. Maitland is our nearest rail town, about twelve miles from MacClaren City. We then traveled to MacClaren City by wagon.

MacClaren City is small but growing fast. The first person I met was Jack Levy, who is Andrew's friend and partner in the mercantile business. Mr. Levy is also the postmaster. A mail wagon makes a regular stop, so there's no excuse for your not hearing from me and I expect a lot of letters from home.

Then we ate a delicious dinner at the home of Doctor Hersey and his wife, Amoretta, who kindly asked us to stay the night. Everyone is very cordial. Andrew is a mighty popular man in these parts.

The next morning early, we drove out to Beauvaise Ridge by buggy, about another twelve miles. I know that when you and the boys come to visit, which I hope will be soon, you will all be surprised by how beautiful the country is. Not at all the desert you feared it would be. It will take me a whole separate letter just to describe the early spring flowers and the grass on the prairie.

And I will try to draw a sketch of the house on the Ridge. It's called Lochleven and is very fine. Big enough for a large family, it looks a little like the farm. So I felt right at home.

Miss Jane, Andrew's foster mother, and his brother Pride made me welcome. Andrew's daughter Snow is very pretty. Cima, the housekeeper, and Taffy Owen, the ranch foreman, were glad to see Andrew home again.

Miss Jane insisted on giving us a big welcome-home party. The guests came from all over the Nation. Yes, Mama, some of them were Indians but nobody was scalped. You have to remember this is *their* country. I'm not a citizen out here any more than the Indians are citizens of the states. And there are a lot of very different people here besides Indians. One of our nearest neighbors is a Frenchman, another an Englishman.

There's so much to see and learn, I am dazzled. I miss you all, but I'm all right and I'm not the least homesick. Not yet, anyway.

My best to you and the boys. Andrew sends his warmest regards.

She started to cross out the *warmest* and then let it stand rather than write the letter over.

She had told the truth, she had just not told the whole truth, and she had gilded the facts a bit. But she was never going to admit that she had not made the right decision to marry Andrew and come way out here. She was too proud to do that ever. Besides, it wasn't true. It was just that everything was a little strange and would take getting used to.

"P.S.," she wrote with a flourish:

I have a new horse, a wedding present from our English neighbor. Her name is Molly May. Oh, and tell Papa that the Chickasaw play a gambling game called *hide the bullet*. A player puts a bullet under one of three pairs of socks. Then he moves the socks around and the other players bet where the bullet is. I don't think the odds are very good. The player who has hidden the bullet seems to be the one who wins most often.

P.P.S. Mama, would you please send me a box of books. I want all the books that are in my room. If it's not too much trouble, I would really appreciate it. As yet there is no library in MacClaren City. The correct address is:

> Mrs. Andrew MacClaren
> MacClaren City
> Chickasaw Nation
> Indian Territory

Most people out here just say *I.T.*, but for our postman back home, I think you'd better write it out. It's still funny to think I'm in a foreign country, but I am. Oh, and one more thing, I'll write Cousin Lucy today and thank her again for the lovely wedding.

She sealed the letter, opened the door from her room and stepped out onto the upper verandah to catch a breath of air. She looked out longingly at the wide plateau of Beauvaise Ridge and then to the east and west grasslands. This was paradise and she was forbidden to enter. Then she happened to glance down and saw Snow on the bottom step of the porch, swinging back and forth from the handrail, sighing and singing softly to herself, a little wordless, hollow tune. The child was as bored as she was.

Reanna wanted to make friends with Snow. They'd started badly, but they had their whole lives ahead of them. They might as well learn to like each other as be enemies. Here was an opportunity to make a new beginning. Reanna went quickly downstairs and out onto the porch.

"Hello," she said. Snow glanced up and saw her. She studied Reanna with a cold, mistrustful gaze. She thought perhaps Reanna had come to scold her. She knew she deserved it for taking Reanna to see the Ponca.

At last Snow replied, "Hello."

"Are you on your own today?"

"Yes, they went off without me."

Reanna smiled. Snow was not as self-assured and confident as she tried to appear. In time, if she was patient, the two of them might even be friends.

"They went off without me, too. Suppose we amuse ourselves."

"How?"

"When I was your age I used to give my doll a pretend tea party."

"What kind of party is that?" Snow asked scornfully. "I never heard of a tea party for a doll."

"You make little mud pies and serve them with tea made from grass." Snow made a face.

"Who would want to eat a mud pie?"

"You only pretend," Reanna said gently.

"I'd rather have real pies," Snow said.

"We could ask Cima to let us have something real to eat, if you'd rather."

"Cima ran me out of the kitchen."

"Then we'll have to pretend."

"Why would you want to play with me?" Snow challenged her. "You're a grown-up."

"Because," Reanna replied as honestly as she could, "we're both lonely, and because there's a lot you can teach me about Lochleven."

"What, for instance?" Snow seemed to think it was a trick, that Reanna's offer of friendship must have some catch to it.

"For instance, you can tell me what kind of tree that is." Reanna pointed toward a large tree in the yard. "I've never seen one like it."

"It's a catalpa tree."

It was a strange tree with leaves as large as elephant's ears and long, green beans hanging from its branches.

"Do you eat the beans?" Reanna asked.

"No, you can't eat them, silly."

"What do you do with them?" Reanna asked, ignoring Snow's tendency to name-calling.

"We can use them as swords and fight a duel." Snow broke one of the beans and advanced on Reanna, brandishing her weapon.

"I don't want to fight with you, Snow, not now or ever. Come on, let's get some water from the well and make some pies." She held out her hand to Snow, who, to her surprise, took it.

As they walked around the side of the house to the well, Reanna saw a pair of doors in the yard that led down beneath a mound of dirt. On top of the mound there was a chimney sticking out. It wasn't a smokehouse. Perhaps it was a springhouse to cool butter and cream. Still, the earth was a peculiar shape.

"What's that?" she asked Snow. "Where does that door go?"

"It's a storm cellar. When the big wind comes, we go down there to hide. And we stay there until the wind blows over."

"Are you afraid of the wind?" Reanna asked.

"Yes, aren't you?"

"No," Reanna laughed. "I like the wind."

"You'll be afraid when a big twister comes."

"I don't think so. I like storms."

"You will, I promise you." Snow seemed sure of her answer, but there was a gleam of curiosity in her eyes, as if she could not wait to test Reanna's words against the reality of a storm. "You'll be afraid, I'll bet you. We all run like rabbits. Everyone does, even my papa and Pride."

Reanna didn't contradict Snow, but she was sure she exaggerated.

She couldn't imagine Pride or Andrew running to hide from the wind in a hole in the ground.

They drew up water from the well, carried it to the front of the house beneath the catalpa tree and sat making pies from red mud and decorating them with sand and pebbles. "It's silly to make something you can't eat," Snow grumbled.

While they waited for the pies to dry in the sun, they sat with their backs against the trunk of the great tree and let the gentle wind blow over them. Lazily Reanna reached up and pulled down a leaf and began to fashion a hat for the doll. She fastened it to the doll's wigged head with a small twig.

"Make one for me, too," Snow begged.

Reanna made Snow's much more elaborate. She overlaid several leaves and trimmed them with blossoms. When she had adjusted it on Snow, she smiled. "You look very pretty, Snow."

"Do I?" Snow's hopeful look betrayed her lack of confidence. Reanna felt as if they had come to a first, small understanding.

"Let's see if the pies are ready," Reanna said. The two of them gazed intently at their handiwork. "What do you think?"

"They're done," Snow said, eager now for the game to continue.

"Well then, let's set the table. We can use leaves for plates and we'll serve our beautiful pies to your doll. What's her name?"

"She doesn't have one." Snow suddenly looked sullen and down-cast.

"Then you give her one and this can be her birthday."

Snow thought awhile and then replied, "I'll call her Catalpa."

"All right," Reanna said, "you serve her tea and pie and we'll sing her a birthday song." She was going to ask when Snow's birthday was when she saw Snow's face go sullen again. Her mouth turned down; her eyes darkened.

"She's only a doll, and I'm a princess. *I* must be served first." If Snow hadn't been so serious, her behavior would have been absurd. Yet there was something poignant in this child's pathetic, quick-silver arrogance. "Are you a princess?" Snow demanded.

"No, far from it." Reanna felt suddenly tired. Perhaps Snow would always blow hot and cold without warning.

"My mother was a princess, and so is Miss Jane." Snow's head was high, her chin jutting out in defiance. She made Reanna think of herself at her most unmanageable and unreasonable.

"Your mother must have been very beautiful." Reanna thought of the pale woman in the photograph.

"I don't remember her." Snow's attitude of belligerent defiance suddenly crumbled.

"I've seen a picture of her," Reanna said, "and you look like her. She was a beautiful Indian girl."

Snow's gaze caught and held Reanna's; her eyes were like Andrew's, turquoise and as cold as the glass eyes of her doll.

"I'm not an Indian!" Snow spat out the words. Reanna was too startled to reply. "My father's not an Indian. I'm a white woman like you. My skin is as fair as yours."

"But your mother was an Indian."

"Not all her blood." Snow remained defiant. "I don't look like an Indian, do I?"

"No," Reanna said.

"I'm not like the full bloods. They're almost as dark as Cima. When I go to town, *nobody* thinks I'm an Indian."

"I would think you'd be proud to be an Indian and a princess," Reanna said slowly, carefully choosing her words. She felt as if she were walking on broken ice.

"Not in the town. In the town they make fun of Indians. They say they're dirty and stupid and lazy. In the town it's better to be white."

Reanna wondered what other currents of pain ran in this troubled child. How did Snow manage to repudiate half of herself? She denied she was an Indian, yet she claimed her royal blood. She looked down on others, yet she was despised by the trash in town who had come to steal her birthright. Perhaps whites could only rob Indians with a clear conscience if they first claimed they were inferior.

"Let's go for a walk," Reanna said suddenly. "We have time before lunch. I want to give Molly May some sugar. I haven't seen her today."

"All right."

They left the doll staring blindly at the uneaten tea party and walked around the house past the storm cellar and the kitchen garden. As they passed by the kitchen door, they called in to Cima that they were going to walk down to see Molly May in the barn. In the barn the smell of warm hay in the loft and the ripe odor of manure made Reanna think of the farm at home. Today she wished she were in Virginia, where she could ride Molly May from morning till night and never lose her way.

She reached in her pocket and found some lumps of sugar, which she put on her palm and held out to the horse.

"Here you are, girl. We can't go out riding today, but I've brought you a present." Reanna was pleased by the great, rough tongue seeking out the last grains of goodness. "You can ride Molly May if you want to."

"I have my own pony, thank you," Snow replied stiffly.

"I only wanted you to know I'd share her with you."

She saw Snow glance up at her slyly out of the corners of her eyes. "Do you want to share a secret with me?" Snow asked.

"If you want to tell me."

"I know where there are berries growing in the woods beyond the barn. We could go and gather them and make a real pie."

Watching the girl, Reanna hesitated. It was a perfectly reasonable request. Yet, why hadn't Snow suggested it before this? And why did she have that strange, intent glint in her eyes?

"All right," Reanna agreed, finally.

They walked through the barn and out the far side to a little wood beyond. It was just a small thicket, but out here trees were a rarity. Set just within the grove was a double log cabin with a dog-trot breezeway running between the two sets of rooms. Sagging from disuse and lack of repair, it leaned away from the strong southern wind. The dry, native stone foundation was uneven; the chinking had crumbled and there were holes in it as large as silver dollars. Some of the rough-hewn planks on the porch were missing. The rough shingle roof, oddly enough, looked sound.

"I didn't know there was another house here," Reanna said.

"How could you? You've never been this way before."

"Does anyone live here?"

"No. Miss Jane did when they first came here from the old Nation. They lived here until Lochleven was built. No one lives here now. It's a storehouse for grain and farm tools. It's full of rats."

Reanna shuddered, an involuntary motion.

"We don't go in," Snow said. "They say it's haunted. That's because Miss Jane's uncle, the old Dog King, is buried beneath the house. The Indians sometimes did that in the old days."

"Beneath the house," Reanna murmured. "I find that hard to believe, Snow."

Snow shrugged. "Believe it or not, it's true. There are lots of things about the Indians you don't know."

"Why would they do that?" Reanna asked.

"The Indians buried their old honored ones under their houses. When they died in battle, the warriors were brought home in white deerskin and buried sitting up, facing west. If they'd been away a long time and their bodies had rotted, their bones were brought back. Our dead were a part of us, always." Snow paused, and then correcting herself to conform with her other image, she said, "They were a part of them always, but when the missionaries came they said that was wrong. They said the dead could only be buried in certain ground, ground they chose and prayed over. Sometimes that ground was far from home." Snow looked wistful and as lost as if she had wandered a thousand miles from home. She seemed bereft, as if something treasured had been taken from her.

"Where is your mother buried? At the mission?"

"Yes." Snow turned away. "She wasn't like those old Indians." Reanna again felt she had fallen into a swift-flowing river where there were dangerous, hidden currents. Snow was like no other child she had ever met. She was much older than her years but without direction. She blew in the wind.

The wood was larger than Reanna had thought. The daylight dimmed, and there were nettles that caught and fastened to her skirt. Small branches flew back, slapping at her face. The ground was soft with pine needles. She could hear the little crackling of dry sticks snapping underfoot. She was glad that Snow knew the way. "Where's the berry patch?" she asked.

"Not far," Snow called back to her. "Just wait and see."

There were living things everywhere: squirrels in the trees, a covey of quail that flew up like doomsday with their wings whirring in the air and made her cry aloud.

"They're only birds," Snow said. "There are bear in here, and cougar, too. Maybe we'll see some." Reanna doubted if that was true. Still, Snow had put the possibility of seeing such creatures into her mind and the edge of fear remained.

There were little white and blue flowers carpeting the forest. She saw an owl's nest; she had heard him questioning in the night. Before she was aware of it, Reanna found herself standing in the thicket, knowing that she had completely lost her sense of direction. Snow turned to look back at her. Reanna had come into the wood because she wanted to please this difficult, sullen child, who now stood staring at her with undisguised dislike.

"How long are you going to stay at Lochleven?" Snow asked. It was such an unexpected question that Reanna wondered if she had heard right.

"A long time, I hope."

"I want to know when you're going home."

"This is my home now."

"Oh no, it's not." Snow was defiant now, her eyes full of malice.

"Why do you say that, Snow?"

"Because I don't *want* you here! You don't know anything about Lochleven. You don't belong here. If I ran away now and left you here in the woods, you would be lost; you wouldn't know how to get back to the house. It's not your home. It's *mine!*"

The woods were suddenly silent. Her shock at Snow's violent hostility left Reanna speechless; she knew Snow didn't like her, but this was more than a child's whim. They stood, two antagonists, facing each other. Then, before Reanna could speak, Snow turned and ran away out of sight into the thicket.

It was a spiteful, vindictive trick; it was so silly that it took Reanna a few moments to realize that Snow really meant to leave her there to find her own way home as best she could. Snow had abandoned her as if she were the wicked stepmother from some fairy tale, some mean, spiteful creature to be left in the woods.

"Come back," Reanna called. "Come back, Snow . . ." But if the girl heard, she paid no attention. Reanna thought she caught a glimpse of a bright flash of blue, and she ran after it. Reanna knew that in time, if she was calm, she could find her way back to the house. She knew north from south; she could get her bearings from the sun. She ran after Snow because she was angry and resentful at being taken in by Snow's incurable slyness, her false warmth.

Yet somehow, part of Reanna's resentment was reserved for Andrew. He'd said she wouldn't fit in out here. He'd said as much before the child; if not in so many words, then she'd caught his mood. Snow was clever, but there was something missing from her character that left her incomplete.

Sometimes Reanna thought she caught a glimpse of Snow, then lost her in the next instant; once she thought she heard Snow's laughter. At last she came out of the woods, not by the cabin but before a wall of gray, granite rocks. They were misshapen and covered with spatterings of old lichen. They looked as if they had been flung about by angry, prehistoric giants.

"This is where the berries were." Reanna looked up and saw Snow above her. She was standing between two rocks looking down on Reanna's confusion. She'd been leading Reanna on, hiding from her, but now it was the end of the game. "It's too bad, the berries seem to all be gone."

"Then we'd better go back," Reanna said, as evenly as she could. She was hot, tired and out of breath. She'd been run ragged, but she would not give this child the satisfaction of seeing her discomfort if she could avoid it.

"They *were* here." Snow would have liked to lose Reanna in the woods. She would have liked to leave her there forever, but she knew she couldn't go home without her.

"Do you want to play hide and seek?" Snow asked.

"I think we've done enough of that." Reanna stared unblinkingly at Snow.

"Are you angry?"

"Yes. Come on, Snow, let's go home now," Reanna said. This cat and mouse game had made her bone-weary. "We can come another time for berries."

Snow smiled. She hadn't managed to lose Reanna, but she'd gotten her angry. She had another idea and it pleased her. Abruptly she said, "Catch me, I'm going to jump down."

"No," Reanna shouted. She stretched out her arms to catch Snow as she jumped. Snow dropped through the air, but she didn't fall into Reanna's arms. Snow had jumped wide and landed between two small boulders. She'd never intended for Reanna to catch her. It was another trick, another way to frighten her father's new wife.

Now Snow stood between the rocks as still as if she'd become a stone statue. Reanna turned away; she didn't want Snow to see how afraid and angry she was. When she turned back she saw that Snow hadn't moved. The girl looked as ashen gray as the rocks themselves.

"Come along, Snow," Reanna said sharply. She was out of patience with the child. At this moment she didn't want to be Snow's friend, she only wanted to be obeyed. But there was no response.

"Snow, are you all right? Have you hurt yourself?" Again there was no answer. Reanna wanted to shake her to make her move, but there was something in the child's face that held her back. As she looked at Snow, she saw her lips begin to move.

Snow didn't speak; instead she made a hissing sound and then a single word slipped through her clenched teeth. "*Shisto*."

"I don't understand you," Reanna said.

Snow stood, her eyes blank and as glazed as a windowpane. She didn't even blink. Once more she said, "*Shisto.*" Then, mingled with the wind in the trees and the beating of her heart, Reanna heard the other sound. It was the faint shaking of seeds in a gourd from somewhere in between the rocks—a thin, ominous sound like the rattle of death.

Reanna's eyes strained and focused on a crack between the rocks. There in the small gap she saw, to her horror, that Snow had landed in a nest of snakes. They were new-hatched, small and wriggling, as vulnerable as Snow. Beside them, coiled and ready to protect its young, was a large rattler; the tail made its lethal warning abundantly clear.

Reanna stood transfixed. She knew she must do something. She couldn't leave Snow there and go for help. She must get her out of harm's way. She heard her own voice cry out as if the words came from someone else.

"Run, Snow. Run to me!"

Snow didn't move. She seemed frozen in granite and deaf from fear. Reanna's one thought was to get her out of danger—take her away from this spot where she was in such peril. She summoned all her courage and made a lunge for the rocks, meaning to snatch Snow up and out of harm's way. As she moved the snake struck, burying her fangs deep in the soft flesh of the child's calf.

Reanna heard Snow's scream mingle with her own. She saw the snake withdraw and slither beneath an overhanging rock. Again and again Snow screamed, as Reanna snatched her up and ran with her in what she hoped was the direction of Lochleven, stumbling blindly through the underbrush. She felt Snow stiffening in her arms. Her eyes were closed, her face distorted in pain. The girl moaned faintly, her face the putty gray of a corpse.

Reanna kept running, calling out for help, hoping that if she ran fast enough Snow would be safe. As Reanna broke into the clearing by the log cabin, she knew she was too tired to run much farther. She drove herself on with the weight of Snow loose and lifeless in her arms. Just as Reanna was about to drop from exhaustion, she saw Cima running toward her. Without a word she plucked Snow from Reanna's arms and began running toward the house.

"How long ago?" Cima demanded tightly.

"Five minutes, maybe ten," Reanna gasped, "I don't know—"

"Better pray there's still time, then."

Reanna followed Cima into the house. Cima shouted at Annoyi to clear everything off the kitchen table. When the girl did not move quickly enough, Cima swept the table clean with one arm, sending crockery bowls, pans of food and vegetables crashing to the floor, and laid Snow on the cleared area as gently as if she were made of spun sugar. Cima turned away and picked a sharp knife from the rack by the cutting block. Then, like a tiger about to kill, she glared at Annoyi.

"Annoyi, you and Rose Dawn hold her. You take Snow's feet and Rose Dawn hold her arms." This time they did as they were told. Cima lifted the iron plate from the top of the stove and stuck the knife into the open flames. When the knife was glowing hot, Cima turned back. "Hold her tight, now, both of you." She looked at Reanna. "You want to help me?"

Reanna nodded mutely.

"Good. Now you hold her head. And if you feel like fainting, you just wait and do it later."

Cima turned Snow's leg toward the light. Reanna could see the twin holes like tiny eye sockets; the skin around them was swollen and discolored. "Got to get that black poison *out*," Cima said, as much to herself as to the others.

Holding the knife steady, she cut—once, twice. Snow's body jerked, she cried out—the low, inarticulate scream of a helpless, wounded animal. After Cima had cut her cross in the flesh, she put her mouth to the open wound and began to suck, spitting out the venom on the floor.

"Now," she said, "keep on holding her. I've got to make a poultice."

Cima went into the pantry and came back with a dark, twisted root which she put into a mortar and pounded into a paste. She put the paste on the wound, laid cobwebs over it and tied it securely with a torn strip of sheeting. Then she took more of the root and brewed it into a medicinal tea.

"Reanna," Cima commanded, "you hold her mouth open for me."

Cima ladled the steeped infusion down Snow's throat. Snow coughed and the tea ran down her chin, but she managed to swallow a portion of it.

"There," Cima said at last. "I've done what I can down here." She spoke to Reanna. "You go upstairs and turn down Snow's bed.

Get blankets from the chest in the hall, you know the one I mean?"
Reanna nodded.

"I'm going to sweat her, to get the poison out of her system.
You girls start heating bricks in the oven. When they're hot
enough, Rose Dawn, you bring them up in the coal scuttle, a
copper boiler, anything you can find. I want you to keep them
coming. Do you hear me?" Cima looked at the girls. They were
both frozen, their eyes round with fright. "Move, both of you!"
She barked out the order. "You too, Reanna MacClaren."

Reanna let go of Snow's head. She'd been reluctant to loose her
grip; she felt in some muddled way that as long as she held on to
Snow, nothing worse could happen. She ran down the hall and up
the stairs, threw open the chest and gathered up a bundle of
blankets.

Cima tenderly lifted Snow up and began to carry her gently up
the stairs, whispering softly, "There there, pretty, there, there."
This child was hers, as her mother and grandmother had been hers.
She had no illusions about any of them, but she loved them all.

She put Snow on her narrow bed, and began to cover her with
blankets. The pile grew higher until only Snow's face was visible.
She looked very small and still and pale.

"Is she going to be all right?" Reanna whispered. She'd been
asking the question silently ever since Cima had found them.

"No way of knowing," Cima said flatly. "Depends on how much
poison I got out of her. And how much the sweating and the
poultice will draw."

"She's so pale." Snow's breath was shallow and faint, as if her
lungs had been paralyzed and each breath might be her last.

"We'll just have to wait and see." Cima crouched down by the
bed. Reanna could not sit still. She walked back and forth by the
windows looking out at nothing, afraid to look back at Snow for
fear of what she might see. Neither of them could have said how
long they waited before they heard the sound of footsteps in the
hall below and then running up the stairs two at a time and Andrew's voice calling, "Where is she? Where's Snow?"

"In here," Cima answered. She rose to meet him. "Be quiet,
now. You want to scare her all over again?"

Andrew hung in the doorway, almost as pale as Snow beneath
his weathered tan. Behind him Taffy and Pride stood, trying to see
into the room.

"My God, what happened?" Andrew asked.

"*Shisto*," Cima said. Reanna recognized the sound that Snow had made.

"Where was she?" Reaching down, he touched his daughter's warm forehead, withdrew the hand as though it had been burned. "How did she come to go off on her own?"

"She wasn't on her own," Reanna said, moving toward him; she hoped he would take her in his arms and comfort her. "Snow was with me."

"With *you*?"

"We went for a walk in the woods. We were looking for berries—"

Andrew was strange and still; his gaze stopped her in mid-passage. "There are no berries now—anyone knows that. What made you take her into the woods?"

"It was Snow's idea. She said she knew where there were berry bushes." Standing before Andrew, Reanna thought, was like standing in a cold wind. "When we got into the woods, she began to run ahead. She ran up into some rocks and when she jumped she landed in a nest of snakes."

"Go on," he said.

"Snow just stood there. I didn't know what was the matter with her. Then I heard the rattle and I saw the little snakes, and the big one coiled ready to strike. Snow was too frightened to move. She kept whispering that word Cima said."

"*Shisto*." Andrew hissed the word in the small room.

"Yes, that one."

"It means rattler."

There was a long silence in the room. Cima turned away to the bed and began to whisper to Snow's inert form. "Poor baby, poor baby, my poor baby girl."

Neither Taffy nor Pride spoke. Andrew was still staring at Reanna, a look that filled her with dread. The idea came to her that they all knew Snow was going to die; they were silent because they didn't want to tell her so.

"What did you do then?" Andrew asked in almost a whisper.

"I—I tried to save her. Snow wouldn't move; I couldn't leave her there. And just as I reached out for her, the snake struck." She feared he might be angry because she'd put her own life in danger, risking it for Snow's. She never imagined he would cross the room in two strides and seize her by the shoulders as if he wished to shake her to pieces.

"You fool!" Andrew shouted. "You should have left her where she was. Snow knew the right thing to do—even a child knows enough not to move at a time like that. If a rattler sees any movement, it strikes in self-defense." He let Reanna go then and pushed her away from him with loathing, as if he could no longer bear to touch her.

"I didn't know that," Reanna muttered. Her lips felt stiff and cold, as if she, not Snow, had been bitten and filled with poison.

"You don't know anything!" he sneered at her. "*You* caused this."

"Andrew," Pride interrupted, "that's enough now."

"You keep out of this," Andrew said savagely.

Pride stepped back, his hands clenched on the brim of his hat, but he said nothing more.

Next it was Taffy who spoke in her defense. "Reanna meant no harm."

"I only meant to help her," Reanna stammered.

"Help her! You maybe killed her. Get out of this room, get out of my sight!"

"But—I want to stay, I can't leave her now."

"Andrew," Cima warned, "I told you to keep your voice down."

But he was past all admonition now. "Get out, I tell you. I don't want to see your face! If she dies, it's your fault! You got that?"

Reanna brushed blindly past Taffy and Pride, the tears in her eyes blurring her vision. She ran into her room, shut the door and leaned against it shuddering, sick with shame and dread. *If Snow dies, it's your fault.* If he was right, how could she live with the knowledge? Even if Snow didn't die, what hope was there now for a loving, trusting future between them? She'd like to weep away her sense of self-pity, but tears wouldn't wash away what had happened. She sat by the window, looking out at the waving prairie grass. The wind had come up stronger out of the southwest. A fine layer of dust had seeped in through the cracks and covered everything with a fine, gritty red film.

She had no idea how long she sat there, her hands clenched together in an effort to keep herself from flying apart. At last she heard someone at the door, but it was only Cima carrying a tray of food.

"I've brought you some supper," Cima said.

"I'm not hungry, thank you. How is Snow?"

"Still too early to tell."

"Is she conscious?" Reanna asked.

"No, but she's sleeping, and that's a good sign."

"Is Andrew with her?"

"Yes." The answer was short, almost curt. Cima set down the tray. "When you didn't come down, Annoyi fixed you some supper on a tray."

"I told you I'm not hungry."

"You have to eat something," Cima insisted. "There's soup and some fresh-baked bread. If you don't eat, you'll get sick. Then I'll have two sick people on my hands instead of one." Cima puzzled Reanna; at first she'd thought the black woman had come to gloat, but now she wasn't sure.

"Andrew blames me," Reanna said, looking directly at Cima. "He says this was all my fault."

"It was an accident," Cima declared. "Snow's not the first child to be bit by a snake, and she won't be the last."

"If I hadn't moved, she would have been all right. That's what Andrew said." Cima frowned; her usually smooth, impassive face was troubled. This was a bad thing that was happening in this house, to her family.

"Maybe yes and maybe no," she said finally. "You don't know that for sure. What was the child going to do—stand there like a statue till doomsday? She had no business playing around them rocks."

"How am I going to face Miss Jane when she comes home? How can I tell her?" Reanna put her face in her hands. "I know what Snow means to Miss Jane. And Andrew."

"Do you, now?"

"I know I could never be what Letty was to Andrew. Her memory still hurts him so, he can't even speak of her."

"Is that what he told you?" Cima said.

"Andrew won't talk about Letty. He says it's wrong to name the dead."

Cima shook her head. "My, my, that Andrew MacClaren is a twister. He ain't told you *nothing*."

"I know they were childhood sweethearts," Reanna said.

"He told you that?" Cima continued to shake her head at her.

"It was only natural that they fall in love and marry. This was Letty's home. She was a part of this house and this land. She belonged here in a way I never can."

(156)

"Now you listen to me, Virginia girl, you got that turned upside down. It was *Letty* who loved *Andrew* from the time they were children. She never had eyes for anybody but him, followed him wherever he went like a puppy dog. And he never even noticed she was there, except to tell her she was in the way and not to tag along. No ma'am, Andrew was never crazy with love for Letty. Half the time Andrew had no use for her—and the other half he paid her no mind."

"But he married her. Why would he marry her if he didn't love her?"

"Because it was what Miss Jane wanted." Cima didn't hesitate. "He knew he owed Miss Jane everything. He come to this house a shirttail kid, an orphan boy that didn't belong. Miss Jane took him and treated him like her own. Sometimes she even favored Andrew over Pride, just so he would feel equal, but that still didn't satisfy Andrew. Oh my, no. To feel equal, he always had to have more than his share."

She raised a long forefinger, brought it down like a rifle barrel leveled. "If he married Letty, he knew, he'd no longer be the orphan boy. If Letty became his wife, she'd be his property. And her part of this house and her head rights in the tribe would be his property, too. That would mean he'd have more than Pride. And *that* made Andrew feel maybe he'd be equal here at last."

Reanna tried to take in what Cima was saying, but it was hard for her to absorb. She'd been so used to thinking of Andrew in another way, as a man who had loved and lost a wife in terrible grief.

"Are you telling me that Miss Jane asked Andrew to marry Letty?" Reanna asked.

Cima laughed. It was a short, hard laugh with no mirth in it. "She didn't have to ask him. Not in so many words. Andrew is as smart as paint. He was able to figure it out for himself. When he told Miss Jane he wanted to marry Letty, it didn't take two eyes to see how happy he'd made her. She took the bundle of calico to Letty. It's an Indian way of asking if a girl says yes, when a man gets his mother to take her a bundle of dress goods. Miss Jane asked the whole tribe to watch them break the ear of corn. Yes sir, that day Andrew had it all."

"And then Letty died."

"Yes." Cima's face twisted suddenly and she looked old and bitter, like the root in the poultice. "I nursed Letty. She was my baby before Snow. When Letty died, they'd both lost something, both Miss Jane and Andrew. And it made an even stronger bond between them. 'Cause then they both had Snow."

"I know you mean what you say," Reanna said. "But I can't believe he didn't love Letty. I know Andrew loves Snow."

"Snow's something else again." Cima didn't change her tone. "You can't fool me about Andrew. No matter what he says, I knew all the time what he done and why he done it. When Letty was gone, he petted and doted on Snow to ease his own conscience." She paused, nodded once. "You doubt what I'm saying. I see it in your face. You think I made this up like a story, because I want to get even with him for marrying my Letty, but it's the truth. I know it and so do you, deep down."

"But why would you tell me all this?" Reanna asked. "You have no reason to like me. You didn't like it when Andrew brought me here."

"You're right as rain. I didn't like you. You're not our kind. But I tell you now," Cima said, standing very straight and looking at Reanna without blinking, "because he's got no right to scream and curse and make you feel guilty for something he done long before you ever met him. He's got no right to make Snow take sides against you and put more trouble into this house. He's afraid, that's why he acts like a bully."

"Afraid of *me?*" Reanna said, bewildered.

"No," Cima scoffed. "He's afraid that if Snow liked anybody better than him or if anything happened to her, he'd lose her head rights and the land she gets from her mother."

"I can't believe that."

"It doesn't matter what you believe, it's the truth and it would be better for you if you took it to heart. You can suit yourself, but it won't change the facts. Listen here, missy, these are my folks and I love them. But I see them clear as crystal glass all the same. And that goes for Snow. She's spoiled and willful. She's a liar when it suits her. You didn't take her into the woods. She took you there to make mischief, and it's come back on her. Taffy and Pride know it's her doing, not yours. They know better than to blame you. Neither will Miss Jane when she comes home. Not when I tell her how it was."

Reanna's thoughts ran a race with themselves. First one opinion won and then another. If what Cima said was true, things were better than she'd feared; yet if what Cima said was true, she was truly in over her head, and she wasn't sure she could ever swim to the shore.

"Will Snow be all right?" she asked again.

"She's got a good chance."

"Thank you for all you did for her. And thank you for what you've told me."

"No call to thank me," Cima said abruptly. "I didn't do it for you. Snow's my baby, my last child to raise. Now you eat your supper, so you won't cause me more trouble." She took the cloth from the tray and left the room.

Reanna ate because she'd been told to do so. She was stunned by the events of the day and by what Cima had said. If it was true, then she knew even less about Andrew than she had before. She was married to a strange, complex man—cold, vindictive, jealous and tormented. For the first time she could see no hope for the future. Nowhere ahead could she believe she would ever find her dream of a life with Andrew.

WHATEVER doubts were in Reanna's mind, the fiercest battle of conflicting emotions was raging in Andrew's heart. He sat beside Snow's bed holding her hand; he wouldn't leave her even for a moment until he knew the crisis was past. In the flickering of the lamp, he dozed. His head came down, and as it touched the patterned coverlet, he roused himself again to watch over her. Snow was everything to him; he truly cared for her. He would have been shocked if he had any idea of how Cima saw his concern for Snow. To him, Snow was his future made secure. He cared for her in a way he'd never cared for her mother. The idea that Snow had been put in danger by Reanna made him wild. If he hadn't brought her here, none of this would have happened to Snow. Sometime after midnight in the small hours between night and dawn, he felt Snow stir. The fever broke and she began to sweat. He called for Cima, who was in the next room, and together they changed Snow's bedclothes and kept watch over her until the fever flushed out the last of the poison. At the end of it, Snow was pale and weak but alive. She was conscious and her eyelids fluttered.

"Papa's here, princess," Andrew said, as Snow's eyes opened. "Papa's here and you're going to be fine, just fine." Her eyes closed again. He was sure she'd seen him and he breathed a sigh of relief.

"She's going to make it back," Cima said. "You go on and get some rest. Why don't you give Mrs. MacClaren the good news? She'll be mighty glad to hear it."

"I won't have time for that." Andrew's jaw hardened. "I have to get on for Texas. I've wasted too much time already because of Mrs. MacClaren."

"All right, then. I'll tell her, if that's the way you want it."

He watched the look of disapproval on Cima's face. "Now don't you start on me. Where's Taffy? I want him to saddle up."

"How can you go without waiting on Miss Jane and seeing what kind of money she can raise?"

"I'm going *now*, I told you. Now, where's Taffy? Or are you meaning to keep it another one of your secrets?"

"He's gone across the river to the Triangle Saloon. That's where he usually goes, isn't it?" She had to take her satisfaction in provoking him.

"Damn his fool hide." Andrew brushed past Cima and stamped down the hall to his room. He meant to get his gear together and go. He had no intention of talking to Reanna if he could get out of it, or of seeing Pride either.

She hadn't slept. Most of the night she'd sat in the chair staring at the blank, dark window, listening to the wind. Every gust was a reminder of what Cima had said, a reproach for what had happened to Snow. At last she'd lain across the bed still dressed, half sick, unable to sleep.

She looked up to see Andrew framed in the doorway. He closed it sharply behind him and began to open drawers, ramming the contents into his saddlebags. She sat up, waiting for him to tell her how Snow was, to give her the comfort of certainty, but he did not speak to her. At last she was forced to ask, "How's Snow?"

"She's alive, no thanks to you."

"Oh, thank heaven." His back was to her, she couldn't see his face. She felt the tension in the room, as if it were a living thing.

"I know you blame me," Reanna said, "but I only meant to keep her from harm. If you'd told me about—rattlesnakes and things—"

Andrew turned. The look she saw in his eyes made her afraid; it wasn't anger now but cold contempt.

"I don't blame you. I blame myself because I brought you here. I shouldn't have married you, but it was what you wanted. You don't belong here. I tried to tell you. I wish for all our sakes I'd never met you."

"Andrew, please don't say that." She went to him then and put her arms around his neck. She couldn't believe he wouldn't relent, embrace her and tell her that he forgave her and that everything would be all right. Instead, he pulled her arms away and, holding her wrists, thrust her from him. The expression on his face was one of loathing and disgust.

"Don't you come at me like that." He spat out the words. "I don't want you anywhere near me. You think you can get around me here the way you did in Washington, but it won't work this time." He turned away and began putting the rest of his things into the bags.

"What are you doing?"

"I'm going to Texas, to buy cattle. I would have gone before if it hadn't been for you."

Her mind was blank with despair. "How long will you be gone?"

"Until I get back."

"What will I do while you're away?" He was going and she would be alone, knowing that he was still angry with her and doubting that she could ever close up the rift that had grown between them.

"I don't care what you do, Reanna. If you're bored you can ask Pride to keep you company. He's good at that."

"Oh, Andrew. That's so cruel."

"But if you're asking me what I want, I'd like it if you were gone when I get back. I think that would be the best for both of us, the best for everyone in this house." She couldn't believe he meant what he was saying. He'd change his mind and say that he was sorry. She only hoped it would be now. She didn't want him to leave her like this. She moved toward him. She meant to try once more to persuade him that, while she'd been at fault and put Snow in danger, she was willing to learn and that she wanted another chance to prove herself; but again he thrust her away, even more rudely.

"I told you not to try your fancy tricks on me. They won't work. You disgust me, you know that? You nearly killed my baby girl. I'll never forgive you for that. Never." He took his saddlebags and his dustcoat and, without a backward glance, he left her alone.

ANDREW rode hard all day up into the northeast, toward
the South Canadian River, pushing the buckskin,
still tense from his fears about Snow, still smarting
from the scene with Reanna. He had the bitter taste of his final
words in his mouth. He was as divided in his mind about her now
as he had been from the very first. He'd told her he'd only married
her because it was what she'd wanted, but that was a lie. He'd
married her because he'd wanted her. He'd told her he wanted her
to be gone when he got back from Texas, when what he really
wanted was for her to stay because she wanted him, not some
western adventure.

From the first their whole setup had been wrong, but since he
had married her and she was his wife, she'd have to abide by whatever rules he set. He meant to be master in his own house. She was
his wife and she'd act like it, or he would send her back East.

Damn her, she had a hold on him, a hold from which he couldn't
escape. He was even jealous of her—he'd known it when he'd first
seen her with Pride. Well, wait till she'd cooled her heels at Lochleven a few months, taking Cima's sass and listening to the wind;
she'd whistle a different tune.

As he splashed through the shallow, sandy-bottomed river and
climbed the far side, he could see the yellow, greasy glow of lanterns and hear voices raised in raucous argument, then laughter and
some off-key singing. Damn Taffy's fool hide, anyway. Taffy was as

fine a trail boss as you could find in all the West. He never drank on the place or on the trail, and he'd be the first to fire any hand that did. But right before a drive, he loved to tie one on.

Andrew hated the Triangle Saloon. It stood for human weakness, for profligacy and loss of control, things he couldn't stand. Yet men made the long pilgrimage with the same fervor as if they were heading toward a camp meeting and certain salvation. Whiskey was against the law in the Indian Territory, but the Triangle was situated across the border in Oklahoma Territory.

The place was notorious. Dutch Kellerman, massive ex-cavalryman and onetime street fighter, ruled with an iron hand, but it was still dangerous enough. Andrew had even heard stories of travelers who stopped for the night and never emerged the following day. As Taffy was fond of saying, "First they take your money, then they take your clothes. After that your boots and the fillings in your teeth." No one had ever claimed the games were honest. At the Triangle no questions were asked, no names ever given. Every lonely cowboy, drifter, renegade or outlaw could purchase oblivion if he had the price.

And on Saturday nights the local farmers and merchants hid their families and valuables in caves or ravines; cowpokes on their errant way home often went on a rampage, merrily looting and shooting up the countryside and one another. Goddamn fools.

Andrew found Taffy's roan gelding at the far end of the post, hitched the buckskin alongside it and offered a scrawny towheaded boy two bits if he'd water and watch over both mounts for him. The kid demanded the money in advance, his palm out. With a wry smile Andrew tossed him the quarter. The kid knew—he'd seen far too many cowpunchers come reeling out of the place too broke to pay him, half of them too drunk to remember they even *had* a horse around someplace. Wondering grimly just how far along Taffy might be by now, he checked his .45 to make sure it was loaded, spun the cylinder twice, eased it up a touch in its holster and climbed the steps.

Taffy Owen saw Andrew come through the swinging doors and sighed through his nose. It depressed him that he could recognize Andrew that swiftly; it meant he was far too sober. The main reason he'd decided to mosey on over here was to get away from Andrew and his cockeyed, runaway temper. The minute he'd found out Snow was out of danger, he'd hightailed it over here for a little peace and quiet.

Fact was, he was cross with Andrew for the way he'd lashed into that lovely lady of his. Blaming her for Snow's getting bit—Andrew himself knew it wasn't fair and it wasn't right; they all did. Why in hell did he *do* things like that? It was as though there were a coiled spring inside him under too much tension, and it kept snapping out of place at odd times. He'd been crazy as a pet coon ever since he'd come back from Washington, as if he wanted to get even with the sun and the moon and the Big Dipper, too. Well, marriage. But it wasn't Miss Reanna's fault, he knew it in his bones. A little green maybe, a little too fine bred, but she'd shape up in time. Andrew was lucky to get her, and that was a fact. He'd better mend his ways, or she'd waltz out of there and leave him high and dry one of these days.

There was a general turning of heads. Andrew never came in here unless it was the end of the world. Dutch Kellerman, behind the bar, ducked his big bullet head and said, "Evening, Mr. Mac-Claren," and Andrew nodded in reply. Sitting at one of the nearby tables, the Starrett brothers watched him like coyotes measuring a mustang, their hat brims low over their eyes. Then Grady slapped the tabletop once with the flat of his hand, to call attention to himself. Andrew glanced at him once, without expression, and looked away.

Grady was the ringleader, the one who thought up all their devilment. They said Jasper Starrett had been bright as paint. Hot tempered, but smart. If so, that strain had bypassed *this* generation for sure. Grady was a bully and a four-flusher, big with his mouth. Bud was quiet, a sneak, always hiding behind Grady. He had no will of his own, but he was obedient. If Grady told him to jam peas up his nose, he'd do it; if Grady told him to knife someone, Bud would do that, too—but in the dark, and from behind. Junior, the baby, didn't have any sense at all. He ran with the pack, growled and showed his teeth, but he was harmless.

Riffraff, Andrew called them, whatever that meant. Andrew said that he had no quarrel with them, that his blood wasn't Beauvaise, that it was up to Pride to settle that score or not, as he saw fit. Yet it was funny. At the wedding party, when Grady was riding up and down playing Chief Crazy Horse and Miss Jane faced him down, Andrew hadn't filled his hand, hadn't even looked like he was fixing to. Wouldn't he back up his own brother? Now and then Taffy found himself worrying about Pride. He believed that the boy meant what he said; he knew there was no yellow streak in him. But he'd have to deal with the Starretts sometime; they couldn't let him alone. He'd have to meet them head-on one day.

"Well, Andrew," Taffy said. He emptied his shot glass with a little flourish. "What brings *you* over Jordan?" This struck him as immensely witty, but Andrew didn't smile.

"Come along, Taffy. It's time to make tracks."

"Tracks? Tracks for where?"

"We're heading for Texas."

"I don't rightly believe I'm ready for Texas." This too seemed like a hugely witty reply and he grinned encouragingly and refilled his glass, but Andrew was dismayingly unresponsive. "Would you care to join me in a spot of red-eye?" he offered.

"You know me better than that."

"Yes. I do." Taffy was furious all at once. Here he was, all relaxed and well in advance of the day, so to speak, and here was Andrew standing over him solemn as an undertaker, telling him to leave this quarter-full bottle of Old Wrangler, simply *leave* it unemptied sitting on this table and go wandering off into the red dust of Texas without so much as a—without so much as a simple *howdy*. It was infuriating! Fact was, he'd come over here to get drunk, and he wouldn't be drunk until the floor came up and met him like a barn door in a cyclone. You'd think Andrew could understand a simple, fundamental thing like that. But no. He was all full of—

"Come on, now. We're going." Andrew reached out and picked up Taffy's hat.

Taffy blinked at him. "God damn it," he said, "that's my hat, Andrew."

"That's right. And you're going to wear it all the way to Texas."

"I told you, Andrew, that is—*my—hat*."

"Do tell."

Taffy watched his hat in Andrew's big hands. He loved that hat like nothing on earth or under it. It was top grade, blue-black felt with a high crown and a band of fancy Chickasaw beadwork Miss Jane herself had given him one Christmas morning. You could water a horse with it, or fan coals, or turn a spooked heifer with it, and it never lost its shape. He was partial to his boots, his blued

Colt .45 and his hundred-dollar saddle, but if he were drowning in the river and had to make a swift and final choice, it would be that hat. Hands could pick him out across two hundred head of milling cattle because of it; yearling riders knew when he was mad, or worried, or pleased as punch from the tilt he gave it. That hat was his badge of honor, the core of his identity.

He threw down another shot and said, "Nobody but me touches that hat."

"All right, then. Come on."

"I'll come when I'm good and goddamn ready, Andrew."

"The hell you will. You'll come with me *now*."

Andrew was mad now, he could tell, standing there in the middle of the room with the whole crowd gawking at him. The thought gave Taffy a touch of pleasure. He stuck out his chin and said, "Take your filthy hands off my hat, you son of a bitch."

Someone behind him laughed, and the pokes lined up along the bar began to turn around to watch the show. Andrew's cheek flexed once; his eyes took on that pale, cold light. He was ready to go toe to toe on this, that was clear. Taffy didn't really want to fight him, not in the mean mood he was in. Before he could make up his mind what to do, Andrew scaled his hat at him and said, "Take your stupid hat. Now, do you want to come the easy way or the hard way?"

Taffy got to his feet, holding his hat. The room was pretty steady, all things considered. He grinned brightly. "Well, now that you've put it like that, Andrew," he said.

There was general laughter, and then a thick, rasping voice said, "Whyn't you pistol-whip him, MacClaren?" Taffy looked around. It was Grady Starrett, standing in front of their table, grinning that ugly, dry-gulcher's grin of his. "Letting him give you that back talk. Whyn't you whip his ass for him?"

"Let's go, Taffy," Andrew muttered.

"Or did some of that Beauvaise blood rub off on you? You know what I mean?"

Taffy turned, holding his hat by the brim with both hands. Bud and Junior had got up too, their eyes shuttling from Grady to Andrew and back again. The room was very quiet now.

"Why, I don't believe you *know* this gentleman, Starrett," Taffy said.

"Gentleman?" Grady laughed, teeth black in his red mouth. "This ain't no gentleman here."

"Next time you talk to Mister MacClaren you call him just that. *Mister.*"

"Taffy, let it go," Andrew was saying hotly.

Starrett laughed again. "You need another drink, Owen. Sober you up. Right?"

The room laughed. Taffy grinned at him—his best, comical, cow-puncher-on-a-tear grin. He dropped the hat on the floor to more laughter, bent over unsteadily to retrieve it—and straightened up with a haymaker that caught Grady Starrett flush on the jaw. Grady gave a grunt of expelled air and flew backward into the table, taking Bud down with him.

"God *damn* it, Taffy!" Andrew was saying.

"*Nobody* bad-mouths you, Andrew," he answered joyfully.

Grady Starrett came up clawing at furniture, his eyes wild; blood was running from inside his mouth. Taffy moved to his left, saw Starrett pause, the hand go back, then the flash of the long blade. Oh, sure. He laughed soundlessly, in pure delight, snatched up his bottle and smashed its butt off against the table edge as casually as flicking ashes from a smoke. This was going to turn out to be fun after all. Bud had his knife out, too. Monkey see, monkey do. In the corner of his eye, Taffy saw Andrew swing a chair with one hand. Grady lunged once, a feint; Taffy slipped left again, holding the jagged bottle low. Next time he—

The roar was awesome, a tunnel blast in the dim, low-ceilinged room. Everything stopped. The Dutchman was standing on the bar holding a shotgun in his huge, blunt hands.

"That's one barrel," he said in his neat German accent. "Who wants the other?"

Grady Starrett sheathed his knife, edging away. Taffy put down the bottle, still grinning. Watching Starrett, he said, "Now why'd you want to kill the party, Dutch?"

"Fight in the street, fight in the riverbed. But not in my place."

"You got the persuader," Taffy agreed. Andrew was pushing him toward the door now. Grady was feeling the side of his face with his hand and nodding.

"I'll remember that, Owen."

"Anytime," Taffy said, and walked backward through the doors and across the porch and fell all the way down the steps.

HE remembered getting into his saddle, and then falling out of it, and Andrew swearing at him. Then he didn't remember much of anything else until he was floundering around in water, lots of water, gasping and hollering, and Andrew was holding him down, half drowning him. Then there was a fuzzy, rock-a-bye time until Andrew was brewing coffee in a fire behind some rocks.

"Don't *want* coffee," he told Andrew. "Want to finish that bottle."

"You broke it."

"The hell I did."

"The hell you didn't."

"I never wasted a shot of rye in my life."

The stuff was scalding. He tried to spit it out, but Andrew kept forcing it into him. At last, Taffy held the cup and drank on his own. When he was finished he said, "To tell you the truth, Andrew, I don't feel so good."

"You should learn to stay out of saloons," Andrew said.

"Don't forget I met you in a saloon."

"I haven't forgotten," Andrew said.

Sometimes it was hard to remember the boy Andrew had been when they first met. Taffy couldn't always recognize that boy in the man Andrew had become. Sometimes he felt he no longer understood him at all. Andrew could be hard. That wasn't a bad thing in this country, but lately Andrew had gotten a mean streak in him that Taffy didn't want to see.

"How's Snow?" Taffy asked.

"The fever's broken. She's all right."

"Thank God for that." Taffy would have taken to Snow more if she hadn't been such a snippy little thing. Just when you thought you had gotten on the good side of the kid and pleased her, she'd act up ugly and say cruel, cutting things that weren't always true. She was Andrew's daughter right enough. Snow didn't favor Letty, that was for sure. Letty had been as sweet and mild as May; she'd never said a cross word to anybody in her life.

Letty had loved Andrew; she'd never had eyes for anyone but him. Taffy remembered the day he'd come up on Beauvaise Ridge for the first time with Andrew, remembered how Letty had been there waiting for Andrew, looking out that high cupola window like a woman on shore waiting for a ship to come. Andrew wasn't a man then—he'd been nothing but a nervy kid trying to act big—but that hadn't mattered to Letty.

"I remember the first time I ever saw you, in that Texas saloon,"

Taffy said. "You'd come to drive Colonel Goodwell's swamp angels up to the Five Nations. You didn't know hair from horn."

"That's right, I didn't." Andrew passed Taffy another cup of coffee.

"But I learned you."

"You did."

"I was Colonel Goodwell's best trail boss. He wouldn't have let them cattle out of Texas if I hadn't been with them. I'm one fine cowhand." Taffy suddenly felt a great wave of sadness for the past that was lost and would never come again.

"You're the best."

"I never wanted to be nothing else but a cowboy. From the day I seen pictures of cowboys in books, I knew that was what I wanted to be. There were pictures in them, all of the wild and woolly West. Nobody I knew had ever seen a cowboy, let alone been one.

"My folks come from Wales. My pa said that he figured he might as well die down a mine in America as down a mine in Wales. He didn't last long. He was already sick in his lungs, I guess, when we got there. My ma married again and her new husband wasn't partial to me. By the time I run off, she had so many other kids she didn't miss me anyway.

"I walked west on railroad ties and kept on going until I come to Texas. I joined up with Colonel Goodwell because they said his was the top outfit. I did every dirty job, took every ribbing the other hands could dish out, but I learned how to cowboy with the best of them. Until I got to be the Colonel's trail boss. That's what I did." Taffy paused. He looked up at Andrew, who was staring at the fire.

"What a sight you were—no lariat and no neckerchief, and scared shitless. You didn't know what to do or how to do it. You couldn't have been more than sixteen."

"Sixteen going on seventeen."

"Just a kid trying to fill up your breeches and walking in a pair of borrowed boots. You were so green, I had to tell you to get in out of the rain." Taffy laughed and his face broke into a satisfied, happy grin. "We were one funny-looking outfit, let me tell you. To ride point we had Jack Levy with his wagonload of bankrupt goods. Good old Jack, out on his own. He was looking for a way to start keeping store. You said, 'Come on with us up to the Five Nations. I'll start you a town and build you a store.' And he believed you.

"God, there was people standing in the street, laughing at you.

You didn't seem to mind what anybody said. You looked as proud as if Jack had the ark of the covenant and you was Hannibal about to lead us over the Alps."

"If we were such a ragtag outfit, why did you come?" Andrew demanded suddenly.

Taffy wanted to tell it again. "I come with you because the Colonel told me to."

"All right, but why did you stay? The pay was poor and the grub was worse." Taffy shrugged.

"*Someone* had to look after you."

"And you elected yourself by a majority of one."

"Could be I stayed because I knowed you were going to be the big cheese around here, and I wanted to throw in with a winning outfit."

"The Colonel was already the best. Why did you really stay?"

"What do you want to know for? It was a long time ago." Taffy looked at the tips of his boots, concentrating on them, as if the answer were in the hand-tooled leather. It was one thing to spin a yarn and another to tell the truth. "I stayed because you needed me and because I found a home. You got to be my folks, my family. It didn't matter if you was a big chief or not."

"Well, I won't ever be a big chief if I don't get down to Texas. The only way to save my hide is to bring up as many head as I can beg, borrow, or rustle, then fatten them on grass and pray the weather holds until I can get them to the railhead."

"You'd better pray the grass will grow and the creek won't run dry."

"When you're sober enough, it's time to ride."

"What does Pride say about the grass?"

"I haven't asked him."

"You're not waiting on Miss Jane?"

"No."

"Miss Jane will be mighty disappointed if you don't wait on her."

"I'm going. Come or stay, as you like."

"You owe them. Miss Jane has done everything for you."

"One way or another, someone always brings that up. It seems to me I showed my gratitude enough by marrying Letty."

Taffy felt stunned by what Andrew had said. Surely he must have misunderstood him. "You cared for Letty. I know she did for you."

"Well, I married her," Andrew said grimly, "and now I've married Reanna, so I don't want to hear any more about Letty."

"You've been mighty hard on Reanna, Andrew, saying all those things to her last night."

"She had it coming."

"She made a mistake. Haven't you ever made a mistake?"

"I made a mistake when I married her."

"Sometimes you're hard to figure, Andrew. You get your tail caught in a crack and you turn plumb mean, you know that?"

Andrew got up and began kicking dirt over the fire. "Well, you've had your say. If I'm that bad, you don't have to come with me. You can leave this outfit any time you have a mind to."

"When I have a mind to go, I will, and that's a fact." Taffy was hurt and angry. He hadn't expected Andrew to turn on him because he spoke the truth. Things were getting bad, and that was a fact. He couldn't see how Andrew could treat Reanna so bad. That girl was something special. He himself would lie down and turn up his toes for a girl like that. If Andrew kept on, something real bad was going to happen. He could feel it in his bones.

"Don't you flimflam me, Andrew. I think you're running scared again, as scared as you were when we first met and you were only a kid."

"Think what you please, Taffy Owen, but this is the last drive. Are you coming or staying?"

"I'm coming. I owe you this one."

"Are you sure you're sober enough to sit on your horse?"

"Yes."

"And, Taffy . . ."

"Yes?"

"After this drive, we're even. You don't owe me anything; we're even and quits."

"If that's the way you want it."

"I wouldn't want you hanging on to an outfit that's going bust."

"Don't talk like that, Andrew. This isn't the last drive."

Silently the two men saddled up. Only the creak of the leather and the rub of bridle chain and the striking of hoofs on hard ground cut the night air. It was so silent and still that they easily heard the approach of men on horseback.

Andrew and Taffy stood wordlessly, listening; then, like the old partners they were, they began to work in concert. Taffy held up two fingers. Andrew shook his head. "Three," he whispered, "there's three of them."

Taffy nodded, knowing without seeing them that Jasper Starrett's boys had followed them across the river. They never came on Beauvaise land except to cause trouble.

They were close enough now that he could see the three of them outlined against the sky. The silver glinted from their bridles, then disappeared as if they'd evaporated into the night.

"It's Starrett's boys all right," Taffy said.

"Yes."

"You want to go for them?"

"No. I've better things to do than chase those bastards."

"Hadn't we ought to tell Pride they're heading his way?"

"Hell, he won't do anything. Pride won't fight with them."

Taffy shifted uneasily in his saddle. "He ought to know they're on the place."

"Then you go tell him," Andrew answered angrily, "but I won't wait for you."

Taffy hesitated. He was divided. He owed Pride and he owed Andrew. Reluctantly he said, "I reckon Pride can take care of it."

"Then if you don't have further objections, let's ride the hell for Texas."

Andrew's horse wheeled and turned and pawed at the ground. To show this was a leave-taking to remember, Andrew drew his pistol and fired into the air. Taffy, catching the spirit of the last big adventure, fired along with Andrew. Then yelling, their hats fanning the air, the two riders galloped toward the Red River and Texas.

WHEN Pride had seen Andrew ride out after Taffy, it had been hard for him to believe that Andrew had really gone to Texas without him. It had been harder to believe Andrew had gone without waiting for Miss Jane to return.

Since Andrew had come home from Washington with Reanna, everything at Lochleven seemed to be out of harmony. When Pride had first seen Reanna in the hallway, holding the Beauvaise cup in her hands, he had felt the earth shift beneath his feet, the old familiar ground struck from beneath him. It was more than her beauty that had unsettled him; he had been seized by the feeling that nothing in this house would ever be the same again.

It was easy to see why Andrew had married her; Reanna was a woman any man might love. But it wasn't so easy to see why she'd married Andrew. Andrew was rude and thoughtless toward her. He'd shamed her and shamed the Beauvaises when he refused to break the ear of corn with her.

Pride had never been ashamed of Andrew before. All his life, Pride had looked up to Andrew. Pride knew that sometimes Andrew would take unfair advantage, but even so he had always felt that everything Andrew did was for the good of Lochleven and the Beauvaises. Now Pride no longer believed that. It made him feel disloyal to his brother, yet it was Andrew who was different.

The old Andrew wouldn't have considered bringing three thousand head onto the grass this dry year, any more than that Andrew would have believed Reanna was to blame for Snow's accident. Even if he'd been angry because Reanna had gone into the woods with Snow, that other Andrew would never have accused her before the others. He would have remembered that Reanna was his wife, a woman of their house, and that he owed her every respect and courtesy.

Pride felt pity for Reanna and shame for Andrew. Here at Lochleven they were all responsible for one another. When Andrew shamed one, he diminished them all. Pride knew that Andrew was worried about what the future might hold, but that didn't alter the hard fact that Andrew had left without waiting to hear what Miss Jane had to tell him.

Pride didn't know how he could help Andrew if Andrew pushed him aside, but at least he could treat Reanna as if she were an honored guest and a sister. To treat Reanna with respect and honor wouldn't be hard. He had been drawn to her as he had been to no other woman.

When she came into the barn, she was wearing a divided riding skirt, a shirt and vest, and boots. On her head was a smart lady's bowler. "I'm sorry I'm late. I had to finish writing a letter home." It had been just a note, really.

Dear Folks,

Andrew has gone down to Texas to get a big herd of cattle. Taffy Owen went with him and Miss Jane is in Tishomingo on business, so I have time to get to know the countryside better. Pride, Andrew's brother, is going to take me out riding today. I wish you were all here to enjoy the fine spring weather. I know both Patrick and Thomas would like the idea of riding for miles and miles with no fences to jump or gates to open. I do so miss you all. I am trying to learn to fit in out here, but it will take time. Cima runs the house and Snow is not quite used to having a new mother. I have so much to learn. Sorry, but I must run. I can't keep Pride waiting.
                              Love,
                              Reanna

Pride had saddled the horses and was waiting, the bridles caught in his hand. He grinned in admiration when he saw her. He was curiously pleased that they had the day ahead of them. He helped her to mount, his strong hands supporting her. He held Molly May as she skittered, and he smiled reassuringly at Reanna as he stroked Molly May's soft nose.

"That hat is mighty pretty," he said, "but you'll need something with a wider brim to keep off the sun. Andrew will skin me alive if I let you get sunburned." Pride handed her a western hat with a drawstring to set beneath her chin. "Here," he said, "I'll trade you even." The hat made Reanna look different. It changed her from a stranger to someone familiar. "You look like an Indian woman in that hat."

She blushed, pleased by the compliment. She might not belong here as Letty had done, but she would try again to fit in.

Reanna had been afraid that they would have nothing to talk about, but now that she was with Pride, she was at ease. No words were necessary for them to know and read each other's feelings. They were safe, complete within a circle of the sky and earth. Being with Pride was so different from being with Andrew. With Pride, the silence nourished and fed her. Even the horses seemed to gentle as they picked up each other's hoofbeats and their gait changed from a rocking canter into a gallop.

They reined in the horses and Pride looked up at the sky, his eyes squinting into the bright sun. He said, "I think we'll go west today."

Reanna's heart soared. She'd come to Lochleven from the eastern side of the Ridge. She hadn't been to the west, which for some reason she thought of as Pride's domain.

They rode down into the waving grass, following a trail she wouldn't have seen in the high grass if she'd been alone. As they rode silently and easily, she felt that Pride was a part of the land itself, a fusion of the elements. He belonged to woods and water, the earth and the sky. She was still alien, but she had for the first time some sense of belonging.

"Andrew thinks it's cattle that will make Lochleven rich." Pride's words came to her on the wind. "I think it's the grass. That is our fortune." He drew up, dismounted and helped Reanna down from the saddle. Together they bent down and sat on their haunches. "See this bluestem grass?" He pulled up a stalk for her. "Its roots go down deep for water. It's this root that holds the soil together. I used to think the roots went down to China." He smiled. "You can graze cattle on this grass till the end of time, but you have to change pastures, give the grass a chance to rest and then come back. If you overgraze, the place will die. Do you understand?"

They walked their horses in the grass, the wind swirling around them, singing in their ears.

"Last year," Pride said, "it was dry, and the year before. This year there still hasn't been enough rain. The grass *looks* the same, but at the root it's wanting for water. If we don't rotate the herd right, we'll overgraze, and then we will have cost ourselves the future."

Listening to what he said, she understood better what his argument was with Andrew, but later, when she thought of that day, she would remember only the way his hands held the stalk of grass, his fingers lingering gently on the long stem. And later, when she thought of him, she'd remember that not only had he touched her arm, he'd touched her spirit. He'd changed forever her way of seeing grass and sky. The earth was a giver, from whom one must not take too much.

As they rode on, the sun rose higher in the sky. They turned north until they came to a low pasture where a few head of cattle grazed. "Is this the old herd?" she asked.

"No, this pasture is for a new strain of grass and cattle. I'm trying to breed up something that will adapt better to this country than the Texas longhorn and be sturdier than the gentle English breeds. Someday I'll get a nick, and the cross will be the right one. It will take time. Look, I have some of Frampton's English stock in with ours." He leaned over suddenly and peered at the grass as if he were reading a page of print.

"What is it?" she asked.

"Three men have been through here. Not our hands."

"How can you tell that?"

"Their horses weren't wearing our irons. They were riding west."

"I don't see anything."

He showed her the print of the horses' shoes. He didn't make her feel stupid for asking. With Pride she never felt diminished. He told her things as if she could understand them, and he never seemed to mind, no matter how many questions she asked. Often he seemed to answer her questions before she asked them, as if he had read her mind. He showed her where the creeks ran into the river. He pointed out the trails that led to the line houses and across the river to Simon Frampton's ranch and Father Soule's mission.

"It's too bad about Frampton," Pride said.

"What is?"

"He won't be able to ranch up there much longer."

"Why not? He's in Oklahoma Territory, not Indian Territory, isn't he?"

"Yes, when Frampton first came out here he leased his ranch on the unassigned lands. Then, when they were opened up to white settlement, Frampton leased again, this time from Washington. They're bound to cancel the lease soon."

"What will Frampton do then?"

"Sell up his stock and improvements and get out. He can't ranch without pasture any more than we can."

"But your situation is so different. This is your Nation, your land. It's so unfair." She knew it was a poor way of saying that she was sorry. "How can the government just come in and take over whenever it wants to?"

She remembered with discomfort the conversation at Cousin Lucy's the night she'd met Andrew. The people in Washington had all been so smug, so sure they knew what was right for the Indians. Her mother and Cousin Lucy had discussed the Indians and their land as casually as if they had been dress patterns or cake recipes.

"How much of Lochleven will you be able to keep when the allotments are given out?" she asked.

Pride shrugged. "It depends. We'll each get a homestead allotment and some surplus land. The number of acres depends on the value the assessor places on the land. It's graded one through ten. The more valuable the land is, the fewer acres we'll get. Our land is still to be assessed and surveyed. There was a work party on the place today. Didn't you see them?"

She shook her head. Pride saw everything, every bird and blade of grass.

"When we get this herd up from Texas, we'll have to stay with them day and night to keep them moving on the grass and to keep an eye out for settlers, surveyors and Snake Indians."

"I've never heard of Snake Indians." She had a vision of the nest of snakes into which Snow had jumped.

"They are mostly full bloods who are against the allotments. They think they can stop the government by coming in and pulling up surveyors' pins, tearing down settlers' fences and frightening as many people as they can." He worried his lower lip with his teeth. "They've been accused of killing people who got in their way or didn't side with them."

"You can't blame them for not wanting to give up their Nation to white settlers," she said emphatically.

He looked at her and shook his head sadly. "What's happening in our Nation is not all the fault of the white settlers. The Indians are also to blame. We let the settlers come in. We paid some of them to come and work for us, to do jobs we didn't want to do or couldn't do for ourselves. When people came in illegally, the tribe was too lazy or too busy arguing among themselves to collect the residence fees. Andrew leased out town lots to Jack Levy and Doc and Amoretta. He thought that we needed a store and a doctor and a post office."

"I believe you think Andrew was wrong to start a town," she said.

"I didn't say that. Miss Jane and he both agreed that going twenty miles to Maitland for supplies was too hard. All I'm saying is that the people we brought here and the people we let stay now want to own their land. I can't blame them. I see their side of it."

"You're always so reasonable. You see every side. Andrew seems to care more about what is happening to your land than you do."

He was silent for a long time, and then he said, "No, Andrew doesn't care more than I do. I just don't show my feelings. The hurt of losing my tribal land and my way of life is too big a hurt to be cured by small measures. Besides, Andrew has a different idea about the land than I do."

"Tell me the difference."

"To Andrew, the land is a living. It is power, place, a position in life. For me, the land is my life. Just as, for me, to carve something out of wood or bone gives me pleasure. To Andrew, carving is useless if I don't make any money for my trouble. To him, I must seem to be lazy or unfeeling, because I won't fight against any of the political factions."

She thought of the Starretts and how Pride had refused to fight them. To her that seemed an act of great bravery.

"There are so many different political factions," Pride said, "so many small, dissatisfied parties, that the Chickasaw have nearly argued themselves to death. One thing almost all parties agree on. They don't care for the Beauvaises. Particularly the full bloods who blame us for letting the whites in."

"I've seen Miss Jane with the people," Reanna said. "No one could be more generous or care more for them than she does."

"The truth is that there are something like fifty families, mostly mixed blood, who control the wealth of the Nation. The rest, the majority, have little or nothing. Either they don't know how to get this world's goods, or they don't want them, because they think everything to do with progress and education and business is against the Indian way. The Indians want to obey their laws and the settlers want to obey theirs, and I know the white men's law is going to win, no matter what we do."

"How soon will you have to give up the land?" she asked.

"I don't know for sure. Next year, if Andrew is right, but we still have it for today." He smiled at her, but there was a sadness in his eyes. "We can still enjoy the land today."

They followed the creek and drew in under some trees. They let the horses drink and then hobbled them loosely to let them graze. They made coffee from the clear creek water and unwrapped a packet of cold ham biscuits and a bonus of crescent-shaped, fried apricot pies.

"That's the best coffee I ever drank," Reanna said.

"It's the creek water."

After lunch they lay down, heads cradled in upstretched arms. It seemed as natural to have Pride lying beside her as the air she breathed. His horse came and nuzzled at his shoulder. She saw his hand stroke the horse's nose, gliding gently and softly over the velvet lips. Suddenly, she wanted him to touch her in just that way. It was a thought that came like a little sliver of light and vanished in almost the same instant. That day they were two innocents together in a world as perfect as Eden.

"You haven't told me your horse's name," she said.

"I hadn't thought of a name," he said, and after a moment's hesitation, "Why don't you name him?"

"Cloud," she said, "Gray Cloud." She had no idea why she chose the name, but it seemed to please Pride.

"You know," he said, "you should learn how to manage your own stock." He turned on his side and looked at her speculatively. "Have your own herd, learn when to buy and when to sell."

She looked at him quickly to see if he was joking. His face was serious and so were his eyes. It was such a strange idea, it turned her head, as if he had given her strong wine. "Andrew would never let me." She felt her lips stiff and dry. "He says I don't know anything about cattle."

"I heard him say that at the table. But you can learn. All our women—Jane, Cima, Letty—all of them managed their own herds and land."

"Cima manages a section?" Reanna was surprised.

"Not now, but she did when she was younger. She could still boss a section if she were pushed. Miss Jane oversees all of Lochleven. Letty had her section, which Andrew took over when they married. She let Andrew run her part, but she knew how. It was hers by right."

Reanna was silent. It gave her something sobering to think about—women who had a right to property of their own, a right to say yes or no, to come and go as they pleased. It was like a lightning bolt to hear Pride say that Letty had given Andrew her share to manage. She hadn't believed all that Cima had said about Andrew's reasons for marrying Letty. It was possible that he had had mixed motives for marrying her. He could have wanted Miss Jane to be happy, and he could have wanted Letty's land. What was most astonishing to her was that Pride should take the rights of the women at Lochleven for granted. He saw her confusion.

"The descent comes through the woman," he said. "A man is the head of the household, and a woman serves him and considers his wishes, but the land and the right of place goes with the woman. It is sensible; a child can always be sure who his mother is, but sometimes the father can be in doubt."

Reanna felt herself flush. A child without a father's name would be an outcast in her world. It was sensible and logical that the woman should own property and that a mother should give a child a family name and land, but to have that right meant accepting power and responsibility. Her own mother ran the farm, but she would go to any lengths to keep her father from knowing it. It would be a shameful thing to the men Reanna had known if a woman had even an opinion of her own, let alone her own money.

Pride rose and looked up at the sun. "It's time to be going."

Reanna felt suddenly bereft; a portion of this special day was already gone. Even as she had listened to Pride, a part of her was saying, "This is the best day of my life." For the first time she had felt completely alive and at one with the world. Her heart almost hurt with feeling so much love for this land.

"You see," Pride went on, "the herd are not smart as individuals, but together they have an instinct to survive. That pull moves them to grass or water. When they're afraid, it drives them to stampede. This year," Pride said, "we'll have to be extra smart for the herd. We'll have to move them, pick the grass that's best and keep them grazing in the right direction. Look," he said. Her eyes followed his pointing finger. "That's the north line house."

Reanna saw a bunkhouse, rudely built, with a friendly curl of smoke rising from the chimney. It was close upon a bend in the river.

"When Andrew and Taffy bring the herd up from Texas, we'll stay out here. Just over the river is Frampton's place. Do you want to ride up today?"

"No." She felt she'd answered too quickly, but she didn't want to share this day with anyone else. By the look on Pride's face, she knew he felt the same way.

They rode on toward the west over rolling prairie. There was no fence to bar their way. "The way west leads to the happy hunting ground." Pride grinned. "That's what the Indians believe. We think that there, beneath the sky, is the home of Breathholder, the Great Spirit, who waits for us. The Cherokee kept the outlet land so that their spirits could have a clear road west. Now it's been opened for white settlement. It's sad to think that the people will have no way to go beneath the sky." He stopped again to pull grass and examine the root, the stem and the head.

It seemed natural that Pride should talk as calmly of death and dying as he dealt with the things of life. It made the seasons of the earth and the years of man all a part of a whole, not a dark mystery of which to be afraid.

Beneath the grass the wild herbs mingled with the dust to make a fragrant bouquet. It had never occurred to her that dust could have a scent that would excite her as if it were a rare blend of potpourri. She felt her blood quicken and her perceptions grow sharper.

As they came over a rise she saw the whole prairie laid out before her. She was filled with a sensation of wonder and something else unfamiliar to her, a rush of poignant happiness. No wonder Miss Jane liked to stay in her cupola room. From her windows she could see this beauty all around her in every season and weather.

"I love this land," she called happily. "I do."

"You shouldn't say that till you've seen it full circle."

"That's what Andrew says. I know I would never want to leave here." She said suddenly, "Are you disappointed he didn't take you with him to Texas?"

Pride looked away. "Andrew and I have a difference of opinion."

"Are you right or is he?"

"There are two sides to the thing. I want to conserve, improve the land and the grass and the breed of cattle. He wants to make big profits while the making is good and we still have the land. He wants it no matter what the risk."

"Then he's wrong. You should stand firm. You can't both be right." As she spoke, she knew she had betrayed herself; without meaning to, she'd already taken sides.

"I think he's wrong. But we're brothers."

"You love him, don't you?"

"Yes. I looked up to him when I was a boy. He is so smart. It doesn't seem I will ever catch up with him. He has strength I lack."

"Strength?"

"Yes, the strength to be hard if he thinks it right. I'm a dreamer. Andrew always keeps one eye open."

"But you have courage," she said.

"Yes," he agreed without hesitation or false modesty. "I have courage, but I don't have the courage to be cruel if necessary."

"It can't ever be right to be cruel, can it?" she asked, and she felt herself being swept into a stream too deep and fast for her comfort. Yet with Pride she would never be afraid, she knew.

"Sometimes you have to be hard if you want to succeed." It sounded like some maxim Andrew had given him.

As they rode south, they passed a ravine cut in the rolling hills. At the far end Reanna saw a small cabin.

"Who lives there?"

"No one. The ravine is a good hideout for cattle when the weather's bad. The cabin is a place I come to when I want to be alone."

"Will you take me there?"

He hesitated; she caught his mood of indecision, as if to take her there would mean a different sort of journey.

"Yes," he said, "one day. But now it's getting late. We'll go home by way of the rock springs. Then you will have made a full circle sweep of the west range."

(182)

As they rode south the terrain changed. The rolling hills of grass gave way to stony, barren soil and then to an outcropping of strangely shaped rocks. Above them in the distance she could see Lochleven high on its rock plateau.

"When you're there you don't realize how high the house is set or how steep the Ridge." She nodded as Pride continued. "It's treacherous in bad weather or at night. If you don't know the place, you can go over the edge." Reanna glanced to the far western rim. It was there she had followed Snow. She must put that day from her mind; it was in the past.

"On this side of the Ridge," Pride was saying, "there are some rock springs. We'll stop there and water the horses."

Reanna could see that Molly May already knew there was water ahead. Then the wind changed and she caught the smell of something unfamiliar and unpleasant.

"What's that awful smell?"

"The springs," he said. "There's sulphur in the water."

She found the odor sickening, as if they had come upon a field of rotten eggs.

The rocks, like sharp dragons' backs, narrowed toward a pool of sand springs bubbling beneath the rocks of the bluff. Kneeling beside one of the springs was a ragged man who seemed as misshapen as the rocks themselves.

"There's a man by one of the springs."

"I know."

Reanna felt foolish for having spoken; she was sure Pride had seen the man long before she did. The man remained bent over the spring.

"He doesn't know we're here," Pride said. "He's deaf."

"You know him?"

"Yes, it's John's Dead."

"That's his name?"

Pride nodded. "It's his earned name. Every Indian has three names. The one he's given when he's born, his secret name that only the Great Spirit knows and the name he earns for himself by his deeds."

She puzzled on this as they drew closer to the springs. From one of the smaller springs the man was skimming up a residue of thick, dark ooze with a spoon and carefully putting it into a wide-mouthed bottle.

"What's he doing that for?" Reanna asked, but before Pride

could answer, John's Dead, seeing the horses' hooves beside him, looked up—and Reanna gasped with shock. The man was hideous. He was cruelly pockmarked; one eye was twisted in its socket. He gave the very appearance of evil.

"John's Dead won't hurt you." Pride made a sign to the man to rise. "He's only here getting medicine. There's an oil slick on the water that the people believe is a magical cure for all ailments."

The man came forward, not toward Pride's horse but to Reanna's. Even Molly May was afraid of this stranger and reared on her hind feet, pawing at the air.

"Why is he called John's Dead?" Reanna asked, as she gentled Molly May.

"Because when he was a boy he had smallpox. He was so sick, his family thought he was dead, and they threw him onto a heap of bodies gathered up in the epidemic. When he crawled out he was a mass of sores. The children, even his own clan, ran from him saying he was a spirit risen from the dead. He's shunned by everyone, but he still hopes for a cure. He comes to the springs for rock oil. He's done that for as long as I can remember."

"I'm sorry," Reanna stammered, unable to take her eyes from the man's terrible face. "Is he all right?"

"He's a little simple, but he's not dangerous. He hasn't the wit to know that he's frightening and ugly and that that's why people shun him. The boys throw stones at him to keep him off, and mothers threaten their children that if they aren't good, they'll grow up to look like John's Dead."

"That's terrible," Reanna said. There was pity in her heart, but her fear was greater than her compassion. The man's hand touched her stirrup. His fingers closed on her skirt and he began to tug at it as if he meant to topple her from her horse.

"What does he want?" she heard her voice, high and unnatural.

"He wants to touch your hair."

"My hair?"

"He thinks that hair with the sunlight in it is an even more powerful magic than the oil. Only the spirit people are believed to have hair like yours."

"I can't," Reanna said, her lips stiff. "I can't let him touch me."

"I understand." His voice was even. There was no reproach in it, but she censured herself for her cowardice. She let her hat slide from her head and hang by its cord onto her back. She reached up and took the pins from her hair and let it fall to within the grasp of John's Dead so that he could touch the ends of her hair. She felt his touch and she heard him muttering, his lips moving as if he said a prayer. She couldn't look at him; that took more courage than she had.

The man looked up at her, dazzled as if she were the noonday sun. There were tears on his marked face that stained his cheeks. He stepped back from her to the spring. He took up his bottles, and still mumbling words she couldn't understand, he disappeared into the cluster of rocks at the edge of the bluff.

"You're a brave girl," Pride said.

Reanna shook her head. She tried to swallow but her throat was dry. "No, I was afraid of him."

"Then you're all the more brave for what you did. John's Dead will live on your magic for a long time."

"But he'll see that there's no change, no cure, and then what will happen to him?"

"Then he'll try the oil again."

"Do the Indians really believe this oil is medicine?" She looked up to the top of the bluff and saw the layers of different rocks that made up the surface. They looked like the layers of a giant cake. The oil seeped out from them in slick, bright ribbons. It must run down beneath the ground to the pools below.

"Yes, they believe," Pride said. "Medicine is about all the oil is good for. Except as a tick dip for the cattle."

"In Pennsylvania they're drilling for oil," Reanna said. "They want it for illumination." She looked at the greenish-purple, stagnant pools below her and doubted if this was the sort of oil to light lamps. "The men who are marketing the oil for lamps and machines sell it by the barrel. They're making a lot of money."

"I know about oil men." Pride grinned. "Some of them formed a company with the tribe to look for oil before the Civil War."

"What happened?"

"They found oil, but there was no market for it and they fought among themselves about what to do with it. Now the government has stopped us from leasing our land for its minerals or grazing until the land can be taken from the tribe and divided."

"Can't you go to court to get the right to drill on your own land?"

Pride shook his head sadly. "I used to believe that what the law had taken the law would restore, but sometimes even the law itself fails us."

"Then you can make new laws, can't you?" A gust of rising wind caught at her hair, blowing it like a flame in the setting sun.

"Maybe I will," Pride said, looking at her in wonder. She was like no other person he had ever met. He felt when he was with her that there was nothing he couldn't do. She gave him a new kind of confidence in himself. All things were possible with Reanna—but then he stopped his thoughts. Reanna was not his, she was Andrew's. He had wanted to go with Andrew to Texas, but now he was glad that Andrew had refused to take him. While Andrew was away, he could spend his days with Reanna. He felt suddenly as rich as if he had discovered gold, not oil in a black, dirty pool.

"Come," he said, "we must head for home."

"If you drilled for oil here at Lochleven, you could be rich enough not to worry about grass or cattle."

"I prefer grass and cattle," Pride said, the smile dying in his eyes. "The oil slick kills the grass and the cattle won't drink the water. Look how barren this place is. No, I wouldn't drill for oil, for fear we might find it."

He turned his horse and she followed. Riding toward home, she thought of how much she had enjoyed the day and of how she would rather stay in the open beneath the sky than go back to Lochleven. It was astonishing that she should feel so fresh after a long day in the saddle or so elated when her situation with Andrew had only been sidetracked, a confrontation between the two of them merely deferred. At first she couldn't for a moment recognize the feeling that suffused her being. And then she laughed, for what she felt was happiness.

At Lochleven Miss Jane and Cima stood looking out the window of the cupola, watching Reanna and Pride come up off the west range.

"They ride well together," Cima said. Miss Jane said nothing. Reanna and Pride were a matched pair. Reanna would make a better wife for Pride than for Andrew. Miss Jane had seen that at first glance, but it was too late for that now and there were other matters on her mind far more immediate. She had gone to the Indian Agent at Tishomingo to find out how much money she could realize in cash. A large sum was owing to her, but she had been made to wait and then given excuses. The government would withhold payment on all claims until a tribal census was taken, the rolls made up and the land divided. It was not right or fair, but it was a fact which must be faced, and it made Miss Jane afraid. Fear was bitter to the taste; it withered the heart.

As Reanna and Pride came into the house, she was in the hall to greet them, and she saw fear of another kind in Reanna's eyes. Cima had told Miss Jane what had happened to Snow. Cima had also told her how Andrew had blamed Reanna.

"I'm so glad you've come back," Reanna said.

"I am happy to be home again." The girl had courage, that much even Andrew would have to admit.

"If I'd known you were coming today, I wouldn't have gone riding with Pride. I would have been here to meet you." She meant to face up to whatever Miss Jane had to say to her. "Cima said there was nothing for me to do here."

"It does not matter." Miss Jane glanced at Pride but she could not read his mind. "I had hoped to be back before Andrew left for Texas. He must have gone in a great hurry. I thought he would be waiting to know how much I was able to raise at Tishomingo." She kept her eyes on Pride. "I am surprised Andrew would not take you with him for such a big drive."

"Andrew thought I would be better used marking out the pastures."

"I see."

"He left in a hurry," Reanna said, "because he was angry. He thought I was to blame for Snow's accident." She spoke clearly but softly, as if she were pleading a case before some high court judge.

"What has happened is a great pity." Miss Jane handed down her judgment. She had already thought out what she would say. "But Snow has only herself to blame. She has been told a dozen times not to go into the woods. She tempted fate and she got what she deserved. She is lucky that it was not worse for her."

Reanna was silent. She found the judgment on her lenient but perhaps harder on Snow than she deserved. She wondered if she could ever be so evenhanded and dispassionate; she didn't think so. She was too passionate, too fierce in her loves and loyalties. Perhaps it was a wisdom that would only come with age.

"It is time for supper. We mustn't keep Cima waiting."

Miss Jane walked ahead of Pride and Reanna into the dining

room. She was no less feeling than she had been as a girl. She had merely learned to keep her face a mask and to do nothing and say less until she had thought things through. How could Andrew have gone without seeing her? Even if he had felt he must save time, the road to Texas ran past the fort; he could have stopped to consult with her there. And why hadn't he taken Pride?

When she was gone, her two sons must keep this place together. The land was Beauvaise land and the management would be Andrew's, but they must be partners. Now that future seemed uncertain. Since Reanna had come to Lochleven, she too must be considered as a part of the future. No matter how difficult for her, one day she would have to run the house and solve its problems. And she would need Cima as her faithful ally.

REANNA looked forward to every day. She enjoyed the sense of freedom it gave her to be with Pride. She couldn't imagine ever being bored, with him for company. They went over the whole ranch and the surrounding countryside. The sight of the two of them together became familiar.

When they rode up to Frampton's, it would have been considered uncivil if they had not stayed the night. Frampton came out to greet them, his rosy, ruddy face aglow with pleasure. He was surrounded by a cloud of yapping hounds. He welcomed Reanna and Pride in, and the dogs came too.

Frampton's house was not as fine as Lochleven, but it was comfortable enough and in spartan order, surprising for this bachelor and the freedom he gave the dogs. They ate by flickering candlelight and afterward drank port. The silver candelabra and the quiet, elegant taste of his house did nothing to solve the mystery of how Frampton came to be there in the West. A scandal over a woman, perhaps? It was possible. Frampton was handsome enough and blessed with charm. Reanna couldn't understand how he had escaped marriage this long; there must be many women who would jump at the chance to marry him.

Had he come out here in disgrace? Did an embarrassed family keep him here on remittance, paying him not to show his face at home again, as Andrew had intimated? Or was he merely an eccentric, or a solitary?

"You must be glad you came out here," Reanna said.

Frampton smiled. "There's no country like it. Some say no one but fools and saints would live here, which makes me think of our old friend Father Soule. He's not been well."

"I've heard nothing about it," Pride said, concerned.

"He denies it. He says he's fine, but at his age it could be serious."

"We'll go to see him," Pride said, "on our way back."

"When you leave here," Reanna said, "I suppose you will go back to England."

"I don't know, I haven't decided. I keep thinking that things will stay as they are, that our lives won't change, even though I know better."

"We would be sorry to see you go."

Frampton was a foreigner, but he had fit in here and he had come to think of the Oklahoma Territory as his home. More than ever, Reanna was determined to stay and to take root.

"What do you hear from Andrew?" Frampton asked. The question startled Reanna. She had forgotten Andrew entirely; for hours on end, she didn't think of him.

Pride made a face. "You know Andrew, he never was one for letter writing."

"No," Frampton said slowly. He seemed to have learned more than he had wanted to know. "I like Andrew, but he can be impulsive and pigheaded." He looked at Reanna. "I trust his judgment more because he had the sense to marry you." He laughed, but the words had been spoken seriously enough.

When Frampton saw them off the next day, he gave her a puppy to take with her.

"It's like giving up one of my children, but the sweetheart's in good hands, I know that. Believe me, if Andrew hadn't spoken for you, I'd give him a run for his money. I hope you know you have a friend here if you need me."

"Thank you."

"It's not just empty words I offer you. I mean it. You may need a friend some day, and you can always count on me."

Reanna rode with the pup balanced in its basket on her lap. After a while Pride said, "He likes you very much. I've never known Frampton to be so easy with a woman."

"I like him." Reanna stroked the puppy's silken ear. "Why *did* Frampton come out here?"

Pride laughed and shook his head. "There are some questions even I can't answer for you."

"I must learn not to ask so many questions."

"Ask anything you want to, Reanna." Pride's face lost its smile. She felt he was on the point of saying something more, but then he stopped himself. Instead he said, "Are you tired?"

"No."

"Then I think we should go to the mission. It's out of our way, but I'm worried about Father Soule."

THE mission was on the north side of the river between Frampton's ranch and the Triangle Saloon. It was set on the highest point of ground, which allowed Father Soule the best view of the Territory and the Nation.

When Father Soule had come there as a young man, the place had seemed abandoned and desolate. He had taken his assignment to the Indians as if it were a penance placed on him for some unknown sin. God had willed him there and he had come, but his heart remained across the ocean in France.

He had begun to build with sticks and mud and stone. He made a little wattle church fit for a martyr, and as he built, the land became his land, the place his place, and the people his people. By his own perseverance and by some miracle, he had built a school, a fine church and a residence, and he had planted his vineyard. It had been years since he had seen the ocean or France, but now he would not willingly leave here as long as there was breath in his body. His first mission children were grown. They had left his school and married, but they had sent him their children and now he was seeing a third generation of babies at the christening font. The grapes were taking hold, adapting to this foreign hillside.

Now, just when he began to see the fruit of his work, suddenly his health had begun to fail him. Time had become his enemy. There were changes in himself and in the Nation that made him afraid he would not finish his work. He would fight those changes, but sometimes of late, he had felt it was a losing battle. There was a shadow falling on him and this place, a darkness after which there would be no day.

He was walking and musing in his vineyard when he saw Pride and Reanna walking toward him.

"My friends, to see you here brings me great joy. I've been hoping for company."

"We heard you hadn't been feeling like yourself," Pride said.

"That is nonsense." Father Soule waved the suggestion aside. "It is only that gossip Frampton who has been talking. You must know already how he exaggerates."

"Then you are well?" Pride asked.

"Yes," Father Soule answered, thorny and tart as a sour grape. "Yes, I can see you have come from Frampton. He is a man for rumors."

"You'll give us dinner, I hope?" Pride asked.

"Yes," Father Soule said, "I would be glad of your company. Though, to tell the truth, I will never get used to calling luncheon *dinner*. It is one thing I have never understood about this place." He led the way into the residence.

After they had eaten, they sat on the side porch in the shade. "You've done wonders here," Reanna said, watching the children playing in the churchyard.

Father Soule sighed. "There is so much left to be done. There never seems to be enough time or money. We are a poor parish."

"You're needed," Pride protested. "Your work cannot be counted in money."

"Tell my bishop that. Money talks even in heaven, or so it seems."

They sat talking of other things until Pride and Reanna saw that Father Soule had fallen asleep. They left him napping in the warm sun and started south again.

As they rode, Reanna thought she had never seen such beauty as this day held. The sky was so blue, its brightness pierced the heart and the eye. The green grass, the red earth beneath, were like banners of life. She'd never known a day to hold so much glory.

"I'm glad you came in the early spring," Pride said, looking at her as if she were the glory and not the day. "I would have been glad for you to come out here at any time, but you mustn't think it's this fine all the year round. The weather is just putting its best face forward for you."

"I don't want this day to end. I want the same weather to last forever," she said.

"Then it will last, just to please you."

AND, as he promised, a fine spell was just beginning, a time when Reanna was full of joy. In her life there wasn't a cloud or a drop of rain to mar her happiness, and it was all because she was with Pride.

If he hadn't asked her to go with him, she would have invented excuses to tag along.

In these perfect days, she didn't think of Andrew. She was too busy, too happy. If for some reason Andrew didn't come back, she knew she could live here happily for the rest of her life. She dreaded the thought that, when he did come back, all the bitter words and feelings would have to be brought out and examined again. But surely then things would be different. When Andrew saw that Snow had recovered with no ill effects, there would be no more talk of his not wanting her. There would be no more pushing her away from him as if the sight of her offended him. He would be proud of her for getting along with Cima and Miss Jane and for learning about the place and the people. Miss Jane was willing to trust her. Cima was more than civil, and Cima had even made Snow be polite. Pride treated her as one of the family. Surely now Andrew would relent, and they could begin to build a life together.

Reanna knew that that was what she ought to wish for, and yet each morning, when she went out with Pride, she forgot Andrew and had eyes and thoughts only for Pride. Everything to do with Andrew had been a source of failure or pain; everything she did with Pride gave her pleasure and confidence. Pride treated her as if she had a brain and not as if she were some useless ornament Andrew had seen, fancied and bought in a Washington shop. For all Andrew believed in her, she could have been another doll for Snow.

To Pride she was a friend and an equal. In a few weeks, he had begun to ask her advice about everything. He sought her opinion as to which cattle they should keep and which they should cull. He had gone from telling her the names of the different grasses to asking her which she thought might be best on which pastures. She saw more clearly every day that Pride was right; the real treasure of Lochleven lay in the land and the increase from it.

She knew how he felt about the land, but never once did he say how he felt about her. She would have had to be blind not to know there was a bond and an attraction between them. With Pride she'd found a deep sense of peace and well-being. Together they were a perfect circle. They could remain so without guilt, because Pride was too loyal to allow those feelings to surface. While those feelings remained a secret, they were safe.

She trusted him to keep up their defenses, never to cross over a line that would open them to censure or shame. She knew Pride's sense of honor didn't require that he shoot an innocent man just to keep to some old tribal custom, but his honor would surely be forfeit if he tried to take his brother's wife. They never spoke of it, but there was an understanding between them more binding than a contract.

Because time was running short, she felt that there was nothing they might not dare to do together. Protected by their innocence, they could go where they liked and stay as long as they pleased. It was a period of grace and total freedom. They were safe as long as they didn't step over the invisible line and touch as lovers.

One golden afternoon they lay under the bois d'arc trees, their heads propped up on blanket rolls. They'd worked hard that day, as they did every day. That morning they'd cleaned out a water tank and set a windmill running properly. The hobbled horses were grazing nearby. Gray Cloud came close enough to nuzzle at Pride's shoulder.

Pride rolled a cigarette. The aroma of the tobacco drifted across the small space between them. She watched Pride through half-closed eyes as he smoked. He lay, his hat half shading his face from the dappled, afternoon sun. His hand, supple and brown, stroked the horse's nose rhythmically. With all her heart she wished that hand would reach out and touch her.

Suddenly, desire flashed through her like sunlight on a polished mirror. She was so startled by it, she felt he must have been aware of the shock that went through her being. She mustn't reveal this passion either to him or to herself. It was too dangerous for both of them. It would cost her dear, but she must be silent and suppress her heart's longing. She'd never willingly do anything to harm Pride. He wasn't a man who could live with trickery or deceit.

He was gentle, a man of such grace that he seemed always to move with the wind and not against it, while Andrew was always fighting a battle with an invisible enemy. Pride was at peace with himself and the world around him. Pride, fair of face and full of grace. She'd almost spoken the old rhyme aloud but had stopped herself just in time. She must guard her tongue as well as her thoughts. As long as she kept her thoughts in her own heart, Pride would be safe.

Pride was a man of ideals. He was a true brother of all creatures of the earth. To him the coyote, the snake, the cougar and the bear all had places at the council fire. If left to himself, he would sit in the sun and carve and play on a deer-bone flute; he would watch the grass and the cattle grow. Yet she knew he was a man capable of swift, sudden action if he felt the necessity to protect, to defend. She never wanted him to feel that he must protect her from Andrew.

There was a great turmoil within her. She'd meant to be a good wife to Andrew. She'd made her bargain, but she hadn't counted on the fact that a bargain might not be enough for a husband and wife. She hadn't known that the marriage might lack everything it needed to endure. She couldn't have guessed that Andrew, for his own reasons, would reject her, mistrust her, be jealous of her when he had had no cause. Now she must never let him find that his worst thoughts of her were true.

She turned her thoughts over and over until they were worn smooth like pebbles in her mind. She slept in the dry heat, slept so soundly that when she woke she had no idea of where she was or how long she had been asleep. She felt a strange sense of unease, as if she had fallen asleep and had awakened in another place and time. Then she heard the sound of a booted heel scrape softly across a rock.

She didn't turn her head or open her eyes, she was so sure it was Pride who had awakened before her and was coming back from seeing to the horses. Then something in her signaled danger. Her senses sharpened so that every nerve was alive. It was not Pride, she knew. There was the same sensation of bound terror she had had when she'd heard the rattle of the snake. She heard the sound of the boot again, then the rasp of uneven breathing; then she caught the scent of sweet, acid sweat, overlaid with the sour smell of whiskey.

She must warn Pride. She must wake him and warn him, but without giving away to the intruder the fact that she was awake. She opened her eyes slightly, peering through her lashes, and slowly turned her head to where Pride had lain, but he was gone. She rolled her head back, opening her eyes slowly, trying not to make a sound.

The shadows of three men were outlined darkly in space above her. She opened her eyes wide and looked into the ugly faces that were peering down at her. They reeked of rot and whiskey. The stench belonged to one of them—the biggest one—more than to the others. He wore it like a mantle of evil. For an instant she was unable to move or to call out.

"You awake, pretty lady?" The sly menace in his brutal face froze her silent.

(194)

A second man spoke. "She's awake all right, Grady."

A rough, calloused hand came close to her face; one finger touched the corner of her mouth, traced the edge of her lower lip. "Open your eyes, pretty lady. We come to welcome you to the Indian Nation."

She sat up in a swift, nervous spasm and looked back at the three of them with as cool and unwavering a gaze as she could manage. The three men were mixed bloods. At first she didn't recognize them. They were ugly men, all of them, with matted, short beards and sweat-soiled hats. Their scent was mingled with a strain of hate. She couldn't imagine what she'd done that any of them should hate her so.

The Beauvaise horses were standing restively, eyeing the intruders' mounts. Where was Pride? She wanted to call out for him, but she had no voice. She didn't know where he'd gone or why he'd left her, but she didn't want to draw him into danger.

"Who are you?" she asked, holding her voice steady.

"Don't you recollect *us?* Why, we're Jasper Starrett's boys, that's who we are." And in the same instant she remembered the three horsemen whirling and rearing at the edge of the gas flares, the lead figure brandishing the rifle and taunting Pride, and Miss Jane pointing fearlessly up at his gaunt, harsh face.

"I'm Grady," the ringleader said. "And this here's Bud, and this is Junior, our little baby brother."

"What do you want?"

Grady grinned at her, his teeth bared like a coyote's. "Well, first off, we thought we'd see who was trespassing on our land."

"Why, it's not your land, it's Beauvaise land—"

"Land the fucking Beauvaises stole from us," Bud said in a surly voice.

"Now, there's no need to go into all that," Grady admonished him with genial malice. "We ain't meanspirited like some folks. We're perfectly willing to live and let live. Why, when we heard Andrew MacClaren was married, we come right over to join the party. We even offered to dance a reel or two with Pride, but he's got no guts for that kind of thing. Like his Pa." His tone changed. "Where is he, by the way?"

She glanced again at the horses, Pride's Winchester still resting in its boot. "I—I don't know," she murmured.

"She knows," Bud said crossly. "She's covering for him."

"No, she don't," Grady corrected him, watching her. "She ain't got idea one. Old Pride's pulled foot, like he always does. Even left his horse and bedroll. See? Hiding over there in some rocks, shaking like a leaf. Ain't he?"

She tried to leap to her feet then. Grady's hand shot out and gripped her shoulder, drove her back onto her knees.

"You haven't let me finish, honey. That's bad manners. See, we only wanted to do the hospitable thing, but we weren't made to feel welcome at all. And that made us downright sad. Downright sad and broody."

He wagged his head with false, forbidding sorrow, his eyes searching up and down her body. "Well see now, when Andrew took hisself one of our Indian girls to bed, we didn't say word one, and now here you are, a white lady, and us Indians want to return the favor. It's kind of a little custom we have out here. Fair's fair, now ain't it, honey? You see how it is."

"Leave me alone," she breathed. She would not show fear; she *would not.*

"And then we saw Andrew leave the home place and we figured you were all alone, with no one to look after you."

"If I had a wife as pretty as you, *I* wouldn't go riding off to Texas and leave her," Junior said. "No sir, not me—I'd keep right close to home, I would."

"That Pride's been sparking her," Bud said sourly.

"No sense in that. A man shouldn't leave a boy to plow his field for him. Especially a gutless tyke like Pride Beauvaise." Grady's hand touched her hair, his wet mouth smiled and she could see the rotted, tobacco-stained teeth. "So we got to thinking, and here's what we come up with. We thought maybe a snotty kid like Pride don't know quite what a man's supposed to do."

His hand moved catlike from her hair to her shoulder, and then to her breast.

"Leave me *be,*" she said between her teeth, shrinking away in spite of herself.

"Sure. Fact is, we've been trailing you quite a spell, and we don't think he's doing right by you. He just don't seem to have the hang of it, you know?"

"All he knows how to ride is a horse," Bud muttered. "Yellow-livered son of a bitch."

"That's it," Grady concurred. "All he can mount is a brood mare." They laughed then, their dark faces cracked with mirth, as if they were sharing a capital joke; then they turned serious again. Reanna tensed her whole body.

"That's why we come by," Grady said amiably, "to give old Pride a lesson in how an Indian takes care of a white woman."

His hand left her breast and ripped open her shirt all the way to her waist. She screamed *"Pride!"* and was silent again.

"Yeah, you do that. You call him, honey. He's out there, listening. Watching, too. Hey, Beauvaise!" he shouted, and the name echoed and reechoed through the rocks. "Hey, come on over and watch how it's done."

He forced her down then and straddled her, let go his grip on her shoulders and began to unbutton his trousers, while his brothers watched avidly, crouched on each side. She twisted and clawed at him in a despairing rage. It was unbearable that Pride had run away, abandoned her to these brutal men; yet she'd seen him turn his back on them the night of the dancing. Or could they have already caught and killed him? Were they playing cat and mouse with her? Anyway, there was no one to help her now. She struggled on in silence, kicking and scratching; her teeth found flesh and bit down, hard.

"Fucking she-cat!" Grady tore his arm away, hit her backhanded across the face, glaring. "Now pin her down," he ordered savagely, "both of you!" Her arms were seized and wrenched high above her head; Bud was forcing her legs apart.

"Going to show you what you been missing, white bitch. Give you what you been wanting all this time, what those shit-eating Beauvaises can't give you. Going to give you all you want and more besides." His eyes were green at their centers, like a timber wolf's; spittle ran in a thin stream from a corner of his mouth. "I'm going first, to show the way, because I'm the oldest and smartest. And then old Bud. And then Junior last, because he's still the baby. Hold her still, damn it!"

She struggled on, panting, felt her bodice ripped apart, her riding skirt pulled above her thighs. He had bent so close she could see the sweat glinting in the stubble of beard, and small, circular raw patches like ringworm. His hand closed on her throat. She caught a glimpse of his sex—a raw, spadelike weapon poised to assault her—and it renewed her rage. If she lived through this, she would make them pay. She'd hunt them down to the very ends of the earth and kill them, kill them all, if it took her—

"All right, now! That's enough!"

The voice was clear and hard, like a knife blade in the dry air. *Pride.* It was Pride's voice. The blunt, harsh pressure against her throat ceased; she felt her legs released, saw Bud roll away behind a rock. Grady, up astride her again, was looking away, a hand on his gun belt. The raw, red spade of his phallus was limp now, pulsing.

"Get away from her, Grady," Pride said flatly.

Her hands were free now. Junior was saying, "We oughtn't a done it, Grady. I told you we shouldn't."

"Shut up, Junior." Grady had twisted around, the heel of his hand still resting on the butt of the Colt. Reanna, panting and dizzy, saw Pride on one knee behind a blue shoulder of stone. His face was perfectly expressionless.

"Go get his gun, Bud," Grady said, watching Pride with his wolf's grin. "Go take his gun away from him. And then he can watch if he's a mind to."

"First man moves on me gets it." Pride still hadn't moved, and his very stillness was utterly menacing. His eyes were slits under the Stetson; there was nothing gentle about him now.

"Go on, Bud," Grady repeated. "Get his iron."

Bud made a curious little contortion with his body. "Gee, Grady, I don't know . . ."

"Shit!" Grady exploded. "What's the matter with you? Can't you see he's just bluffing? He won't do nothing, he never *has*." He rolled away from Reanna and stood up, his legs spread, his sex still hanging from his open fly, the very stance contemptuous, insulting.

"*Reanna,*" Pride said with sudden, low intensity.

She scrambled to her feet and started toward him—realizing in a flash that she mustn't block Pride's view of the Starretts, his line of fire—and swerved away behind a low rock outcropping near him.

"All right," Pride said. "Now get off this land. And stay off."

Grady laughed, rocking on his heels. "You going to *make* us go, Beauvaise? That it?"

"Grady," Junior said in a whining tone.

"Stop your fool blubbering!" Grady shouted at him. "What you worried about him for?" And to Pride, "Why didn't you open up on us a few minutes ago? Why's that?"

"Because I don't shoot people in the back, Grady."

"No—you don't shoot at all! You couldn't do it then, and you can't do it now. You ain't got the guts to pull the trigger. You never did."

"*Then try me.*"

There was a short, hard silence. Reanna could hear a hawk's shrill hunting cry beyond the ridge, the sizzle of an insect in the baked earth.

"What the hell do you care?" Bud said in his surly voice. "Shit, she ain't even yours."

"Shut your stupid face, Buddy!" Grady snarled. "He's nothing. He's a gutless, four-flushing little—"

The gunshot tore the high stillness. Reanna saw a bright flash of metal as the piece of spur flew away from Grady's right boot. He cried out and gave a little dancing stagger, his face pale now under the stubble.

"OK, Grady," Pride commanded, "all of you, drop your gun belts. Then get off this place and don't come back. Ever."

Before he had finished, Junior was running for their horses, his gun belt floating out behind him; Bud had backed away, his guns falling at his feet. Grady roared at them, looked back at Pride, who was standing up now, the Colt in his hand, its barrel smoking faintly. Grady gazed down again at the shattered spur, let his gun belt fall, then hurried away behind the others. In silence they mounted and rode off to the north, toward the river.

"Oh, Pride," Reanna murmured. She started to button her shirt, but the buttons all were missing. Her hands were shaking so badly she couldn't do anything, her whole body was shaking. She was crying then, sobbing soundlessly, and then his arms were around her. That was all that mattered now, all that mattered on this earth. He was soothing her; his hand was stroking her hair, her neck, as though she were a child.

"I was so afraid," she sobbed, holding on to him as if he were all of her life.

"I know," he was saying. "I was down by the pond when I heard them coming. There was no way to warn you. I'm sorry."

She tried to speak, but she couldn't find the words for her tears. His arms were links of unbreakable iron. Slowly he lifted up her face and wiped away her tears. They stood looking into each other's eyes. Her first fear had vanished, and now they began to read something in each other's eyes that would hold them prisoners forever.

"You would have killed them, wouldn't you?" she whispered.

"Yes."

"You would have done that for me." He nodded. "You would have killed to defend my honor, but not your own."

"This was different, Reanna, no empty vendetta code. This was you. You know what you mean to me, Reanna. You've known from the beginning."

"Yes, I know."

They stood for a long time, holding each other. The wind ran in the trees and the grass; it played over them like a blessing.

"I love you, Pride," Reanna said, "and because I love you, nothing can ever be the same again."

"Yes," he said.

"Even if we try to deny it, everything has changed for us." Once she could have stopped the words, but now she could not. The two of them had come together as lovers, and now nothing on earth or in heaven, not even the wind, could keep them from each other.

ROM the crest of the Ridge they heard a rumbling sound like thunder, but the sky was clear blue and cloudless. The earth seemed to shake, as if an army of giants were on the march. Reanna looked up from their work on the watering trough to Pride, thinking he'd have the answer. Suddenly, without a word, he mounted Gray Cloud and galloped over the Ridge.

As she came up beside him, the scene took her breath away. From the south over the eastern range there rose up a mighty wall of red dust. It was twisting and spiraling into the blue sky. From within the curtain of red dust she could hear again the persistent sound of thunder.

"What is it?"

"It's Andrew," Pride said. "He's come home and brought half the cows in Texas with him." His face betrayed no emotion, but she could see his eyes snapping with anger.

Cima came toward them from the house, riding hard. She drew up by Pride and Reanna. "How many head do you make it?"

"I can't say yet."

"Make a guess." Cima looked worried.

"Three thousand, maybe more."

"Just where does Andrew think he'll find grass and water for that many?"

"That's what I'm about to ask him." Pride galloped toward the oncoming herd.

Reanna glanced at Cima. The black woman's face was hard with consternation as she said, "It's time Pride stood up to Andrew. If they're going to run this place together, then Pride should have an equal say." Cima clapped spurs and galloped after Pride, signaling Reanna to follow.

TAFFY, riding line, was utterly whipped. He'd watched in wild amazement as Andrew had bought up everything with hide and hoofs in the state of Texas. He'd been like a gambler who wouldn't leave the table until he or the house was broke. What Andrew was using for money to pay for the critters Taffy didn't know; he'd had cattle in every feedlot and corral for fifty miles. When the cattle got so many they overflowed out of the towns and onto the range, Andrew wanted them all trail-branded. That was a job for a month of Sundays, but Andrew wanted it done overnight. When Taffy protested, Andrew demanded that he cut the dewlaps of every single head.

"I want everybody to know they're mine," Andrew had said. "I don't intend to lose a single head. You get that straight."

To do the kind of job Andrew wanted would have stretched even a big outfit. They had come down to Texas with four of the five Beauvaise hands, Dub Wilgress, Tiny Bentham, Frank Pettis and Dan Penland. Taffy had left Slim Dress up on the place to look after the home stock. Slim was stove in and ailing. A heifer had kicked him and broke three of his ribs. Nobody was surprised. If there was an accident going, it would happen to Slim Dress.

Outside of Slim, the Beauvaise hands were as good a bunch as you'd find. They worked clean and fast and there was no better rope, tie and brand team anywhere than Tiny Bentham and Dub Wilgress. To watch Tiny throw an overhead heel catch was a beautiful sight to behold.

Tiny, in the way of cowboy wit and humor, was a big man, six feet and solid as a mountain. It was a wonder cow ponies didn't buckle under him, but he sat a horse as light as air. Tiny and Dub had come on the place about the same time, and they'd got to be saddle buddies right off. Dub was as small as Tiny was big; the other men called them the long and the short of it. When Dub stood behind Tiny you could plumb lose sight of him altogether.

Dub was the joker in the outfit. There was nothing outside of his snakeskin boots that he liked better than to play a prank on

Tiny. There was not a day complete for Dub if he didn't put one over on Tiny. It wasn't hard to do; Tiny believed everything Dub told him. If Dub said the sun was coming up in the west tomorrow, Tiny would fight any man who said different.

Whenever the rest of the gang hee-hawed at Tiny, he would just sit there, his brow furrowed, not seeing the joke but trying hard to figure out what was so funny. Then pretty soon, just to be friendly and show there were no hard feelings, he'd give a sheepish grin and say, "Well, I guess that's another one on me."

On one drive they'd had a real mean cook who wouldn't let the hands take even an extra helping of sugar off his wagon. Dub knew how big Tiny's sweet tooth was, so he told Tiny that the cook had said the first man in the morning to get his bedroll in the chuck wagon could have all the sugar he wanted. The next morning Tiny was up early, had his bedroll slung in the chuck wagon and was reaching for the sugar for his coffee when that cook saw him and blessed Tiny out. Boy howdy, that cook had a tongue as sharp as barbed wire.

Tiny just stood there looking down at the cook, and then he picked him up and carried him to the nearest tree and hung him upon a high limb by his coat and left him wriggling and shouting while Tiny went back and put all the sugar he wanted into his tin cup of boiling hot coffee. No sir, there wasn't a fish story too big for Dub to tell and have Tiny swallow it—hook, line and sinker.

On the other side of it, Tiny could drive you crazy singing. The cattle liked it fine. All Tiny had to do to quiet them, even in the worst storm, was to make a kind of high yip and tiyee at them that sounded like a cross between a coyote howl and a wolf whine. They'd gentle right down. On a night full of thunder and lightning, Taffy had known Tiny to sing at a herd all the night through. What Tiny did wrong was to try and sing with the boys when they was all sitting around a campfire. He only knew one verse of one song, "A Cowboy's Life," and he sang it over and over. And he couldn't carry a tune in a bucket.

But the boys had almost rather hear Tiny sing than hear Dub tell the story one more time of how he got his boots. Dub purely loved those boots. He could tell you the day, the hour, the date, the month and the year he'd first seen them boots down in Austin, Texas. A dreamy, faraway look would come over little Dub's face and he'd say, "Did I ever tell you boys about the time I was down in Austin, Texas, and first saw these here snakeskin boots of mine?"

The men would all groan and say yes, they'd heard it before and didn't want to hear it again. Only Tiny would sit listening, all ears, like it was all original news.

The way Dub always told it, he'd cottoned to those boots at first sight and he'd followed the fella wearing them, a fella about his size, down the street in Austin and asked if he could buy the boots off him. The fella understandably said no, they was his boots, and he meant to keep them, which made Dub sad and down at the mouth. But then later that night, as luck would have it, Dub was doing some drinking in a saloon when the fella with the boots came in and got hisself shot. Dub followed right after the corpse to the undertaker, bought the boots and left the dead man the ones he'd been wearing to be buried in. The way Dub saw it, it would have been a sin and a pity to have those snakeskin boots nailed away in a coffin.

Dub never worried about wearing a dead man's boots, but he sure fretted over the weather and how the cold or the heat might affect them. One winter there was a cold snap. It was cold enough to freeze the balls off a brass monkey, and Dub kept worrying about them boots freezing in the night.

Well, damn and dang if Tiny didn't take them two boots to sleep with him under his big belly, just like he was a mother hen and they was his best eggs. It was kindly of Tiny to do that, because Dub was not known to take a bath more than once a year and he'd never been known to change his socks.

It was the year of that big cold spell that Frank Pettis had come looking for work. He was the kid of the outfit. He'd come in half starved, riding crowbait. He looked about sixteen and said he was twenty. Taffy felt sorry for him and gave him a job just so Frank could get a square meal. They'd all sat around watching the kid eat, waiting for him to get full, but he just kept shoveling it in. Several platters of ham and eggs disappeared, a pan of biscuits and a whole dried apple pie. They'd all agreed afterward they didn't know where the kid put it. He kept on eating like that every day and never put on weight; that boy was as skinny as a catalpa bean.

Frank was a good-looking kid with big ears and big eyes and he was catnip to the ladies. Maybe they fell for him hoping to fatten him up on love and home cooking. One time Frank took up with a girl in town, a pretty little thing, all pink gingham and blue eyes and yellow hair. He'd courted her awhile, but when she began to get serious on him, Frank got spooked. He persuaded Dan Penland to go and tell the girl that Frank Pettis had gone north to Kansas and died on the way.

She was real tore up over it. She cried and cried and damn near bawled her eyes out, but she would have got over it in time if Frank hadn't have forgot and gone into town.

First crack out of the barrel, he met her on the street. She looked at him real hard and said, "I thought you died."

"No, ma'am," Frank said, right back at her, "that was my brother."

She took another real hard look and said, "I'm sorry to hear that, because your brother was the best of a mighty sorry family."

Dan Penland always liked to tell that one, when he wasn't talking about the ranch he was going to buy. What he intended to use for money for this dream spread, nobody knew. Dan had never been known to save a penny of his thirty a month. Playing cards for money in the bunkhouse was against the rules, but Dan would bet on anything. All anybody who wanted spending money to tide him over to payday had to do was to make a bet with Dan Penland, because he was sure to lose. As you took his money Dan would say, "Listen, when I get settled on my ranch you're more than welcome to come and visit anytime."

It was funny about Dan. He couldn't remember what card had been played last, but he was the best tally man the outfit had ever had. He could count cattle in a holding pen at one look-see and rarely be off by a couple of head.

Taffy had set the four Beauvaise men to trail-branding cattle, but to get it all done Andrew had had to hire on more hands. Andrew had sent Taffy two brothers, Zeb and Zack Easter, saddle tramps and drifters, but it was late in the season to find good hands and they were both willing to go up on the Chickasaw for a long, hot summer. Andrew had also sent in a Mex remuda man named Paco, whom Taffy set to chousing up horses, and a China cook whose name Taffy couldn't say straight. The closest they could any of them get to it was Chang.

Taffy set himself to get them all used to working together as an outfit before they started up the trail. He didn't like a new bunch of cowhands any more than he liked to drive a mixed herd.

In an effort to get the line going and keep it going smooth, Taffy had strung out the herd. There was enough beef to feed Coxey's army. The long column of cattle merged from lot to lot, from range to range, until you couldn't see from one end of them to another as they headed north from Texas up across the Red River toward the Indian Territory.

Andrew insisted on riding point, setting the pace and expecting Taffy on drag to keep up with him. It couldn't be done. Andrew cursed Taffy, the hands and the horses. With that kind of a mixed line, there was bound to be trouble.

They could only trail from water to water. It was best, that late in the spring, to travel at night and then stop at dawn to let them graze; they'd lose less weight that way. At best they could make only twelve agonizingly slow miles a day. They went like a plague of locusts, a scourge upon the land, plodding on, pond to pond, creek to creek, drinking them dry and grazing the ground bare.

Any given season, this drive would have been hard. This year it was a bone breaker and a cow killer. The pickings were so poor, the animals soon grew lean and restless. There was the dust, heel fly and grub worm. No one in the outfit, including the cattle, could sleep more than four hours at a stretch. Every hour they were awake and on the move, they complained and competed for the front place, out of the storm of dust.

Every herd had its trail leader. Andrew, determined to pick up the pace, rode point. He'd tied an ox bell onto his saddle, and at each tolling of the bell the tide had to move forward. The steer who chose to walk the point was no easier to get along with than Andrew. He wouldn't stay on the trail; he wandered, leading the line with him, weaving like a snake while Andrew cursed him and threatened to shoot him, as if the poor dumb thing understood or cared what Andrew wanted.

As always, there were trail pals. Two of the older cows, born troublemakers, began butting and horning in left to right. It gave the others ideas. The animals, once pals, wouldn't be separated, any more than any Tom and Harry who had decided to ride together, bunk together and eat together.

The worst trial of all was the cook Andrew had hired. He was meaner than a case of saddle sores. He wouldn't hear of dipping into the molasses barrel or give a third cup of coffee to Jesus Christ himself without skinning the hide off a man with his heathen tongue. His biscuits were rocks and his bacon had no lean. Nobody rode easy or slept easy or ate without a bellyache a single mile of the long way.

There was a fight a day, mostly Zeb or Zack Easter arguing about anything. But no one argued with Taffy that riding drag was the worst. There they ate dust, if nothing else. Every drag hand was fighting, cursing, kicking and bawling, inch by inch, trying to drive the weak on, to keep up with the loco point steer and an even crazier boss.

When they came to the Red River, at first it seemed a sign that their troubles were nearly over. The river was low, and that was a blessing. Crossing the Red when its banks were full was a passage to disaster. Yet this year the weather had played its tricks, and the wet sands were quick and shifting. Treachery lay in a wrong step. When some of the cattle panicked and floundered, they went down. As they sank, their eyes rolling, white stubble eyelashes spiked toward the sky, they bawled out for help that wouldn't come. Andrew rode up and down with no thought for his own safety, cursing, roping, loosing line and cow and then blaming God and man.

Beyond the river things were no better. The grass was poor and the water low. In a week, ribs began to show like barrel staves; flanks grew lean. Eyes were so dry they couldn't close. Tongues were swollen and hung out of parching lips. When they did come close to water, the herd set up a din of bawling and moaning. No amount of persuasion or skill could keep them in line. They broke and ran for the water in a stampede. It took an extra day and night to round up the strays.

Then, to add to their woes, the buffalo soldiers kept them company to be sure they kept the line moving across the assigned trail lands. The buffalo soldiers were black, their officers white. Both men and officers were vultures waiting for the feast. Taffy saw Andrew give one lieutenant a sack full of gold coins, letting them fall, one by one, like drops of yellow rain into the officer's outstretched hands for taking longer to move the herd than the law allowed.

Even on the best days, they went at an uneven pace. The cows couldn't keep up with the steers. They dropped a calf and stayed behind to hide it out. Andrew, not wanting to lose a single head, kept a pair of wagons busy going up and down the line, gathering calves, coaxing cows to follow with teasings of hay and the plight of their young muddled together, all bawling for help on the wagon floor.

There were days and nights when Taffy thought they would never see home again. In the beginning, he'd been afraid of what Miss Jane would say to Andrew when he showed up with more cattle than any sane man would have under contract. Now Taffy no longer cared for anything but a tub to wash in and a bunk to collapse in. If this was to be the last great drive, he'd wanted to be in it, but he wouldn't be sorry when it was over and no more than a memory in a story or a song about the not-so-good old days.

Taffy hadn't thought past the moment when they would get the beasts up onto the Beauvaise grass. A knot of apprehension tied his stomach as he saw Pride riding out to meet Andrew, followed by Cima and Reanna.

As they approached, Andrew pulled himself erect in the saddle and pulled the bandana from his face. He was worn thin with exhaustion and leathered by the wind, but his aquamarine eyes glittered, blinking away the grit. There was something ruthless and defiant in him.

"You the welcoming committee?" he asked Pride, ignoring Cima and Reanna. They all three stared at him. Their horses pawed at the ground, ears back, nervous before this seething mass of cattle; it was hard to hold them in rein.

"You expect a welcome—with *this?*" Pride shouted at him over the bawling of cattle. "So this is why you wouldn't take me with you."

Andrew smiled a cold, supercilious smile. "Long, hard ride, little brother."

"Oh, no, it was so you could go ahead and do what you wanted to do all along, without me being in the way. Isn't that right?"

"I know what I'm doing."

"The hell you do! Not in this or anything else."

"*Pride,*" Cima said in warning.

"If this army isn't broken up right away, it'll grind the whole range to pieces, and you know it," Pride pushed on.

"Miss Jane wants to see you," Cima said coldly to Andrew, her face betraying nothing. Andrew's eyes held on Pride.

"I see you've been keeping Reanna company." It was question, statement and accusation all in one. Reanna saw a flush spread across Pride's face. She wanted to tell Andrew that, two days before, Pride had saved her from the most vicious violation, perhaps even death, that she felt a bond to Pride that she could never feel for anyone else. But she was silent; Andrew would never understand.

What had happened that day was between herself and Pride. It belonged to no one else.

"Snow's missed you," she said instead. "She's all well and happy again."

"Who's taking care of her?"

"She's with Miss Jane," Reanna said.

"I'm glad to hear that."

"And Miss Jane sends to tell you, Mr. Andrew," Cima repeated, "that she wants to see you. And *muy pronto*." Then, signaling to Pride and Reanna to turn for home, she headed back to Lochleven.

That evening in the dining room, they waited for Andrew to appear. Miss Jane was at the head of the table. Pride was on her right hand, Reanna across from him and an empty place beside her. Snow had been sent to bed early with the promise that her father would come to tuck her in when he finished supper. Cima paced by the sideboard on the pretext of seeing to the meal. The silence was uneasy for all of them. The ticking of the mantel clock grated on their nerves.

When Andrew finally did come, he stood hesitantly in the doorway, waiting for Miss Jane to speak him welcome and give him permission to enter. The grime of the trail was still on him.

"You are come," she said at last.

"I am."

"We have waited for you, Andrew. And for Taffy."

"Taffy was needed to stay with the herd." Andrew sat by Reanna and looked at the fresh-laundered tablecloth and the platters and bowls filled with food.

"It looks like you've killed the fatted calf for me."

"Are you the prodigal son?" Miss Jane asked him.

"Oh, he can't be the prodigal son," Pride said, looking at him with a steady, cold resentment. "The prodigal came home empty-handed. Andrew has brought the thousands and the tens of thousands with him." Andrew flushed as Cima laid down the large platter of fried chicken.

"How many head have you brought up from Texas?" Miss Jane asked. A muscle in Andrew's sunburned cheek gave a twitch. Tonight there would be no waiting till the meal was over before they talked business.

"About three thousand. Give or take a few." There was silence.

"I said one thousand, and you left Lochleven before I came back from Tishomingo. How could you know how much cash money I would be able to raise?"

"I knew about what the government owed you. I figured you'd get at least half that."

"Even if I had gotten the full amount, it would not have been enough to buy three thousand head." Miss Jane still betrayed no emotion; she merely set out the facts—hard, and without comfort. "Knowing Colonel Goodwell, I doubt he gave you the remainder."

"I got some from the Colonel. And I dickered and dealt for the rest."

"What did you use for cash?" Miss Jane asked quietly.

"I gave the Kansas City Cattle Company my personal note for the rest."

Pride muttered something inaudible, and Reanna saw Cima's eyes roll white in amazement. There was a long, uncomfortable silence while Andrew went on eating.

Miss Jane said, in the same soft, implacable tone, "How are you going to pay them for the cattle?"

"When I take the cattle to market."

"And when will that be?" Pride said, looking at Andrew with angry disbelief. The risk involved more than the fate of Lochleven and the loss of the grass pasture. If Andrew didn't make good on the note, the cattle company could well look to the Beauvaises for payment.

"We'll take them to market in the fall," Andrew answered coolly. But Reanna noticed that he avoided Miss Jane's eye.

"And what if there's not enough grass to last until fall?"

"With a little rain we can get three stands of grass."

"And now you control the weather, I see." Pride's eyes were snapping with anger. "Along with everything else."

"It'll work out."

"If you drive them to the railhead half-starved, you won't make enough to pay for them. And the grass will be gone forever."

"How do you know *that*?"

"Because I know grass, and I know we're in a dry cycle. Any goddamned fool knows that. But no, you decided *you* were right— and the rest of us could all go to hell in a handcart."

"It's going to work out all right, I tell you!" For the first time, Andrew raised his voice. Then he set down his fork and leaned forward on his elbows with a quizzical smile, his eyes cold. "All right," he said. "I've got the courage to gamble, little brother. How about you?"

"This has got nothing to do with courage. It's plain, stupid selfishness!"

"Pride," Miss Jane murmured, but he was past warnings now; the issue was out at last.

"There was no agreement on three thousand head! It was only you who wanted to—"

"I tell you, this is our last chance to make a killing."

"It's our last chance to destroy ourselves, that's what it is!"

"If you weren't such a weak-kneed dreamer, you'd see my—"

"Yes, I'm a dreamer; I've got dreams for Lochleven, and they have nothing to do with any folly like this white man's greed. You're *wrong*, and you're—"

"*Be silent, both of you!*"

Miss Jane's voice cut through the quarrel like steel, imperious and clear. Both men stopped. Miss Jane was sitting very erect, her fine hands clasped in front of her, her eyes flashing from one son to the other. She was formidable; Reanna had never seen her this angry, not even when she had defied Grady Starrett. Even Cima looked cowed.

"Pride," Miss Jane said, "that is a thoughtless and cruel remark. Andrew is your brother. You will withdraw it. Now."

Pride looked down at his plate; his fist, resting beside his water glass, was clenched white. "I apologize for what I said," he murmured. "I had no right to say it."

"Good." Miss Jane turned her proud gaze to her other son. "Andrew, there was a decision reached at this table, in council. You have broken your word to that decision. What have you to say to that?"

"Situations alter decisions, Miss Jane," Andrew said; his face was flushed. "They're overstocked down there; I got a good price per head. Look, this is the last chance we'll have to make a profit for ourselves before we have to take our allotments—something for the future before the government takes it all away from us." His voice gathered force as he talked. "We've worked long and hard. We deserve this chance to lay something by for the future. Who knows what it'll bring? I'm your man of business, Miss Jane. I've never let you down."

"Not until now," she answered, and the words rang in the room.

"Well, it is done," she said after a moment, with quiet finality. "The arrow has been loosed. We must deal with the condition." Andrew moved suddenly, as though to get to his feet, and she turned to him again. "Now you hear me, Andrew. You have been arrogant, and you have been rash. You do *not* know whether there will be rain or whether the grass will hold. Only Breathholder knows what is in store for us. You did not wait for my return from Tishomingo, because you did not want to hear what I would say. What you did was unworthy of you. And of us all, as Beauvaises. If the word is broken, the world falls. From this day you are not to take *any* action on your own authority. Is that clear?"

Andrew stared at her, his lips working under the sweep of his mustache. "Yes. It's clear."

Andrew shoved back his chair and nearly leaped to his feet. "I'm going out on the line," he said to Pride harshly. "I'm going to need your help. Now, are you going to see this thing through with me or not?"

Reanna was unable to look at any of them. She'd never felt like such an outsider, not even on the first day. And now she was hot with shame at Andrew's behavior. He didn't seem to care whom he hurt, as long as he could do what he wanted to. Even Miss Jane's rebuke and warning hadn't touched him.

"The herd's on the southwest section," Andrew went on. "I think we ought to hold them there for two days, and then start them circling counterclockwise around the Ridge. Do you agree?"

Pride watched him without expression. "I agree," he said formally, after a moment, and Reanna could see what the reply cost him. "I'll help you until they're ready for market."

"Good," Andrew said, and flung down his napkin. "We'll be staying on the pasture till I say different. Are you coming, then?"

"You will stay the night," Miss Jane said. It was an order.

Andrew stared at her. "I don't want to leave Taffy on his own. Besides, he's due for a rest."

"You will stay the night and go early in the morning. You have not seen your wife in weeks." It was an order and reprimand all in one. Reanna saw him flush.

"Maybe it *is* a good idea," he said. "I want to see Snow. And I could use a bath and a soft bed, for a change. It's a long, dusty way from Texas."

Reanna rose and said, "I'll go up and see to a bath for you."

She avoided looking at Miss Jane or Pride. Once again she'd been humiliated by Andrew's indifference. Andrew wouldn't have stayed the night if Miss Jane hadn't insisted; they all knew it. Andrew had left her in anger and, now that he'd returned, he was still determined to exclude her from his life. She couldn't read for sure what was in his mind, but she knew that she'd changed. She'd been happy without him. She'd come to love Pride. Even so, Andrew was her husband. Nothing had changed that.

She saw to Andrew's bath and avoided looking at him while he soaked in the tin tub. When he'd put on his nightshirt and gone into the sitting room next to their bedroom, she cleared away the bath water, red with dust, and prepared for bed. Then she slipped between the sheets and waited for him to come to her, as was his right.

When he came, she stared sightless into the darkness. They lay side by side, not touching. She waited for him to turn to her, to take what was his. She was rigid with the strain of not touching him. She tried to breathe normally, as if she were deep in sleep, but he must know she was still awake. Finally, he put his arms behind his head and sat propped against the pillows.

At last he said, "I'm surprised you're still here. I thought you'd go while you had the chance." He hadn't changed toward her; she shouldn't have expected it.

"I'm not going, Andrew. I've learned a lot about Lochleven while you've been away. Miss Jane has made me feel at home."

"And Pride, has he made you feel at home?"

"Yes."

"I guess you think I should thank him for that?"

She was suddenly very tired and sad. The joy of the last few weeks had vanished.

"I want things to go well between us, Andrew. I want us to have a good life together. I've tried to be what you want. I'd hoped you'd change your mind about me while you were away."

"I haven't changed my mind or my feelings toward you. It's a mistake you came out here." His voice was low and rough. It made her feel like a child who had been punished for something she hadn't done; she wanted to cry out for comfort. But she wasn't a child, and this wound he'd made would heal.

"Andrew, I'm here and I mean to make a go of it." There was a long silence, then he said:

"How do you figure to do that?"

She waited for him to say more, but there was nothing in the night now except the silence between them.

He fell asleep quickly, but she couldn't. She lay on her half of the bed, in this enemy territory. He wouldn't reach across the boundary line to touch her, and for the first time, she didn't care. When she awoke in the morning, Andrew had gone without a word. She wasn't sorry. She didn't miss Andrew, but she found that without Pride, every day seemed to have a hole in it, like a tooth that wouldn't stop aching.

In the days that followed, no one at Lochleven saw either Pride or Andrew. Taffy rode in every week to check on the household and to see what was needed, but no one in the house rode out to the pastures.

Cima kept the house running smoothly. After a few rebuffed attempts to help, Reanna didn't try again, and after a few more offers of friendship to Snow, Reanna didn't try to keep her company. There was no open hostility between Snow and Reanna, but there was a distance between them that neither could or would cross.

Reanna had a letter from her mother.

Dear Reanna,

Of course your Papa, the boys and I would very much like to come for a visit. We'll try to find a time that is best for the whole family. We're delighted to hear that you've been so well received out there, but I do worry over your being some place we've never seen. When you are in the sun, remember to carry a parasol. Sun and wind can be so aging. Your books have been sent. Hope they arrive safely.

Your loving mother

Reanna thought it unlikely that she would ever be able to explain any of the realities of her life here at Lochleven to her mother. She'd been attacked by violent men, nearly raped, and all that concerned her mother was her carrying a parasol.

Reanna wrote back.

Dear Mama,

Andrew has come back from Texas with a big herd of cattle. To keep the grass from being overgrazed, the men have to stay out on the range. My books have arrived. Thank you.

(214)

I'm not homesick, but I do miss you all very much and I hope you'll come out soon. There's plenty of room, and Miss Jane will be glad to have you. You'll be waited on hand and foot. I'm just a lady of leisure here. I have nothing to do but read and write letters and help Miss Jane, which I like very much. She has been so kind to me.

Love,
Reanna

Miss Jane had treated Reanna like a daughter. She'd taught her how to do the accounts and insisted she learn all the business of Lochleven. She expected Reanna to help her welcome every visitor and petitioner who came to Lochleven. Reanna soon got to know many of the tribe; more than their names and faces, she came to know their needs. When she was free of her duties she tried to escape, riding Molly May up and down the Ridge.

It was easy to know where the herd was at any time; above them a vast cloud of dust rose from the parched ground. It did no good to pray for rain. The gods were deaf. The grass was going dry; she could do nothing but scan the sky with anxious eyes for a sign of rain clouds. She thought of Pride every day; somewhere out there in the midst of that milling, bawling, grazing multitude, he was fighting for the life of the land he loved.

In the long evenings after supper, Reanna sat with Miss Jane and listened as Miss Jane talked. Sometimes it seemed that Miss Jane was speaking not to Reanna but aloud to herself, trying to remember the accumulated wisdom of a lifetime in the space of a few weeks.

Reanna liked doing the accounts best of all. She was fascinated by the columns of figures.

"You have a head for figures," Miss Jane said, watching Reanna tally the week's expenses.

"Thank you," Reanna said, flushed with pleasure at the compliment.

"That will be useful when you have the responsibility of keeping the books and accounts for Lochleven."

Reanna looked up, dismayed. "Andrew would never let me do that."

"Why not?" Miss Jane seemed genuinely surprised.

"He doesn't think I can be trusted with pocket money, let alone business. He would never let me keep the books for Lochleven."

Miss Jane was still puzzled. "But it is the woman's right. Just as it is the woman's right to have her own land and cattle. Every Indian woman has a right to her portion of the tribe's wealth. If it were not so, who would see to the children? The child has its name and takes its place at the campfire through the mother. You must learn to run your own land and affairs." It was what Pride had said to her, that she had a right to land, to place and responsibility. She had the right to money, if she could earn it and be smart enough to keep it. It was a new way of looking at the world, and one she admired and envied.

"But," Reanna protested, "I'm not an Indian woman."

Miss Jane looked at her in astonishment. "Not by blood, but even though you will have no allotment of land because you are a white married to an intermarried citizen, you have married into our family. You are one of us now. That is a tradition. I hope those ways may never change."

The cupola became a haven to Reanna. She liked the great brass bed with its colorful hand-loomed coverlet. She liked the old, battered rolltop desk, its pigeonholes crammed with papers. She found peace in that room, sitting in the deep comfort of a large leather chair. She had a sense of accomplishment as they worked and talked. There was peace here and tranquillity and excitement, the kind she had never experienced before, except in Pride's company.

Late one night, when they'd worked until their backs ached and their eyes were tired, they sat, two women alone together, one young and one old. Miss Jane sighed and began to speak. Once more, it seemed that she was talking to herself. "Soon the land of the tribe will be divided. We will each have an allotted place where we must live and stay forever. We will no longer be free to come and go in our own Nation. The rest . . ." She stopped, her mouth working as if she had a thorn caught in her cheek. "The rest they will give to the settlers. It will be a sad time then, and everyone will weep."

"What will you do, Miss Jane?"

"I will try to keep Lochleven together. To do that, I will sign for the Ridge, Andrew for the east pasture nearest the town and Pride for the west where the grass is best. Snow will have her portion on the east, and Cima will be entitled to land of her own. It will not be much. Forty acres, but it will be hers. She wants her land to lie alongside Pride's."

To Reanna it seemed wrong to make a division at all. Perhaps there was no other way, but this meant that the tribe would never again be one people of one land. As if Miss Jane had read Reanna's mind, she said, "Then there will be no more Nation forever. We were promised this land for as long as the sun shone, the rivers ran and the grass grew. Now there will be nothing left for us to call ours but the wind."

Again there was a long silence.

"Have I showed you the things for the women's dance? I keep them in a chest here beneath the bed." Miss Jane pulled out the chest and opened it. "Here are the terrapin rattles and my dress of white deerskin. They will be yours one day. I will give them to you, and in turn you will give them to Snow." It seemed strange to think that Miss Jane would put her before Snow. It made Reanna feel a new sense of obligation to Miss Jane, and to Lochleven and what it stood for.

"Have I shown you how to resew the beads on the deerskin?" Miss Jane asked.

Reanna thought Miss Jane looked tired. Sometimes she looked as fragile as the delicate bone and shell beads. "No," Reanna said, "but there will be plenty of time to teach me that another day."

Miss Jane shook her head. "No, I will show you now." She took up a porcupine quill and a bone needle and began to repair a bare patch. "I must show you everything now. There is so much to be done and not enough time. It will be New Year and then time for the green corn dancing before you know it."

"New Year?" Reanna asked, thinking Miss Jane must be confused.

"Our New Year comes in the late spring, about the time of the strong wind. At New Year we take out the old fire from the house and bring in the new. It is the time to set the house in order. That is what I am doing." She looked at Reanna, her eyes dark and unreadable. "I am setting my house in order."

The next day they began a thorough housecleaning. Top to bottom, not a room or closet was overlooked. Reanna had seen her mother at such times, but Miss Jane excelled even Mrs. Lovell's ability to seek out dirt. Every window was washed, every bed turned, every carpet beaten. Each hearth was cleared; every chimney swept clean.

When everything was finished and met with Miss Jane's approval, the last fire in the house, from the kitchen stove, was taken into a clearing before the house. A new fire was made according to ritual and then taken to the kitchen. The spirit of the house was rekindled.

Cima began to prepare a feast. The first new vegetables were taken from the sprouting garden. Little lettuces were made into a salad. Poke was cooked and flavored with ham. There was new-risen bread. On New Year there must be a fine table set with good things. This day all debts must be canceled, all old grudges settled. It was the rule that there should be friendship and forgiveness to all guests of the house.

Neither Andrew nor Pride came in for the feast. They sent Taffy to say they couldn't spare the time. The herd had to be turned for grass and could not be left to drift. They'd found nesters running fence on their range, and there was constant trouble with the government surveyors. At Lochleven there were only women at the table. It was the first time Miss Jane could remember that neither of her sons had been in the house for the New Year.

"Why haven't they come?" Snow asked. "Is it because of her?" She pointed at Reanna, and for her rudeness she was sent from the table. Reanna interceded on Snow's behalf, and Miss Jane relented and let the child come back again in time to hear some of the New Year's songs. Miss Jane sang them softly. And then they were silent for a time, before the four women went to separate, lonely beds.

When Taffy had said that the men were not coming, Reanna knew she should have thought of Andrew, but she hadn't. That night it was Pride's face she saw in her dreams.

In the morning Miss Jane said at breakfast, "Surely both Andrew and Pride will come for the green corn dance." Reanna hoped she was right, but it would be months before the green corn. July seemed a lifetime away.

For Reanna there was a sameness to the days. She tried to pay attention as Miss Jane told the stories of the "little people" who haunted the woods or recited the list of the clans and how they came to have their names and their place at the council fire, but she couldn't keep her thoughts from wandering to Pride.

It was a bittersweet spring. She saw how the new year had begun, but she couldn't guess how it would end. The weather was fine, without a cloud in the sky, though each day they looked for rain.

"May is our rainy month," Miss Jane said, once more reading Reanna's thoughts. "If we do not have the rain in May, it will not come."

"I'm sorry," Reanna said, "I was woolgathering."

(218)

"I have told the stories before," Miss Jane sighed. "It is only that I hope you will remember them to tell to your children." Reanna looked away, uncomfortable with the thought that she and Andrew would ever have a child.

"I'll remember the stories," Reanna said, "and tell them to Snow if she'll listen. I sometimes wonder if she'll ever accept me as you have done."

"She will change when she is older," Miss Jane said, and then shrugged regretfully. "She will change, if she has any sense. You are a good daughter of this house and as much a part of it now as if you were my own." Tears came to Reanna's eyes. She reached out and put her hand over Miss Jane's. Her hand felt dry to the touch, as if it might crumble to dust.

"Why have you been so kind to me?" Reanna asked. "I've done nothing to deserve it."

"At first I was not ready to receive you as my daughter." Miss Jane spoke softly and with regret. "I did not like it that Andrew had brought you here without my permission. But then I saw something in your face. It made me think of a white woman I had met long ago when I was a child on the journey from Mississippi to the Nation in the West. All of us were tired and hungry and far from home—a home we would never see again. That woman was kind to us. She gave us food and medicine, but her best medicine was to be kind. If I have been kind to you, perhaps it was to repay that woman."

"I'm not so noble or fine as that. I don't know if I would have helped you if it had meant being made fun of. I don't know if I have courage or not."

"You will find that you have courage when you need it. You have not been tested yet. I know what I see. You will always stand your ground, even if you stand alone."

Reanna was still not sure she deserved Miss Jane's confidence in her. She felt she should speak to her about her feelings for Pride, that not to do so was disloyal and deceitful, but she didn't know where to begin or what to say. "I must tell you how I feel," Reanna began once. "I must tell you how I've changed since I've been here at Lochleven."

"You do not have to tell me what you feel," Miss Jane interrupted gently. "What is in your heart is yours to hold. What you do will be another thing entirely. I know that you will do what is best for all this family."

It was a strange reply. It didn't give Reanna the relief of unburdening herself to Miss Jane, of saying that perhaps she had come here out of her own desire for adventure, not because she'd wanted to be Andrew's wife no matter where he lived, that Andrew felt she'd tricked him into marrying her. Reanna was sure that if she hadn't pursued him, he would have come back to Lochleven without her. She had reached out to him, not he to her; now she was bound by duty to live with her choice. Only now that she was here, she didn't think she could do that, not for a lifetime. She couldn't live out a lie, because now that she had met Pride, she could picture clearly what it would mean to be a real and loving wife. It was like a revelation, a streak of lightning in the sky. It was right, as everything with Pride was right. Yet, much as she wanted to, she couldn't find the words or the courage to say any of those things.

She went to bed and lay awake listening to the lowing and bawling of the cattle far away to the north and to the tremulous moan of the wind that thrust down from the north and then changed direction at a moment's whim. She felt suspended in the loneliness of the bed, as if she were on some far desert plateau, a prisoner in exile from all she wanted most.

In the morning her heart ached as though it were in some vise. Her hand kept going to her breast, as if to soothe and ease the pain. She felt bruised by the spring; it hurt her eyes to watch the flowering and feel so unfulfilled herself. She was grateful for Miss Jane's kindness and for Cima's new civility. It seemed to signal a new climate, the possibility that she would feel at home, and yet the pain remained. There were times when she had to get away from them all, to run from the house. She wanted to hide, when there was no hiding place. She wanted to flee, when there was no reason for flight and no one to run to.

She had written her father.

Dear Papa,

I hope you and Mama and the boys are really going to make plans to come out. They say the summer weather here is dreadful and I know you have lots to do at the farm. Andrew will not be taking the cattle to market until autumn, so I guess it will be best to make plans for the fall, but any time would be all right for you to come.

I need you. I want to see you and talk to you. There is so much to say and it's so hard to write. I got my way, Papa. I got what I wanted. I love this land and everything about it. But still, life can be full of surprises. I need you, Papa, and your advice.

Love,
Reanna

As always, when she felt she could bear the house no longer, she saddled up Molly May and rode to the far end of the Ridge. Sometimes before she returned, she'd stand at the far end of the Ridge alone, looking out at the multitude of cattle in the swaying, glittering grass, the miniature riders mounting guard over them—Andrew's red checked shirt and Taffy's high-crowned black hat, and then Pride kneeling over a sick animal, his buckskin shirt dark with dust and sweat—and she would feel as if all this existed only in her imagination, suspended in space.

This afternoon her loneliness seemed almost naked, illuminated beneath the bright sky; she felt faintly dizzy, her senses disordered. The world seemed to share her sense of trembling vertigo. Everything, everywhere was out of tune. The barn cat had screeched like an owl, arched her back and spat at nothing in the air. Molly May was skittish, rearing back from a twig as if it were a snake. No amount of sweet talking or petting calmed her. She refused an apple and reared away from Reanna's hand. Reanna stood at the edge of the Ridge, the light hurting her eyes. It was not precisely the brightness of the sun, but the harsh distortions in a world that was out of focus. Something prickled at her spine, some warning in the far reaches of her mind. It was nothing she could identify. The sky, the entire atmosphere, seemed blurred, opaque and diffused, as if it were slipping under water. It was some time before she could move; she seemed to be caught in an inexplicable lethargy.

When Reanna came up on the home place, it looked as if it were already dusk, although it was mid-afternoon; a haze had descended like a blanket to shroud the earth. The overcast was thick and sullen gray; it made breathing difficult. Even Molly May blew, laboring as if she were struggling up a mountain, not cantering along the flat top of the Ridge. The leaves hung drooping without a breath of wind to ruffle them. In the barn the chickens had gone to roost.

Reanna had never known a day like this. Her arms and legs were heavy and didn't function as they should. She unsaddled Molly May and put her in her stall. She gave her some water and hay, but Molly May refused both as she had the apple. Reanna wondered if

Molly May were sick. She'd have Taffy take a look at her next time he came in off the range.

When she came out of the barn, she saw that the sky had darkened still more. To the south there was a solid, dark cloud, moving like an impenetrable slate wall in the direction of Lochleven. A few large raindrops fell, spattering on the dusty ground with force, leaving marks as large as quarters.

Reanna ran, then, and entered the kitchen where Cima was plucking fowl and the girls were cutting up greens for salad. Cima, her face beaded darkly with sweat, was saying crossly to Snow: "No, I told you *no*, princess! It's too all-fired hot for baking anything, let alone pies."

"It's raining," Reanna said, and Cima looked up.

"Rain?" she murmured. "Praise God and little fishes. Break this heat."

"Cima, can you come outside a minute? I want you to look at the cloud."

Cima scowled at her; her strong, mahogany arms were bristling with hen feathers. "Can't it wait?"

"No, I think you'd better."

Cima stared at her a moment, then wiped her hands and arms on the dishtowel tied around her waist and followed Reanna out the back door. The cloud had darkened still more, and the wind had shifted, coming off the bare pasture to the southeast. The heavy raindrops pelted down, each drop a separate force. The dark cloud seemed cunningly independent of the rest of the boiling sky. Cima stood silent and still, glaring upward. Reanna thought Cima was going to scold her for bringing her out on a fool's errand, but Cima only muttered faintly, "Sweet Jesus, oh Lord, sweet Jesus."

"What is it?"

"Sheet cloud. That's more than rain. There's hail in that cloud, and maybe a twister. We've got to go to the storm cellar. I'll get the girls and Snow. You go ring that bell on the back porch, so the hands will hear it and take cover. Keep on ringing it! In a big wind even a ditch can look like heaven."

She scurried back into the kitchen. Reanna ran up the porch steps, untied the lanyard and began to ring the big brass bell; its piercing clang sounded feeble and thin under the rising rush of the storm. In the distance the great cloud was boiling within itself like some evil genie. Cima burst out of the kitchen again, leading a frightened Snow by the hand and carrying a basket. Rose Dawn followed her, a loaf of bread under each arm.

"That's it!" Cima shouted into the rain. "Keep on ringing that bell! I'll leave the door open for you. I've got to draw some water."

"What about Miss Jane?" Reanna cried.

"I've sent Annoyi." She vanished around the corner of the house in a spinning swirl of rain and wind.

In place of the troubled lethargy of the past hour, Reanna now felt a wild, almost savage excitement. The bell clanged crazily, the rain came in sweeping silver torrents, the catalpa tree flailed like a willow whip in the gale. The sky darkened to twilight, to an almost-dark, though along the horizon strips of milky light played fiercely, glowing and fading. She was soaked to the bone, her ears ringing. She laughed once—a gasp of breath—pulling wildly, her feet braced. Pride was out there somewhere, drenched and gasping, too, hat jammed low over his eyes, glaring into the washing sheets of rain; he couldn't hear her, but she'd keep on ringing until he *could*, and then he'd come riding back, his yellow slicker whipping around him like a battle standard.

A figure was running from the house, hands over her head—a slim, awkward figure.

"Annoyi!" she called. The girl turned in a brief comic dance of indecision, then began to make frantic little sweeps with one arm. "—cellar!"

"*Miss Jane!*" Reanna screamed. "Where is she?"

The girl gave a swift, forlorn gesture. "She won't come."

"What?" Reanna let go the lanyard and ran to her. The roar of wind and rain was immense now, an almost concrete force. She seized Annoyi by the shoulders. "Why didn't you bring her?"

"I told her! Miss Reanna, she won't *come* with me."

Reanna released her with a low cry and ran for the house through pelting, smashing torrents of water. The door, when she lifted its latch, slammed back into the room like a gunshot, and water volleyed into the great hall. Reanna stumbled on the third step and went to her knees, thrust herself up again and raced along the upstairs hall to Miss Jane's study.

Miss Jane was standing erect and motionless by the cupola windows, her figure clearly outlined against the savage panorama of the sky. "It's coming fast," Miss Jane said in an almost dreamy tone, "fast as the wind can carry it." She stood without turning.

(223)

"We must go to the storm cellar," Reanna said. She did not understand why, if Miss Jane had seen the cloud, she hadn't gone with the others to take cover. "Annoyi says you—"

"You go on," Miss Jane said. "I'll stay here."

"Cima says we must hurry. She thinks it may be a twister."

Miss Jane turned then; she had a smile of anticipation on her face, as if she had been looking toward something she had wanted for a long time, a prize of great value.

"Do you know what lies behind the cloud?" Reanna shook her head. "Behind the cloud, beneath the sky, Breathholder is waiting for me." Reanna felt a chill run in the corridors of her mind; this was no time for Indian legends, this was a time for action.

"Please come, Miss Jane! We must get to the cellar, where we'll be safe."

"Safe." Miss Jane smiled faintly. "I will only be safe when I am with my Pride again." All at once there was a sound of terrible hammering, a million mailed fists battering at the roof. The old house creaked and groaned like a ship foundering. "Hail," Miss Jane said. "After the hail, it will come. I am old and tired. I am ready to answer Breathholder's call. I have waited for a long time. A very long time."

"You *must* come!" Reanna cried and took her hand. "You don't understand."

"Oh yes. I understand." The tower room dipped into almost total dark, and the wind took on a new treble shriek. Miss Jane drew back and said, "Go, now. You must go."

"No—I won't go down without you!"

"Child, you have your whole life ahead of you."

"No," Reanna said, the words coming as if torn out of her, "you have *given* me my life—you've made me feel valued, and important—you've taught me what a woman can be. I won't leave you here!"

The wind's high scream swallowed up space and time; the house shivered once, as if hit by a gigantic battering ram. Then, without warning, the wind fell away, and the rain; there was only this curious, oppressive weight that made it hard to breathe and that unearthly light, pulsing and fading around them.

"It's over," Reanna said in amazement.

"No. Now it will come. See, there."

And following Miss Jane's finger, Reanna saw from the cupola window a slender, dark serpent that looked as if it had grown down out of the cloud, swaying and spinning, borne on an eerie, sub-terranean roar.

"There is no more time," Miss Jane was saying to her with soft urgency; Reanna could barely hear her. "You must go."

"No."

"I am head of the Beauvaises. I *order* you to go!"

Reanna felt tears sting her eyelids. "I can't—I can't obey you! You're more important to me than Lochleven or the Beauvaises or the Five Nations . . . I will stay with you."

"Stubborn girl," Miss Jane said, but she smiled at her fondly. "Then I will come."

As they went down the stairs, there was a roaring like a thousand runaway locomotives, and the house shook terribly, quivering throughout its length; in the kitchen something crashed to the floor.

"Hurry!" Reanna called, drawing the older woman along; the pressure in her eardrums was unbearable, her vision was blurred. "Cima said she'd hold the door."

"Wait."

"What's the matter?"

"The Beauvaise cup." Miss Jane moved toward the mantel where the big silver cup gleamed dully. "We cannot leave it here."

"There's no *time*."

Miss Jane reached up for the cup, Reanna moved toward her—and the world came to an end. There was one thunderous, all-encompassing explosion, and then everything around her lifted and shattered and splintered, whirling off into insupportable chaos. She had the sensation of floating almost pleasurably through a surf-surge of chairs and plates and curiously unidentifiable objects. She was falling, falling away from life, into a tumultuous oblivion that would not release her. Something struck her in the forehead, the small of her back. She said, *"Pride"*—one intensely affectionate thought that was like a prayer in the midst of this unbearable surf-like crashing; and then everything slipped off into darkness.

THERE was a pattering, the gentlest pattering, cut through by cries, faint and faraway, like children playing. Rain. Rain, and someone calling. She tried to move but couldn't. Something was pressing down upon her from a great height. Groaning, she worked one arm free. Miss Jane was pinned beneath her; the Indian woman's face was white and drawn, but curiously peaceful. A voice was calling—Cima, shouting Miss Jane's name over and over.

"Here," she cried—a call that was ridiculously faint. Something had her body, her legs pinned. *"Here."* There was nothing but jagged, broken ends of things, pain in her forehead and the rain's soft patter. But how could it be raining inside the house?

"Don't try to talk, Miss Jane. Please rest and be quiet. They will come soon."

They were pulling at timbers, pieces of wreckage. Cima was calling, "Hold on, you two, we're coming, we'll get to you," her voice hoarse with exhaustion.

"Promise me that you will hold the Beauvaises together, on Lochleven."

"I'll try."

"No—promise. Give me your word on it."

"I promise."

The great weight was drawn away, in a sound of grating and a clatter and tinkle of glass. Cima was bending down to her, her proud, black face soaked in sweat and red with dust, contorted with fear.

"Where is she, my own sweet lady, *where is she?*"

Reanna struggled to her feet with a gasp. Her back hurt, but she could move, she could move her arms and legs, her whole body. She was standing here. Alive. Rain falling on her face and hands. She was standing in the open, in the rain. There was no great parlor, there was no Lochleven any more. The girls were staring at her with dazed, frightened faces.

"Your head," Annoyi shrilled.

She put her hand to the painful place on her forehead; it came away smeared thickly with blood.

"*Help* me, all of you," Cima cried. She was crouched over, tearing at the splintered timbers in a frenzy. The four of them worked in desperate silence, lifting away shattered pieces of beam, bits of stone and mortar, gasping with the effort. When they'd uncovered the small, broken body, Cima gave a low, animal groan.

"Oh no, oh no no," she kept saying, over and over, a low terrible keening. *"Ala ala a-ree."*

"Don't move her," Reanna said suddenly.

Cima looked up wildly. "*Got* to move her."

Miss Jane's eyes opened again; her face still had that tranquil expression, as if she'd been set free from an interminable bondage.

Her hands, clutched together, extended the dusty, dented cup.

"Reanna," she breathed. "I cannot give you land, but I leave you the cup. Keep it safe."

"What are you saying, Miss Jane?" Cima moaned. "You going to be all right."

"Take it," Miss Jane whispered. Reanna put her hands over Miss Jane's and together they held the Beauvaise cup.

"You'll be all right, my Princess Jane."

"No," she said, the word defined and clear. "I have stayed beyond my time. Today Breathholder will take me to Pride. He is waiting there, at the end of the sky." She closed her eyes and gave one long, shuddering sigh.

When Reanna was sure that Miss Jane was dead, she gave a great cry that would have astonished her mother. Grief was vulgar, never to be displayed in public. None of those rules mattered to Reanna now. She was outraged, as one is when death has come and will not leave empty-handed—a faceless, invisible enemy who will not accept defeat. She cried out because Miss Jane had gone and left her alone with a burden she hadn't asked for and could never carry.

Reanna stood holding the cup. It was dented, scarred, streaked with dirt and Miss Jane's blood. It was her legacy, a legacy she couldn't forsake.

Cima was rocking Miss Jane as if she were a small child who had been given into her safekeeping. "Cima going to take care of you, Missy. Cima going to lay you out nice. You'll see."

"Shall I ring the bell?" Reanna asked.

Cima looked up, her eyes full of desperate scorn. "What bell you talking about? There ain't no bell. There ain't nothing left here at all."

Reanna looked around her blankly. The house had gone down, smashed beyond repair. All that was left were the fragments of the chimneys, standing like shards of great earthen vessels. There was no barn, no chicken house, no corral; even the wellhead had been razed. A few chickens ran pathetically here and there and the horses all were gone, save one who lay on its side in the mud, screaming in fear and pain; its left hind leg was bent in a grotesque shape. She must get a gun, if she could find one, and put the poor beast out of its misery.

She hoped Molly May had run away into the woods and survived. As she looked southeast, she could see the milewide path the storm had cut through the grass. Everything in its way had fallen before it. When it had reached the Ridge, it had narrowed into a funnel, the tip of which had struck down Lochleven. Mindlessly, it had jumped and skipped in a pattern of random choice, leaving some parts of the Ridge stripped and others standing whole and intact as if there had been no storm at all. Down the west slope lay a welter of planking, smashed furniture and clothing and other debris.

There wasn't the simplest thing left to make a new life with. Everything they had always taken for granted was gone. There was no bed to sleep in, no kitchen to cook in, not a table, nor a chair. Cima looked as bewildered as she herself felt.

A mute, crude witness to the absurd whim of fate was the old log cabin at the edge of the woods; it remained completely untouched. The cabin had been hastily built, ill cared for, abandoned. It was so near collapse a strong arm could have broken through the chinking—and yet it had stood, while all that had been well built, substantial and valued was gone. The catastrophe seemed more terrible in the rain than if the sun were shining upon it. Death seemed more final in the rain. This was the death not only of Miss Jane but of Lochleven. Yet they must live on, and they must bury their dead.

"Ah ah," Cima moaned tonelessly, sobbing now, rocking and rocking, still clutching Miss Jane's body. "Ah, my sweet Mistress Jane, you gone, ain't nothing left, nothing. Can't do nothing any more."

Reanna looked at her. Behind her, Annoyi and Rose Dawn had caught Cima's grief and were wailing and wringing their hands. Snow stood beside them, a slender little figure turned to stone. She thought again, *Pride*. Where were the men? Were they even alive? Anyway, they had their hands full with the herd. She couldn't count on them now.

The cabin. The cabin was the answer. Ramshackle or not, haunted or not, it *was* a dwelling, a roof over their heads. There wasn't anything else.

Reanna watched the others for a long moment, and then her mouth hardened, her head came up. "Annoyi," she said sharply, "I want bedding—blankets, coverlets, sheets, anything you can find. Follow the twister's path down the slope, there—*listen* to me!" Cima was staring up at her dully; the girls were frozen into silence.

"Blankets?" Annoyi faltered.

"Go *on*, now, gather up bedding, clothes, everything you can find, and take it to the cabin there. Now move along! I mean it."

Annoyi glanced fearfully at Cima, then hurried off down the slope through the trail of wreckage.

"Rose Dawn, you hunt around for any food you can find."

"But Miss Reanna—"

"Do you hear me?" She shook the girl; it made Reanna's head throb so violently she groaned aloud. "Check the root cellar, then look under the—where the smokehouse was. Look for hams, salt pork, corn, greens—anything you can find—and take it to the cabin, too. You understand?"

"Yes, Miss Reanna."

She walked up to Snow, who was still standing there perfectly motionless. "Snow, I want you to go into the woods and catch one of the horses. Your Picaunli, or Starlight or Molly May. And ride into town for Doc and Jack Levy. Tell them a twister has hit Lochleven, that we need staples and—and clothing, anything they can spare."

She broke off. Snow still hadn't moved; she was staring at Cima and Miss Jane, her eyes glazed. Without thought, Reanna slapped her across the face, hard. She saw the child's eyes flicker once; then her face contorted and the tears began to stream down her face.

"You hit me," she sobbed, and then to Reanna's amazement the child clutched her around the waist with all her might, catching her breath in long, shuddering gulps.

"All right, Snow," Reanna murmured. "All right now, honey. Now you must help. We've got big trouble and everyone must help. Go find Picaunli now, find a horse and ride for town. You can do it."

"All right."

The child stopped sobbing and walked off toward the woods. Reanna went over to Cima and knelt beside her. Cima glanced at her and then bent over Miss Jane again, moaning and muttering.

"Cima," she said softly. "We're going to need a fire. Cima."

The black woman wagged her head desolately. "Don't nothing matter no more. Miss Jane gone, my sweet mistress lady, no sense in nothing."

"Cima," she said gently. "We've got to go on living."

"What I'm going to do? Where I'm going to lay to rest my sweet lady?"

Reanna put her hand on Cima's shoulder. "We'll take care of

her. We'll bury her with all honor. You'll see. But first we must work out food and shelter." She said intently, "*Cima*. Start a fire in the cabin hearth. It'll be dark soon."

Cima turned her head slowly, her amber eyes glinting. "You giving me orders?"

"Yes. *Now build me a fire*."

"What gives you the right to tell me what to do here?"

"This does." Reanna held out the cup. "Miss Jane gave it to me. You saw her. I'm mistress here, now she's gone." Cima looked at the cup and then back at Miss Jane.

"We've got to make this place as fit as possible for Miss Jane's funeral," Reanna continued. "I don't want to shame her before the whole tribe. She was a Beauvaise, a princess of the royal clan, and we will do her every honor, as is her right. But now we need food and a roof over our heads. You know that."

For a moment Cima wavered, hesitating; then slowly she released Miss Jane and got to her feet. Her hands were bloody from digging; her face was ashen.

"Tell me what you want," she said.

"I want to get that cabin livable. Build me a fire; we're going to have to boil our water for a time. And we'll have to rustle up something to eat. Then we'll tend to Miss Jane, I promise you."

In an hour or so they'd made the cabin habitable; the roof leaked in two places, but there was no help for that. Reanna and Cima salvaged parts of two bedsteads from the debris at Lochleven, and three torn mattresses; the hearth served as a cookstove. Annoyi brought in blankets and odd bits of clothing. Rose Dawn found hams and a partly crushed cheese and the canister of coffee, and some of the iron pots and skillets had survived. The tornado had left its customary capricious mementoes; the Dresden teapot was unbroken, with only its top missing; they found an oil lamp perched on a heap of wreckage, perfectly intact; and Miss Jane's hand mirror was unearthed under the shattered remnants of the great dining table, not even cracked. Reanna took it as a good omen.

In the gathering darkness, they dug out the great front door, propped it on trestles and laid Miss Jane on it. While the girls rigged a flimsy lean-to to shelter the frail, broken body from the rain and wind, Reanna and Cima washed her and combed and braided her fine, steel-gray hair. Reanna found Miss Jane's personal trunk, overturned and half crushed. She brought the white deerskin dress over to the makeshift bier and said, "She must wear it."

Even Cima looked troubled at this. "It supposed to be passed down, Miss Reanna. To you, and then to Snow. That's the custom."

"No." Reanna shook her head. "Miss Jane must be richly dressed, so that even Breathholder will know she is a royal personage, the granddaughter of a queen." Cima was staring at her in amazement. "If in time Snow decides she wants to wear the dress of her mother's people, I will have one made for her. This is Miss Jane's. Now help me with her."

"Yes'm," Cima said.

Later—much later—the two women sat together on one of the cornshuck mattresses and gazed into the fire, stupid with exhaustion, too tired to sleep. Cima had dressed the cut in Reanna's forehead; Reanna had bandaged Cima's hands. The girls were fast asleep on one of the pallets. The rain had let up, but the wind still moaned softly under the sill.

Reanna said, "Do you think they're all right?"

Cima nodded; she knew Reanna meant Andrew and Pride, and the ranch hands. "Pride's got the Indian nose for weather. He'd have smelled it and got the herd into the big ravine before they spooked and stampeded. He'd have things in hand even if that Andrew . . ."

She broke off in embarrassment, biting her lip. Reanna smiled grimly. "Go on."

"I didn't mean to say that."

"You're right, though. Even if 'that Andrew' is too headstrong and selfish to see *anything* beyond his own nose."

They laughed softly in the late silence.

"I wonder if Snow made it to town. I guess I made a mistake, sending her off alone like that."

"No, you done the right thing. Better to get her away from Miss Jane, standing around brooding. She's too little to help here, anyways. Poor little tyke; first her mother, then her grandma."

"It's such a long way to town. She's so young."

Cima snorted. "Don't you worry about that one. She can find her way through a swamp of fire-breathing panther-crocodiles, come out the other side wearing a fancy leopardskin shirt and alligator high-button shoes. God help the poor helpless man she sinks *her* hooks into."

They laughed again and fell silent. The embers in the banked fire snapped, rain dripped soddenly on the swept earth floor.

"Well, we seen it all now, ain't we?" Cima said. "Lord, lord . . ." She turned and looked at Reanna. "I was wrong about you. I sold you short, believed what I wanted to believe, not what was there in front of my staring eyes. Thought you were too fancy-frilly for this country. It breaks 'em, you know. Year in, year out, it breaks 'em under the wheel. Only ones that pull through are tough—good tough and mean tough. Miss Jane told me you had sand, and I wouldn't believe her." She put her hand on the younger woman's shoulder. "You really loved her, didn't you?"

"Yes. Oh, yes."

"I knew it. You took hold like a wonder."

Reanna felt tears start in her eyes. "Thank you, Cima."

"I mean it. You're mistress, lady of Lochleven. Even if there ain't no Lochleven left any more. And you can count on me right to the bottom of the well. I won't let you down like that again. That's a solemn promise."

"Thank you. I'll need you, more than you know. I was scared—half to death. The whole time."

"I know. That's why you can count on me. Always."

And to Reanna's amazement the tall black woman embraced her once, hard; Reanna felt tears on her cheek. Then Cima released her and rose, sniffling noisily.

"Let's get some sleep while we can. Tomorrow's going to be a long day."

IT was nearly evening before the three men came in, riding hard. They'd been driving cattle from a bed in the river when Pride had read the danger signs and hurried the herd under the bluffs. From a high point later, he and Taffy had seen the deadly funnel. They hadn't known for sure that the storm had struck at Lochleven, but they'd taken no chances and ridden straight in, back-stringing extra horses, riding first one and then the other.

Pride's first thought was for Reanna. He had to make sure that she was safe and unhurt before he could think of anything else. He was stunned by his mother's death, but he could accept it as her desire. His relief over Reanna was so great he wanted, at the same time, to cry aloud his thanks. Reanna, his love, was alive in all this chaos and desolation!

Taffy wanted to know what he could do to help. His attention was concentrated on seeing to the needs of Reanna and Lochleven. This was his place, his fence to mend. These were his folks; it was for them he worked and for them he worried. He found it impossible to accept the fact that Miss Jane was gone. She had always been there, the linchpin, the wheelhorse, the heart of the place. He kept expecting her to appear, to take over the disheartening job of clearing away the sea of wreckage. He began work on a coffin for Miss Jane, to take his mind off things.

Andrew's first thought was for Snow. He was enraged when he heard that Reanna had sent her off to town for help; he cursed her, called her heartless and vindictive, even accused her of trying to abandon her stepdaughter. Even Cima's angry defense of Reanna and Pride's heated intercession made no difference. He remounted and rode off in a raging fury, only to meet Jack Levy coming out from town with a wagonload of supplies, Snow perched happily on the seat beside him. She'd caught Picaunli and ridden to town bareback to find herself the center of attention. Andrew petted and praised her. She was immensely pleased with herself.

Even then he wouldn't let up. "Snow tells me you sent her to the cellar and then stayed behind with Miss Jane. What possessed you to remain in the house?"

Reanna stared back at him. "I *told* you, Miss Jane wouldn't go down."

"Why in hell was that?"

Reanna bit her lip. "She—wanted to stay, that's all. I just got her to come down with me when the twister hit."

"And now she's dead. If you'd only—" But he saw something in her eyes then; he broke off and moved away.

She watched him wandering through the ruins, poking aimlessly at something. If he planned to blame her for Miss Jane's death, she would fight him, before the whole household. Something in her had blown away on that tiger wind. She had changed; she was determined not to let him hurt her as he'd done in the past. That was over. A great many things were over.

On the morning of the third day, people began to arrive, by ones and twos and in great families. The word had spread that the twister had touched ground on Beauvaise Ridge, destroyed Lochleven. As Reanna went out to greet them, she was touched by their sympathy. They had genuine concern for her and offered her their kindness and support.

A few, who had been wiped out themselves, came to the Ridge

empty-handed, but most brought some gifts: an oil lamp, a hand axe, a down pillow, a sack of beans.

Most of all, she was grateful for the help the women gave to Cima and to her. She knew it was something else Miss Jane had left her; perhaps it was a legacy of even more value than the Beauvaise cup.

Andrew kept wandering through the crowd like a man in a daze. He kept saying over and over again, "All gone. It's all gone. There's nothing left." He kept stopping and turning around, as if when he turned, Lochleven would still be there in all its glory, and the storm would all have been an evil dream. Reanna was shocked at his reaction. It seemed to her the loss of material things meant more to him than Miss Jane's death.

Then he would all at once come alive and turn on her again. "What do you thing you're doing, trying to feed all these people? We're ruined; we can't afford it."

"We can't afford *not* to do Miss Jane honor." She had half expected he would take this attitude; she had her answer ready for him. "What would people think if we let her go like some poor relation? All we have is because of her. I will not shame her before her friends, her people! No one will leave Lochleven without being fed." She looked at the cauldrons full of bubbling hominy and beans, the kettles filled with hot grease for the fry bread. "We will offer the same hospitality as if Miss Jane were here."

The sky had begun to clear; the rain had stopped and the fires had been lighted against the chill evening winds. The wrecked chimneys cast their shadows over them.

Father Soule came from the mission, traveling together with Frampton; they, too, brought a wagonload of supplies. Doc and Amoretta came out from the town with a loaded mule. Neighbors and the ranch hands arduously cleared away the debris, stacked the shattered timbers, repaired broken chairs and chests, salvaged curtains and silverware and a few dishes.

Then the women swept the cabin and the yard clean, as if this were another New Year. In its way, it was a new beginning. The fires burned high all night, but not high enough to warm Reanna. The wailing of the women and the slow beat of the drums only heightened her grief, her sense of loneliness and loss.

She'd been glad to be busy. Many wanted to talk, to tell their troubles as they always had to Miss Jane. Now they began, in halting English mixed with Chickasaw, to pour out all their woes to

Reanna. She didn't understand one word in three, but it didn't seem to matter. What was important to them was that she listened, and she knew it.

In the night the men of the tribe fired round after round from their rifles in the air where the house had stood, to drive away the spirit of the dead if it had remained behind, and to scatter any evil from the place. At sunset and sunrise Pride joined with the men to sing a chant for the dead; he cut a lock of his hair to show he had entered into a state of mourning. Tomorrow at noon Miss Jane would be buried, and then the more traditional would not say her name again.

It would, Reanna thought, take more than a few rounds of rifle fire to drive evil spirits from the place. The bitterness inherited from the past blazed up as hot and bright as the funeral fires.

There was a heated argument between the brothers over where Miss Jane should be buried. Andrew said there was no house left to bury her under, and Pride retorted that burial at the mission church was an insult to her Indian beliefs and traditions. Finally, at Reanna's and Cima's urging, they compromised; Miss Jane would be buried at the end of the Ridge, where her husband Pride had been killed and interred with only a cairn of stones to mark the deed and the day. Andrew hotly ridiculed the idea of a Catholic priest speaking the service, but Pride wouldn't let his mother go to rest without the blessing of her old friend Father Soule.

At noon, at the graveside, the men began covering the coffin with red earth. Reanna felt that she too was in the coffin with Miss Jane, boxed for all eternity into a situation that she hadn't made but that had been forced upon her by a dying woman's last wish. The dirt filled the grave, and no reprieve came.

Walking back from the Ridge, Reanna felt Andrew's hand on her arm. She heard him say, as if from a great distance, "I have to go back to the herd. I'm taking Taffy and Pride and the hands with me."

She looked at him numbly, barely able to understand the words. He was going, she understood that, and she would be alone. She hadn't expected him to stay, but to go so abruptly was cruel. He might not care for her feelings, but he should have shown more respect for Miss Jane. All he cared about, it seemed, was the cattle and what could be recouped of their fortunes.

"I've arranged for you and Snow to go into town with Amoretta and Doc. You can stay with them for a while. I'll send Cima with you to look after you. You can stay there until I decide what's best to do with you."

She stared at him through tear-brightened eyes. He must think she is a child or an idiot to talk to her in that fashion, as if she were a parcel that had been inconveniently left in his care. She shook his hand from her arm.

"I'm not going to town or anywhere else." The gulf that had always been between them widened. "I'm going to stay here."

Andrew was dumbfounded. "You don't know what you're talking about! This whole thing has been too much for you. You aren't thinking straight."

"Oh yes, I am. I'm staying here at Lochleven."

"You can't stay here," he said. "There's no place to stay."

"I'll stay in the log cabin. It's still standing."

"It's not fit to live in."

"Then I'll make it fit." Her eyes blazed at him. "It was good enough for Miss Jane when she first came out here. It will be good enough for me."

"I'm ordering you to go to town, where there will be somebody to look after you."

"I can look after myself."

"What will you do for food? I can't be running over here all the time to get supplies in from town."

"There's time to plant another garden."

He struck his thigh in exasperation. He knew she could be difficult and stubborn, he'd had plenty of proof of that; now he desperately wanted to find an argument she'd accept. She didn't belong here at the best of times; how could she cope now?

"Look, this is your chance to go back East. Go home. Who could expect you to stay after a tornado, when there's no house, no place for you to live?" He'd played his ace; he was sure it would carry the hand. She'd know her family couldn't condemn her over an act of God.

"No, Andrew." She stared him down. "You haven't been listening to me, have you? I'm not going anywhere, not to town, nor back East either. *This* is my place and I'm staying on it."

"You'll starve," he said. It was the first real fear that he had voiced; if things went on like this, they might all starve. "I can't spare you anybody."

"Yes, you can. You'll give me two of the hands, for one full week. And I won't starve. You seem to think I'm some fragile piece of porcelain that will break at the first hard tap. Well, I'm not fragile—I know that now. I'm a woman but I won't starve, nor will any of mine. Not as long as I have these two hands." She held them out before him, worn and crudely bandaged, as if they were positive proof that what she said was true.

For the first time, he knew she would never leave this place or him. That in some way he could not define, she had triumphed over him.

"I only wanted you to be safe," he said lamely and turned away. But he knew it was far too late for that.

REANNA wrapped the Beauvaise cup in a shawl and put it away in a battered trunk. Andrew had ridden back to the herd, taking Pride and Taffy with him. Pride was reluctant to go, but Andrew had left her Dub Wilgress and Tiny Bentham for a few days. They were his best hands and she was grateful. A few neighbors and friends remained behind to help them pick up the pieces. When the cabin was swept out, the chinking replaced, the fireplaces cleared, the roof repaired and the windows set with glass, it was livable enough.

It was a double log structure of four rooms, two on each side, with a dogtrot breezeway in the center, running front to back. On the right was the kitchen and behind it a room for Cima and Snow. Across the breezeway, opposite the kitchen was a room for Reanna and behind that the girls slept. Two rooms had fireplaces large enough to keep them cozy in winter, and if there was a breath of cool air in summer, it would certainly be found in the shaded walkway of the house.

The two ranch hands rounded up the horses and made a corral and a lean-to for a barn. Reanna was happy to see that Molly May had survived; it meant she would have something left that was hers alone, as well as a way of getting off the place on her own. After a week of hard work, there were pigs in the pen and wood for the stove, and the well was working again. They had stalled a cow, who soon freshened and gave them milk. Cima and Snow caught what chickens came home to roost. When all that could be saved and salvaged was set to rights, the neighbors went away to tend to their own homes. Jack Levy was the last to leave. Reanna sent a letter by him to her folks.

Dear Mama and Papa,

I'm sorry this letter is so rushed, but we have had some bad things happen here. A tornado has blown down Lochleven. It came so quickly, right out of a black cloud. I could see it coming and then, when it had passed over, the house was just rubble—splinters.

Miss Jane was killed, pinned beneath the house. She was the spirit of this house. It seems impossible that both are gone. We were not the only place hit by the twister, but all our neighbors have been so generous and helpful. They came for miles to pay their respects to Miss Jane and to help us get started again.

Andrew, Pride and Taffy were on the range when the storm struck. They got here as fast as they could. It's fortunate they and the cowhands were all unhurt. The herd was not touched. We've lost everything, but when the cattle go to market and sell, we can rebuild. For now, we're lucky there's a cabin nearby, where the family lived before Lochleven was built, so we'll have a roof over our heads.

You know I wanted you all to come out this fall, but I'll have to ask you to postpone that, because we have no place to put you. It will be more convenient if you wait to come until we get on our feet again.

I know you'll understand that I am bitterly disappointed. Oh, it's so sad to be here without Miss Jane. Now, don't worry about me. I'll be just fine, and I love you all.

Reanna

P.S. Jack Levy has been especially kind.

Jack Levy's wagonload of supplies was a godsend. A sack of flour was a treasure and a packet of spices worth a ransom. The first time she smelled gingerbread baking in the kitchen of the cabin, the aroma of cinnamon and molasses mixed with ginger was more aromatic and pleasing than a rare perfume. If she didn't glance toward the shell of Lochleven and the outline of the old foundation, she was content, for this house was as comfortable as the ones most of the families of the Nation lived in.

She had to start with the very basics of life. The success or failure of this new adventure depended on her ability to get the others to work as hard as she did. She couldn't expect enthusiasm for such backbreaking toil, but she did expect the work to be done, share and share alike, and no shirkers.

She had to see to all the stock and the household, as well as plant a fresh garden. She worked sunup to sundown out of doors and came in for the evening meal. Often she kept the others waiting while she finished some last-minute chore, but none of them dared sit down to table without her. Sometimes she rose from that table so tired that she was barely able to stagger across the breezeway to her room, where she fell on the bed without taking her clothes off and lay like a stone until morning.

She had barely enough energy to read the letters from home.

Dear Reanna,
It is terrible news about your house and Miss Jane. Of course, we understand and we wouldn't think of imposing on you when you are unable to receive us. I am sending a box of things by freight that I hope you will be able to use. We are so glad you're safe.

The boys, of course, are dreadfully disappointed about not going out West, but they're young and they'll get over it. Your Papa says he will write under separate cover.

Ree, don't mention that I told you, but your Papa has had a little financial upset. Just temporary, so it's really more convenient if we do come another time.

> Love,
> Mama

Dear Ree,
Golly, I wish I'd been there to see the big storm. We miss you a lot, and I said I missed you more than Patrick, and he hit me. You never know about Patrick.

> Love,
> Thomas

Dear Sister,
I did not hit Thomas. Thomas is a child. I do not strike children. Sorry for your trouble.

> Your brother,
> Patrick

Reanna saved the letter from her father for the last.

Darling Girl,
I so wish I were there so we could really talk. I wish, too, I had

some advice to give you other than time has a way of making things come right. Don't tell your mother, but things are not going well for me just now. I am pressed by my creditors. A speculation I had great hopes of did not work out. So it is really better that we all come another time.

That won't stop me from thinking of you always and wishing I could help you.

Your adoring Papa

God knows she needed help.

She'd told Andrew they wouldn't starve as long as she had two hands, but she found she needed a dozen pair of hands and as many legs as a centipede for all that had to be done. She'd never hitched a plow or broken ground or planted seed or hoed a row of corn. She'd never fed pigs or chickens or milked a cow before. Now she did all that and more. She shared out the work, but if she wanted it done properly, she often found she had to do it herself. She alone planned what had to be done and worried over the outcome.

She fought not only the wind and the limitations of her body, but a caprice of nature; after the drenching rains of the tornado, a dry spell set in. It was so dry that each plant had to be watered, bucketful after bucketful, from the well. She formed the girls into a bucket chain. Snow cried and complained of being put upon.

"I never had to work in the fields when Miss Jane was alive. She never let me stay out in the hot sun. I used to take a nap," Snow sobbed.

Reanna's voice rose in anger. "I told you—if we don't work, we don't eat." Cima came from the lean-to where she had been mending harness.

"You're too hard on Snow; she's only a baby. She should get out of the sun."

"She's *not* a baby. It will be a lot harder on her if she starves sitting in the shade."

The sun was unremitting; it scorched the crop as the wind blew in out of the south. To keep the wind and sun from blistering her, she wore a straw bonnet. It was the one she'd worn as a bride, but no one would have recognized it, set flat on her head, held down with an old scarf; it made a long bill brim that shaded her neck and face. It had been rained on, mashed out of shape and discolored; still she preferred it to a sunbonnet. It was the last vestige of her ties to home. She'd promised her mother she would never wear a sunbonnet like a farm woman, and she had at least kept that one promise.

She labored like an animal. She washed clothes in the yard, bent over a tub. She boiled the bedclothes and work clothes in a heavy kettle and rinsed them in another, and then hung them on a bush to dry. Sometimes, when the wind was blowing strong enough, the first batch of clothes she put out were dry before she had finished with the last. On those long days, she was too tired to speak at the table in the evening and could barely taste the food she ate.

She knew she couldn't let up. She was the wheelhorse for them all, a donkey harnessed to a treadmill that never stopped. She'd promised Miss Jane to keep the place together, and if she didn't go on like some dumb brute, one foot before the other, she'd break and leave. She wouldn't be defeated, not by Andrew or Snow or these idiotic, shiftless girls. She wouldn't be beaten by anyone.

She learned with angry amazement that she not only had to fight people and weather for a garden crop, but had to struggle to save what was coming up. Every seed was precious; when the new plants put forth their pale green shoots, she nurtured and watered them. For every stalk of corn, she could count the buckets of water, the chops of the hoe; and as they grew she had to fight cutworms, blight, locusts, grasshoppers, deer, rabbits and foxes. They all came to eat her garden, steal her corn or raid her henhouse.

One blistering hot morning, Reanna was weeding the garden when she looked up to see a freight wagon circling up into the clearing. It had come to deliver a box from her folks in Virginia. Inside there was a note from her mother.

Dear Reanna,
Here are some things your Papa and I hope you will find useful. Cousin Lucy has been here for a visit. The pair of mauve kid gloves are from her. She says they don't match her new traveling costume. Now, Reanna, it really hurts me to think of you so far from home and in need of castoffs, but I'm sure Cousin Lucy meant to be kind, and as I have always told you, a lady is known by the quality of her gloves.

Love,
Your Mama

Reanna unpacked the contents of the box, with Cima and Snow looking on excitedly. There were six hemstitched linen sheets, six luxurious warm blankets, a dozen huck towels and a beautiful batavia-worked tablecloth with napkins to match.

Reanna was truly grateful for the sheets, blankets and towels. As for the tablecloth, they had not sat down to a properly set table since they had moved to the cabin. Perhaps at Christmas. Enclosed was a neatly wrapped box in which Thomas had sent her a felt pen wiper he had made and Patrick had sent a painted cardboard hair receiver. Her father's special gift was a little ivory fretwork fan that had been his mother's. Reanna let Snow use it and was rewarded by a whole day of passably good behavior. That evening, after the others had gone to bed, Reanna wrote to her folks.

Dear Mama and Papa,
The box arrived today. Thank you for the sheets, towels and blankets. They are much appreciated, and what a beautiful table-cloth.

When you lose everything all at once as we did, the funny thing is you sometimes forget it's all gone until you reach for something you need and find it's not there.

We're all doing fine, considering the weather. It's been very dry. We have a big garden and everyone pitches in to help.

The men can't get home often. They need to keep the cattle grazing from pasture to pasture so as not to eat the grass down too short. But the cabin is so small that we'd be mighty cramped if they were here. Cima is my rock. She makes my day-to-day life possible. I couldn't do without her.

A special thank-you to Patrick and Thomas for the pen wiper and hair receiver. So thoughtful.

I have written Cousin Lucy about the gloves. Yes, Mama, I re-member your always saying that a lady is known by the quality of her gloves.

Dear Papa, I will treasure the fan.

Love,
Reanna

I think every day about you all in cool, green Virginia. Surely the heat here will break soon.

But as the days went on, the dry wind blew unremittingly, like a demon that wouldn't leave them until it had possessed their souls. It blew without stopping, night and day; it blew until she felt her mind go blank. She began to feel she was in a constant stupor, waking or sleeping.

She had no choice. She stayed at it when her back ached, her hands were red and blistered, the blisters themselves broken and rubbed raw. She stayed when the perspiration ran in rivulets down her back and between her breasts. She stayed when she loathed the way she smelled of sweat and of the sulphur she had put in her shoes to discourage the chiggers and ticks from eating her, as the other pests ate the green stalks and leaves. She stayed when she was thirsty and bone-weary.

She wouldn't allow herself to sit in the shade, even for a brief rest, for when she did her mind ran on ahead; there was always more and more to do. The tasks were greater than her strength. There was more to do than there were hours in the day. Her face was burned despite her hat; her body was worn thin. She felt she was wandering aimlessly in an endless desert with a hoe in her hands and the wind ceaselessly blowing in her vacant mind.

Cima became more and more concerned; she watched Reanna hoe the same row of corn twice, unaware of what she was doing or where she was. If she kept on like this, the girl would drop in her tracks, and that wouldn't help any of them. "You're so tired, you don't know what you're doing. You come in and rest now. You hear me?"

"I can't rest. There's too much to do."

"If you don't sit down, you're going to fall down." Reanna stared back at Cima, her eyes vacant. "I tell you what you're to do." Cima spoke gently, in the voice she'd used when she talked to her Letty. "You come on in and get you some clean clothes and that cake of store soap and lavender water. Then you go down to the creek and get in it. Wash your hair. I never thought to see you like this, your hair all a-tangle and your skin burned up like a peach pit. You don't look one bit like the girl that came out here."

"I can't. There's too much I must do," Reanna said tonelessly, but the temptation of cool water, the prospect of being clean, of smelling of lavender and not sulphur was a powerful lure. She longed to free herself of insect welts. She hated the ticks more than any other tribulation of this life; she loathed them boring into her, sucking at her blood. She was more afraid of ticks than of snakes.

Even so, she wasn't sure she had the energy to get herself down to the creek. It seemed almost a waste of time and energy to go and get clean; she would only have to come back again and pick up her hoe and start all over again at the other end of the row.

"Listen," Cima said, "before you came we managed without you, and we'll manage to get along without you now for a little while. Take a day or two, get away, go see Father Soule at the mission or visit Frampton. They'd be glad to have you."

"I can't leave. There's too much to do." Reanna spoke the words, but there wasn't much conviction behind them.

"You've done the work of ten women," Cima said. "You deserve time to yourself." She couldn't have said anything more surely calculated to appeal to Reanna than the thought of time alone to herself. And then, as if to put a cap on the argument, Cima said, "There'll be plenty for you to do when you come back, if that's what's worrying you. Even if *you* don't want to go, you ought to take Molly May out for a run, or she'll forget she's a saddle horse."

Reanna thought of the peaceful atmosphere of the mission, the laughter and pleasant civility at Frampton's; she longed so for touches of grace, for easy, cheerful conversation—and lodged deepest in the bottom of her heart was the thought that she might catch sight of Pride. She'd missed him more than she would have believed it possible to miss another human being; he was always there. She'd built a secret shrine in her heart's core where she could worship him. As long as she did not speak of her feelings for him, she still believed herself safe from any harm.

Gratefully she obeyed Cima. She took her clothes to the creek, looked for the deepest fishing hole at the bend and sank into the cool water. She came out of it feeling as though she'd been baptized into another woman, one almost like her old self.

She knew she wasn't a girl anymore. She'd lived through violence and sudden death and bitter privation, and had come out of the experience alive. Yet she knew she was still empty, incomplete. Now she found she had a real woman's needs and hunger. She dried her hair and soothed her skin with oil. She smelt clean and of lavender. As she drew the clean, crisp clothes over her head, she found they were too large for her; she'd lost weight in the furnace of the sun. She left the old clothes in a bundle by the steps and went to the lean-to to saddle up Molly May. The little mare whinnied with pleasure and anticipation. It had been a long time since the two of them had run free in the wind.

As Cima and Snow watched Reanna ride off toward the west range, Snow narrowed her eyes. A look of envy came over her face.

"Where's Reanna going?"

"Visiting," was Cima's curt reply; it could cover several days and any number of situations.

"Why didn't she take me?" Snow demanded.

"She don't need you tagging along." Reanna had not ridden toward town; wherever she was going, it wasn't to visit with Amoretta and Doc. Well, what Reanna did was her business.

"She don't need us and we don't need her," Cima concluded. "What do you say we make us some taffy. It's been a long time since we had a good taffy pull."

"It's too hot!" Snow began to sniffle. "I want a lemonade, that's what I want." Cima felt full of pity for the child. Nothing ever satisfied Snow; she wondered if anything ever would.

"What you want and what you git are two different things, child. You won't never be happy if you don't take pleasure in what you hold in your hand. Don't you know that?" Even as she said it, Cima knew she was wasting her time; Snow was a born discontent.

As she headed westward, off the Ridge, Reanna realized for the first time that she'd never considered any destination but the presence of Pride. He could be anywhere under the sky on that big range, but she would trust to luck to find him. Her very being was drawn along by a force greater than her will.

All along the way, her mind was alive with poignant memories of the days they'd spent together before Andrew had come back. Here they'd ridden together, here they'd stopped and he'd said words to her that she remembered as if they'd been engraved in stone. It was there she'd first felt his hand over hers, and there he had held her as he lifted her down from her horse. In that place they'd shared a cup of water, and on that little rise of grass, beneath that tree, she'd sat watching him as he'd carved a cottonwood flute he gave her.

As she rode farther and farther to the west, fear seized her, a fear greater than any she'd ever known, even in the heart of the cyclone. She was in a panic that she might not find him. He might be with the other hands, or gone to town for supplies. No. He'd be rounding up strays, or checking grazing land ahead of the herd. He'd be by himself—she knew it in every heartbeat. She felt all hollow as she rode on, putting spurs to Molly May as if her life depended on finding this one man.

Reanna had been riding an hour, perhaps more, when she saw a figure lost in the gray-green distance before her. The solitary rider retreated, then vanished; perhaps he'd been something she'd imagined out of her terrible longing. Still prayerful, she galloped after, following this will-o'-the-wisp. At the top of a small rise, she again caught sight of horse and rider, just as they disappeared into a ravine.

She rode on, obsessed with finding him, but with no clear idea of what she would say to him if she did. None of that mattered as she pushed on at a hard gallop. She felt her heart beating as fast as the horse's hooves. It was the ravine where he came when he wanted to be alone. It must be Pride, it had to be, and then she saw, with a relief so deep she could have drowned in it, that it was Pride. He was riding Gray Cloud toward a cow, a calf slung over his saddle; the calf was bawling for its mother.

She reined in and walked her horse then, as if she had all the time in the world and the very stars in the universe would wait for her. She knew he'd heard her coming, but he didn't look up from the calf he had set down by its mother until she reined up beside him. Then he turned, bewilderment in his eyes. He held up his hand to shield them, as if she were too bright, like some sudden, sharp burst of sunlight.

"You are come," he said, the traditional Chickasaw greeting, which might mean everything or nothing.

"I am come," she said, and she held out her hand to him to help her down. She slid into his arms, knowing that once she was there, he wouldn't let her go. He held her in his strong embrace as sure as if it were the most natural thing in the world for him and it was every day she came to him. Everything he did was right and easy. It seemed as if time had reversed itself and then stopped at the moment when he had held her in his arms after saving her from Jasper Starrett's boys. It was then they'd both known that they could not deny what they felt for each other. But she had drawn away, as if it would erase what she'd felt for him and seen in his eyes. She thought to feel as she did, for any man other than Andrew, was wrong; but now Andrew had forfeited her love, and she had come to Pride of her own free will. Nothing was more right than for her to be here with him; it was where she belonged.

"Reanna," he murmured, like an incantation.

He took her hand then and turned it palm up, peering at the blisters and calluses. She was so drawn, so tired and thin. She looked whipped, near the end of her endurance. He traced her cheek and touched her lips. His hand lingered on the curve of her throat before it fell to her breast and lay there covering it, caressing it. His look, his hands sparked into flame the passions that had been buried for so long; she seemed made of fire.

She'd never been cold by nature. She'd been willing to make a loving marriage with Andrew, but he'd turned her away, and now she realized that she'd never truly loved him. What might have been, he'd killed with his initial selfishness, and then his indifference and jealousy. Pride's kindness and tenderness, his companionship and affection had carried her into passion. This was the first day of a love that would last as long as she lived.

Andrew had accused her of being a romantic, as if that were a crime, or some fault that must be rooted out of her nature. But she *was* a romantic; because of it, she followed Pride to the line house as if he were taking her to cool water.

Inside the cabin, he shut the door behind them and they stood in the cool half-light. She felt herself trembling, her legs so weak that they were barely able to support her. She was not afraid of Pride, only of herself.

She felt him holding her to keep her from falling. She heard him whispering words of comfort to soothe her fears; and then, in a rite older than any other, they began the undoing of clothes, the lying together free of constraint. Man and woman, they lay naked before heaven, twining themselves into one flesh and one heart and one mind.

Their lovemaking was green with adventure; she plunged through depths she'd never dreamed of, soared in bands of iridescent light, drenched in sensation; she heard a moan, then a cry of pure felicity wrenched from the very core of her—a sound over which she had no control. When at last they lay still, she couldn't believe that such a sense of joy and peace was possible, or that it wouldn't last forever. This was a gift from heaven. It couldn't perish or be destroyed. She had no words for what had happened. It was not that they'd become lovers—she had loved him long, long before this moment. They were, simply, a part of each other, two sides of one coin; without him she would be bereft. They'd joined together and nothing would ever part them. There was no prison, no force, no might on earth that could take from them what they had. They lay in the deep silence of that knowledge, listening to the singing of the cicada. It had gone from day to night, and they hadn't noticed the passage of the sun. It was Pride who broke the spell.

"We'll go away," he said. She didn't answer. Pride took her hand

and held it tight, as if he meant to weld her to him in some kind of unbreakable pledge. "Andrew must let you go. He doesn't love you as I do."

"I don't think he loves me at all."

It was not the answer Pride had expected. She'd come to him as a dream comes in the night or a spirit in the woods. Once she was lying there in his arms, he couldn't think of letting her go, no matter what the obstacles. They would weather any storm. She was his, not Andrew's. "You can't stay with him," he pressed. "You belong to me, not to him. You know that." There was a silence deeper than before, and Reanna drew away from him.

"I don't belong to either of you. I belong to myself." She hadn't known how she felt until then. She loved Pride and she didn't love Andrew, but she couldn't think now of belonging to anyone. She'd found a freedom here in this soaring moment of rapture, a belief in herself. She'd felt, even as a girl, that she wouldn't be her mother's property; even now, when she'd given herself to Pride so freely, she retained her independent right to make each gift a separate thing. She wasn't willing to be a lifetime grant, not even to the man she'd married.

"Andrew thinks I belong to him. He would never let me go, although a part of him would like to be rid of me, as he's told me often enough. He didn't want to marry me, but now that I'm his wife, he thinks of me as his possession, like his gun or his cattle. But I'm not a possession. I'm not some object that has his name, his brand on it."

"The world is a big place. We'll go far away."

"He'll come after us. We'd always be looking over our shoulders. Besides, I can't go, not because of Andrew but because it's my decision."

"I don't understand." Pride sat up. He'd been sure of her and now he was lost, with no idea of why Reanna would refuse to go with him. "Are you afraid of him?"

"No, I'm not afraid of Andrew," Reanna said. It was almost true. "I'm afraid, though, of what would happen to you if you left here. This place is yours much more than Andrew's. You're rooted here, like the grass."

"There's grass other places in the world." He spoke with quick bravery, but she knew what it would cost him.

"You're tied to this land," she said. "It's yours. You can't leave it, you belong here. And I belong by marriage to Andrew."

Pride looked at her in disbelief, hurt and bewildered. "Then why did you come? Why did you hold out hope to me, only to take it back? I can't stay here and watch you live with him. Not when he treats you as he does."

"I can't go away with you," she said, like a final promise.

"I won't share you with him!" Pride felt sick with the thought of losing her. "I can't let you go back to him."

"I have to go back."

"Why?" he asked in anguish.

"I tricked Andrew into marrying me."

"I don't believe you. I know you—you couldn't be anything but honest."

She sat up too, pulling the bedclothes about her, and shrugged in regret. "I always used to think so. But I tricked Andrew into marrying me because I wanted to come west. He didn't want to marry me, God knows; he said as much. But I forced him into the marriage, and I can't walk away now just because it suits me. I can't escape my responsibility to him or to Miss Jane."

"What has Miss Jane got to do with it?"

"When she was dying, I promised her I'd keep Lochleven together and see that you and Andrew ran the place as equal partners. I won't break my word to her. I won't let you leave—or see Andrew go—because of me."

"And what do you expect?" Pride was angry now, his hurt breaking out in a flash of fire. "That I'll share you with him like a pasture?"

"You know I don't mean that. I love you and I'll always love you."

"But you're going back to him."

"Yes."

"And you expect me to let you go and say nothing."

"Yes."

"Why did you come to me today, if you meant to go back to him?" She didn't answer. "Why?" He was shaking her now, as if he could force another, better answer from her.

"I came today because I had to. I didn't plan this. I didn't start out to come here. I won't tell you that I regret it or that I'm sorry I came. This day and every day we've spent together is more precious to me than the rest of my life could ever be." She looked up at him fearlessly. "I'll treasure this day; it's changed my life. I won't lie and say it shouldn't have happened, or that I think it's a sin for which I'll burn in hell. But I won't do something which will make you or me regret what we've done and what we've been to each other."

"Not what we have been," he pleaded, "what we *are*."

"I won't cost you your birthright," she said. "If I went away with you and took you from here, you would regret it always."

"Let me be the judge of that."

"I will not break my promise to Miss Jane."

"What do you expect me to do, just let you walk away from me? Watch you and Andrew live out your days as if there had been nothing between us?"

"Yes." She reached out and held him. "We have had this time together. We have loved each other utterly, without reserve, and that is more than some people have in a lifetime. Don't spoil it or destroy it. Let's be grateful for this and not ask for more."

He shook his head. "I want you and I want you forever."

She drew away then and began dressing.

"It's no good running away," he said doggedly, watching her. "I won't change my mind. I'll stay until the cattle are sent to market; I promised Miss Jane I'd do that. And then I'll come for you."

"I won't go with you, then or ever."

"I'll come to you and ask you. You can't stop me. Think what it would be like here, the rest of your life and mine—with only this one day to remember."

"Then I'll stay today and tomorrow," she said, "and perhaps even the day after that."

"I want you to stay, but even if it were to be three days and not one, it's not enough to last your whole life or mine. I want you always," and he did want her always and forever.

Yet, when next day she said she must go, he didn't try to stop her. He helped her to mount, but before he let loose the reins he said,

"I'll come for you when the cattle have gone to market."

"I will not go," she said. "I promise you."

"I'll come," he repeated, his face drawn with grief, and she rode away thinking that she would never have anything so hard to do again as long as she lived.

BACK at Lochleven she didn't say where she had been, and Cima didn't ask. In a week it seemed those precious days had only been a dream, a chimera which had vanished in the harsh light of the sun. If she'd had a struggle before, now it was a Herculean task just to get through each day. The sun beat down, the wind blanched and dehydrated and seared them, turned them all short-tempered and crazed. It took an agonizing effort just to hold what they had. A blight shriveled the beans, foxes killed several hens, a cloud of locusts ate half the crop before they could drive them off with flails. The cow went dry, and the well was poisoned by some underground flow they couldn't trace or identify; each bucket of water had to come now from the dwindling creek. And still the wind blew, the sun beat down on their heads, day after cloudless day.

Reanna was determined to see this nightmare through, to endure. She'd forced Andrew to bring her here; she'd given her word to Miss Jane. She wouldn't escape the consequences of her own actions, but in her dreams, both waking and sleeping, she longed to run away and find Pride. She knew that, as he had said, he'd come for her when the cattle had been shipped to market. She made a fantasy play in her mind of saying yes to him, of running away, her hand in his. There must be a place where they could begin again with no thought of the past. But even as she dreamed, she knew it was not so.

In the late afternoon of the sixth week since their meeting, dark clouds came out of the north and met the south wind. The skies opened and hail fell, crushing the green plants, and just as swiftly disappeared. The sky turned empty blue again. The sun's unrelenting eye began to warm, to bake and then to scorch. The wind fanned out from the south like a blast from hell. By the end of June, the drought was the only fact of life; the sun in the empty, blind, blue sky searched out every growing thing and shriveled it down to dusty, withered death.

Through it all, Snow never stopped complaining; the girls fretted and whined. Cima worked doggedly, struggling with Reanna to save what little was left to them.

As they went up and down the rows pouring the treasured creek water, dipper by dipper, on each plant, only to see it sucked into the parched earth before their eyes, Reanna felt a sudden nausea and a sense that she was about to faint. Crossly, she shook it off; she had promised Andrew she would never faint again. Yet she had no conscious control over this weakness. She sat down between the corn rows, her heart pounding, dazed by a feeling she had never experienced before.

She tried to search out half a dozen causes, but even as she rummaged about in her mind, she knew as sure as that sun was overhead that she was going to have a baby. It had been six weeks since she'd come back from her stolen time with Pride, and she had missed her period. She had put it down to too much hard work and the shock of the storm, but all the while she'd had the suspicion that she was pregnant. Andrew hadn't touched her when he'd come back from Texas, or since. She sat there hidden from Cima and the girls, facing up to certain truths that would soon be self-evident.

When she did begin to show, Andrew would know the child wasn't his. All her fine, high-flown resolutions about never seeing Pride as a lover again, about keeping the place together, collapsed, and she watched them vanish like the water swallowed by the famished earth.

She was going to have a baby. When Andrew discovered it, he would not only guess whose child it was that she carried, he would take a revenge too terrible to think about. Andrew adhered to a code of honor the opposite of Pride's. For Andrew, it would be an eye for an eye.

She had meant to save Lochleven for Pride, and now she'd cost him everything. Andrew might well kill them both and feel within his rights. She didn't half care what he did to her, but she must think of what was best for Pride, and for the baby. It seemed to her like a dream that one day the seed she carried within her would be a child. This hard-earned land would be her child's inheritance only if Andrew believed the baby was his, and gave it his name. It was one thing for Miss Jane to say that name and place came through the mother; it was not the way of the white world. Soon all this western country would be more white than Indian. Whites wouldn't be as easy and forgiving as the Indians about a nameless child; there would always be a shadow of dishonor over hers. She herself could give it nothing but bitter herbs.

If today she followed her heart and went to Pride and told him the child was his, he would insist that she go away with him. She would have cost him his place and the land that he loved and that was his birthright. Worst of all, she would have broken her word to Miss Jane. She had enough on her conscience without that.

She lived the next days in torment, her mind rubbed raw with the wind and the dust that blew into everything. It was in her clothes, in the food; it gritted in her teeth, worked its way under her nails and in the roots of her hair; in her bed at night there was a film of red dust, like dried blood. Her nerves quivering, she had to clench her hands to keep from screaming at Snow, who never stopped whining and crying, accusing her of being cruel, of keeping her beloved father away from her.

As she worked in the fields, she felt her spirit become tempered by the furnace of the wind. Her will turned hard as steel, her heart as unrelenting as the stones on the parched ground. She was fierce in her determination not to let Pride or his child suffer for what she had done.

The night Andrew had returned from Texas, she had sworn never to give herself to him again; but now she knew she must send for him. The only way she knew to save them all was a way as old as Eve; she must get Andrew here and into her bed. She must send for him. He'd said he would never touch her again. What if she sent for him and he wouldn't come? She was sure he wouldn't come if he thought it was for her alone. She must give him some good reason to leave the herd.

The water from the creek was bad; no matter how they boiled it, it still had given them all fever. Snow was afflicted worst of all; for two days she had lain on her shuck pallet, complaining about the heat, and her belly and the flies.

Andrew would come in for Snow, if he'd come in for anyone.

"Ride out to the herd, and tell Mr. MacClaren to come in as soon as he can," Reanna said to Annoyi.

"Come here?" the girl asked blankly.

"Yes—where did you think? Tell him Snow is ill and needs him."

Snow looked up at Reanna, that mischievous glint in her eyes. "When my Papa comes, I'll tell him how you treated me! How you made me work in the fields."

"When he comes, you can tell him anything you like." She looked up to find Cima watching her intently.

"He ain't going to do that child no good."

"Probably not."

"He'll only be madder than a yellow jacket."

Reanna said, "It's time he came home," and went out on the breezeway. She didn't know what Cima suspected and she didn't care. It was Andrew, not Cima, she must put on a show for.

Even using Snow as bait, she couldn't be sure Andrew would come in. If she was having a bad time here, he must be having a worse one. The grass was going as dry as the creek. It was eaten down to the nub; to get a second growth, the grass had taken every drop of moisture from the topsoil.

She knew that despite his braggadocio Andrew was wild with fear that the grass might not last and the cattle would starve and die, but she could do nothing for her baby or for Pride now but wait.

She was unable to think what she would do if he refused to come; the thought was so terrible, she felt paralyzed by it. She had always been impatient. Now she had learned to wait, to bide her time, and if the conditions of her life had made her strong and hard, the waiting had made her determined to do what she thought necessary, without wavering.

In the morning she stood on the porch looking out toward the range, waiting. She stood there again in the evening and then, late on the third day, just as she'd nearly given up hope, she saw him far in the distance, coming up from the east. He sat his horse slouched, hunkered down in the saddle as if he wished to make himself smaller to avoid the wind. Snow, who'd been up and chattering with impatience ever since Annoyi had ridden off, broke away from Cima with a happy cry. Reanna caught her, drew her back and said, "No. You wait, now."

"But *why?*" The girl struggled ineffectually in her arms. "I want to meet Papa. I always go to meet him."

"No," Reanna repeated, holding her firmly. "Let him come in. You need to save your strength." Cima was still watching her with that wary, hooded glance.

Andrew rode slowly up to the cabin. Reanna could see how weary he was from the way he dismounted and passed the reins over the hitching post. As he came into the breezeway, Snow twisted out of Reanna's grasp and ran to him, her arms out.

"Oh, Papa—you're home, you're home!"

"Snow, honey."

"She wouldn't let me run to meet you," the child added, with a furtive glance at Reanna.

He swung her up on his shoulder and looked at Reanna. His face was gaunt and tanned to leather, his aquamarine eyes glittered feverishly. Dust lay on him in a foul red film; his bandana had faded to a pale pink, his shirt was worn through at the elbows.

"Now what's this all about?" he demanded.

"It's Snow—" Reanna began.

"Annoyi said she was sick. She doesn't look very sick to me."

"She *has* been," Reanna said.

He still hadn't taken his eyes from her. "Is that right?" he said with a trace of his old, mocking skepticism.

"Course it is," Cima broke in crossly. "You think we'd make up something like that? *Look* at the child—she's still as gray as pork fat. You been three days getting here."

"We've all been sick," Reanna said quietly. She didn't dare look at Cima. "It's the well water. How are you getting on out there with the herd?"

Andrew bent over and set Snow down. Reanna could feel his exhaustion in the way he straightened again and arched his back.

"We eat dirt and pray for rain," he said flatly.

Reanna hadn't realized how she would feel at the sight of him. She was filled with an almost physical revulsion. She wished them both dead, beyond all the pain and anger that was between them; but at the same time she was filled with a terrible, unshakable determination to save this baby, its good name and the land that one day would belong to it. "Wash up and come in," she said brightly. "Supper's ready."

She'd cooked the things she remembered he liked best, pork chops with pan gravy, biscuits and summer beans and fried okra, even a dried apple pie—the best they had to offer. They'd done without frills for months. Cima's eyes had rolled up in amazement when Reanna had started cooking.

He ate hunkered down over his food, as he had sat his horse. Fatigue grayed his features.

"Mighty good feed," he said to Cima. "I haven't eaten food like that in a month of Sundays. You lose all track of time out there."

"She cooked the supper," Cima said, pointing at Reanna. "Thank her, not me."

Andrew looked at Reanna; the trace of a smile, grim, without warmth or humor, teased his mouth. "Well, I see you haven't starved, anyway."

She wanted to strike out at his face with her nails. Instead, she said pleasantly, "I'm glad you enjoyed it, Andrew. I've heated water for you to take a bath."

He scowled at her. "I have to get back. There's too much to do for me to loll around in a tub of water." But she knew a bath was something he hungered for more than food.

"I wish you'd stay," she said softly.

He shook his head and rose.

"How long has it been," Cima demanded suddenly, "since you've had a warm bath, slept in a comfortable bed?" Again he shook his head.

"Oh, please stay, Daddy," Snow cried.

"Can't stay, honey."

"Who says?" Cima pursued. "You boss of the outfit or not? If you're boss, you can come and go to suit yourself. You work harder than the others, and you deserve it. You owe it to yourself."

He stared at the black woman in dull amazement.

"Please stay," Snow begged him. "Papa, please! I never see you any more."

"Well . . ." He shifted his feet; one boot was cracked across the toe. "I don't suppose it makes much difference if I stay the night and ride out in the morning."

"Now you showing some sense for a change," Cima said.

"I'll get the tub filled for you." Reanna went to the door. "It's in the room across the way." She avoided the word *bedroom*. She felt acutely nervous, her whole body tense and on edge.

There was a copper cauldron boiling in the yard. She helped the girls carry it inside and pour the steaming water into the tub she'd placed behind a screen so Andrew could have his privacy. From across the way, she could hear Snow's voice unrolling a long litany of her grievances.

"She made me work in the fields like a common hand! She makes me do chores every day; I haven't had a new dress or ribbons for my hair in a long, long time. I thought when you came, you'd bring me a present. You've *never* come home without bringing me a present before."

"I haven't been any place where they had presents for little girls," Andrew said. His voice was hoarse. "But next time I'll bring you a present, princess."

Reanna walked quietly back across the breezeway.

"You promise?" Snow's arms were around his neck, her face close to his.

"I promise."

Reanna had never seen him look at anyone with that same tenderness. Well, she'd take help from any quarter this evening. Even Snow.

"Will you come again soon?" Snow pressed him for an answer.

"I'll do the best I can." He looked up and saw Reanna watching them.

"The tub's ready, Andrew. If you'll put your dirty clothes over the screen I'll have them washed for you."

He nodded, stretched slowly and painfully. Like a man old before his time, he plodded slowly into the bedroom and shut the plank door behind him. It was a fool's gesture to shut a door in this heat, but it was a way of showing he meant to keep her out.

When she knew he was undressed and in the tub, she went in to get his clothes. As she entered, she heard the splashing in the tub stop. It was as if he had gone on alert, expecting an enemy attack.

"I've just come to get your clothes," she said hastily. "When you're through, there's a nightshirt for you. You'll find some whiskey on the nightstand."

There was a long silence. She didn't know whether he had heard her or not, and then at last he said in a dry, guarded tone, "You seem to have thought of everything."

"It's your home, Andrew. You have the right to be comfortable." She felt as though she would choke on the words.

She oversaw the girls while they washed the clothes and put them out to dry; then she sat on the front steps and began to clean and polish his boots. She listened, wanting him to have ample opportunity to finish his bath and drink from the precious bottle of whiskey Jack Levy had brought them before she went in to him. Behind her, she could hear Cima moving in the kitchen. She didn't turn around. Sitting there in the fading twilight, she bent over, her knees touching her chest. She felt sick, as if something had caught deep in her throat. She had once told Andrew that she never lied. Now she was living a lie, and before the night was over, if she was lucky, she would add yet another and far greater lie to the scarlet list.

She wasn't proud of herself, but this crisis was of her making. She mustn't add cowardice to her catalogue of faults. She had no one but herself to blame. The least harm would come to them all if she took the responsibility for her own actions. It might scorch the very heart out of her, but she must do it.

She waited, listening. She heard Andrew step out of the bath and cross the room, and then there was a silence. She heard the clink of glass on glass. She relaxed a little. That would be a help. At last she heard the bedstead creak. She waited for him to blow out the light, but he didn't, and in a few minutes she heard him snoring.

She tiptoed into the room. The bottle by the bed was emptier by a large glassful; the tumbler was empty. She wondered if that was enough to make him fuzzy-headed. She didn't know much about drinking or the effect it might have on a man. She stood looking at the shadows from the lamplight playing across his face. He was a handsome man with his rugged, clear-drawn features, the fine, sweeping mustache. Most people would consider him more handsome than Pride. She'd been attracted to Andrew because he was different from any man she'd ever met; now she saw he was ruthless and hard, mean in spirit—even to Snow, the one person he seemed to love.

Cima had said he hadn't loved Letty. Perhaps some woman somewhere could change him, turn him loving and kind, but she knew she would never be able to, just as she knew he would never let her go to live with Pride. He didn't want her but she was his, and he valued his property above any human feeling. *Pride*, she thought, with a dart of pure anguish. When she had lain with Pride, the world called it adultery, but lying with Andrew was the real sin, then and now. What she was about to do would break her heart if she thought about it any longer.

She blew out the lamp. A shaft of moonlight fell across Andrew's sleeping form. She prayed for strength to do what she must do. She let her nightgown fall from her shoulders to the floor. She stood there naked, shivering in the warm night. Then she lay beside him.

She listened to his slow, labored breathing. It seemed he drew away from her, but in truth it was she who kept her distance from the animal warmth of his body. She knew she must make the first move. She let her hand touch lightly on his bare shoulder. He hadn't bothered with the nightshirt; he must have been sure she wouldn't come to him. He didn't stir as she let her hand slide down his chest over the flat of his stomach. She was trembling now, her heart quaking like a ceremonial drum. As she touched his groin, she felt herself go weak with loathing, but she willed her hand to go lower.

Her touch roused him, pulsing and swelling hugely. His breathing changed; he stirred. She forced herself to stop trembling by an act of sheer will. In the next moment he'd turned to her and mounted her roughly, his breath hot and foul against her throat. Without warning he thrust deep within her. Even prepared for the customary discomfort of his entry, remembering the other times— her wedding night on the rolling, jolting train, and the infrequent grapplings at Lochleven—she nearly cried out from the sharp pain of his dry, harsh entry. She realized that he simply wanted to hurt her, but she bit her lips and thrust in rhythm, thinking *Pride, Pride* in a whirling, dark pool of misery. But she didn't weep. He gripped her fiercely, driving and grinding his way, a far longer passage than any she could remember, and she decided it must be because he was so tired. Finally he released himself, panting, and lay heavy on her, quite still. After that she heard him groan, as if for the first time he were fully awake and knew where he was.

He drew away from her, then, and said in a voice thick with fatigue and whiskey, "Damn you. Are you pleased with yourself now?"

He fell asleep again, quickly and easily, but she lay awake feeling she was cursed and damned forever. When she was sure he wouldn't wake, she went into the kitchen and washed herself again and again as if she would never be clean. She heard Cima stir and knew she was awake. She sat in the kitchen until daylight, listening to a chuck-will's-widow, and a lonely coyote somewhere, and the wind.

When Andrew came in, he ate quickly. He said nothing and didn't look at her; when the others came to the table, he barely acknowledged them.

As he rose to go, Reanna asked, "When will you be back?"

"I don't know," he muttered.

"Will you be home for Thanksgiving, Papa?" Snow asked.

"I can't say."

"For Christmas?"

"I don't know, I tell you!" He'd never spoken so harshly to Snow. Her eyes filled with tears.

"But you *have* to come for Christmas, Papa. It wouldn't be Christmas without you." He relented then and picked Snow up, stroking her hair tenderly.

"Of course," he said to Snow. "I wouldn't want to have Christmastime without my girl."

"When you planning to go to market?" Cima asked. She wasn't looking at Andrew but into the tin coffee cup she held between her hands.

"When I'm good and ready." Andrew glared at her. "Herd's down too fine. All this drought and not enough pasture."

"Do tell," Cima said grimly. "Tell Pride and Taffy they should come in once in a while, get a good feed. We'll keep a place set for them."

Andrew scowled. "I can't spare them. I need all my hands."

There was an uneasy silence in the room. Andrew set Snow down, took his hat and headed for the door. Snow and Reanna went out to see him off.

As Andrew mounted his horse, he looked at Reanna. "Is there anything you want me to tell Pride?" he asked and paused before he added, "Or Taffy?"

She shook her head. "When do you think you'll be back?" she asked. She pressed her hands against her stomach.

"I told you I don't know," he said, "but it shouldn't matter to you. What happened last night won't ever happen again. You understand me?"

She heard herself gasp; the cruelty in his saying this in front of Snow shocked her.

"Do you understand me?" he repeated. "If I come in again, it will only be to see Snow."

She raised her eyes. She knew she looked pale, but she felt a kind of savage exhilaration; he didn't know that when he hurt her like this, it made her own guilt easier to bear.

"Yes, Andrew," she said slowly and distinctly, "I understand you." She understood more than he could imagine. He would never touch her again, but she'd made the child safe. Last night he had done all that she would ever require of him. She didn't wave good-bye as he rode away.

She knew he wouldn't come at Thanksgiving, but he'd come at Christmas because it would please Snow. It was a long time until then, and she had work to do.

It was work that kept her sane. When her day's work was done, she didn't have time to think of what might have been or what the future might be. She did only what she had to, to keep this family and herself alive.

The summer was a cauldron, a crucible in which Reanna managed to endure the fires of July and August before her pregnancy began to show. When Reanna first saw Cima looking at her knowingly, she stared back and waited for Cima to speak, but Cima only shook her head sorrowfully. Cima could count as well as the next one, and she knew when Andrew had paid his last visit.

When the girls took notice, they giggled, but Snow was oblivious to the facts of life. One evening in late August, as they ate supper by the flickering lamplight, Snow said, "Don't give Reanna another helping, she's getting fat." Both Cima and Reanna looked at Snow, waiting for another remark to follow, but there was none.

When harvesting began, Reanna stood, holding the small of her back with her two hands, rubbing, trying to undo the strain of carrying such an unaccustomed weight. She felt fragile, on the edge of collapse. She looked up to see Cima looking at her. Reanna raised her head high, as she had done when she was a girl and wanted to defy her mother, but Cima came toward her. In a soothing, crooning voice like a mother will use to a hurt child, she said, "Don't you punish yourself so, you hear me? You did what you had to. You have to see that baby comes into the world safe. You have to keep going on by *yourself*, the rest of your life."

The words were so unexpected, so near the heart of her worst fears, that Reanna couldn't believe she had heard Cima. She thought it was herself speaking aloud. She didn't know—and this was her worst fear—if she would be strong enough to hold this secret to herself. She didn't know what she would do when Pride came and saw her with child. She wondered if, when she looked into his eyes, she would have the courage to lie and say it wasn't his child. If he believed her, she would be alone then for the rest of her life. The thought of the years stretching ahead of her, empty and lonely, made her break into sobs. She buried her face in her hands and wept as she had never wept before in her life.

Cima put down her hoe and took Reanna in her arms, cradled and rocked her back and forth as if she were a child of her own.

"There, there," she said over and over. "There, pretty, there. I know you'll do what's best for the baby and for both of them. Men." She spat the word out. "What do they ever know? Nothing that you don't tell them."

"Yes," Reanna sobbed, "but what about *me*? It won't be best for me."

"Then tell Pride the baby is his. He loves you, you know that."

Reanna shook her head doggedly. "I promised Miss Jane I'd hold this place together. I promised her Pride and Andrew would run it together. I gave my word. I can't break it."

Cima drew in her breath through her teeth. "When did you promise her that?"

"When she was dying. I can't go back on my word," Reanna repeated.

"No," Cima said sadly, "you'll keep it. Because you're a lady. Miss Jane knew it first time she saw you. But my precious, you taken on an awful burden to carry all your life long."

"I know. I don't know how I'm going to do it, Cima."

"You got me," the black woman said. "I won't ever leave you. No matter what."

The bond that had been made between them the day of Miss Jane's death became even stronger. They were bound together by a secret in a tie that would never be broken.

Together they brought in the harvest—or what the locusts and weather had left of it. What they could gather must last them for the winter ahead. The drought had baked the corn to small, shriveled ears. They salvaged enough to grind into meal and cut some hay for the animals. They dried vegetables and fruit, cured hams, smoked a turkey and salted some beef. They had molasses and sugar and coffee only because Jack Levy brought supplies out to them along with the mail from home. Reanna read and reread the letters and dreamed of a soft Virginia autumn far away.

Andrew didn't come off the range to help them. He didn't come because he didn't want to, and, because *he* didn't come, he wouldn't let Taffy or Pride come in either. To be fair, Andrew hadn't time or supplies to spare. He already had all the trouble he could handle, with the survey teams and the settlers from across the river in Oklahoma Territory coming in, eyeing property they meant to fence and make theirs. They were the land-hungry from every state in the Union, hoping to get in on what looked to be the last homestead land in America.

But the worst trials of all were the weather and the lack of grass. The grass was thinning and drying down, just as Pride had predicted it would. They had to keep the herd continually on the move so that there would be some chance of regrowth. The weather was a torment and a tease. Clouds would appear as if they meant to rain—and then go on by like a coy flirt who promises everything and gives nothing, leaving only anger and frustration behind.

In September, Reanna began to look for autumn as she would have done at home, but the temperature was still at ninety and more. This was an endless summer.

"When will they take the cattle to market?" Reanna asked Cima as they stood scanning the ranges.

"They usually go in October."

"Then they'll be here by Thanksgiving." Reanna was trying to prepare herself to see both Andrew and Pride; she wouldn't be able to hide her condition from them when they came.

"He'll go to market later this year. The weather's holding and there's some grass yet. Andrew's got to get all he can out of that mob of cows."

"But it will soon be winter."

"Not out here. Sometimes we don't get winter till after Christmas. Sometimes the whole winter is mild. You can't count on weather in the Nation."

"That a fact?" Reanna answered tartly, and the two women chuckled.

At Thanksgiving there was a cold snap; a white frost like spun sugar came down in the night. Reanna thought Cima had been wrong, but after a three-day spell of cooler winds, the heat came again. It seemed strange to get ready for Christmas in such weather.

This year they were so pinched that there could be nothing store-bought or grand; they must make their own presents. To keep their presents secret, at night each worked in a separate corner of the kitchen, or in the attic. At least at night it was cool enough for a fire in the kitchen, which raised their spirits a little.

Reanna prepared a Christmas box to send home: two flutes Pride had carved and two terrapin rattles for the boys, a handworked cowhide wallet for her father and a pair of deerskin gloves for her mother, who set such store on a lady's gloves. And knowing she could not put it off any longer, she wrote them about the baby.

Dear Mama and Papa,

I sent off a Christmas box to you all this week. I hope it gets there in good time, but I wanted to add some special good tidings. I'm going to have a baby in March. I haven't told you before, because I didn't want you to fret over me. I am feeling very well and so must the baby be, because it kicks like anything.

I just wanted you to know you'll be grandparents in the new year and Patrick and Thomas will be uncles.

Now, knowing you, you'll want to get on the first train and come out here, but I'm fine, I really am. Doctor Hersey, who will deliver the baby, is an excellent doctor, and Cima is very experienced at taking care of babies. It will be much more convenient for you and for me if you come later on, after the baby is born. Merry Christmas to you all. This will be my first Christmas ever away from home. I won't think of that or I'll puddle up. Just think of me on Christmas day, as I'll be thinking of you.

                              Love,
                              Reanna

Reanna worried mostly about what to give Snow for Christmas; in the end she made her a corn dolly. It was nothing like the fine doll Andrew had brought Snow from Washington, but it had a sweet face and Reanna made it a cradle and some clothes. She wished she could get Snow a new pair of shoes; even her best were too small and wearing thin besides. It was terrible to be poor like this. It put a blight on everything. She had known what it was to pinch and do without, to hold your head high to keep up appearances, but this kind of poverty was a different thing. This ate into you and clung like a tick. It went beyond mend and make do.

Reanna went through every trunk salvaged from the storm and managed to find some flannels. She cut up and hemmed an old blanket for the baby. It made her feel she had done something. Again she thought of how it would be when Pride and Andrew came back. She tried to imagine the scene, but she couldn't.

It was easier to cook, to clean and to make the cabin festive. They baked a Christmas cake and brought in cedar branches and mistletoe to decorate. They cut a tree and decorated it with strings of corn and holly berries. She found some tinsel paper and made a star for the top of the tree and let Snow hang it.

The weather remained a mockery, like her pregnancy. She'd be as big as a side of the old barn by the time the men came. She'd counted with care; if she was right, the baby would come in February. She must be careful not to say anything to give herself away. She must remember that, to the world, this baby was not due until late March. She'd find a way when the time came of making them think the baby had come prematurely. There was no use in borrowing trouble; she had enough trouble as it was to last her a lifetime and then some. She knew for certain that she was doing what was best for everyone.

A letter arrived from home with a big parcel of Christmas presents.

Dear Reanna,

You're having a baby and you didn't tell us at once. Why? I never did understand you, Reanna, and now less than ever. If you'd let me know *earlier*, there is so much advice I could have given you.

You say not to worry about you. Of course I worry about your being confined and my not being there with you. I am sure the doctor you mentioned is a qualified man, but at a time like that, a girl needs her mother.

I don't see how I can come out until after Christmas. The boys need me at the holidays and so does your papa. And, of course, late winter is the worst possible time to travel. I'm just at sixes and sevens about what's best to do.

Now, Reanna, whatever anyone tells you about getting up after the baby arrives, you must stay in bed at least ten days. Labor is the hardest work a woman ever does. How I wish I could bear the pain for you. Afterwards you will need *rest*. It may be hard for you to lie there and be waited on hand and foot, but believe me, it will make all the difference in your regaining your strength. I know the care and feeding of the infant is a mother's first duty, but just at the beginning she should think of herself as well.

I am sending only a few things for the baby's layette. I know you'll be having baby showers, and you must already have dozens of receivers and wrappers and flannel navel bands. I am sending some soakers my sewing circle crocheted for the baby and the christening dress we used for all of you. I feel confident your father and I won't have any more children, so by rights it should go to the first grandchild. If later you want to pass it along to the boys when they have their families, I'm sure it will be appreciated. At the moment, I sometimes think those boys will never grow up. They are making a frightful racket with those flutes and terrapin rattles you sent.

We opened your Christmas presents early. Thank you for the gloves. They're not kid, are they? Some sort of Indian work? I was debating if they would do better for gardening or what? I decided they would do nicely with my winter coat for informal calls. Your father likes his wallet very much.

Do get lots of rest, Reanna. Rest is so important and, if you can, get a really reliable nurse for the baby. I know Cima will be with you, but you need someone just for the baby. Merry Christmas, my dear.

> Love,
> Mama

Both her father and the boys enclosed notes of their own.

Dear Reanna,
I know things are not going well for you. With so many things needed, you must be pressed for cash, a condition with which I am not unacquainted. Just remember, keep your chin up. After a run of bad cards, your luck is bound to change. Here's a gold piece for

luck. I always kept it in my watch fob pocket, but I think you may need it more. You can keep it in your shoe.

About this baby, I am so proud you're making me a grandfather. You know, they say a man is always supposed to want a son, but when you were born I was so pleased that it was a girl and that the girl was you.

Your loving Papa

Oh, and thank you for the beautiful leather wallet. It is excellent work and so very thoughtful of you. I am now going to try to fill it with money.

Dear Reanna,

Patrick and I made some ornaments for your first Christmas tree away from home. We didn't know what to send the baby if it isn't there yet, so we made it a kite. You said there was a lot of wind. Patrick made most of the kite, but I put on the streamers and wound the cord on the spool. I wanted to put the baby's name on the kite, but Patrick says we don't know what it will be. He says it doesn't matter whether it's a boy or a girl. But if I get a choice, I would rather it was a boy, because we could play with it. You have to be so careful of girls or they cry.

Love,
Thomas and Patrick

And Patrick added:

Thank you, Sister, for the flutes and the terrapin rattles. It was good you sent two of everything so Thomas and I wouldn't quarrel over them. I would very much like to see some Indian dancing when we come West for a visit.

Even when the package and the letters had come from home, Christmas and the baby both seemed remote and unreal to Reanna. And then suddenly it was Christmas Eve afternoon, and Pride and Andrew and Taffy came riding up out of the northwest—like the Three Unwise Men, as Cima said sardonically.

They looked fearfully frayed and worn, men and horses alike, as if the wind had scorched away layers of their clothing and finally their hides. Their hats were bent down at front and back, to protect faces and necks from the endless sun. Their chaps were torn, their dusters and shirts in tatters. Dust outlined the deep wrinkles around their eyes, which seemed to be half shut in a perpetual squint.

Reanna felt her heart beating, the echo pounding in her ears.

Beside her, on the porch waiting to greet the men, Snow stood on one side of her, proudly wearing a blue ribbon in her hair. Reanna had found it in one of the trunks, pressed it and given it to her. Cima stood on Reanna's other side, tall and resolute, always on guard.

Andrew was the first to see her condition, as she knew he would be. He started, then straightened and kicked his mount into a gallop, right up to the house. The others might think that he was in a hurry to be with her and home again, but she knew he only meant to confirm what he'd already seen. Reanna was glad Andrew had ridden ahead of Pride and Taffy; they didn't have to see the look that came over his face, a mixture of disbelief, anger and scorn.

She waited, sick with fear, for what he might say or do. If he meant to deny the baby was his and denounce her, this was the time for it. She watched him dismount and throw the reins loosely over the hitching post. She watched as he walked toward her, his cold, aquamarine eyes measuring her to make sure this was no joke, no new fashion in full skirts.

He nodded then, one quick jerk of his head as he accepted the fact. He didn't stop staring at her, even when Snow broke away and ran toward him. Absently he picked her up, but his eyes were still on Reanna. As she waited, Andrew walked slowly up the two stone steps. Snow, oblivious to the whole situation, was chattering on at Andrew.

"I've been looking for you to come, Papa, hanging out the window, waiting." Her face was shining with pure joy. "Have you brought me a surprise?"

"What do you think, sugar?" he answered, but he was still looking at Reanna, sifting the possibilities. He was still undecided how to react to what he'd seen. "People always give surprises at Christmas, don't they? But nobody's fuller of surprises than Reanna."

"Merry Christmas, Andrew," Reanna said softly. She didn't know how to take his remark. Was he making a cruel joke at her expense, or had he accepted the situation? For an instant she felt like running away, but there was no place to go. She had to stand her ground.

"We been waiting on you all," Cima broke in firmly. "Snow's been tallying every day till Christmas." She stressed the last word, as if to remind Andrew of the season.

"Well then," Andrew said with a harsh laugh, "no sense in waiting any longer, is there? Now we're here, Christmas can begin." He brushed past Reanna, carrying Snow into the kitchen. Cima and the girls quickly followed them. Reanna took a deep breath. She'd passed one hazard—if she had; now she must face another.

Taffy had waved a greeting and was leading the horses toward the lean-to. Pride walked up to the steps and stood below, staring up at her.

"You are come," she said gently, in Chickasaw.

He made his reply. His eyes were shining, dark with the most jubilant amazement. Then, as he watched her, his expression faded into consternation, then immense hurt and disbelief. She could have wept forever.

She'd hurt him irreparably, this man she loved, the only man on earth she wanted to make happy. She had wounded him as surely as if she had taken a knife and thrust it in his heart.

"Why didn't you tell me?" He'd figured it out now, or thought he had.

She lifted her head high, as she always did when she meant to defy or deny. "There was no reason to tell you anything. This baby had nothing to do with you." She'd once blamed Andrew for using a knife to sacrifice a steer for the Ponca; she'd even called him a savage.

"No reason?" he whispered. He looked like a man who had lost a huge amount of blood and was in shock. "No reason?"

"This had nothing to do with you, Pride. It's between Andrew and me." She had hurt him to keep the baby safe, and now she must hurt him again to drive him from her life forever. "This baby isn't a Beauvaise, it's a MacClaren."

It was the one sure way to turn him away forever. She felt the ground move beneath her. Uttering the words had made her physically sick. She thought she must recant now, now—to save herself from this fire of hell, this kind of death in life—but she held as silent as Pride, while the gulf widened between them. Soon it would be so deep there would be no way for either of them to cross it to reach the other.

Taffy came round the corner of the house, saw her clearly and started beaming.

"Well, Miss Reanna—well, congratulations, now! Ain't that something. I hope and trust it's a boy."

"It is." She tried to smile. She stood watching Pride walk away toward the well. She was trembling with shame and fear, wanting to run after him, knowing that she wouldn't.

"Come in," she said to Taffy. "You'll be ready for dinner, I expect."

Inside, she moved from the stove to the table, glad to be busy, grateful not to have to make conversation. She served up turkey and beans, potatoes and cornmeal bread, a pumpkin pie after a pan of biscuits. They all ate silently, intent on the feast of food. She had to make herself swallow each mouthful; she couldn't meet Pride's eyes.

When they had done eating and it was time to clear, she heard herself say, as if some perverse part of her spirit had entered the room, "Well, at least we didn't starve, did we?"

There was laughter from Snow and Taffy and the girls; they'd all eaten as if none of them had ever seen food before and might never do so again. Cima grunted in pleasure, and even Andrew smiled his thin, sardonic smile; if he remembered his dire prediction, he gave no sign of it.

They began to open their presents. In the box from Virginia there were presents meant for all of them: a Smithfield ham, a fruitcake soaked in brandy, sweaters and mufflers and, from Thomas and Patrick, the pretty kite for the baby. After Reanna folded away the wrapping paper and wound the ribbon up to save for another time, she finally allowed herself to look at Pride.

He was still silent. His eyes probed hers; it was clear from his expression that he remembered when Andrew had come home last. What Pride couldn't understand, she knew, was why she was trying to deceive Andrew and him. Perhaps he'd never understand that.

In the warmth of the kitchen there was laughter and the singing of carols. Taffy, after downing a tumbler of whiskey, sang "We Three Kings of Orient Are" in his husky tenor, and instructed Rose Dawn in the intricacies of the Virginia Reel. Cima took a drink herself and sang a melancholy song about a woman betrayed by her lover, a riverboat gambler.

This was Christmas; it was the time to be happy and to forget the cares that lay outside the room. Cima had made fudge from some of the zealously hoarded sugar; there were handknit socks, horses and birds carved by Pride, even six oranges Andrew had picked up on a ride to MacClaren City.

Finally the singing and hilarity wound down, the little room returned to silence; then the subject that burdened all their minds couldn't be put off any longer. It was Cima, characteristically, who voiced it. "Well, Christmas has come and gone. When you meaning to drive the cattle to market?"

Andrew took his eyes from Reanna and said curtly, "When I'm ready and not before."

"I realize that, Mister Big Trail Boss. Only when's that going to be?"

Andrew was silent, his pale eyes overbright, always a dangerous sign. But Cima wouldn't be put off. "You should have been gone a month ago," she said.

"The weather is holding fine."

"So far, yes. And the grass, is that holding fine too?"

"Ask Pride." Andrew turned away from Cima. "He's the man who knows the grass. Knows all the answers, I believe."

The silence in the room seemed to quiver like a bowstring. Reanna, tense and unhappy, realized dimly that Cima had another purpose; as long as Andrew was thinking of the cattle, he couldn't be thinking about Reanna and Pride.

"Nobody's ever held cattle this late, Andrew. Not in my lifetime," Cima said.

"There's never been weather like this before," Andrew retorted blandly, staring at her. It was true; there had only been that one cold snap, and then it had been like Indian summer again. The grass might stay green the whole year round.

"It won't last," Cima said implacably.

"It might. And if it does, I can hold the herd till spring and pick up a calf crop. It would mean more money, and we need all the cash we can get."

"And what do you say, Pride? Will the weather hold? Will there be grass in the spring?"

Pride looked into Cima's dark, hooded eyes. "What are you badgering *me* for?" he said querulously. "You know what I think. We'll get a norther—this weather will breed it. And the grass won't hold; the taproots are withering now. You know how I feel about it—and so does he." He glanced hotly at Andrew. "What difference does it make *what* I think? He'll do what he wants, anyway. He always does."

"I don't see why," Cima protested. "I thought this was a family council, we talked it out and then we voted."

Pride laughed once. "That was when Miss Jane was alive," he said bitterly. "And even *then* he lied to her."

"The hell I did," Andrew shot back.

"The hell you didn't! You broke your word to the council, and you know it!"

"Are you calling me a liar?" Andrew said in a soft, ominous voice.

"Now hold on, boys," Taffy broke in. "There's no call to get into a hassle. It's Christmas—"

"You know what I think?" Andrew went on with soft ferocity; the skin around his lips was white. "I think your nose is out of joint. That's what I think."

Pride kicked back his chair and got to his feet. He was sick of the whole rotten business—that monstrous, ungovernable herd, and the drought, and the dying grassland, and the unnaturally hot weather in December, and Andrew's headlong, destructive will. All he wanted was to get out of this room, away from this house. He'd never in his life been without hope. He'd been utterly sure in his heart's core that when this miserable drive was over he would come for Reanna and she'd leave with him. She loved him as he loved her—without fear or reservation—and when he'd seen her with child his heart had leaped. She would leave now; she would have to go away with him.

And then she had said—what she had said.

All through dinner and the rude festivities he had watched her, her eyes like a stranger's. His beloved. It was more than he could stand. He could not stay here another minute without shouting in all their faces that he loved her, he would always love her, come what may; that the child was his, he knew it in his bones; that he didn't care for that matter whether the child *were* his or Andrew's or had been fathered by the devil himself; that he wanted Reanna, he wanted to live with her forever, his whole topsy-turvy life depended utterly on her simply saying *yes*, and taking his hand—

He looked down at Andrew with hot contempt. "Who cares *what* you think," he said. "I'm going back to the herd."

"Well . . ." His brother watched him with mocking surprise. "I'm glad to see you've come to your senses."

"Now wait a minute, you two," Cima said.

"Nothing to wait *for*." Andrew was already on his feet and buckling on his gun belt.

"But it's Christmastime!" Snow began to wail, pulling at his trouser leg. "You can't go off on Christmas!"

"It's all right," Pride said to her somberly, nodding. "Taffy and I will go back; your Daddy will stay home with you."

Andrew was glaring at him, one hand on the child's curly fair head. "You telling me what to do?"

"Yes, for a change. You're needed here at home for a spell. I think that should be obvious to you."

"Now you hold on," Cima said harshly. "There's got to be a decision about this herd, we got to—"

"Then you put a gun in his belly and tell him," Pride shot back with an angry laugh. "It's the only thing that'll work. Come on, Taffy."

"I'm sorry you must go so soon," Reanna said to him formally, but her voice was shaking. "I'll put up a poke for you," she said to Taffy.

"Thank you," Taffy said, "that'll be right nice. It was one fine meal and we're mighty grateful."

Pride stood in the lean-to saddling the horses. He knew she would come to him. She wouldn't, couldn't let him go away without speaking to him; there were too many words left unsaid.

In a few moments she came out of the house carrying a tow sack filled with leftovers. He waited, trying to think of what he could say to her to make her leave here with him. If she didn't come today, his hopes for the future would be smoke. Watching her approach, he had a swift, indescribable rush of joy. Then she was there standing before him, and he saw that in her eyes there was a new and different look, a look as sharp as knives.

"You can't tell me this baby is Andrew's," he said.

"I do." Her look never wavered; she spoke in a clear voice. "That's just what I do tell you."

"I don't believe you."

"You can believe what you like, but the child is Andrew's."

He was nearly sure that she was lying. At last he said, "It doesn't matter whose child it is. I want you to come away with me."

She suddenly looked very tired, as if the strain of the day had worn her down. "I've already told you, I won't do that. I can't tell you more plainly. My place is here."

"You don't love Andrew, you love me."

"I'm staying with Andrew," she flared out at him. "I'm staying because he's a man, and you're a boy to talk of loving."

"You're lying to me," he cried softly, "just the way he does."

She struck her fist against her thigh. "You're a fool to think I'd leave my husband for you! Think what it would mean for a woman like me to be married to an Indian. The days of the Nation are over;

soon this will be a white man's land. I want my children to be white, not Indian."

His head went back, the old terrible rage caught him; then he locked his hands together. "You must want me to go very badly, for you to say such cruel things," he murmured. "Those are not your words. Not one of them came from your heart. If it means that much to you, I'll go. But I'll wait for you. I'll wait for you to come to me. I am yours, for as long as the sun shines, the grass grows and the rivers run."

He took the reins of his horse and Taffy's and walked away from her. She followed, knowing that she'd won. Pride would not claim the child as his. And in the winning, she'd lost everything. If she'd touched him at that moment, she would have gone into his arms for good and forever, no matter how terrible the consequences. She'd never imagined such pure anguish of the heart.

As they came from the lean-to, they met Andrew and Taffy and Cima. Andrew's eyes told her nothing, but she was sure he'd seen her go to meet Pride.

"I see you got Pride fixed up," Andrew said. Again his words could have meant everything or nothing. She did no more than nod. "Maybe he should stay and I go?"

"No," she answered evenly, "there's no need for that." She'd stood her ground with Pride; now she was standing up to Andrew. No matter how he tried to break her, she would stand like a wall of stone.

"You'll want to stay until the baby comes," Pride told him.

"When will that be?"

"I figure March," Reanna answered.

"You can't always tell with the first one," Cima put in quickly.

Taffy said, "We'll manage. If anything comes up we can't handle, one of us'll ride in. Don't worry," he went on earnestly, "we'll be fine without you."

Andrew glanced quickly at Pride. "I'll stay a few days anyhow. I've got some business to attend to."

"WHY didn't you tell me?" Andrew said to her later, as Cima and the girls were feeding the stock. His eyes were as green as glass in winter.

"You were busy," she said coolly. "You're too busy these days to care what happens to us here at Lochleven. You've as good as told me so."

His eyes narrowed. "Or did you want to pay me back, shame me in front of Pride and Taffy? It's embarrassing for a man, not to know his wife is carrying a child."

The idea took her by surprise. "The baby is hardly a secret."

"I would have had time to hear this kind of news," Andrew said, cross and sour. It seemed to Reanna that he was relenting, as if the idea of a child somehow pleased him.

"I knew you couldn't think of anything else until you got the cattle to market. Why *haven't* you taken them to the railhead before now, by the way?"

He looked at her with pity. It seemed she could learn nothing about the business. And then he relented a little. She was, for all she had done here at the place, only a woman. "I won't take the cattle to market while the grass is still holding." He spoke patiently.

"If the grass goes, their weight will drop off and you stand to lose everything. Why not take them now?"

"Since when did you become such an expert on grass and cattle?"

She faced him, her head high. "A child fresh from the city could tell you that much."

This new Reanna took him off guard. She wasn't the person he had watched across that Washington drawing room. She was no longer a girl he could bring to tears with a frown. Well, they said some women got that way, like a bossy cow carrying a calf. "I say the grass will hold," he declared in a hard, stubborn tone. "I'm betting on it."

"I never took you for a gambling man, Andrew. I thought you only bet sure winners."

"I'll win." He made himself grin at her in the insolent, arrogant way he knew would torment her. "Now that I have a family to think of."

"You can't always win," she said, turning away wearily. This had been a long, terrible day and she wanted to see the end of it. She still had the rest of the Christmas season to get through, and a lifetime after that. Yet she couldn't resist one more question. "Why not quit while you're ahead?"

"It's not that easy. The mortgage on those cattle is in my name. I signed the notes for them. I have to take them to market fat to make a profit, or else Colonel Goodwell and the Kansas City Cattle

Company will have a lien on everything I own or ever will own." He glared at her. "It's a fine time you picked to have a baby."

"I didn't pick the time," she said. She was near tears now, but she wouldn't let him see. She turned away from him, and now her voice left no further room for argument. "Don't let it worry you, Andrew. You don't have to worry about the baby any more than you ever worried about me."

That night she wrote to her mother. As she read over the letter, she realized more clearly than ever how little she could tell anyone in Virginia—even her father—of what her life here was really like.

Dear Mama and Papa,

Thank you all for all the splendid Christmas presents and for your dear letters. The christening dress is beautiful. The soakers were especially welcome. Thank your sewing circle for crocheting them. Now again let me say, *please* don't worry about me. I know you want to be with me, Mama, but your place is with Papa and the boys. I will be just fine. Remember, in addition to Cima, I have two girls, Rose Dawn and Annoyi to help with the housework. Tell the boys I'll hang the kite on the ceiling until the baby is old enough to fly it. I wish I could have sent you all more this Christmas, but until the cattle go to market, we have to economize. I hope you had a merry Christmas and will have a happy New Year.
                                                    Love,
                                                    Reanna

THE January weather was oppressive. The terrible heat had gone, but the days and nights were unnaturally warm. Andrew went about in shirt-sleeves. They saw the buds on the trees, the day lilies sprouting up green as if it were May. Andrew pointed out to the range.

"Look, what did I tell you? There'll be January grass. There's nothing better or richer than winter grass." But he didn't seem happy about it; he only looked balked and angry.

At night, when the baby turned and kicked, she lay unable to sleep, listening to Andrew lying in the cot he'd put into their room. She had known he would not want her, and she had no idea of ever letting him touch her again; still, she'd been surprised when he insisted on sleeping alone. His words had been as cold as his eyes when he said, "I don't want to disturb you with the baby."

She always felt there was a veiled threat in everything he said, but she couldn't be sure it wasn't just her conscience bothering her.

It was February, and still the weather held. Each day Andrew woke up in a worse temper and prowled the place, looking out toward the ranges, longing to be there. Then he came inside and raged at them all over trifles. The girls stood with their aprons to their eyes wailing, and Snow sobbed as if he'd broken her heart. Cima lashed back at him like a tiger, and he stormed outside and split wood in a frenzy, the axe going deep into the block like gunshots.

When Rose Dawn got sick, it only made everything worse. The girl was running a high fever, and there were curious little eruptions about her waist and under her arms; she had no appetite at all.

"Think it's hives?" Reanna said.

Cima shook her head worriedly. "This is something else. I never seen nothing like this before."

"It's nothing," Andrew broke in roughly, "just an upset stomach, food poisoning. She'll get over it."

Cima stared at him for a moment, her eyes like bits of obsidian. "You always had a mean streak in you, Andrew. A mean streak a cloth yard wide." She said to Reanna: "I want to take her in to Doc."

Andrew cursed under his breath. "That drunken old fool—what does he know? All right, I'll ride in and get him. What's the problem?"

"The *problem* is it may be catching," Cima told him with ominous softness, "that's what. I don't want to take any chances, with the child on the way. I want to take her in to Doc."

"All right," Andrew shouted, "go on then! Take both girls, Snow too. I'm double-damned if I'm going to go on listening to a bunch of wailing women. Take the buckboard."

Cima glanced at Reanna. "What do you think?"

"It's best," she answered, though she felt a first, faint ripple of dread. "I'll be all right."

Snow was ecstatic. Going into town was a rare treat, even more than her Papa coming home. And Annoyi had been begging to go home for a visit. There was a small, quick exodus. Cima and Reanna got Rose Dawn in the wagon bed, and Snow sat up front with Annoyi. Reanna hated to see Molly May used for anything but a saddle horse, but she couldn't ride her now anyway.

When they'd gone, the place was silent, strangely empty. She wasn't used to being alone with Andrew. She cooked, they ate at the kitchen table, she fed the chickens, he looked after the stock. They might have been any farm couple. They didn't quarrel because they didn't talk. Each day the buds grew fuller, the grass greener, the baby nearer to being born. She was sure he'd come soon. He was as active as an acrobat.

In three days she'd lulled herself into a false sense of security; she couldn't believe that the worst wasn't over and done with. The sun shone; the wind was mild. She was amazed to think what a gentle country this could be in winter and remembered the hard snows at home at this time of the year.

On the morning of the fourth day, she saw Andrew peering up at the sky in a different way.

"What's the matter?" she asked.

"I don't like it."

"I can't see any change," she said, but looking off to the north-west she was conscious of a gray, metallic glint in the sky, the palest of shadows. The wind had fallen away.

"There's weather coming."

She waited for what she knew he would say next.

"I've got to go."

"I didn't think you would leave me in this condition. What if something happened while you were gone?" She hadn't realized till then how much she'd counted on his being there, on his knowing what to do.

"The baby isn't due until March, isn't that right?" She nodded dumbly. "Cima will be back in a day or so. There's nothing to worry about. I have to get out there, Reanna. I can't take a chance on it."

"I see." She felt herself caught out. She couldn't object to anything he said. "Sure," she said, trying to sound self-confident, but there was an edge to her voice. "I'd like some time to myself anyway." It sounded as though she didn't want his company; she hadn't meant it that way.

He looked at her irritably. "Well, make up your mind. If you want me to stay, say so. Do you want me to stay?"

She bit her lip. "It's up to you."

"Reanna, be reasonable. What do you want me to do, sit here and hold your hand?"

She was suddenly tired, too tired to argue with him. She knew he'd go no matter what she said. She only wanted him to go away and leave her alone. "I've learned not to expect anything from you, Andrew. I don't care whether you go or stay."

"Well"—he looked off at the far horizon again—"I've got to go anyway."

She watched him hurry toward the lean-to, whistling up his horse.

* * *

ANDREW rode hard up to the northern line house by the river. Before he'd saddled up and left the Ridge, the sky had steeled over and the wind had freshened out of the north. By the time he was within sight of the line house, the clouds had built into a slate-dark wall beaten hard by the wind. The temperature had dropped more than twenty degrees and now light snow was mixed with rain. He could see the great mass of the herd; they seemed to be drifting with no fixed destination. Inside the cabin, he found Pride and Taffy, with Dub Wilgress and Tiny Bentham, huddled around the stove with tin mugs in their hands. Dub was in his stocking feet; his snakeskin boots sat near the fire. Pride and Taffy were wearing fleece-lined jackets and macintoshes, their hats pushed back on their heads.

Frank Pettis and Dan Penland were playing a cutthroat game of checkers, and Zeb and Zack Easter were arguing with the Chinese cook, Chang, who was spouting back at them in Chinese. On one of the top bunks, Slim Dress was asleep, snoring. He'd had a bad fall the week before and was still on the mend. Paco was alone in the corner, coiling rope.

Andrew could see the worry and fatigue in their faces, but it wasn't the time to be friendly or pretend a cheerfulness he didn't feel. He'd left the move to market late, maybe too late; now he had to drive the herd to market whether he wanted to or not.

He was the boss here and he'd have to light a fire under them. He strode to the stove and poured himself a mug of coffee; he knew it would be bitter and laced with unsettled grounds. "I see you've kept the place nice and warm for me till I got back." His voice lashed out and stung the men, as sharp as the wind outside. Heads snapped around; eyes fixed on him, full of resentment.

"We've just come in," Pride said wearily. He knew what Andrew was up to; he'd seen him attack before, when he wanted to get the men to do an unpleasant job.

"So you left the herd to fend for themselves," Andrew said, "that it?"

"There's snow coming, Andrew," Taffy said, quietly, "best to let them drift."

"No." Andrew's voice raked over them all. "I'm not going to let them drift it out. I'm going to drive them to the railhead and ship them to market."

Taffy stared in disbelief. "You can't drive them twenty miles in this weather."

"That a fact? I want you to get these men saddled up. We'll head off the herd and run them over the east end of the Ridge toward Maitland. We've no time to lose. By the look of them, they've already turned tail to the north wind and started to drift into open range. If they move much farther west, we won't get them together until spring."

"Drifting's best for them, if it comes on a norther." Taffy stood his ground, puzzled by Andrew's order. It was what they had always done with a big herd in a storm. "Looks like a big snow might be in those clouds."

"You listening to me, Taffy?" Andrew said harshly. "I want you to turn them and move them over the east end of the Ridge to the railhead."

"You can't drive that bunch in snow! They're a mixed herd—cows, steers and heifers."

"They were a mixed herd when we drove them up from Texas."

"That was spring and this is winter." Taffy was furious at the order. Andrew had got a hair up his ass again. "It was bad enough then. I never liked a mixed herd. But now it's not only the weather; a lot of them cows is fixing to calf. You try to turn and drive them now, they'll fight you."

Andrew said in a cold, hard voice, "We're going to find them, turn them and take them over the Ridge."

"You'll never get them to the railhead in snow," Taffy came back at him.

"No? We'll see about that."

"If you're damned and determined to drive them," Pride broke in, "then the best place to shelter them is in the ravine. They're closer to that than the Ridge."

"The hell with that." Andrew didn't even look at him. "I mean to get them to the railroad. I mean to go, and right now. I can't take a chance of holing them up in that goddamned ravine of yours. There's no grass there now."

Pride faced him. "After this storm, there won't be any grass anywhere until spring. You should have sold long before this." The room was very quiet now under the rising moan of wind, the patter of sleet on the shake roof. The hired men glanced at one another uneasily. It was the first time Pride had said before the hands that he disagreed with what Andrew was doing. It was no surprise to them that he felt this way, but it was a shock to hear him say it.

To challenge Andrew's authority was to rock the foundation of their small world.

"I am by God going to *drive them over the Ridge to the railhead*," Andrew half shouted. "You can stay here and sit by the fire and suck sugar-titty, but I'm going!" Andrew looked around the circle of men for his support; he found little in the worn, troubled faces to encourage him. "What *are* you—afraid to go out in a little weather? Afraid it might freeze and break off?" He knew he had to whip them up to this night's work. For a moment, watching them, measuring their sullen resentment, he thought he'd gone too far.

"You're asking a lot of the boys," Taffy said quietly. He'd gotten over his anger now and was thinking about snow. "They've been pushed pretty hard all summer and fall, Andrew."

"Those who come will get a bonus. Those who don't can saddle up and ride out."

There was no response to this. Andrew knew most of them owned their saddles but no horse. They rode ranch stock. If they left tonight, they'd have to leave afoot, carrying their saddles and tote. Andrew stared at them defiantly; he had the dismaying sense that he'd played his cards wrong, and yet he couldn't see how. He turned to Taffy and said, "When you've finished talking it over, you'll find me outside," and he went out into the cold. The wind had risen; it was driving hard from the north and the sky had darkened. Night was coming on and it was much colder. He leaned against the palomino's warm belly, fidgeting, wondering what Taffy was saying to the men, and most of all, what the men were saying to Pride. They felt they could always talk to Pride and tell him their troubles; he was always taking their part.

In the line house the men were silent, waiting for Taffy to speak. A log hissed in the potbellied stove and broke and fell.

"OK," Taffy said, "you heard Andrew. You know what he's asking."

Still they said nothing, avoiding his eyes and each other's. Then Slim Dress woke, sat up suddenly, yawned and said, "What's happening? What's goin' on?" The tension broke and the men began to relax.

"Andrew's got his tail in a crack over this herd," Taffy said. "You all know how bad things are. He didn't mean to sound off." He looked quickly at Pride to support him.

Pride looked around the circle of sullen faces. "You're a good bunch, the best. If any of you want to stay back, then say so and I won't think the less of you for it." He had given the men a choice; now it was up to them.

Dub looked up at Pride. "I don't take kindly to Andrew calling hell down on us. I don't want to go out and get my boots froze. I guess Tiny and me both just about had enough."

Tiny cleared his throat. The deep rumble made Dub stop short. "But," Tiny said, "that don't mean we'll let Andrew down. We're in."

That was two men Andrew could count on. Pride turned to Frank Pettis and Dan Penland. "Frank?"

There were two red patches on Frank's baby-smooth cheeks, a sign of his anger and resentment. "Well, me and Dan have a real good game of checkers going." He looked over at Dan and Dan nodded. "On the other hand, I already took all Dan's money, so we might as well both go along to keep you company."

Dan nodded again.

That took care of the old, loyal hands. Pride was not sure of the new men. "What about you, Zack?"

Zack Easter's bushy eyebrows almost met as he frowned. "No need to stay inside, when I can go out in the snow and get paid for it."

Then it was Zeb's turn. He banged on the deal table with his fist. "I'm not staying behind with the Chinee," he declared. "I'm going with Zack."

Chang was already packing up grub into sacks. Pride never knew what Chang understood and what he didn't, but he seemed to know what was going on now right enough. That left Paco. "Paco?" Pride waited.

The Mexican looped up his strand of rope and grinned. "The horses wouldn't be happy without me, so I go."

"Well, that's settled then." Pride nodded at Taffy. "You can go tell Andrew he's got what he wanted. The men are coming."

"And me too." Slim Dress clambered heavily down from his bunk. "I'm coming too, damned if I'm not."

Outside, Andrew waited, stomping his feet in the light dusting of sleet and snow. At last Taffy came out. He stood staring at Andrew as if he were seeing him for the first time.

"Well?" Andrew demanded. He was in no mood for waiting.

"They'll come." Taffy looked at him quizzically. "They've got nowhere better to go. They're a good bunch. They've stayed with you so far."

"Hell, they'll go out in any weather if the money is right."

"They won't come just for the money," Taffy said tightly. "You know that."

"We can't stand around any longer," Andrew said. His feet were already cold in his boots. "I want all the remuda. I want a chuck wagon and a wagonload of hay." The wind whipped his words away.

"You can't get a chuck wagon through snow, let alone a wagonload of hay," Taffy protested. "If it ices up, even oxen can't pull them."

"Then get sled runners on both wagons. Start out with the oxen. I've got to have the hay for the horses, and the men will need something hot if they're going to ride this woolly bugger out. Tell the Chinaman to cook up a bucket of soup, along with the coffee and corn bread. Tell him to put in a barrel of whiskey."

"Whiskey!" Taffy was going at him, incredulous and angry. "We've never had no drinking on the trail, Andrew—"

"We've never had a problem like this. That sky is closing in. I think we're in a blizzard."

Pride came out and stood, the men clustered behind him, shifting uneasily, staring stonily at Andrew.

"You sure you won't think again on what you're doing?" Taffy asked.

"No," Andrew said.

"Well, you're the boss."

"That's right."

"It was your decision to buy the cattle and then to hold them," Pride said. "You knew that grass in January was too good to last. But what happens now affects us all."

"The cattle are mine, and it's *my* decision what to do with them." He made himself grin at his brother. "How about you? You coming, or are you going to sit by the fire and whittle?"

Pride bit at his lips. "I think a big snow is coming. A very big snow."

Andrew said loudly, "We're wasting time standing here talking. I can't afford to lose even one head."

"You're bound to lose some, Andrew."

"You take the drag and I'll take the point. Taffy will ride the line."

"You're going against everything you ever taught me," Pride said into the wind, watching Andrew's face. "The Chickasaw have the

right word for you, Andrew. *Haksi*." It meant crazy, deaf or criminal, depending on the inflection one gave it. At this moment, Andrew sounded like all three.

"If I made the rules, then I can break them." Andrew swung up
into the saddle, beating his free hand against his thigh. "Now, let's
go."

THEY rode after Andrew, nearly blinded by the queer half-light,
into a snow fierce with sleet and from the north a punishing wind.
It was nearly dark when they found the herd. It took every man to
turn them toward the Ridge. The cattle bellowed and bawled their
displeasure; it was herd instinct to turn tail to the wind and drift
until the storm blew itself out. Now these men on horseback turned
them, unraveled them from their comforting safety and strung
them out into a thin line. Andrew gave his commands for the stations they each would ride.

"I'll take the point," he yelled over the wind, waving his lantern.
"Keep up with my pace."

The snow began to fall, thick, white and silent, a shrouded curtain that kept them isolated when they were sixty feet apart. Eating
in shifts, they managed one hot meal from the cook wagon. Andrew
ordered the hay wagon up to the point. It was a place of safety, and
it was also a lure to the lead steer; he took the scent and followed
the bait. Andrew began to move the whitened sea of cattle forward.
All night they struggled. Andrew led them, cursing the wind, the
snow, his bitter predicament, God and especially Reanna. The men
followed, cursing him and everything else. Andrew was their only
compass. He held up the lantern that was their only point of reality.
During the night, the cook rode the line, putting coffee into cans
tied to saddle horns, pressing sandwiches into hands chafed raw
with cold. To add to their troubles, the cows and heifers had begun
to calve. They strayed from the line, trying to find a place to lie up,
and the hands had to keep whipping them back into line again.

At first light, Pride broke from the drag, cantered up to Andrew
and called, "You're moving too far west."

"The hell I am." Andrew glared at him, his mustache caked with
ice. "I know this goddamn range."

"So do I. Better than you, Andrew." And as if to settle the quarrel, the snow lifted, and there was a curious yellowed patch of light,

a clear rift in the sky overhead. They were still in the west; they'd wandered in a lazy half circle, doubling back on themselves. They were heading west again, not east.

"We're almost back where we started from," Pride said calmly.

"Goddamn it, I can see where we are!" The Ridge was still obscured in this whirling white wilderness. "It's all right. We can make up the lost time."

"This storm isn't over," Pride said. "There's a lot more to come."

"And just how do you know that?"

"I just know, that's all. I can feel it. Andrew, take them into the ravine. They'll be safe there. The snow's already piling up. If it starts to drift, they won't make it."

"They'll make it. They *have* to make it. We're going on."

"Why?" Pride demanded. "What will you prove?" His words were lost in the wind. The sky closed in; the snow began to fall once more. This snow fell dense as a winding sheet, enveloping them all.

They went on, knowing it would be a long day. If they did find the west end of the Ridge and work around its high rock wall, it would still be a long, long way to the railroad. As the day began, some of the cows began to drop calves. Every instinct drove them to hide out, to nurse their young away from the herd. Some of the young heifers, frightened by the storm and near exhaustion, aborted. The older cows broke and birthed without trouble, but then they refused to leave their calves in the snow. Andrew rode back from the point, shouting and cursing Taffy.

"Damn you, keep that line moving."

"They won't leave their calves," Taffy shouted back.

"Then kill the calves, throw them up on the hay wagon! It's the only way to keep those cows following the herd."

"*Kill them?*" Taffy repeated, his mind blank with a numbness that had nothing to do with the cold. The only way to keep a new-birthed cow in the herd was to make her follow the scent of her calf. He'd heard of cowmen killing calves, but he'd never been a part of it. He knew Andrew was desperate—if he lost this herd he was bankrupt—but this was a crazy man who cried out his orders as if he thought he was some god of the wind.

"Kill them, I said!" Andrew roared. He drew the Winchester from its sheath and began to fire round after round into helpless little white faces.

Pride heard the shots, curiously muffled in the snow. He rode out from the drag along the line toward the point. The men were hunched down in the saddles, cursing, burrowing deep in their mackintosh collars for warmth, praying for an end to this trail of misery. They'd been in the saddle nearly twenty-four hours. Andrew had used up all the hay; the horses were going to give out soon, perhaps before the men.

Pride rode through the swirling, deepening drifts, nodding the barest greeting to Dub Wilgress and Tiny Bentham. Dub had long stopped worrying about his boots. His mind was on his feet. They felt like two great lumps of ice.

"How long are we going on?" Dub yelled at Pride.

"Ask Andrew."

"If you see Paco," Tiny called over the wind, "tell him we need fresh horses."

"Right." Pride rode on; there was nothing more to say. He passed the hay wagon, now piled high with corpses. Blood dripped onto the snow. One old cow, crazy with grief, butted her head against the wagon, bawling out her lament. The lines of blood in the snow formed crazily laced patterns, red on white.

Another cow, trailing a blue chain of afterbirth, nosed in the slaughter pen, trying to find the calf that was hers. Beyond the wagon a knot of cows followed, too spooked and crazed to have any sense of direction. Their eyes rolled in their heads; their tongues were lolling from their mouths in shock. The snow was beaded white on their white eyelashes. They staggered in their tracks, their heads jerking up and down, frantic to find relief from this endless agony.

Pride spurred Gray Cloud. He knew the horse's heart would burst before he'd let him down, but Pride could feel the animal tiring. He pulled even with Andrew and caught at his bridle.

"You're going too fast, Andrew! The drag can't keep up on the line."

Andrew glared at Pride from under the soaked rim of his hat. "Take your hand off my bridle! If you can't keep up, then go on home. We don't need boys to do a man's work."

"I'm no boy, Andrew, and you know it. Turn them back or let them drift! Even if you get them to the Ridge, there are the bluffs beyond. Let them drift; let them find shelter if you won't give them any."

"I'm going to the Ridge and God damn you to hell!"

There was nothing more to be said. They went on through the last of the day. Toward dark, trying to move the herd in *any* direction was almost impossible. They'd surge forward a few hundred feet and then draw back again; each time they swung back, they changed direction. When the wind shifted, it was worst of all. Each hour the snow grew deeper, blowing into long swales and ridges. The wind howled like a horde of demons. The cows bawled pitifully for their dead. A rogue steer took the point and gave Andrew a contest over who would be leader.

The men crouched, swaying over their saddle horns, roped on so they could sleep without falling off. They'd been on the trail a night and a day. There was no way to relieve themselves without the risk of lagging behind and getting lost in this white wilderness. Some had lost control, and the steam rose from their chaps, their thighs were raw. Since noon they'd had nothing to eat or drink but a tin mug of whiskey.

Their faces were swathed in handkerchiefs pulled tight over their noses and mouths. Their collars were drawn up to meet their hat brims, leaving only a thin, narrow slit for their eyes. Their hands, even in lined gloves, had frozen around the reins. With the onset of the second night, they'd lighted lanterns up and down the line to keep from getting lost forever in this universe of aching cold and stinging, whirling snow.

Dub tried to stick close to Tiny, but he kept losing sight of him. From somewhere ahead he could hear Tiny singing. He could catch only a fragment of the song, but he knew the words. Tiny had sung them often enough—a verse from the "Kansas Line."

> The cowboy's life is a dreadful life,
> He's driven through heat and cold;
> I'm almost froze with the water on my clothes,
> A-ridin' through heat and cold.

Frank Pettis' face, crusted with snow, made him look like an old man. He hunched over, shivering, wishing he'd never left home and thinking of his mother. Zeb and Zack Easter cursed the cold and Paco for not bringing in new horses, as their own stumbled in the drifts. Nobody had seen Slim Dress or Dan Penland. They had evaporated into the white night and the idea of a chuck wagon or hot food was long forgotten.

Back on drag, Pride felt the land rise beneath him. He could see nothing, he only knew as sure as he drew breath that Andrew had missed the east passage, that they were going up the slope onto the west end of the Ridge and to the bluffs beyond. He galloped forward, crying, "Stop, Andrew! Stop and turn them." His voice sounded shrill and faint against the wind. "You're heading up the west end of the Ridge. It's the wrong direction."

Andrew was crouched low in his saddle, lighting a torch soaked in pitch from the lantern. "It's the right way—I'm going against the wind."

"It's shifted. For the love of God, turn them! If they go up the Ridge, they'll be even with the bluffs. There's that big drop on the far side."

"God damn it, shut up!" Andrew roared at him. "I know what I'm doing."

"The hell you do! You're—"

"Get back on drag! When I give you the signal I want you to light a fire under them. Burn their asses if you have to—I want them to *keep on moving.*"

"No!" Leaning out, Pride snatched the lantern out of Andrew's hand. "You're wrong—you're wrong and you're crazy as well. You'll destroy the whole herd—listen to me! Turn them, let them drift! I'm not going to let—"

He stopped, shocked into silence. Andrew had whipped the rifle from its boot and was pointing it at him. "You try and stop me now, I'll blow you in two. I mean it!" With rifle in one hand and smoking, blazing torch in the other, he looked like some night rider out of the past, gaunt and vengeful and mad. "Now *get back on drag!* We're going to drive them through." He raced off down the line, swinging the torch low in the snow-caked, panicky white faces.

Hide and hair were singed; the stench filled the cold air. The herd began to turn, to surge up over the Ridge. It was like no stampede Pride had ever seen. They couldn't have run more surely up the Ridge if there had been arrows pointing the path. Up and up the sea of cattle went, one mass of heaving shoulders, swaying horns. Nothing could stop them. Two riders—one of them looked to Pride like Tiny Bentham, with Dub Wilgress calling after him—were on the leading edge, borne backward, frantically waving their hats, shouting something. Then they vanished as though they'd never existed, and the herd rushed on.

Pride watched in gathering horror as the very earth beneath the snow began to tremble. Up the Ridge they ran, across its narrow plateau, onto the southern rim, where he knew there was a deep ravine. There was a brief, panicky jostling at the herd's leading edge as the first steers saw the danger. And then wave after wave of them plummeted into the abyss.

They piled on one another; above it all was the high scream of terror that faded into a hollow, sonorous moaning. It sounded like the burial of the world. And finally there was a near silence.

Pride found Dub Wilgress—he knew it was Dub by one of his snakeskin boots—a battered, mangled scarecrow of crushed bone and torn flesh and rags, unrecognizable, no longer human, already mercifully coated with snow. Sickened and despairing, he turned away. Tiny Bentham was nowhere to be seen; he must have been carried over the rim in that first terrible rush.

Standing at the edge of the precipice, holding a lantern over the drop, Pride peered down through the driving snow. He felt himself go weak with horror. Far below them was a quivering, steaming mass of blood-soaked, shattered carcasses. Here and there a horned head stirred, a hoof kicked feebly. It seemed as if the world itself had stopped in its turning, that everything was suspended, frozen before this hideous carnage, seeking to hide it under a dense, white mantle.

Beside Pride stood Frank Pettis, crying, the tears freezing on his face. "I seen them go. Tiny gone and Dub was hollering for him to stop."

From the curtain of snow the others began to drift up to the edge. Dan Penland, Paco, Chang—they stood, their eyes wide, staring at the stark tragedy.

"What about Zeb?" Dan Penland asked.

"I'm here." Zeb's voice was cracked and hoarse. "I'm here, but Zack's hurt bad." Zeb had walked in, leading his horse with Zack slung over the saddle.

Slim Dress kept shaking his head back and forth. "I was right there with 'em. It could have been me, but no, I'm in one piece. Me, the one who always has the bad luck, and they're gone."

"Oh, my Jesus," Taffy was muttering. "Oh, my sweet Jesus."

Andrew stood beside him, staring hollowly into the ravine. His hat was gone; his face was smeared with pitch and smoke. He kept rubbing his nose with one hand.

"Let's go round them up," he said.

Pride stared at him. "Round *what* up?"

"There are strays. Some of them broke off, down the east slope. I saw them. We can—"

"You've lost two of your best men," Pride said grimly. "Let the cattle *go.* Let them drift, find shelter if they can, where they can. Haven't you done enough damage as it is? Come on," he said to Taffy, "let's see to Dub and . . ." He couldn't say Tiny's name; it hurt too much. "We'll do what we have to here, and then we'll get the men we've got left back to the bunkhouse. Then I mean to get home. I want to find out how Cima is making out in this."

"Cima isn't there."

Pride turned around. Andrew was still gazing slack-jawed into the arroyo. "Cima *isn't there?*" he repeated.

Andrew shrugged. "She may be back by now."

"What the hell are you talking about?"

Andrew stared at him; his eyes were so pale in the lantern's glow they seemed made of glass. "She took Snow and the girls into town to see Doc. Rose Dawn was sick."

"Annoyi, too? But *why?*"

"She thought it might be catching."

Pride seized him by the collar. "You left Reanna there *alone,* so near her time? Is that what you're telling me?"

"I had to."

"With the baby coming and this storm on the way?"

Andrew shook his hand off; the snow beat and beat in their faces. "How could I know we'd get a blizzard like this?"

"And you left her. *Alone.*" Pride was filled with rage—a rage born of mounting fear.

"I had to. I had to save the herd."

"You goddamned fool!" Pride shouted. "You haven't *got* any herd. You haven't got anything at all! We're going back there. Right now."

"The hell we are! We're going to round up strays."

Pride had the sense, crouched here at the edge of the cliff in this universe of stinging snow and biting wind, that he was dreaming. At any moment, he would wake up in his bunk at the line house and swing his stockinged feet to the floor and all this would be a silly nightmare.

"There's nothing we can do, Andrew," Taffy was saying dully.

"Of course there is! Half the herd, I saw half the herd—"

"There ain't any herd left at all."

"There's got to be!" Andrew cried, waving one arm. "There's got to be *something* left!"

"Couple dozen steers, maybe more. You even *find* 'em, you won't be able to do anything with 'em. Snow's higher than the horses' hocks now."

Pride found his voice then; he bent close to Andrew. "You son of a bitch! She's there alone in this storm, and you stand here talking about rounding up strays."

"Yes, and I'm going to get them! All of them!"

"You're crazy," Pride said softly, watching the pale, glazed eyes. "You know that? *Haksi*. Stark, raving mad."

"I know what I'm doing!"

"Sure. Sure you do. Come on," Pride said to Taffy, "let's get out of here. We'll ride and tie. We can get through if we move out."

"The devil you will!" Andrew shouted. "You're staying, Taffy! You got that? I need every hand."

"Boss, he'll never make it back alone. Nobody on earth—"

"You owe me, Taffy!" Andrew cried out in the wind. "You owe me, and you stay."

Taffy looked at Pride, then back to Andrew. He looked utterly whipped. His beard was matted with ice; his eyes were almost closed with pain and fatigue.

"All right," he said grimly. "You're the boss, and I'll stay. I'll see the men back to the bunkhouse, but this wipes the slate. From here on in we're quits. You understand that?"

Andrew said nothing. He rubbed at his nose with his gloved hand.

"I'm going then," Pride said and swung up on Gray Cloud.

"And I tell you you're staying!" Andrew shouted at him.

Pride looked at him with contempt. "You going to pull a gun on me again? That your plan? You and your guns."

"She's *my* wife, you got that? Mine!"

"The hell she is! She never was—you threw her away. You're not good enough to hold her stirrup, you selfish, cold-blooded murderer!"

"That so?" Andrew laughed savagely, his chest heaving. "Running home to Mama!" he jeered. "Just like always. Haven't the guts to stay and do a man's work."

Pride reined up then; he had never in all his life been this angry. "You want it, don't you?" he screamed over the howling wind. "Kill us all, destroy everything—that's what you want! Isn't it? Then you won't look like such a cold-hearted, lying son of a bitch to yourself!"

"You'll never make it, anyway!"

"And you'd like that too, wouldn't you? It'd solve all your troubles."

Andrew danced up and down in the snow with rage; then, "You run out on me now, Beauvaise, and that's it—you hear me? We're through. Don't you ever come running to me again!"

"You can go to hell, big man."

Pride rode off westward; in twenty seconds they had vanished— the cliff and Andrew and Taffy and the hands, the whitened mounds of dead cattle. It had turned into a gale of ice now, each pellet stinging like flung sand, cutting any exposed skin, burning it raw.

Gray Cloud fought his way through the deep drifting snow. They were enveloped in whiteness. Pride had never known it to be so cold. The storm was fierce, utterly impenetrable. He had only the wind to go by, and his old, hard-won sense of terrain.

He rode on, praying to the Great Spirit to keep him safe until he found his way back to Reanna. She was near her time; the baby was his. He knew it with every beat of his heart. He made a promise to the gods of wind and winter that, if she was safe, he would accept any sacrifice.

The wind kept shifting, now from the west, now from the north again. He kept beating his hands against his thighs; he'd lost all feeling in his left foot, and this frightened him. He'd lost all track of time and distance. He was half blinded by the wind.

Gray Cloud struggled on gamely, one hour after another, floundering in the drifts. Pride could see his nostrils flared wide and hear a terrible rattling groan deep in his lungs. Pride threw away his saddle bags and bedroll, his rifle and lariat, jettisoned everything he could to lighten the load. He knew he ought to dismount, but the snow was nearly up to Gray Cloud's shoulders and Pride needed every mile the horse could give him. The horse had to carry him as far as he could. And Pride knew he'd do it.

"Come now, boy," Pride said. He could barely move his lips. "Help me."

The horse toiled up a little rise, fought his way down an endless swale of pastureland—slipped suddenly sidewise with a low cry. Pride heard a sound like the breaking of a twig. The horse stopped and held there, motionless and swaying, and Pride knew without question what had happened. Yet even then, Gray Cloud refused to go down; he wouldn't throw Pride.

Pride slipped into the snow and put his hand against the horse's side. He was trembling terribly, lathered with sweat under the sheath of snow and ice, his head down, drawing long, shuddering breaths. Pride drew his revolver from under his coat and put it to Gray Cloud's ear.

"Forgive me," Pride whispered. The words were lost in the flat sound of the gunshot and in the silence that followed. He knew he was crying, because the tears froze on his face like diamonds. He wrapped himself in the saddle blanket and began to walk on. Before he'd gone fifty feet, the still, low mound was buried in the lashing snow.

He didn't know how long he'd walked before he caught sight of Reanna and smiled in sheer joy. She was there in the snow, beckoning to him. Laughing, she held out her arms to him, but as he came closer to her, she faded and then disappeared in the swirling white mist. She'd vanished, and there was nothing but snow and ice and the moaning, pitiless wind. And now he was mortally afraid for himself, as well as for Reanna.

WHEN Andrew had ridden off, Reanna had determined not to be afraid. She told herself Cima would be back that day or the day after; there was nothing to worry about.

It was a kind of luxury to have time to herself. It had been many months since she'd had a day when she didn't have to think of the others' needs. No matter how long the days or how tired she was, she'd had to tend to the house, the crops and the stock, look after Snow and the girls. Cima was a great help. She couldn't have managed without her, but in the end, all the responsibility was Reanna's.

As the baby had grown, the unusually warm days and the constantly running south wind had siphoned off her strength. Cima said that Reanna carried well, because she was tall, and that since the baby rode high, it was bound to be a boy. Reanna didn't care where the baby rode within her, she only wanted it to be born. She wanted to be free of it, to be able to do as she pleased without always having to consider this alien being who had invaded her privacy, who it seemed would never leave her for a life of its own.

Now, alone in the cabin for the first time in months, free of Andrew's irascible bullying, she had time to think. She enjoyed the novelty of it, the quiet. After the tornado had destroyed Lochleven, the cabin had become not only a place of refuge but her home. She'd found a sense of pride in making it neat and habitable. The kitchen was warm and sweet-smelling, with echoes of the spicy fragrance of Christmas baking and the aroma of winter evergreens.

All at once, the weight of the baby and the closeness of the air made her sleepy. There was something irresistible about the idea of taking a nap in the morning. There was no one there to scold her for going back to bed. She put down the dishcloth and walked across the dogtrot to her bedroom. The last quarrel with Andrew had left her bone-weary; she fell on the bed in a sort of stupor.

Despite the unnatural warmth of the day, she felt a chill. She pulled the coverlet over her, making a cocoon for the baby and herself. For a time she lay there, shifting about, trying to find a comfortable position. The baby had a way of turning somersaults; just when all seemed quiet, a tiny foot would kick, a hand try to explore. She felt possessed, as if a monstrous stranger had taken her identity; she no longer mattered, only this giant thing called baby. At last, as if by some unexpected blessing, she fell into a deep, fathomless sleep.

When she woke, she knew at once that something was wrong. She was shivering with the cold. She drew the quilt closer around her, but the most ominous aspect of her discomfort was not the cold but the silence. It was an omnipresent, layered thing that hung over her like a great weight. It was foolish to lie there shivering in this strange, dim light, not knowing whether it was evening or morning or how long she'd slept. She rose, pulling the quilt around her for a robe, and went to the window.

The sky was dark and threatening; the clouds were made of flawed pewter. A peppering of icy rain beat against the windowpane, sharp as needles. From Cima's bedroom, she heard the Lochleven clock striking the hour. Five strokes. She'd slept the day away. Only five, but there was something in that grim, leaden sky, the fast-fading light that made her uneasy. In only a few hours, the world had rushed from spring to winter.

She was cross with herself. She'd have to feed the chickens and milk the cow, and she didn't feel like doing chores any more than she'd felt like doing the housework. She called once but there was no answer. She stepped across the passage into the kitchen to find the dishes still unwashed. The fire in the stove had gone out long ago. She could feel the cold under her feet and in her hands. The temperature must have dropped at least thirty degrees while she'd been asleep.

She milked the cow and fed the chickens. She walked quickly

back to the cabin, missing Cima. The icy sleet grated and crunched underfoot, a white, granular film over the ground. The sun had disappeared so completely, it seemed as if her world had lost its light forever. The last thing she saw clearly before she went inside were the first flakes of snow. Cima would be back tonight, she told herself, or if not tonight, next morning. Perhaps Rose Dawn had been more ill than they'd thought. Twice she thought she heard the buckboard come into the yard, but when she went out to look the snow struck at her face, pecking at her like little beaks. It was much colder. The sky was a dark mirror that reflected nothing.

This snow would surely let up soon, but just in case it should last the night, she went to the woodpile and brought up several armloads to the porch. The exercise made her less apprehensive, and she was suddenly filled with energy. She set about putting the kitchen in order. She fastened the shutters, laid a fire in the fireplace and another in the stove. She soon had the kettle boiling and a pot of tea brewed. While the kitchen slowly warmed, she decided against trying to keep a fire in her bedroom as well as the kitchen. She went across the dogtrot to the bedroom for quilts and pillows; she would sleep in the kitchen. If Cima and the girls came home late, they'd have a cold supper and a colder bed.

She heated some soup, took one of Miss Jane's books down from the shelf and propped it against the base of the lamp to read while she ate. It was the first time she'd really been alone since she was at home on the farm, and even then it had been rare. She felt as if she were playing hooky from school. She could eat when she liked, sleep when she liked and read as late as she liked, with no one to scold her.

She dawdled over supper and the washing up, then read for a while longer, lulling herself in the rocking chair, before she settled for the night. She dimmed the lamp, opened the shutters and looked out. The snow had changed to larger flakes; it was no longer a mere dusting but several inches deep. It had begun to drift at the corner of the steps; the wind, which she had tried to ignore, was driving hard and relentlessly from the north. She had to face the fact that Cima was not coming back tonight; she wouldn't leave town in this weather. She was going to be alone all night, but she had plenty to do to keep her busy. There was some sewing she'd meant to finish for the baby; the shelves above the soapstone sink needed fresh paper, and the dresser drawers should be turned out.

She had to admit that she was glad Pride had left when he did;

if he'd stayed, she would have betrayed her feelings, and Andrew's suspicions about the baby would have been confirmed. Andrew might not want her for himself, but he'd kill any man who tried to take her from him, and he'd have prairie law on his side. A minister of the gospel had pronounced them man and wife. In the sight of God's law she was his till death did them part, and that was an end to it.

Yet that was not the end of her feelings. She loved Pride; she hungered for him. When he was in her presence, her heart and her hand went out to him. She ached to touch him, to have his arms around her. When they were together, her eyes swung to him as if he were true north. And when they did, she found he was looking at her. She *belonged* to Pride; not because of any law of God or man, but because she had consented in her heart to be his.

She didn't think Andrew had any notion of the depth of her feelings for Pride. He was a jealous man and inherently suspicious, but he was too preoccupied with the cattle, too obsessed with proving his superiority over Pride to really care what she felt. Times were bad. But even if they had been smooth and Andrew had been at home with her all day long, she knew that he wouldn't have changed his feelings toward her. He didn't want her; he'd said so. If it had been anyone but Pride, Andrew might have let her go; he had urged her to leave him more than once. But because it was Pride she loved, Andrew would make certain he was the one man she could never have.

The wind was whining under the sills and rattling the dried-out chinking between the logs. Looking out once more, she saw the snow was rapidly accumulating, but she had no sense of foreboding; instead, she was curiously elated. Even after all the work she had done, she was wide awake and full of energy. She ought to get in some more wood, just to be on the safe side. This time the trips to the wood pile were not as easy as before. The wind raged around her, tore at her skirts; this snow was not going to blow over in a hurry.

She was surprised to find out how much strength the work had cost her. She was glad to sit in Cima's rocker and drink another cup of tea. The baby moved within her, suddenly active, stirred by the effort of her carrying the wood. One of its tiny hands unfurled its fingers and poked and prodded, as if exploring a possible exit from its confinement.

Reanna lay before the fire, watching the flickering of the flames and the fall of burnt wood into ash. She hugged herself around the baby, drawing herself up as if she were a child surrounding a child and the cabin a great wooden womb. In the morning when the storm was over, maybe she should go into town to stay with Doc and Amoretta. There was the old buggy Taffy had repaired, and she could hitch up Picaunli. It might be a wise thing to do. She had misled Doc about the date of her last period. This baby would come soon; it had changed position, she was sure she hadn't imagined it. There was no real discomfort, but she was aware of herself being transformed, as though her body were waiting for the next step. She hid away the thought that even she couldn't predict the true date of the baby's birth. She wasn't sure of the exact date of her last period and she'd lied so often, she no longer knew the truth.

She slept fitfully. This time when she woke there was a deep silence; even the wind was muted, the way it often was just before the dawn. She built up the fire in the fireplace and made breakfast. She was reluctant to look out. Then her resolve gave way, and she flung back the shutters to see snow still falling as steady as rain. The wind was whipping it into lazy peaks and valleys. There was nothing but snow left in the universe. It lay high against the side of the lean-to; the chicken house was only a vague shape iced in white. She couldn't go out in this. The animals would have to fend for themselves until Cima got out from town.

Reanna stood on a chair, trying to see beyond the yard, but as far as she could look, everything was cloaked in white. She was a prisoner of the snow. There was cream from yesterday's milking, but she ate the oatmeal with salt and butter, the way her father had used to do. It made her feel closer to home. She felt like a child; she wanted her mother to tell her what to do.

She was suddenly angry with Andrew for not being there. It was his duty to be there. Even if he didn't love *her*, he should have thought of the child. Perhaps that was being unfair. He couldn't have known there'd be such a storm; yet she knew he would always have favored the cattle over her or the baby. He'd suspected there was a storm coming; why hadn't he made sure she wouldn't be alone?

Toward the evening, she began to have symptoms that she couldn't ignore. As the last light faded from a dull, gray sky, she was forced to accept the unthinkable. Cima wasn't coming; the girls weren't coming. Andrew wasn't coming back. She was here alone in this howling waste of snow. She was going to have this baby now, and she would have to manage on her own.

She heard herself cry out. There was no pain, only a burdensome ache that began, and stopped, and came again—an ever-tightening rhythm. Labor. She was coming into labor, then.

She must be calm. Perfectly calm. What good would panic do her now? An hour later, she felt water running from her, and gasped in sudden fear; surely she wasn't as frightened as that, to disgrace herself in a childish accident. But when she cleaned herself, she saw it was a thick fluid, another signal of what was to come.

Suddenly all her anger was against the baby, this being who would come soon, even if she was unready or unwilling. There was nothing she could do to stop it. It was her time, and soon she would be brought to bed, but for as long as she was able, she would stand and walk and be her own mistress. She longed for Cima, for her mother, even for Amoretta; she wished with all her heart that she had more experience of these things and knew what to expect.

She must think what to do, while she still had some control. Soon she would be unable to make any choices. The thoughts which came to her were beginning to be brief fragments between the rhythmic parting of her body. If she was going to survive this night, and with the baby, too, she would have to gather what was needed now. She'd lined a drawer in the cupboard earlier. Now she put in dishtowels for a mattress with an afghan for a coverlet; it would make a fine crib. She'd hemmed flannel bands, and the water was boiling on the hob. She must have a clean, sharp knife and some twine. She'd heard her mother talk about these things. She had plenty of bedding from the night before. She would make a lying-in pallet before the fire.

She made her list, walking around and around, knowing that as long as she could walk, she was still a thinking human being and not an animal. Yet any animal would have been wiser, could have trusted its instincts to see it through. She felt the contraction of her muscles widening her channel, making way for the new life. She was not the first woman this had happened to, and she wouldn't be the last. Other women had labored and borne a baby alone; what they had done, she could do. She wouldn't be beaten by her fear and ignorance. She wouldn't cringe or whimper in a corner.

In her moments of remission from this thing that was happening to her, she slept a sort of shallow half-sleep. Once she dreamed of a summer, not here, but at home. In her dream she was an audience to herself, as she used to be. She saw herself running in the fields. It was green and cool, and she went wading in the brook. She heard herself laughing to think how cross her mother would be with her for taking off her stockings. The water was so cold, her feet felt frozen. She must put her stockings on again, but she couldn't find them. There was an animal prowling in the thickets; she became afraid that she would have to stay here. She would never get home again; she would never be warm, but always trapped in this cold stream.

She woke to find the cold was real enough. The fire was dead. The wind was gusting down the chimney and the ash blew uneasily on the hearth. The house groaned as the logs shifted. The storm outside had gained new force; sleet battered at the house in mounting waves. Slowly and painfully she began to build up the fire again. Everything she did was more difficult now; every movement required greater effort. Her time of siege had come. Now with each painful contraction, she had to rest; it was very uncomfortable to stand. She lay down and prepared herself. After each assault she lay panting, straining with the effort to expel the baby, push it from her. She heard a sound, a moan so low, so like a brute thing, that she looked about to see who else might be in the house.

There was a great, all-engulfing pain; she was parted, wrenched asunder. Dimly she felt the head, the shoulders emerge, and then this bulking form separate from her. There had been no sound but her own groans and labored breathing. Then had come a mewing, as the new lungs took in the alien air and gave a first, lusty cry.

The one thought crowning all others was that she must cut the two of them apart. The knife was already beside her, and the twine. Driven by necessity, she did what she had to, and did it carefully and well. She'd been afraid that she would be a coward, that she would panic and do something for which she'd be ashamed. Now the worst was over and she had survived. She was elated; her spirits soared up like fire.

Before, she had been anxious to get the baby born; her only thought had been for herself and how she might rid herself of a burden. Then all that changed. From the moment the child left her body, all her concern was for it. She reached down and brought the baby up to her. Never in her life had she felt such joy. She had done it! And she had done it alone. She had given birth to a son.

Gently she cleaned him with oil, counted his fingers and toes. She swaddled him and held him to her, thinking how beautiful he was. She was astonished by the stark intensity of the love she felt for him. She was too exhausted to clean and care for herself. She reached out from her pallet to throw wood on the fire. She must keep the house warm for him. She lay triumphant, waiting for the first light of day.

She hadn't expected the next series of spasms. This pain was worse than anything that had gone before. She'd never experienced anything remotely like it. She felt her stomach; it was still swollen. The pain ripped her, tore through her; it wouldn't leave her alone. It was her companion, for life or death. Faintly she heard the baby cry. She didn't know whether she should feed him, but there was nothing she could do while this new agony gripped her.

The spasms came again, and again; the pressure within her was unbearable. She bore down, gasping and panting, disgusted at the animal cries she heard herself making. When she thought she could bear it no longer, the cries came again. And always there was the pain.

She felt the blood flowing from her. The sight of it transfixed her with terror. She was cold, as cold as death itself, but she couldn't keep up the fire now. She couldn't do anything at all. She thought she had escaped all danger, and here she was, screaming in fear and unendurable pain. "Help me, oh help me!" she heard herself shrieking over and over again, and then she heard nothing at all.

How long he'd been walking, Pride had no idea. The snow was up to his chest in places; the wind blew in gusts that tore the breath out of his throat. Reanna had appeared again, laughing at him and teasing, and the hallucinations frightened him more than the pain in his eyes or the numbness in his left leg. He knew that if the snow didn't let up, his chances of reaching the cabin were very poor. After Gray Cloud had broken his leg and he'd had to shoot him, he knew those chances were even slimmer. All night he'd been certain he'd been moving in the right direction, but with early light he wasn't so sure. He'd lost nearly all feeling in his hands. The snow's resistance, its sheer, burdensome *weight*, was awesome; he kept losing his balance and falling, forcing himself to his feet, and falling again. He'd gotten rid of everything but the saddle blanket, which he was using as a poncho, and some strips of jerky that he doled out to himself every few hours. Once the snow had let up a little, and he'd been shaken to look back and see his tracks fading back in a long half circle. He was wandering. He was lost, and he knew it. Only the thought of Reanna sitting alone in that cabin kept him going, putting one foot after another, dragging through this malevolent, buffeting wilderness of white.

He was very near the end of his strength when he stumbled onto a small, angular mound buried in snow. He recognized it as the ramshackle lean-to John's Dead had built by the oil springs—and knew exactly where he was. He clawed a pathway inside, cleared a small space and lay there for an hour or more out of the wind, napping fitfully, gathering strength. It was a sign. Reanna had leaned down and let John's Dead touch her flaming red-gold hair, and Breathholder had remembered. Reanna was all right; he would reach her now, he knew it without question. Then, afraid of freezing to death if he stayed any longer, he got up and went on, keeping the Dragon Rocks on his right, past the woods where he cut wood for his flutes and where Snow had tried to lose Reanna and been struck by the rattler, on up the long slope, step after agonizing step, to the cabin. The drifts were terrific; he had to break a path for a yard or two with his body, trample that snow down, and break more open all over again. When he finally saw the cabin, he was sobbing with exhaustion.

The storm had transformed it into another, alien place. Snow had piled against its sides, molded it into a series of mounds and scoops; only the tops of the windows were visible. There was no smoke coming from the chimney. The cabin looked as abandoned as some arctic graveyard. The closer he got, the more afraid he became. He spent the last of his strength in one great paroxysm of effort and finally reached the doorway. He heard a shriek that made his blood stop, then again that awful, unnatural silence. In a frenzy he kicked and swept the snow away and forced open the door.

"Reanna." He bent close to her. "It's Pride. I'm here." She was moaning softly, as if the sound gave her some comfort. In a box beside her was a baby swaddled against the cold. The fireplace was dead ashes; the room was freezing.

"Reanna," he bent close to her. "It's Pride. I'm here." She was past hearing him. Her eyes were closed and she was as pale as the frost on the windowpanes.

Beating feeling into his hands, stamping his feet, he built up the fire and set a kettle on to boil. Kneeling down beside her again, he spoke to her. He wasn't sure she knew he was there. The baby began to cry fretfully, and Reanna's eyes fluttered open, but without focus. She moaned again, feebly. He'd never felt more helpless. He didn't know what to do for her. She'd delivered the baby herself, and it seemed well, if hungry, but something had gone wrong. Suddenly she was seized by a spasm of pain and cried out—a faint, exhausted cry. Something was very wrong.

"You'll be all right," he told her with a confidence he was far from feeling. "I'm here. I'll take care of you." Then he drew back the quilts. "Oh, my God," he heard himself mutter.

She was in even worse condition than he'd feared. The afterbirth had not come as it should. He watched her bear down, as if in pitiful mimicry of her labor. She was so weak. If the afterbirth was not expelled, she could contract childbed fever. And then the chances were she would die. He would have to force her to expel the afterbirth. Holding her, sweating with fear in the damp cold, he coaxed and pleaded and threatened her to make one great final effort; he shouted and prayed.

She heard him now; her eyes opened, held on his with an agonized, passionate intensity. Her breath sang between her clenched teeth. Together, with his hand applying pressure to her lower abdomen, they rocked and struggled. And when with one last terrible shriek it was over, she was so spent, he was terrified that he had lost her.

He made her as comfortable as possible. He held tea made from *wahewah* root to her trembling lips, wrapped her gently; then there was nothing for him to do but to wait and to pray. As she slept, he warmed milk and put a twisted flannel rag into milk and sugar and gave it as a pap to the hungry baby. He heated and ate the remains of the stew, fought his way out into the gale and brought in several armfuls of firewood. Then he sat looking at Reanna, rubbing his frostbitten foot and listening to the wind howling outside, until he fell into a troubled half-sleep.

When he awoke with a start, the sun was blazing on the upper windowpanes. Reanna was sleeping deeply and peacefully; the fever was down. When he touched her forehead, she stirred, sank back again in sleep. Outside, the wind glazed the snow's surface or whipped it into miniature cyclones of crystal. He got a shovel and cleared a working space in the yard, freed the woodpile from its heavy mantle of snow, plowed his way to the lean-to and henhouse and fed the stock and poultry. The drifts were four and five feet in places. He knew no one could get through to them for days.

They were prisoners in a brilliant, frozen universe and, in spite of his fears for Reanna, he felt a deep, furtive joy. No one could get into their private world, not this day or the next. For a little time, they would be the world for each other.

She slept until afternoon. When she woke, it was to a warm fire and a room filled with sunlight, the smell of corn bread baking and stew bubbling in the big iron pot. Pride was dozing by the fire, and the baby was asleep in his makeshift crib.

"Pride," she murmured, as if to make sure he was real and not a dream. She reached out to him, put her hand in his and held it as tight as she could. She was very weak; the pallor of her face glowed in the light of the fire. "Is it really you?" she whispered, smiling. "I thought it was a dream."

"I am come," he said in Chickasaw.

"My baby." She rose up on one elbow suddenly. "Where's my baby?"

"In his box, fast asleep."

"Is he all right?"

"Yes. You have a fine, healthy son."

"I have a son." She lay down again and her eyes closed. He saw she was trembling beneath the quilts and he drew them over her shoulders.

"How do you feel?" he said.

"All right. I'm all right now. I remember the baby coming, and then I don't remember anything more. Except the pain." She opened her eyes slowly and looked at Pride as if she were seeing him for the first time. "How did you get here?"

"I left the—the herd." He saw no point in telling her now about Andrew's madness or their common ruin.

"You came, through all that snow and wind. How did you ever get here?"

"Breathholder took pity on me," he said with a smile.

"You saved me once before. And now you've risked your life again, to save my son."

He smiled again, but not sadly. She had read him like a track in the snow. She always knew his thoughts. But she'd thought of the baby before she'd thought of herself. She would always think of the baby now before anything else.

"I risked nothing," he said simply. "You *are* my life."

Tears brightened her eyes. "I'm sorry for the cruel things I said at Christmas."

"That's all behind us," he said. "What matters is that you're safe and that we're together. What matters is now, today." He got to his feet. "Are you hungry? I've made some stew."

"You're limping," she said. "You've hurt your leg . . ."

"Touch of frostbite. It'll get better."

"It must have been terrible. Out there in all that ice and wind. I thought of you. How are Andrew and Taffy and the others? What did you do about the herd?"

He turned away. "We'll talk about it later."

She raised herself on the pallet with an effort. "I can face it, Pride. It's bad news, isn't it?"

He looked at her then and saw her face change. "Worse than anything you can imagine."

"After the past three days," she said quietly, "there's nothing worse than I can imagine. I want to hear it now."

She listened in silence as he told her, her fine brown eyes widening in horror, then darkening subtly as her jaw set.

"Of course," she said finally, flatly. "I should have foreseen it. He's so enraged at the whole world now, he wants it all to smash. You, me, Lochleven, the range—even himself. There are none left?" she cried softly. "None of all that tremendous herd?"

He shook his head. "Thirty, forty head maybe. And *they* broke away up on the cliffs. There's no shelter there. I doubt if any of them will survive this. Eat your stew, now. You need it."

When she'd finished nursing, she slept again. Later they ate their supper by the firelight. The wind had finally died away, and they could hear the house shift and settle beneath the weight of the snow and ice. They were alone together, and he'd never felt more calm or serene.

"We're snowbound," he told her. "We can't go out and they can't come in. Are you afraid?"

"No." She shook her head happily. "How long will it be before they come?"

"A day or two. Three if we're lucky."

There was no constraint between them. They could have spoken any words, told any secret, but instead they talked of ordinary things, as if they had a lifetime ahead of them. They had all they needed to be happy; they were a man and a woman alone with their child. Their greatest pleasure was in the commonplace, as if they both knew how rare it would be for them.

They were so close that Pride began to feel as if they were one person. He'd never been so happy. And yet he sometimes had the feeling that he wasn't there at all; he was on the outside looking in at them, an observer of some infinitely precious world that couldn't last. He saw with sad, wise eyes how frail and vulnerable they were. With a terrible clarity, he saw that soon Andrew would come in that door. Then Reanna would have to act, and so would he.

Reanna only knew that she loved Pride and he loved her, and that together, for this moment, they shared this miraculous child. There was no way to keep the world out forever. Her husband would return, and all this would be over. She watched Pride as he stood staring down at the baby.

"What are you doing?" she asked.

"Trying to decide who the baby looks like."

"He looks like himself," she said defensively.

"He has your red hair, and I think his eyes will change to brown like yours."

"Perhaps. All babies have blue eyes in the beginning."

"He will have Andrew's name."

"And mine, Lovell MacClaren." She said it like a judgment.

"He doesn't look like Andrew."

"No."

"Will Andrew love him?"

"I hope so."

"A boy should have a father to love him. A father who will teach him what is important for him to know." Pride paused and his eyes went from the baby to Reanna. "Andrew is too impatient; he will have no time for him. A son needs a father to teach him about the clans and in what order they should sit at the campfire. A son needs a father to show him the different kinds of grass. He must have a father to teach him the dances and the songs."

"A mother could teach a son those things. Besides, he will go to school to learn."

"You cannot learn such things at a white man's school. Father Soule can teach him to read and write and do sums, but for the rest, he needs another kind of father."

"I'll see he learns those things. When he is older, I want him to go East to school. It's a big country, the Nation is only a small part of it."

"You would send him away?"

"When the time comes."

"But now there is so much to learn, and he's so small." He picked up the baby and held it to him, rocking it gently as if his arms were a feathered cedar bough gently rocking in the wind. "Will Andrew know how to care for him? When he is sick, will Andrew make him a *pishofa* feast or call the doctors who know how to cure an owl sickness?"

She felt tears rise in her eyes. Pride was making his case, and his plea was based on love. "I'll keep him safe," she said. "I'd kill to keep him safe."

"I know. You have great courage. You are *tashka*, a warrior. I always knew it. They will come soon," he said, holding the baby and watching the melted snow rain emeralds from the eaves.

"When?"

"Tomorrow, I think." He looked at her. "Are you afraid?" he repeated.

"No," she said, but he knew she lied.

"I'm afraid. Shall I tell you why?" She nodded. "When they come, we will break apart. We will be like a nation that has lost its way and forgotten its own language. If we met again, we'd be so changed we wouldn't even recognize each other. We'd meet as strangers."

"I'd always know you, always. And you'd know me."

"And the baby? Would *he* know me if we met again?"

She looked away then. What he said was true, and she couldn't argue with him anymore.

"They'll come tomorrow," he said, watching her intently. "Do you hear me, Reanna? After tomorrow, there will be no turning back." He knew, despite what he'd said, that she was the only woman he would ever love. He'd known it from the first time he saw her standing in the hall at Lochleven, holding the Beauvaise cup in her hands. She'd change her mind; he had to believe that.

NEXT day, just before noon, Andrew and Taffy broke through from the southeast. When Andrew flung open the door and saw Pride standing by the fireplace, his face gave a curious little quiver.

"Well," he said. "You made it all in one piece."

"That's right," Pride answered.

Andrew forced a grin. "I figured we'd be digging you out along about spring." He turned to Reanna; then he caught sight of the baby in its drawer-cradle, waving its tiny arms, and his jaw dropped. "So soon?" he murmured.

"They come when it's their time to come," Pride said.

"You have a son," Reanna told Andrew quietly. "A fine, healthy son. And his name is Lovell."

Andrew stepped over to the cradle and peered down at the baby, as though he couldn't believe it. His eyes, narrowed with snow glare and exhaustion, kept flickering at Reanna and Pride. His macintosh was torn and blackened with soot. His mustache and hair were soaked with melting snow; sodden snow dripped from him onto the floor in little, dirty puddles. He said in the old airy, arrogant tone, "I want to call him Andrew."

Reanna rose then. "I *told* you, I've already named him Lovell." She fixed her eyes on his, unwavering. "You weren't here when he was born. I have the right to name him. And that is all there is to it." She picked the baby up and carried him into her bedroom across the dogtrot and shut the door.

Taffy said, "Now what'd you want to do that for, Andrew? I never even got to see the little feller."

"Well," Andrew said loudly, "this calls for a little celebration. Wouldn't you say, Taffy?"

Taffy glanced uneasily at Pride, who was still standing by the fireplace. "Well, I don't know, Andrew."

"Course you do." He rummaged around in the compartment under the dry sink and drew out the whiskey bottle, peered at it and then took a long drink while the two men watched him. "A little celebration over the happy event." He handed the bottle to Taffy, who looked at it unhappily. "Birth of a son and heir doesn't happen every day," Andrew went on, watching Pride. "Does it, little brother?"

"Oh yes, there's a lot to celebrate," Pride said tightly.

"Sure there is. For instance, here you are, safe and sound. The old Chickasaw scout. The pathfinder. Here we all are, all together again. In one tight little cabin. That's something to celebrate, isn't it?"

"And the herd," Pride said in the same low, ominous voice. "Let's not forget the herd. Did you round up all that wonderful Texas stock again?"

Andrew turned his back on him. "Some of them," he said carelessly.

"I'll bet. How many, Taffy?"

The trail boss shifted his feet. "Maybe a hundred head—most of 'em stiff as a board under three feet of snow."

Andrew swung around angrily. "We'll find more of them in time."

"Sure. And they'll all be frozen stiff, too," Taffy said.

"Of course, *we* didn't go riding off to rescue the lady. Who seems to have made out perfectly all right on her own, for all your—"

"You don't know anything, see?" Pride burst out savagely. "She was *dying* when I got here. She'd have been dead in three hours, and the baby too—that's how much you know, big man! She'd have been dead right now, and you would have killed her."

"What the hell are you talking about?"

"And that would have given you satisfaction too, wouldn't it?"

"Boys," Taffy said, "now let's let this drop."

Andrew took a step toward Pride. "You remember what I told you? Out by the bluffs?"

"Yes. I remember, and—"

"All right. That's it! You're at liberty to leave, any time you have a mind. I don't want you in this cabin."

"Yes, I'm leaving," Pride said. "And I'm taking Reanna with me."

There was a brief, taut silence. Andrew's face was frozen in furious amazement. A log snapped in two and dropped into the ash and burning coals. Watching both men, Taffy set the bottle carefully on the table.

"You aren't taking her anywhere!"

"You don't give a damn about her, you never did. You care more about your cattle than Reanna."

"She's my wife, and she stays with me in my house."

Pride said, with soft ferocity, "She never loved you. She hates your rotten, selfish guts! She loves me, and I'm taking her with me."

Pride's words hit Andrew hard. He'd been jealous of Reanna since the first time he'd seen the two of them together. Now he knew for sure he'd had true cause. He struck back at Pride with the sharpest weapon he possessed. "Reanna doesn't love you, boy. It's Lochleven she loves. She'll never leave Lochleven for you."

"Liar."

In the midst of his rage, Andrew forced a thin, contemptuous smile. "If you want to take her, you'll have to kill me first, little brother. And you won't do that." The smile broadened, but his eyes were hard as jade. "Because you haven't the guts for it. You couldn't kill the men who gunned down your own father! You sure as hell won't kill me."

Without warning, then, he lunged out and caught Pride on the side of the head. Pride blocked the next blow and hit Andrew full in the face. Then Taffy had driven in between them and was saying, "All right, now! That's enough."

"*Well.*" Andrew was dabbing at his nose, which was bleeding faintly, staining his mustache; his eyes were glinting. "He *will* fight, after all."

"If you're set on a fight," Taffy told them, "then go outside. You want Reanna to be a party to this?"

"Fine," Andrew said, "let's go." The brothers locked eyes. "Call the stakes."

"Reanna," Pride said without hesitation.

"Reanna." Andrew nodded agreement. "For who stays and who goes. Winner take all."

"However you want it."

They went out to the clearing Pride had shoveled, and Andrew shrugged out of his coat and threw it on the woodpile.

"All right," Taffy said. "No low blows, no boots. No choking. Everything else goes."

"Not today," Andrew said; the steam whipped away from his mouth on the wind. "You fight an Indian, you use his weapons." Reaching down, he drew the hunting knife from his boot top and hefted it, watching Pride.

"Oh, no," Taffy protested. "Not knives."

"To a finish," Andrew said, smiling through his teeth.

"You agree to this?" Taffy asked Pride.

"If that's the way he wants it."

Taffy said, "Hand me your gun belt, Andrew."

The tall man turned to him angrily. "Why, for Christ's sake?"

"Because I don't like the look on your face," Taffy told him flatly. "*Give me your belt.*"

Andrew glared at him for an instant, then shrugged and unbuckled his gun belt and handed it over. Then he flung the knife into the center of the circle. It struck the film of ice and quivered there.

Slowly and deliberately, they began to circle the knife, whose pommel glittered in the cold sunlight. Their arms were outstretched, held low; each was looking for a purchase on the knife, an advantage over the other.

Pride moved awkwardly, and Taffy saw that he was limping. He started to say something, and at the same instant Pride slipped on the ice. Swift as a field hawk, Andrew pounced on the knife. He plucked it out from the ice and now began circling again, tossing the knife lightly from one hand to the other, waiting for an opening.

Taffy watched, unhappily wondering how he could put a stop to this. He didn't like the look in Andrew's eyes. He wasn't at all sure he'd be satisfied with cutting Pride, who was still moving awkwardly on his bad foot, his face expressionless. Andrew lunged then. Pride dodged catlike, sideways, and Taffy saw a line of red stain below the slash in Pride's shirt.

If Pride was hurt, he didn't show it. The knife slashed again, glittering, and cut Pride on the forearm. Both men were panting now, steam rising from their bodies. Taffy wondered if perhaps Andrew was right and Pride lacked the nerve to kill; he was too gentle, too compassionate to go up against Andrew, who liked violence, the fury and the pain of it.

Pride slipped and fell again. Andrew leaped at him with a long, sweeping thrust, and slipped himself. The blow missed and Pride rolled away onto his feet, frantically brushing snow out of his eyes. His forearm was bleeding badly now.

"All right," Taffy shouted. "That's enough. You've cut him. Let it go, now."

Andrew paid no attention. He continued to stalk Pride round and round, the knife held higher now, farther forward. Pride's face was contorted with pain and tension. Taffy moved forward to break it up. Andrew lunged deep, and Pride, twisting away, with one swift, sure kick knocked the knife out of Andrew's hand; it flew high in the air, glittering, and dropped out of sight in the snow beyond the circle. With a snarl Andrew rushed him then, and the two began hammering away at each other with their fists. With a grunt of pure relief, Taffy stepped back. Andrew would beat Pride senseless, but at least there was no more danger of killing.

For a long—a surprisingly long—time, they traded blows, gasping and flailing, tramping the area into a rust-dark bog of snow and mud. All at once Pride sank to one knee; Andrew hit him again, and he dropped to his hands and knees, swaying.

"No boots, now!" Taffy called in warning.

Andrew looked over; he was cut over one eye and his nose was bleeding thickly, but he was grinning his harsh, superior grin. "Don't *need* to stomp him, Taffy," he panted. "What ever gave you that idea? Get up," he said savagely to Pride, standing over him, his big fist cocked. "Going to take Reanna away, are you? Takes a *man* for that. She needs a *man*—not a snot-nosed, dreamy boy. Come on, get up," he taunted Pride, who was looking up at him doggedly, his face smeared with blood. He looked all done in. "You can't, can you? Because you're yellow. Like every Indian that ever lived. Yellow-livered, gutless—"

Pride moved so fast, it surprised Taffy. He got his feet under him and drove his shoulder into Andrew's belly; the tall man lost his footing and fell flat. Pride jumped away before Andrew could grab hold of him, and as Andrew got to his feet, Pride was on him in a raging fury, raining punches. Andrew hit him twice, very hard; the blows had no effect at all. Pride caught him full in the throat and in the face, again and again. Andrew's whole head and shoulders snapped from the impact. He hadn't ought to have called him that, Taffy remembered thinking, and then Pride had bent Andrew almost in two with a blow to the belly that sent him sprawling in the snow. Pride rushed on him raging, fell astride him, gasping, pounding and pounding at Andrew's bloodied, misshapen face.

Then Taffy had reached them, locked his arms around Pride's neck and was pulling him away, crying, "No more! Stop it, Pride! Hear me? Stop it, or you'll kill him." Pride looked up numbly at Taffy; he didn't know where he was. Taffy said gently, "You could have killed him."

"I wanted to kill him."

"They'd only hang you, and you still wouldn't have Reanna." Pride sat up and packed snow against his face and the long cut on his forearm, staring now and then at Andrew's body lying still in the trampled mud.

"Is it deep?" Taffy asked.

"No. I must go away," Pride said. "You understand, I can't stay here. I'm going away, and I'm taking Reanna with me." He got to his feet, swaying, and plodded toward the house.

REANNA was resting in bed, the bed she'd shared with Andrew. The baby was asleep beside her. Pride had poured whiskey on his arm and bound it up, and cleaned himself up as best he could, but his cheek was laid open and one eye was nearly closed. Reanna had heard the quarrel in the kitchen, and sounds of the scuffle outside. She looked at him, sick with sorrow, her eyes filled with tears, and waited for him to speak.

He knelt beside her and took her hand. "I'm going away now, and I want you to come with me."

With infinite gentleness she touched the swollen, battered face she loved, and then shook her head.

"No," she said.

"Reanna, you love me. I know you do."

"Yes."

"Then come."

"I can't go with you." This was the moment she had known would come. She'd thought to set herself to it, to make herself strong enough to say the words she knew must be said, but she felt as if she were passing sentence on herself for a lifetime of loneliness.

"Why not?" Pride pleaded. "Tell me why."

"Andrew is my husband."

"I told Andrew you loved me. He doesn't want you. He's given you up. I *won* you, in a fair fight."

She gave a groan of pure anguish, of outrage. "But what about *me?*" she cried. "Doesn't what *I* want mean anything? Listen to me. I promised Miss Jane I'd keep Lochleven together. I gave my word."

Pride felt suddenly cold. "Andrew said Lochleven meant more to you than I did."

"He's wrong, but this is your land, your place."

"I can't stay here."

"You once said you loved this land more than your life."

"I love you more than land or life."

"I won't go with you, Pride. I won't make Lovell pay for what I did. Not now or ever. Andrew is my husband; I'm bound to him by law."

"Now Andrew knows you love me. If you stay, what will your life be like? He will make you pay dear. You know what he's capable of. He forfeited his right to you when he left you here to die. Come with me. We belong together."

"I must stay."

"And if I stayed, I'd kill Andrew," he said tonelessly. "I came close out there. Too close." He shivered. "I must go. I couldn't bear to watch the two of you together."

"What about your inheritance?"

"We'll file for our separate allotments. It will be settled between us. Now and forever."

"Where will you go?" she whispered.

"To Muskogee, to the Agency. The Dawes Commission is there;

(314)

they're the men in charge of dividing our tribal land. There I can be of some use. Many don't know how to file the papers for what is theirs by right. They'll need help."

"When will you be back?"

"Never!" His answer was as final as hers had been to him.

"Then what will you do?"

"Study the law."

"The law? Why the law? You're a rancher."

"I must learn the law." His eyes flashed at her hotly. "The law that says we must divide our land. The law that says you belong to him. What the law has taken, the law must return."

"And then where will you go?"

"I don't know." He gripped her hand, hard. "Wherever I am, I'll wait for you."

"I will not come."

There was a finality to her words, like the tolling of a mission bell. Something of tremendous importance in her life had ended. She felt as if the very heart had been torn from her and the open wound cauterized with lye.

"That won't stop me from waiting for you."

The long silence between them was a torture. "There's nothing more to say, then," she said finally.

"No, nothing."

How superficial physical hurts are, she thought, watching his battered face, the blood-soaked bandage on his arm, thinking of her labor; they are only shadows of the true pains we feel.

"I'll go now. *Uno ihullo ishno.* I love you."

He released her hand and got to his feet. He still couldn't believe she would let him go without her. It was a wrong that could never be right, a denial of life. He couldn't trust himself to speak again. For the two of them, there could never be a word called goodbye.

In the kitchen, Pride found Taffy setting Andrew's nose with pieces of shingle. Andrew was slumped in a chair. One eye was completely closed, his face was a misshapen, discolored mass of flesh; blood had soaked his mustache and shirt. He looked up through his good eye, his hands clenched on the chair arms.

"Come to crow it over me?" he muttered.

"No."

"When are the two of you going?"

"Reanna won't go."

"Why not?" Andrew squinted at him suspiciously.

"She says she's your wife. She will be loyal to you, and to your son."

"That's what she said?" Pride could see him puzzling over it, trying to figure out what the catch was.

Pride smiled at him bitterly. "It seems you won, after all. I'm going, Andrew. I will not come back. I'll take my allotment on the west. You can take the Ridge and Snow the east."

Andrew was still watching him narrowly. "What if you change your mind and want to come home again?"

"I will not come back. You have my word."

Andrew looked away, then nodded. "So be it."

"So be it. Goodbye, Taffy."

"No." The trail boss looked up at him imploringly, his eyes bright with tears. "I'll only say so long for now. God bless you, lad."

Pride looked once more at Andrew watching him implacably, gripping the chair arms. Then he went out into the snow and wind.

*I*T cut Taffy up bad to see Pride go. It hurt him even more that Reanna never spoke his name to Andrew, or Andrew to her; it was as if Pride had died for both of them and, in the Indian way, was never to be spoken of again.

Taffy took care of Andrew, rubbed tallow in the cuts and put ice on his smashed cheekbone. He did it willingly enough, but it sometimes seemed to Taffy that Andrew didn't try as hard as he might to get on his feet again. It was as if Andrew considered his beating as some eerie kind of punishment. As long as he was stove in and laid up, he had an excuse to stay at home and not go out and face the ruin that lay at the far end of the Ridge.

Cima arrived the next afternoon in the buckboard with Snow and the girls, wild with anxiety. She couldn't get over the baby. She was jubilant and fearful and relieved all at once, heartsick that she hadn't been with Reanna when she needed her. "How in Caesar's ghost did you ever manage?" she kept saying, holding Lovell, shaking her head in awe at Reanna. "I couldn't have done it, I *know* I couldn't."

"You do what you have to," Reanna answered. "That's what you've always told me. Pride was with me at the end," she said quietly. "The worst part. Pride saved my life."

"Ah." Cima cut her eyes over at Andrew. "*You* don't know the kind of wife and woman you got, Mr. Cowman. That's what's wrong with you. Out riding around, playing Colonel Highpockets

Goodwell—shoot, you don't know what real trouble is . . ." She studied Andrew's face, the splinted nose, the broken, discolored cheekbone. "Well. Been *some* kind of scenery round here, I take it. *Some* kind of goings-on." She'd figured out exactly what had happened, Taffy could tell; Cima could read sign like nobody he'd ever met. He tried to signal her to back off, but she was having none of it; relief had turned her garrulous and aggressive.

"Well, *I'm* back here now," she declared, glaring at Andrew, her eyes deep as onyx. "And here I'm staying. No matter what, hear?" She put her hands on her hips. "I hear there was a little stampede trouble," she went on implacably, watching him. "It's all over town. Hear that big, get-rich herd Goliath multitude of yours is long gone. That so?" Andrew said nothing; he was holding Snow on his lap, passing and repassing a bruised hand through her thick, curly hair. Cima turned to Taffy, as he knew she would. "That the slant of it?"

"Lock, stock and barrel," he said simply, nodding, " 'cept for a few strays. We're cleaned out, Cima."

"Uh huh." She gave Andrew one last, withering glance and turned away. "Well, we been there before. We'll manage, I reckon. But everyone better pull his weight from here on in, or he's getting hisself cut right out of the herd."

Taffy took over the room behind the kitchen to use for Andrew and himself. Reanna stayed in the front bedroom with the baby. The girls went up in the loft above the kitchen. Cima and Snow remained where they'd been, in the room behind Reanna's.

For the benefit of Snow and the girls, the story was that Andrew's injuries were a result of his being caught in the stampede during the blizzard and that Pride had left for Muskogee on tribal business.

Everyone kept his thoughts to himself. It was a way of surviving in close quarters. Andrew said nothing, but Reanna felt him looking at her, his eyes full of cold reproach. At last she said, "All right, Andrew, if you have something to say to me, say it now."

"Say about what?"

"About Pride and me. I know he told you I love him."

"That doesn't signify." Andrew spoke contemptuously. "I knew you'd never leave Lochleven for Pride. Lochleven means more to you than anything or anyone."

Reanna stared at him. He knew nothing of her heart. He never had. "If you believe that, Andrew, you're a fool."

"What do you want me to do, Reanna? Say I forgive you for loving my brother?"

"Don't you care how I feel, Andrew?"

"Not much, but there's something you should remember, Reanna. You're mine. You're my wife from now until the day you die. No way you'll ever be free."

There was a terrible silence in the room and she could hear Lovell in his cot, his tiny hands fluttering against the blanket. "Then we just go on," she said, "day to day."

"That's it, Reanna. We just go on until death do us part."

For a few days the sun shone and melted away the snow. The land was exposed, green and benign, and the wind was mild, as if the blizzard had never happened. There was a February thaw followed by an early spring. The first prairie flowers—mallow, gaillardia and wild violet—rushed color into the season. Only sometimes, when the wind was from the west, there was the faint, sweet odor of rotting beef.

Their first visitor was Jack Levy. Reanna was glad to see Jack. It gave them all someone to focus on besides themselves. And now she'd be able to get him to mail the long letter she had written to her folks about Lovell and what a remarkable baby their first grandchild was.

Dear Mama and Papa,

You are now grandparents and the boys are uncles. I had a fine, healthy boy, born during a snowstorm in February. I have named him Lovell. He is so pretty and so sweet. I am astonished by how fiercely I love him. No one told me I was going to feel this way about a baby.

He seldom cries, and he always smiles when he sees me. Cima says that's only wind that makes him smile, but I know better. He is so dear with that toothless, little grin. I wish I had nothing to do but sit and watch him grow and kiss the back of his neck. It's like velvet.

The fact is, I have some bad news to go with the good. The snowstorm developed into a blizzard, and we lost the cattle, all the big herd. It's been a bitter blow to us, coming on top of the tornado. It means we're nearly wiped out, with only a few head left.

I'm telling you this because you know I had so wanted you to come for a visit, but I can't ask you to come just now. At present we're going to have a hard time just getting on our feet.

Still, no hardship can take away the joy of having Lovell. He is perfect, and I want you to see him as soon as possible.

Love,
Reanna

It gave Reanna great pleasure to watch Jack Levy make a fuss over Lovell. He talked baby talk to him, and Lovell crowed with delight. Jack should really have a family of his own. He had a talent for being a father.

When Lovell finally had fallen asleep in Jack's arms, and Reanna had taken the baby and put him in his cot, Jack was able to get down to the reason for the visit. He had heard rumors of a fight between Pride and Andrew, but Jack had discounted them. Now, watching Andrew, he wasn't so sure. He was shocked by Andrew's appearance. He'd always been lean and active. Now he was stooped and slow, and much of the old fire had gone out of him.

While Reanna cleared away the supper dishes, the men sat around the kitchen table.

"When will you have some idea of what your situation is?" Jack asked Andrew.

"I'll have to wait and see what we can round up off the open range."

"Can you salvage any of the herd?"

"I've been out looking for strays," Taffy broke in.

"How many, then?"

"One, two hundred head." Taffy's voice was low, almost inaudible. "It's a touch better than we thought."

"Two hundred," Jack murmured.

"Jack, say it right out. I'm ruined." Andrew spoke to Jack, but he looked at Reanna. "I need cash to pay off the cattle company, and I've got no place to get it."

"There's more, I'm afraid." Jack hesitated. "The wholesalers want their money."

"Won't they wait? We've always been good for it."

Jack shook his head. "I've been looking for some way to raise the cash."

"How much do we have now?"

"About half."

"You mean *you* have half. It's my half that's missing." Andrew grinned; it was only a pale copy of his old, cynical arrogance. "What you need is a new partner."

"Don't talk like that, Andrew. We've always been partners." Again he hesitated. "I was thinking maybe you might want to sell out."

"Who would consider a dry goods store in MacClaren City as a good risk?"

"Lots of people are looking to come in here, now that statehood's on the way. We could pay off the wholesalers and you'd have a few dollars left over."

"What good would a few dollars do me? I owe thousands. Only the weather has kept the Kansas City Cattle Company from coming down on me before this. They're in no big hurry; they can squeeze me any time it suits them."

Jack shifted uneasily in his chair. "There's one way you could get them off you."

"What's that?"

"You could go into bankruptcy."

"I don't much like the idea."

"You're not supposed to like it."

"Besides, what real good would it do me? If I sell up all I have, I couldn't pay off ten cents on the dollar."

"I'm not saying you should pay them anything now."

"I don't follow you."

"First you put all your assets in Reanna's name, *then* you file for bankruptcy. That way the cattle company and your other creditors can't take what you don't own. They can't attach or sell what's not yours."

Andrew's eyes shot over to Reanna, darted away again. "I've done a lot of things I regret," he said thickly, "but they've all been aboveboard and legal."

"*This* is legal. I'm not asking you to break the law. I'm trying to show you a way to save yourself, now when it counts. When you're able, you can pay off what you owe. When you raise the cash again, you can pay them a hundred cents on the dollar, not ten. Look, if there weren't bad times all over the country, you might persuade them to wait; but right now they're going to press you to pay, because the banks are pressing *them*. You need time to get back on your feet. This'll give it to you."

"I may never have the money to pay them."

"I never expected to hear you talk like that. You're just going through a bad patch. Every cattleman has a bad year now and again. You'll come back. Think about it, Andrew. If you put everything in Reanna's name—the house, the cattle, the store and the land—she could hold it free and clear of any attachment. Give it to her as a gift by deed."

Andrew glanced at Reanna again; when he looked back at Jack, his lip curled, his aquamarine eyes glinted in his forbidding, supercilious way. "Just what's your angle?" he said.

"Angle?"

"What's in it for you? What are you figuring to get out of it?"

"Now see here—" Cima broke in, but he ignored her.

"You're pretty slick, Jack. You're not doing it for nothing. I suppose you've fixed it up, the two of you. You and my wife."

"Andrew!" Reanna said in a voice of iron; she was standing straight as a ramrod, her hands clenched at her sides. "That's a vicious remark; it's insulting and it's untrue. You have no right to say it!"

"I can see when a—"

"Jack's your best and oldest friend." Her voice rang in the silence. Jack Levy was staring at Andrew in shocked amazement; a deep red flush had spread over his neck and cheeks. "*I know you didn't mean that, Andrew,*" Reanna went on, and the naked scorn in her voice was like a bullwhip's flicking. "You will apologize to him, do you hear?" she whispered fiercely, bending toward him. "You will!"

There was a dead silence in the room. Furious with Andrew, feeling for Jack, shamed above all for Reanna's having to take this from her own husband in a roomful of people, Taffy could have broken a chair over that stupid, suspicious head of Andrew's. What in Christ's name had gone wrong with the man? He was turning on everyone like a wounded snake.

"That's right, Reanna," Andrew was saying nastily, trying to grin. "Wait till they're down, then kick them."

She drew herself back up then, coolly. "You know that's not true. You owe Jack an apology in full, and that's all there is to it."

Andrew looked down, fiddling with a table knife. The silence grew. "I'm not myself, Jack," he said heavily. "I had no call to say that. It—just took me by surprise, that's all." He paused. "I want to apologize."

"It's all right," Jack said awkwardly; he was rubbing his chin. "I know it's a hard thing. For any man."

"But especially for *me*." Andrew looked around the room with quick, angry defiance, then subsided. "All right," he muttered. "I'm between a large rock and a very hard place. I'll do it."

"Only thing," Jack said, "what about the allotments? They haven't been taken yet, have they?"

Andrew looked savagely at Reanna. "It's all decided," he told Jack harshly. "Pride Beauvaise gets the west range; I'm to take the Ridge. The east range is for Snow. We each are entitled to a homestead and the rest is surplus land." He grinned at Cima without mirth. "Cima is entitled to forty acres as a freedwoman."

What about Lovell? Taffy thought. What about the little shaver? As the child of an intermarried white and a white woman, he'd get nothing. And he looked instinctively at Reanna, but she shook her head in reply. She'd decided for reasons of her own that it was a poor time to mention it, maybe.

"Then let Cima choose her allotment now," Reanna said. She was determined to make Andrew do the right thing; Taffy realized with a start that she wasn't as afraid of him as she once was.

"Choose, Cima," Andrew said in his patronizing manner. "Take your forty acres and make your mark. Or I'll sign for you, if you want me to."

Cima turned from the stove; there was no trace of emotion in her face. "I already filed for my allotment, Mr. Andrew."

"What?"

Taffy saw Andrew's jaw harden and that angry vein beat in his temple. He couldn't believe he had heard correctly. Cima had filed for land he'd always believed was his to give or take forever.

"I filed for my land." Cima's gaze defied him to say any more. She knew she was within her rights.

"And just where *is* your land?"

"I took the ravine up there on the northwest. You know, it's where Pride used to hide the cattle out, in bad weather." It was as if she were staring through him. "It's not the best land maybe, but it has a little improvement on it. That old line house."

Taffy felt himself smile grimly. It was a challenge, that's what it was, a challenge to Andrew over his bad judgment. A cool reminder that if he'd done as Pride had wanted, the herd might still be safe, or most of it.

"Forty acres of rock and a beat-up old shack," Andrew was saying contemptuously. "I don't know what you wanted with that parcel. If you'd asked me, I'd have given you a better place where you could have grown a little garden."

Cima's eyes glittered once. She started to say something, then stopped herself. *It wasn't for you to give me nothing*, is what she wants to say, Taffy thought. That tough old gal was something.

"That's mighty kind of you, Mr. Andrew," she said in a voice soft as silk, "to want to give me a better piece of land. But it seems you have troubles enough of your own. Anyway, I done made my choice, so I'll just be content with it. And now if you'll excuse me, I'll get on with the chores while you fine folks talk."

Taffy would have liked to have excused himself as easily. His conscience pricked him a little. Nobody knew he had homesteaded a hundred and sixty acres north of the Canadian River. He'd have to live on it a little and make a few improvements, and then it would be his. It was a claim another man had wanted to sell because he was going back to Kansas. Frampton had put Taffy on to the opportunity.

The land lay right by the river crossing. It had surprised Taffy to find he wanted a little place of his own, a little part and parcel of what was going. He knew he'd never marry, and he'd meant to leave the land to Pride, because it bordered on Lochleven. But now he thought it should go to Lovell, especially since Andrew was not providing for the boy. This baby of Reanna's was a cunning thing, a pretty baby with his red-gold hair. He could see nothing of Andrew in the baby so far, and thank God for that, too.

"Well then." Andrew made a gesture of resignation. "I guess it's all settled. Bankrupt it is, and let them I owe try and find me."

"It will buy you time."

"Help me write out the deed, will you? Only thing is, if I haven't filed for my allotment, how can I give my wife what I haven't got?"

"Simply make out a deed to her for all your property, real and otherwise. That sounds legal enough. Then, whatever you get on homestead and by surplus grant will come to her in her name." He paused. "What about Pride? When he comes back from Muskogee, where's he going to live?"

"He won't come back; we have an understanding," Andrew said flatly. "Pride won't come back to Lochleven to live."

Jack started to say something more, but Taffy gave him a small shake of his head.

With Jack's help, Andrew wrote out a quitclaim that made all his property, real and otherwise, a gift by deed to his lawful wife, Reanna Lovell MacClaren. Cima and Taffy witnessed his signature.

"I hope you'll find a buyer for my half of the store," Andrew said, handing Jack the papers. "Reanna will need the cash, and I haven't any to leave her. I want to go off to Texas free and clear."

His statement brought a wide stare from Reanna and a grunt of shocked surprise from Cima. "Texas!" Cima exclaimed.

"That's right, Texas." Andrew looked pleased. Caught us off guard, Taffy thought; how that man loves to play cat and mouse. "I can't stay here. The vultures would be sure to tie me up with a lot of legal rope. In Texas I'll look around to make a fresh start."

"It's the first I've heard of Texas." Reanna had shut her lips into a thin line. Paying her off, Taffy decided morosely, for this hassle with Jack. Married life. He's given her Lochleven by deed and now he's going to turn it into a ticket of leave.

"I don't expect you to go to Texas with me." Andrew was clearly enjoying this, especially before witnesses. "I think you and the baby should go back East."

"Don't bring that up again!" Reanna snapped at him. "I'm tired of hearing you say that. I'm not going anywhere, and you know it."

"Then suit yourself, Reanna. I should have known better than to try and talk sense into you." He turned to Jack Levy. "I'll depend on you to record the deed. I'll stop by Tishomingo on my way to Texas and file for my allotment."

"When do you figure to go?"

"Why, I'll just get my poke together and I'll be ready to travel."

Reanna took the deed from Jack and looked at it. "Won't you have to file this yourself? Can Jack do it for you?"

"Sure. It's been signed before witnesses." Andrew grinned. "Don't think you're rich. You couldn't get five cents an acre for the place in these times."

Taffy got up and stood by the door. The worst part of it all was that Andrew seemed to be enjoying what he was doing to her, and to the rest of them, too. That Andrew MacClaren was a hard man.

"It was a joke." Andrew was smiling again, but there was no warmth in it. "You hang on here, you could get a fair price for the place."

"I won't sell Lochleven," she said to him, "not now or ever." And Cima banged an iron spider down on the dry sink, as though to emphasize the words as forcefully as possible.

The silence in the kitchen was now acutely uncomfortable. Jack

Levy rose and said awkwardly, "I thank you for the fine meal, Reanna. I hate to eat and run."

"Why not stay the night?" Andrew asked hospitably.

"Can't, I reckon."

"Then hold up and we'll ride along with you. Taffy and me."

"You're going now? *Today?*" Jack couldn't believe his ears. At one time they'd been close, but this man was a total stranger.

"Might as well go if we're going," Andrew said. "Now this legal business is all decided, there's nothing to keep me here." He didn't look at Reanna, but she looked as if he'd struck her in front of all the world.

"I ain't going with you, Andrew," Taffy said. He'd gone a long way with Andrew, but this was the end of the trail.

"What are you talking about? Of course you're going with me! We've always ridden together."

"Nope. I'm needed here." Reanna was looking straight at him, her face excited and warm, and for some reason it pleased him immensely.

"Oh, come on." Andrew looked perplexed and sunk. "You owe me, Taffy."

"Not no more. I said I'd stay with you till you took them critters to market. That day on the Ridge, when you pushed me to—well, never mind that now. I told you *then*, the slate was clean. The way I see it, the tally's even."

Andrew watched him for several seconds. He knew better than to go on. Taffy was a man of his word.

"If that's your decision."

"It is."

Andrew turned to Reanna. He had to admire the way she had carried herself from the moment he told her he was going. Other women would have cried a river or run for the railroad and headed home to mama, but there she stood, holding her ground, not a tear or a whimper.

"When I find work and make a little ahead, I'll send some back. I know you won't listen, but if you were wise, you'd go home."

"That's right. I won't listen."

"I think you know I meant to do better by you than this."

"It doesn't matter now what you meant." She set her shoulders and stood straight.

"No. It doesn't matter now."

"If you get strapped . . ." He hesitated. "Jack and I own some town lots. They might be worth something."

Nothing more was said. There was nothing worth saying. Reanna and Cima fixed Andrew a poke. He went away with a horse, a saddle, a five-dollar gold piece and some cold bacon and biscuit. Andrew rode off without saying goodbye to Snow. He told himself that parting from her would hurt them both too much, but he knew that wasn't the plain truth.

REANNA was overjoyed Taffy had stayed; she needed his strength and his experience and his company. She was now a woman of property, but she was also a mistress of loneliness. Sometimes she was sure she could hear Pride's voice in the wind, but when she turned to look, there was no one there. To keep herself from thinking of him, she drove herself and everyone else. She'd worked them before, but now she ran them ragged and wouldn't listen to their complaints. Now she had not only the house and the garden to see to, she had the running of the whole place.

"Taffy, I want you to round up every head of cattle we have and sell them for whatever you can get."

"You won't get much. Let them graze out the summer."

"I want them sold. And then I want you to let the hands go."

Taffy was dismayed. They'd always kept their top hands, good times and bad. "I could maybe let Zack and Zeb and Paco and Chang go, but we ought to keep Frank and Dan and Slim. You won't get that good again."

"I'm sure that's true, Taffy. But if we don't have any cattle, we won't need any hands. We can't afford to keep them on to do nothing. I have to get enough cash ahead to pay the taxes and to hold as a hedge, in case things get worse."

In a few weeks, Jack Levy came back with letters for her from home, which Reanna read at once. She had found it difficult to write her folks to say that both Andrew and Pride had gone. But putting the words on paper had made her see clearly how much she must now depend on herself alone.

Dear Reanna,

We have just had a letter from you saying both you and the baby are well. Your papa and I both wish we could have been with you, and as soon as you are able, please write more about Lovell. Your papa says he is drinking a toast to his first grandson. I believe your papa was even more worried about you than I was. It is too bad about your weather, and we are so sorry to hear you lost your livestock. Nothing has gone right for you since you got out there. I wish you'd never gone so far from home. Now, in your second letter, which came today, you say Andrew has gone to Texas. Reanna, I don't mean to criticize Andrew, but for him to go off and his brother to go away at the same time and leave you with only the foreman and Cima and those girls to look after you and the baby and Snow seems to me to be *very* irresponsible. Your papa and I are anxious to come out as soon as we can to see for ourselves that you are all right. Of course, the boys are in school and they will insist on coming too, so our visit will have to be in the summer. Your papa has just said to tell you that he wants to see you.

We have had dreadful winter weather here, too, this year. Old Mrs. Bryson fell just after Christmas and broke her hip—trying to rescue her cat, I believe.

Love,
Mama

Dear Sister,

We were very glad you had a baby and that we are now uncles. Please send us a picture of the baby soon, so we'll know what he looks like, and one of you, too. It's been so very long since we've seen you.

Your affectionate brother,
Patrick

Dear Reanna,

A boy. Just what I wanted. Thanks.

Uncle Thomas

Dear Reanna,

Late at night in my study, and I am thinking of you. Dear, dear daughter. Thank you for my grandson named Lovell. I've a dram taken, but I am sober enough to know a great thing has happened. I wish I could send Lovell the moon. I do send him a grandfather's love instead.

Your Papa

When Reanna had finished reading her letters, she looked up and smiled at Jack.

"Everything OK at home?" he asked.

"Yes," she said.

"Well, I believe I have a little more good news for you."

"I could use it."

"I've been able to satisfy the wholesalers, at least for the time being."

"How did you manage that?" Reanna asked in admiration.

Jack flushed. "Well, I had a little put by. And I borrowed a bit from Doc and Amoretta."

"That means you're carrying Andrew."

"He's still my partner."

"It's not fair."

"He'd do the same for me."

She didn't think Andrew *would* do the same for Jack, but she said nothing; instead, she made over her half of the store and two town lots to Jack outright.

"You don't have to do this." He looked at the deeds in embarrassment. "I'll be all right until Andrew gets back."

"You don't know when that will be. He could be gone a long time."

"You can't keep a man like him down. Andrew will make good again."

"Maybe not."

"He wouldn't leave you on your own."

"He's done it before."

Jack wouldn't quarrel with that. In the end, he accepted the deeds. It was what Reanna had thought was fair. In fact, he'd paid out a good deal more than what they were worth to the wholesalers in Kansas City.

"You'll stay for supper?" she asked.

"Yes, thanks."

After supper, when Cima and Snow had gone to bed, Reanna and Jack sat in the kitchen over an extra cup of coffee. She looked at him carefully. He was a nice-looking man, and everything about him was a testament to loyalty and friendship. But she realized that, in fact, she didn't know much about him.

"Andrew always told me I asked too many questions, so if I get out of line, stop me."

He looked up at her, puzzled. "OK, shoot. What do you want to know?"

"How did you get out here to the Indian Territory?"

"I came up from Texas with Andrew, peddling a bankrupt stock."

"I knew about that. I guess I mean, how did you get to Texas? Where was home for you?"

He sighed. "I was born in a village on the Russian-Polish border—the youngest of ten. My mother died, and my father moved on to Austria. I don't know why. He was a poor man, not a practical one. He kept leaving his children first with one relative and then another. I ended up with an uncle who wanted to come to America, and when he couldn't locate my father or anyone else who would be responsible for me, he took me with him. I was six, nearly seven, when we landed in New York.

"My uncle went into business—buying, selling, doing what he had to to keep us both. Then he died of typhoid and I had to get out on my own."

"How old were you?"

"Fifteen."

"A baby."

"How old were you when you married Andrew?" He grinned.

"Eighteen, nearly nineteen."

"A baby."

"When you went out on your own, what did you do?"

"I got a job selling on the road for a line of ladies' dress wear. I wasn't good at it, but I had a lot of energy."

"And that's how you got to Texas?"

"Yes. It wasn't the best job in the world, but I traveled and met a lot of people, and I made a little money. When I got to Galveston, my job folded up on me and I got another, still selling, this time a line of shoes and notions. By the time I got up to Fort Worth, that job had played out too, and with my savings I bought a bankrupt country store and decided to take it up to the Indian Territory, where I thought I could turn a profit. That's when I met up and fell in with Andrew, who was going back up, driving cattle. He knew the Nation, and he wanted to start a town. A town would need a store." Jack stopped. "Well, that's it. That's my story."

"And you're glad you came?"

He thought for a while and then said, "Yes."

"You must have been lonely up here."

"I've made some good friends."

"You know what you need?" she asked.

He thought she was going to offer him another cup of coffee.

"What?"

"You need a wife," she said earnestly.

He threw back his head and started to laugh. He laughed so hard, she had to shush him to keep him from waking Lovell.

"I don't see what I've said that's so funny."

"Reanna." Jack put his hand over hers. "I can't afford to pay the wholesalers, let alone afford to keep a wife."

"Maybe someday you'll marry," she persisted.

"Maybe someday." Then he looked at her, his eyes large and kind as he said, "You must be lonely, too."

"I have Lovell," she said defensively. "And I have a lot of good friends."

"Have you heard from Pride?"

"No." She felt her face go stiff and her heart began to beat.

"When do you expect him back?"

"Andrew told you, Pride's not coming back." Saying the words aloud was like the harshest of medicines. It gave her pain, but it was a part of a hoped-for cure.

"Why did Pride go to Muskogee?" Jack asked. "Did he and Andrew have a falling out?"

Reanna looked Jack square in the eye. "Pride went to work for the Dawes Commission. He means to stay and study the law." Her gaze was cold, forbidding him to ask her anything more.

Jack backed away. "Well, I can't blame him for getting out of ranching. The way things are this year, the law is bound to be an easier way to make a living."

Later, he spread the word around town; it became the official reason for Pride's leaving Lochleven.

REANNA lived without word from Andrew or Pride. She went for weeks without thinking of Andrew; she wished she could say the same about Pride. There was never a day when she didn't think of him. She ached for him; at night, alone in her bed, the coarse sheets were a rack for her desire.

In the day she dreamed of him, thinking of where they'd walked and what they'd said; she kept turning old memories in her mind like pebbles until they were worn smooth. Sometimes she imagined she could see him riding far to the west. She was glad he couldn't see the ranges. With the spring, the grass had come back, but it had been overgrazed, as he'd feared, and was sparse and patchy; the raw earth lay exposed. When she rode out looking for she didn't know what, her mind often played her tricks and she could see Pride riding toward her, coming from the river, but it was only some stranger passing through. She would turn away and ride home, pretending dust had got in her eyes.

Sometimes Cima rode out with her. She'd been a fine cowgirl and a superb horsewoman in her day, but she was getting old and a day in the saddle laid her up for two afterwards.

Together they lived and endured. For Reanna, there was no joy in life but for Lovell. They stayed on the place, rooting in the dirt for their dinner and chasing chickens for Sunday. They got through another blast furnace of a summer.

Snow was as discontented as ever. When she learned her father had left for an indefinite time and without even saying goodbye to her, she became hysterical, accused Reanna of driving him away, and was inconsolable for days. She refused even to eat.

"I declare, child, happiness is where you're *not*," Cima told her once crossly; and indeed, it did seem to be true. She would complain of the heat, the flies, the wind, claim she was overworked and maltreated, and then all at once beg for candy and ribbons and other pretties. On the other hand, Snow was growing up, and she only wanted what most girls wanted.

Reanna refused to give in to these incessant pleas for finery. She did without and she expected others to do without as well. She scraped and saved every cent. She begrudged herself postage for a letter home and only wrote when it was necessary.

Dear Mama and Papa,

This summer's weather is worse than last year's. It's just about impossible to keep cool. In the afternoon, I take Lovell out and put him in the shade of the catalpa tree under a cheesecloth netting. I bathe him in rainwater and baking soda and put cornstarch on his neck to keep him from getting heat rash. They were all Cima's suggestions. She knows everything about babies.

Lovell is generally such an easy, goodnatured baby, I hate it when he does fret. Cima says she thinks he is cutting a tooth.

We all take turns minding him. Just at first, it was hard for Snow to get used to the idea of not being the only child in the house, but even she loves him, and Lovell adores her. He holds on to her like she was gold. I am enclosing a picture of Lovell and Snow. A photographer came by with a camera, so I had a picture of the two of

(332)

them taken. You can see how big he's getting. I was in my gardening clothes and didn't have time to change, so you'll have to wait
for a picture of me. Besides, it cost a lot.

I am so glad you're not thinking of coming out here in this heat,
but if the weather will only break and a little luck will come our
way, we'll all be together soon. Perhaps you can come in November
for Statehood Day. The boys would miss school, but it will be very
historic.

Yes, Andrew is still away. No word from him. I hope no news is
good news.

My love to you all.

Reanna

Dear Reanna,

It was a grand picture of Lovell. We have it framed. The little
girl, Snow, looks younger than I had imagined. What a sad-faced
child. Maybe it's just the light in the photograph.

Now, Ree, I wish, as do your papa and the boys, that we could
come out for Statehood Day in November. *But*—and this is just to
be between the two of us—your papa is still having some serious
money worries. Don't think I mean to criticize your papa. I wouldn't
change him for any other man, but I must tell you that it's hard
when the bills pile up and there's no hope of paying them.

I had to write this to you, because I don't want you to think we
don't want to come. We can't afford it at present. So, to make your
papa and the boys feel better, I just said I think it's inconvenient
for *you* if we come before you are more settled.

Your loving Mama

Dear Papa,

I am sitting in the kitchen. It's late and the house is quiet. I'm
sorry I can't ask you to come out just now. What's worst about
money is not having any. Sometimes it seems I'll be poor forever.

I hate to whine. Most days I put one foot in front of the other
and just go on. But at night I get to thinking—trying to see a way
out. And it's so dark.

Papa, tell me something to hang on to. What do you do when
you can't win for losing?

I read this over and I'm ashamed of complaining, but I've already
addressed the envelope and put the stamp on it, so I'll mail it.

Love,
Reanna

Dear Girl,

I am glad you mailed the letter. Of course I know what it's like to have a bad run of luck and feel down, but stay in the game, don't fold. It helps to have good cards, but if you don't have them, bluff. And when you do get dealt a decent hand, bet the pot.

I love you, dear girl. If you still have that gold piece, spend it on something pretty for yourself.

Love,
Papa

But she could not spend the money. She had come by what she had the hard way, and it was the only defense between her and a vast, threatening world.

Whenever she felt tempted to spend something on the house or herself or Snow, she'd take the chest from its hiding place and count out the money. It added up to nearly five hundred dollars. This small fortune was her reserve, her buffer against disaster; it was money to be saved and not spent. Besides, she could spend it to the last penny, but it wouldn't buy her what she truly wanted.

Cima knew that Reanna was laying some money by. She understood saving for a rainy day, but still she thought that some small part of it should be spent now. The children were ragged. She began to voice her complaints aloud in front of Reanna, as if she were talking to the air. "Look at Snow," Cima would say absently. "The girl's growing up, growing up to be a young lady soon. Look at the poor thing going barefoot. She needs a pair of shoes."

"It won't hurt her to go barefoot. I used to like to go barefoot when I was little."

"That's 'cause you didn't have to," Cima would mutter.

"I'll get her a new pair of shoes, next time we go to town."

"And when will that be? Do I dare ask?"

"We can't go gallivanting into town any time we take a fancy."

"Well, we'll have to go in November."

"Why November?"

"In November we'll go for Statehood Celebration Day." Cima looked grimly determined. "The Twin Territories will become the sovereign State of Oklahoma."

"Oh that." Since her folks were not coming, Reanna did not consider the event a cause for celebration. "Lot of foolish nonsense. Cigar smoke and speeches. I've heard them." Rounding the side of the house, Taffy and Snow could overhear the end of the conversation.

(334)

Snow ran toward Reanna, crying, "Please say yes! Say we can go. Pretty please."

"We'll see."

"Can't we go, Taffy?"

"Sure we're going," Taffy said. "We're all going to climb in the wagon and go to town for the big day." He grinned at Reanna slyly. It was like pulling hen's teeth to get Reanna to go anywhere. She'd let them go to the green corn dance last July, but they had none of them been off the place since then, except to work. They all needed a day off, especially Reanna.

"Who will look after the place?" she asked him crossly, because he'd promised without asking her. "We can't just go off and leave it."

"Why not? Nobody's going to come and carry it off. Everybody's going to be there."

Reanna was still undecided. She hadn't been to town since Andrew left. She felt safer here at home. She didn't want to face a lot of prying eyes or answer a lot of questions.

"*You* may not care about statehood," Taffy went on smoothly, "but now think about Lovell. When he's a grown man and you have to tell him he missed the single biggest day in history, he's going to hold it against you. He's bound to."

She knew she was being flimflammed. "Lovell's only a baby." Reanna tried not to laugh. "He won't remember it anyway."

"You don't *know* he won't," Taffy pressed her. "Lovell's quick as a wink. Anything he sees, he remembers."

"Say we can go," Snow begged. "Please."

"All right," Reanna agreed grudgingly. "Since you all seem to be so set on it."

"Now you're talking!" Taffy shouted, and he uttered a blood-curdling rebel yell, which Snow imitated, clapping her hands. Even Cima was grinning, her gold teeth glinting in the sunlight.

Seeing them all so happy touched Reanna strangely. She'd made the right decision. And anyway, it was time she took Lovell to town and let the world have a look at him.

TAFFY hadn't exaggerated. It seemed everybody in the entire county was in MacClaren City to celebrate statehood. Reanna was amazed at how the town had grown. There were two more churches, another school, and a town full of strangers. She was glad to see Amoretta and Doc, familiar faces in the boisterous crowd.

There were so many changes. There were actually sidewalks, and the main street had been extended by several blocks. There were new storefronts, a newspaper, a cafe and a boarding house—all that since she had come as a bride.

Everyone was bent on seeing that statehood did not go unwelcomed. There was a band and a parade with veterans of the Civil War, both the blue and the gray, though there were more of the gray. The men were getting to be old. Reanna thought of her father and wished he were here.

There were turkey shoots and horse races. Reanna noticed two of the old ranch hands, Frank Pettis and Dan Penland, spurring their cow ponies to the quarter-mile limit. They tipped their hats, but they didn't come to pass the time of day with her or with Taffy, which hurt him; she felt sorry they'd been let go, but they all knew the reason was the loss of the herd and Andrew's departure.

Reanna knew they looked shabby next to the town folk. One glance at them was enough to show how things were. She'd done all she could to put them into their best, but they had nothing new, only mend and make do, patch and pretend. Even her bonnet, which she'd tried to refurbish and clean with cornmeal, looked bedraggled.

She tried to take her mind off their ratty appearance by paying attention to the speeches and looking at the flags. They watched the mock wedding between the Twin Territories, in which Frank Pettis, as the cowboy, married the Indian princess, a friend of Annoyi. They stuffed themselves on fried chicken, hams, pies and cakes and drank gallons of iced lemonade and tea. Taffy passed this last up in favor of a sip of whiskey with Doc. There was no stopping the men, and after they'd settled in, there was no finding them.

After the speeches and fireworks, Jack Levy opened up the store. As Cima picked out a new pair of shoes for Snow, Reanna and Amoretta had a chance to visit.

"What do you hear from Andrew?" Amoretta asked, holding the baby. It was a reasonable enough question, but Reanna felt a sudden rush of anger. It wasn't right of Andrew to go off and leave them and not even send a postcard to inquire how they might be or tell them where he was.

"Oh, the usual snips and scraps," she said. "Cattle and weather. Andrew was never much of a correspondent."

(336)

Amoretta jiggled Lovell up and down, patting him on the back. Her rouge glowed above the flush of her cheeks. "Andrew ought to get back here. Times are changing fast. Doc and Jack went up to the capital to see about getting a charter for a bank. Think of that, a *bank* for MacClaren City! Andrew should be here to see it. They're going to build it on one of those lots we bought from you. And there's talk the railroad might run in a spur line. A railroad! Now that would *make* MacClaren City."

"I'm glad about the bank," Reanna said, wondering how Andrew would feel about it; nothing had ever been done in town without his permission before. "It will be handy not to have to travel twenty miles to get on a railroad."

Amoretta's color deepened. She gave a nervous cough and blurted out, "Have you heard from Pride?"

Reanna looked away, taken off guard. "No."

"Somebody told Doc they'd seen Pride up in Muskogee." She waited, but Reanna said nothing. "They said he was fixing to study law. We surely do miss him." Amoretta hurried on, "And Andrew too, of course." Her face was now the color of fire.

Reanna was sorry for Amoretta's discomfort. None of their old friends could discuss Pride or Andrew without embarrassment or curiosity about their quarrel. But before Reanna could think of something polite to say, Snow came running up in her new shoes, wanting them to be admired. The child begged for a little rabbit muff she'd seen.

"No," Reanna said, "we can't afford it, Snow."

"I want it so! I *need* it, to keep my hands warm."

"No. I said no and I mean it."

Amoretta shook her head. "Snow's growing up and no mistake."

"Let me give it to her as a present," Jack offered.

"Thank you, Jack, but no," Reanna said. "We can't take what we can't pay for."

Snow began to wail, and Jack gave her an all-day sucker. Bending down, he whispered in her ear, "Maybe Santa Claus will bring you a muff." Snow stuffed the jawbreaker in her mouth and was silent.

"She misses her father," Cima said, and, as if it were a cue to leave, they all said their goodbyes.

Amoretta hugged Reanna. "Why don't you come in more often? A visit now and again would do you good. Come and stay for Sunday and church. I'll fatten you up a little; you're thin as a rail."

"I'll try. I will." Reanna knew she wouldn't come, and so did

Amoretta. "Now help me find Taffy. It's time we headed for home."

The two men were out back of Amoretta and Doc's house, hiding out in the barn; their loud, off-key singing afforded a neat indication of the stage they'd reached.

"My, my," Amoretta said, rolling her eyes, "I don't know where Doc learned songs like that."

It took Cima and Annoyi and Reanna, with Amoretta's help, to hoist Taffy into the back of the wagon. At the end of town, Reanna saw John's Dead in a new checkered coat. On one side of him was a city slicker with a gold watch chain and a new derby, and on the other a fancy woman with piled blonde hair. They were leading John's Dead along as if he were a dancing bear.

"Did you see that?" Cima demanded hotly. "*That's* what comes of statehood. The law says John's Dead can't sell his allotment land for twenty-five years, but the law also says he's an incompetent. So they appointed him a lawyer who can buy or sell or lease or anything he pleases. I ask you, is that right, is that fair?"

"No," Reanna said, "but tell me what's right or fair about a lot of laws."

"I don't like this new state. If Pride can thread his way through these legal shenanigans, more power to him."

Snow had been dozing on a pallet beside Lovell and Taffy, who was snoring almost as loudly as he'd been singing. "Why wouldn't you buy me that muff? If it was Lovell, you'd buy him the moon."

"Go to sleep, Snow. I've got a good deal more to worry about right now than you and that rabbit muff." Still, in her heart, she knew Snow was right. For Lovell, Reanna would have stolen the moon and strung the stars. For Lovell, she had to find a way to make a better living. She didn't want him ever to feel poor when they went to town. She'd felt poor that day and no mistake; it wasn't a feeling she meant to repeat. She had a plan working in the back of her mind that would change all that, a plan to make them rich. All she needed was the right occasion and a little old-fashioned, country luck.

There was nothing on earth she wouldn't do for Lovell.

EVERYTHING about Lovell delighted her. He slept in her room where she could watch over him. The drawer had been replaced by a cradle and then a cot. She woke every morning to find him smiling blissfully at her. His first tooth was an event; the day he first pulled himself up and stood was a time for celebration. However, he didn't stand again for another three months. It was a portent of his stubborn and independent nature. No one could coax Lovell to do something he didn't want to do.

Not that he ever acted ugly about it. He seldom fussed or cried. He didn't speak words for a year and some, but everything Reanna said to him pleased him; he babbled back happy gibberish. He seemed to love Reanna and everyone else. He rode Taffy's leg, listening in fascination as Taffy sang of the Old Chisholm Trail and Barby Allen, or jogging merrily up and down as the trail boss chanted, "Hot and dusty, goin' to 'Gusty . . ."

Taffy would have died rather than admit that Lovell was the joy of an errant life, though he would say he felt partial to the little critter. Before Lovell was able to walk, Taffy had sat him on a horse in front of him. Taffy taught him everything about Lochleven, its weather and its grasslands. When Lovell was old enough to toddle, he walked beside Taffy, holding tightly to his finger and his heartstrings. When Reanna looked out the window at the two of them, she could see Taffy's jaw moving up and down and Lovell nodding ardently, smiling that warm, beatific smile. She wondered if Lovell understood a word, if he would remember any of it. Then she would see him gently stroking the cat, or holding a stem of lupine to the light, and her heart would catch at her. His eyes had darkened, but his hair and skin were as fair as her own. She'd tried to be fair and not show how much she loved Lovell, but there was no fooling Snow.

"When is my daddy coming home?" the girl would demand sullenly.

"I don't know."

"It's *your* fault he went away."

"Snow, that's not true."

"You hate him, you *wanted* to be shet of him."

"When you're older, you'll understand."

Snow turned even more defiant than before; when she thought no one was looking, she would bedevil Lovell and make him cry. Once she pinched him so hard, she left a mark on his arm. Reanna wanted to slap her, but she checked herself; she was afraid if she once hit Snow, she'd strike too hard. When it came to Lovell, she couldn't trust herself to be fair.

"Don't ever do that again!" Reanna shook Snow and let her go. Snow's eyes were round with satisfaction; she'd gotten some response at least. Next time she'd provoke Reanna more.

"I'm doing my best," Reanna told her. "I give you everything I give to Lovell." She stopped herself; it wasn't true, and Snow knew it. "I do care for you, Snow, as much as I'm able." It was all Reanna had to offer, and it wasn't enough to satisfy Snow.

"I hate you."

"I'm sorry. I hoped we could be friends."

No matter how much Snow tormented Lovell, he worshipped her. He followed her around and babbled all his secrets. He would share his toys and, on the rare occasions when he had any, his store candy.

The Christmas after Andrew left was the leanest ever. She sent a box home of just what came off the place: pecans, a wreath of mistletoe and gilded bois d'arc apples. It was so little to send, but she couldn't spend when she didn't know what lay ahead.

The preparations at the cabin were what Cima considered niggardly; she continued her habit of talking aloud to herself. "Poor babies, nothing in the poke for their Christmas. Old stagers like

Taffy and me, it don't matter none. But a baby and a growing-up girl, they deserve better."

Her arguments failed to move Reanna; she'd learned to keep close what she had. There would be no one to help her if she failed; it was up to her to root, hog or die, and she knew it in the marrow of her bones.

The Christmas weather further depressed her spirits. This year was as bleak and raw as the year before had been mild and fair. She tried not to think of last year, of the men coming in caked with dust and sweat, of the look on Pride's face when he saw she was going to have a child, or of Andrew not sure if this baby was his, but with no way to prove otherwise. This year Pride wouldn't be coming home, and there was still no word from Andrew. In an effort to make up for Andrew's absence, she'd asked Jack Levy to come out and play Santa Claus, bringing the rabbit muff he'd promised for Snow. Jack, Taffy, Cima, Snow, the girls and Reanna, with Lovell on her knee, sat down to Christmas dinner. There was enough but not a feast. When they opened the box from Virginia, the presents were lavish in comparison to what she had sent home to her people. There was a blue velvet skirt for Snow, a paisley shawl for Cima, an embroidered vest for Taffy and a silver mug for Lovell. For Reanna, they had sent a dressing gown of cashmere.

How like her family to be so generous, when they had done it all on credit. And Reanna thought of what it must be like at the farm—the wide hall full of lighted candles, the banisters twined with a rope of cedar and holly, the tree trimmed, a pile of presents beneath it. And in the dining room, the punch bowl full for company from all over the county, and laughter in every room. No matter how poor of purse her family was, they had always entertained at Christmas, while here even the singing of carols and Taffy's spirited rendition of "Red River Valley" did little to raise their spirits.

No matter how they had tried to be festive, the day had been lackluster. Reanna was relieved when it was over and she and Jack were alone.

"Jack," she began tentatively, "there's something I've been wanting to talk to you about."

"What's on your mind?"

"Have you heard anything about the oil play up around Tulsa?"

"Some, why?"

She stopped picking up the Christmas clutter and sat facing him. "Jack, I think there's oil here at Lochleven."

"Here?"

"Yes, down at the seep springs."

He thought for a moment. "That could just be surface oil."

"Maybe."

"I thought I'd come into town and read back newspapers about what's been happening in oil in the area. But you are always in town. A lot of people from all over come into the store and the bank. You could keep your ears open."

Jack grinned. "I could certainly do that." He hesitated. "I was thinking of going up Tulsa way on business. I'll have a look around."

"Thank you." She grinned back at him now, knowing he had caught some of her enthusiasm. "If we struck oil, you would be able to afford a wife."

"Stop trying to marry me off." Jack hesitated again, unsure he should ask her the question that was on his mind. He took a deep breath and dived in. "When I'm up at Tulsa, I could come back down by way of Muskogee and see Pride."

She sat very straight, staring at the fire.

"Anything you want me to tell Pride? If I see him?"

"Just tell him we're fine and hope he's all right."

"If you wanted to send him a letter . . ." Jack left the question open.

"No."

"Just asking. It's my job to deliver the mail. I'm still postmaster."

"Thank you, Jack. I know you mean well, but some things are best left as they are." She stood up. "Now, can I get you anything else, another piece of mince pie?"

"No, I ate too much as it is. That was a fine dinner."

"Well, good night then. I hope you'll be comfortable by the fire. Sleep well." She walked toward the door. She could hear the wind blowing and whistling in the chinked logs. She turned back to Jack. "This is my second Christmas out here. Sometimes it seems like a hundred years. Things have to get better, and I'm going to make them get better soon."

By Lovell's birthday the weather had improved. Reanna killed a chicken; there was a six-egg cake with icing, and presents wrapped in silver paper.

"My birthday cake wasn't as big," Snow grumbled.

"No, but you had more candles," Reanna answered.

It was an answer that satisfied no one. Snow flew into a tantrum and Reanna sent her to her bed. Cima continued to complain out loud about all this pinch-gut living, and Taffy disappeared for a three-day drunk across the river.

It was a hard winter with all seven of them cooped up in the little house, bumping into each other, rubbing each other the wrong way. Reanna's best times were when she and Lovell were alone. She was never too tired to sing him a song, never too busy to find an hour for a story before bedtime. He was the bright star in her crown.

"Everything's going to turn out all right," she whispered, rocking him, holding him close. "I promise you, honey. I don't know just how, but I'll make everything right."

At last, just when they'd given up hope, the south wind came and warm rain. It seemed a good omen. Reanna planted an early garden, and within the month the shoots came up, strong and green.

Taffy noticed with relief that Reanna wasn't so tired all the time; she was much less impatient with everyone. She was full of good humor, as if she were expecting a longed-for guest. She seemed to be holding herself in readiness for something. Taffy didn't think it was for Andrew's return. There had been no word, which probably meant he was still a dollar down and a day behind. She'd gone into town with him twice and spent hours in the newspaper office reading back issues; then she'd been closeted with Jack Levy in the back of the store while Taffy waited outside. Whatever was on her mind, she wasn't telling and he wasn't about to ask. He knew it wasn't Pride she was waiting for; that race was run. He wasn't coming back, and she wasn't leaving Lochleven. That was a puzzler, when you thought about it.

Then, one evening when they were sitting on the porch, rocking and passing the time of day, Cima said, "Company," and Taffy saw two men driving down the Ridge from the east. As they drew nearer, he could see it was two strangers in a hired buggy; they were dressed in city suits and had derby hats on their heads.

"God Almighty, it's lawyers, duded up like that. They're coming to serve you with papers on Andrew. I'm going to get my gun belt."

"Be still," Reanna said softly. He looked at her in surprise; she was bent forward a little, her eyes shining with that funny, eager expectation. "It's all right." She put aside the beans she'd been shelling.

"Could be worse than the law," Cima said, her hand over her eyes.

"What's worse than the law?" Taffy demanded.

"Hired guns from the cattle company. *That's* worse."

"They're not dressed like gunmen. And they'd be riding," Reanna said serenely. "Let's wait and see what they have to say."

The two men hitched the buggy and came toward the house. They were a nice-looking pair, neatly dressed. Both wore black suits, white shirts and bowler hats, which they took off politely as they came near the porch. The thing about them that struck Reanna was that, while they wore city suits, their complexions were weathered and their hands red and coarse from hard work. One was tall and craggy-featured, the other shorter and as round-cheeked as a cherub, but what they both had in common was a look in their eyes like two foxes dressed as gentlemen, come calling at a hen-house.

The taller, thinner one spoke for them both in a soft, deferential tone. "Evening, folks. My name is Wade, and this is my partner, Mr. Wardell."

"How do you do?" Reanna said, rising, polite but cool.

"We were just driving past and we, ah"—Mr. Wade paused to clear his throat—"why, we heard from a Mr. Jack Levy about this fine seep springs where we could water our horses." His eyes shifted from Reanna to Taffy to Cima.

Taffy went on his guard at that. Those two hadn't any need to water those horses, and any damn fool could see it. And they hadn't been just driving by, either. They had something on their minds, and it was probably so crooked you'd have to screw it into the ground.

"We found the spring," Mr. Wade was saying. He hesitated. "Out by those cliffs, ma'am. It's very interesting, very unusual."

"It's what they call a medicine spring," Taffy volunteered blandly. Reanna shot him a sharp, disapproving glance and he shut up.

"The Indians think it can cure most anything," Cima said. Reanna was staring at her, hard, but Cima didn't pick it up. "You folks wouldn't be snake oil salesmen trying to buy up John's Dead's supply, would you? If so, it's not for sale."

"Cima," Reanna said quietly.

"That oil is already spoke for," Cima went on.

The two men looked back and forth at each other then. They both seemed a bit confused.

"My, no," Mr. Wade said. "We're not looking for medicine oil." He hooked his thumbs in his vest pockets. "As a matter of fact, we were wondering if we might arrange a lease from the owner of that land. Liberal terms, of course. We might be interested in doing a little drilling."

"Drilling?" Cima said with a laugh. "Drilling for what? Rattle-snakes?"

"Cima," Reanna repeated, and now there was no mistaking the edge in her voice. "Would you gentlemen care to come up and sit a spell?" she said sweetly. "We could offer you some cool butter-milk, can't we, Cima?" And before you could say *jackrabbit*, the two men were up on the porch and sitting in rockers with glasses in their hands.

"What part of the country do you fellas hail from?" Taffy asked.

"Pennsylvania," Mr. Wade said.

"That's right," Mr. Wardell added. "I guess you've heard about the oil fields up in Pennsylvania."

It was news to Taffy, and Cima was still glowering at them, but Reanna nodded.

"Yes," she said, "I've heard of them."

"Well, the thing is," Mr. Wade continued, "we've seen your spring and, now the allotments have gone through and the land is under individual ownership, we'd like to take a lease on that prop-erty. Purely speculation, you understand."

"I see," Reanna said. Taffy couldn't read her at all.

"Do you think your husband might be interested in leasing the land?"

"You want to dig a hole for oil?" Taffy couldn't believe his ears. "You raise oil and the grass won't grow. The cattle can't drink it. That stuff's poison."

"Taffy," Reanna said in a tone that stopped him in his tracks, "if you don't mind. My husband isn't here at the moment," she went on, her voice as smooth and cool as the buttermilk they were drink-ing, "but the property is in my name. You gentlemen can do busi-ness with me."

They glanced at each other shrewdly, and Taffy knew exactly what they were thinking. The right to lease in this new state was not a straightforward, clear thing on some of these Indian homesteads. The principal being a woman might give them an advantage.

Mr. Wade cleared his throat. "Well, I'll tell you what's usual in these deals. This offer is standard practice. We want a five-year lease on the property directly around the springs, with the option to lease more land—say another five hundred acres—if we find oil."

"What advance in cash are you offering?"

"Why none." Mr. Wade looked as surprised as Taffy was himself; the trail boss stole a glance at Reanna, but she was smiling pleasantly at Mr. Wade.

"No ma'am, we aren't offering any bonus." Mr. Wardell was definite.

"When would you begin drilling?"

"Beg pardon?" Mr. Wade looked downright flustered now.

"By what date would you begin drilling?" Reanna repeated.

"Well, we'd drill at our discretion," Mr. Wade said.

"And how would I be paid, for both the lease and the oil?"

Mr. Wade cleared his throat again; the Lochleven dust seemed to be bothering him, in spite of all that good buttermilk.

"We're prepared to offer a sixteenth of the profits on every barrel."

"Is that on both oil and gas?"

"Gas isn't worth anything to us," Mr. Wade said, frowning. "If you get gas, you need a pipe to ship it."

"I see."

"They're talking about five hundred acres of your good grazing land, Mrs. MacClaren," Taffy couldn't refrain from saying. "Oil and cattle don't mix."

"Mrs. MacClaren," Mr. Wade said, in his softest voice; there was honey on his tongue, all right. "That five hundred acres was just a figure, a figure we can work out in the future. Right now all we want is to lease the land around the seepage. There's oil there already, so the cattle won't be affected any more than they are now. And maybe we could afford just a token payment in advance of royalties."

Reanna nodded, as though she'd just remembered something she'd left simmering on the stove. "Well," she said, "I certainly want to thank you gentlemen for your offer. It comes as a surprise. I'm sure you understand that I'd like to think it over for a day or so."

Wade and Wardell looked very troubled at this. It wasn't at all the answer they'd expected. Taffy suppressed a grin and shifted his plug. This was turning out to be more fun than a good night at the Triangle.

"We'd hoped we might reach some kind of agreement . . ." Wade was saying in a faltering tone.

"I do thank you again," Reanna interrupted him sweetly, her eyes wide, the lashes fluttering, "but I can tell you now, so as to save your wasting any more of your valuable time, that I'd want to give you no more than a six-month lease. A test well would have to be completed in that time. And certainly, for a well you already have so much confidence in, I would expect a—what did you call it—a bonus."

"We might consider a bonus," Mr. Wade said grudgingly.

"A small bonus," Mr. Wardell added, "but we'd want a year's lease, minimum."

"And," Reanna went on, "I'd consider a one-eighth royalty on every barrel to be fair." She hadn't once stopped smiling. "Take it or leave it, gentlemen."

Mr. Wade and Mr. Wardell looked as if they'd just run up against John D. Rockefeller himself. Reanna was still watching them pleasantly; Cima's face was inscrutable, but her eyes were glittering. It was all Taffy could do to keep from yipping out loud. Talk about draw poker! What'd she have—a full house or a busted flush? So *that's* what all those sessions with Jack Levy had been over. Oil! She'd been studying up and biding her time. She'd had Jack spreading the word about the oil springs. Hot damn, he was proud of her! These two city fellas had been so sure they had the horse in the barn. Well, she'd suckered 'em in slick as a whistle, and then she'd turned them every which way but loose. She was a hummer, all right. Why, hell, Andrew wasn't in her class. The look on the faces of these two was a pitiful sight, a pitiful sight indeed.

"The fact is," Mr. Wade said finally, in a hollow voice, "we don't have cash in hand just at the moment. You see, we're actually drillers by trade. We were just passing through town, and we'd heard about those oil springs. And then, when we saw them for ourselves, we had a hunch this property could prove out in time." He grinned weakly at them. "That's what this business is all about, playing your hunches."

"Drillers?" Now it was Reanna's turn to stare. She's misplayed her hand, Taffy thought, but he couldn't figure how.

"Yes, ma'am," Mr. Wardell said awkwardly. He was sorry if

they'd got the wrong impression; he'd never liked pretending to be more than he was.

"Just passing by, you say?"

"We're on our way to Tulsey town, to a drilling job."

"I'm sorry," Reanna said, "but without the capital to lease or drill, I don't see how we can do any business."

Taffy could read how disappointed she was. She'd been raising and raising in this hand as pretty as you could ask, and when she took the pot, they couldn't cover it. He could see her thinking fast what she could do, and getting nowhere. Then she swallowed her medicine.

"If you'd like to stay on for supper, we'd be glad to have you. It's a long way back to town."

Mr. Wade and Mr. Wardell thanked her kindly for her most generous offer, and those two four-flushers were inside the house and tucking into some feed before you could say *snake oil*. But Taffy knew Reanna well enough to know there was a method in her madness.

"The thing is," Mr. Wade said expansively—it was wonderful how a square meal picked up a man's spirits—"to get into this oil game, you've got to have assets. You've got to have money, or know how to get it. Now, nobody knows drilling like Wardell and me, but we don't have the land, and we don't have the cash to lease the land. We *know* there's oil out there by those springs. This country out here is going to boom, and we want in on it so bad, we can taste it. It's going to make Pennsylvania look like a pea patch. You remember what I said, when some of these big fields come in."

Reanna wiped the corners of her mouth with her napkin. "What will you do for drilling equipment when you get to Tulsa? Is your rig—isn't that what you called it, a rig? Is it already there?"

"Why no, ma'am," Mr. Wardell spoke up proudly. "Blue Racer—that's the company that hired us—is shipping out a rig on the railroad."

"Do you drill rotary or cable?" Reanna asked softly.

"Cable."

"I believe I read somewhere that they used rotary at Spindletop."

Taffy had to stifle his laughter. So that's what she'd been reading up on at the newspaper office—oil wells.

Mr. Wade looked startled. "That's right, but we believe cable is best for this country. You see, it's all a matter of what rock and sand formation you expect to find. Spindletop was a salt dome."

"How deep do you think you'd have to drill to find oil down by the springs?"

"Nine hundred feet; it could come in at six hundred, but I wouldn't count on it."

Reanna looked pale, but her eyes were bright. "I see. And just where is this rig of yours now?"

"It's at the rail junction over beyond MacClaren City. We'll meet it there and ride over to Tulsey with it. We came on ahead on the passenger line to Maitland, thinking we'd scout around a bit on our own."

Reanna smiled again, a smile as bright as sunshine, and Taffy thought, Oh *no*, she's thought of something else; here we go again. This poker game ain't over yet.

"Mr. Wade, Mr. Wardell, won't you have another piece of Cima's fresh apple pie and some more coffee?" she said. "I think perhaps we should look at this matter from an entirely different angle. We all want the same thing. We only need to find a way of *expressing* it."

"That's true, ma'am."

"Mr. Wade, what if you were to speak to the freight agent at the Maitland junction and ask him if he'd be willing to let you take the rig off there for just a few days? If you're so sure there's oil there, you could drill here *first*, before you go on over to Tulsa."

Mr. Wade's loaded fork had stopped in mid-passage from plate to mouth. Mr. Wardell's hand had locked on his coffee cup.

"I'm sure even a month's delay wouldn't interfere with the other well, would it?"

Wade and Wardell looked at each other nervously, and Taffy could tell right off what was eating them. They wanted a stake of their own and they wanted it bad; they'd seen what kind of money oil could bring. They didn't dare to say yes, and they couldn't bear to say no.

"It might take more than a month to drill," Mr. Wardell said guardedly. "If pigs could fly, we could make a hundred feet a day, but you can't count on it."

"How much longer?" Reanna asked.

"Let's say six weeks."

"All right, let's say two months," Reanna agreed. "For the sake of argument, let's look at it this way. I have the land and the oil under it. I want to hire you to drill a well for me, just as you'd drill a well for someone in Tulsa. You have the rig, or you can get it, and for that I'll pay you no salary, but *I* will give *you* one-eighth of everything we find."

A stunned silence followed. Mr. Wade and Mr. Wardell looked stricken. Even Cima's mouth was open. Taffy had only just been able to follow her. She'd been seller; now she'd turned buyer, without batting an eye. That woman was a humdinger, and no mistake.

"That's not the way things are usually done, ma'am," Mr. Wade was saying in a small, awed voice.

"Possibly not," Reanna agreed amiably, "but this is an unusual case. A once-in-a-lifetime opportunity, wouldn't you say? Your business is drilling for oil. Am I right?"

"Yes, ma'am."

"Then it seems to me that we have a perfect partnership. I have the land and you have the knowledge, plus the rig."

"Well, it isn't exactly *our* rig," said Mr. Wade with regret.

"I don't understand."

"The rig belongs to the company in Tulsey. They bought it and shipped it out here. We're only drillers hired by the company that *owns* the rig."

"But you know where the rig is, don't you?"

She's a born gambler, Taffy thought in pure amazement, and I never even saw it. She won't let go; she'll keep on raising the ante until she brings it in. Why those sharpshooters over at the Triangle are rank amateurs; she'd clean them all out in three hours.

"Yes, we know where the rig is. But even if we could manage to get it off the railroad and drill in six weeks or less, how would we get the rig over here? How would we find a crew, and how would we pay them?"

Reanna was all smiles again. "If that's all that's bothering you, Mr. Owen and I could take the wagon over to the Maitland junction and help you haul it back. Couldn't we, Taffy?" Her eyes held that fierce, expectant glare. He didn't know what she was getting herself into, and he didn't think she did either. A goddamn *oil rig*.

"You gentlemen are welcome to spend the night. We'll all get an early start in the morning. As for the crew, you can leave that to me." She rose from the table as if it were all settled, and none of them could at that moment think of a good reason to deny that it was.

* * *

(350)

THE more he thought it over, the more Taffy decided it was one wild, harebrained scheme. Only his devotion to Reanna could have made him find himself driving the wagon with Reanna beside him on the seat, preceded by two strangers in a hired buggy heading out to the junction. He kept hoping she'd see that this was all pure foolishness, a king-sized dose of wildcatter's fever, and tell him to turn for home, but she didn't. She'd dressed up in her best dress and put new ribbons on her shabby bonnet. She looked as pretty as a girl going to her first party, but beneath that pretty exterior was a calculating turn of mind and an iron determination that scared him. What in Tophet were they getting themselves into?

The rig had come in all right; it was resting on a flatcar on a siding. But there appeared to be some difficulty. Mr. Wade and Mr. Wardell were talking to the freight agent, Horace Green; they were doing a lot of gesticulating and their faces were agitated. Taffy followed Reanna over.

"Good morning, Mrs. MacClaren." Mr. Green tipped his visored cap politely.

"What seems to be the matter, Mr. Green?" she said.

"I knew it was too good to be true," Mr. Wade answered for him dejectedly. "We can't have the rig."

"Why not?" Reanna asked.

"There's freight due on it to be paid by the consignee in Tulsey," Mr. Green said with a self-important air.

"I'm sure there must be some mistake." Reanna offered her most charming smile. "These men have been brought out here to drill for oil. They can't do that without a rig, can they?"

"No, I reckon they can't, but I can't let this rig off the line unless the freight's paid."

"If they paid you now, could you let the rig go?"

"Yes, certainly."

"Then it's not a matter of their not having the *right* to the rig. It's merely a matter of money." She put her query in such a way that money seemed the very least of all their problems.

"That's right."

"Mr. Green, I wonder if I could speak to you in private?" She nodded to Taffy to stick with her. Reanna drew Mr. Green to one side, out of earshot of the drillers. "Mr. Green, you know me and my husband. You know he'd be good for the charges, but Andrew isn't here right now. Now, I think the best way out of the difficulty is for these men to pay you out of their profits."

Mr. Green looked dubious. "How do I know there will be any profits?"

Reanna shrugged. "Well, of course there's a small element of risk, as there is with everything in life. But when a well comes in, it can make a lot of money."

"But supposing it doesn't come in? What then?"

"Oh, but *you* wouldn't have any risk, Mr. Green. The worst that could happen is that the rig would come back to you here in, say, a week or so, and you'd just ship it on." She paused a moment and added casually, "No one would be any the wiser."

"What if they didn't come back, Mrs. MacClaren? What if those two turn out to be fly-by-nights?"

"Why, *I'll* be right there, you see?" Reanna laughed lightly. "They'll be working for me. And I trust them, and you trust me. You see?"

Horace Green said nothing to this. He looked as if the plug he was chewing had gone bad on him.

"Mr. Green," Reanna said in almost a whisper, "I know I shouldn't be telling you this, but I know I can trust you to keep this quiet. I'm going to drill an oil well, and I need that rig. I'd be very grateful if you could oblige me. You know how often shipments can get, oh, put off on a siding somewhere and delayed for a week or two." She lowered her voice still further; Taffy could barely hear her. "Just think, this is a chance for you to get in on something big, without putting up any risk capital whatsoever. The ground floor! Think of how surprised Mrs. Green and the children will be when you make a killing!"

Mr. Green grinned all at once—a quick, furtive grin—and began to pull at the corner of his mustache in a frenzy. He's hooked, Taffy marveled; he's hooked and wriggling. Old Horace wasn't giving a thought to Persis Green and the loving kiddies. Not one. Every train that passed through, he thought about scrambling aboard and riding into the sunset—and all by his lonesome. He'd always hankered to travel and to see the ocean. He'd long since given up hope that his dream would ever come true, but now here it seemed not only possible but almost within his grasp. Wildcatter's fever was catching. She made it all seem so—likely. Taffy could feel his own toes begin to tingle. Just supposing—

"It would be our secret?" Horace asked, his eyes bright. "You wouldn't say anything to Mrs. Green?"

"Not a word."

"I guess," he said slowly, "if this rig didn't move out of here for a week or two, it wouldn't hurt nobody." Reanna started to thank him, but he stopped her. "All the same, I'd feel just a tad better if I had a little something in writing."

"And you shall have it!" Taffy could see it was a lead-pipe cinch to give up a part of what you don't at all have. "But let's make it a gentlemen's agreement between ourselves. We don't want to bring lawyers into it; that could attract a crowd trying to buy up leases. And if the news of it got out, it would spoil your surprise for Mrs. Green. Do you see?"

"Certainly, Mrs. MacClaren."

"Good." Reanna wrote out an agreement on the back of an envelope for Mr. Green to keep hidden away safe in his wallet. He was to get one percent of the proceeds from the first well drilled. Reanna signed it with a flourish and they shook hands, while Wade and Wardell watched them in bewilderment.

The rig was a heavy, ugly monster, but loading cable drums, the steam engine and pipe and drilling tools wasn't the end of it. Reanna made Taffy go round up lumber for a derrick and wellhouse and more six-inch casing that Mr. Wade said they needed, which meant hiring two more wagons to haul the stuff. He knew now that they were in over their heads; he knew in his bones that this was going to take a lot more than any two weeks.

It took three long days just to make the long trek back to the place, pitch tents and unload out by the springs.

"What about a crew?" Mr. Wade demanded. "I told you we'd need a crew."

"I'll get you a crew," Reanna told him firmly. "How many men do you need?"

"Four at least and six is better. That'll give me three shifts, with me and Wardy. And don't get me any cowboys. They don't know anything about running pipe and stringing tools."

Taffy glared at Mr. Wade, who glared right back.

"I'll get them." Reanna began to saddle up Molly May.

"Where are you going?" Taffy asked her. You couldn't tell *what* she was up to these days.

"To get a crew. What did you think?"

"And where do you intend to get them?"

"Across the river at the Triangle Saloon."

Taffy was aghast. "You can't go *there*."

"Why not?"

"It's a cesspool of human iniquity."

"*You* go there."

"That's how I know! It's no place for a lady."

"Out here, if I only went to ladylike places, I wouldn't go anywhere at all," she said.

"You can't go there alone!" Taffy seized her bridle.

"I'm not going alone." She grinned down at him. "You'll be with me. I need you to show me the way."

Taffy rode alongside Reanna to the Triangle Saloon, arguing against the project all the way; by the time they'd forded the river, he'd given up. She walked into that gin mill as if it were the First Episcopalian Cathedral and stood calmly inside the swinging doors, trying to adjust to the dim light, the shifting clouds of tobacco smoke. Jack Muldoon, holding up the far end of the bar, put his fingers over his eyes as if he'd started hallucinating; there was a general commotion and craning of heads, and even Dutch Kellerman, whom nothing and no one ever fazed, stared at her wide-eyed and said, "Madam, you've made a mistake."

"No mistake." Her voice carried clearly the length of the saloon. "I need some men," she said. "Some good men."

This provoked a torrent of lewd rejoinders and laughter. Taffy started forward to do battle, but she caught his sleeve and held him.

"Silence!" the Dutchman ordered in his cavalry sergeant's voice, and the room quieted down.

"I'll pay three dollars a day and found."

There was complete silence at this. The sober ones thought they were drunk; the drunks thought they'd gone to heaven. Then there were a few derisive chuckles.

"*Too much,*" Taffy whispered to her under his breath, but she paid no attention.

"How about it?" she said.

"Doing just what?" The question came from a tough-looking customer with a round, red face and a blue stubble of beard. Taffy had never seen him before.

"Doing what you're told," Reanna answered in a level tone.

"I ain't taking orders from no woman," the man declared to general approbation and applause.

"What's your name?" Reanna asked him.

"Mitcher. Ward B. Mitcher."

"Well, Mr. Mitcher, you'll take orders from a foreman, not from me."

(354)

"What will we be doing for this three dollars a day?" He was still suspicious.

"Digging holes."

"Yeah, and what else?"

"Whatever else you're told. You'll stay on the place, no drinking, no days off. If you don't want to work hard, don't sign on. You'll earn your money, I promise you."

There was another silence, while everybody digested these terms. Then a hard-luck old homesteader Taffy knew named Nat Gibbons said, "I'll scrub out the bottom furnace in hell for three dollars a day," and Mitcher said, "Okay, where do we sign on?"

"Right here." She handed him the paper she'd prepared in advance. Taffy rejected Jack Muldoon, who couldn't stay sober for four hours, let alone two weeks, and took Mitcher against his better judgment. They signed up six men. The best, in Taffy's opinion, was the old-timer Nat Gibbons. He looked simple, but at least he was sober. They rounded the men up and headed back across the river again.

At last, when the men were at a safe distance, Taffy exploded. *"Three dollars a day!* Are you crazy? Where are you going to get the money to pay them? You don't have to tell them where it's coming from, but *I* want to know."

"I've got three hundred and ninety-one dollars left from the sale of the cattle after wages and bonuses." She shot Taffy a look. It still galled him that she'd been so generous. "And I have another hundred scraped from this and that. In all, I've got close to five hundred dollars."

"And?"

"And that's it."

"Good God Almighty, you're going broke. You've spent half that already on pipe and lumber and supplies."

"Not me. I'm going to get rich, by God."

And she began to laugh with such sheer excitement that after a while there was nothing to do but to laugh right along with her. When they finally ran down, she said, "I know how you feel, Taffy. That was cattle money and it should go back into cattle. But believe me, if this well comes in, it will be a way out of all our troubles. If it doesn't come in, we'll be stony-broke. I've given no cash to the drillers or Mr. Green. I saved the cash for food, labor and supplies. This is a gamble, and I'm going to take it. My father was a gambler. I never used to understand why he took risks, but now I do. Sometimes gambling is the only possible way to change your life. So it's all or nothing. Do you see?"

She wrote to her parents.

Dear Folks,

The spring comes much earlier here than in Virginia. It's already warm. A few days ago, we were sitting out on the porch, Cima, Taffy and I, when two men, strangers, came by and stayed to talk business.

Now, I don't want to get your hopes up too high, but they made me a business proposition which, if it works out, will be so profitable that all our financial troubles will be over.

I don't want to put a jinx on this by telling you too much, too soon. Just cross your fingers and wish hard. Oh, if it will only work out, we'll have money to spend for whatever, whenever we please.

Love,
Reanna

SHE moved them out to the seep springs to be near the well site, the whole kit and kaboodle—Cima, Snow, Lovell, the girls, Reanna and Taffy, along with Mr. Wade and Mr. Wardell and the crew. To look at them all living out there under lean-tos and canvas, you'd have thought they were a circus on tour or a zany band of gypsies. At the beginning, it was like a field day; there was a note of festivity, of bright anticipation in the air that made Taffy feel like he'd been smoking locoweed and drinking green whiskey all at the same time.

Reanna insisted on picking the drilling site herself. She chose a spot near the seepage where she'd first encountered John's Dead. Wade disagreed with her. "The place you picked is low and hard to get at. The one I have in mind is better. After all, I have experience and you don't."

She faced him, smiling. "Well, it's my land and my money. And I say we dig here." Wade shrugged; whoever paid the piper could call the tune.

"OK," Wade said to the crew, "you can spud in here, and we'll poorboy down." He still thought he was right and Reanna wrong. "Though to tell you the truth, nobody knows exactly where the oil is. You drill by guess and by gosh, and if luck is with you, you hit a pool."

The equipment was catch as catch can, just like the men who

ran it. Wade had to train the raw crew; Reanna felt that the crew took advantage of that. The men were dumb louts, but not too dumb to know that the slower they worked, the longer they'd get paid. Mitcher had appointed himself ringleader; he made them slow down. It drove Reanna to near distraction to watch them dawdle over the simplest task.

There was a lot of work to be done and all of it from scratch. They had to build a platform, raise a derrick, set up the steam engine and cut and stack the wood to run it. They set in a crown block and pulley at the head of the derrick; then they threaded it with cable and attached a walking arm. They strung the tools onto the block and, to case the wellhead, they ran six-inch pipe to below water level. They drilled foot by hard-drilled foot.

The crew was inexperienced and ignorant, but they earned their three dollars a day. Taffy laid down the law. They were to work around the clock in twelve-hour, two-man shifts. No man was to leave the place. No man was to drink while he was there; there was enough danger of accident without running the extra hazard of drunkenness. The men had agreed to the terms, but they began to grumble in short order. Taffy knew he'd have to watch them; he'd never seen a more rag-tag-bobtail lot in all his misspent life.

Cima agreed to cook for them, but she called them trash all the same. She kept the children and especially the girls close, and took to carrying a wicked twelve-gauge shotgun, which made the men mighty polite to her at all times.

Reanna was around Wade and Wardell like a gadfly; she asked a thousand and one questions. By the time they'd drilled a hundred feet, she knew almost as much about drilling oil as they did. She was amazed at how fast she learned. Soon she could distinguish wellhead casing from drill pipe and a bit from a drill stem. She could tell crown block and pulley from gin pole; she knew drift from bedrock and sand from shale.

She found she'd come to thrive on this hunt for oil; there was a thrill, a challenge to the work. But all the time she had the feeling that she was racing the clock. Time was money, and she was squandering it every second of every hour of every day. It drove her wild.

Even on the best days, it was slow going. The men were often wet and cold. They were always hungry and demanding to be fed. They complained and malingered and cursed the day they'd signed on. It made them curse the more when they saw that Reanna was up earlier and slept less than they did. She noticed Taffy had taken to wearing his .45. She didn't mind the cursing or the rough life. She was sure she'd hear a lot worse before the well was finished.

Some days she doubted that day would ever come. She hovered over Wade, stood by his elbow and watched him. Over and over she asked the same question. "Mr. Wade, how much longer will it be until we strike oil?"

He shook his head glumly. "Your guess is as good as mine. We've come a long way from Titusville, but this is still one hell of a way to make a living. You'll pardon my language." He wished she'd leave him in peace. "Why don't you take a rest, Mrs. MacClaren? We can manage for a while without you."

As they drilled down, foot by arduous foot, the gray mud came up, ran down a sluice and fed into an earth-ringed slush pit. It wasn't a pretty thing to look at, and it gave off an odor of sulphur and rotted slime. Snow and Lovell loved to wade in the slush; it was the best game they'd ever played. As the mud oozed up through their toes and caked and dried on their legs, they squealed with delight. Cima scolded them, and she washed and cooked and badgered the girls nearly to tears, and worried that supplies were running low.

They kept drilling from the end of a rainy May into a hot, sultry June. In the heat, tempers began to erupt, but Reanna refused to let up.

"How many feet now, Mr. Wade?" she said, and, "Show me the sand samples." Wade sighed and did as she asked. There was no keeping her away from the well; they'd just have to put up with her.

She wouldn't leave—she couldn't; she was growing desperate. Time was running out and that precious reserve in the chest under her bed was dwindling away. She put them all on short rations, fed them beans and more beans. She counted every cup of coffee, each biscuit. She hated it when she saw Wade coming toward her; she knew he'd be bringing some fresh complaint from the men, and some new demand. Just when she was most discouraged, he told her, "We're going to need more cable."

"How much more?"

"Two fifty, three hundred feet. Maybe more. And we'll need pipe when we hit pay formation. Nine hundred feet of pipe ought to do it. We had a good show of oil yesterday. We're getting close."

She nodded. Her heart gave a great lurch. Pipe was sixty cents a foot. She couldn't trust herself to speak.

"And the crew's got to be paid." He was watching her closely. "You do have enough money to pay the men," he asked, suddenly suspicious, "don't you?"

"Of course." She didn't have the money; she couldn't pay for the pipe. She'd charged the last hundred and fifty feet of cable. Jack Levy was carrying her for supplies and she couldn't pay wages.

"Tell me now, Mr. Wade," she said coolly, "how much money will we need to finish this well? We're almost down to nine hundred feet. You say we have a show of oil. How much money and how much longer?"

He shifted his feet and hitched at his trousers. "That's hard to say."

"This is no time for vagueness, Mr. Wade. Give it to me straight, so I'll know how much to withdraw." She hoped fervently he'd believe she had a bank account.

"Another two weeks," he said reluctantly. "A little more or a little less. By then we'll know whether we've got oil or a dry hole. We'll need another thousand dollars, just to be on the safe side."

He'd named a sum that made her knees go weak.

"Without pipe and replacements for other equipment, we can't drill," Wade was saying, still watching her. "And without wages, you'll lose your crew. They aren't much, but they're all you've got."

"You'll have the money tomorrow," she said. "Get the pipe and give them my personal note. There's nothing to worry about." She hoped her smile gave Mr. Wade a sense of confidence she herself didn't remotely possess.

She saddled up Molly May and rode back to the cabin. The place had been deserted for only a few weeks, yet even in this short time it looked wolfish, overgrown. The fowl were running wild; the garden was choked with weeds. She went to her room and dragged the iron chest from beneath the bed, unlocked it and took inventory. There was only twenty dollars left, and the Beauvaise cup wrapped in its sleeve of cloth. She held it to the light. Its dented, tarnished surface reflected her face—a dull, misshapen reproach.

"May God and Miss Jane forgive me," she whispered. God might forgive her if she failed, but Miss Jane never would. She felt as if the ghost of the Dog King was about to rise up from his grave beneath the cabin and confront her. But this was the way it would have to be. She had only one place to turn. This was her legacy, and she must accept the responsibility.

She wrapped the cup again in its faded flannel and jammed it

(359)

deep in her saddlebag. She washed and changed and put up her hair, making herself as attractive as she could under the circumstances, and rode north toward the river.

AT Simon Frampton's ranch, she was greeted by the raucous bugling of hounds. Frampton came outside, roaring at them; he was delighted to see Reanna. "Well," he said, blinking with surprise, "what an unlooked-for pleasure!" He caught her as she dismounted and embraced her awkwardly. He was deeply tanned, burned brown by the sun and wind. His complexion set off his clear, pale blue eyes.

"Hello, Simon." She untied her saddlebags and slung them over her shoulder while he watched her.

"Is there something wrong?" he asked.

"Wrong? Why should something be wrong?"

He became apologetic. "Well, I heard you were drilling out by John's Dead Springs, and I thought . . ."

She laughed, partly by design, partly out of genuine pleasure at seeing him. "I don't need a disaster to make me want to see you; I just felt like paying you a visit. Is that so strange?"

"Yes, a little," he replied, smiling.

"Oh Simon, you're so incorrigibly English."

"All Englishmen are incorrigibly English. It's the secret of our failure."

Laughing, she entered the cool, tidy, handsomely appointed room, thinking of her childhood and the old house in Buckingham and her father's warm, winning smile. The sense of loss and self-reproach grew during dinner, amid the pewter candlesticks and Lowestoft and fine old silver. Had she really taken leave of her senses, as they all thought? Was she forfeiting Lochleven and all it stood for, chasing this fata morgana sunk deep in the bowels of the earth? The ancients believed hell lay down there—the inferno and the dolorous city of Dis, where damned souls suffered to the very end of time.

"Well, we're down to nine hundred feet," she heard herself say brightly, as if of course he would understand what a tremendous accomplishment that was. "What do you think of that?"

"I—I don't know quite what to think," he said and laughed his hearty English laugh. "I'd think it wasn't the *distance* actually, so much as finding the oil."

"You do have a way of coming to the point."

"I'm sorry. It's the John Bull in me."

"Of course, you're absolutely right. The problem is to find the oil."

There was a little silence. Frampton said, "Are you pleased? I mean, with the progress you're making."

She grinned at him wryly. "I *have* to be. I chose the spot!"

"I see. And Andrew—how does he feel about it?"

"Andrew doesn't know anything about it. At least I don't think he does. The well was my idea."

"Ah." Frampton fiddled with his wineglass; he seemed a touch embarrassed. "I knew—that is, I heard—he'd left for Texas."

"True enough."

"When, ah, does he plan to return?"

"I really couldn't say."

He became alert at this; the genial interest in his eyes deepened to something more intimate. "He's a fool," he said simply. "I always thought so, and now I know it. To cut out on someone as fine, as utterly charming as you."

"Oh, we're all of us running out on something," Reanna replied airily, and then realized what she'd said, and broke off. Frampton flushed beneath his tan; his blue eyes slid away. "Look at me," she went on in some haste. "I was wild to get away from my mother and all she stood for, and I snatched at Andrew like a drowning soul. He didn't stand a chance, poor man. I suppose you could say I've drawn my just deserts."

He shook his head stubbornly, watching her. "You deserve better. You always did. You're the kind of woman who needs to be appreciated."

She laughed nervously; this whole conversation struck her as fantastic in the light of her present situation. And there was that faint click of attraction that Frampton had struck in her before. It was not the innocent surge she'd first felt with Andrew, nor the fierce, all-embracing passion she'd known with Pride, but it was there. And he was attracted to her deeply, she knew.

"Simon," she said in a very different voice, "I'm drilling this well on my own. All the property at Lochleven is in my name, now. Andrew's declared himself a bankrupt."

"Oh, I say . . ." Frampton bit at the underedge of his mustache. Then he laughed over his embarrassment and said, "So you're an heiress!"

"If you want to call it that." She paused. "I'm sorry if it makes you uncomfortable, hearing this. But I want to make certain you understand my situation. I'm asking you for help."

"Of course, dear lady." He flushed this time with sheer pleasure. "I told you when you first came out here, if you ever required anything—anything at all—you need only come to me."

"Simon, I need to borrow some money."

He nodded, as if it were a request for a second cup of coffee, but he looked troubled. "I'll be happy to do what I can. This is a difficult time for me, actually."

"It's not such an awful lot of money, but it might as well be a million dollars as far as I'm concerned. I need enough to finish drilling. I'm sure you know it's a gamble, but if this well comes in—and I believe with all my heart it will—we'll be rich. All of us."

"You're risking so much, dear girl. On such a long shot. It troubles me no end."

"I know you're waiting for the right buyer here. It's not a matter of time, anyway. We'll win or we'll lose in short order. And if the well comes in, I'll pay you back double on your loan."

"Double or nothing," he murmured with a soft, sad smile.

"Yes, that's right. And I'll give you a major share in the royalties. Twenty percent." She held him with her eyes. "I'll be able to rebuild Lochleven, restore it to its old glory, and you'll be able to go home to England in style!"

He gave her a sharp, frightened glance. "How d'you know that's what I want?" he stammered.

"I—just know, that's all. Say you'll do it, Simon. I'll give you a pledge as security."

His big, capable hands were gripped tightly together; he was staring down at them. "I'm not a gambling man," he said softly.

"I know. They say you never even play poker for petty stakes. I know you don't gamble, but try to understand what this means to me, why I'm willing to throw everything into hazard for something I've set my heart on." She put her small hand on his shoulder. "Try to see my side of it, can't you, Simon?"

To her surprise, he leaped to his feet and went over to one of the windows. "Nobody understands anyone else," he muttered in so low a voice that she had to strain to hear him. "I know about gambling," he went on grimly, nodding, his back to her. "I know *all* about it. Believe me."

Reanna watched him, her heart sinking. If there was anything she did not need at this moment it was a moral lecture on the destructive nature of gambling. She had pinned all her hopes on Frampton. Doc and Amoretta had no cash to lend; Jack Levy was over his head with creditors and wholesalers; Father Soule was out of the question.

Slowly she got to her feet. "I'm sorry I came to you with this," she murmured. "I had no right to, I know."

"Wait," he said, turning; in the evening light, his face looked much older, lined and rather hard. "You don't understand. I came out here to the Territory because I was a gambler. I once played for high stakes, very high stakes."

"And you lost," Reanna sighed.

He cried softly, "No, I won! That was just the trouble. I'd never had such a run of luck; it was uncanny. They couldn't believe it, they *wouldn't* . . ." He paused and said flatly, "I was accused of cheating."

"Oh no," she breathed. "You never cheated anybody in your life."

"How the devil do you know that?" he said in great agitation.

"I know."

He laughed harshly, gripping and ungripping his big, red hands. "Try telling *that* to the Marquis of Wrentham," he said, "especially when his Lordship has had a drop too much to drink, and when his two closest friends have lost upwards of twenty thousand pounds sterling. They were highly convincing. And everyone chose to believe them, it seemed. Friends and neighbors—even family, finally." He looked at her unhappily. "I've never told this to anyone before, anyone in America. I don't know why I'm telling you, now."

"There's more that you haven't told me, but that's your secret. I thank you for confiding in me." She smiled softly. "One day you can tell me the rest of the story, if you want."

"Are you so sure there's more, and that I'm innocent?"

"Yes, as sure as I am that there was a girl in the story. A girl you wanted to help, as you want to help me now."

"I never told you about a girl."

"You didn't have to."

Frampton seemed fastened to the spot; he was gazing far beyond her to another time. When he finally spoke, it was in a low, reflective tone. "Yes, I'll help you. I'll do what you ask." He turned and went to the squat, black iron safe. "How much will you need?"

She told him. He took out a thick stack of paper money and put it in her hands.

"We must draw up a contract," she said. "I want this to be a matter of record."

He shook his head. "I set no store in contracts or solicitors. You'll pay me back the money when it's convenient."

"I must give you some security. You must have my pledge that I'll repay you." She placed the money very carefully on the table. It seemed odd to her to treat paper with such respect. Yet those sheets of paper could mean the difference between success and disaster.

She drew the Beauvaise cup from the saddlebag, handed it to Frampton and watched as he unwrapped it and saw what it was. "I can't keep this." He thrust it back toward Reanna. "You don't know what you're doing."

"I can't borrow the money unless you keep it as security. I know exactly what I'm doing. It's all I have in the world that's mine; Miss Jane left it to me as my inheritance. As long as the Beauvaises have this cup, they will not fail. I'm gambling my future, my honor and the honor of my son. Surely you can understand what family honor is worth."

"Oh yes," Frampton said slowly, "I understand family honor. I'll keep the cup until you come for it."

"I'll come soon." She gave him back the cup. "And now I must get back."

"You're so tired. Won't you at least spend the night?"

"Thank you, I can't. Things are in a state of crisis. Shall we keep our secret?"

"Yes." He took her hand and held it to him. "I promise, honor bright." He leaned down to kiss her on the cheek.

"Friends for life?" she asked.

"Friends for life."

"That girl in England is very lucky. I hope she knows that."

Frampton blinked at her, his eyes bright. "Bless you, darling girl."

"Goodbye, Simon, and thanks," Reanna said. She hoped she hadn't made old wounds bleed; she'd never do anything to hurt him. She owed him the promise of her future; she would keep safe his secret.

* * *

It was late when Reanna started back toward the well site. She'd never ridden alone at night, but there was a moon. She hoped that she could slip into camp without a lot of fuss and questions. She liked being alone in the dark, with the moon and the stars to guide her. It gave her time to think. She wouldn't permit herself to dwell on the possibility of failure. She knew the chance she was taking, but when she imagined the future, she saw a far different life for Lovell than if he were raised on dirt, out here on the prairie. As she rode, she felt tears on her cheeks. Here in the dark she could weep for Pride, and no one would notice.

At the edge of camp she dismounted and walked Molly May in. She looked into Wade's lean-to. He and Wardell were gone; Wade had left her a note saying that they would be back tomorrow with the pipe. Cima's tent was dark, as was Taffy's.

She could hear the donkey engine as it popped and sputtered and the deeper rhythmic thump as the drill pounded through, into the lime and sandstone far below. Yet something felt wrong; it was nothing she could put her finger on, but she felt it. She hurried around the engine toward the derrick platform. The crew were sprawled on the platform, sound asleep. Ward Mitcher was sitting on the steps, and Snow was perched on his knee with her arms around his neck. For a moment Reanna was paralyzed by shock, unable to move.

"I'm a princess." Snow's voice was low and breathless with excitement. "A real princess."

"Is that a fact?" Mitcher said thickly. He looked down unsteadily, and Reanna saw the glint of the bottle at his feet. Mitcher leered at Snow. "Say, highness, how about a little royal loving?"

Snow squirmed softly and slapped at him, laughing. "Oooh, mustn't do that."

"Why not?"

"Because I haven't told you you can. You must say please."

"Hell, I'll even say pretty please, with syrup, all over it." Mitcher grinned, an eager, obscene grimace.

"Oh my God," Reanna heard herself say. "Oh my God." She clenched the riding crop in her hand and went up to Snow and Mitcher. When they saw her, Snow gave a little cry and Mitcher stumbled to his feet.

"All right, Snow," Reanna said quietly, "go to your tent."

"I don't want to." Her voice was slurred and unsteady.

"Do as I say."

"Why should I?" Snow said with sly defiance. "You don't care what happens to me. You aren't my mother."

"I don't want to hear you say that again." Reanna was surprised to find her voice so steady and level. "I'm your stepmother, and if you don't obey me, I'm going to whip the very hide off you."

Snow smiled maliciously. This was even more fun than sitting on silly old Mitcher's lap and teasing him. Reanna was angry. And better than that, Reanna was upset about *her*, not Lovell or that pokey old oil well. She lifted her chin and said, "No. I won't go."

Slowly and deliberately, Reanna raised her free hand and slapped Snow. She heard the sound her open palm made on Snow's cheek and saw the dark shadow it left there. The action and the sound seemed to take place in slow motion, in a dumb show, but then the illusion was shattered by Snow's wail. Some of the crew began to stir heavily.

"Now *go find Cima,*" Reanna said, and Snow, sobbing and wailing, ran off toward the tents.

"Mitcher, you have three minutes to get your gear together and clear out of here. Or so help me God, I'll make you wish you'd never been born."

"Now hold on, Mrs. MacClaren," Mitcher whined accusingly. "She started the whole thing, I swear it. I didn't mean no harm. She come and set on my lap, and then she began making up to me."

The fact that he could easily be telling the truth made Reanna want to do him some great harm.

"She *asked* me for a drink, I didn't offer it."

"She's a child, for God's sake," Reanna shouted, "a mere child!" She began to beat at Mitcher with her riding crop, striking him again and again, following him across the clearing while he gasped and cringed. She couldn't stop herself, even when she saw the welts and the blood score his face.

The camp was wide awake by now. Heads popped out of the crew's quarters; Cima came running, the shotgun in her two hands. "Now what's going on here?" she demanded.

"Snow and that man were—together," Reanna stammered.

"Did you lay a finger on my precious child?" Cima said in a whisper so fierce that Mitcher gave way. "Did you?"

"He gave her liquor to drink," Reanna said. "He says she came to him."

"She did, Mrs. MacClaren, I swear." Still he stood there, unable or unwilling to move.

"Well go on, get out of here!" Reanna cried. "What are you waiting for?"

"I want my wages."

"Your wages?" Reanna stormed at him. "You're lucky to get out of here alive!" She struck him again, and Cima raised the shotgun until it was pointing at his oversized belly.

Mitcher gave a cry of outrage. As he ran away and they lost sight of him in the night, he called out, "I'll get you for this!"

Reanna whirled on the men by the derrick. "What are you all staring at? Get back to work, if you don't want to join your friend."

The men began to move slowly back to their abandoned tasks. Cima and Reanna went to look at Snow, who was sprawled on her cot, sound asleep.

"That girl is just plain drunk, if you ask me," Cima said.

"Where's Taffy?" Reanna asked.

"Gone with those two snake oil merchants to get pipe."

There was a silence between the two women. Reanna said, "What am I going to do about Snow?"

Cima shook her head. "I can't tell you nothing, except we're going to have to get a very big dog to watch that girl."

In the morning light everything looked better and brighter. The men came back with the needed pipe. Taffy was furious he hadn't been there when Mitcher had pulled his little stunt. Reanna paid out wages and the hands were happy. Snow was actually rather contrite, though Cima said she thought most of that was hangover. The wind died down, and the sun was warm but not brutal. The sand pulls were promising; they had another show of oil. Wade and Wardell looked excited. For the first time in all the hard weeks of work, success looked not only possible but likely.

To celebrate the occasion, Reanna gave all hands the night off and had Cima cook broiled chicken with rice. After the evening meal, Reanna said she was going straight to bed and advised them all to do the same. It had been a long two days, she told them, with a wry glance at Cima, and they had a big week ahead of them.

Taffy put Nat Gibbons on duty at the derrick. Nat was slow, but he pulled his own weight. Taffy told him he'd relieve him at two and turned in for forty winks, dreaming of pools of blue-black oil that turned magically into rye whiskey. He was splashing about in the whiskey happily, laughing at Andrew, who was standing at the sump's edge, afraid to get his feet wet.

He woke with a start, staring sightlessly up at the canvas above his head, listening. The sound that had waked him came again—a curious *clunk*, sharp over the engine's erratic murmur, a sound he couldn't identify. He checked the old alarm clock Cima had given him. One fifteen. He rolled out, pulled on his boots, clapped his hat on his head and moved quickly and noiselessly down the dusty path behind the tents toward the drill site. Nat Gibbons was silhouetted high on the derrick near the block, his arms raised, working at something.

"Want a hand, Nat?" he called softly.

The figure started, then his hand went back over his head, and Taffy realized it wasn't Gibbons. There was that same *clunk* sound, of iron hacking at iron. Then the cable let go. There was a racketing crash as something plummeted away down the shaft; Taffy gazed upward in consternation as the severed cable swung crazily away up into the crown block and began to whip round and round against the night sky, a steel ribbon in a windmill. He heard an awful grinding of gears; the engine wound up, screaming, then quit with a pop. And in a flash of raging certainty, Taffy knew exactly what had happened.

"Mitcher!" he shouted. "You hold it right there."

Then Mitcher scurried down the ladder, and dropped heavily from the platform to the ground. Taffy ran toward him, thinking, *Gibbons, what's happened to Gibbons?* Mitcher ducked behind the toolshed, broke away on the far side and cried, "Stay away from me, Owen."

Running hard, Taffy saw him stop and turn, caught the dull glint of light running up the rifle barrel; he dove to his right without thought and hit rolling. The Winchester crashed, and something *whunked* into the ground a scant foot from Taffy's head, kicking dirt in his face. He gasped in fear, rolling over again, and came up on one knee with his hand filled. The rifle fired again, a monstrous flash in the near dark. Taffy brought up his arm, the .45 kicking high with each round. Mitcher gave a high, hoarse scream and fell sidelong. There was an instant of complete silence; then, panting as if he'd run for his life up the entire north Ridge, his ears ringing, Taffy could hear calls and cries and the thump of people running.

He stood up and walked carefully toward Mitcher, watching the rifle. The roustabout was lying on his back, his legs oddly twisted and his arms flung wide, his mouth gasping; blood had already soaked the front of his shirt and was spreading blackly underneath him. His eyes stared upward glassily. As Taffy knelt over him, Mitcher made an odd little sucking sound deep in his throat, strained upward, then fell back with a low, shuddering sigh. Taffy stood up again and looked distantly at the dreamlike crowd of shouting, gesticulating figures.

Reanna was pulling at his sleeve. "What happened?" She was crying, her face wild. "What *happened?*"

He gazed at her vacantly, nodded toward the drilling gin. "Cut the cable. I saw him. No-good son of a bitch."

"Oh, *no* . . ." She whirled and ran off toward the platform.

"It's Mitcher," Cima said in surprise, bending down. "Dead?"

Taffy nodded at her. "I knew he was trouble. That kind always is."

"Well, he didn't get away with it." Cima picked up the rifle and ejected a round from the breech with an almost contemptuous competence. "Well," she said again, and Taffy could see her eyes glittering at him. "Kind of like old times, Taff."

"Yeah," he echoed, still bound in a dreamlike strangeness, watching Wade and Wardell crouched over the wellhead, fussing frantically with something. Several of the crew crowded around Nat Gibbons, helping him to his feet. "Kind of like old times."

He began to shake, then. Looking down, he saw the revolver still dangling loosely against his leg and shoved it in its holster, fumbling badly at it because of the trembling, which was getting much worse. *Too old,* he thought, for the first time in his life, and clamped his hands under his armpits hard to make them stop shaking. *Too old for these damn hijinks. And that's a fact.*

THEY worked right through till dawn, trying to measure the extent of the damage. When the cable had been cut, the string of tools had fallen into the well. There was no way to continue drilling until they were removed. They all watched fascinated as Wade and Wardell took turns fishing with a long line and grapple, trying to secure a purchase on the twisted cable and dredge the lost tools from the pipe.

They made drop after drop. The tension and frustration rose to what seemed unbearable limits. Then at last, sweating and flushed with success, they pulled up the bent and battered bit from the wellhead. As they pulled the string to the surface, the crew gave a shout. But as Wade came toward Reanna, holding a frayed cable in his hand, she saw something more serious than fatigue in his sober expression.

"Well," he said, "there's the story."

"How bad is it?"

"Bad enough. Those buggers had gone clean down to China."

"Now what?" she demanded.

He shifted his gaze from hers. "Sorry, Mrs. MacClaren."

"Sorry? But I don't understand. You got the tools out."

"Yes, but the casing is whacked up bad, and the sand's beginning to cave in."

"What do you do now?"

"I don't do anything." He wiped his moist forehead with a grimy handkerchief. "There's too much damage for us to ream her out. The well is a goner."

She heard herself gasp. "It can't be. You must do something."

"There's nothing I can do."

"What do you suggest?"

"Abandon the well."

"I can't do that."

"Drill another hole."

"That's not possible. I've staked everything on this one. We haven't time, the money—"

"I'm sorry, Mrs. MacClaren." Wade shook his head sadly. "There's no way we could even shoot this well in."

"I don't know what you mean, shoot the well."

"To shoot a well, you put a can of nitroglycerin down the hole. When the torpedo explodes, it brings the oil out of the sand. If the oil's there."

"You said there was a show of oil yesterday."

"Yes, but that was before all this happened. Now the picture's changed."

"How?"

"You can't go on drilling in a shifting hole. This is it. We're finished."

"If the oil was there yesterday, it's there today," she said doggedly. "I say shoot the well."

He went pale beneath the dirt that encrusted his face. "It's not that easy, Mrs. MacClaren." He was bone tired, and a thin whine had crept into his voice.

"But you know it can be done. You've seen it done."

"Yes, I saw Red Fallon shoot a well back in Pennsylvania, but he was an expert moonlighter. The best in the business."

"What's a moonlighter?"

"An independent, a man who travels with torpedo equipment and nitro."

"Well, then, let's get a moonlighter."

"It's too late for that. By the time we got in a shooter, this well would have plumb caved in."

"Then you must do it."

"I told you, I can't."

"If you know how it's done, why can't you do it?" There was a silence. Wade stood with his head bowed. "You're an experienced driller. There's always a first time."

Wade raised his eyes to hers. "The next time Red Fallon shot a well, he was blown to pieces. If you spill a drop of the stuff, you go sky high. If you hit the torpedo against rock formation on the way down, it's goodbye to everybody on the location. Once you get the torpedo set, you have to send down a go-devil to detonate the charge." His voice had risen another note, shrill in the morning air. He broke off and looked away; Reanna saw a thin film of sweat under his hat brim.

"Do we have any nitroglycerin?" There was a short, uneasy silence. "Do we? *Answer me.*"

"No." Wade's voice was a hoarse whisper. "We couldn't keep it on the place. It could explode at any time!"

"Then go and get some." She turned to Taffy. "You must know who sells the stuff."

Taffy nodded. When she had her mind made up, there was no changing it. "Lester Bowles has a nitro wagon. We used him when we was blowing water wells on the ranch."

"Then go get him," she cried at Taffy. "We're wasting precious time."

"You don't understand—" Mr. Wade broke in.

"I understand that if there was oil in the sand yesterday, there's oil there today, and I mean to get it out."

Taffy sighed. "I'll go for Lester. It could take a while to find him."

"I'll wait," she said grimly.

It was late afternoon before she saw a wagon headed toward them from the direction of MacClaren City. Taffy was riding along-side but at a respectful distance. As the wagon approached, Reanna could make out a thin, hollow-eyed man holding a tight rein on a pair of black geldings.

He looked a little like an undertaker with his black wagon and black horses. She didn't find comfort in that image or in the sign painted in bold red and white that said DANGER, NITRO-GLYCERIN.

The wagon rolled forward at a slow and even pace. Reanna waved the crew and Cima and the children back from the well as the wagon came closer. She walked toward the driver as the wagon halted by the derrick steps.

"Mr. Bowles?"

He raised his hat politely. "Yes ma'am."

"You've come to shoot the well?"

"No ma'am. I haul and I sell, but I don't shoot."

She couldn't believe she had heard him right. "But why come, if you aren't going to shoot the well?"

"Because Taffy Owen told me to. He said you wanted nitro; he didn't say nothing about shooting no well."

"You must do it, Mr. Bowles."

He shook his head emphatically. "Not me."

"You can name your price."

"No ma'am, I can't do it. It's too dangerous. This stuff can blow you to kingdom come."

"But you haul it. Isn't that just as dangerous?"

"It's risky, that I will admit, but not like putting it down a hole. No ma'am, I'm an old man with a young wife, and I don't mean to make her a widow."

Reanna turned to Mr. Wade. "Then you must do it, Mr. Wade."

He looked as if he was going to cry. He shook his head. "Sorry, Mrs. MacClaren, but I told you I wouldn't. I don't even like standing next to the stuff."

She was filled with a cold, implacable anger. She couldn't lose it all now. She could not. "Then I'll do it, if you won't."

"You gone haksi," Cima was saying; she was holding Lovell, who was smiling happily, chuckling and reaching out toward Reanna. "Clean haksi, crazy. You know that?"

"Shut up, Cima."

"Now, you can't do this," Taffy was pleading. "I ain't going to let you."

She stared at him. "I can do it," she said, "and I will. We are just about at the end of our resources. We have enough money to finish this job, and that's all. We have no other choices."

"For the love of great God, Reanna—"

"Be quiet, Cima! Go and fetch my hat. I want to keep the hair out of my eyes." Cima handed Lovell to Taffy and half ran to her tent. Reanna faced Lester Bowles. "Now tell me exactly how to do this."

"You ever seen a can of nitro before?" He was watching her out of the corners of his eyes.

He doesn't think I'm going to do it, she thought in hollow surprise, looking at the ring of faces. None of them does. They all think I'll back off at the last moment. "Just tell me what to do," she said grimly.

"How far down have you drilled?"

"Nine hundred and eighty feet."

"I'll measure out nine hundred eighty feet of wire. Put it on this big spool and attach it to a winch. At that depth you'll need one torpedo. It's already loaded with gunpowder and nitro. Six quarts of the stuff, that ought to do the job. Take this torpedo to the wellhead, hook the bail handle onto the wire, then lower it down the well till your wire's played out. Remember, you can't spill any or bump this critter too hard, or she'll go off and kill everything that's big enough to die. When the spool is plumb played out, then send down this here go-devil device so it will hit the cartridges at the head of the torpedo. As soon as you send down the go-devil, you turn and run like hell." She was silent, staring at him. "You want me to repeat that?"

"No. I understand. It would be a help to me if you'd set up the winch and spool of wire and go-devil at the wellhead for me. I'll handle the rest for myself."

"Sure," he said. "I reckon I can do that much."

Reanna opened the flap of the wagon and looked at the box of nitroglycerin torpedos. There were four of them neatly and carefully packed in well-padded compartments. She drew a deep breath as her hand went to lift the nearest torpedo from the crate.

(373)

"Give me that," Taffy said.

"No, I'll do it."

"Look, if you're bound and hell-bent on this, I'll do it. I ain't about to—"

"You can't, Taffy," she told him quietly. "You're unsettled." He looked down unhappily at his hands trembling and said nothing.

Cima came from the tent, carrying Reanna's bonnet. "You better change your mind, lady."

"It's my well and my land," she declared, though her throat had gone dry as she watched Lester Bowles carrying the wire and go-devil toward the drilling platform. "I'll do what I think is best."

"Best for who? For Lochleven? For me and Taffy? For Lovell?"

She turned away. She wouldn't think of Lovell now. *She would not.*

Cima gave her the bonnet. She looked at it a moment, then put it on her head and tied it securely in place with her scarf. It was the hat she'd worn the day she'd come out here as a new bride; the wind had swept it away and she'd laughed, watching Andrew chasing after it in the high grass.

"Well, then," she said aloud, "here goes." She was pleased to hear her voice perfectly steady. She looked at them all—Cima, Taffy, Snow and the girls, then at Lovell, who was still beaming merrily in Cima's arms and waving one tiny hand. No. This was for Lovell, for him alone. She wouldn't fail, because of Lovell.

"Now stand back, all of you. No matter what happens, don't come near the well."

"Please, Reanna," Taffy pleaded. "It ain't worth it."

"Oh yes," she said, "it's worth it." His face was all broken up in wrinkles; he looked old and unsure. To her amazement, she found she was smiling at him. "I know I can trust you to manage, if you have to. Now stay with the others. No matter what happens, see they all stay where they are."

He nodded and herded them all farther off; they seemed to back away reluctantly, still facing her, as though they could save her by staying near. Cima's lips were moving steadily; she was gazing skyward. Why, she's praying, Reanna thought with distinct pleasure, she's praying for me. Taffy had his hands clasped under his arms. Wade and Wardell were crouched on their hams, staring at her without expression. Snow was holding on to Taffy's sleeve, looking cowed and remorseful. That's a welcome change, Reanna thought. She gave one last fierce glance at Lovell, turned away and walked to

Mr. Bowles' wagon with its waiting load. Slowly, carefully, she took hold of the bail handle and pulled the torpedo up from its padded nest. It was heavier than she'd expected. Holding it with great respect, she began her long walk toward the derrick. Halfway there she met Mr. Bowles coming back to the wagon. They paused, standing aloof from each other.

"Is everything ready?" she asked.

"Yes. I measured out the spool and the go-devil is there beside it. Be extra careful when you first clamp on and lower the can down the hole. You don't want no sudden snap when she falls into the hole!"

"I'll be careful."

"Now, if you'll excuse me, ma'am, I'm going to get the hell out of here, because your blast could set off the rest of my nitro. Good luck."

"Thank you."

As she turned, she heard him mutter under his breath, "You're going to need all the luck you can get."

She walked on toward the derrick, all her senses keyed to a high, screaming pitch. She felt the handle bite into the palm of her hand. She was aware of each pebble beneath her feet and every small rise in the ground. She came to the platform and started up the steps. Thinking that she was close to her goal and that she had made it there safe, she hurried; as she came to the last step, she misfooted and felt herself falling. From behind her she heard a gasp from the watching circle and Cima calling her name. It was an act of will that made her find her balance.

On the platform she saw the spool of wire and the go-devil Mr. Bowles had made ready for her; holding the torpedo with one hand, she reached out for the hook at the end of the wire. As she fastened them together, she heard the click of metal touching metal; it seemed as sharp and loud as a rifle shot. She grasped the handle with both hands and raised the canister over the wellhead, aware of an even louder, more persistent noise. It was, she was surprised to discover, the beating of her own heart. As she held the torpedo above the small opening of the pipe, the wind rose and swung the wire to and fro. It was still swaying as she began to lower the torpedo into the well mouth.

Hand over hand, she played out the slender cable wire on the winch. The torpedo went down foot by foot until it disappeared into the darkness. She reached the four-hundred-foot mark on the cable and then the six and the eight. She had no notion of how long it took; she had lost all sense of time. She was only aware of the pain in her hands, the tension of the muscles in her back and arms, and the deadly weight at the end of the cable. Her mouth was dry. She began to feel dizzy, looking down into the seemingly fathomless hole, a little the way she had before she'd fainted. There was a ringing in her ears; the wind made a thin, whistling sound as it passed through the wooden fretwork of the derrick.

She took a deep breath. She must be calm and control her emotions. She must keep her hands steady. One false, sharp movement and it would all be lost. She took another deep breath, gasping the cool air into her lungs. She let out the line evenly, until at last she came to the end of nine hundred and eighty feet of wire.

She let go of the winch handle and looked at her blistered hands. Again the wind sang through the derrick, moving the dangling, slender wire. The wind was playing tricks on her. In the buckboard that first afternoon with Andrew, she had laughed at the wind. She should never have done that, she knew that now. No one could defy the wind. No one.

She wouldn't give up. She was so tired, her nerves had been stretched so taut, that she felt herself shaking as if with a fever. It took all her control and concentration to pick up the go-devil and fasten it to the wire holding the torpedo. She took another deep breath and then, precisely and deliberately, she dropped the go-devil down the wire. For a second she felt she was fastened to the spot. Then she turned and ran down the steps toward Cima and the others. She took Lovell from Cima's arms and hugged him to her, crouching low, waiting.

An entire lifetime passed in silence—a silence that made her think they might have all gone deaf; then there was a first, slight tremor. It was followed by another. Now the earth seemed to shake in constant agitation. From the wellhead a shower of rocks and sand and pipe flew high in the air and smashed against the crown block at the top of the derrick, shattering it.

The earth continued to shake. A rust-red column of water and debris erupted upwards, blowing into the air like a Niagara driven skyward. The water was mingled with great, dark blue gouts. And then—like a crazed black fountain—oil, under pressure of gas, burst into the air.

The oil showered down on all of them, pelting them with greasy black torrents until they were strange, slick creatures caught, shrieking and singing, in a danse macabre. Wade and Wardell were dancing a reel, their arms interlocked; Cima was waving her long, black arms to heaven; Taffy was sitting in the muck, giving his rebel yell and holding his precious hat high aloft, as if to catch it all. They looked like a demented sect of Holy Rollers, bathed, baptized and anointed, children of the great god of oil.

Only Lovell lamented this coming of a new age. He screamed in fear and outrage, wagging his little, round head, watching friends and loved ones transformed into capering strangers. Reanna held him close to her as she danced round and round, as she crooned to him in the slick, alien rain.

"There, there, don't cry, Lovell. Everything's going to be wonderful. Don't cry, Lovell, look at the oil! We're going to be rich! By God, we're going to be rich!"

AFTER this day, whenever a well blew in against all odds and flowed a gusher, people would say it was a *Reanna* wind that had brought them luck.

Reanna, watching the spectacle, was suddenly sobered by the sight of so much oil going to waste. All along, her vision had only extended to the possibility of finding oil. Now that it was here in an abundant reality, she didn't know what to do with it. She went to Mr. Wade and shouted over the roar of the cascade, "What do we do now?"

"What?" he shouted back.

"What do we do with the oil?"

"You put the well on pump and sell the oil to a refinery."

"How much will they pay me for it?"

"It depends on what grade oil it is. And this is good grade for sure," but she wouldn't take his word for it. She wanted to hear it from an impartial source.

When they had cleaned up, Wade, Wardell, Taffy and Reanna went into MacClaren City. It was past midnight when they got there. Reanna rousted Jack Levy out of bed and added him to the delegation that went down the deserted main street to see Doc Hersey. Doc was used to people knocking on his door in the dead of night, but he was surprised to see Reanna and the others; he was even more surprised by the reason for their visit.

"Here." Reanna thrust a bottle of oil into his hands. "I've drilled an oil well, and I want you to tell me what grade of oil it is."

Doc looked at the bottle and said, "You folks better come in. Amoretta will make us some coffee."

They all hovered around the kitchen table as Doc made a great show of tasting, smelling and rubbing the oil between his fingers. Then he poured the contents of the bottle into the base of a new lamp and struck a match and lit the wick. The oil began to burn as bright and clear as if it had already been refined.

"It's high-grade oil," Doc said, "no doubt about it."

"I told you so." Mr. Wade felt he had been vindicated.

Their shadows were cast large upon the walls of the kitchen, making them look like a circle of conspirators. Reanna looked at each of them in turn. "I want to keep the news of my well quiet for as long as I can. When the word gets out, we'll have every wildcatter in Christendom coming in on us. Before that happens, I want to line up a refinery and get busy signing up leases on the surrounding area. If you all want to do a little leasing on your own, I think it's worth the gamble."

"Agreed," Doc said.

Jack nodded. "I'm with you."

"Besides, I can't go on drilling with a borrowed rig." She turned to Mr. Wardell. "Mr. Wardell, you and Mr. Wade go on up to Tulsa with the rig as planned. When you get there, scout out some rotary rigs. Cable's just too slow. And to keep the crew from blabbing this strike around in saloons, I'll keep them on salary and busy out on the well site. Taffy, you'll go back and ride herd on them so they won't go running off."

"Where will you be?" Taffy asked.

"Tulsa."

Amoretta bustled from the stove to the table. "Come on, you all, and drink your coffee and eat your breakfast while it's hot." She took the lamp away so she could set the table. "Whatever you all get up to, you'll do it better on a full stomach."

Reanna rode up to Tulsa on the train with Wardell and Wade. She found a refiner who agreed to take whatever product she could ship. She made her way home, talking to farmers who were more than happy to take her money just for signing a lease form. Even with leases at fifteen cents an acre, this new activity would strain her resources. She'd need more men, more equipment and wagons to haul her oil to market. She needed time, but there was no way to keep what she was doing a secret much longer.

The news of her strike came from an unexpected quarter. Mr. Green, the freight agent at Maitland junction, sent his boss a telegraphed message. "Have struck oil. Am quitting job and leaving for parts unknown."

The news of the *Reanna One* went down telegraph wires all over the country like wildfire in an electrical storm. The word was out that there was oil play near MacClaren City, and people came from everywhere. They came on foot, by train, by wagon, in buggies, on bicycles and on horseback. Some even came by automobile. There was a flood of drifters, drillers and get-rich-quick charlatans. Lawyers with printed lease forms rubbed shoulders with roustabouts and pipe fitters. They all came running, wild with oil fever, and all of them had one thing in common—they were sure they'd make their fortune out of oil.

Overnight, MacClaren City became a boom town. In the countryside, a tent city sprang up and spread out its canvas wings. In town, they charged a dollar for bacon and eggs and another dollar for a glass of water. It was romp and stomp, hoot and holler, twenty-four hours a day. The crews worked twelve-hour shifts and made good money, which they spent before they lay down to sleep three in a bed.

There were flashy gamblers and fancy women. There was rotgut whiskey and hellfire preachers. There was shooting and stabbing; thieves broke in everywhere and took anything they could grab and carry off. Jack Levy had to sleep in the store with a loaded shotgun just to keep stock on the shelves.

Reanna wrote home to her folks.

Dear Mama and Papa,

The business proposition I wrote you about has worked out. I drilled an oil well, and it's come in a gusher. There is so much oil play here that I can't leave just now. But as soon as I get things going, I want to see you all and you to see Lovell. The trouble is that if you come out here now, when the place is so crowded, there'd be no place to put you, so what I propose is this. When I can and if it suits you, I'll bring Lovell and meet you all halfway at Memphis. I'm sending some cash for tickets and travel expenses and to spend for whatever you please.

Love to you all,
Reanna

* * *

REANNA brought in a second well and began drilling a third. When it came in, she headed up to the cabin for a bath and a change of clothes. She had already sent Cima and the children home from the *Reanna One*. Cima had been more than ready to go, but Rose Dawn and Annoyi had made faces. They had liked the freedom from regular chores. Reanna had sent them back despite their protests, because she could take no chance of a second incident with Snow.

She came up to the cabin late. The place was dark and she tiptoed to her room quietly so as not to wake the household. Lovell was fast asleep in his cot. There was a narrow beam of moonlight across his sweet face. She'd missed Lovell cruelly. She didn't like to miss a day of his growing up.

She stripped off her outer garments and let them fall in a pile on the floor. As she began to unbutton her chemise, she suddenly felt a chill on her neck. Her nerves began to prickle; she had the feeling that she was being observed. Her first thought was that some animal had found its way in and was watching her. Fear for Lovell seized her, and she made herself turn to face the danger.

As her eyes became accustomed to the dark, she saw the shape of a man sitting in the shadows of the far corner. She heard herself gasp as she realized it was Andrew. "What are you doing here?"

"That's not much of a welcome home, is it?"

He drawled out the words softly, as he rose and walked toward her. He didn't try to embrace her, but she felt herself shudder. The memory of their last night together in this room, in this bed, came back to haunt the present.

"Aren't you going to ask me how I've been?" Andrew's eyes glittered cold and pale in the half-light.

His apparent calm infuriated her. "If you had wanted me to know how you were, Andrew, you could have written. I haven't had a word from you in nearly two years."

She spoke with a sharpness that was new to Andrew. "I'm not much of a hand at writing." With one finger he touched her bare shoulder. "You're looking good, Reanna."

She drew away from him. "What brings you back?"

He hesitated a moment and then said, "There wasn't as much opportunity in Texas as I'd hoped for, so I decided to come on home. You know what they say, 'there's no place like home.'"

Andrew had taken the advantage by surprising her. Now she let

(381)

him grow uncomfortable in silence. At last he said, "I hear you've been busy."

"I've not been idle." She would give him no satisfaction if she could help it.

"I heard the news about your strike in Texas."

"When did you get back?" Her tone was flat and dull, but her heart was racing.

"I rode in last week."

"Why didn't you let me know you were here?"

"I didn't stop, because I could see that you were busy. So I went on into MacClaren City on business."

"What kind of business?" She felt a sense of wariness. She knew he was up to some trick. He was being altogether too amiable.

"Yes sir," he said, "everybody in town seems to be interested in oil. It was sure good to see Doc and Jack and hear them talk about the leases they've been getting." She was alert, sensing danger. He took another step toward her. He didn't raise his hand or touch her again, but it was a threatening step all the same. "You must be right proud of yourself to have found oil."

"I've worked hard and I've been lucky."

"Unlike some?"

Every question he asked seemed to be a test that she must pass. "What does that mean?" She still could not tell exactly what he was up to.

"Some folks might say that when my luck ran out, yours came in."

She felt her anger overpower her good sense. She knew she should be calm, but she could not. She flared out at him. "It was your decision to drive those cattle instead of sheltering them in the ravine. That wasn't bad luck, Andrew, that was bad judgment." She saw a muscle in his cheek tighten.

"I went broke in the cattle business, but believe me, I can't lose now there's oil on the place."

She had to bite her tongue to keep from shouting at him. She knew now for certain that he'd come home because he meant to cause her trouble. "You used not to have a very high opinion of oil." She heard Lovell stir in his cot and whimper. Andrew didn't seem to notice, but it heightened her sense of uneasiness.

"I've changed my mind about oil," Andrew said. "I changed it when I noticed that you'd drilled the first well on the west by the seep springs."

"That's right." She was puzzled by his words.

"Did you talk it over with Pride?" There was a hard edge to his voice. "Did you fix it up between you?"

She stared at Andrew in disbelief. "I haven't seen or heard from Pride since you left."

"Maybe," he said slowly, "maybe you were hoping to open up an oil field on the west and make Pride a rich man."

"Pride has nothing to do with this. I didn't drill on Pride's land. I drilled on Lochleven homestead land. Pride had nothing to do with those wells." She disliked being put on the defensive. "I drilled there by the seep springs because that's where the oil was. If the field spreads onto Pride's land, that's not my doing."

"I tell you what I think, Reanna. I think you all meant to put one over on me. You and Doc and Jack and Pride. Well, I have something to tell you that's going to put a spoke in your wheel."

She saw he meant to hurt her, that her pain would somehow give him pleasure. For the first time she fully realized how much he hated her. Before there had always been some part of Andrew that was still balanced and rational, but now he'd slipped over the line. He smiled at her, but there was no warmth in it, only the deadly chill of a long winter. "Can you guess what I did, Reanna?"

"No," she said, "but you're going to tell me, aren't you?"

"When I went to file for my allotment, I filed for the Ridge and the land on the west. The west is mine, not Pride's."

"You did what?" Her lips felt stiff, and she heard her voice like a leaden echo from a long way off.

"I filed for my allotment on the west."

She knew that Andrew was capable of anything, but still it took a moment for the full implication of what he had done to penetrate her consciousness.

"But you can't do that. It was agreed that you'd take the Ridge and Pride the west."

"I filed for the Ridge and the west and took Snow's allotment on the east. I got the land assessed low so I'd get a big holding. It cost me, but it's done. Now who's the smart one, Reanna?"

"And Pride?" she asked, her voice a whisper. "What about Pride?"

"Let Pride take care of himself." His eyes narrowed and his lip curled in mocking satisfaction. "All of this place is mine."

"When did you file?" She wanted to know, not that it would change the facts.

"Before I went to Texas. So you see, Reanna, it's been my land all along."

"But how could you get them to let you have Pride's allotment? Everyone knows this is Beauvaise land." Andrew was silent. There was something sly and self-satisfied in that silence that made Reanna sick with shame. "What did you do?" she asked. "Did you bribe them to let you have Pride's land?"

Andrew shrugged. "Let's say I did a little trading. That's the way things are done in this world."

"That doesn't make it right. You cheated Pride out of his land. You robbed him of his inheritance. You're a cheat and a thief."

Again Andrew smiled. "Let's just say I took this land, and Pride had to file for his land somewhere else. But I thought you would have known that by now. You two were always so close."

"The west was Pride's. You have to give it back to him."

"It's too late, Reanna. It's all signed, sealed and delivered."

"And what about Cima's forty? Have you taken that too?"

His jaw tightened. "Cima had filed for her forty before I went to enroll. Her measly forty acres in a dead-end ravine doesn't bother me one way or another."

"Doesn't being a thief bother you? You stole from your own brother." She saw his fist clench as if he meant to strike her.

"Can you say he never stole anything from me? Can you swear he never took anything that was mine?" Andrew's words were a two-edged sword that cut at her again and again.

"Give Pride's land back to him." It was a demand, not a plea.

"Can he give me back what was mine?"

"You have to give him back his land."

"No I don't, Reanna. I don't have to do anything."

"Why, why did you take what was his? There was enough land for both of you."

"Pride nearly killed me, Reanna."

"He had cause. You know it and so do I."

She shivered, remembering the snow and the storm howling around her winter prison. She'd been abandoned and alone. "You left me here, knowing what might happen to me."

"And you think Pride is some kind of hero, because he came through that blizzard to rescue you while I stayed with the herd."

"You didn't care what happened to me or to the baby. Pride saved my life and Lovell's."

(384)

"He took my place here in my house. He took what was mine, and now I own the land."

She felt rage sear through her like lightning. "You don't own me, Andrew, and you don't own this place. You may have filed for Pride's land, but if so it's not yours, it's mine. You seem to have conveniently forgotten that you put everything you owned in my name. The land and the wells are mine by deed."

He stared at her, as surprised as if he'd seen her for the first time. "That was just on paper. I signed that paper just to keep the creditors off my trail. Jack Levy talked me into it. It wasn't a true gift. I never considered it binding. It was just a way to keep me from being sold up as a bankrupt."

For the first time since they had begun the argument, she had Andrew at a disadvantage. "You meant to cheat your creditors and steal from your brother, but you've outsmarted yourself. The wells and the land are mine."

Andrew scowled darkly. "It was all a setup from the first. You all meant to cheat me—my brother, my friends, my wife. I asked Jack what he was going to get out of it, remember? Well, now I know why Jack was so anxious to help me."

"No man ever had more loyal friends."

"Where did you get the money to drill the wells?" Andrew demanded.

"I sold the cattle and . . ." She hesitated. She would not tell him about Frampton. It was a matter between Frampton and herself. Andrew mistook her hesitation for an admission of guilt.

"You gave Jack my share of the store and the town lots. Jack and Doc have their bank on my lots now. You cheated me, and my friends helped you do it."

She couldn't believe his perceptions were so far from the truth. "Jack only bought you out because you'd left him with debts and we were in want. Jack has carried us."

Andrew ignored her. "I mean to get back at them and at you. I'll take you to law."

"You won't win."

He shook his head. "Maybe not, but no matter what, I'll always have the east."

"Only until Snow comes of age."

"Or for as long as she is declared an incompetent under the law. Snow will have to prove competency before she can handle her own affairs. I'll see to it that Snow's my ward for life."

Reanna gasped. To take Snow's land was perhaps the worst wrong of all. Long ago, Cima had told her that Andrew had only married Letty for her head rights. Now he had them in Snow's portion of the land. Reanna stared at him, wondering what she'd ever found to care about in this hard, ruthless man.

"You'd do that to Snow?"

He nodded.

"Then take Snow's allotment, but get off Beauvaise Ridge. I never want to see you here again. Get off my land."

"Your land." His lip curled upward in derision. "You make me laugh. You may have a deed, a piece of paper that says this land is yours, but since you set such store by a piece of paper, I have another piece of paper that says you're my wife."

The thought of being Andrew's wife in name or fact filled Reanna with revulsion. "I'll never be your wife again." As she said the words, she knew that they were true. This was the end for the two of them. Their marriage was over and done with. Andrew had forfeited all rights to her and to the land by what he had done. "I'll never live with you again."

"The law says different. In this state a man is the head of the household. I have the right over you and Snow and Lovell."

When Andrew spoke of Lovell, Reanna felt sick with dread. Andrew would do anything to get back at her. He would even try to use Lovell, as he had used Snow. Without considering the consequences, she said, "You have no right over Lovell. Lovell isn't your son."

Andrew had backed her into a corner. He'd forced her to say it aloud. Now it was done, and she couldn't take back her words. The look on Andrew's face told her that if he had suspected that Lovell was not his son before now, he had not known for sure. Her confession had struck at him hard.

"Lovell isn't yours." Her voice was low, but it echoed in the room. "Lovell is Pride's son."

There was a long silence. Andrew blinked as if he had something sharp in his eyes.

"Does Pride know Lovell is his?"

"No."

"You haven't told Pride, but you've told me?"

"Yes."

(386)

"How do I know it's true? You'd say anything to have me off the place."

"I'm not lying," she said quietly, "and you know it."

Once, long ago, she'd told him she never lied. Then she'd been a beautiful girl in an apple-green dress, a girl he'd desired against his will.

"Let's say it's true," he countered, but the words came hard. "Say Lovell isn't my son; what do you expect me to do about it?" Even now he hoped that she might deny what she had said.

"I want a divorce."

"You want me to let both you and the land go?"

"Yes."

"You believe I'll go into a court of law and say Lovell isn't mine?"

"No!" The word rang out like a shot. "I want a divorce, but you'll leave Lovell out of it."

"How do you figure that?"

"You've already claimed him as your son. He has your name. You won't stand up in court and say that he's not yours, because that would make a fool out of you and you don't want the world laughing at you. But you'll give me a divorce."

"No, Reanna, that's where you're dead wrong. I won't ever give you a divorce, no matter what you do."

"Why? You don't love me! You never did."

"I won't give you your divorce because you'd go to Pride. I won't ever let you leave me to be with Pride. You say I don't want to look a fool, but I'll call your bluff. You won't try to get a divorce, because you don't want Lovell to be branded a bastard. Even if I could never prove he wasn't my son, *bastard* isn't a pretty name. Once said, it would stick like a burr." Andrew stepped toward Lovell's crib and the sleeping child.

Quickly Reanna put herself between Lovell and Andrew. "Don't touch him."

"Touch him!" Andrew laughed, but the sound was dry and sharp as wire. "I wouldn't touch your bastard, but that doesn't mean I don't have the right to. He has my name. I'm his legal father. I can do what I please with him, just as I can do what I please with you because you're my wife."

He reached out for her. His hand fell on her bare shoulder, traveled to the top of her chemise and ripped it down the front, leaving her naked and exposed. The sight of her blurred his senses. His hands went on stripping her bare.

She tried to hold off his assault, to beat him back from her body, but he was too powerful. She raked at his face with her nails, leaving a track of blood on his cheek. She struck at him with all her might, but he hardly seemed to feel the blows as he pinioned her hands, holding both of hers with one of his. The raw, brutal force of his attack had taken her by surprise.

She cried out, but Andrew's mouth on hers muffled the sound. As they struggled, she fought not only for herself but for Lovell. She had to keep Andrew as far away from him as possible. She wouldn't give way to Andrew without marking him as he meant to mark her. She beat out against Andrew as he bent her down to her knees before him. He wouldn't be satisfied until he had been able to subdue, humiliate and break her to his will. She threw herself to one side, struggling to keep him from falling on top of her and thrusting himself within her.

She was so engrossed in her desperate conflict that she didn't hear the sound of the door opening, but both Reanna and Andrew heard the small, ominous snap as the safety catch on Cima's shotgun was released. Both of them froze, caught in a shaft of light from the doorway. They looked up at Cima and her shotgun.

"Let the lady go, Mr. Andrew," Cima said, her eyes never wavering. "Let the lady go, or I'll blow you in two."

Andrew swallowed hard. He'd been in physical danger before, but this was a different kind of jeopardy. He hesitated. If he turned Reanna loose, he'd have no advantage left. In the moment he hesitated he saw Cima's finger tighten on the trigger.

"Let her go," Cima spoke again, and this time Andrew knew better than to tempt his luck. He let loose his hold of Reanna. She slipped from beneath him and, pulling a quilt around her, she went to Lovell. She saw that he was still sleeping, but he was restless, as if he were having a bad dream from which he couldn't escape.

She must make sure that Andrew never had another opportunity to harm Lovell. She watched Andrew as he buttoned up his shirt and tied his string tie. He pretended to be calm and take his time, but she saw that his fingers were trembling, while Cima's were still steady on the trigger.

Reanna kept her voice even as she said, "Get out of my house and off my land. You're never to come near me or my child again.

(388)

You have no right over me or anything that's mine. If you try to take my land or my wells, I'll fight you through every court in the land."

He stood looking back at her with deepening hatred. "I'll go, Reanna, but you'll be sorry for tonight. I promise you that. I'll never give you a divorce. You'll be my wife as long as you live. For all I care, you and your bastard can stay here until you die and rot in the wind."

"Harm Lovell and I'll kill you."

Andrew smiled as if she had just given him a compliment. "So that's how we leave it, then. Either you get me or I get you."

She nodded. "That's how we leave it."

He walked across the room. At the door he turned and tipped his hat to Reanna. It wasn't the polite gesture of a gentleman taking leave of a lady. It was a challenge to do battle for a lifetime.

"I'll get my own back, Reanna, you can depend on it." He turned and disappeared into the darkness.

There was an uneasy silence; then Reanna picked up Lovell and held him close to her. He began to cry, fretting at having been so abruptly taken from his sleep. Looking over his head at Cima, Reanna said, "Thank you."

"Nothing to thank me for. That Andrew's a mean one. He's going to hurt you if he can." Cima hadn't lowered the shotgun or taken her eyes from the door, as though she half expected Andrew to return.

"Whatever he does, I intend to give better than I get." Reanna spoke sharply. "If it's war he wants, I'll be waiting for him. He won't surprise me again."

CHAPTER 16

REANNA could not let the matter stand. Andrew had taken Pride's land. Since she now owned all Andrew's property by deed, the only honorable thing for her to do was to give Pride back what had been taken from him, but she needed advice on how to go about it. She saddled up Molly May and rode into MacClaren City to see Jack Levy. The town was mobbed.

Jack wasn't in the bank, but she found him at the store waiting on a customer. When he saw her, one look at her face was enough to tell him that she had not come in just to pass the time of day or buy a spool of thread. He quickly turned the customer over to a clerk, excused himself and came toward Reanna.

"What is it? What's the matter?"

"Andrew's back."

"I know, he came into town last week. He was looking real good." As Jack spoke, he saw the tears well up in her eyes.

"Andrew has done something terrible."

"Come in, you need some tea." Jack took Reanna's arm and walked her toward the back of the store to his living quarters.

She sat straight, her hands in her lap like a child, as he busied himself with the samovar. "My first night in MacClaren City, Andrew brought me here to this store. If I had known then how things were going to turn out, I would have left and never come back."

Jack handed her a glass of steaming hot tea. As she sipped it, the color began to come back to her cheeks. "All right," Jack said, "now what's all this about Andrew?"

"Andrew came out to the ranch last night. He said and did things that . . ." She stopped, then took a deep breath and went on. "We have separated for good, Andrew and I."

"I'm sorry."

"Don't be," she said bitterly, "I'm not. The worst is not what Andrew's done to me but what he's done to Pride." She looked at Jack, her eyes large and troubled. "Andrew took the land that Pride had chosen for his allotment. He has stolen Pride's land."

"I can't believe that." Jack shook his head. "I can't believe Andrew would do such a thing."

"Believe it. And because I hold Andrew's property by deed, I want to give the land back to Pride."

"Are you sure Andrew was telling you the truth?" Jack found what Reanna had said hard to believe. "He says things when he's angry that he doesn't mean."

"Andrew said it was what he had done. He accused me of drilling my wells on Pride's land to make Pride rich. You know that's not so. I drilled on Lochleven homestead land, but if a field develops to the west, Pride's land will be worth a fortune."

"There must be some misunderstanding. When Doc and I saw Andrew, he never said anything about the land or the wells. Andrew was friendly, all smiles, like he'd never been away. He seemed pleased at how good things were going for Doc and me." Jack shook his head, "Andrew must think we've all been against him all along."

"Don't waste any time feeling sorry for Andrew," Reanna snapped. "Pride is the one who's been wronged. Do you know if Pride is still in Muskogee?"

Jack nodded. "He's working for a law firm, Mason and Jackson. I haven't seen him, but I've heard from him, a card or two, and he never mentioned his allotment."

"I want you to go to Muskogee and see him. Tell him, explain to him that I knew nothing about what Andrew did and that I want to give him back his land. It's his. It's his birthright."

Jack was stunned. "You want me to go? Why don't you go see Pride yourself? It would come better from you than from me."

"I can't leave here." She was in a panic at the mention of going to see Pride. "I don't know what Andrew's planning to do next."

"You think he plans to do something?"

"Yes. Andrew won't let this rest. I don't know what he'll do, but I know it will be something. Andrew will never give up what he thinks is his."

Jack rubbed at his forehead, thinking. "Reanna, you say I shouldn't feel sorry for Andrew, but you can see that from where Andrew's standing, it must look like all of us have made a profit at his expense. I think what he's done about Pride's land is wrong, and I'll go see Pride. I can take the next train out of Maitland. I've been planning to go up to Tulsa on business for the store anyway. It will suit me to go early. But Reanna, you're coming with me. I'm not doing this on my own."

"I can't go." She was trembling. "You don't understand."

"I'll go up on the train with you. I'll stay there and put you on the train back here before I go on to Tulsa. I'm willing to be your chaperone, if that's what you want, but giving the land back to Pride is something I can't do for you."

She was quiet for so long that he thought she was not going to answer him. Then she looked up and said, "I can't go looking like this."

Jack sighed with relief. At last, here was a problem he could deal with. "Pick out anything in the store, but don't take more than half an hour." He patted her shoulder. "Now go and choose something pretty and let me pack."

Jack packed his worn leather gladstone with a change of linen. Then he and Reanna headed for Maitland by buckboard to catch the Katy. As they sat side by side on the hard coach seats, Jack thought he saw tears in her eyes, but the day was hot and the windows were open. It could have been that a cinder had caught in her eye. He knew she looked mighty pretty in a new ruffled shirtwaist.

The trip took longer than usual. They were on the milk and market run. There were two layovers; it was morning before they pulled into Muskogee. Jack asked directions to Pride's office from a baggage handler. As they started the walk up from the station, the streets were already crowded with people.

When they found Pride's street, Reanna stopped at the corner and put her hand on Jack's arm. "You'll have to go first," she said. "I can't walk in and surprise him. He'd misunderstand why I've come. He'd think I've come to stay." She was trembling.

Jack had never seen her in such a state. "All right, go and sit over there by the courthouse on one of those benches. But stay there, you hear me? Don't you go running off on me. You promise?"

"Yes, I promise."

Jack watched her walk across the wide street. She looked as if she might break in two, she was so thin. Then he opened the door to Mason and Jackson, attorneys-at-law. Pride was sitting at a table in the outer office. There was a pile of leather-bound law books on either side of him. He was busily writing down notes from one of the books onto a sheet of legal paper. Pride did not look up until Jack spoke his name, then he stared at Jack as if he were a ghost who had appeared out of thin air.

"Jack?" Pride asked tentatively, to make sure his eyes were not playing him tricks.

"Hello, Pride."

In a flash Pride was up out of his chair, around the table and embracing Jack. "Let me have a look at you. I can't believe it's you. Jack Levy, you're a sight for sore eyes."

"You look pretty good yourself." It was true. Pride had always been a good-looking boy, but he had matured into a fine-looking man.

"What brings you to Muskogee, Jack?"

"I just came up for the day," Jack hedged. This was more difficult than he had thought it was going to be. "I'm between trains on my way to Tulsa." He hoped it sounded less lame than it was.

Pride blinked. "This is the long way around to Tulsa, Jack. Why are you here? Is there something wrong at home?"

"No, no, nothing's wrong. Everybody's fine." He coughed nervously. "What time can you get away from the office?"

Pride looked at Jack hard. "I can get away any time."

"Some kind of law firm you work for, to let their help go any time they feel like it." He was trying for a little humor to lighten the moment, but he wasn't doing well. Not well at all.

"Mason and Jackson have been good to me," Pride said, trying to figure out what had brought Jack so far out of his way. "I'm reading for my bar exam, and in the meantime I work cheap and I stay late. You want to go get some breakfast?"

Jack looked down at his shoes and held on to his bowler hat. "The thing is, Pride, Reanna's with me." Without waiting to hear any more, Pride started past him to the door. Jack had to reach out and hold him back. "She wanted me to come in first and make it plain that she hasn't come to stay. She's just come up because she has something to discuss with you. She's going back today on the noon train."

"Oh." Pride looked like he'd been hit with a pole and was hurting. "I see," he said slowly. "I understand now why you came. Where is she?"

"Over there." Jack pointed out the window. "She's over there by the courthouse. I tell you what; I'll go have my breakfast and I'll be back by noon. Is that all right?"

Pride looked at Jack, his eyes dark with hurt. "Since I don't have a choice, I guess it will have to be."

As Pride came up to Reanna, she turned her head. The look in her eyes made him feel like the sky had fallen down on them both. He had dreamed of the day when she could come. He could not have imagined that when she did come at last, it would only be for an hour or two.

He sat beside her without speaking, not knowing what to say or how to begin. They both stared ahead, as if they were strangers who had never met and only chance had put them there, side by side.

At last it was Reanna who spoke first. "It's so crowded here. There are so many different people. Where have they all come from?" Her voice was clear and steady. She was in control of herself. She had promised herself she would not cry.

"There were a lot more people the day I came here. That first day, I felt like I had left one nightmare for another. There were thousands of people speaking different tongues, all milling around like it was the end of the world. For most of them, it was the end of their world. The tribal governments were being disbanded. The tribal rolls were closing, and the last of the allotments were being taken.

"That first morning, I'd had it in my mind that I would get a job with the Dawes Commission. But as I was walking up the street toward Agency Hill, I saw the law offices of Mason and Jackson. They had represented the Beauvaises in the past, so I went in and asked them for a job. I had no experience of the law, but they hired me anyway. They needed someone who knew tribal languages, who could read and write and who would listen to the complaints of clients. There was already a long line of them that went halfway around the block. Some of them had been sleeping out all night, just to have a place in the line and a chance to be heard.

"I began working that day. I listened, I wrote reports, I ran papers from one law office to another. I went from the Agency and the Dawes Commission to the courts and back again. I began to learn something about the law. I slept at the law office. There were no rooms to be had at any price. I ate in cafes and bathed at the barber's."

"Pride," Reanna cut in, "Pride, listen to me. I came here to tell you something. I came to tell you that I know now that Andrew took your allotment."

Pride was silent.

"Oh God." She put her hands over her face. "How could he do that? How could it have happened?"

"It happened to me like it happened to a lot of other people."

"I don't want to know about other people. I only want to know about you."

"I didn't file for my allotment when I first came here."

"Why not?"

"There were so many people needing help." He remembered them all—case after case, claim after claim. Indians whose land had been stolen by greedy whites or by the courts or by absentee Indians, Indians who had never lived in the Nation but who'd come in just to grab a piece of free land. "I became so involved in all their problems, in all the plats and surveys and assessments and litigations, I never got around to filing for my own allotment.

"Then, as the deadline for filing came closer, one day I went to see the allotment agent about a claim for a client. I thought while I was there I might as well attend to my own business, but as I looked at the survey map for Beauvaise Ridge, I discovered that I, like hundreds of others, had lost my land. What made it hardest to bear was that the land had been taken not by a stranger but by my own brother."

"And you did nothing."

"I gave myself the advice I had given others. I'd told them to accept the loss, to let go of their old land and to take another allotment. For if they went to court, they might lose their case; even if they won, the title could be clouded for years to come. I'd said to let go of the old and get on with a new life."

"And that's what you did."

"And that's what I did. I took another allotment. I began to read the law. I went on working at Mason and Jackson. When I sit my bar exams, they will sponsor me. I live in a nice rooming house. I get up in the morning and I go to bed at night and I eat three meals a day."

She rocked back and forth, holding herself with her arms as if she were a mother comforting a child. "Oh! Oh, my God. I didn't know what Andrew had done until I saw him yesterday—or was it the day before? I want you to believe that I didn't know."

His eyes closed, then opened slowly. "I didn't think you knew. I didn't think you were a party to it."

"I don't even know how Andrew managed to get the land. How did he do it?"

Pride stood up and reached for her hand. "Come on, let's walk."

"What about Jack?"

"We won't go far." Holding on to her, he crossed the street to a small park and a circle of trees. They stood in the shaded shadows. He put his arms around her and drew her close.

"Tell me," she said, "tell me now what Andrew did."

"I can't prove it in court, but I'm almost certain that on his way to Texas he went to the appraisers and persuaded them to revalue the land, claiming that, because the grass was gone and the tornado had destroyed the improvements, the place had been set at too high a figure. He got the land scaled down to ten, the lowest evaluation. Then he went to the allotment agent and presented himself as Miss Jane's heir. He took her homestead allotment, his own allotment and Snow's land, plus land from the MacClaren City townsite that was his. He signed up for all that, plus the surplus land. He did very well. He got more land than we had looked to receive. The only thing he did wrong was to leave me out of it."

"He lied and he bribed someone, you know he did."

"I have no proof."

"You know he did, or else he couldn't have gotten the land."

"It doesn't matter what I think, only what I can prove in court."

"It matters that he took your land. I mean you to have it back again. Andrew was a little too clever before he started for Texas. To avoid bankruptcy, he put all his property in my name. Now I can deed you back what's yours."

"No." He stepped away from her. "No."

"Why not?"

"It's done. Let well enough alone. Miss Jane wanted you to keep the place together, and you are doing that."

"She meant for you and Andrew to run it together."

"That's never going to happen now."

"Andrew will never get the land from me. I promise you. Andrew and I have separated. I'll never live with him again. Never."

He reached out for her. For the first time he had hope. "Then divorce him. Come to me."

"No, he would never let me divorce him to live with you. I'm staying on that land. Besides, I've another reason to stay. I've drilled some oil wells. I want you to take your land now, because if oil is discovered on it, it could be worth a fortune."

"I don't want money or oil. I want you."

"I want to keep Lovell." The words tore out of her. "If I tried to divorce Andrew, he could try to get custody of Lovell."

"Then keep the land." Pride's voice was hard. "Keep the oil. Keep it all with my blessing as an inheritance for Lovell. Keep it all, but tell me, what am I to have if I can't have you?"

He might as well have hit her with his fists. She began to cry, great, ugly, wracking sobs.

"Oh, my God, don't cry, Reanna, don't cry." He held her close again. "I never meant to make you cry." He turned her face up to his, and with the fingers of one hand he gently wiped away the tears and then began to trace the outline of her face, the arch of her brows, the shape of her eyes and the line of her throat. It was as if he were trying to make a pattern of her that he could remember when she was gone. At last he touched her lips before he kissed her.

"I can't let you go," he said.

"I can't stay."

"Will you come again?"

"No, it would be too risky, too cruel. It hurts too much to see you and then to leave. Will you ever come home again?"

"No. What am I to come for, if I can't have you?"

They stood, his arms around her, like a statue carved from one piece of stone, until Jack Levy came for her.

Pride saw him first. "Is it time?"

"Yes," Jack said.

"Shall I come with you to the station?" he asked Reanna.

"No, no, please don't. No more goodbyes, no more partings." She walked away from them down the street, turned the corner and disappeared. Jack and Pride watched her go.

"Will you take care of her, Jack?"

"I'll try. I'll try. You write to me when you get a chance, and I'll see that she knows how you are." Then Jack ran after Reanna, and Pride was left alone beneath the trees.

JACK and Reanna waited on the station platform for her train to Maitland and his to Tulsa. She was so pale and still, he began to worry that she might collapse. He was by nature a quiet, retiring man; all this running up and down and drama had been too harrowing for him. Certainly it must have been hard for Reanna.

"Listen, Reanna," he said, "I don't like to leave you in this state. If you want me to, I'll forget going to Tulsa and go back down home with you."

"No," she said, "I don't want to take you away from your business."

"Well, it's not so much business as a personal matter." He felt himself beginning to go red in the face as she looked at him questioningly.

"Personal, Jack?"

"Well," he hemmed and hawed, "I have an engagement for dinner tonight in Tulsa."

"Jack, you're blushing."

"No, I'm not."

"You are."

She smiled a faint smile, the first he had seen from her in two days.

"Jack, you sly thing, you're not going to Tulsa on business, you're going courting."

"Well, I'm not too old for that yet." He felt cornered. "Besides," he said, on the defensive, "it was you who put it into my mind. You told me I needed a wife."

"Who is she?"

"Her name is Lillian. Lillian Bauer."

"Have you asked her to marry you?"

"No."

"Why not?"

"I'm not sure she'd have me."

"You're a catch, Jack. A merchant, a banker and the postmaster."

"I'm giving up the post office. That's a full-time job now."

"But you're going to ask her, aren't you?"

"I don't know."

"Why not? Is she pretty?"

"She's beautiful."

"Then what's stopping you?"

"I'm poor. Her folks are well-to-do."

"Oh well, Jack, if that's all. I thought maybe she was too tall or had a squint. Now I find out that all that's wrong with her is she's got money."

Reanna was beginning to get him hot under the collar. Her train was pulling into the station, and she was going on at him about why he wasn't married.

"If you love her, ask her, Jack."

"This is your train, Reanna, get on it. I'll be back Monday. Whatever Andrew is up to, he can't do much before Monday morning."

Reanna hugged him. "Thank you, Jack. Thank you for everything. If you love Lillian, ask her to marry you now. Don't wait until it's too late for happiness."

All the way to Tulsa, Jack kept thinking about Pride and Reanna. There seemed no way for her to be happy. His train was late, but still he got to Tulsa in good time for dinner.

The first time he'd gone up to Tulsa, he'd come to look over the oil play situation for Reanna and to see a new store, Arnheim's. When he'd been on the road selling, he'd tried to do business with Arnheim's in Atlanta. They were too big and fancy for his line, but one of the brothers, David, had been nice to him and had let him down easy.

Jack had heard that David Arnheim had opened up a branch in Tulsa. Jack had gone to the store. It was a nice place, not as big as the Atlanta store but a cut above anything else in the state. David had remembered him, and when they'd finished visiting, he'd surprised Jack by asking him home to dinner. Jack had accepted at once. Better a home-cooked meal than supper in a cafe.

Jack hadn't expected that they'd be joined by a clerk from the store. "Lillian Bauer," David said, "this is Jack Levy from Mac-Claren City. Lillian is my wife's niece who lives with us."

Her hand was cool. She was of medium height, her light brown hair curled around her face. She had doe eyes and a flawless peach complexion. She spoke in a soft southern drawl, and her hat was a masterpiece. Jack complimented her on her hat. She smiled. "It's one of my creations."

(399)

"Lillian," David Arnheim said proudly, "is in charge of our hat department and ladies' ready-to-wear."

The Arnheims' modest house was on a new street with half-grown trees in the yard. Everything about Tulsa was new and raw, but it had a look of vitality, like a town ready to explode. David Arnheim had chosen a good place to begin a business.

Mrs. Arnheim, Belle, was a plump, cheerful woman who made Jack as welcome as if he had been expected. She asked him to make himself comfortable in the living room. There was a piano in the corner and a music stand by it. He saw a collection of family pictures on the piano. He sat thinking how peaceful it was to be in a real home.

Lillian had gone up to change before dinner, and she came down hatless and radiant. Her hair was thicker and more luxuriant than he had imagined. She was wearing a cream-colored, fine lawn dress with ruffles at the neck.

Before dinner they assembled in the living room. Mrs. Arnheim placed a lace shawl over her head and lighted two candles. She began the Sabbath prayer. First in Hebrew, "Baruch Atah Adonai Eloheinu melech ha-olam asher kidshanu b'mitzvo-tav v'tzivanu l'hadlik neir shel Shabbat." Then in English, "Praised be Thou, O Eternal! Our God, King of the universe, who didst sanctify us with Thy commandments, and command us to light the lamp of the Sabbath."

The ancient words and the spirit of the prayer evoked memories in Jack that he thought were long forgotten. It had been years since he had observed any form of his religion. This night, the words made him feel as if something lost had been miraculously restored to him.

The dinner table was set with fine china and old silver. The dinner was delicious—a baked hen, brown and succulent, with roast potatoes and, for dessert, a sponge cake with fresh strawberries. The meal was as pleasing to his palate as if he had been served manna and milk and honey.

He felt a child again, and a picture flashed in his mind of his mother at the table on the Sabbath evening. His emotions were too near the surface for comfort as he tried to make conversation with David Arnheim on the progress of the growing town, or as he stammered his thanks to Mrs. Arnheim for the fine dinner and her kind hospitality.

All evening he kept looking at Lillian, serene and poised, and when after dinner she sat at the piano and began to play, he felt that that accomplishment was more than she needed to make her perfect. When the Arnheims had retired, he and Lillian sat on the porch in a glider swing. He was unable to say much of anything, but he was eager to listen to her.

She had been born in Atlanta, had gone to school there and then to a music conservatory, but her real interest was fashion. She liked design and color. As they swung back and forth, she asked if he had read Thomas Mann. He said no. She asked if he liked music, and he said he didn't know much about it. He had nothing to contribute to any conversation, certainly nothing that would interest a woman like Lillian.

At last he blurted out like a kid, "Are you engaged?"

"No."

"Don't you want to get married?"

She smiled. "My mother keeps asking me that."

"And what do you tell her?"

"That I like people. I like working in the store and seeing different people every day. They wouldn't let me work in Atlanta. I was lucky when Aunt Belle and Uncle David hired me so I could stay out here."

After the evening was over, he went away in a daze, promising to come back again soon. He came as often as he could make the time and sat, evening after evening, in the glider swing like one hypnotized. He watched and admired Lillian in an array of dresses, thinking she looked lovelier in each of them. But he never proposed. He held back, not wanting to be refused, afraid to speak.

But now was the time for him to act.

All the way from Muskogee to Tulsa, Jack kept thinking about Reanna and Pride and Andrew and what Reanna had said about waiting too late for happiness. If he was going to propose to Lillian, he must do it tonight. Tomorrow might be too late. Someone else might come along and take her, someone better and braver than he.

He arrived in Tulsa with enough time before dinner to walk from the station to the Arnheims'. With each step he tried to collect his thoughts and gather his courage. As always, the Arnheims and Lillian greeted him warmly. As always, the dinner was delicious, though if later someone had asked him what he had eaten, he could not have told him. And, as always, after the Arnheims had retired, he and Lillian sat in the glider swing. But this night was different from all other nights. He felt his heart pounding. He must speak now or count himself a coward.

He took a deep breath and said, "Lillian, Miss Bauer, I want to tell you about my assets. As you know, I have a country store, a small store. I am a partner in a bank, the smallest bank in the county. This morning as I was shaving, I looked at myself in the mirror and I saw a man who is going a little bald. I know I should lose a few pounds, but even if I did, I would not be able to call myself handsome.

"I want a home and a family, and I want to marry you. If you are wise, you'll refuse me. The only prospect I have of being able to give you the things you deserve in life is the chance that some of my oil leases may work out. Then I'd be able to offer you more in marriage than life in the back of the store."

He had said it all in one breath and waited for her to ask him to leave. She sat rocking back and forth in the glider as if she had not heard him, and then she said, "Mr. Levy, Jack, I'm a spinster. I work for a living and I would like to work in a store of my own. If I may say so, your hair and weight are, in my opinion, quite acceptable, and I love you because you are a very dear man. I'll make you a home wherever we live, and I'll give you children if I can. My dowry, if you want to call it that, is that I think I know what women will buy to wear and what they won't."

He sat stunned, unsure of what she had said. "Does that mean you will marry me?"

"Yes."

"When?"

"Soon, I think, for if I don't marry you now before you're oil rich, you might always think I married you for your money."

"Then it's yes?"

"Yes, it's yes. I've already said yes."

He stopped the swing. "Lillian, I don't even know a rabbi."

"Fortunately, Mr. Levy, I do."

And as he leaned forward to kiss her for the first time, it seemed to him at that moment that life was full of nothing but agreeable surprises.

CHAPTER 17

NDREW was full of surprises.

Neither Jack Levy nor Doc Hersey expected him to turn up at the bank on Monday asking for a loan. Only a few days before, they'd greeted him like a long lost brother; now they sat silent and still-faced in the partitioned office of the small, granite bank, unsure of how to answer him.

Andrew stood facing them, grinning. "Let me make this easy for you boys. I've come, hat in hand, to borrow money."

Jack cleared his throat. "We know you've been strapped for cash."

"You also know I don't have any collateral. I don't have a store or lots or cattle. My wife's got all my property in her name." He waited for a response.

Jack flushed red to the rim of his hair, and Doc reached for the jug of whiskey beneath his desk. "Jesus, Andrew," Doc said, "we can't talk business empty-handed." He poured out generous shots for both Jack and Andrew. Neither touched the liquor; after a polite pause, Doc drank his down in a single gulp.

Andrew continued to grin, as if he were enjoying their discomfort. "I know what I'm asking is a large amount for a small bank."

"You can say that again!" Doc poured out another splash. "It's almost our entire capital!" He exchanged an uneasy glance with

Jack. They had both taken out substantial personal loans for a flyer in oil leases.

"The nice thing about small banks," Andrew continued, "is that they can always borrow from a bigger bank upstream. Like a small fish sucking onto a bigger fish."

Jack sighed. This was uncomfortable for all of them. "We could ask St. Louis or Kansas City, but they'll want the loan secured."

"Tell them whatever they want to hear," Andrew said. "I'm giving you my word as collateral. My word is still good around here, isn't it?"

"Of course," both men hastened to reassure Andrew.

Andrew grinned again. "You helped Reanna so much while I was gone, I was sure you'd want to help me."

They were being hijacked. All three of them knew it.

"We were glad to help Reanna," Jack said. "What are friends for?"

"That's what I say," Andrew agreed affably. "Maybe I can do the same for both of you one day real soon." Andrew's sarcasm was lost on both Jack and Doc. Neither heard the threat behind his words; they only saw the smile.

"Mind if we ask what you want the money for?" Doc inquired.

"I'm going to drill an oil well on the east range."

"Jesus!" Doc took another drink.

"Does Reanna know?" Jack leaned forward as if to hear Andrew better.

"Reanna and I are quits. Hadn't you heard? She's drilled her wells, and now I'm going to drill mine."

Jack and Doc were too stunned by the news to ask any more questions. They wrote up the loan at a fair rate of interest, hoping they could lay it off with a bigger bank.

As Andrew left, the cash safe in his pocket, he said, "I won't forget what you boys did while I was away. When my well comes in, I'll pay you back for everything twice over."

After Andrew had gone, Doc sat morosely, holding his empty glass. At last he broke the heavy silence. "Why don't you say something, Jack?"

"Like what?"

"Like what are those two up to?"

Jack considered carefully, then shook his head in wonder. "I'd say we've just seen the beginning of the great MacClaren Oil Wars. By the way Doc, this may come as another surprise, but you might tell Amoretta I'm getting married."

It was a surprise to Taffy to see a derrick going up on the east range. He rode hell-bent for Sunday to find Reanna. "Look'ee there!" he cried, pointing east. "What's that?"

"It's an oil well," she said. Her mouth looked as if she had bitten down on a green persimmon.

"Who's drilling?"

"Andrew."

"He's no oil man."

"He is now."

"What's going on between you two? Ever since Andrew got back from Texas, he hasn't said hello or how are you to me."

Reanna gave a short, dry laugh. "He didn't say anything to me when he took Wade to drill his well for him."

Taffy's eyes went wide. "Wade's gone? You're funnin' me."

"No."

"Why did he go?"

"Come on, Taffy, you weren't born yesterday. He went for the money. Wade's going to get twice as much from Andrew as he did from me, and he won't have to share it with Wardell. Plus which, he's going to drill with a rotary rig. Let's see if I can remember his exact words: 'The faster you go down, the faster the oil comes up, the faster the money comes in!'"

Taffy shook his head in dismay. "This is bad business, real bad."

Business wasn't bad for Andrew. Drilling with a new rotary rig, he had his well down to pay formation in twelve days. Reanna watched from the Ridge as the *MacClaren Discovery Well* came roaring in to outproduce her *Reanna One* by five hundred barrels a day.

Reanna had eight producing wells in the field. Though she could ill afford the time, she decided to take Lovell to Memphis to meet her family.

She enjoyed her time alone on the train with Lovell; she so seldom had the uninterrupted pleasure of his company. Lovell enjoyed the novelty of the journey. He was walking—and running—on his own now, and was able to scoot away from her down the aisles. He made a new friend of everyone he met. At twenty months he didn't have too many words at his command. *Hi* was his favorite and *Bye* was another. Lovell might not be much of a conversationalist, but he was a good listener and always ready with a big smile to show off his new, tiny, white teeth.

Reanna had reserved a suite at the Peabody for all of them, with a big sitting room where they could be comfortable. The Lovells had already unpacked when Reanna arrived. They greeted her and Lovell with exclamations of joy and fierce hugs. In two years, the boys had grown so much bigger. Patrick at fifteen was still the polite authoritarian. He said, "How are you, sister, and how was your journey?" While Thomas at twelve was, as always, the more affectionate and outgoing. Her parents were delighted to see her, of course, but their real point of interest was Lovell.

"Well, this is some boy," her father said, beaming as Lovell beamed back at him.

"Why, he looks like the Lovells," her mother said. "All that red hair." And she began a stream of baby talk to Lovell, which made him laugh. But when Mrs. Lovell tried to pick him up, he squirmed to get away, eager to explore the fascinations of the sitting room. He trotted over to his grandfather and grasped Mr. Lovell's finger, pulling him from one side of the room to the other to inspect each object.

"You know something?" Thomas said. "This hotel is my very favorite in the whole world."

"You've never stayed in a hotel before." Patrick spoke with scorn.

"Well, it's my favorite now," Thomas said. "There's a fountain downstairs in the lobby. Did you see it? If you're there at the right time, a gong sounds and men in white coats come to feed the ducks. What a wonderful hotel, to have ducks in the lobby. Can we see them before dinner?"

"Yes, of course," Reanna said. "We can do whatever we want."

They all changed for dinner and arrived in the lobby in time for the ritual feeding of the birds. "You mustn't let Lovell stand too close to the ducks," Mrs. Lovell said. "They might bite."

But Lovell had other ideas. When he saw the ducks waddling along in a line, he crowed and chortled with delight. "Hi ducks, hi. Ducks mine." He did not want to leave this wonderful place for the dining room. He would have gladly taken one of the ducks with him to dinner, if his grandfather had not diverted him.

Mr. Lovell insisted that Reanna put Lovell's high chair next to him and fed him the choicest morsels from his own plate. He talked to Lovell as seriously as if he were the most fascinating and intelligent person he had ever encountered.

"He was like that with all of you," Mrs. Lovell sighed. "He treated you like you were grown-ups, not babies."

"Well, this is a very unusual child," Mr. Lovell said seriously. "Reanna, you'll want to get him in a good school."

"Yes, Papa," Reanna said, laughing. "But with so small a vocabulary, who would take him?"

"Not now, of course," Mr. Lovell said, "but for later. I hear the Tennessee Academy is a very good boarding school. It's run on the English plan. The headmaster is a friend of mine. I'm sure they'll take him."

"I still have a few years to think about it," Reanna said.

"You don't want him growing up wild and running with the wrong crowd," Mrs. Lovell put in. "The right sort of friends is so important for a boy."

"Yes, Mama."

"I can teach him how to play baseball," Thomas said eagerly.

"Lovell's too young for baseball," Patrick said. "He's only a baby."

"Maybe we can get him a ball tomorrow." Reanna smiled at Thomas. "Not a baseball, but a rubber one."

"I just happened to bring one with me." Thomas grinned back at her.

The meal over, they went upstairs to the sitting room. On the way up in the elevator, Thomas whispered to Reanna, "You know, Ree, we don't have to get dressed and go downstairs for breakfast. We can have it brought up to our suite. It's called room service."

"What a wonderful idea." Reanna gave Thomas's hand a squeeze. "That's just what we'll do."

"Thomas has already been ordering from room service," Patrick said. "Very expensive things, like strawberries out of season."

"We can afford it, can't we, Ree?" Thomas asked earnestly.

"Yes, Thomas, order whatever you want."

Upstairs in the sitting room, Reanna, her mother and her father sat watching, while on the floor, Patrick and Thomas took turns rolling Thomas's ball to Lovell, who good-naturedly rolled it back again. At last, Reanna said, "This oil well I wrote you about—the fact is I've drilled eight wells. A big field is opening up out there, which I believe will make me very rich."

Her mother frowned. "Reanna, you don't know anything about oil, or wells or business."

"But I'm learning, Mama, I'm learning. The thing is, I've already made quite a lot of money and I'll be making much, much more. So now I want you to pay off your debts and start buying back all of the farm you had to sell. I want you to put the place on a first-class basis."

Patrick looked up, his eyes wide with interest. "Does that mean we can rebuild the stables and buy up some bloodstock?"

"Yes, if that's what Papa wants to do." She turned to her mother. "I know, Mama, you've been wanting to do over the house. Now's your chance. What I propose is to give you a check to put in the bank when you get home. Then I'll send you another check every month." She named a figure that made her mother gasp.

"That's very generous, Reanna," her father said, blowing his nose. "It will help to settle one or two outstanding accounts."

"This is very thoughtful of you and Andrew," her mother said.

"Andrew doesn't come into this," Reanna said coldly. "You might as well know, Andrew and I have separated."

"Every husband and wife quarrel. It is a part of married life," Mrs. Lovell said, looking distressed.

"This is more than a tiff, Mama. We're separated. We'll never make it up or live together again, and that's final."

"But you have Lovell to think of, Reanna. He needs a father. What can Andrew have done that makes you so set against him?"

"Minnie, don't pry," Mr. Lovell said. "It's Reanna's business." He looked at Reanna. "Whatever you decide, Ree, we'll stand behind you."

"Are you really going to be rich?" Thomas asked.

"Yes," Reanna said, "I am."

"Then will we see you more often?"

"Yes, I'll see you as often as possible."

"And now can we come out to Oklahoma? I want to come and so does Patrick."

"And I want you all to come, but because of the oil boom, there's no place for you to stay. I don't want you to have to sleep in a tent."

"I wouldn't mind sleeping in a tent," Thomas said.

"And," Patrick added, "I'd like to see the Indian ponies. They say some of them are very fast."

"At the moment I don't have much time for entertaining. I'm very busy. In the oil business, you have to stay on top of things. It all changes so fast. There is so much work to do every day."

"Reanna, surely," her mother put in, "now that you have money, you can get someone to do all this work for you."

"Mama, it's my field. I have to run it, my way. This field is going to get bigger fast. I have to be there. That's why I can only stay a week in Memphis."

"Only a week, Reanna? What kind of visit is that?"

"Minnie," Mr. Lovell said, "I think Reanna wants to get back. She likes her work. It's not really work when you like what you're doing."

"That's right, Papa. Thank you for understanding."

"Well, I'm sure I don't," Mrs. Lovell sniffed.

Later that evening, when Reanna was getting ready for bed, her mother came in to say good night. "Reanna," Mrs. Lovell said, looking distressed, "I didn't want to say anything in front of your Papa, but I don't believe that you were wearing a corset."

"That's right, Mama, I wasn't. Good night, Mama."

For the next week they all went shopping and saw the sights and played with Lovell in the park. But half the time Reanna's mind was not in Memphis but in the oil patch. At the end of the week, she was more than ready to get back, and she knew with certainty that Oklahoma was her real home now, not Virginia. She had transplanted herself west and she had put down deep roots.

REANNA came home to find that, after Andrew's stupendous strike, he had become the bank's biggest depositor and that as such, Doc and Jack had felt it was only right to put him on the bank's board of directors. Andrew found the position agreeable, for now when he wanted to borrow money, he had only to sign his own name on the note.

His friends all agreed that ever since he struck oil, Andrew had seemed much more cheerful. Still, they worried over him, Jack in particular. "Can't you patch it up between you and Reanna?" Jack asked.

"No."

"Every married couple has their ups and downs."

Andrew gave Jack a hard, cold look. "There's nothing like a new bridegroom for giving advice to a married man. And how is Lillian?"

Jack flushed. "It's just that I'm partial to you both." He stopped short. He could see he was talking to a stone wall, just as Doc and Amoretta felt they were up against one whenever they suggested that Andrew might be overdoing his borrowing. Every time he was challenged, Andrew merely smiled and said, "There's nothing to worry about. We're in oil. Besides I need the money to play catch up with Reanna. When she puts down one well, I mean to put down two. If she gets one lease, I'll have three. I'm going to match her, derrick for derrick, and then some. The way to keep in the oil game is to expand, keep growing. Look what oil's done for Mac-Claren City."

Looking out the bank window, all Jack could see was a main street where everything horse-drawn or motor-driven was hub-deep in mud.

REANNA was outraged by what she saw from the Ridge. Every well Andrew put down was offset drilled from the Reanna pool. He lined them up against her like soldiers ready to do battle. There were five new wells in a month, one hundred and fifty in a year. Wardell estimated that there would be over two thousand before the pool was drilled dry.

The only way to get her share of the oil was to drill more and more wells with no attempt to conserve or restrict production. The gushing, flowing oil was pumped into earthen dams, into wooden storage tanks; when there was nothing left to contain the oil, it seeped onto the prairie to become a shallow lake of oil that killed the grass and marred the landscape. Over the sound of the pumping wells and the odor of decaying crude, the gas flares burned twenty-four hours a day, wasting a resource that no one valued.

Long gone were the days when the Eastern crowd had said there was no oil in the West. The fool who had boasted that he would personally drink every barrel of oil found west of the Mississippi regretted bitterly the statement he could never live down. Ever since Ford had made his flivver cheap enough so that every man could own one, the demand for oil had become insatiable. The East was now looking, begging, to buy all the production it could get hold of. They were even desperate enough for oil to do business with a woman.

Reanna had the crude to sell. Every well of hers was a producer, not a dry hole on the field; the rub was the going price—a dollar a barrel. It cost her ninety cents to get it to market, and it took forever to haul it there.

When she did get her crude to Maitland junction for shipment by rail to the refinery, she and the other independents found there was a shortage of tank cars. Competition for the few available was as stiff as the shipping rates caused by Standard's rebates. Half the time she had to dump her product or cart it home again.

She faced Taffy in the field, her eyes blazing. "If I keep on selling oil at these prices, I'll go broke." She had a man's black felt hat jammed over her red hair. She was wearing whipcord trousers, a plaid shirt and a worn leather jacket. It had been a month of Sundays since she'd worn a dress or had time to look in a mirror. "The only way to make a profit is to ship from MacClaren City. Now that Andrew has got the railroad into MacClaren City, he can get his oil out at half my cost, or less!"

Taffy shifted uneasily. "To get to MacClaren City, you'll have to cross Andrew's field."

"So?" She lifted her chin in defiance.

"So, Andrew may not take kindly to that."

"Then Andrew can lump it. I have to ship from MacClaren City or go under. I want you to get every wagon, barrel and mule you can find. Hire on all of those freeloading cowboy cronies of yours that you've been feeding down at the bunkhouse."

Taffy bristled, his face puckering up in dismay. "Frank and Dan and Slim are my friends. They're cowboys, they ain't muleskinners."

"They've driven cows, they can drive mules."

"I think I ought to tell you, cows and mules is different animals," he said tartly.

"Don't argue! We're going!"

As she spoke, the spring rains began to fall. And as the long, heavy wagon train set out for MacClaren City in a red sea of mud, the heavens opened up and still more rain came pouring down. They went inch by inch; hub-deep for the wagons and knee-deep for the mules. The creeks rose and flash floods swept down gullies, tilting the wagons and scattering the barrels, which broke apart as easily as if they were eggs. Everywhere the oil lay wasted on the soggy ground.

When they got to the boundary where the road crossed onto the east range, Reanna could not believe what she saw ahead. She wiped the rain from her eyes, but the sight remained the same. Andrew had set up a barricade. A high mound of barbed wire in sinister loops barred the way and cut off her access to the rutted road.

On Andrew's side of the barbed wire were his men on horseback with their guns. On Reanna's side were a train of wagons and her men with their guns. It was a Mexican standoff. Andrew faced her across the barricade, and to make her rage even deeper, she saw he was smiling that insolent, sure smile that made her want to kill him.

"Move that wire," she said, "and let me pass."

"No." He shook his head.

"I'm going to the railroad."

"Not this way. You have no right to trespass on my land."

"You drill from my pool."

"That's legal. Ask any lawyer. It's called rule of capture. I can drill for as long as there's oil to be had."

"Damn you. I mean to get my crude to that railroad."

"Then you'll have to go the long way around. But take my advice and save yourself the trouble, Reanna. There are no tank cars available for months to come."

"Why?"

"They're leased to me. So you go on home. Forget being in the oil business. I've got you boxed in."

"I'm going to sell my oil one way or another," she said grimly.

"You can always sell it to me."

"Sell you my crude?" She couldn't believe he'd made such an offer.

"That's right. I'm always looking to buy, if the price is right."

"And you'd set the price?"

"That's business, Reanna. Supply and demand. I'll buy from you and the other independents."

"Never. I'll get to the railroad if I have to go to Tulsa to load out my crude."

He smiled. "That will cost you nothing but money." He'd made a joke at her expense. The men behind him began to laugh; even Andrew chuckled, enjoying her predicament.

She didn't mean to let him enjoy it for long. She drew her rifle from its sheath and aimed it at Andrew. She heard the laughter stop and a murmur of shocked surprise from the men behind her in the wagons. She heard Taffy call her name. She raised her rifle slowly and took a bead on Andrew. His eyes flickered, and she could see he was having second thoughts. "Get the wire out of my way." She signaled Taffy and Dan Penland to move it. They hesitated for a moment and then rode up, swinging their lariats overhead. They threw wide, caught the wire and began to pull it away from the road.

As the way was nearly cleared, from somewhere behind Andrew a shot rang out. That shot was answered from Reanna's side. Suddenly Andrew rose up in the saddle. He held up his hand, shouting, "Stop, hold your fire." Both sides were silent. The battle now was one of wills, not bullets. It was a contest to see whether Reanna or Andrew would back off from the situation. She didn't mean to yield.

"Go home, Reanna, before somebody else gets hurt." He spoke to her, but his eyes went beyond her. She turned to see Taffy holding his arm. The blood was showing dark red, dripping down from his sleeve. She heard Andrew say, "Sorry, Taffy, I didn't mean for this fracas to get out of hand." Taffy's mouth twisted in a grimace of pain.

"Damn you, Andrew MacClaren." Reanna fought the tears as she tried to keep Molly May from rearing away from the sharp barbed wire. "You don't care who you hurt, do you?"

"I warned you, Reanna. I told you it was you or me. Now go home, and when you're ready to sell your oil at my price, you know where to find me."

"I'll never sell."

"We'll see. Never is a long, long time."

ANDREW had made her back off. He'd made her a laughingstock before his men and hers. He'd humiliated her. Reanna fumed as she paced the kitchen floor, while the rain continued to beat down and the oil to overflow onto the range. She felt as though she were drowning in a sea of oil.

Taffy sat holding his arm in a sling and watched while her temper got worse. "What are you going to do," he asked, "besides wear out the floor?"

"I'm going to get my oil to the refinery."

Taffy shook his head sadly. "How do you figure to do that? There aren't enough wagons and mules in Oklahoma, let alone barrels, to get the *Reanna* field to market."

She wheeled on him. "Then I'll build me a pipeline."

"All by yourself?" He had meant to make a joke of it, but Reanna didn't laugh.

Her sense of humor had vanished on the road to MacClaren City. She bit at her lip as she unrolled a map on the kitchen table. If she built a line north toward the river, she could go across Frampton's and then mission land. That would bring her closer to market and get her out of this box Andrew had put her in.

She'd need Frampton's permission and Father Soule's. She'd also need to cross a corner of Cima's allotment and Taffy's homestead land. She'd also need money, a great deal of it. To get that money, she'd have to be able to guarantee a steady, predictable flow of product. To get that much crude on a deliverable basis, she'd have to rope some of the independents in on it. If they made an agreement to stick together, they could control overproduction and cut costs, as well as keep prices up.

"I'm going to Frampton's," she said to Cima and Taffy.

At first Taffy was dead set on coming with her, but she refused to hear of it. His blood had already been shed for her. If she got her plan going, then she'd ask him to ride shotgun and risk his hide again.

She went to see Frampton alone. As always, he greeted her warmly. By now he was used to her coming in at all hours.

"Simon, I need your help again."

"What can I do for you this time?" He was so solemn and serious that they both laughed as they embraced. It was a relief, after all the recent strain, to be with Frampton.

"I want to get a bunch of the independents together here at your place. If I do it on Beauvaise land, Andrew will send one of his hired hands to spy. This way I might keep it a secret for a little while."

"You're always welcome to my house."

"And," she said, "I want an easement to cross your land. I have to get my oil up to Tulsa and the refinery by pipeline. Andrew won't let me come into MacClaren City unless I sell him my crude."

Frampton frowned. Everything he heard about Andrew these days was a surprise, and none of it pleasant. This new Andrew was a man he didn't know or like. "Yes," he said thoughtfully, "a pipeline is a good idea. It's not easy country, but I think your best route is from Cima to Taffy to me, and then onto mission land to the north."

Reanna hugged him. "You never argue; you always make things sound so easy and possible."

"Why not, my dear? You always manage to do what you want, one way or another."

"Do you think Father Soule will let me cross mission land?"

"You'll have to ask him, of course, but I think he will be very agreeable. Only"—Frampton hesitated—"I think you should get his permission soon."

"What do you mean?" she said, noticing the grave look on Frampton's face. "What is it? What's the matter?"

"The Church is going to close his mission. They say the school is no longer of any use. It means that his work and his school are finished. Father Soule is an old man, Reanna. He has no heart to go on."

Reanna gasped in surprise. "They're wrong. Don't they know what the school and the mission mean to the people here?"

"They say it's time the children went to school in town."

"Can't something be done to change their minds?"

"No, Father Soule has done his best to convince his bishop, but he won't listen."

Reanna thought otherwise. "I'll bet you a shiny silver dollar that if I take a lease on the mission land, they'll let him stay on. I'll put it in the lease—no Father Soule, no oil."

Frampton smiled. "It might make a difference, although I must warn you before you go to see him, you will find him greatly changed."

FATHER Soule was in the winery when she arrived. He came to meet her with only a counterfeit of his old warmth. He tried valiantly to pretend to a spirit and energy that he no longer possessed.

"Well, well," Father Soule said, his hands held out to touch hers. "It's about time you came to see me. I've been trying to decide on this new grape. I've crossed it with one from the Rhône. Try it and see what you think." Reanna gravely tasted the grapes and nodded her approval. It was all playacting. She didn't know one grape from another.

"I'm flattered you came to see an old man." Father Soule looked at her sideways. "I know how busy you are."

"Yes, I'm busy. The truth is I wanted to see you, but I've also come wanting a favor. I'm sure you've heard that Andrew won't let me bring my oil into MacClaren City. I want an easement for a pipeline to cross mission land. Will you give it to me?"

Father Soule considered. "You know I'd give you the moon and the stars, but it's not up to me. I must ask the permission of my bishop."

"How do you think your bishop would react to a nice, long oil lease, with a bonus thrown in for good measure?"

"I think he would sing hosannas." For the first time, Father Soule smiled.

"Then I'll lease the land and pay a good price, with the condition that you stay on here. I don't mind drilling for oil and making your bishop rich, but I wouldn't like to have it on my conscience that I'd destroyed any of your vineyard."

Father Soule regarded Reanna as he might a religious vision. "How long a lease will you take?"

"I was thinking of five years."

Father Soule held up his hands in the air as if to accept a gift from heaven. "Five years. That will be more than enough time for me to see if this new strain will take and bear fruit. My dear, five years is a lifetime." He hesitated, but only for a moment. "If, of course, the bishop agrees."

ON her return to Frampton's, she found a parlor full of men, all of whom had been and still were her competitors. These wildcatters and independents were a breed apart. They were all as different from each other as day and night. There was Galvin Taylor, who had grown up with drilling in Pennsylvania, and Virgil Kemp, who had left a safe, solid family business and run away to join the oil patch fun with the same spirit as a boy might run away to join the circus. There was Duard Hesketh, who had put down fourteen dry holes before he made his first strike, and "Moon" Mills, who never began drilling except in a full moon. They were all different, but they had one thing in common—the passion to find oil and to sell it without asking anyone's permission.

As Reanna faced them, she found her knees were shaking. "I thank you for coming all this way to hear what I have to say. I asked you to Frampton's because it seems to me we're in the same boat. We've struck oil, and we can't sell it at a fair price. It's like being dressed up and having no place to go."

She'd been nervous about speaking to them, but she was encouraged to hear a little laughter and to see Duard Hesketh lean back and light up one of his monster cigars. She was the only woman present; that alone was usually enough to make men look grim. God knows what her mother would have thought about it. Not that anyone could have stopped her from trying to beat Andrew at his power game.

"Many of you find it hard to get your oil to market because of the location of your wells. Some find it hard to haul, because Andrew MacClaren insists that if we go through MacClaren City, we have to sell to him at a price he sets and deliver no more than he wants to buy." She spoke Andrew's name as if he were a stranger she'd never met. If the men were uneasy because she was Andrew's wife, that was their lookout, not hers. "What we must do for our mutual good is to form an association to move our oil to the refinery by pipeline. We'll share the expenses, and we'll share the profit. We'll guarantee product, and we'll sell at a price we can all agree is fair."

She waited for a response, but the men sat as silent as if she had offered them a surefire producer and no dusters for life; then they erupted into a babel of different opinions. In the end they voted to accept her proposals. Only two mavericks declined; Taylor and Mills both wanted out of this field. They were going to try their luck near Bartlesville. All in all, it had been a good night's work. She went home triumphant and exhilarated, only to find a problem there that she hadn't anticipated.

Reanna had taken it for granted that if Frampton, Father Soule and Taffy gave her permission to cross their land with the pipeline, Cima wouldn't object. She found she'd been wrong.

Cima sat at the kitchen table shelling peas, her black face set hard as stone. "Sure, I'll give you permission to cross my land," she said, "on one condition."

"Name it."

"I want you to drill me an oil well on my allotment." Cima had made a demand as firm as if she were the chairman of Standard Oil.

Reanna was astonished. "Your land lies mostly in a ravine between two piles of rock."

"I know where my land lies as well as you do." Cima continued filling a saucepan with fresh peas and discarding the shells.

"There's been no show of oil up there," Reanna said. If Cima hadn't been so serious, she would have laughed at the idea of drilling in the ravine.

"That's doesn't mean there isn't oil on my land. You're going to drill on mission land, why not on mine? I want an oil well like everybody else. So the way I look at it, no well, no easement."

"That's blackmail," Reanna said.

"I'm a black woman with a black heart." Cima gave a thin, pinched grin and rose to put supper on to cook, but her eyes were dark and serious.

"Then I have no choice, do I?"

Cima shook her head.

"All right, I'll drill you an oil well, but not now, not until I can afford it. Right now, Cima, I'm in over my head in oil I can't sell." Cima was silent. "I'll drill in a year, agreed?"

Reanna had made her final offer. Cima nodded and they shook hands. Cima wiped hers on her apron first, but Reanna felt Cima's palm was still slightly moist—whether from the peas or oil fever, Reanna couldn't be sure.

Taffy was leery of the whole idea. He said, "You know there's going to be more trouble when Andrew finds out what you've been up to. He thinks he has the market sewed up. He's been telling it everywhere that he's got you in a corner. He's riding high."

"I know that."

"Andrew will do his damn best to keep you out of the market and him in it. Where are you going to get the men to dig the pipeline? It's already hard to get crews. Men know if they work for you, they'll never work for him. To keep even with him, you'll have to keep digging in, boring down, and moving oil from now to kingdom come." He fell silent, waiting for her to answer. It plumb wore him out, all this talking.

"Don't worry about it, Taffy. I'll be fine. For the first time since Andrew came back home, I've got a few surprises for him."

WHEN the pipeline was completed, Reanna stood on the Ridge with her field glasses trained on the pattern of welts that made the prairie look as if a giant mole had been burrowing its way north to the river.

Laying the pipeline had taken nearly six years. There had been delays and extensions as the field grew; there had been legal wrangles over right-of-way. But it was finished. She had overseen the work to the river, and beyond to join with the other independent carriers. As a result, she had a lot of facts in her head that she had learned the hard way. She knew that six-inch pipe, lap-welded in fifteen-foot sections, at a grade of fifty-five feet a mile, would carry crude seven miles without the use of pumps. She knew that costs had been higher than she'd expected, but at eighteen thousand dollars a mile, it was worth every penny and all the backbreaking effort, because now she could ship at five cents a barrel into the larger, always expanding skein of gathering lines.

As she lowered her glasses, she saw Taffy looking at her disapprovingly. He didn't like the sight of her in men's breeches. She knew he was bothered by what people were saying about her—that she was as hard as a man and that she drove her crews to exhaustion. They also said that she was lucky that every lease of hers had crude beneath it. Even Cima's allotment had opened a new stratum and proved a winner. But luck be damned; she had earned everything she had.

For six years she had worked hard, taking only a few weeks off each year to go with Lovell to visit her family in Virginia. Every day she had gone out to match Andrew, lease for lease, field for field. All over the state, she'd sat in hotel lobbies with the boys and talked oil. At night she'd sat in smoke-filled suites and played poker with them. Once, on a bet with Duard Hesketh, she'd smoked one of his monster cigars. She'd won the bet and the lease she was after. People had gotten used to seeing her as she drove up and down the oil fields. She had no fear of being on her own.

Next to Lovell, her car was her greatest pleasure. The first car she had bought was a Model T. It had come to the house on a wagon. She'd put it in gear and taken off down the Ridge. It had never occurred to her to read the manual. She'd figured that if she didn't have the sense to master a piece of machinery, she shouldn't have it in the first place. As she drove, she had experienced a sense of freedom and exhilaration she'd never known before. She was in control. She was in command. It gave her the vision to see how people all over the country would soon be able to go where they liked in their cars, and they would use her oil to do it.

The day she'd driven out into the *Reanna* field, driving circles about the derricks, bumping along the rutted tracks until she got the hang of stopping and starting, had changed her life. That car was the best thing that the world had offered her in a long time. It gave her pure pleasure to drive along a pipeline under construction. She could arrive at any time, without warning, to oversee the progress on the pipeline or to supervise the drilling. Sometimes she was out in the field for days at a time.

It took working around the clock to beat Andrew. He was supplying himself from his own fields, and he was refining. His great, ugly refinery sat out on the east range, where she could see it belching out smoke and burning off waste gas. Next he'd be setting up his own retail outlets in Oklahoma and Texas and Arkansas. He was buttering up the big boys in the East, and if he got their blessing, he could still drive her and the independents to the wall. She needed another pipeline to the Gulf of Mexico, to ships and a world market. Once again, it was to Frampton that she turned for advice.

She sat in his ranch house, dressed in jodhpurs, boots, and a leather jacket. A modified Stetson that had seen a lot of service rested on the table beside her. She relaxed with Frampton and drank a pot of strong tea. Her hair flamed red and gold in the firelight.

"I don't know what I'm going to do," she said. It was an admission she'd never made aloud. "I think Andrew is going to get big enough to swallow me. Now that he's playing up to the Eastern crowd, he'll get enough backing to run the independents out of business."

Frampton had seen her worried before, but he'd never seen her look more beautiful. She had no idea of how she looked; her lack of vanity was one of her attractions. Yet, in his opinion, it wasn't right that a woman like this should have to lead a man's life. It wasn't right that she had no one to cherish her. If he had made such an observation to her, she would have laughed at him. Whatever her reasons—and he could only guess at her secrets as she guessed at his—she would go on fighting the world.

If she was to win, she needed friends with power. "There's a group I've heard of in England who are interested in petroleum."

"A fat lot of good men in England will do me."

"Hear me out, Reanna. They want to expand into the world market. They already have interests in North America. They might just be willing to listen to your ideas about a pipeline to the Gulf. If you and the independents can offer them enough production, they might give you a better price than you'd get elsewhere."

"I'd like to meet these men," she said thoughtfully. "As things are now, I've got Andrew ready to devour me on one side and Standard on the other. It's lions and tigers wherever I look."

"I hear the government is going to bring an antitrust suit against Standard to break it up into smaller companies."

"Yes." She made a face. "But no matter how many new names they give those new companies, the same dog will come running when Standard whistles."

"Then why go on with it? You don't have to keep working like you do. You have enough money." He spoke gently, but with feeling.

She shook her head. "It's not just the money I'm working for. When a well comes in, for a moment I get a big thrill out of it." She sighed. "But I must admit that sometimes I feel like the more I get, the more I lose."

"I don't understand."

"I miss the way things were, the way they might have been. I miss seeing friends like Doc and Amoretta and Jack and Lillian. I have no time for anything but business."

"And Pride?" he asked abruptly. "Do you miss Pride?"

She felt her breath catch in her throat. She knew she must have gasped. She made herself meet Frampton's gaze. "Yes, I miss Pride.

I always will." She felt as if he were probing at an old wound to make sure it had healed properly.

"I hear he came through the bar exam with flying colors and has set up his own law practice. I know you must be proud of him."

"Yes," she said softly, "I am. The tribe needs a lawyer they can trust." She couldn't bear to say Pride's name again. It hurt too much. She rose. "I must be getting back."

"I never like to see you go."

"More work to be done." She forced herself to smile.

Frampton walked her out to her car and held the door for her. "You know you always have me for a friend, don't you? Now and always."

"I know." She touched his outstretched hand, then let it go and quickly set the car in gear. "I've always got you and I've got Lovell. No one will ever take Lovell away from me." She pulled away down the drive and left Frampton staring wistfully after her.

As she drove down dusty back roads toward home, she thought of Lovell. Lovell was her heart and abiding joy.

At eight he was a winning little boy with soft brown eyes, red hair and a gentle curve to his cheeks. It gave her a painful kind of pleasure to look at him. Everyone said he looked like her because he had her coloring, but she could see Pride in the structure of his bones and in the curve of his cheek and in his eyes. Sometimes, when he looked at her as they rode into the morning sun, she could see Pride looking out at her from Lovell's eyes.

Cima said Lovell had Reanna's willfulness. Without a doubt, Lovell was a stubborn child. Once he'd made up his mind, it was like pulling hen's teeth to change him, but it was more than her willfulness that had formed his character. Like Pride, Lovell did not care what others thought of him. He judged himself. He walked his own path, and he marched to the beat of his own drum.

Reanna could not fault him even for that. She adored Lovell. He could make her laugh as no one else could. He was fine company and a good companion, as they drove to the back of beyond and home again. Lovell liked that car and he liked being with her. As they drove up and down the muddy, rutted oil field roads, she felt him warm beside her.

When the sky was blue and the wind calm, the world belonged

to them. They shared hours of gold as they ate their cheese and crackers, sitting on the running board, or drank cold water from a farmer's well. On those days, she told him all about leases and railroad rates and the cost of pipe per foot. Like some cat, she hoped she could teach him to hunt in her jungle.

She took him with her when she went to buy leases from farmers. Before she went up to the place, she'd stop out of sight of the house and change whatever she was wearing for a straw hat, work shoes and a worn dress. "Why do you always do that?" Lovell asked, eyeing her gravely.

"Do what?"

"Change clothes."

"When you want to do business with people, you have to make them feel at ease. If I came dressed fit to kill in my Sunday best, they would mistrust me as they do all strangers. They trust people they know. If I come as a friend and a neighbor, I have a much better chance of getting their lease at my price."

Lovell frowned. "You mean that you do all this changing of clothes so you can get the lease cheaper?"

Reanna was both annoyed and amused. "Yes, in a way," she said. "Most of all, it's a matter of their having confidence in me and not in the competition."

That day when she had changed and they were walking hand in hand up to the farmhouse porch, Lovell had given her hand a squeeze and whispered, "Anyone would rather do business with you than Andrew MacClaren."

She was caught off guard. She never knew what Lovell would say or what he was thinking. Lovell seldom mentioned Andrew. When he'd first asked her why Andrew lived in one place and they lived in another, she'd said, "We had a quarrel."

"Because of me?"

"No, Lovell, it was nothing to do with you. You were only a baby when Andrew and I separated."

"Snow says my father wants to come home but you won't let him."

"Andrew doesn't want Snow, or you or me. He wants the oil. That's why we quarreled—over land and oil. We are business rivals; that's why he keeps to his oil patch and I to mine. Do you understand?"

"Yes," he said, but she was not sure that he did or what a father's absence cost him. She'd tried to make it up to him. "I'm getting these leases for you, Lovell," she had said. "One day I'll build us a refinery bigger than Andrew MacClaren's."

For a moment she thought Lovell hadn't heard her. Then he said, looking up at her as if he saw through her to the marrow of her bones, "Will that make you happy?" She felt exposed, like a nerve caught on the raw.

"I want to build you the best. I've been thinking it's time I rebuilt Lochleven. I've put it off so long, but now I want you to see the house as it was before the tornado."

"Does that mean my father is coming home?"

She looked at Lovell sharply. She could never be sure when he was testing her. "No," she said, "Andrew is still going to live in town, and I'll live at Lochleven with you and Snow and Taffy and Cima."

"Is he going to marry someone else?"

"No." Rumor had it that Andrew saw a different girl every week and that as he got older, they got younger. Poor, silly things if they thought he would ever get a divorce to marry any of them.

"Are you?" Lovell asked.

"Am I what?"

"Are you going to get married again?"

"No. Why do you ask?"

"I just wondered." He looked away.

She couldn't fathom his reason for asking such a question. "Do you miss having a father at home?"

"No, I don't miss my father." But in his heart he had always thought it was somehow because of him that Andrew had gone away. If he only knew what he had done, perhaps he could change and be the son Andrew wanted. But he could not tell Reanna that. Instead he said, "I'm fine. I don't miss Andrew. I have Taffy and Dan and Frank and Slim."

"Indeed you do." Reanna frowned. Lovell spent more time with Taffy and his saddle tramp friends than he did with her. Taffy was still feeding and housing an assortment of cowboys down at the bunkhouse. There were no cattle on the place. They'd only come to freeload. Lovell was out there more than she thought was good for him. If she wanted Lovell, she had to go out and fetch him. He was always reluctant to tear himself away from the singing and the storytelling. They were filling his head with stories of a West that had never been. They'd made legends out of the long drives and the great blizzard. But it was more than that which disturbed her.

Once she had gone down there to fetch Lovell up to the house and found him carving a bird from a piece of wood. As he cut away the shape, he was whistling a tune she had never heard from anyone but Pride. The sight of him and the sound of the tune had shaken her. Lovell had Pride's gifts, for all to see. They had come to him by birth, in his blood, like a legacy.

"Who taught you to whittle?" she had demanded.

"No one." Lovell had looked up, startled by the sharpness of her tone.

The circle of men had been silent, looking at the boy and then at her. She'd felt herself flush; she'd jerked Lovell up and dragged him away.

"Yes," she said aloud now to Lovell, "that's what I'll do. I'll rebuild Lochleven. There's no sense in having all this money if I don't spend it on you."

She hoped that when they all had a proper house again, things would be different and Lovell would stay at home more. Amoretta and Doc had a grand new house, a two-storied brick, at the end of a wide drive on MacClaren Avenue. Jack Levy and Lillian had a house and a new store, bigger than anything south of Tulsa or north of Dallas. Andrew, folks said, was building a marble palace outside of town. He'd actually imported a lot of Italian workmen and had them shipped over with the marble from Italy. He was putting in greenhouses full of native wildflowers, fountains and God knows what else. Well, if that was what Andrew wanted, let him have it. She'd see Lochleven rise again.

The idea of Lochleven took root in her mind. She was too busy to oversee the work, but Cima could. Cima would remember every nook and cranny of that old house. It would be good for Cima to be occupied with the rebuilding. It would give her something to fret over besides Snow.

As Snow grew older, she grew more restless and sullen. She was also a bigger flirt, shining up to anything in pants. There was no dog big enough to watch that girl twenty-four hours a day. Reanna had tried to keep an eye on her, but she wasn't at home enough to act as a policeman and, when she was there, Snow ignored her. Things had never been easy between them, and time had not improved their relationship.

Cima said that Snow was pining for Andrew, that Snow still waited for the day when Andrew would come and take her to live with him. Maybe Cima was right, but if Snow was waiting for Andrew to rescue her like some white knight on a charger, then Snow would have a long wait.

Reanna didn't know what to do for Snow. Snow should be sent away to school. She'd tried to talk Snow into going to Ward Belmont, where they accepted Indian girls, but Snow wouldn't hear of it. Reanna knew she had Lovell's education to think of as well. Her father kept insisting that she send Lovell to boarding school. She had written to the Tennessee Academy. Her father's friend, the headmaster, was more than willing to accept Lovell. She knew Lovell must learn to wear something besides boots and chaps and speak in something other than a country twang, but for now she couldn't bear to let him go. For a little while at least, she'd try to keep him with her.

No matter what she did, Reanna could not keep the world from changing. Just when she had finished rebuilding Lochleven, and was expecting her family for the housewarming, Frampton drove over to tell her that Father Soule had died.

They sat in the little parlor off the hall. There was a bee buzzing at the windowpane; the small sound was magnified in the silence of the room. At last she said, "I knew that he was ill and that it was only a matter of time, but I had hoped . . . When did it happen?"

"Last night." Frampton held her hand gently in his. "He died in his sleep. He went without any pain."

"I can't imagine the mission without him. It's selfish of me, I know, but I keep thinking I had just sent him an invitation to the housewarming and now he won't see the new Lochleven."

Frampton shook his head. "No, but perhaps a new Jerusalem."

FATHER Soule was buried at the mission in the little cemetery just down the hill from the church. The spot had been chosen to protect the graves from the wind. That day, wild spring gusts twisted and howled around the mourners.

People had come from miles around—the old and young, Indians and whites, the rich and the poor, all of Father Soule's children. The bishop seemed surprised at such a large showing, especially when he'd seen so few in church on his Sunday visits.

For this one day, even bitter enemies declared a truce. Andrew and Reanna stood in divided camps—Andrew with Jack and Lillian and Doc and Amoretta across the open grave from Reanna and Lovell, Cima, Taffy, Snow and Frampton.

Reanna looked for Pride, but she didn't see him in the crowd. Even after all this time, she didn't know, if they came face to face, whether she could hide her true feelings.

As the service drew to a close and ended with a prayer for Father Soule's soul, suddenly from the crest of the hill came the sounds of an Indian deer-bone flute. The thin, piercing notes were like a human voice crying out a lament. The Indians who remembered the old way began a chant for the dead. The women cried, "*Ala, ala, ala*" for their friend Father Soule, who had been taken from them when they still had such great need of him.

Reanna looked at the shadowed outline of the figure standing at the top of the hill. Pride had come after all. She might have known he'd find a way to do Father Soule honor and yet not create any embarrassment by his presence. She felt cut in two by the sharp sound of the flute. Her heart pounded as if it would escape from her body and fly up to him. She stood transfixed, looking up until the song was finished and Pride disappeared from her sight. When he'd vanished, it seemed to her that he might have been an illusion, only a figment of her imagination, a dream longed for and lost.

When she turned back again, she saw Andrew staring in her direction. At first she thought he was staring at her, but then she lowered her eyes to the angle of Andrew's gaze. He was looking not at her but at Lovell. In his expression she saw pure, unalloyed hatred. In a maternal gesture, as involuntary as breathing, she turned Lovell toward her and pressed his face into her dress so that he might not be harmed by Andrew's basilisk eyes. She watched, trembling, as she saw Andrew walking toward her. As he came closer, he must have heard her heart pounding.

Ignoring the others, he spoke to her. "Well, Reanna, you're lookin' good. I hear you're doin' good too, just a-pumping oil down that pipeline of yours ever' which way." Andrew smiled. "I just want you to know my offer still stands. I'm willing to buy your crude any time we can agree on a price."

She tried to keep her voice steady. "This is neither the time nor the place to talk business."

"It's always the time for business, Reanna. Just name your price."

"You'll never have enough money to buy me out, Andrew."

He shrugged. "I'm a very patient man, Reanna. I've waited six years, I can wait a little longer. I'm going to Washington on business. We'll talk when I get back."

"My answer will still be no."

"We'll see. You may not want money, Reanna, but you have a price." His hand reached out to touch Lovell on the head. It was as if Andrew had put a mark on him. "Everybody has a price, Reanna. It's just a matter of finding out what it is. We'll talk again."

Reanna drew back; still holding Lovell to her, she turned to Frampton. "Please take us home." She'd been afraid for Lovell before, but now she realized exactly what great danger he might be in if Andrew decided to use him as a weapon to get possession of her oil. She knew Andrew would stop at nothing to have his own way.

As they turned to leave, Snow tried to break away from Cima to run after Andrew, who was striding off in the opposite direction. There was a struggle, but by the time Snow had broken from Cima's grasp, Andrew was gone and Snow was left. Ignored by Andrew, she shouted at Reanna, "Why won't you let me go with my father? He wants me, but you won't let me go! You hate me."

Reanna felt torn between fear and anger. Snow was devastated by Andrew's refusal to speak or recognize her in any way, yet rather than blame him, Snow had fastened all her resentment on Reanna.

"Come, Snow," Reanna said gently, "it's time to go home."

THE long procession of automobiles wound its way south from the mission across the *Reanna* field to the Ridge and up the wide drive to a perfectly restored Lochleven.

All the way home, Snow sobbed while Lovell sat quiet and fearful. He had seen his father for the first time, and his father had touched him. He knew from that touch that whatever he had done, his father had never forgiven him. No matter what Reanna might say, it was something to do with him that kept his father away.

As they stopped before the house, Snow burst from the car and rushed past them all up the stairs to her room. The sound of her door being slammed shut reverberated down to the hall. Embarrassed, Cima and Taffy invented excuses to make themselves scarce.

When they were alone, Reanna looked at Frampton apologetically. "Poor Snow, nothing ever seems to go right for her. I keep hoping she'll make friends and be happy, but everything I do seems wrong." She looked about the hall. "I thought perhaps bringing this house back to life might make a difference. I know this is not the time for a housewarming, just after a funeral, but my mother and father are already on their way from Virginia with my brothers, Patrick and Thomas. I was planning to give a big party for them and the house and to ask the Nation, the way Miss Jane would have in the old days."

"I think Father Soule would approve," Frampton reassured her. "It will be wonderful for you to have your people here. I'm looking forward to meeting them. We'll all give them a big welcome."

Reanna had been more upset by Andrew's demand to buy her oil than she cared to let Frampton know. The way Andrew had looked at Lovell had made her afraid that he would use Lovell to get at her. She must send Lovell away, and soon. She was glad that Andrew was going to be in Washington while her family was in Oklahoma. It seemed to her that even before they arrived, there was a cloud overshadowing their visit.

The night before their arrival, she had trouble at one of the well sites. She stayed out on the rig until morning. There was no time to go home and change clothes. There was barely time to race into town and meet the train.

Fortunately, her friends and the town had turned out in style. Doc and Amoretta headed the welcoming committee. Jack and Lillian were there beside them, Lillian looking stunning in a mauve shantung suit and a hat trimmed with summer roses. Frampton stood a little apart, looking aristocratic in an impeccably cut suit and waistcoat. Taffy had lined up the cowboys to ride a guard of honor beside the limousines. Their silver spurs and leather saddles were shined and oiled for show.

There was a band and banners saying WELCOME. There were flags waving. School had been let out for the day, and the children were cheering as if it were a royal occasion. It couldn't have been a better planned, more lavish reception if it had been for the Queen of England—and there Reanna was, running down the platform, out of breath, in dirty whipcords and an old felt hat. Her own mother stepped down from the train and she didn't recognize her. She started to pass Reanna by without a glance, but her father knew her at once and began to cry out, "There she is. There's my girl." Patrick and Thomas shook hands with Reanna formally, and then they hugged and kissed her.

Patrick couldn't wait to tell her that the farm was running at a profit for the first time. Thomas was at Charlottesville at the university, where he boasted they were teaching him to be a Virginia gentleman and an all-round hell-raiser. As Reanna looked over Thomas's broad shoulder, she could see her mother's familiar, disapproving frown. Some things never changed. And she knew that all the flags and bands and bouquets from smiling schoolchildren would never make up for the way she had come dressed to meet them.

"I'm sorry," she said to her mother. "I had trouble at a well." Her mother's mouth pursed up, but just as she was about to make some reproving comment, Frampton saved the day. He took Mrs. Lovell's hand and kissed it, and then led her and the entire party to line up for the photographer.

As Reanna squinted at the eye of the camera, she felt sure that her late arrival was only a portent of the way things would go from here on out. It was entirely possible that she would always be a little late and a little out of control.

Snow and Cima were on the steps at Lochleven to welcome the Lovells to the house. Lovell was beside them, jumping up and down in a state of ecstatic excitement. There were more introductions and embraces and kisses. And then suddenly the house was full of people and noise and luggage being brought in. Cima had hired a bevy of girls to help out. There was a lot of running up and down stairs and through the halls and shrieks of laughter from Snow and the boys and Lovell.

Snow had taken a fancy to both Patrick and Thomas. Lovell clung to first one uncle and then the other. And he was made a fuss over and approved of by his grandparents. Even Reanna's mother seemed to find Lovell highly acceptable.

Reanna had been especially worried about how her mother and Cima would get along. Both of them were used to having their own way in the running of houses. But for some reason Reanna never fathomed, Cima took to Mrs. Lovell on sight. By dinnertime, Reanna found Cima and her mother together in the kitchen comparing recipes for rosehip jelly.

Reanna had given up the cupola room to her parents, but still, in cramped quarters in the box room, she'd managed to make herself clean and tidy.

Cima's first dinner was a triumph. Everyone ate and laughed too much. After dinner, when they'd calmed down, Reanna said how glad she was that they were all there together. She told them of the raft of parties and entertainments that were being given in their honor. There had been a flood of invitations. Every day of their visit was to be filled with at least one or more engagements. Her mother said that it was kind of people to think of them and that she hoped they wouldn't be in the way or too much trouble.

Then Mrs. Lovell began to yawn. They were all tired from their long journey and the excitement, so they went to bed early. All slept soundly except Lovell, who woke Reanna up in the night to ask could he please have a rodeo, just a little one, in the corral for his uncles. She said she'd think about it, but only if he went back to bed. He couldn't remember where he was supposed to sleep, so she gave him a pillow and a quilt from her bed and told him to sleep on the sofa.

The next day the official entertainments began. Reanna took her mother into town, where Amoretta was giving a silver tea to raise money for charity. Reanna smiled and shook hands with a lot of women she didn't know. She drank tea and ate frosted cakes and watched the satisfaction that it gave her mother to be the center of attention.

The following day Reanna took her mother to a fashion show that Lillian had arranged to benefit the young musicians' fund. They looked at clothes, all shapes and colors, and listened to music both new and dissonant and old and familiar. Her mother was asked to award prizes for fashion and musical effort; she handed them out as if she'd been born a duchess.

The men were taken riding and hunting and were treated to Lovell's home rodeo. She had warned Frampton to keep a special eye on Snow and the boys.

When Reanna and her mother got back from the fashion show, Mrs. Lovell went up to rest and Reanna went looking for her father and brothers. They were nowhere to be found. At last she discovered her father down at the bunkhouse with Jack, Doc and Lovell. They were playing poker, using a stack of matches for money. They were also drinking bourbon, which Mr. Lovell had brought with him in case there was a shortage in Oklahoma. She didn't dare ask what was in Lovell's glass. When her father looked up and saw her standing in the doorway with her hands on her hips, he smiled his old roguish smile and said, "Well, Reanna, someone has to teach the boy to play cards."

She prayed for strength. As she looked up toward the house, she could see Snow and Patrick and Thomas cantering toward the barn with Taffy and Frampton in dogged attendance. Thank God for Frampton, who stayed to dinner and enthralled her mother with stories of Queen Victoria and Edward VII. He caused Mrs. Lovell to beam with pleasure by saying she greatly resembled the present Queen Mary.

The next day Reanna herded them all into cars for a tour of the oil fields. The day was hot and dry, her family hot and bored. Her mother kept fanning at the dust as if it were there only to annoy her. After an hour, Reanna gave up, brought them all back to the house and told them to do as they pleased for the afternoon. She overheard her mother saying to Snow that she had not known that oil was so dirty a business. Reanna forbore to say that it was dirty oil that supported them all.

As Reanna was dressing for the housewarming party, her mother came in. She sat on the edge of the bed and eyed Reanna's gown. Reanna had been avoiding any heart-to-heart talks with her mother. She felt it would be wiser not to allow herself to be provoked and lose her temper.

"Reanna, I want you to know how we all appreciate what you've done to make us welcome and to show us a good time."

"Why, thank you, Mama." Reanna softened. Perhaps she had misjudged her mother's intention to complain and find fault.

"But there are one or two things I've been meaning to speak to you about."

"What things, Mama?" Reanna could feel her jaw getting tight.

"Why can't you ask Lillian Levy to take you in hand? Now, she has real style. I have noticed that some of the things you wear are almost—well, mannish. Lillian is such a charming woman. We know some of the same people in Atlanta."

"Is that all, Mama?"

"Well, there is one more thing. I know Mrs. Hersey would be more than happy to get you into some of the women's clubs; they do so much good civic work. She was telling me about it at the picnic."

Reanna prayed for patience. "I work, Mama. I don't have time to go into town to club meetings, and you don't wear tea gowns in the oil fields."

"Well, of course, if that's the way you feel." Her mother looked pained. "But I would have thought that Andrew made enough money to support you."

"I've told you, Mama, at least once a year for the last seven years, Andrew and I are separated."

Mrs. Lovell ignored what she did not want to hear. "Well, I can't see how he could let you go out there in that dirty, rough place with all those men."

"I think, Mama, this conversation must end now. I have to get downstairs to my guests."

Mrs. Lovell sighed. "We never seem to have the chance to really talk."

IT was the biggest party ever given at Lochleven. People came from miles around. It was no longer possible to illuminate the yard with the gas flares that had been used at Reanna's bride's dancing. The drilling in the fields had caused the gas pressure to become erratic, though the gas fissures still honeycombed the Ridge. So Reanna had hung the trees with Chinese lanterns and had decided on a display of fireworks as a suitable end to the evening.

There was food to please all palates and music for all tastes— three fiddlers and an orchestra and Indian drums and flutes. The music began as the people started to pour in—by car, by wagon and by horseback, but mostly by car. Doc and Amoretta came in an Essex and Jack and Lillian in a Chandler. Frampton came in a Ford, but it had been modified with special upholstery.

Reanna stood on the porch steps with her family to receive guests. Her mother took each greeting and each compliment as a personal tribute to her. Lovell stood between his two uncles, looking up at them as if they were tall trees. Lovell was a good host. He kept introducing the neighbors and friends, saying, "I'd like you to meet my grandmother, my grandfather and my uncles, Patrick and Thomas." Even Snow was smiling; she looked happy, if just for the evening.

Reanna had to be everywhere, overseeing everything. She shook hands, smiled and greeted people she hadn't seen in years. It was a success; nothing had been left to chance. She went to find Cima to congratulate her on making the evening one to remember. She stood by Cima, telling her how much she appreciated all she had done, when she saw Cima's eyes shift from her to a point beyond her shoulder. Reanna turned to follow Cima's gaze. To her shock and outrage, she saw her mother standing at the far end of the verandah with Andrew. They were talking, unaware of anyone around them, their heads close together.

She could not remember ever having been so angry. The rage seemed to explode in her brain and color her vision with a red haze. "That low-down man," she heard Cima say. "I'll get Taffy and we'll run him off the place."

Reanna reached out and held Cima back. "No, I don't want to cause a scene. No one else seems to have noticed that Andrew is here. I'll go. I'll get rid of him myself."

Reanna walked toward the porch as casually as if she were going for a cup of fruit punch. She went up the steps. She kept her nails dug into her palms, fighting for control of herself and her voice. As she reached Andrew and her mother, Andrew turned and smiled. He was pleased, by the look of that smile, pleased with himself and his being in her house.

"Reanna." He held out his hand, but surely he did not expect her to take it. "I'm real glad I got back from Washington in time to see your folks before they left. This is one fine party; the place looks real good, and so do you." His hand went down to his side. His eyes were as cold as the smile was false.

"Andrew and I have been having such a nice talk," her mother said, "and Andrew agrees with me that you work far too hard and that you spend too much time with those oil wells."

For a moment Reanna was so overwhelmed with her anger that she could not speak. Above all, she did not want to call attention to the three of them.

"I promised your mother," Andrew said, "that I'd do everything I could to see that you didn't wear yourself out. I even said how glad I'd be to take over your oil, if it would mean that you could stay home with Lovell more."

"Don't talk about Lovell. Leave him out of this."

Andrew shrugged regretfully and turned back to Mrs. Lovell. "When Reanna and I separated, I let her keep custody of Lovell, but if I didn't think the boy was being looked after right, I'd want to have custody of him myself. I'm his father. A father has a right to his son."

Reanna felt as if she had been struck with a bolt of lightning. Sick with the shock and the fear of what he might do to take Lovell from her, she held up her head and set her shoulders. Andrew had come for her oil at Father Soule's funeral and he had come for her oil here at Lochleven, trespassing into her house; she would not give him a third chance. She would not let him use Lovell as a weapon to get what he wanted.

"Mama, I know you've enjoyed seeing Andrew, but we do have some business to discuss. Will you excuse us, please?" Andrew stood, not moving. At first she was not sure that he would come with her as she asked, but then he bowed to Mrs. Lovell.

"My regards to Mr. Lovell in case I don't have the chance to see him." And he walked with Reanna around to the back of the house, away from the guests.

"I want you to go, Andrew. I want you to go now. You know what I'll do if you stay."

"What," he asked, taunting her, "what will you do? Get old Cima to hold a gun on me?"

"No, Andrew, if you don't go quietly, I'll kill you myself."

He looked at her, his head on one side, figuring his odds. And then he went, disappearing into the shadows, walking down the Ridge toward the road and his waiting car.

SHE thought the evening would never end. She could not remember who she'd talked to or what she'd said. Her mind had been racing around and around, making plans.

The fireworks exploded, showering burst after burst of color. Then, when it was dawn and the last guest had gone, Reanna was alone in the hall with Frampton. They stood before the fireplace, a copy of the portrait of the first Pride Beauvaise above the mantel looking down on them.

"I asked you to stay after the others had gone up because I have something to say to you. I wanted to thank you for lending me the money that made it possible for me to drill the *Reanna One*, to rebuild this house and put the Beauvaise cup back where it belongs. I was going to make a ceremony of it tonight at the housewarming, but then I decided that this moment should really be just between the two of us."

She took the cup from the iron box. She had shined it up for the occasion. As she set the cup carefully on the mantel beneath the portrait of Pride Beauvaise, Reanna hoped the spirit of Miss Jane would be at rest. She'd done all she could to keep this place together, and if she hadn't kept all the land as Miss Jane had wished, then part of the blame at least must lie with Andrew.

"And now I have something to say to you," Frampton said. She knew before he spoke what he was going to say. "I'm going home. There's going to be a war, and I want to be in England."

"Is it all right for you to go home again?"

He nodded. "Yes, quite all right. The reason I came away no longer exists." Frampton hesitated. "My family matters are settled. My brother, Lord Carding, has died, and his son, my nephew the new Lord Carding, has written to invite me home."

"Do you want to tell me more than that?" Reanna asked softly. She was sure that no matter what his reason for coming out here or how his situation now had changed, it was still a painful subject to him.

"No, not tonight. Someday I'll tell you the whole story."

"Will you be happy to go home?"

"It's my duty." Frampton stood erect as a soldier. "And with the money you have made me, I'll go home in style."

"There would have been no fortune for either of us if you hadn't helped me." She heard her voice break. "Oh, I will miss you so, dear friend."

"Then why not come to England with me?" He took her hand and held it to his heart.

She shook her head. "I can't see me in England. This is where I belong."

"There are influential men in England, men interested in oil, men you should meet. Say you'll think about it."

"I'll think about it."

"The war, when it comes, can't last forever."

"When are you going?" she asked.

"A week or two. There are a few odds and ends to settle. I must find a home for my hounds. They're used to this country and wouldn't be happy in another climate."

Reanna took a deep breath. "There's something else," she said. "I'm sending Lovell away to boarding school. How old were you when you went away to school?"

"I was eight."

"Were you homesick?"

"Yes, I thought I would die of it, but I got over it."

"I'm going to send him east with my family when they go. My father can take him to the school in Tennessee to meet his head-master, who's a friend of Papa's."

"And you're sure you want him to go?" Frampton asked.

"Yes." She was grateful that Frampton didn't ask her any more questions. She knew what she must do. If Lovell was out of the state, Andrew could not take custody of him.

Telling Frampton that she was sending Lovell away to school was one thing. Telling Lovell was another.

"I won't go," Lovell said, his eyes blazing with indignation.

"You will."

"No, I won't, and you can't make me."

"Yes, I can." Reanna was firm. But seeing his crestfallen expression, she softened. "The Tennessee Academy is a nice school, it really is. You'll have lots of boys your own age to play with, and you'll learn lots of things you'll need to know. You see"—she held out the school's brochure to him—"here are some pictures of the place. Your grandfather will take you to the school and see you settled. He knows the headmaster."

"I'd rather not go, please."

"What would you do if you stayed here? You'd only spend all your time down at the bunkhouse with Taffy."

"No, I wouldn't." His chin went up in a gesture she knew he had copied from her. "Do you want me to go?"

"Yes."

His eyes were bright with tears. "Will it be easier for you with me away?"

"Yes. When I sent you to the local school, you played hooky. Don't bother to deny it. I've seen you out riding your pony when you should have been at your books."

"If I stayed, I could take care of Father Soule's vines."

It wasn't the answer she'd expected. It caught her unawares, and she stared at him.

"They say the vineyard will die because there's nobody to look after it, just the way the grass is dying here."

"The vineyard is not for you to worry about." Her voice was not as strong or as forceful as it had been. Lovell made a jelly of her heart with his sweetness. She couldn't bear to let him go, but she couldn't run the risk of Andrew's taking him from her.

SHE saw Lovell and her family off from MacClaren City, no bands this time or flags waving. Cima, Snow and Taffy had said their goodbyes at home, and on the train her family had tactfully made themselves scarce so she could have the last moments alone with Lovell.

He sat huddled in a corner of the compartment, his hands palms up on either side of his eyes like blinkers on a horse. He was eight, but still child enough to believe that if he couldn't see Reanna, she couldn't see him. He didn't want her to know that he was crying.

He was ashamed of his tears. Reanna had told him that when he was a baby and the *Reanna One* had come in, he'd cried. She'd made fun of him for weeping when everyone else believed the coming of the oil would make everything wonderful. He didn't think this day was wonderful. Somehow, because of the oil, he was being made to leave all he knew and loved. He would be far away, and she'd still be free to drive out in the car and buy up leases. She'd get richer and the field would grow bigger, so that when he came home, the range would have shrunk. The chance of the cattle and the grass coming once again would only be a distant dream, like the stories Taffy and his buddies told around the fire.

When he came home again, everything would be different. He too would have changed. He heard the conductor cry out, "All aboard," but he still refused to turn or say goodbye. At last she went away and left him in his misery. The wheels began to turn and the train moved away from home, taking him to some strange place where he'd never been and didn't want to go.

He couldn't bear to leave. He wanted to stay at home where he belonged. He made himself a promise, a promise he would keep. She could send him away, but he would never stay in some far-off, foreign place. Wherever she sent him, he'd come home again, like a lost dog following a scent to the place he was meant to be.

REANNA missed Lovell cruelly, but she knew she'd made the right decision. She couldn't forget the look of hatred and greed she had seen in Andrew's eyes. If Lovell was out of the state, perhaps Andrew would have to concentrate on some other means to get her oil. He did.

The pressure on her to sell Andrew her crude increased. Not a week went by that someone acting for Andrew didn't make her an offer. When she refused, a rash of costly, unexplained accidents plagued her fields. She had no proof, but she was sure that Andrew was behind every pipeline leak and drilling delay. She doubled her security, but the accidents continued.

The latest was a fault in the valves at one of her tank farms. She and Taffy stood regarding the damage, as the overflow ran, wasting itself on the prairie. She turned to Taffy. "Was it an accident or not?"

"Could be." He was noncommittal.

"And it could be that somebody jammed the valves."

Taffy said nothing. Ever since she'd sent Lovell away, Taffy had been more taciturn than ever.

"All right," she said, "let's get this mess cleaned up and hope it won't happen again."

As they drove to another crisis spot, Taffy sat silent beside her in the car, staring straight ahead. At last she could stand the silence no longer. "Why don't you say what's on your mind? Spit it right out. You think I was wrong to send Lovell away."

"Yes ma'am, that's what I think. I think you shouldn't have sent him away." Taffy still didn't look at her, but she felt the tension begin to lessen.

"Lovell had to go to school to learn something."

"He's smart enough already. Book learning can't teach you to be smart."

He put her on the defensive. "Maybe I wouldn't have sent him away if he'd spent more time on his lessons and less with you and those cowpoke buddies of yours down at the bunkhouse. What are they doing on the place anyway? They don't work for me anymore. How long do you intend to be a charity for every down-and-out cowboy between here and the Pecos?"

"It ain't my fault there's no work for good men." He rolled down the window and spat a stream of tobacco juice into the wind and along the roadside.

"Disgusting," Reanna said. She meant both the tobacco and the cowboys. Taffy gave her a baleful look, and she softened. She really shouldn't blame him because she was afraid for Lovell. "It really is disgusting," she said.

This time he knew she meant the Climax plug. "So's all this oil and such," he said, and spat again.

"What do you mean by 'and such'?"

"You running around the countryside doing whatever. You know what they say about you."

"I don't care what they say."

"What about you and Andrew and this feud? How long is that going on? You've both got enough money now to last you."

"There's no such thing as enough money. Besides, I'm not doing it just for the money."

"Then what are you doing it for? Where's it all goin' to end up? When you've killed each other off, dead in the street? You tell me cowboys is out of style, well so is feudin' and gunfightin'."

She knew it cost him to say all of that, but it didn't change the facts. "I have to keep looking for oil," she said. "There's a war coming and the country is going to need oil."

"In a war," Taffy muttered, "a lot of innocent people get themselves kilt."

Reanna didn't intend to be one of the casualties. She meant to defend herself against Andrew and to survive and win. But it was getting harder all the time. There was a new phase in their private war. Overproduction had cut the prices down again. There were new legal wrangles over the use of pipelines. Commissions were formed and investigations were made into the common carriers. There were findings and whitewashings, but little was actually accomplished.

In a cutthroat business like oil, no matter how strong the independents' association became, it was still every man for himself. Wildcatters were loners by nature. When it was to their interest, they all drilled and pumped oil as if they were convinced that their wells would dry up on them if they stopped. No wonder the price of crude was down, but a war would put the price up again. And before that, she must at least try to get the independents to agree to some voluntary proration. She must also take great care that Andrew didn't sabotage her fields. It was a new word, but she thought the meaning exactly fitted her situation.

SHE found it was easier to control the price of oil than to control Lovell. She had sent him far from home, but he had a mind and a will of his own. He put all of his energy and intelligence into finding ways of getting home again.

At his first school, he didn't work at all. He sat staring out of the classroom window, dreaming of Lochleven. He remained inert as a stone, refusing to read or write or speak when spoken to. Reanna was summoned by the headmaster to talk sense into the boy. She left a state senate hearing on conservation to go to his school in Tennessee.

When she arrived, Lovell wasn't even on the campus. He was at the stockyards, sitting on a fence, talking cattle prices and market futures with some cowmen from Denver. When she railed at him, he said that he didn't like school and that all he wanted was to come home. She insisted he stay. He bucked and reared and pinned his ears back like a wild colt. Reanna put the spurs to him. "Well," she said, "if you won't take the smooth, then take the rough."

She put Lovell into a military school in Virginia known for discipline, a hard academic course and cold baths. Feeling she had Lovell settled at last, she went back to Lochleven and business.

She had a telegram waiting for her when she got home. Lovell had run away from the military school. No one had any idea of where he might be. She was frantic trying to find him. She hired detectives to follow his trail, as if he were a rustler or a bank robber. They gave chase and at last ran him to ground, flushing him out at the line house up in Cima's ravine. He'd been hiding out at home for weeks.

Reanna accused Cima of helping him. "You knew where he was, didn't you?"

"No, I didn't." Cima's eyes were blazing with indignation. "But even if I had known where he was, I wouldn't have told on him."

"Did Taffy know where he was?"

"You'll have to ask him that." Cima's mouth pursed up like she'd sucked up alum.

"Somebody knew something. Someone helped him. He had no money. Not a penny in his pocket. How did he get across the country? How did he get food, clothing and shelter? He had to have money for railroad tickets. If I find out either of you have been helping him, I'll skin you both alive!"

In fact, neither Cima nor Taffy had helped him or known what his plans were. It was Snow who had sent him her pocket money and gotten him supplies when he came back. Reanna never suspected Snow. It never occurred to her that Snow and Lovell were friends. Reanna still suspected both Cima and Taffy, but she blamed Taffy the most for putting impossible dreams into the boy's head. If given his way, Lovell would turn back the clock to the time of the tall grass and the longhorn.

Taffy stayed well away from Reanna and her wrath. When he had something important to talk to her about, he came up on the porch and shouted it in the windows.

Lovell was not allowed out. She didn't want Andrew to know Lovell was home. He was under house arrest and Reanna was his jailer. His only company was Snow. They whispered, giggling, heads together, out of sight. Reanna determined that next time she would send him so far away, he couldn't get home in a week of Sundays. She summoned Lovell to the dining room for a royal decree.

"This time I'm sending you to a boarding school in New England. I've given them instructions to watch you like a hawk. They're to put a guard at the railroad station and on the roads. The Yankees are to keep you there until you graduate and are ready for college." She waited for him to say something in his own defense, but he said nothing. She could see his mind was already working on a plan of escape. "I mean it, Lovell. If you run away, I'll only send you back. If you're wise, you'll stay up East and study your lessons."

Snow had been listening at the door, peering through a crack. When she thought Lovell might be about to cry, she burst into the room. "Why do you keep on sending Lovell away when he doesn't want to go? If you sent me away, I'd be as happy as a rabbit in the moonlight. The day I leave here will be the happiest day of my life."

Reanna had to bite at her lip to keep from answering Snow. She'd offered to send Snow away to school, but Snow had refused. The only place Snow really wanted to go was to Andrew.

Lovell had collected himself and met Reanna's cold stare with an unwavering one of his own. Today he was no match for her. But she saw in his boy's eyes the reflection of the man he would be. Secretly, she was amazed by his stubbornness and more than a little proud of him for having the gumption to get up and go when he didn't like the school she'd sent him to. She loved him more, not less, with every year, even though it broke her heart as he began to look more and more like Pride. His brown eyes and red hair might fool the unobservant, but she would have known he was Pride's son anywhere. She could have picked him out of a throng of boys and said, "This one belongs to Pride. This boy is a Beauvaise."

Every time Reanna looked at Lovell, she felt a rush of memories. It seemed when Lovell smiled at her that it was a trick he played to trap and catch her heart in a snare. It was because she loved him so that she said, "You'll go to school up East, Lovell, and this time you'll stay until you're ready for college. Then we'll talk about your future, but not before. Do you understand me?"

He nodded. He knew she meant it. If he came home, she'd only send him back. "I understand."

"And me?" Snow said. "What about me? What will you do with me? Am I always to be your prisoner here at Lochleven?"

Reanna sighed. It took more out of her to try to be a good mother than to string pipe to hell and back. "I haven't time to argue, Snow. I'm busy now. I have to pack Lovell up once more." She turned to Lovell. "This time you'd better take two trunks, because you're going to be away for a long, long time."

Once again she took Lovell to the railroad station at Maitland and put him on an eastbound train. This time he didn't cry, but there was something sadder than tears in Lovell's look of resignation.

This parting cut her deepest of all. She couldn't face going back to Lochleven just yet. She stopped in at one of the wells to sort out a dispute between the driller and the crew. Here, under the gas flares in a field of derricks with her wells all pumping deep, the war in Europe that had gone on for nearly three years seemed very far away. But when America came into it—and she was sure America would—then she must have a supply in reserve to fill the demand.

She felt grateful that Lovell was too young to fight, grateful too that he was settled for the next few years. As for Snow's problems, they would have to wait; just now she must think of business and not children.

It was a week before she got back to Lochleven. She hadn't let Cima know she was coming. The house was strangely dark and quiet. There was no one on the porch or in the hall. The dining room was empty and the kitchen stove was cold. There was something ominous in the quiet, as if Reanna had stepped aboard a ghost ship. She ran up the stairs, sure that something was very wrong.

At the top of the landing she saw that the door to Snow's room was open. That in itself was odd. Snow usually closed herself in. Cima was sitting in a rocker by Snow's bed, her arms clasped around her chest, holding and rocking herself as she had once held and rocked Snow. There was no sign of Snow.

Reanna hurried to Cima. "What's the matter?" Cima continued rocking. Looking at her, Reanna realized for the first time how old Cima was. Her face was lined and pinched with pain. She looked as withered as a dry cornstalk after a long drought. All the life force seemed to have gone from her. Her eyes were sunken and dull. Cima had been old for a long time, but it was easy to forget her age because she had a youthful vitality and spirit that made everyone think of her as a young woman. Now she seemed as one dead who had been brought back from the grave.

Her lips moved soundlessly, wordlessly, as her rocking continued. The strike of the rocker on the bare floor made a sound as grating as fingernails across a slate.

"What is it?" Reanna demanded sharply. "You must tell me."

"It's Snow." Cima's eyes never wavered or closed. She stared straight ahead.

"What about her?"

"She's gone."

(444)

"Gone?" Reanna repeated. "Gone where?" Reanna didn't understand what Cima was trying to tell her, but Cima's voice had the sound of a tragedy in it. Each word carried the ring of a funeral bell. "Is Snow dead?"

"No." Cima's eyes closed and she made a quick intake of breath. "No, Snow's not dead, but she might as well be. She's run off."

"Where has she gone?"

"I don't know."

"Then how can you be sure she's run away?" Reanna sought to put some order and calm into Cima's mind.

"I'm sure. My sweet baby's run off with a piece of oil field trash."

Reanna knelt down beside Cima, trying to think of what she might say to comfort her. It seemed that they'd come a long way, only to find themselves back where they'd started. All along they had feared Snow would take up with one of the drifters, and now, like a prophecy, their worst fears had become a reality.

"Do you know who the man is?" Reanna held Cima's dry, thin hand in hers.

"His name is Cecil Bell. They call him Digger, but it makes no difference knowing his name when Snow's gone."

"When did she go?"

"I'm not sure. She left this on her pillow." Cima handed Reanna a piece of crumpled notepaper on which were the words, "This is to tell you I have gone with Cecil Bell. He says he means to marry me, so don't worry. I'll write when we get settled." Snow had signed her name, but she hadn't added "Love" or any other farewell, and she had given no address.

Cima put her hands before her face to hide her grief. "She's gone."

"She'll be all right," Reanna said gently. "Don't worry about her. I'll get the detectives after them. Remember those men we used to find Lovell? Snow shouldn't be hard to trace. They can't have gotten far."

Cima took her hands from her face and looked at Reanna, her eyes bright with anger. "I don't want no detectives. I don't want strangers chasin' after Snow."

"That's their job. They're used to looking for silly young girls who run off with the first man who asks them."

"Snow's young and she may be silly," Cima defended her, "but she's never been happy since Andrew went off and left her. She was always dreaming for him to come back. She had it in her mind that

Andrew really wanted her to come and live with him, only you wouldn't let her go."

"That's not true and you know it. Andrew abandoned her. He left her here without a thought for her, just as he abandoned the rest of us when he went to Texas."

Cima stared past Reanna. "Snow kept saying he was coming for her. That one day Andrew would come and take her with him."

"You know as well as I do, Andrew was never coming for her. He made his fortune off her land. He took her allotment and leased it to himself, and he never paid her a penny. He never came to see her, because he was ashamed to look her in the face, or he should have been. He didn't even speak to her at Father Soule's funeral."

Cima was silent, her hands working together as if she were kneading a batch of bread. At last she said, "No matter what Snow played like, she knowed all long he'd never come, not after she wrote to him."

"She wrote to him?" Reanna hadn't expected that. "When?"

"After Father Soule's funeral. She wrote to tell him how unhappy she was, and she begged him to come for her. But he never even answered. So, rather than face up to it, she run off with a piece of oil field trash."

"You don't know he's trash," Reanna said. Cima began to rock again, as if the motion might bring her closer to Snow. "I'll ask around the oil fields. Someone must know him. Maybe they'll know where he's gone with her. What did she take with her? What kind of clothes?"

"She didn't take much. She just had a little suitcase and some trinkets not worth nothin'." Cima began to cry. The tears flowed slowly, silently down her withered cheeks.

Reanna had never felt more helpless. "I'll go look for her," she said. "Would you like me to do that?" She had no idea of where to begin, but she'd try anything to get Snow back again and to make Cima happy.

"No!" Cima said savagely. "I don't want you to go look for her. Even if you found her and begged her on your knees, she wouldn't come back."

"Then what can I do? Tell me and I'll do it."

A low cry escaped from Cima. "I want Andrew to go find her. He's the only person she might listen to. I want you to go and talk to Andrew and make him go find Snow. He's her father. It's time he acted like it."

Reanna didn't know what to say. She'd sworn she'd never see Andrew again. She didn't think she could trust herself to be in the same room with him. She was afraid of what she might do to him or he to her. They had come close to killing each other before now, and even after all this time, nothing had changed between them except for the worse.

"I'll go," she heard herself saying. "I'll go, and I'll take Taffy along to ride shotgun."

SHE found Taffy at the bunkhouse jawing with his pals. She said, "Taffy, will you step outside, please. I want to talk to you."

When they were out of earshot of the bunkhouse, she told him, "Taffy, I want you to go someplace with me."

"Where?"

"MacClaren City."

"Why?"

"I don't trust myself to go alone."

"What are you going to do in town?"

"See Andrew."

Taffy backed away from her. "No ma'am, not me. Count me out of this one. I'm not gettin' in the middle again if you're fixin' to tangle big with Andrew."

"I need you." She gave him her most appealing look. "I really do, or I wouldn't ask."

In the end he went with her, as she knew he would. He didn't like her mood. She drove too dang fast, right down the middle of the road. He peered ahead of him, squinting into the sun, worrying the tobacco in his lip and praying they wouldn't meet too much oncoming traffic.

He made her more nervous than she already was with his silent disapproval. At last she said, "I purely hate that old cud of yours."

Taffy didn't take his eyes from the road, where danger might appear at any moment. "There's a lot of things I hate these days," he growled.

"What do you mean by that?" She was in a mood to pick a fight with him. If she had it out with Taffy, perhaps she could avoid a confrontation with Andrew.

"What do I mean? You have eyes, look around you. Why would anyone in their right mind cotton to the look of all that?"

Outside the car window, she could see derricks growing as thick as a forest. Just ahead was Andrew's refinery, belching out steam and chemical stench. Clustered around the refinery was a tank farm, each tank with MAC OIL printed on it in black and gold.

The ground that had once been rich pasture was dead in a coating of black oil. As they came closer to the outskirts of MacClaren City, they drove along a high, stone wall, which ran for miles ahead of them.

"That's Andrew's new spread," Taffy said. "He's building hisself a marble palace to live in."

"Yes," she said dryly, "I'd heard." The whole state had heard about Andrew's palace—how big it was, how much money it was costing, how long it was taking to build. Three years, and still it was nowhere near being finished.

"You want to turn in the gate so you can have a look at it?"

"No."

"They say it's going to cost him a million."

"A million before furniture," Reanna said.

Taffy shook his head in wonder. "What does he want a place like that for, away out here?"

"He wants to show off."

"He could do that in town. Why build a million-dollar house on the edge of a dirty oil patch?"

Reanna gave a short, dry laugh. "He wants to make sure the world knows he owns all this. That's why he's putting up gasoline stations all over three states with MAC OIL written on big signs. One day Andrew wants to have stations coast to coast."

"Does that mean you're fixin' to sell gas at every corner?"

"Maybe. I'll see. That's why he wants my oil. He's beginning to hurt for product to fill those gas pumps."

"You just won't quit, will you?"

"No." She gave Taffy a warning glance, a signal to change the subject.

"And what about the little shack Doc and Amoretta have built on MacClaren Avenue?" Taffy asked. "Have you seen that?"

"Yes."

"Doc and Amoretta's house has fifteen rooms and a three-car garage with a servants' quarters over it. There've been a lot of changes in town. Yes ma'am! At least Jack Levy and Lillian have kept their house small, that's something. It's nice to know at least some people who ain't gone plumb crazy with the oil."

She looked up at him sharply. "Do you think it was crazy to re-build Lochleven?"

"Never said that." Taffy shuddered as Reanna swerved to miss an oncoming car.

"Do you come into town often?" Reanna asked.

"I come in to see Jack and Lillian and Doc and Amoretta when they ask me, but I'm not for towns. I don't know why they stay in town. It's all different now. They've got enough wherewithal so they could live anywhere they wanted."

"They want to live in MacClaren City. MacClaren City is their home. I remember some good times in that town."

"Yeah. Well, those good days are long gone. We won't see them no more." Taffy was morose. He'd been putting off the one question he most wanted to ask. "Are you comin' to see Andrew because of Snow?"

"Yes."

"Figures."

They were in town now on the wide, brick-paved main street. Reanna pulled into a parking space before the MacClaren Building, a square, brick edifice six stories high. Across the street was the brick MacClaren Hotel, also six stories high.

"They've paved the main street," Taffy said, as if Reanna might not have noticed it on her own. "You can't drive cattle down pavement. It's bad on their feet." They sat in silence, and then he said abruptly, "Well, what do you think of progress?"

"I think Andrew must have gotten a good buy on brick." She sat fiddling with her purse, not moving out of the car.

"Do you want me to go in with you?" Taffy asked.

"No, I'll do this myself."

"Then I'll go over to Jack Levy's and do a little swap and shop with him. I like that Lillian; she dresses real ladylike." Taffy looked at Reanna, trying to read her mood. He didn't want to leave her if she needed him. This whole trip into town was a bad idea. It only stirred things up and did no one any good. Snow was gone. No amount of talking was going to change that.

As Reanna rode up in the elevator to the sixth floor of the Mac-Claren Building, she felt as though she were Daniel heading for the lions' den. She hadn't expected that coming to see Andrew would be easy. In fact, she hadn't expected ever to come to see him hat in hand at all.

She got off the elevator and walked toward the double glass doors with *MacClaren Oil* printed on them in bold black letters. The offices were surprisingly modest. A girl with a skirt short enough to show her ankles sat behind a desk pounding at a typewriter. When she saw Reanna, she stopped and frowned and spoke in a voice as warm and sweet as poured molasses. "Can I help you?"

Reanna wondered idly if Andrew had slept with her, if he'd had any joy of it. God knows he hadn't found much pleasure in their marriage bed.

"I'd like to see Mr. MacClaren."

"Do you have an appointment?" Butter wouldn't melt in her mouth.

"No."

"I'm afraid Mr. MacClaren can't see anybody this afternoon. He's very busy."

"He'll see me," Reanna said.

"You can't see him," the girl said with a simper of satisfaction. "He's out."

"Where will I find him?"

"I don't know." The girl began to fill a fountain pen from a bottle of Carter's blue-black ink. She was a snippy girl who needed to have that simper slapped right off her silly face.

"I'm Mrs. MacClaren." The pen made a suction noise as if it had inhaled and choked. The girl went pale as she laid down the pen. There were ink stains on her fingers and the blotter. A fiery blush stained her cheeks.

"I'll ask if they know where he is," she said, her eyes wide. She thinks I'm here to make trouble for her, Reanna noted with satisfaction. She was sure now that Andrew had tampered with the girl. She wasn't surprised that Andrew had found companionship elsewhere, but to do so with a girl younger than Snow she found distasteful.

The girl hurried back and closed the door to the inner office carefully behind her. Her hands were trembling. Andrew had probably told her that Reanna was a witch. "They say he's over at the hotel."

"Thank you," Reanna said, politely. She considered that she was behaving very well. She was being exceedingly ladylike. Her mother would have been proud of her. She hoped her good behavior would continue when she met Andrew face to face.

WHEN she walked into the lobby of the MacClaren Hotel, a silence fell over the men sitting in a circle of leather chairs. They were seemingly rendered dumb by the sight of her. Their mouths remained open, their cigars unlit. They looked trapped in amber.

She knew most of the men well. Independents like Moon Mills did business with her, pretending they had no time to truck with Andrew. They'd clearly never expected to be caught out.

Andrew was sitting with his back to her, but sensing something of importance was happening, he turned to face her. She had to admire the way he kept his composure. He hadn't expected her, but he betrayed no surprise. She might have come in every day at this hour.

"Hello, Andrew," she said. "I wonder if I could speak with you for a moment?" The circle of men seemed to be holding their breath, waiting for an answer. "Hello, boys," she said, making a general greeting and meanwhile imprinting every face and name in order. She'd remember them all, and well they knew it. They looked as foolish and embarrassed as if she had followed them to the men's room and found them with their pants down.

"Certainly, my dear." Andrew stood up. "You'll have to excuse me, gentlemen. It's not often my better half comes into hotel lobbies looking for me." Reanna flushed and hated herself for betraying her feelings. She remembered as well as he did what had passed between them long ago in Washington. "This isn't much like the Willard, is it?" he asked, grinning at her discomfort.

"No."

He took her arm, and they walked out of the lobby into the street. Behind them she heard a sudden buzz of voices. The two of them would be the number one topic of conversation, but then, when had they not been the target of speculation and gossip? As they walked down the street in the bright sunlight for all to see and remark, Andrew said, "I know why you've come, Reanna, and the answer is no."

She felt her arm tense beneath his hand. "Are you sure you know?" she asked.

He nodded. "And I'm not giving in to you or the independents.

You can lobby all you want to up at the state capitol, but I'll fight this new legislation. It's not to my advantage to see regulation or limiting of production."

She stopped and stared at him. "No, I'm sure it's not. You want to go on overproducing until you drive the price of oil so low we have to sell to you or go broke." She was angry with him and with herself. He thought of nothing but business, and he had made her lose her temper while he still had his in control. She took a rein on herself.

"I didn't come to talk about oil," she said, "and I don't want to stand out in the middle of the street. Let's sit in the car."

He laughed. "What's the matter, Reanna, don't you trust me indoors?"

"I wouldn't trust you anywhere, Andrew," she said, as evenly as she could manage. At least sitting in the car she was on her own property, even though she was in his territory. Yet, when they were beside each other in the car, both staring straight ahead like statues, it was Andrew who spoke first.

"Well, what is it? If it's not oil, it must be something right important to bring you into my town."

"It's Snow. She's eloped with an oil driller named Cecil Bell." She stopped, waiting for him to react to the news. He showed no emotion at all.

"What do you want me to do about it?"

"I want you to find her and bring her home. She wouldn't listen to Cima or me, but she would come home if you asked her."

"Why do you think she'd come home, if she's already married?"

"She's a child, Andrew. She's underage."

"She's nearly as old as you were when you married me."

"I want her home."

"Why did she run off in the first place? Did she have to get married?"

"You mean is she pregnant?"

"Yes." Andrew looked uncomfortable. She couldn't tell whether it was shame or anger.

"I don't know whether she is or not. I think she just ran away with the first man who asked her."

Andrew was silent, staring out the car window. "Have you heard from her?"

"If I had, Andrew, I wouldn't need your help to find her." A

(452)

sharp pinprick of suspicion nagged at her. Andrew had known all along that Snow had gone. He knew and he'd done nothing about it. "No," she said slowly, "I haven't heard from Snow, but you have, haven't you?"

"I had a letter," he admitted grudgingly.

"From Snow?"

"From Digger Bell."

"Why did he get in touch with you?"

"Why do you think?" Andrew's tone was scathing. "He wants money. He wants control of her fortune. Why else would he have married her? I asked if she had to get married because I wondered if he'd been smart enough to get her pregnant first."

Reanna was repelled by Andrew's suggestion. His brutal attitude should not have surprised her, but it had. "Did you send him money?"

"No."

"And you won't go after her? You won't try to bring her home?"

He shook his head. "No, she's made her bed and now let her lie in it." He turned to Reanna. "Besides, this is your fault."

"How do you figure that?"

"You never looked after her the way a mother should. If you'd kept an eye on her, she wouldn't have run off on you."

"Sorry I troubled you, Andrew. I should have known better. It's not to your advantage to have her back, is it? It's more convenient for you to have her be considered irresponsible and incompetent." She leaned over and opened the car door. It was a gesture and an invitation that needed no words.

Andrew got out of the car without protest. He closed the door and stood looking at her through the glass before he turned to walk away. Then she realized that in her anger she had let him go too easily. She rolled down the window and called out to him. "Andrew, you'll have to crank the car for me."

He turned and grinned. "It's nice to know you still need me for something—right, Reanna?" He took hold of the crank handle and began to turn it, twisting it like the neck of a chicken. He turned it over once, twice—the third time was the charm. Andrew stood erect and came back to her, still grinning. "Anything else?"

"No." She hated being beholden to Andrew for anything. Then she reconsidered. "Yes. Andrew, where was the letter from?"

"What?" He leaned closer, not sure he had heard her.

"The letter you had from Snow's husband. Where was it from? There must have been a postmark on the letter."

"New Orleans," he said.

"Where in New Orleans?"

"Somewere on Calvados Street."

"I want the street address."

"I want your crude."

"You won't get it."

He shrugged. "Maybe not today, but one day. It's a matter of time till I find the right price."

"And if I don't sell you my oil, you won't give me Snow's address?" she asked wearily. "Is that it?"

He thought for a moment and then made his decision. "It was 37 Calvados Street." He turned and walked away. This time there was no need for her to call him back.

She sat, shaken by the encounter with Andrew. It had been more unsettling than she'd expected. Then she drove over to Jack Levy's to collect Taffy. She passed the time of day with Lillian and sent her regards to Doc and Amoretta. Then they headed out of Andrew's town for the Ridge, doing forty-five miles an hour, dust blowing behind them, spiraling upward in the savage wind.

Taffy held to the seat with both hands, his knuckles showing white. He'd seen Reanna angry before, but never like this. She plumb scared the horseflies off him. "Next time you want me to drive with you someplace, I aim to be too busy to go! That is, if I'm still alive to make that decision." He didn't dare ask her how she'd made out with Andrew; she'd probably run them off the road altogether.

CIMA was waiting for them in the hall. She looked so fragile and vulnerable that Reanna wished there was some way she could make the news easier for her to bear.

"Well?" Cima demanded.

Reanna shook her head. "Andrew won't go after her."

Cima sat down abruptly, as if her knees had given way beneath her. "I see."

"It's not all bad," Reanna said confidently. "Andrew knew where she was. He'd had a letter from her husband. Don't worry, I'll find some way to bring her home."

Cima looked up. "Where is she?"

"New Orleans."

"I see," Cima said again.

"Andrew had the address, 37 Calvados Street. Now we know where she is, I'll get her back. It's too late to do anything tonight, but in the morning I'll decide what's best to do. I promise."

IMA allowed herself to be led upstairs and put to bed. She hadn't argued with Reanna, but she had no intention of waiting for morning before she went to find Snow. If Andrew wouldn't go, then it was up to her. There was nothing that Reanna could do or say that would bring Snow back. Right or wrong, Snow blamed Reanna for all her unhappiness.

Cima lay with her eyes closed until the house was quiet. Then she got up, took a worn carpetbag from the top of the cupboard and packed it with a change of clothes and some necessities. She dressed in her Sunday best, a neat black crepe dress, black broadcloth coat, a black straw hat with a ribbon rosette and her black kid shoes. Dressed and packed, she stood in the middle of the room thinking about money.

On the day her first royalty check had come in, Reanna had told her that she, Cima, was going to be a rich woman. She opened an account at the bank in Cima's name and deposited the check for her. Cima didn't like banks, but rather than make a fuss she'd continued to deposit the checks. Then each month she withdrew almost as much as she deposited. She hadn't wanted Reanna to think she was ungrateful or contrary, but she liked to keep her money where she could see it, in her own room. She'd put her gold beneath the floorboards and the paper money in the mattress.

Now she must decide how much to take and how to carry it. She had no idea of how much she'd need. She filled her purse with bills, then pried up a floorboard and took out gold coins to sew in the lining of her coat and to fill a worn money belt that Taffy had used when he carried large sums of cash money to buy cattle.

When it was done, she put the planks back in their place, smoothed out the bed, blew out the lamp and tiptoed downstairs to the dark hall. She telephoned for a taxi hack to come out to Lochleven from Maitland and meet her at the end of the drive. At that hour of the night, a taximan could be sure of a large tip to come out to Lochleven.

She'd worried over how to let Reanna know where she was. She printed out the words "GONE TO FIND SNOW" on a large sheet of paper. She was too tired to write more. Besides, there was nothing more to say.

She'd decided to take the train from Maitland instead of Mac-Claren City, because there was less chance anyone there would recognize her and try to stop her. She was nervous and uneasy about the venture. If she was sweet-talked, she might back out at the last moment. She'd never traveled by train before. As a girl, she'd never been out of the old Nation. New Orleans was a long way off; only the prospect of finding Snow made the journey worth the risks.

At the station she walked erect and resolute to the ticket window and boldly asked for a ticket to New Orleans. "Which way do you want to go?" the ticket agent asked. "Down to Dallas and over, or over to Memphis and down?"

"I want to go on the first train." As she paid for the ticket, counting out the money from her purse, she saw the ticket agent eyeing her suspiciously. She must remember to be more careful in the future to keep her money out of sight.

She sat down wearily to look at her ticket. It was as long as a spool of ribbon. Trying to figure out the timetable was confusing. She'd take the morning train from Maitland to Fort Smith, then to Little Rock and on to Memphis, where she'd transfer from the Rock Island to a southern line. All along the way there were complicated stops and starts and changes she didn't understand. She was so engrossed in the puzzle that at first she didn't hear the ticket agent's raised voice. It took another moment to realize that he was shouting at her.

She looked up, startled to see him standing over her. His face was red, the cords in his neck standing out like rope. He looked like a man about to suffer an attack of apoplexy. "What are you doing in here?" he shouted.

"I'm waiting for the train."

"Waiting for the train?" he repeated sarcastically.

She nodded. "You just sold me a ticket." He seemed to be out of control. Perhaps he was *haksi* and she should try to humor him.

"Well, you can't wait here. What kind of stunt are you trying to pull?"

For a moment she thought it must be something to do with her ticket. Perhaps she hadn't paid him enough. "I'm just trying to figure out the ticket," she said politely.

He exploded with rage. "You can read, can't you?"

She nodded. "Yes."

"See that sign?" He gestured wildly at a sign on the far wall. "If you can read so good, read that!"

She adjusted her glasses and looked first at the man. His face was mottled and distorted by rage. Then she looked over at the sign. It was old and yellowed, but the words were still visible. Waiting Room—Whites Only! She sat, stunned and sickened by the shock.

"You know what the words mean? You understand?" He was still shouting as if she were deaf. "You aren't white. You're a nigger woman. The waiting room for the coloreds is around the back."

She was untraveled and inexperienced, but she was not so far out of the world that she hadn't heard about Jim Crow. It was simply that, in all of her life, this was the first time Jim Crow had been applied to her. It fell on her like a lash, and the pain was nearly insupportable. She felt as if she'd been poisoned by his words. The evil had infected her so that she was paralyzed, unable to take any action. It seemed a lifetime before she rose unsteadily to her feet.

He had called her a name she would never answer to. He had humiliated her—a man she wouldn't have let on the place. He had taken her dignity, as surely as if he had taken her clothes and left her naked and ashamed. The only revenge was to refuse to answer him back. She must turn the other cheek and leave in silence. It was the Christian way.

She walked to the door and on toward the other, smaller, colored waiting room. She went meekly into the dingy place and sat trembling, her lips moving, as she mumbled the words, "Oh Lord, oh Lord, Jesus!" But then, suddenly, she realized that she was too angry for prayer or for silent forgiveness. She had never in her heart considered meekness a useful virtue. When she'd encountered wrong in her life, she'd fought back and righted it.

She stood up. "I won't let him treat me that way. You folks

either." She turned to the waiting passengers. Instead of admiration and encouragement in their eyes, she saw only fear. "He should have his hide nailed to the barn." She spoke clearly. "He shouldn't be allowed to get away with treating people as if they were no account. Who does he think he is? He's only here to sell tickets, not to holler and make rules. I mean to tell him so to his face, and now!"

The black faces all around her had become masks of terror. They were her sisters and her brothers, but they were cowards all the same. Perhaps she would have been too, if she'd been poor and had a family to protect. She didn't have their compromises to make. She'd lived her life free at Lochleven. She'd always been treated as a friend and had a place at the table. Before she had time to prove her words to herself or to the others, she heard the sound of the eastbound train pulling into the station. Once aboard, everything would be different.

THE train proved to be no better than the station. She was put into a segregated car. She'd paid the same price for her ticket as the whites, but the conditions of the coach were far from equal. Her car was old and drafty and the upholstery was stained and torn. The railroad car was not fit for cattle. Her fellow passengers sat as far away from her as possible. She'd been outspoken, and that made her a threat. They averted their eyes from her or they looked through her, as if she were invisible.

She rested her cheek against the glass and looked out the window at the passing landscape. She could see her own dim reflection in the grimy surface as proof of her existence.

She determined to forget everything but her true business. She was going to find Snow, and she would let nothing stop her, not even hunger. By noon the passengers all around her had taken out food from parcels and baskets. The mouth-watering aroma of chicken, ham and fried pies filled the car.

Cima reckoned that in her time she must have packed up a thousand pokes, but she'd been in such a hurry to leave Lochleven, she'd taken no thought for herself. It had never occurred to her that there would be no food on the train. It was clear that no one was going to offer to share his meal with her.

It was afternoon before the train stopped at a station long enough for her to find a little rundown grocery and buy cheese, crackers and an apple. She had to be content with that and to drink from a half-empty watercooler in the car. The water had a brackish and bitter taste.

She had slept a little before they reached Fort Smith, but in the night, while the others slept, she was awake, unable to stop her mind from darting this way and that. What if Snow wasn't in New Orleans? What if she'd gone somewhere else? What if she refused to come home with her? If she didn't stop her worrying, she'd wear herself out, and that would do no one any good.

At Little Rock, all the passengers she had begun the journey with were gone, and the car filled up with a new crowd bound for Memphis. They were not a rowdy bunch, but more talkative and open-natured. They didn't know she was a dangerous woman who spoke her mind.

In Little Rock she would have liked to take a day's layover to rest. She was bone tired, but she'd been told that not many places catered to coloreds. Those that did didn't like to take in a stranger for a meal and a bed, and if they did, the food was poor, the bed lumpy and the prices outrageous. It would have been easier if she'd belonged to a church or a lodge. But she belonged to no one but herself and to no place but Lochleven. She had lived her life free, doing a free woman's work for a free woman's pay. In a hostile world away from home, she faced up to another night of discomfort on the way from Little Rock to Memphis.

There wasn't much rest possible; there was a lot of stopping and starting and more and more passengers getting on the train, so that at last some whites, if they wanted a seat, were forced to come into the Jim Crow car. The conductor ran up and down in a state of agitation, muttering, "The blacks are in with the whites. The whites are in with the blacks. Get on board and we'll straighten everything out later!"

Cima looked at a white couple at the far end of the car. They seemed less concerned than the frightened blacks who outnumbered them. The blacks began to silence noisy boys, to hush crying children in an effort to be silent and invisible, to call no attention to themselves, as if to become visible was to invite disaster.

By Memphis, Cima had had enough of traveling in close confinement in a world full of cold, frightened strangers. She took down her valise from the rack above her seat, got off the train and walked out of the station. She saw a taxi with a colored driver at the end of a queue and headed for his cab. But when she tried to get in, he turned on her. "Get away, mama, I'm waiting for a fare."

"You for hire?" She was soiled and tired, but she believed she still looked respectable enough to hire a cab. "I'll pay you."

He eyed her warily. "Where are you going, mama?"

"New Orleans, but before that I want a good meal, a hot bath and a clean bed. I want you to take me to a decent hotel."

He stared.

"How much?" she asked. He named a price that was highway robbery and she said, "I'll pay it."

She started to get into the back seat, even though he hadn't gotten out to open the door for her as she saw other taxi drivers were doing for their customers. As she put her hand on the door handle, he said, "Don't you sit back there. Sit yourself up in front. I can't have you sitting in the back, mama, not for any price. I drive white folks in my taxi, and they won't never ride with me no more if they thinks I carry black folks."

His words were the last straw; she almost heard the snap of the camel's back. She began to shout at him, "This world out here is crazy. You know that you're all crazy. You tell me the front of this and the back of that. You say sit here, drink there. You all say crazy *haksi* words." She took a roll of paper money from her pocket. She held it out in front of him like a carrot before a balky mule. "You want money, then take me where I want to go!"

"I'll take you, mama," he said, his eyes round with greedy delight, "but you'll still have to sit up front with me. This here is Memphis."

She opened her mouth to berate him again, and then she thought better of it. She had no strength or time to waste. She wanted to rest more than she wanted to argue. She opened the front door of the cab and sat down wearily beside the driver. She looked at him dispassionately.

His black face glistened with nervous perspiration. He was a man of no particular age. He wore an old, battered straw boater set jauntily on his head. The gleam of white teeth showed bright as his face broke into a wide smile. He was smiling, she knew, because he'd seen her money. He might have been a well-trained black dog who had learned to obey and do clever tricks for tips. Yet for all that she despised him, she understood him better today than she would have yesterday, before she'd seen that to act the part of a mindless idiot was a way of being safe.

As he drove toward the black section of town, they traveled beside the wide river. As she watched the water flowing calmly past, a plan began to take shape in her head. She didn't want to stay in Memphis any longer than she had to, and she definitely didn't want to get back on the train. She turned to the grinning baboon of a driver. "Sonny, how would you like to drive me to New Orleans?" He was so startled by her question that he turned the wheel suddenly and the car swerved up onto the curb.

"I can't do that, mama. What do you think I am? I don't own this cab."

A dozen alternatives came flooding into her head. She could buy him a cab, if it came to that. But for now she was too hungry and tired to properly organize the next stage of her journey. When they stopped in front of the colored hotel he had chosen, she got out and said to him, "You'd better come in too. I'm going to be here awhile."

"No, ma'am. This is no place for me. This is as far as this nigger goes."

"Then wait for me," Cima commanded him. She saw the look of indecision on his face. He still didn't know what to make of her. "When I've finished here, I want to go find a riverboat going to New Orleans." She took out a twenty-dollar bill and tore it in half. His eyes widened and his mouth gaped open. "If you wait, you can have the other half for a tip when I comes out." Without stopping for his answer, she turned and went into the hotel.

She had a bath and a nap. She ate a reasonably good hot meal. When she'd finished, she found her driver obediently waiting to take her to the landing where she could board a steamboat called *Water Lily*, bound for New Orleans. He got his tip.

CIMA was obliged to buy her passage in the stern of the boat, close by the moving paddle wheels. There were no private cabins available for the colored, but she was able to rent a chair in a small, dark saloon. If the weather was fine, she could bring it out and sleep on deck. At least for this leg of the journey, she had thought to buy food and a warm shawl.

As the *Water Lily* cast off from the landing, the aft deck was crowded with passengers. They were far more agreeable and friendly than those on the train had been. They shared food, gossip and laughter. They sang and danced as if they were all on a picnic or going home to loved ones. Perhaps they felt easier on the water because there was no conductor walking up and down the aisles to oversee what they did. And they were not confined in four walls. Here there was the sky above and the water below. Both the sky and the water were free.

Something stirred in Cima as she listened to the old refrains. She felt as if she had always been here on the moving river. She was a hundred years old and as strong as the changing currents. She remembered all the stories her mother had told her of slavery and of a country they had come from, a country far away that neither had seen. She felt joined to those women, then, now, forever, as she was lulled by the singing and the turning of the paddle wheels.

An old woman and a little girl shared their basket of food. The woman was taking her grandchild to New Orleans to her mother. Cima showed the woman the address she was looking for. The woman didn't know where it was exactly, but she was sure it was in the old section called the French Quarter.

"Thank you," Cima said, relieved. It gave her hope to think the street really existed. She spent her time resting and dozing in the warm sun and watching the river being churned up by the great paddle wheels.

As they drifted southward, the landscape changed. The giant trees with their drapery of hanging moss were a strange sight. They looked haunted, filled with their living cobwebs. In the fields, the cattle were a new and different breed, and each seemed to have its own white egret as a companion. She counted little wooden landings along the banks where she saw colored families fishing together. She turned to the old woman. "It's fine to see folks have time to fish."

The old woman laughed a toothless, soundless laugh. "They has to fish for cray or cat or anything they can get. They has to fish to live."

Cima frowned. "Cain't they live off the land?" Beyond the riverbank, visible through the oak and cypress, she could see rich fields.

"Darkies don't own no land. They works for white folks, harvest to harvest, and still they has to fish jes' to keep body and soul together."

Cima said no more. Still, it seemed to her that those families by the river looked happier than others she had seen inland. At least here something of interest was always doing. There was cargo to be delivered or loaded aboard and different passengers getting on and off the boat, and always the river flowing by. If she had to make a choice of where to be, other than Lochleven, it would be on the river.

THEN, on the morning of the third day, just as she'd gotten used to being on the water, the boat tied up at a levee landing by the French Quarter. Cima said goodbye to the old woman and the child and walked down the gangplank into the crowded, teeming market, alive with hawkers crying out their wares between rows and rows of stalls displaying a seemingly endless variety of goods. She was dazzled by the sights and sounds and unfamiliar smells. The people pressing in on her from all sides were all different shades of white and black and brown. They spoke in accents as rich and singular as their colorful clothes.

She felt dizzy. She needed time to find her bearings. She stopped at a stall and bought a sweetbread called a beignet. It was like a doughnut, only in a different shape, and with it she drank a cup of milky, bitter coffee. Then she wandered from the market into the well-marked Jackson Square, surrounded on three sides by low, graceful buildings whose balconies were bordered in ornate ironwork railings. At the far end of the square was the Cathedral of St. Louis. She saw other coloreds walking in and out of the church, so she went through the crowd of jugglers and beggars and vendors and buyers toward the church's great, welcoming doors.

Inside there was a mass being said. The church was dim; the shimmering light filtered from the stained-glass windows was reflected by the candles on the high altar and on the smaller shrines. The musty smell of incense filled the air. Cima found the shrine to Saint Anthony. She remembered that Father Soule had said that Saint Anthony was the patron of the lost. She lit a candle and placed it in front of the little altar. On her knees, her eyes screwed up tight, she said her brief prayer. "Please, please help me find Snow."

Then she went outside again and, as her eyes became accustomed to the light, she saw a tall, graceful woman walking in her direction. The woman was not dark or light but of some mixed blood. She was wearing an elaborately wrapped bandana, which sat on her like a crown, and a bright blouse and long skirt, like a gypsy's. In her hand she was carrying a shopping basket. She looked as if she was at home here in the Quarter.

(464)

Cima stopped her. "Please, can you help me? I wants to find this Calvados Street." Cima showed her the address she had written down on a piece of paper.

The woman looked at it and then at Cima. When she answered, she spoke in a voice that was slightly accented. "Why you want to go to that street?"

Cima was about to make her a short answer but decided the woman had not meant to be rude. "I'm looking for a girl. Someone I knows."

The woman frowned and shook her head as if she was undecided how to answer. "Are you sure this is the right address?"

"Yes," Cima said firmly. She had no other.

The woman shrugged. "If you are sure this is the house—you go down Pirate Alley. You see it there by the church. The street you want is not far behind it."

Cima thanked her and made her way through the throng toward Pirate Alley. As she turned into the narrow passageway, she glanced back and saw the woman who had given her the directions still watching her. Cima had the fleeting impression that the woman was about to follow her, but then she was lost in the crowd.

Cima walked uneasily on the rough cobblestones into a jumble of streets behind the cathedral. To Cima they were a maze of shops and houses, at the sides of which were iron grillwork gates that led into dim courtyards beyond. The air was close with the damp rising from the river and the smell of unfamiliar herbs. There was a low roll of thunder. Cima felt heavy-limbed; even the lightly packed valise was a burden to carry.

Cima clutched at the piece of paper in her hand, looking for the right street and number. The streets twisted and turned so that she lost direction and walked back the way she had come, until by accident she discovered that she was on Calvados Street. She stood directly across from number 37.

Now that she was here, she hesitated, afraid to cross the street and go in. If Snow was not there, what would she do then? She would have no idea of where in the wide world to find her. The strain of the long journey suddenly hung on her as heavily as the humid, fetid air. She set down the valise, her heart beating unevenly in her chest.

She must act. She couldn't stand there staring at an unfamiliar house. She must find the courage to go in. She gathered her strength, walked slowly across the street and reached out to open the gate. As her hand touched the handle, the cool, moist iron seemed almost as painful to the touch as a glowing hot brand.

The gate creaked shut behind her. She walked unsteadily down the dark way into the courtyard garden. She could hear the splashing of a fountain and smell the cloying fragrance of flowering vines.

The L-shaped, two-storied house had a gallery that ran the length of it. The doors to all the rooms led out to the cool of the garden. As Cima stood, unsure of what to do next, a woman appeared on the gallery above her.

She was in a faded silken wrapper. She looked as if she'd just awakened and it were morning instead of evening. She had thick, curly hair dyed a startling red. Her face was painted a dead white, her eyes outlined in black and her mouth and cheeks heavily rouged. She blinked at the light and then, as she glanced down, she saw Cima. "What the hell are you doing down there?"

Cima looked up, not knowing what to say.

"Who do you think you're staring at?"

"I—I'm sorry," Cima stammered, "I thought this here was 37 Calvados Street."

"That's right." The woman's eyes narrowed suspiciously. "What do you want?"

"I'm lookin' for a girl."

The woman gave a short, unpleasant laugh. "You came to the right place for that, but I don't run octaroons."

Cima felt her breath catch in her throat. She ignored the woman's words and their possible meaning. "I'm looking for a Miz Cecil Bell. She live here?"

"Mrs. Bell?" The woman leaned over the railing and peered down at Cima.

"Miz Cecil Bell. Her name was Snow MacClaren, but she married with a Cecil Bell."

The woman's eyes narrowed again, and her red lips straightened into a thin, sharp line. "I don't know anybody by either name. You've made a mistake. Go look somewhere else."

The woman was lying. She knew something she wasn't telling; Cima was sure of it. "Mr. Bell, he wrote a letter and gave this address." Cima stood looking up, her gaze steady. "I cain't go until I've found her."

The woman's eyes turned hard and cold. "You're leaving here, and right now!"

Cima didn't move. Now the woman began to shout. "Reba! Reba, you come here!"

A black servant appeared from the rear of the house. She was not young or old, somewhere in between, but she looked pinched and old as if life had used her hard. She wiped her hands on the apron that covered her maid's dress.

"Yes, Madame?"

"This woman is looking for a girl named Snow she says was here calling herself Mrs. Cecil Bell. She claims this Mr. Bell is the girl's husband. I told her there was no one here by that name, but she won't take no for an answer. Now I don't want trouble, but I want her out of here. Understand?"

The woman turned and disappeared through the French doors behind her. There was silence in the garden save for the splash of the water in the fountain. Reba stood staring at Cima. The woman was servile, Cima thought, but there was a shrewd cunning in her eyes. "You heard Madame Fleur. There's no one here by the name of Bell."

Cima stared back at her. "I cain't believe that. You know somethin' and this Madame Fleur knows somethin' you're not tellin'. Why?"

"I don't know nothin'." The woman was surly, as if she were the victim of a punishment she didn't deserve.

"This girl I'm looking for is young. She's seventeen—nearly eighteen." The woman looked away, but Cima persisted. "Her name's Snow."

The woman's eyes flickered; she looked up quickly at Cima and then away again. "She's a runaway?"

"Yes. How come you know that?"

"I've heard this story before." Her face widened into a mirthless, toothless smile. "This Snow—she ain't your daughter?"

"No."

"Then why you care where she is?"

"I raised her." There was a moment's hesitation when Cima thought the woman was about to speak again. "I wants her back home. I'll pay to find her."

"How much?" The woman's eyes suddenly focused hard and bright on Cima. The bargaining had begun.

"Whatever it takes."

"Would you pay a hundred dollars?"

Cima nodded. She felt her heart hammering in her chest. "Yes'm. I'd pay a hundred dollars." It was a price she might have paid for an animal.

The woman sucked air through her lips. "How I know you got that kind of money?"

"I can get it." Cima knew she must be careful not to seem too eager. She saw the woman trying to make a decision as she glanced furtively at the balcony.

"You have to go now. If Madame Fleur comes back, she be plenty mad if you still here."

"I won't go without findin' my Snow. She was travelin' with a man named Cecil Bell. They come here from Oklahoma. She was from the Indian Territory."

Suddenly the woman's expression changed. She began to back away from Cima. "She was a real Indian, this girl?"

"Yes." The woman was clearly frightened of more than Madame Fleur. "You know somethin' about her, please God, tell me."

"Maybe I know, but I can't tell you nothing here. If Madame Fleur finds you still here, she'll skin me alive." Then, as if they were old conspirators, she lowered her voice. "This girl, she claim to be a princess?" Cima nodded. She could say nothing; her mouth was dry with excitement. "You get me a hundred dollars, and I'll tell you where to find her." She began pushing Cima from the courtyard.

"When?" Cima held to the woman's sleeve.

"You go to the end of the street," the woman hissed. "I'll meet you there as soon as I can get away. You wait for me, and you be sure you have the money. You hear?"

"Yes, I hears you. I'll be waitin' with the money." She found herself being forced past the outer gate as the woman raised her voice and made a great show of shouting, "You go on. You nothin' but trash, and you got no business in a private house. You go on off, or I'll have the law on you." Then she whispered in Cima's ear, "You wait for me."

CIMA stood in the shadow of a doorway at the end of the street, waiting. She was prepared to wait until the last trumpet sounded for word of Snow, but Lord she was tired. The small valise was too heavy for her to hold. She set it down beside her. She felt sick with apprehension. She wasn't worldly, but it wasn't hard to see what kind of place Madame Fleur kept. She knew why women would stay there and what men would pay them to do. What she didn't see was how any man could have brought his wife there, even if he'd thought it was a good place to hide. It was the only reason she could think of for such vile behavior, and it didn't satisfy her or make her any easier.

The world was a strange and terrible place, and she was alone in the dark shadows as night and mizzling rain began to fall over the Quarter. The lights showed in the houses. The street lamps were lighted. Black jazzmen carrying their instruments passed her on their way to their night's work. No one noticed her. Once more she was invisible.

She heard shouts of raucous laughter from the end of the street, as a band of sailors went past on the prowl for a good time. She stood shivering in the shadows, waiting for an hour, then two, until at last she'd lost all track of time. Finally she saw the woman Reba come out of Madame Fleur's gate and walk in her direction. As the woman came even with her, Cima drew her into the shadows beside her.

"Well?" the woman demanded, as if it were she, not Cima, who had been kept waiting. "Do you have the money?"

"Tell me where my Snow is, tell me."

The woman shook her head. "I know enough not to tell what I knows until I see the money."

Cima had the money in her hand, ready. She held it out just beyond the woman's reach. Greedy for the prize, the woman began to speak quickly, one word running into another. "In the first place, I can tell you this girl you lookin' for—she ain't no Mrs. Bell."

"How do you know that?"

" 'Cause I know Cecil Bell, and he already got hisself a wife."

"But he called her Mrs. Bell. He said he married her."

"You can call a pig a horse, but that don't make it so. You payin' me to tell you what I know! If you don't want to believe me, then that's your lookout."

"Go on."

"He brought this Snow to Madame Fleur's. He say he wanted to lie low till her rich pappy sent money for her. He say they ought to keep out of sight 'cause certain people might be lookin' for him. Which knowin' Cecil, they mos' usually was."

"He was keeping her against her will?" Cima asked.

The woman laughed. "Don' you believe that. She loved that

man. Doted on him. They stayed here eatin' and drinkin', and Mistah"—she exaggerated the word *Mister*—"*Mistah* Bell doin' whatever it pleased him without his sweet wife even knowin' what was goin' on. Until one day Madame Fleur, she got tired of carryin' him. Madame, she had a talk with him and tol' him she don' think this Snow has no rich daddy who is goin' to send money or come lookin' for his little girl. An' she tol' Mistah Bell he'd pay up or else."

"And did he pay up?" Cima's mouth was dry. The woman came closer. Cima could feel her breath on her cheek.

"What he goin' to pay with? That Cecil, he skip. He gone, an' he left his wife or whatever you call her to settle his account."

"But how could she, if she had no money?"

The woman stared, round-eyed. "You dumb, or you jes' pretend to be? Madame Fleur, she say this Snow can work for the money and she take what she owe her out of her wages."

"What work? What was Snow to do?"

"You want it spelt out for you? She whorin', but she no good at it."

"It's a lie." Cima choked out the words.

"Madame, she tried everything to get that girl to act sweet. She got her drunk, she gave her powders, but that girl, she won't do nothin'."

"What powders?" Cima heard the words as if they had come from someone else. She wanted to know everything, and at the same time she wished she were deaf.

"Powders you put in girls' drinks, makes them feel so good they don't mind what they do or when or where."

"Oh God."

The woman cackled. "God, he too busy elsewhere to care what's goin' on in the Quarter. Now I tol' you what you want to know, I want my money." She reached for it, but Cima still held it from her grasp.

"First you tell me where she is."

"She gone."

"You said you knew where she was. You're a cheat and a liar."

"Who you calling names?" The woman was indignant. "I ain't finished. She gone 'cause Madame Fleur got tired of her lyin' there doin' nothin' for the gentlemen, so she sold her into Storyville. She there now. See, I tol' you I know where she is. She there in Show Street."

"I don't believe you." Even as she spoke, Cima knew it was true.

"Suit yourself."

"How do you know it's the same girl?"

"Only one girl call herself princess. It's the same girl all right. You go see for yourself." She reached out for the money.

"Where is Storyville?"

"You in Storyville now."

"How do I get to Show Street?"

"Show Street," the woman laughed. "Show Street is straight on. You can find it quick enough. All you have to do is follow the sailors. They all know Show Street."

The bargain had been made and kept. Cima put the money in the woman's hand. She wanted to be rid of her, to be alone. She didn't want to show her feelings before a stranger. The woman counted the money, licking her thumb against her tongue before she turned the notes. Then she backed away. "Remember, all you have to do is follow the sailors." She laughed again; the laughter echoed down the cobbled street until she had disappeared in the dark.

CIMA had made a long, hard journey to find Snow. She'd prayed and lighted a candle to Saint Anthony, but now that she was near her destination, she found it was not what she wished for or wanted.

As the woman had promised, she didn't have to look for a street sign. All she had to do was follow a gang of sailors. They were unsteady, weaving back and forth, holding on to each other for balance. Like a band of apes, they led her to the narrow, mean place that was Show Street. It was an alley more than a street, narrower even than Pirate Alley. It was a place of small houses with brightly lighted windows. In each sat a girl displayed like merchandise.

At each door Cima saw a vendor there to dicker for the highest price for the girl's services. When a sum was agreed on, the customer entered. The blind was drawn and, when the time paid for was spent, the business began all over again. Each girl in this competitive market advertised a different specialty. Everything from French Lessons to Strict Governess was offered, something for every taste and palate. It was halfway down Show Street that Cima found Snow.

She was sitting upright in the center of a window, staring straight ahead. Her face was painted with streaks of red and white and black. On her head was a tawdry Indian headdress, something a child might use in a play. The bedraggled feathers had been dipped in different garish colors. Her costume for this charade was a mockery of an Indian maiden's ceremonial gown. The scraps of cloth were decorated with beads of every description. Pasted to the window was an ill-lettered sign that read, "SEE THE INDIAN PRINCESS, SHARE HER ANCIENT SECRETS IN A PAGAN LOVE RITUAL."

Cima suddenly felt dizzy, as if she were about to fall. There was a pain in her chest, and for a moment her eyes wouldn't focus properly. She wished for the earth to open and swallow her. Until this instant, she hadn't truly expected to find Snow in such a place. The idea was unthinkable. She felt dead, but knew she was alive, for she had never experienced such pain.

She sat upon the curb and tried to breathe. She couldn't run; there was no hiding place. She couldn't stay, she couldn't bear it. Yet somewhere in between the waves of horror was the knowledge that she must get Snow away. She must make a plan that couldn't fail.

To call the police would be useless. If they weren't blind, they already knew what was happening here and had condoned it for a price. Besides, this rescue must be done without calling attention to Snow. There must be no notoriety. The best plan would be to leave New Orleans without anyone knowing that Snow had come or gone. One more lost girl wouldn't matter here. In a month, no one would remember she had existed. And as for Cima, the secrets of this place, which she had paid so dearly to learn, would go with her to her grave.

In her purse she had the golden key that would set Snow free. She had money. In the world beyond Lochleven, there was nothing that money wouldn't buy.

She rose and walked to the man standing at the entrance to Snow's display. He wore a plaid vest, a bright yellow shirt, the sleeves caught with red garters, and a black derby hat set at a rakish angle. For what he'd done and was doing now to Snow, she would gladly have killed him, but she also had the sense to see that if she hoped to buy Snow out of her bondage, this was a man who would sell.

She stood in front of him. With her voice steady, as if she were doing her morning marketing, she said, "How much?"

He was startled, taken off his guard. "What?"

"How much?"

He looked at her with scorn. "What's that to you?"

She held out money. It was something she had learned to do well in these last few days. It was the one gesture that hadn't failed her. "Nothin' to me," she said, her voice almost inaudible, "but this person I works for is very interested."

He looked down at the amount of money, his eyes large. He wasn't a quick man, but he made a rapid calculation. The sum total made him smile. "Who's this generous person?"

"He's a very big man, very important. If he come hisself, you sure to recognize him."

"I could turn a blind eye," the man laughed. "I've looked the other way before. Believe me, in this business it don't pay to see too much."

Cima cut him short. "This person, he couldn't afford to be seen in this street. You understand." She found she had a talent for lies that she hadn't recognized in herself before. She was full of guile and deceit and glad of it, for now she needed all her wits.

"I want you should let the girl come with me."

The man scowled and shook his head. "I can't do that. The girl can't leave here."

"I kin make it worth your while." She began counting out money into his outstretched hand. She counted on and on. She counted until she thought it was more than enough and hesitated, but he didn't take the bait.

"I can't," he whined, his face perspiring. "I'll get into trouble—bad trouble."

Cima now had less money in her hand than he had in his, but she felt the balance of the scale begin to tip in her favor. "No one would know," she said softly. "You goes to get a drink, you stays away an hour, two. What you don't see you don't have to know. You make up a story to tell. Say there was a fight and that the girl was stole." Once she began invention, it seemed easy to tell a plausible tale. "That sort of thing happens? A fight, a girl stole away—who kin blame you if she was taken?"

He shook his head slowly. She'd given him an idea, one that would make him richer than he was now. He held out his hand. "No one, I guess."

Cima began to count again. And the thought came to her, sharp and clear, that she could buy back Snow, but not the time Snow had spent here in this hell. Money could buy everything, but the thing Cima wanted most was to have Snow undamaged—to have her home again, whole and untouched. When she had counted out the last of the money, she said to the man, who was counting it once more, "Go on. Get away from here. Now you come into money, you kin go and do whatever you please."

He stared at her and at the money in his hand, then he turned and went in the opposite direction, half running, half walking until he disappeared around the corner.

Cima took a deep breath. She went up the steps into the small, fetid room where Snow sat as motionless as a carved wooden statue. Cima drew the blinds to shut out the world beyond and then bent down by Snow. In an unsteady voice she said, "Snow, it's Cima."

Snow's head turned slowly; her eyes were open, staring straight ahead. The pupils were dark and dilated, and she gave no sign of recognition. She'd been drugged, and for that Cima was oddly grateful. Oblivion for Snow was a blessing.

"Snow baby, it's Cima. I've come to fetch you home." There was no response. She might as well have been talking to a girl who was blind and deaf. "You're comin' with me. We're goin' home."

She took a handkerchief from her purse and began to wipe the paint from Snow's face. Beneath the greasepaint she was pale as death. When her face was clean, Cima removed the headdress and tried to help Snow to her feet. "Stand up, honey. Stand up, baby." Snow was limp as a rag doll. She leaned against Cima; although she was pathetically thin, the dead weight was almost more than Cima could support.

"You can't go home in that outfit," Cima said sternly, speaking as she had when Snow was little. "We got to get you into some decent clothes." She stripped the wretched rags from Snow. She opened her valise and took out a clean shirtwaist and skirt that hung on Snow like a tent, but at least was better than the thing of beads and patches that lay at her feet. "Now, be patient. I'll tie this skirt up high with a belt and then you gonna look fine, jes' fine." She did her best to make Snow look presentable. She couldn't claim that she was in fashion, but at least she would do.

After she put her own coat and hat on Snow, she pulled the shawl around her own shoulders and tied a scarf into a bandana about her head. She surveyed her image and Snow's in a cracked mirror. They looked reasonably like a girl and her mammy. No one would take special notice of them in the street.

"Now, my sweet baby, we goin' home. We goin' to Lochleven, and when we gets there, we ain't ever leaving again, not as long as we lives."

Cima felt Snow stiffen as she tried to guide her gently toward the door. Snow stopped suddenly and wouldn't move. "I can't go home. I can't go back there again."

"Of course you kin, baby. You kin go home. You all right. You with Cima now."

"I'm so tired." Snow began to cry soundlessly, the tears welling from her eyes and flowing down her cheeks. "I'm so tired and dirty."

"You fine," Cima tried to reassure her. "You feel better when you get home."

"I don't have a home. I ran away." A note of panic was in Snow's voice.

"You have a home. You live at Lochleven. You remember Loch-leven?"

Snow shook her head. "Lochleven is gone. It blew away in the wind."

"But it's all built back again just the way it was. Your room is there just like it used to be. You come with me and you'll see."

Still Snow hung back, trying to pull away from Cima. She whispered, as if it were a secret, "I can't go back. Nobody wants me there."

"I do," Cima said fiercely. "I want you." Once more she tried to get Snow out of the hateful room, away from the house before they were stopped.

"No," Snow was sobbing, "you don't want me, nobody does. I'm dirty." She began to wipe at her face, as if the paint were still there.

"I want you, child. I come all this way to get you, didn't I?"

Snow was suddenly very still; she stood, looking for the first time directly at Cima. "I don't know you. I don't know who you are."

It was an arrow in Cima's heart, tipped with poison. "I'm Cima. You know me. I'm your Cima and I come to take you home. We has to get away from this bad place, where the wind don't never seem to blow. This is a sick, bad place, not like home."

Snow began to tremble, shaking as if there had been an earthquake and her whole world had fallen down around her. "Nobody wants me. Not even Papa. I wrote my papa, but he never answered. He doesn't want me anymore." Snow slumped against Cima as if her legs had given way beneath her.

"Get up!" Cima said sharply. She had to get them away from there before that man came back. This was no time to try to comfort Snow. "We're going home. You hear me? All you have to do is walk down the stairs, and then we'll get on a train and go home. Cima's here. I want you and I won't leave you."

"I can never go back."

"Come with Cima and I'll give you a pretty present." Cima was coaxing her as she had when Snow was little, wheedling her into taking one step at a time. Still Snow hung back.

"I can't go. I'm afraid."

"Why?" Cima was losing patience as the time ran out.

"I have to wait until Cecil comes back. He made me promise," Snow whimpered. "He hit me and hit me."

If Cecil Bell had been in that room at that moment, Cima would have killed him. "Cecil ain't coming back. He's gone for good. You'll never see him again."

"I'm so alone." Snow began to cry again, as if she were a child alone in the dark.

"You're not alone. You're with Cima. You may not know me, child, but I'm the only one you got in the wide world, and I'm taking you home. Now hurry."

It was easier for Cima to get Snow all the way back to Lochleven than it was to get her down the stairs. She had to force her into a taxi and hold her while she ordered the driver to take them to the train station. She spoke with absolute authority. Even in this strange world, she'd gotten used to giving orders and to being obeyed.

At the ticket office, it was a simple matter for a black maid traveling with a white mistress to arrange for a double compartment. No one questioned her right to make the reservation or to stay in first class with Snow. But Cima was whipped; she'd used up all her courage. She needed help now to face going home. She sent a telegram to Pride to meet her in Memphis.

At Memphis, Cima looked out of the compartment window, searching the platform for a sign of Pride. She could not leave Snow to go out and look for him. She felt the time passing by. Soon the train would be leaving again. Then, when she had just about given up hope, she saw him. She began to rap on the compartment window to attract his attention.

She stood guardian at the compartment door, waiting for him. "Thank God, oh thank God you come."

"Of course I came. But you didn't say in your telegram why you wanted me."

She put out her hand and he took it. "It's Snow."

"Snow?"

"She's in there. She's sleepin'. You can come in, but if she wakes, she may not know you."

Pride went into the darkened compartment. He saw Snow curled up asleep. There were dark circles underneath her eyes, and she looked thin and very ill. "What's happened to her? Why is she on this train with you? Where have you been?"

Cima's mouth set in a hard line. "I don't want to tell you nothin' you don't have to know. It's best for her and for you. I sent for you because I couldn't take it no more. I had to have someone from home, some kin, who cares for her."

Snow stirred; her eyes opened. She saw Pride and sat up. Pressing back against the berth into the corner like a frightened animal, she began to whimper.

"It's all right, Snow. It's all right," Cima said, "it's your Uncle Pride. He won't hurt you. He's come to take you home."

Snow put her hands over her eyes and began to tremble.

"She doesn't know who I am." Pride was incredulous.

"No, she don't know you from Adam, but she believes me when I say you ain't goin' to hurt her, and that's something to be thankful for."

"She needs a doctor."

"No." Cima was adamant. "No doctor. We goin' home and you goin' to take us there."

Pride tried to get something more from Cima, but she would say nothing that gave him any idea of where they had been or why. Cima had locked what she knew away in her mind. She would not tell him anything, and Snow could not.

At Maitland, Pride hired a car and drove them to Lochleven. It was March, and the roads were slick with a film of ice. As he made his way up the Ridge to the house, he had to drive with care. He had not seen Lochleven since it had been rebuilt. He felt as if time had turned around and brought him back full circle. He was a stranger in his own land. He had not seen the oil fields or the billowing smoke of the refinery that had made a horror of the landscape.

It was late when they arrived at a dark house. Pride had to hammer at the door before Rose Dawn and Annoyi came to let them in. They stared wide-eyed at him and at the change in Snow, until Cima sent them running to fetch this and carry that. Then she ordered them to their rooms and told them to stay there.

"You help me get Snow upstairs," Cima said to Pride, "and then leave us be while I gets her into her own bed."

Pride did as he was told and then wandered back down the corridor, feeling like an intruder. The house seemed empty, with no sign of Reanna or Taffy or Lovell. He looked through the open door of the cupola room. In the half-light his eyes and heart played him tricks, and he thought he saw Miss Jane there in the window, staring out, waiting for Breathholder to call to her.

He went downstairs into the hall and stood before the restored portrait of his father. He touched the cold silver of the Beauvaise cup, and as he did he was caught up in a mindstorm of memories so vivid that when the outside door opened, he almost thought it was Taffy and Andrew coming in from the range. Then he heard Reanna's voice.

"Who are you? What are you doing here? What do you want in this house?"

Pride turned and she gasped.

"Pride?" Her first impulse was to go into his arms.

"Yes." His first thought was to hold her. It would always be the same for each of them. Nothing could change or diminish their longing for each other.

"Why are you here?"

"I came back with Cima and Snow. Cima sent for me."

"Snow's back?" Reanna looked relieved. "I was so worried. Where are they?"

"Snow and Cima are upstairs."

THEY went up together to Snow's room. Snow was sitting in bed in a ruffled nightdress, looking like a child's doll, staring sightless into an endless void. Cima was patiently brushing Snow's hair.

"She's all right," Cima said when she saw Reanna. "She's all right now. I goin' to look after her. I goin' to take care of my Snow. She won't be no trouble. She won't run off no more." She stopped, her lips working painfully as if she had something sharp caught in her throat.

(478)

"What about her husband?" Reanna asked.

"There ain't no husband. Ask me no questions, I tells no lies." Cima was close to tears.

"All right, Cima," Reanna said, "I won't ask any questions, I promise, but one—is there anything I can do? Just tell me that."

"No." Cima shook her head. "You go on away, both of you. Go away and leave us be. I thanks you both, but there's nothin' more you can do now."

They went back down the corridor, aware of how close each was to the other. As they accidentally touched, Reanna shied away as if burned. "Have you had any supper?" she asked abruptly. "Can I get you something to eat?" She was behaving like a polite hostess with an unexpected guest.

"No, thank you."

"It's late. If you are staying the night, I'll have a room made up for you."

"I'll stay, but I must leave in the morning. I'm going away. I had already made my plans when Cima's telegram arrived."

She stopped and looked at him. "Where are you going?"

"France."

"We aren't at war."

"We will be in a month."

"And you rushed to enlist?"

"Yes."

"And you're going to fight?"

He shook his head. "I'm too old for heroics. They don't need me for a soldier. They've made me a captain, and I've been assigned as counsel from the Judge Advocate's department to a group of American businessmen who want to make sure their property and the loans they've made to the French and British will be protected if we go in as allies."

"How long will you be gone?"

"I don't know. No one knows how long the war will last. The British and the French have been in it since 1914, and now they're stalemated in the trenches. We are supposed to come in and save the day, but we're unprepared." He stopped, looking around him, suddenly aware that they were standing in the shadows of the hall where they had first met so long ago. He felt the memories begin to rush again and overpower him. He felt suffocated. "I can't stay here in this house. There are too many ghosts, too many memories. Get your coat and let's go outside."

They walked onto the verandah. A gust of sharp March wind shook the leafless catalpa tree. There was a little, silver moon half hidden by high-flying clouds. He drew the collar of her coat up around her neck. Then, with his arm around her, her head on his shoulder, they began to walk toward the old cabin.

From somewhere in the woods beyond, there came the cry of an owl and the sound of night creatures scurrying in the underbrush. They stood in front of the cabin, holding each other.

He said, "I never thought I would be here again with you. I want to stay. I want to be with you." He waited, thinking she would never answer.

"We'll go in and build a fire."

In the old stone fireplace the kindling crackled and burst into bright flame. He watched it glow as it began to warm them.

"Everything is the same as it was before," he said.

"Nothing is the same," she answered.

"We have not changed, and you know it." He held out his arms to her.

The first time they made love, it was with the rough passion of those long starved of love. The second time, it was a feast to be savored and treasured for long years to come.

In the morning, the fire had died down. There was no time to build another and no time left for them. Reanna walked Pride to the car.

"I'll tell Taffy you are sorry you missed him."

"And Lovell."

She looked away and then back at him. "Lovell is not here."

"Where is he?"

"At school at Harringtons in Massachusetts."

"He's eleven. That's young to be away."

Her chin went up in the old gesture of defiance. "I sent him away to keep him safe from Andrew. I will never let Andrew take him. I will never give him custody of Lovell or my oil."

"It must be hard to have Lovell so far away."

"It is worth anything to keep him safe."

He looked at her until he could look no longer. "Will you write to me?"

(480)

"Yes, I will write, but I can't say goodbye." She turned to walk away. He called her back once more.

"Take care of yourself, Reanna, and of Snow and this house."

Then he was gone. She watched him go, as women everywhere in America would soon watch men going to war, and she waited to hear from him so that she would know he was safe.

PRIDE's first letter was postmarked New York.

Dear Reanna,

Confusion has been the watchword of this mission so far. They have been wrangling over our points of procedure, but nothing is decided. I believe some of the men are only along to get to France and into top places before war is declared.

Mr. Desmond of the Ohio Cable Company, who is the nominal head of the mission, took me aside the other day and said that he had had it on the best authority that it would be wise to wait until he got to London to have his uniforms made, because the British had the best tailors. I said he must do what he thought best, and I took the opportunity to ask him just what he felt my main contribution to this mission was going to be. He said, "You speak French." I was too stunned to laugh. It's true I speak a little French, but it is French with a Chickasaw accent. Then he said, "Of course, you'll be expected to write all our reports."

While the mission met and argued, I went up to Boston to meet with some bankers who have outstanding loans abroad. I took a half day and went to Harringtons to see Lovell. I thought it would be a shame to be so near and not see him. The school authorities met my request with some suspicion. I am writing you this because it is bound to get back to you that I was there. You can rest easy knowing that they are looking after Lovell very well indeed.

They said they could not let me talk to him because it was class time. The class turned out to be a game of lacrosse. I was allowed to watch in the company of one of the staff. It was strange to see Indian stickball played so far from home. Lovell is a good player and a fine-looking boy. I was glad I saw him. I can see why he means so much to you. You know what you mean to me.

I send my love to you all. I will write from London. And I will try to get in touch with Frampton while I am there.

We are sailing tomorrow on the ——————. We had been sworn to secrecy about the ship and the date. We were reminded of the dangers of U-boats and the sinking of the Lusitania; then there was an article in one of the New York newspapers: "American

Businessmen Brave the Perils of the Sea to Protect Our Interests Abroad." So much for security and censorship.

I doubt I will take to the sea. I am too much of a landsman.

Love,
Pride

Dear Reanna,

In London you see evidence of the war everywhere. There are shortages, balloons to deter the zeppelins and the grey, strained faces of people who have been fighting a long, very hard war. So many men in uniform.

Our mission is at the Savoy. No shortages there. We hold meetings with delegations and with the American ambassador. Everyone asks us what is happening at home, now that we are in the war.

We were at sea when the news came through on a marconigram. We drank a toast to America and to President Wilson, who had won the election because he had kept us out of the war and now must serve as the President who led us into it. And we drank to our allies.

I tried to get in touch with Frampton, only to learn that he is in France. His nephew, Lord Carding, who had been invalided home on leave, was very kind. He says he feels he knows us all, because Frampton has spoken of us so often.

Lord Carding took me to the theater, to see George Robey in *Zig Zag*, and to supper at his club. He was badly hurt—walks with a cane and is in pain—but he does not complain. He says he is anxious to get back to his men. Over brandy, he did say he hopes that the Americans will place their army under British command, because the British have had the experience of this war that the Americans lack.

I was saluted for the first time yesterday. I felt like a fraud, as if suddenly I might be arrested for impersonating an officer.

Mr. Desmond and most of our mission are now in uniform. There is a lot of discussion about the proper way to wear the Sam Browne belt and who will be our commanding general. Pershing is favored to get the post, although he is not everyone's first choice.

I was right to think I would not take to the sea. The sea didn't care much for me, either. Now a channel crossing lies ahead, but at least it will be short.

My love now and always to you all.

Pride

Dear Reanna,

Paris. We are now at the Crillon. A war *de luxe*. The feeling in Paris is much more subdued than in London. There are no young men. They are all at the front. There are acute shortages, and you see in their faces what it is to be French and to have the war being fought on their soil.

We met with American businessmen and the American ambassador. No one yet seems to have a clear picture of what will happen next. As soon as the ambassador gets one set of orders from Washington, they are countermanded by another, but Colonel House seems always to have the last word. The commanding general is to be Pershing. That is official.

The French I talk to are as anxious for the Americans to put themselves under French command as the British were eager for us to fight under their orders. So far there are no American troops for anyone to command.

Tomorrow the mission is going to a sector near Châlons, where we are to see a factory financed with American money.

We get around in two cars, a Mercedes and a Packard. Our drivers are Americans. The Mercedes was captured from the Germans, and I don't know where the Packard came from. Both cars break down on the road. The drivers get out to tinker and we sit and listen to Mr. Desmond of Ohio pontificate about our American role as the savior of Europe.

Love,
Pride

Dear Reanna,

As we got closer to the western lines, I was appalled by the destruction. Because the Germans knew there would be a spring offensive and that the British and French would attack from two sides, they destroyed the sector in between before they withdrew. Everything is laid to waste. The land is bare—no trees, no farms, no bridges, nothing but debris, abandoned tanks and, by the road, dead horses and mules.

We were all sobered by the sight. No one is speaking now of playing savior to this kind of a debacle. The motto of Verdun was They Shall Not Pass. It is hard to imagine who would want or dare to come this way again.

The French are still here. All the way, we saw men returning from the French sector. They looked exhausted. The wounded are a grievous sight. The men were too exhausted to wave or pay us any notice.

When we reached the factory, we found it had been destroyed, nothing left but a pile of rubble. We have had our first example of the war and of the lack of communication. We'd been told the factory was standing.

(483)

We dined that evening at a nearby château. There have been wars in this part of France for generations, but the château still stands. It should be a sign of hope. I excused myself early from the toasts and the speeches and went into Châlons for the night. I stayed at a hotel and spoke with people in the town. The one thing everyone asks is, When are the Americans coming? I have no answer.

Pershing arrived today, June 13th. There were crowds everywhere. The police have taken every precaution to be sure he is well guarded. The air force was on patrol against a German raid. I suppose his arrival could have been kept a secret, but morale has been given a great boost. The war-worn have a new hero to look up to, and the Germans have been put on notice that there will be a reckoning.

The Gare du Nord was decked out in flags, and there was a great reception. Everyone who could manage it was there. I saw him at a distance. They say he is cold and detached. He may be, but if I had lost a wife and three of my children, I would maintain as thick a hide and as hard a surface as I could to keep out the sorrow. It is not a bad thing to have a man who is detached at the head of this chaos.

I love you all. I love you.

Pride

Dear Pride,

Your first letter came and then two at once. I am glad you saw Lovell. Yes, he is fine. Thank you for telling me that he was being well looked after. I am always afraid that he may be abducted. That's my fear, that Andrew will take him.

Taffy was sorry to have missed seeing you. He comes in every day to see how Snow is. He just stands there at her door, and then he bolts down to the bunkhouse and has a drink or more. I can't blame him for feeling at loose ends. His cowboy pals had gone off even before the war, and I know he's missing them and Lovell.

We all miss you.

Cima is so strong; she's like a rock. She just goes on, day to day.

Snow has fewer bad dreams than when she first came home, but it will be a long time before she is right again.

Here, when the news came that we were in the war, there was a storm of patriotic fervor. There were flags and speeches, and people began to hoard sugar and collect bits of rubbish that they said would be useful if it was a long war. Everyone is enthusiastic about this war, even those who are going off to fight. Enlistments are up. Most of the boys from here are being sent to Camp Bowie. Two of our doctors are gone, and Doc Hersey is delivering babies again.

Both Doc and Jack are heading the local committee to sell war bonds. Every time I see anyone from town, the first word I hear is *committee*. Amoretta has organized a canteen to serve coffee and doughnuts to the boys at the station, and there is a committee to knit and one to make up parcels for the boys at camp.

Lillian makes talks to the women's clubs about why skirts should be raised to save cloth for uniforms and why we must give up high-buttoned shoes for low ones to save leather. And she has organized a unit to train nurses for the Red Cross.

My war work is to get oil and gasoline to the military. So far no one has called me a profiteer. Andrew has not been so lucky. There was an article in an Oklahoma City paper saying he had set exorbitant prices for his war contracts. Andrew will do well from this war, but then so shall I. But only if you are safe.

You said your mission was not going to be in any danger, but I cannot think that near the front is the safest place in the world to be.

I think of you every day. We all think of you. Be well. Be safe.

Love,
Reanna

Dear Reanna,

What I do puts me in no real danger. I only write reports to Washington. I might as well be dropping them in the sea in a bottle. I send the reports but I never get a reply, at least not to any of my requests or questions.

I have been assigned to G2. I am to gather information. Now that the weather is improved and summer is here, all along the way to the French and British fronts the French countryside is green and rich. It is so lovely. My driver and I stopped yesterday at a little village with a small, very old church. They were holding a funeral service for an aviator. We thought it polite to pay our respects. As we knelt down during the mass, we could hear the distant sound of the artillery.

It is hard to grasp that, not many kilometers away, there are men in trenches. Now that I have seen the trenches, I know I would rather go facedown into a latrine than spend a winter or a summer in one of them. I don't wonder there is a lack of morale. What I wonder is how the men live day-to-day and still manage to fight a war.

The men coming back from the frontline trenches have wounds so shattering they cannot be mended. Even if they could, infection has already set in from the filth of that mud and dirt. They are doomed, done for, long before they get to the hospital.

My driver is a keen young mechanic. After we left the village, he stopped the car to let the wounded pass. He put his head down on the steering wheel and wept. He said later that, despite the funeral we attended for the aviator, he will try to get himself posted into the flying corps. The sky is so clean.

If anyone at home asks what kind of war this is, in which an army cannot advance twenty miles in months, then tell them to come and try to go forward faster themselves. They are welcome to my share of it.

July, and our troops have landed. They are encamped at Saint-Nazaire. They are not prepared for what they will have to face. Many of those boys have never fired a gun.

And as we drove on, we saw shelling ahead and an airplane over the area, dropping down destruction. The sky can also be deadly. As we hurried ahead to see if we could be of any use, we were passed on the road by an ambulance unit that nearly ran us into the ditch.

The shelling was of a Red Cross hospital, clearly marked. The sight of the wounded being so hard used by the Germans was awful. Men on stretchers being moved, men screaming, the dead left where they were. I went toward an orderly to ask what we could do when I heard a voice boom out behind me, "You Yanks—come three years too late and then you stand about doing nothing!"

The orderly went red with embarrassment and then blanched to see two grown men hugging each other like bears. It was Simon Frampton. He had passed us on the road with his ambulance unit. I helped him unload supplies and move men to a safer location, if such a place existed. Much later, when he had the situation in hand, we sat in his tent drinking brandy and anything else that came to hand. He asked for you all at home, but especially for you. He said you had sent him the ambulance unit. It is put to good use.

I cannot remember ever having drunk so much. Sometime before first light, we stood holding each other up, waiting for the sun. Simon said something I know he would not have said if he had been sober. He said that what he was most afraid of was not being killed but being wounded. I knew what he meant; there is a kind of horror in this war far worse than death.

By the time I had left him, new supplies were streaming in—a truckload of hip baths, when what they had ordered was stretchers and more morphine.

He sends his love to you and everyone at Lochleven, and so do I. I'll try to see him again, at least by Christmas.

Love,
Pride

Dear Pride,

When you see Frampton again, please give him all our best. Particularly mine. I think now is a time when everyone says things that they would not have said if it had not been for the war.

I was at a rally to sell war bonds. I was with Amoretta, and I said that I was glad that Lovell was too young to fight. Amoretta said that if only she had a son, she would even be willing to send him to war. Amoretta had never mentioned being childless before. I don't know if she would have said anything about it even then, if we had not just seen Lillian. Lillian and Jack are going to have a baby at last, a war baby. Lillian is very serene about it, but Jack is a perfect fool.

After a lot of bonds were sold, we had a sing-along. We sang "Over There" and "There's a Long, Long Trail A-Winding" and "It's a Long Way to Tipperary" and "Pack Up Your Troubles in Your Old Kit Bag." I don't want ever to hear any of those songs again. And then we sang "Auld Lang Syne" and all went home thinking of old acquaintances and those gone far away.

Cima has Snow busy, which is good for her—good for both of them. They are rolling bandages. There is a little circle of country women that meet at Lochleven. It may do good and it can do no harm. Oh, my dear, my dear. The winter is coming. Will you be warm enough, and where will you be at Christmas?

Love,
Reanna

Dear Pride,

I've had no letters from you, but then, I have been away. I am in Washington. It is cold and inconvenient, and everything that goes wrong in the shops, in the hotel, in the streets—every rudeness is blamed on the war.

I'm here because of the war. I can't fill my contracts if I can't get tank cars, and I can't get tank cars without clearance. I can't find the proper authority for that clearance without coming up here and arguing with the damn bureaucrats and fighting miles of red tape. No wonder they don't answer our letters or read your reports. They cannot read or write. Oh, what's the use of complaining!

I am going to Virginia and the farm for Christmas. I'll see Lovell

(487)

there and stay for his birthday, as I've done every year since he went away to school.

We have sent you a big box from Lochleven of what we hope are useful presents. Some for Frampton, too. And a Christmas cake in a separate parcel. I hope they all arrive on time and that you have a merry Christmas and a happy New Year.

What I really mean is that I wish you were home.

Love,
Reanna

Dear Pride,

We had a very nice, quiet Christmas.

My brother Patrick is married and was home on leave. My brother Thomas is on his way overseas. My father is running the farm with catch-as-catch-can help. My mother is complaining, but there is nothing unusual in that.

We went to church and sang carols. There were a lot of men in uniform and some women in mourning. My heart this Christmas was not in Virginia but somewhere in France.

Lovell at nearly twelve is between child and young man.

Where has all the time gone?

It is the season to be jolly and the season to be sad. When a telegram came for me from Taffy and Snow and Cima just to wish us a merry Christmas, I saw my mother's face. She thought it was news of Thomas. Oh dear, oh dear, I was sorry I had ever thought a mean or hard thought about her. We just sat and held hands by the fire.

Where were you?

Love,
Reanna

Dear Reanna,

The box arrived in good time for Christmas, but not the cake. Frampton and I managed to have the day together at a hospital near ——————. The shelling was less—a present from the Germans—and Frampton and I gave a party for the wards. Frampton had somehow gotten Christmas "crackers," something very dear to the English—party favors, we'd call them at home. They snapped open and were filled with whistles and paper hats. Then Frampton turned out the lights and came in with a big platter of raisins doused with brandy and set on fire. Snapdragons, he said they were. We sang carols here too.

That day I saw my first case of burns from mustard gas and my first case of shell shock. What a world, what a war.

After we had put the ward to bed, Frampton and I went out and sat in the snow and drank. He said what can one expect of a war in which all the generals' names sound like battles and the battles like generals. We began to expound on the theme—the offensive of Joffre, the siege of Foch, the battle of Haig. And then we laughed, though nothing was funny, at General Verdun and Field Marshal Metz. We roared so at our wit that by the time we got to Knobelsdorf, we couldn't decide whether he was a battle or a terrible condition like the clap.

It was so cold, so still; then from somewhere in the German lines there came the chatter of a machine gun, just one gun, like boys trying out a Christmas toy.

Frampton said it was not a very Christian thing to do—to shoot at people on Christmas. I agreed. He said it was a pity we were too old to fight, or we would show them all a thing or two. I agreed.

And then, before I could stop him, he had gone over the wire, crashing across the empty space of no-man's-land toward the machine gun. I felt I had to go with him because he was my friend.

We took the machine gun and the gunners as our prisoners. Frampton said it was the element of surprise that made the thing a success. That was only partly true. We had no guns. I just picked up the nearest rock, held it in my hand and told the Germans it was a grenade. Frampton ordered them to stand with their hands on their heads. It never occurred to the Germans to disobey the order of a superior officer. So up they got, and we marched them back to our lines.

Of course, if we had been sober, we never would have done it, at least I wouldn't have.

The French have decorated us, the British have reprimanded us and the Americans deny that anything ever happened.

It is still very cold, and I love you very, very much.

Pride

Dear Reanna,

March. A year since I saw you. Can that be? Frampton and I saw each other once after Christmas. I have not seen him since the British Fifth Army was destroyed. But I hear he is fine.

Frampton was right, you know. What can one say of a war in which the battles sound like generals and the generals sound like battles? We came into the shooting war in October, and I can't yet see quite how we will get out of it.

I saw American soldiers without warm uniforms or proper shoes. Their feet left a trail of blood in the snow.

I write reports. It is not enough.

Love,
Pride

* * *

AND for the rest of the war, Pride wrote of battles—Château-Thierry, Belleau Wood, Soissons. He wrote of Saint-Mihiel and the Argonne, and of it being October and still no cake had arrived.

And Reanna wrote him of the telegram that had come about her brother Thomas, and of the weather, and of her mother bearing up and of Patrick home out of the fighting early because of the flu which had added to casualty lists at home.

And he wrote her of the flu in the trenches. Then in November, the long war, the war to save the world, was ended; there was an armistice. He wrote how he and Frampton drove to Paris together to see the dancing in the streets and hear the singing.

Dear Reanna,

Well, it's over and done with, all but picking up the pieces. I go to Germany soon to see after the condition of our prisoners of war and to help them get home.

I won't be coming back for a few months. The tidying up and the treaties will take awhile. There will be talk and more talk about boundaries and reparations. Someone will be needed to write a report that will be filed and never read.

When I come home again, I want to come to you. This war has changed so much, I want you to tell me it has changed things for us. I want you to consider a divorce. After all this time, Andrew will let you go. Please say you will think about it.

Love,
Pride

Dear Pride,

The world may have changed, but nothing has changed for us. Lovell is not of age. Andrew could still sue for custody of Lovell if I tried to divorce him to marry you.

I think you know what I am going to say. It is that I think we should not write anymore. I know we cannot see each other when you come home. If we kept teasing, tantalizing each other, holding out false hopes and dreams, it would be wrong. A clean break is best.

My love always,
Reanna

Dear Reanna,

I would ask again and again, but I know you won't change your mind. I have been so grateful to hear from you, to have seen you, even once. For all the bad things in the war, it gave us a little chance to be close again.

Love,
Pride

He did not write to her again. In December, a year after she had sent the cake, it was returned to Lochleven, marked Incorrect Address.

It was hard as granite.

A YEAR after Pride had looked for the Christmas cake, he was in England with Frampton.

"What will you do now?" Frampton asked him.

"When I've finished writing my reports?"

"Yes."

"I'll go back to practice law."

"And Reanna?"

"I can't say. I know we won't see each other. We only wrote because of the war."

"What will we do now, when we can't blame everything on the war?" Frampton asked. Pride had no answer.

That night Pride put all Reanna's letters on the fire. Reanna, who had the most at stake if Andrew read the letters from Pride, tied them in a blue ribbon and put them in the drawer of her desk at Lochleven. She wrote to Lovell to say that she hoped he was happy and doing well at school.

WHEN America came into the war, Lovell had been eleven. Like all schoolboys, he'd cursed the Kaiser and said his prayers in chapel for the brave soldiers at the front. He'd traced the River Marne on his schoolroom map and learned to pronounce the names of strange, faraway places like Ypres, the Argonne, the Somme and Château-Thierry. And all the while he'd waged a private war with Reanna, fighting to come home.

It had been a losing battle. She had adamantly refused to consider it. She'd ordered him to spend his short vacations with one of his teachers and the longer holidays in Virginia with her family. He liked his grandparents and his Virginia uncles and cousins, but he'd felt like a prisoner of war being shifted from camp to camp.

The farm was a lovely place, all rolling hills and green forests. When Reanna had gotten her oil money, she'd bought back the farm to its original boundaries. She'd encouraged her mother to refurnish the house as it had been in its glory. Now that his grandparents were old, his uncles oversaw the running of the place, though Reanna said her father had never been a man to farm or keep accounts.

On her annual visits, when Lovell was there, she'd rarely stayed more than a few days, even at Christmas or birthdays. She'd blamed that first on work and then on the war, but Lovell had always had the notion that he was not as interesting to her as her oil wells.

Even when she wrote to him, there was little news of home or of Taffy, Cima or Snow. Her letters might as well have been censored. The only way he could endure his fierce longing to be at Lochleven was to live in his dreams.

Lovell had never seen the high grass or the big cattle drives— they were only stories told by Taffy and his saddle buddies—but those days were more real to him than his own hand. In his dreams, he rode to the crest of the Beauvaise Ridge and stood tall in his stirrups as he looked over paradise. In his dreams, the oil wells had miraculously vanished; the high bluestem grass rippled in the wind, revealing red cattle grazing in the golden pasture; and high above in the cloudless, azure sky, a single red-tailed hawk wheeled and glided toward the far horizon. He could feel the wind in his face, the sun warm on his back, but as he tried to ride on, he was suddenly powerless to move. Crying out in protest, he awoke in a frigid New England dormitory, felt the shock of cold linoleum against his bare feet and saw the rows of white cots filled with sleeping boys.

He'd said nothing to his schoolmates about Andrew. For Lovell, it was as if Andrew didn't exist. He sensed, as he always had, that there was some mystery surrounding Andrew. There were so many things that he didn't understand, so many questions that had always gone unanswered. He wasn't an orphan, but he felt like a fatherless child.

He had only seen Andrew once that he could remember, at Father Soule's funeral, and then Reanna had kept them apart, as if she were afraid for them to meet. He remembered his father's eyes, staring at him. His father's touch, like a curse, not a benediction. Andrew had never come to Lochleven. When Lovell had asked Reanna why, she had said that they had quarreled over oil. Lovell still believed that he was the reason Andrew had abandoned them.

When he had asked Snow, she had said that it was all because of her, because Andrew wanted to take her away with him and Reanna wouldn't let him. As a child, Lovell had loved Snow. He'd followed her like a puppy. No matter how she teased him, he believed every tale she told him. But this piece of news had bewildered him. "Doesn't Andrew want me, too?"

Snow had laughed at him. "Why would he want you? You're only a baby."

Still, he'd followed her, holding on like a brier. "What about Uncle Pride? Why doesn't he ever come to Lochleven?"

Snow had looked at him with scorn. "Pride Beauvaise isn't your uncle, he's mine!"

Lovell didn't understand. The truth was a dark mystery which he must bring to light and solve. When he got home again, he'd be old enough to ask questions and demand answers. Of one thing he felt certain—whatever the riddle or the answer, he, not Snow, was at the center of it. Till then, he must bide in the alien corn and live in his dreams.

As the months and years went by, he came to feel that if he'd never left Lochleven—that golden, magical place—he would never had had the measles or colds in winter. If he'd stayed at home, he would have had no growing pains or trouble with geometry and Latin. It seemed that school, like the war, would never end.

He knew that when the glorious day came, he'd leave school and the East without a backward glance. He was popular enough, but he'd made few friends that he'd miss. He was a quick, bright student, but he'd learned nothing that he wouldn't be happy to forget. In 1923, at seventeen, he earned his diploma but no prizes. They gave none at his school for carving in wood or for learning to endure with patience.

AND there was no way Reanna could keep him from returning home. To his chagrin he discovered that he was the only passenger on a private train deadheading from Boston to a siding near Maitland. It belonged to an oilman friend of Reanna's. It embarrassed him that she would have asked such favored treatment for him. He was uncomfortable being waited on hand and foot like some Balkan prince returning from exile. Yet he would gladly have endured any indignity to be home again.

As he looked out of the compartment window, watching the passing landscape, he felt like a lover traveling to meet his sweetheart. His mouth was dry, his palms moist and his heart beat faster. When the train crossed the Arkansas River and came into the State of Oklahoma, he imagined he could hear the earth singing beneath the rails. He swore to himself that, no matter what, he'd never go East again as long as he lived.

Taffy was there to meet him, walking up and down beside the track like an expectant father. When he saw Lovell, his wrinkled, weathered face broke into a big grin. He came running toward

Lovell on his bowed cowboy legs, grabbed at him and held him close, pounding on him as if he were a sack of feed. "Well, look at you, boy. You plumb growed up. Six feet and skinny as a post. We'll have to put some meat on them bones. How in the Sam Hill are you?" He stood back and stared at Lovell with pure joy.

Lovell looked up and down the siding platform. "Where's Reanna?" Lovell had always called his mother by her first name, through no lack of respect. Her name was like a title by which the whole world knew her.

"Ah, well . . .". Taffy shifted uneasily from one foot to the other. "She's in the City—up at the capital." He ducked his head down to his chest. "The governor sent for her. She had to go—it was real important—you understand."

"Of course," Lovell said stiffly. "I understand."

"Now don't get all crossways, boy. Your ma didn't know exactly when you was coming in. Private trains don't have no set schedules."

"You're here to meet me." Lovell applied logic to the facts.

Taffy looked sheepish and grinned. "I've been here the best part of a week."

Lovell grinned back. "Camping out at the siding?"

"Close enough. Come on, let's get you home. They've been waiting for you at Lochleven like you was the second coming."

Lovell's grin faded and his face darkened. "I'm not sure Reanna wanted me to come home."

Taffy was pained by the suggestion. "You're wrong there, dead wrong. Reanna's missed you most of all." He caught Lovell by the arm and headed him across the tracks toward a waiting limousine.

At the sight of the impressive car, Lovell stopped short. "What's that?"

"That's what they call a Rolls-Royce," Taffy said proudly.

Lovell whistled. "You travel in style these days."

"Not me. It's your ma's."

"Where did she get it?"

"Frampton sent it—a kind of return present. Your ma outfitted an ambulance unit for him when the war first broke out."

"How did Frampton get it here?"

"The Royal Navy brought it to Galveston, if you please, and then it come overland by train. It's even got a driver with it. Davies is his name. He says he speaks English, but I can't understand a word of it. Whatever he's jabberin', as long as he keeps the Rolls-Royce going and drives the dang thing, it saves wear and tear on your ma's nerves."

"How's Frampton?"

"Getting rich, I hear. Not as rich as your ma, but rich. He's in with a British oil crowd. They don't dig for it over there. They just control wherever it's dug in the rest of the world."

"I'm glad Frampton's rich—but a liveried chauffeur!" Lovell shook his head. "That must cause talk."

"Around here, yes. Up in the City or Tulsey, they're used to putting on the dog. Rich oilmen every which way you look. Lots of changes these days."

"What kind of changes?"

Taffy hawked and spit. "You'll see soon enough."

"Tell me one change." Lovell was eager to know everything.

"We've got a telephone. It don't work half the time, but we got it. Wires strung all across the Ridge, and we got water running inside the house."

"What else?" Lovell asked, knowing Taffy had more on his mind than plumbing and the telephone.

Taffy looked uncomfortable. "Like I said, you'll see soon enough."

THEY rode over newly macadamized roads, heading south.

"The highway's improved, that's a change for the good," Lovell observed.

"Yeah, but it won't last long." Almost as soon as Taffy spoke, they bumped off onto a gravel and hard-packed dirt road that made the Rolls' well-sprung frame a blessing. The dusk lengthened out. The sun hung behind a streak of flame-colored clouds on the western horizon, then abruptly disappeared, and it was dark.

Lovell regretted coming home at night. He wanted to see everything. In the deepening darkness, he heard the sound of the pumping wells, and in the distance he saw the flares of wasted run-off gas casting their amber yellow glow over the MacClaren refinery. "The *Reanna* and *MacClaren* fields are still running," he said. "That hasn't changed. The refinery looks bigger. Is it?"

Taffy didn't answer, but as they came onto the Ridge and headed up the wide drive toward the house, he pointed to the porch.

"Cima's been looking out for you. She's waiting to see just what's become of you up North."

Before the car came to a halt, Lovell had opened the door and was running toward the steps and Cima. He picked her up in his arms and whirled her about. She weighed no more than a feather. It seemed that while he'd grown, she'd shrunk. He carried her up the steps, inside to the hall, and set her down at last so that they stood facing each other.

Cima looked up at him, her head shaking from side to side. "Look at you! Just look at you. We've missed you like a front tooth."

"Do I pass muster?" he asked as he glanced about him at the familiar furniture, the portrait of Pride Beauvaise and the Beauvaise cup beneath it. He was home again, and Lochleven was better than a dream. He wanted to shout for joy, but his throat was too tight and it ached so, he was afraid he might cry. "Where's Snow? I can't wait to see her."

Cima reached out and put her hand on his arm. There was a look of warning in her eyes. "She's coming down, but before she does I have to tell you . . ."

"Tell me what?"

"You'll find her changed." There was something sharp and imperative in her voice.

"Changed how?"

"Snow's been sick."

"What was the matter with her?"

Cima avoided his eyes. "She's better now, but sometimes she's a little slow to answer. Take no notice. She's been looking forward to you coming home. Just be patient with her."

As Cima spoke, Snow appeared at the top of the stairs. She came down slowly, holding on to the banister as if she were afraid she might fall. She was much thinner than Lovell remembered. She looked as fragile as if she were made of spun glass, and she looked at him without a sign of recognition. He was shocked by the dullness of her eyes. The spirit seemed to have gone out of her.

He went up to her and held out his hands. She stared blankly at him, then drew back, as if she were afraid of him. "Snow, don't you know me? It's Lovell."

She caught her breath; her eyelids fluttered. She seemed as unsure as if she'd stepped from the dark into glaring light. She looked questioningly at Cima and asked, "Is it Lovell?"

"Yes." Cima nodded. "It's Lovell. You remember, honey, I told you he was coming home."

Snow shook her head, as if trying to clear away cobwebs from her memory, and then a small smile touched her lips. "Lovell." She looked at him hopefully. "Is this really you?"

"Yes, Snow—yes."

A wave of relief swept over her face. "Oh, Lovell, I've missed you so. I'm so glad you're home."

"So am I." He took her in his arms and held her close. She was skin and bones. He felt the sharp edge of her shoulder blades. The change in Snow was so dramatic that he felt stricken by it, as if he too had been ill. He wanted to ask a dozen questions, but again he got that look of warning from Cima. He began to talk, saying any old thing, to fill in the awkward silence.

"I've missed you all." He stepped back from Snow, letting go of her gently. "But you know what I've missed the most?" He didn't wait for a reply but answered his own question. "What I've missed most is Cima's cooking."

Cima beamed. "Supper's on the table."

Lovell bowed gallantly to Cima and Snow and held out an arm to each of them. "Lead the way, ladies. I'm starved."

"Didn't they feed you up there?" Cima asked.

"Not like home. You wouldn't believe what Yankees call food. They don't know how to chicken-fry steak or barbecue beef or make a decent pot of chili."

"Whatever do the poor folks eat?" Cima was round-eyed with wonder and pity.

"Salmon and creamed peas for the Fourth of July. Baked beans, clam chowder and codfish balls every chance they get."

"Mercy!" Cima shook her head. "Just think of it, all them years without grits or greens. It's a wonder you're alive to tell the tale."

"Well," Lovell conceded, "I did get better victuals in Virginia, but even there it's not like eating your home cooking. It's good to be back where people know peas from *pishofa* and a Chickasaw from a Chippewa."

"Then let's eat," Cima commanded, calling out for Taffy to hurry in and join them.

Lovell looked around the dining room. The table was set and laid out with the main meal. The dessert was on the sideboard. "Where are the girls? Where are Rose Dawn and Annoyi?"

"They're long gone," Cima said.

"Gone—where?"

"They've gone to get married and raise their families," Taffy said as he crossed the room to join them. "That's another change you'll have to get used to around here. People growing older and goin' away."

Cima frowned. "Snow and I run the house with some daily help coming in to do the heavy work. Don't worry, you won't starve."

Lovell laughed. "I'm sure I won't."

They sat down to a feast of fried chicken, cream gravy, black-eyed peas, greens and corn bread. It seemed Lucullan to Lovell. As they ate, Lovell talked and talked. He made them all laugh; even Snow began to smile. And when he mimicked Yankee accents, she clapped her hands and laughed out loud.

But when the meal was finished and Cima and Snow had cleared away, Snow abruptly excused herself and left the room. Lovell started to follow her, hoping to have a moment alone with her, but Cima motioned him back. "Snow's just tired. We're used to going to bed early here."

Lovell waited, but no further explanation of Snow's mysterious illness was given, and he couldn't find a polite way of asking questions.

"Well, then," he said with an exaggerated stretch, "I'm for bed, too. It's been a long trip home. I'm going riding in the morning. You want to come along, Cima?"

Cima looked shocked at the idea. "What you take me for? My riding days is over."

Lovell turned to Taffy and grinned. "What about you, Taffy?"

Taffy grinned back. "You didn't think you'd get off without me, did you? I've got a brand-new pony broke and waiting for you."

LOVELL and Taffy rode out before sunup, walking the horses slowly along the northern edge of the Ridge. Only the creak of leather, the jangle of bit and spur and the sound of the horses breathing deeply through flared nostrils broke the morning stillness. At the rim of the Ridge, Lovell reined in and sat looking to the east as the sun rose up over the *MacClaren* field.

The sight he saw before him struck him like a blow. His eyes darted back and forth from east to west. Everywhere he looked, in both fields, he saw the same terrible ruin of his dreams. The earth around the wells had been scraped bare, the topsoil eroded in great, crooked, ugly gashes. Dark-stained weals of buried pipe erupted every few miles into a nest of tanks. A few trees and patches of grassland were left, not by design or plan, but by some whim of cruel, random chance. This might have been some European battle-field, not the precious, sacred land of his home.

Since he'd been away, the wells had multiplied three times over. The MacClaren refinery had grown like some iron monster, a hostile alien form that befouled the ground it sat on and poisoned the air above. There was nothing left here of his dreams of grass or cattle. All that remained was a living, waking nightmare.

At last he turned to Taffy. "Oh, God, it's worse than I remembered."

"It's bad," Taffy agreed ruefully.

"There are no cattle anywhere."

"There ain't been cattle for a long time," Taffy said softly.

"I remember cattle." Lovell was defiant.

"You remember wrong."

"No cattle at all?"

"Oh, there's a few head—wild strays hiding out."

"We could round them up, couldn't we?"

"What for? So we could lot-feed them at Lochleven?"

"We could start a new herd."

"Talk sense. There's no grass."

Lovell felt sick and betrayed. "Well, at least we can ride back by way of the bunkhouse and visit with the boys. Do they know I'm home?"

Taffy looked crestfallen; his face puckered up as if he were on the point of tears.

"What's the matter?"

"The boys are gone."

"Gone?"

"That's right." Taffy's voice was barely audible.

"Why didn't you tell me?"

"How could I tell you?"

"You could have written me a letter."

Taffy shifted in his saddle. "I ain't no hand at letter writing. Besides, I don't fancy telling bad news, and if it wasn't for bad news, I wouldn't have had no news at all."

"Where did they go?"

"Dan Penland and Frank went off and joined up with Miller's 101 *Wild West Show*."

Lovell started to laugh. He felt a great surge of relief. "This is a joke, right? You and the boys made it up between you to guy me. You're pulling my leg."

"It's no joke," Taffy said soberly.

"Come on. It's a joke—it's got to be. No cowboy from Lochleven would go off to a sideshow, not if Geronimo and Buffalo Bill both begged them pretty please with sugar on it."

Taffy's eyes were red-rimmed. He blinked against the wind. "It's the truth. They went off to the sideshow. They was over in England when the war broke out. The British government took the horses and the mules for the war, and that was the end of the show for good. The Cossacks went home to Rooshia, and the cowboys like to never got back to the U.S.A. When they did finally make it, Dan and Frank went to work for the army buying up horses. Nobody ever knew horseflesh better than them two."

"The war's long over." Lovell's gaze was fixed on Taffy. He still half expected that this was a story they had invented to fox him. "Where are they now?"

"Dan and Frank went west to Colorado, or maybe it was Wyoming—some damn place like that. They figured to start up a small spread and run a few head."

"And Slim Dress?"

Taffy shook his head sadly. "Slim went to live with a married daughter up in Salina, Kansas. Well . . ." He cleared his throat and looked out over what had been open range. "You can't blame 'em really for getting out. No man can cowboy forever."

Lovell's eyes blazed with anger. "They'd be here still, if it weren't for Andrew's oil." He pointed to the *MacClaren* field as if to indict it.

"The country needed oil for the war."

"Andrew wanted the oil so he could get richer."

"You can't blame Andrew for everything, son. He didn't start the war. He ain't the Kaiser."

Lovell threw back his head, his face turned to heaven. "Oh, God. I wish . . ." He stopped and fell silent.

"What do you wish?"

Lovell flushed. He'd been about to say that he wished Taffy was his father, not Andrew MacClaren, but instead he said, "I wish Andrew had never drilled the first well."

(501)

"He didn't drill the first well," Taffy reminded him reasonably. "Your ma did that."

"But Andrew went on drilling, so she had to drill more and more to keep up with him." Lovell bitterly resented Reanna for keeping him at school, but he would never bring himself to believe that she'd been responsible for the ruin of the land. It was Andrew who was in the wrong, just as it was Andrew who was at the center of the mystery. Lovell looked at Taffy. "You and Andrew were friends, weren't you?"

"Yes," Taffy admitted, his jaw tight. "Me and Andrew was good friends and that's a fact."

"You liked him a lot then, didn't you?"

"That I did." Taffy's face might have been set in stone for all that he betrayed his feelings.

"But when Andrew went to town to live, you stayed at Lochleven instead of going with him."

"That's right."

"If you were his friend, why did you stay?"

Taffy took his time before he answered. "Because your ma needed me."

"I'm glad you stayed." Lovell put out his hand to touch Taffy's arm. "I needed you too."

Taffy blinked and rubbed hard at his eyes. "Your ma'll skin me alive if we don't get back. She'll be home by now, sitting up in Miss Jane's room talking on that dang telephone. I never saw a person talk so much on a phone as your ma."

LOVELL ran through the hall and bounded up the stairs. For all his hurt and anger, there had never been a time when he didn't love Reanna. He was eager to see her. Now that he was home, he was prepared to forget the past and make a new beginning.

As Taffy had predicted, Reanna was in the cupola room sitting behind her desk, talking on the telephone. When she saw Lovell, she held up her hand in a warning gesture which stopped him at the threshold and silenced all he meant to say.

"Yes." She spoke sharply into the telephone. "Yes, I understand you've got trouble, but this job must be completed on time and that's final. I have to make delivery by Thursday or the contract is canceled. Don't ask me how to do it, just see that it's done. No, I can't come out there. You're in charge, it's what I pay you for."

There was a silence and the faint, garbled noise of a reply from the other end of the line. Reanna looked up at Lovell and frowned, as if his presence was somehow an unexpected, inconvenient interruption. "Make the delivery on Thursday—and no excuses." She hung up the receiver with a loud bang.

She rose at once and came toward him, her arms outstretched to embrace him. She was tanned from the wind; her red hair made a bright frame around her face. Her costume was as original as ever. She was wearing one of her outlandish outfits, a pair of old jodhpurs with puttees wound down to a pair of dust-caked short boots. She had on a man's shirt open at the throat with a bandana tied around her neck. The ensemble was a hasty collection of colors and materials put on with a total disregard for style or fashion. On any other woman it would have been ridiculous, but for Reanna it was right. At school Lovell had met other boys' mothers. They'd worn nothing like this, but then they hadn't been as alive or as vibrant.

After a moment she released him and stepped back. "Sorry not to meet your train," she said, looking him up and down in an appraising glance.

"That's OK." He tried to sound as if it hadn't mattered.

"Have a good trip?"

"Fine." How could he complain about such luxurious isolation?

"You've grown again."

"It would be pretty funny if I hadn't. It's been over a year since you've seen me."

She frowned. He hadn't meant to rub her the wrong way. Somehow they always seemed to be at cross-purposes.

"Is your room comfortable?"

"Yes, thanks."

"Well, if there's anything you want while you're here, just say so."

"While I'm here?" He didn't understand her. They spoke in such short sentences, they might have been communicating by telegraph. "I hear you've been busy," he said.

"Yes, very." Again she frowned.

"That's good, isn't it?" he asked.

"Good and bad." She motioned for him to sit in a leather easy chair facing her desk. He felt young and clumsy and out of place in this room.

She walked brusquely behind the desk and picked up a sheaf of papers. "These are just some of the new orders for crude I have to

(503)

fill. The country is begging for gas and oil. There are over two million cars on the road now and more coming. Nobody can deliver enough crude to the refineries."

"And that's good." He tried to sound interested.

"It's a whole new game. To be in the oil business today, you have to be producer, refiner, shipper and marketer all in one."

"Andrew seems to be doing it all." As he spoke, he saw her flush beneath her tan. "I saw his refinery," he added lamely. "It's very big."

"Yes," she said bitterly. "Andrew's climbing to the top, up there with Sinclair and Marland and Phillips. He won't rest until he's as big as Standard."

"Sinclair was a crook, wasn't he? Wasn't he in with that Harding gang on the Teapot Dome swindle?"

"He went to jail for it. He was after proven production. Lots of men do worse than Harry Sinclair."

"Are you defending him?" Lovell was astonished.

"No, but he's always been straight with me."

"Do you want to be as big as Sinclair or Standard?"

"Lord, no! I just don't want to stay so small that Andrew or anyone else can gobble me up. Andrew's already swallowed a lot of small fish. He has a way of getting what he wants. He's just got a new lease on tribal surplus lands. It's an open-end lease and on his terms. No drilling date, no completion restriction and the price—when and if he finds oil—to be negotiated."

"How did he get the lease?" Lovell asked. "Surely the tribe wouldn't agree to terms like those."

"The lease was granted by the Department of the Interior. He had *special* consideration."

"Are you saying he bribed them?"

"I'm saying it was a sweetheart deal."

"But that's not right."

She shook her head and sighed. "The competition for product is fierce. Everybody is looking for an edge—an advantage. When I walk into the Petroleum Club these days, I feel like I'm walking into the lion's den."

"You don't have to worry. You're the best wildcatter in the state." He meant to reassure her.

"Thanks, but the wildcatting days are long gone, my dear. Now if I want to find oil, I have to hire geologists and petroleum engineers and a team of seismologists."

"What do they do?"

The lines around her mouth deepened. "They blow holes in the ground and draw graphs and present reports. They take the joy right out of the day."

"Do they find more oil than the old top-of-the-ground way?"

She sighed. "They say so, but they cost more and they use at lot of four-bit words. I have to meet with a new geologist tomorrow and listen to him gibble-gabble. I'm glad you're here. You can come with me."

He looked up quickly. If she'd been paying attention to him, she would have seen his disappointment. "Tomorrow?"

"Yes, we'll get an early start, just the two of us in the car together, like old times."

It was no use pretending that things hadn't changed for him too. He was no longer a little boy to sit quietly by her side. "I'm sorry," he said, "I can't tomorrow." He raised his eyes to meet hers and held his chin high in a gesture of defiance, a gesture he had inherited from her.

"Why not?"

"I've made other plans."

"Cancel them. While you're here—before you go off to college— it's important that you learn as much about the oil business as possible. You only have a few months before the fall semester begins."

"I'm not going to college." He spoke quietly, but each word was measured and weighed. "I got one diploma. That was our bargain. And now I have other plans."

"What plans?" She was angry. He hadn't been home a day, and already the two of them were in a contest of wills.

"I'm going to round up some strays."

"What for?"

"I want to start a herd again."

"That's foolish. Where would you put them?"

His chin went even higher. "There must be some land left in the State of Oklahoma that doesn't have oil wells on it. I believe there might even be a little left here at Lochleven."

She stared at him. "I thought it was understood that you'd go to college."

"No, I mean to stay."

"Here? For how long?" She could have bitten her tongue. If this were a matter of business, she would have been adroit and tactful. But this was a matter between mother and son, and she had never been wise where her heart was concerned. "Is Taffy going out with you?" she asked. "Is he going to look after you?"

Lovell stood up. He was straight and stiff as a soldier. "We're going together, but I'm grown up now, Reanna. I can find my own way. I can look after myself."

She couldn't explain to him that she was still afraid for him to be alone and unprotected in Andrew's part of the world. "I just want to know where you go and what you do."

"I'll give you a full report."

She had handled it all badly, and she didn't want to make matters worse. She shrugged and said in an overcheerful voice, "Well then, you go looking for your strays. Perhaps you'll come with me another time."

"Perhaps." He stood his ground.

"I'll ask again."

REANNA often asked Lovell to go out with her into the field or to a meeting, but something perverse and stubborn in his character always made him find a reason to refuse. He spent his time with Taffy or out on his own, wandering the countryside. He rode his new pony or drove in Reanna's old Model T. Everywhere he went, everything he saw made his heart grow heavier.

The people he'd known as a child had been dispossessed to make way for the age of oil. Many had been cheated of their allotments. Those who had been clever or lucky enough to keep their land had leased it out to strangers. They had abandoned their farms and ranches and gone off to live in town, where they spent their royalty checks buying things they didn't need or want and where the new life separated them from their children and their tribe. He found houses deserted, surrounded by oil wells and storage tanks. On one there was a crudely printed sign on the door, FAMILY GONE AWAY.

There were some people, like the Beauvaises' old enemies the Starretts, who hadn't filed for their allotments. The enrollment, the signing, even by mark, had been too bewildering for them. They knew the land was theirs; they felt no need of a commission to give them their own land back again. They wandered homeless, living on charity, with no strong tribal government to guide them. Tribal life seemed to have vanished or was being run by outsiders appointed from up in Washington. Lovell hoped that somewhere out of sight, hidden in the backland, there were still people who kept the old ways, but he couldn't find a green corn dance or a *pishofa* feast.

The people who had come to work in the oil fields, sure that it would make their fortunes, were, in Lovell's opinion, not much better off than the people they'd evicted and supplanted. The best off made good wages but spent as much and more to live. They never seemed to get a grubstake ahead. The less fortunate were maimed, burned, left hideously scarred and broken by the terrible accidents that were part of the job. If they were hurt and unable to work, there was no compensation. Unless they had a benevolent employer, they were on their own.

But the worst of all for Lovell, even more terrible than the ruin of the land, was finding John's Dead's abandoned lean-to near the polluted springs by the *Reanna One*. Taffy said that John's Dead had been living there, a pauper, cheated of his head rights, and had died waiting for a miracle cure, a miracle that never came.

As Lovell went up and down the countryside, he thought his heart would break as one wrong multiplied against another. In his judgment, Andrew and his greed were responsible for all the squalor, the ruin, the misery and the defilement of the precious, sacred land. Others had done as much and worse, but it was Andrew's wrongs that Lovell focused on. He made a list of Andrew's crimes and added them up like a bill that one day he meant to present to Andrew for payment in full.

Like a man possessed, Lovell began to hunt up strays. He rode out early and came in late. He went into every dry ravine and into every thicket of scrub oak. Taffy rode with him, trying to talk sense into the boy's head. "Let 'em go, Lovell. Let 'em go! If you try to pen and worm 'em, you'll stress 'em too bad. They can't take any setback. They're too used to the wild."

"I won't give them up." Lovell rode on. He was deaf to good advice.

One morning he found a newborn calf trapped in the oil slick of gray shale water in an unfilled slush pit. The calf was sinking, with no strength to fight the mire. Taffy watched, scowling, as Lovell tried to throw a rope on it. The cow who had just calved stood at a distance, bawling for her calf. She was a poor, gaunt, half-starved thing, her bones showing, her eyes sunken in her head. The calf made a few, weak bleats in return and then gave up the struggle and lay still.

Lovell wouldn't give up. He waded into the filth, hip deep, lifted up the calf and brought it out to its mother. Despite her pitiful condition, her teats were strutted with milk. If he could get the calf to suck, it might have a chance. She licked at the small body with her rough tongue, then, as she caught the smell and taste of the sulphur, she backed off from the calf. She loped away, leaving the calf to die. Try as Lovell would, he couldn't drive her back. "Damn him," Lovell shouted to the heavens. "Damn him to hell."

"Now what's eating you?" Taffy was bewildered.

"Damn Andrew MacClaren."

"No need to curse Andrew."

"This is his fault, all this—the oil, the waste." Lovell hung his head so that Taffy couldn't see the sudden rush of tears to his eyes. "I hate him. I'm ashamed to be his son."

"Well, that's bad enough, but you've no call to curse him or go taking out how you feel on your ma, like you do." Taffy had been wanting to say that ever since Lovell had come home again. "It hurts her when you won't spend time with her or go nowhere with her when she asks. She needs you."

"If she needed me so much, she could have let me come home before now." The words were no sooner spoken than Lovell was ashamed of them. His emotions were all at crosscurrents. They were quicksilver, as close to the surface and turbulent as the spring weather. "If she needed me so much, she shouldn't have sent me away."

"She thought she was doing what was best."

"Best for her, not me. If she wanted to send someone away, she should have sent Snow. Look at Snow. I couldn't believe it was the same girl. What's the matter with her? She never goes out. She acts like a frightened rabbit. All the spunk's gone out of her. It's not good for her. She ought to have boyfriends." He had made his case and he waited for Taffy to reply.

Taffy sat in the saddle, silent and still-faced. Lovell felt he was facing a stone wall. "Snow can't still be pining for Andrew. She can't still believe Andrew is going to come and take her away," Lovell said. Taffy still didn't answer him. "Why doesn't she have any boyfriends? She's pretty enough. She could get herself any husband she set her cap for. At least she should get away from here. She could go anywhere she wanted; Lord knows she's rich enough."

Taffy shifted uneasily in his saddle and looked off into the distance. "Snow ain't rich."

Lovell thought he hadn't heard correctly. He stared up at Taffy in disbelief. "What do you mean Snow's not rich? She's got her royalty money." He began to wipe the tiny calf with a handful of dry buffalo grass.

"Snow's got no money."

Lovell shook his head in disbelief. "Snow must have a fortune in her own name."

"Nothing," Taffy said bitterly. "Snow's got nothing."

Lovell stopped and looked up at Taffy. He saw Taffy was convinced that what he said was the truth. "Why not?"

Taffy cleared his throat; it was hard to talk about things that hurt so deep. "When Snow got her allotment, she was underage, a minor. Andrew put her on the rolls and he was her guardian. When the oil came in, she was still a minor and he leased her allotment to hisself. He's never paid her one red cent."

Lovell stood up slowly and stared at Taffy. "Snow's not a minor now."

"She's still Andrew's ward."

"How come?"

"Because she's got no certificate."

"What does that mean?"

"It means she's an Indian, and to handle her own legal affairs and run her own business, she'd have to have a certificate of competency."

"Then why doesn't she get this certificate?"

"Andrew won't let that happen. Besides, you've seen Snow. She ain't in no fit shape to go to court."

"It can't be legal for Andrew to keep Snow's money."

"Oh, it's legal all right, just like getting a new drilling lease on tribal land," Taffy said, his mouth twisting around the words. "Everything Andrew MacClaren does has a lawyer in it."

"I don't understand. Explain to me how it can be legal."

Taffy frowned. "I don't know all the ins and outs of any of it."

"Don't know, or won't say?"

"Don't know," Taffy mumbled.

"If you can't tell me, who can? Who does know the straight of it?"

"Jack Levy does."

"Jack Levy wouldn't tell me anything," Lovell said bitterly.

"Why not?"

"He's Andrew's friend. They're in business together. They run the bank. Doc and Jack and Andrew."

Taffy's eyes narrowed. "Jack Levy is Reanna's friend too, and don't you forget it. Jack and Reanna—they never had a cross word."

"All right, then. I'll ask Jack Levy." Lovell bent down and picked up the calf. He wrapped it in a saddle blanket and slung it before his saddle horn.

"What are you going to do with that peaky calf?"

"I'm going to take it home to Lochleven. I'm going to take it back where it belongs, and then I'm going to begin asking some questions I should have asked a long time ago."

WHEN they rode into the barnyard, Lovell left Taffy to stable the horses as he carried the calf to the back porch and shouted into the kitchen for Snow. "Get out here, Snow, and hurry."

Snow appeared at the kitchen door, looking frightened and bewildered by the summons. She came out hesitantly, wiping her floury hands on her apron. "What is it? What's the matter?"

"This!" Lovell thrust the calf toward her.

Snow backed away. Then curiosity got the better of her fear, and she lifted a corner of the blanket. "Oh, the poor thing." She looked at Lovell, her eyes glistening. "Where's its mother?"

"The cow refused it. If someone doesn't take care of it, it will die." As he spoke, he pushed the calf into her arms.

"I can't be responsible for it. I don't know how."

"You'll have to clean it up, get the oil off its hide, put it in a warm place and feed it every four hours. Even so, it's only got a fifty-fifty chance. It won't have immunity from its mother's milk. It might die, but if you don't take it, it's a goner for sure."

As he spoke, Snow had begun to edge toward the kitchen door. "Ask Taffy to bring me a box with clean straw. I'll keep the calf by the stove. That ought to be warm enough."

"I'll tell him," Lovell said, grinning at Snow. "And while you see to the calf, I'll get cleaned up for town."

By the time Lovell bathed and came back down to the kitchen, Snow had already washed and fed the calf. She was sitting on the floor by the box near the stove, watching it sleep. The calf was breathing deeply, its white face stained with milk and the tip of its pink tongue just showing. Snow's expression as she watched the sleeping form was full of tenderness. She looked up shyly at Lovell and smiled. For the first time since he'd come home, he saw some of the old spark in her eyes.

Crowding behind her, Cima and Taffy were beaming like proud godparents. "I think the heifer might make it after all," Taffy said.

"Of course it's going to make it," Cima added fiercely.

"I gave her some honey with the milk," Snow said, "and she liked it. She has the sweetest, whitest face I've ever seen. So I'm going to call her Daisy." She smiled again. "Thank you, Lovell, for bringing her to me." Snow's hand reached out to touch the sleeping calf on the head.

"It's only a calf." Lovell spoke brusquely. "But it's a beginning."

"You've done a good deed." Cima's face was shining. "You'll get stars for your heavenly crown."

"Don't make over him so," Taffy grumbled, "or he'll get a swelled head and want to bring home everything with four feet." No matter what Taffy said, Lovell could see that he too was pleased.

"Well," Lovell said, "now that I see Daisy's in good hands, I'll be going."

Cima was instantly alert. She looked sharply at Lovell. "Where are you off to?"

"To town."

"What for?"

"Business."

"When will you be back?"

"When I get here."

"Shall I hold supper?"

"No." Lovell opened the door. "I may be late." And before Cima could ask him any more, he had gone.

Driving down the road to MacClaren City, Lovell felt he was coming closer to the heart of the mystery that surrounded Andrew. All his life he'd been put off with excuses and half-truths, but now he meant to have the whole truth. Nothing else would satisfy him.

It was late in the day when he got to town. He asked for Jack Levy at the store and was told he'd find him at the bank. At the bank, the blinds were drawn. Lovell had to pound at the door until a teller, working late, let him in.

Jack and Doc Hersey were in the president's office bent over a pile of papers and ledgers, their heads together, absorbed in serious conversation. At first they didn't notice Lovell standing in the doorway; then Jack glanced up, blinked and shook his head, trying to make sure of Lovell's identity before he spoke. At last a big smile broke on his face and he came toward Lovell, holding out his hand in welcome.

"Lovell MacClaren! I didn't recognize you at first. We heard you were home. Well, you've surely grown up into a fine-looking young man."

It pleased Lovell to have Jack call him a man, not a boy. Seventeen was limbo, somewhere between the two. He shook Jack's hand and then Doc's. "I see you're busy," he said. "Maybe I should come back later. I need to talk to you, Mr. Levy."

The two men glanced at each other, a brief exchange but a significant one. "You've come on a bad day," Jack said, "but your leaving won't make it get any better."

"We're just finishing up," Doc said ruefully. "I have to be getting home. Amoretta's expecting me. You come by and see her, you hear? She'll never forgive me if I let you leave town without her getting a look at you." They shook hands again; then Doc turned to Jack. "Maybe things aren't as bad as they seem."

"No," said Jack bitterly, "they're worse."

When Doc had gone, Jack stood for a moment, rapt in thought. Then, as if he had suddenly remembered Lovell was there, he motioned him to a chair. "Sit down, Lovell, sit down. Well, what can I do for you?"

It was hard to begin. Lovell had tried to decide how best to ask his question before he came, but now that he was here, he found it more difficult than he'd expected. "Mr. Levy," he blurted out, "I need your help."

Jack smiled ruefully. "You want to borrow some money?"

Lovell shook his head. "No."

Jack leaned forward. "Is it about a girl?"

"No."

"Then perhaps you'd better tell me about it."

"I want to ask you a question, and I want a straight answer."

Jack pressed the tips of his fingers together. "This is serious then?" he asked.

Lovell nodded.

"Ask your question."

"Why has my father never paid Snow any royalty on her land?"

Jack was silent. He looked at Lovell as if he were trying to pick his words carefully before he answered. Lovell was impatient. He wanted more than a cautious dismissal.

"I know you're my father's friend, but I must know. I can't ask him. I haven't seen him since I was a child. He never comes to Lochleven. Is it because he's afraid to face Snow—afraid he might have to pay up what he owes her? Please answer. You're the only person I can ask."

Lovell stopped. He'd bungled it, made a fool of himself—gone too fast, asked too much. He felt as if he were talking into the wind. He waited. He knew he was so close to the truth that he could almost reach out and touch it. And he sensed that the truth was as dangerous as fire in dry grass.

In the silence, Jack turned away from Lovell and stared out the window. Lovell could hear the ticking of the wall clock and the beating of his own heart. Then, just when he thought he could bear the silence no longer, Jack turned back to face him. "You say I'm your father's friend. I thought I was. I've believed it for more years than you've been alive. But if you expect me to help you understand why Andrew MacClaren does anything, you've come to the wrong man on the wrong day!"

Lovell felt his disappointment as keen and sharp as if he'd been dealt a blow. He rose and said stiffly, "I'm sorry I bothered you. I'll go."

"Sit down." Jack looked suddenly very tired; his shoulders sagged. "None of this is your fault. You have a right to an answer to your questions. It's just that today Doc and I have had to make up a considerable deficit here at the bank, out of our own pockets. A deficit caused by Andrew's insane borrowing. We're overextended in our out-of-state, upstream loans by several million dollars." His voice had sunk to a barely audible whisper.

"Several million?" Lovell repeated Jack's words to be sure he'd heard them correctly.

Jack nodded. "As directors of the bank, we're liable for all loans. We've had to come up with the money out of our private funds."

"But why couldn't Andrew put up his share? He's a rich man, richer than either you or Doc." Lovell flushed. He'd presumed too much, but what Jack had told him was incredible and it had taken him by surprise. "I'm sorry, I shouldn't have said that."

"Why not?" Jack shrugged. "It's true, but when we asked Andrew to make good on his loans—at least to secure the interest—

he said it wasn't convenient to convert any of his holdings to cash. He said he needed his capital to expand his business." The words seemed to taste bitter in Jack's mouth. "He's used this bank like a private account. He's even borrowed to build that marble folly of his. Have you seen it?"

"I saw it on the way to town. It's as big as a palace."

"It's a monster. He's poured money into it for years—like pouring sand down a rat hole. The grand opening is a month away, and he's invited the whole state to the housewarming."

"But it's not fair that you and Doc should pay up for him."

Jack looked sharply at Lovell to see if he was making a joke. "Fair! I don't think the idea of fair has ever entered Andrew MacClaren's head. He says Doc and I should be more than willing to pay up for him, because he made our fortunes for us."

"What if you didn't pay up for him?"

Jack shrugged, a gesture of hopeless resignation. "We have to make good or see our depositors suffer. Andrew knows we won't let that happen." Jack laughed, a short, dry rattle of a sound. "He's had a sweet revenge for whatever wrongs he thinks Doc and I have done to him."

Lovell was thoughtful. "What you're saying is . . ." He spoke slowly, measuring out the words. "What you are saying is that Andrew's cheated Snow and now he's cheated his friends."

"Why not?" There was a sharp cutting edge of anger in Jack's voice. "Why shouldn't we expect Andrew to cheat us, when he's already taken his own brother's land?" He stopped short and stared at Lovell, his mouth still open. "Oh, God," he said at last, "if I could take back those words, I'd ransom them with gold."

Lovell was stricken by the words. There was a ringing in his ears. His mouth was dry and he felt weak, as if he'd had a fever. He'd wanted the truth, but now that he was this close, he wished he could run away. But he couldn't move. He was trapped, caught between two high walls and they were closing in on him. "You can't stop now. You must go on."

"There's nothing more to say." Jack looked at him, pleading for a mercy he felt he didn't deserve.

"Tell me the truth, please. I want all of it."

Jack sighed. He'd opened a door, and now there was no turning back. "The year of the big blizzard, Andrew lost his herd. His creditors were after him. On my advice, to stay clear of bankruptcy, he put his property in Reanna's name. The Dawes Commission was making allotments to the Chickasaw. Andrew and Pride settled between them what portion of the Beauvaise land each would ask for their allotment." He stopped, and then knowing there was no way out, he went on. "Only, when Andrew went to sign up for his land, he took it all. The east range—that's now the *MacClaren* field— was Snow's portion. The rest—the Ridge and the west range—he kept for himself. The joker was that by deed all the land Andrew had filed on for himself, the west and the Ridge, belonged to Reanna, not to him. He'd already deeded them to her."

"I still don't understand." Lovell felt as if a cold, north wind was blowing in his mind. "You say Andrew filed for the land that should have been Pride Beauvaise's and that my mother had it by deed . . ." He stopped, not wanting to go on. He'd caught fire in his hands and he couldn't let it go.

"That's right," Jack said.

"Then my mother—knew all this." Jack didn't reply. "Did she?"

"Yes."

"If she knew and did nothing, then she's as guilty as Andrew."

"No!" Jack's voice cracked like thunder. "She tried to give it back. You can't blame your mother for any of this. I shouldn't have told you about Pride and Andrew. I regret it with all my heart. I never would have told you, but you came on a day when I wanted to strike out and hurt Andrew. And now I've hurt you instead. I ask you to forgive me."

"Oh, I got what I came for. I wanted the truth and I got it. I'll always be grateful to you."

"Grateful?"

"Yes. For now I don't have to feel guilty any longer. When I was little, I used to think that the reason Andrew never came to Lochleven was because I'd done something to drive him away. I thought that I'd somehow failed to be the son he wanted. And that I was sent away to school as punishment."

"Oh my God." Jack was shocked by what he'd heard. "And you've been carrying that around with you all this time?"

"Yes." Lovell was pale and trembling. "But Snow's carried an even heavier burden."

"You must never blame yourself or your mother for what Andrew did."

Lovell stood up. He held himself erect and spoke in a formal manner, as if he'd been coached in the words. "You've been very kind, Mr. Levy, and I thank you. I mustn't take up any more of your time."

"Don't go—not yet."

"I'm sorry, but I must be getting home."

"You said you were grateful to me for telling you the truth. If so, please remember that Reanna isn't to blame for what Andrew did. She didn't take Pride's land, Andrew did."

"No, I understand. My mother didn't take Pride Beauvaise's land, but it was my mother who kept it. And now, sir, if you'll excuse me, I must go home and ask her why."

CHAPTER 22

REANNA sat at her desk in the cupola room. The lamp-light cast shadows against the far wall as she studied a geological survey map. She'd learned to read them because they were necessary to her business, but she resented every hour she spent at paperwork and out of the field. She frowned and bent closer, tracing an anticline with her finger, when suddenly she felt she was being observed. She looked up to see Lovell standing in the doorway staring at her. She had no notion of how long he had been there. He looked pale and young and very vulnerable.

"I want to talk to you," he said.

"To what do I owe the honor? Usually it's I who want to talk to you." No sooner had she spoken than she regretted the words. Why did she always have to say the wrong thing to Lovell? She could charm the birds from the trees. She could wrap the hardest, sharpest lease trader around her little finger, but with Lovell she was forever inept and clumsy.

She loved him with all her heart, and yet it was as if she was compelled to alienate Lovell from her—as if by keeping him at a distance from her and from Lochleven, she could protect him from harm. She'd sent him away for his sake, and when she couldn't bear the loss of him, she'd run East to visit him. She'd rarely stayed above a week; if she'd stayed longer, the parting would have been too painful. Now that he was home there was a gulf between them, a barrier she couldn't seem to bridge.

"Come in and sit down." She motioned him to the easy chair.

"I'd prefer to stand, thank you."

"As you like."

He stood straight as a soldier on inspection parade.

"What do you want to talk to me about?"

"You and my father."

She felt as if her heart had stopped.

"I know about you and my father."

It was the thing she feared most, that one day Lovell would find out the truth about Pride. She had imagined the scene a hundred times. She'd rehearsed a dozen different answers, but now that the moment was here, she didn't know what to say to him.

"Is it true?" he demanded.

"Is what true?" She felt she was standing on the edge of a precipice.

"Is it true that Andrew MacClaren took Pride Beauvaise's land?"

A great wave of relief swept over her. She wanted to laugh out loud. This was something she could deal with, something she could handle.

"Is it true?" Lovell repeated.

"Yes." The word slipped out like a sigh.

"And you knew about it?"

"Yes."

"You knew it and yet you drilled the *Reanna* field on his land?"

"When I drilled the *Reanna One*, I didn't drill on Pride's land, I drilled on homestead land. I didn't know then that Andrew had taken the land from Pride."

"But when you found out what Andrew had done, you went on drilling."

"Yes."

He looked stunned, as if she had struck him. "Then you're to blame for cheating Pride Beauvaise as much as my father."

"I'm sorry you think that."

"Well it's true, isn't it?"

"No! Andrew had put all his property in my name. It was mine by deed. I didn't know what he'd done until it was too late."

"Too late!" Lovell's eyes blazed. "You got the land by deed; why didn't you give the land back to Pride by deed?"

She turned her head away so he couldn't see her eyes. She didn't want to betray any more to him than she had to. "I tried. It wasn't possible."

"It seems simple enough to me."

"It's more complicated than you know."

"Then explain it to me."

"Why?" She met his anger with her own. "Do you intend to be my judge, jury and executioner all in one? Are you wise enough for that?"

He stood his ground. "I want an explanation. I deserve that much, don't you think?"

Suddenly she felt very tired. The weight of the years rested on her. "By the time I found out what Andrew had done, Pride had already filed for another allotment." She hoped that much might satisfy Lovell and keep him from going on with his inquisition. "Who told you about the land? Was it Taffy?"

"No." Lovell shook his head.

"Who then?"

"Does it matter? What matters is that for you or anyone to keep Pride Beauvaise's land isn't right. You must give it back to him."

If he hadn't been so young and so serious, she would have laughed at the idea. "If it were that easy to make things right, I would have done so long ago. You're very young. You can't understand things that happened before you were born."

His chin went up. "I'm not so young and ignorant that I can't see that Andrew took his brother's land and that you kept it and made a fortune off of it."

"That will be enough."

But he'd just begun. "My father is a thief, a liar—a spoiler of the earth. He's opening that great marble folly to the people for a big, statewide housewarming—just Andrew and a few thousand of his closest friends—and all the time the truth is he's cheated Snow, his family and his friends. And now he means to cheat the people."

"Stop it, Lovell, stop it!" She couldn't believe he felt so deeply or had kept so much bottled up inside himself.

"It's all dishonest, everything he does. Keeping Snow's royalties and Pride's land. Pride Beauvaise is a lawyer. Why didn't he take Andrew to court to get his rights?"

"Pride had his reasons."

"No matter what the law says, Andrew cheated his brother and he should be made to pay for it. It's because of what you and Andrew did that Pride never comes here, isn't it?"

She felt herself trembling. "There's more to it than that. Pride and Andrew quarreled long ago."

"At first I couldn't believe that you'd be a party to it. But it's true, and the worst of it is, you've gotten rich at Pride's expense."

"You only know part of the truth." She lashed out at him, trying to stop his attack on her. "What I've done, I've done for you."

"For me!" His hurt and bitterness welled up and burst out in a new torrent. "What have you done for me? You sent me away. Was it because you were afraid I'd find out what you and Andrew had done?"

"I sent you away because I wanted you to be safe. I wanted to protect you."

"You only let me come home again because you ran out of excuses to keep me in the East. You keep pretending that I'm going to college or that I'm going into the oil game with you. But I'm never going to be an oilman. I don't want the oil or the money."

"What do you want?"

"I want this place as it was. I want grass and cattle and clear water. I want the people as they were before the oil ruined all their lives."

"You don't know how hard that old life was," she said bitterly.

"It must have been better than this. Look out the window. What do you see? No cattle, no grass. The land has nearly been destroyed."

"It's not cattle that give us our living, it's the oil."

"I hate the oil. I hate what it's done to this place, but most of all I hate—" He stopped abruptly and didn't finish. He looked pale and shaken.

She knew he'd been on the point of saying that he hated her too. She felt as if she could weep a well full of tears. At last she broke the terrible silence and said, "I don't expect you to understand, but long ago I made a promise to Miss Jane to keep the Beauvaise land together. For good or bad, I've tried to do that. It's cost me dear. I can't turn back the clock, not even to suit you. I can't plug the wells and fill in the holes. Like it or not, we're in the oil business and that makes us richer than you'd ever get on cows and grass. This place is your inheritance. Take it, learn to accept it and be grateful for it."

"No!" It was a long, loud cry from his heart. "No, I won't accept it. I want to make this place what it used to be."

"And how do you plan to do that?"

(520)

"I don't know, but I'll find a way."

"What's done is done. Face facts. You're not a child. You can see it's impossible."

"That's your answer to everything, isn't it? To say it's impossible or that I don't understand because it happened in the past. You won't do anything, will you?"

"Do what? What can I do?"

"Give Pride Beauvaise back his land."

"No, I won't do that, because I can't."

He stared at her for what seemed an eternity. "Then," he said at last, "I must."

"Must what?"

"I must try to make right the wrongs you and Andrew have done." He turned and went quickly out of the room and down the stairs. She ran after him, calling out his name, but he didn't stop. When she reached the front porch, she heard the sound of a car pulling away, speeding down the wide, gravel driveway.

She stood on the porch for a long time before she went back into the house. In the half-light of the hall, she could see the portrait of Pride Beauvaise and, beneath it in the shadows, the Beauvaise cup.

She went to it and took it in her hands. It was cool to the touch. And after a time she heard herself saying, "If I had it to do again, Miss Jane, I'd let the land blow away in the wind before I'd let Pride go. Love is worth more than the land—worth more than any promise."

It was Pride Beauvaise's habit to come in from his ranch to his office in Muskogee very early in the morning. He got half his day's work done before court convened. Even at dawn, it didn't surprise him to find someone waiting for him, camped on his doorstep. Many of his clients were country people for whom the trip to town was a long journey. They weren't the sort to stay in hotels.

To the people Pride served, his office was a refuge, his ability to defend them their last hope. They believed in him because he was a Beauvaise, a man of the blood, and because he didn't charge them more than they could afford. Some believed he was a Chickasaw wizard who could talk to the Great White Father in Washington. To them he was a figure of supreme authority. The wings of gray at his temples lent him an air of great dignity. The slight stoop of his shoulders suggested he was able to carry the cares of the world, and his serious expression promised wisdom beyond his years and compassion for others' suffering.

Despite all his disappointments and setbacks before the bar, he was still optimistic enough to believe that the one constant hope of the world was the law. What the law had taken, the law could restore. The law took time, more time perhaps than he would have in his life, but in the end the law would prevail and right would be done.

This morning, as he drew closer to his office, he saw the figure of a boy curled up in the doorway like a hedgehog, his head pillowed on his knees. He touched the boy's shoulder and shook him gently. The boy stirred and raised his head. As he looked up and Pride saw his face, he felt as if he had had the breath knocked out of him. This boy was so like her that he could not be anyone else but Reanna's son. He stared at the boy as if hypnotized.

After the war, Reanna had insisted they make a clean break and not write nor see each other again. She had said she was doing it for Lovell's sake. Like any break, it had been painful, but he had knit and healed. The old wound only bothered him now when the weather changed or he thought of her. But when he saw this boy's face, suddenly all the old pain returned.

The boy stared up at him, rubbed his eyes and blinked and said, "You're Pride Beauvaise?"

Pride nodded. He could not trust his voice that pleaded so eloquently for others to speak for him.

"I'm Lovell MacClaren." The boy stood up. He was taller than Pride and very thin. "I drove all night to get here. I know it's early, but it's important that I see you. I'm sorry. I guess I fell asleep."

"Won't you come in?" Pride fumbled with the key. His hand was unsteady as he opened the door. He led the way inside the dim office. He put the case containing his briefs on the desk and pulled up the blind to let in the early light. He needed time to recover his composure.

"I suppose you're wondering why I came?" The boy asked the question as if it were a challenge.

"I'll wait for you to tell me." Pride discovered his hands were still not quite steady. Whoever had spread the story that Indians were a stoic, unemotional people had told a ridiculous lie. As he looked at the boy more closely, he saw he had Reanna's hair and brown eyes, as well as her mannerism of lifting her chin to defy the world.

Lovell returned Pride's appraising look. "I've seen the copy of your father's portrait in the hall at Lochleven. When I was little I used to think that because you were Snow's uncle, you were mine too."

"How is Snow?"

"She's not been well, but she's better now."

"I'm glad she's all right."

"She'd be better still if you came to see her."

The boy's gaze was so direct and penetrating that it made Pride uncomfortable. He felt as if he were on the witness stand and were being cross-examined. "It's not always possible to do what one would like," he said. He knew, as he said them, that the words sounded false and hollow. "Won't you sit down?"

As he sat, Lovell continued to stare at him as if he couldn't yet make a judgment about him. Pride waited, trying to prepare himself for the next line of questioning. The question, when it came, caught him off guard.

"Is it true that my father took your land?"

Pride willed himself to answer carefully, as if he were under oath. "It is true that Andrew filed for his allotment on the land that I had spoken for." He could not yet see what conclusion the boy had in mind.

"It was your land, wasn't it? It was Beauvaise land?"

Pride nodded.

"Then why did you let him have it?"

"He filed for his allotment before I did."

"But that's not right. You're a lawyer. Why didn't you take him to court to get it back?"

"I took other land for mine." It was an evasion, but Pride hoped it would divert the boy. It did not.

"Was your allotment equal to Andrew's?"

Pride shrugged. "The commission believed it to be fair."

"Did you have oil on your land?" Lovell persisted.

"No."

"Then your land was not equal to Andrew's."

The boy was leading the witness, putting words in his mouth. Pride felt he must object. "I sold my allotment and bought a ranch near here. I have a good ranch. I have a small herd of highbred cattle and some good grass and water."

"But you have no oil."

"No."

"Then you should be entitled to the royalty from the oil drilled in the *Reanna* field. You could still bring a suit for the land and make a claim for your property."

Pride still could not make out the boy's motive. "The land was allotted a long time ago. I have some experience in cloud-on-title suits. They're difficult at best and almost impossible to prove."

"It's worth trying, isn't it? To see justice done? It's not right for Andrew to have filed for your land."

"What he did was legal."

"It was wrong for him to take the land and for my mother to keep it."

"Your mother had nothing to do with Andrew's allotment."

"She got the land by deed and she kept it. What she did was wrong."

"What she did was within the law."

"Then the law is blind to true justice."

Pride smiled. The argument was flawed, but the boy was sincere and full of passion. "You must be a lawyer to be so sure of the meaning of the law."

"No." Lovell flushed. "I'm seventeen. But I know the difference between right and wrong."

"Not many people can say that."

"Don't patronize me."

"I didn't mean to." Pride regarded the boy's discomfort and was sorry for it, but he still couldn't read him. He felt it was time to cross-examine. "Are you interested in the oil?"

"No!" Lovell reacted as if he had been accused of a capital crime. "I hate the oil business and everything to do with it."

Pride was unprepared for such vehemence. "I see."

"Do you? You'd have to be blind not to see what the oil has done to the land and to the people. They are like children with Christmas toys they don't understand. They drink because they can't manage the money or the changes it has brought to their lives. They were farmers and ranchers; now they're nothing. They don't know how to live in town. They make fools of themselves. They all dance to Andrew or some other oilman's fiddle."

Pride shook his head in denial. "Not all the people who got oil money are fools. Far from it. Many of them manage very well indeed. They've used the money to build houses, hospitals and schools to educate their children. For them it was a blessing, a deliverance." Pride believed what he'd said; still he felt a little like the devil's advocate.

The boy looked as if he was close to tears.

"I thought you of all people would understand. They told me you were a champion of the people. I thought if I came to you, you'd see that you must make Andrew do what is right, not only for them, but for you and for Snow."

Pride leaned forward. "What does Snow have to do with this?"

"Andrew has cheated her as he cheated you. He uses her land and pays her nothing for it. He keeps her as his ward, because under the law she's a legal incompetent."

Pride felt a rush of fury sweep through him. He held the arms of his chair until his knuckles went white. The wrong Andrew had done him was nothing compared to the wrong he had done to Snow. It made him sick with shame to think of it. He said, "I didn't know Andrew's greed had carried him that low. If Andrew has cheated Snow as you say he has, then Snow should sue Andrew. She should hire a lawyer to represent her."

"Why don't you represent her?"

"It's not always a good idea to represent relatives. There are many good attorneys closer to Lochleven than Muskogee."

Lovell's face showed all his disappointment. "You haven't been listening to me. You're like all the others. You don't care."

"I care about Snow."

"Do you really?" The boy looked at him with contempt.

"Yes."

"But you'll do nothing for her. You say she needs a lawyer, but it's just a convenient excuse to get rid of her. If you had ever come to Lochleven, you would have seen just how much she needed you."

"I told you, it's not always possible to do what one would like to do."

"That's only another excuse. You didn't come because you didn't care."

"You couldn't be more wrong. I do care for Snow, as I would for anyone who has been kept from their rights, but I happen to care more for her because she is my blood."

"Then prove it. Come home and fight for her."

"I can't."

"Why not?"

"There are reasons."

"What reasons?"

"What's past is past."

"That's what my mother says."

Pride felt an ache in his heart. "Does your mother know you've come here?" It was easier to say "your mother." He still couldn't trust himself to speak Reanna's name aloud.

Lovell flushed a deep scarlet. "No."

"Does Andrew?" It was a question Pride had wanted to ask from the beginning.

"No! Coming to see you was my idea. I'm old enough to make my own decisions."

"I didn't mean to suggest otherwise."

"I came on my own." He hung his head. "I can see now that it was foolish of me to ask your help. I've wasted my time and yours."

"Not at all. I know you meant well, but believe me, it's no good stirring up ashes. Let the past alone."

"You mean, let Andrew do anything he pleases. Just because he's rich and powerful, let him get away with mocking and twisting the law."

"No, I don't mean that. I meant what I said. Now let it alone, Lovell." It was the first time he had called him by name. "It's best for everyone."

"I don't believe that." There was anguish in the boy's voice. "I don't believe it's best for everyone that Andrew keep land or royalties that don't belong to him. I don't believe it's best to let him go free and clear. Too many people have suffered because of Andrew. He's taken the land. He's taken the black gold and left nothing but a barren waste. How many more people will you let him cheat, now that he's taken a lease on the tribal surplus land?"

Pride stood and faced Lovell, who rose to confront him. "The tribal lease is a matter for the courts to decide." Pride's tone was soft, but it sent a chill through Lovell. "That lease will never stand up in a court of law."

"He'll buy the courts like he's bought everything else. He got the surplus land on his terms—an open-end lease to drill when he likes and set a price he chooses. He gave no cash bonus. It's worse than the Teapot Dome. He's bribed someone in Washington. He's paid their price to get the prize."

"I promise you the courts will deal with it."

"Why should I believe you? It's all happened before. It will happen again. Your law let him rob you and Snow. It did nothing to stop him. You'll do nothing to stop him."

"I can't prosecute him in court on this, not even if I wanted to."

"Why not?"

"The case would have to come before the Federal Court of the Eastern Division here at Muskogee. It's a federal case. I'm not a U.S. attorney."

"And if you were, would you prosecute then?" He waited. Pride didn't answer. Lovell looked at him with scorn. "It's just another excuse for doing nothing."

"Listen to me." Pride was suddenly angry. "I don't owe you an answer, but here it is. Yes. If I were a United States attorney, I would indict Andrew and bring him to court. But I'm not, so that ends the matter."

"Could you get a federal appointment?"

Pride shook his head. "No."

"Why not?"

"United States attorneys are appointed by the president. They're recommended by the senior senator of the state to the president—a senatorial courtesy, it's called. And I won't be recommended."

"Why, because Andrew owns the senator?"

"You're very young to be so cynical."

"I have cause."

"Have a little faith."

"I want to. I want with all my heart to believe there's hope for a decent future for the people and the land. The tribal land is the precious, sacred ground of their being. How can you, a Beauvaise, stand by and let Andrew destroy the spirit of the tribe's life?"

Pride was shaken by what Lovell had said. They were words he himself had spoken. The Indians believed that the earth is the mother who gives freely to all men. That the earth is sacred and must not be defiled.

As Pride stood looking at Lovell, Lovell mistook his silence for rejection and began to back away from him. "I'm sorry. It's useless to try to talk to you. I'm sorry I bothered you. I've taken your time. You can send me a bill for it." He turned to the door.

"Stop!" Pride couldn't let him go like this, empty and disappointed. He saw something in the boy that made him want to reach out to him. Long ago, he'd wanted to believe that this boy was his son. He'd been sure of it, but Reanna had made him believe otherwise. No matter whose son he was, he was a boy to be proud of. Pride couldn't see him hurt by events the boy hadn't caused and couldn't change. "You say I don't care for the land. I say that's out of line. If you could see my ranch, perhaps you might change your mind."

Lovell hesitated, studying Pride, and then said, "I'd like to see your ranch. When may I come?"

"Any time that suits you."

"What about today?"

Pride was caught off balance. He hadn't expected Lovell to be so eager.

Lovell took another step back. "You didn't mean for me to come at all. You were just being polite."

"No! I wasn't being polite. I want you to come very much." To his surprise, he found it was true. He wanted to show Lovell the place he had made for himself. He wanted it more than anything he had wanted in a long time. He made a rapid survey of his office calendar. "I have to walk some papers over to the courthouse, and then I have the rest of the day free."

As they walked away from the federal courthouse, they kept easy step together. They might have been old, familiar companions. Pride found himself wishing he and Lovell might become friends. Then, as swiftly as the wish came, he killed it. He mustn't allow himself to become attached to Lovell. He musn't see him again. It wouldn't be good for the boy, and Reanna wouldn't like it. She'd broken them apart and left no hope of mending them. Abruptly, he turned to Lovell. "Have you a car?"

"Yes."

"Then you can follow me out to the ranch, and you'll already be headed south on your way home."

To Lovell it was a cool dismissal. He had somehow thought they'd go together. He shrugged, trying not to show his disappointment. "I'll follow you, then, if that's what you want."

PRIDE drove slowly down the dusty back road, glancing in his rearview mirror to be sure Lovell was still following. He'd decided to come down to the ranch from the east. It was from that approach that one got the best view of the whole place. It was a surprise to him to discover just how important Lovell's good opinion of the ranch was to him. He'd done a lot with the property. Almost every moment not given to the law was spent here. His work and the land filled the wide, empty spaces in his life.

This was a perfect day for Lovell's visit. The sky was a clear, crystal blue, the grass was as green as winter wheat and a cool, spring wind was running fresh from the south. This was a spring day without a flaw. Against his will, Pride found he couldn't hold back a rush of poignant memories of another spring and the sweet days he had spent with Reanna. The remembrance of those other days struck at him like cold air on an exposed nerve.

He parked his car by a section line fence and waited for Lovell to join him. The expression on Lovell's face when he saw the rolling pasture was like an accolade. His eyes sparkled, his cheeks were flushed and the wide smile on his face reflected pure delight.

"It's a fine place."

Pride opened the gate and they walked across a cattle guard into the high waving grass. "It wasn't like this," Pride said. "When I took title to it, the topsoil had been destroyed by homesteaders plowing the bluestem and the land was badly eroded."

"Where did you start? How did you begin to make the new grass take root?" Lovell began to walk faster, and then he ran to the center of the field. He stopped and stood with his head thrown back in the bright sun. "Oh, this is wonderful, truly wonderful. I know you didn't have an oil slick over everything, but still, to do all this . . ." His arms stretched out on either side of him to encompass the whole pasture.

Pride was enormously pleased by the compliment. They were words he wanted to hear. "Thank you. I've had good luck and good weather."

"What did you do first?"

"I let the land lie fallow while I limed the acid soil and put on a cover of manure. Then I planted in crested wheatgrass. The Russian strain makes pasture come back as quick as anything I know. Next, I tried a dozen different grasses mixed with blue grama, because the grama withstands drought.

"I wanted to develop a strain that would combine the old bluestem strength with newer mixtures for nutrients. In pasture, you need a balance of phosphorus, nitrogen and potassium. I got the nitrogen from the vetch and the balance from rye, fescue, midland Bermuda and clover."

"What about alfalfa?"

"It's a soil builder, but it can bloat the cattle. That's only my opinion, of course. I tried just about every combination before I came up with this."

He led the way to the next pasture, holding the barbed wire apart for Lovell to climb through. While Lovell looked at the high grass, Pride said shyly, "I think I may be getting close to something. I'll show you some of the pulls."

Pride took a handful of grass, grasping it close to the bottom, and pulled it up, dusting it against his boot, letting the red dirt fall from the long roots. He gave the sheaf to Lovell, who bent over it, studying the roots, the stem and head of each blade as if he were examining pure gold.

"Oh my," Lovell said at last. "Oh my! This is something. You're more than close. You've got yourself a new strain for sure. You've developed a Beauvaise Bluestem." He looked up admiringly at Pride. "Taffy always said you knew more about grass than anybody."

Pride glanced away quickly, afraid to betray his pleasure. "I have a long way to go before it's weather proved, but I think I'm on the right track." He glanced back at Lovell and was blinded by the sun. It shone behind Lovell so that the boy's red hair was like a flaming halo. For the first time since he had left Lochleven and Reanna, he had to admit that a son like Lovell was more important than the life he and Reanna could have had together. He would have done anything, given anything he owned, for a son like Lovell.

The realization of how much he'd been drawn to him in this one day made Pride suddenly afraid. He'd been so lonely for companionship that Lovell had cast a kind of spell on him. Now he must, for both their sakes, turn him around and send him home, before it was too late and he wouldn't be able to let him go.

Gruffly he said, "I've talked too much. Once you get me going on grass, I don't know when to quit."

"You couldn't talk too much about grass to suit me. I want to see everything you've done here. I want to know everything you know." He reached out and put his hand on Pride's shoulder. "What you have done here, I want to do at Lochleven. I know I can't stop the oil wells pumping, no matter how I'd like to, but there must be some way to ranch and pump oil at the same time.

You can tell me how to begin to clean up the mess, how to begin to grow grass again."

Against his better judgment, almost against his will, Pride began to answer questions as they walked on in the waving grass. "You can plow under the oil slick, and then put in a series of holding crops. You'll have to experiment until you find the right combination to enrich and revive the soil."

"How long will it take?"

Pride shook his head. "I can't tell you that." He saw the boy's face go dark with disappointment. "You can't expect miracles. Going back to prairie grass takes time, but there are only a dozen grasses that produce all our forage. The trick is to find the right mixture for each pasture and climate. It's all changed because the water table has been altered by the drilling."

Lovell nodded. "This new Beauvaise Bluestem—how long a grazing season will it give?"

"April to October, and then you'll need a cool season cover to see you through the winter."

"What about conditioners?"

"Sensitive Briar—try that. It's a strong tonic that has lots of protein, and the cattle like it green or in hay."

"What kind of cattle are you running?" Lovell asked.

"Hereford." Pride grinned. "Is there another breed?" It was a cattleman's joke. As he stood smiling at Lovell, suddenly Pride saw, as if it had appeared before him, the view of the old west pasture from the top of Beauvaise Ridge. In his memory he could see the tall, waving grass and the drifting herd of red cattle. The vision came and disappeared again, leaving him bereft.

"Do you still have Herefords at Lochleven?" He felt his throat ache; the words were hard to say.

It was a long time before Lovell replied. "Only wild things. I brought in a stray calf yesterday for Snow to raise."

The smile twisted on Pride's face as if a hook had fastened in his cheek. "The Beauvaise women used to run their own herds." Once again, he felt the awful ache for all he had lost, for all he could never have again. He knew he couldn't be any part of this boy's dreams, any more than he could go home again.

"Come on," he said abruptly. "I can't send you home without showing you my new bull. I brought him over from England."

The massive, powerfully built, white-faced red bull stood on a hillock in a green field. He was surrounded by a herd of cows contentedly grazing on the rich grass and waiting for his attentions. He was without a doubt the king of all he surveyed.

"He's magnificent," Lovell said soberly, as he admired the beauty of the beast. "And he's pure polled."

"That's right. I'm counting on old Rowley there to knock the horns off everything he covers."

Lovell turned to Pride. "You have it all—the land, the grass and the cattle."

Pride shook his head. "No man has it all."

"You have everything I want. You know everything I want to know." He reached out and held Pride's arm. "Come to Lochleven and help me get started."

Pride drew back and Lovell's hand fell away. "No! I can't do that." Pride's voice was harsh and cold.

"Why not?" Lovell was bewildered by the sudden change in Pride.

"I can't come to Lochleven now or ever."

"Tell me why."

"There are things you're too young to understand."

"I've heard that all my life." Lovell was more angry now than puzzled. "I understood why you wouldn't sue Andrew to get your land back. I understood why you had no need of it or royalties from the *Reanna* field when you had this fine place. I even understood why you couldn't try a federal case for the tribal land. And I saw, too, that it would be best for Snow to have an attorney represent her who's not a blood relation. But not to be willing to come to Lochleven to help me start a new stand of grass—that's something I don't understand at all." He waited, hoping Pride would answer him. "You'll have to tell me why. You'll have to spell it out, if I'm so ignorant and so stupid."

Pride felt he'd been asked for bread and had nothing to give but a stone. "I've told you I can't come to Lochleven. Now let it go. It's for the best, believe me."

"I was beginning to believe you," Lovell said. His eyes accused Pride of betraying him. "I won't make that mistake again." He looked at Pride, still hoping for a different answer. "Shall I tell you why I think you won't come to Lochleven? Not because it's best for everyone, but because it's best for you. Up here, you're king of the mountain. Here, you've got it made. Why should you care what happens to the rest of us?"

"Is that all?"

"No, I think you won't come because of Andrew MacClaren. You wouldn't fight him in the past and you won't fight him now. And the simple reason is you're afraid."

Pride clenched his jaw tight, trying not to show how deep the words cut him. He wanted this boy's acceptance and approval. He wanted Lovell's good opinion so much he was tempted to plead his case, make a defense of what he'd done and why, but it would have meant bringing Reanna into it. He couldn't do that. At last he said, "I fought Andrew once. I won't do it again."

"Because he beat you?" Lovell's tone was full of scorn.

"No, I won the fight, but the winning cost too much."

Lovell was brought up short. He waited for Pride to say more, and when he didn't, he felt again the sense of mystery that surrounded anything to do with Andrew MacClaren. Even when he thought he had reached the end of it, there was more, always more.

"I'm sorry," Lovell said. "I guess you're right. I don't understand, but I know that if you won't fight Andrew, I will."

"Don't try it." Pride's tone was sharp.

"I have to. I can't let him run over the people or the land. Someone must stop him." The boy stood straight, his chin lifted in defiance.

"You can't win," Pride said. "Andrew's too big. He's riding too high."

"Then he's riding for a fall," Lovell said, "and someone must bring him down."

ANDREW was riding high, wide and handsome as he led his big parade down the main street of Mac-Claren City. His horse was a splendid palomino, his spurs were silver and his saddle was made of Spanish leather. Strapped to his waist, his six-shooters had handles of polished ivory.

Behind Andrew came a cavalcade of marching bands, brightly decorated floats, old-time chuck wagons and buckboards, a line of new-make automobiles, assorted chapters of Elks, Masons, Rainbow Girls, DeMolay and Eastern Star, Veterans of Foreign Wars and an impressive array of horse quadrilles shooting off their pistols into the morning air.

Andrew squinted up at the cloudless sky. A thin wisp of a smile marked his face, as he made sure that no rain would fall on his parade or mar the barbecue to follow. This was his day. All around him flags rippled in the Oklahoma wind and the draped red, white and blue bunting fluttered as he rode past the MacClaren Building, the MacClaren Hotel, the MacClaren City Bank and on out west toward his marble palace.

As he passed Doc Hersey's house on MacClaren Avenue, he looked up and saw a curtain in the upstairs parlor window move. A figure hastily retreated behind the velvet drapes. Amoretta, probably. She'd cut him dead in the street, but if he knew human nature, Jack and Doc would turn up at the powwow just to show he hadn't got the best of them. He'd evened the score and he'd lost his old friends forever, but he had a host of new ones. The crowd on either side of the street roared his name.

AMORETTA turned away from the window to Reanna, and Lillian said, "I wish you'd look at that. They're following after Andrew like he was the Pied Piper of Hamelin."

"If he paid them enough, they'd follow him to hell," Reanna said.

Amoretta looked shocked. "Reanna, your language."

"Sorry." Reanna smiled ruefully. "I'd forgotten how genteel you town ladies have become."

Amoretta bridled then and shook her head so that her new marcel quivered like an agitated washboard. "If you came into town more often, you might see that Lillian and I are trying to set the tone, promote good manners. The town is full of that rough oil field element. We have to make a stand against them. You should join some of our clubs. There's the Twentieth Century Circle and the Literary Historical Guild and the Garden and Music Society."

"Thank you, Amoretta," Reanna said dryly, "but I'm still working for a living out in the oil patch. The bigger Andrew gets, the more I have to run to stay in place. He's always on the lookout to get my crude. I only came into town today because I wanted to see the big show."

"And to see Lillian and me, I hope." Amoretta cast Reanna a quick glance.

"Yes, I always like to see you, and catch a glimpse of Vera Sylvia." Jack and Lillian's daughter was, at five, a particular favorite of Reanna's.

"Are you sure you don't want to go out to the palace and see it for yourself?" Amoretta asked.

Reanna shook her head. "No, I wouldn't give Andrew the satisfaction."

"Nor would I," Lillian said. "They say he's imported every tree and bush and shrub, that he brought in a whole trainload of rolled-up grass sod to make the lawn and that he's dug water wells and dammed up the creek so all those marble fountains can spout water even in a dry summer."

"Andrew never was one to do things halfway," Reanna said.

"He's got three acres of greenhouses filled with Oklahoma wildflowers. I can't see that at all. What's the point? Why not leave them in the wild?" Lillian persisted.

"He couldn't control them in the wild." Reanna checked herself. "To be fair, Andrew always liked wildflowers."

"Andrew? Well, still it's a funny thing to do if you ask me. I can't imagine three acres of wildflowers."

"What about you, Amoretta?" Lillian asked. "Are you sure *you* don't want to go and see Andrew's marvels for yourself?"

Amoretta looked as if Lillian had insulted her. "Not on your life. You couldn't drag me out there with a team of wild horses. I'll never set foot in his house, not after what he did to Jack and Doc." Her eyes narrowed with suspicion. "Is there anyone from Lochleven going?"

"No, Cima and Snow say they have a lot of canning to do today. Taffy made a show of riding fence, and Lovell's gone off downstate to a cattle sale. And I"—Reanna smiled—"I came in to see you."

"I'm glad you came." Amoretta poured out a cup of coffee from a silver pot. She handed the cup to Reanna. "Did you know that Andrew, after all he's done, had the gall to send Pride a handwritten invitation?"

Reanna set the cup down and some of the coffee spilled into the saucer. "Is he coming?"

"You know better than that." Amoretta looked offended. "It would really be a cold day in July before Pride came to any play party of Andrew's. None of the old crowd are going."

"Doc and Jack are going."

Amoretta glared in defense of the two men. "Yes, but that's because they want to see what they've got for their money."

"Men!" Lillian said.

ANDREW MacClaren had spared no expense to make this day one Oklahoma would remember. He'd hired a circus—elephants and all. He'd built a bandstand so every band could take its turn showing off for their home folks. The gardens, like the town, had been festooned with flags and bunting. Opposite the circus was a Ferris wheel and pony rides, and around the walled gardens were stands dispensing watermelon, ice cream and lemonade, just to make sure that no one went hungry before the big barbecue.

Out in the field beyond the garden, Andrew had ordered a hundred beeves for the barbecue. There were beans on the boil and biscuits on the bake. He'd set up grandstands for the crowd to watch a Wild West show and quarter horse races. Near the stables he had an ample supply of bourbon being poured, away from the disapproving eyes of the preachers and the WCTUers.

Lifting a tin cup of whiskey, Doc said to Jack, "Here's to bread and circuses."

Jack shook his head. "What I don't understand is, if Andrew's so all-fired proud of this place, how can he let in this bunch of galoots to stomp on the grass and tramp through his house?"

"That's easy. He wants them to think he's just a good ol' boy, just like one of them, only he happened to strike oil—something they all sincerely believe could happen to every one of them any day in the week. He wants them to think he's their friend. Lordy, he'd let them burn down his barn if they were friendly about it."

"This has cost a bunch of money." Jack shook his head in wonder.

Doc took another swig of bourbon and held up his cup in mock salute. "Then we might as well enjoy it, because we paid for it. Come on, Jack, let's go find the son of a bitch."

The two men walked unsteadily toward the garden, holding on to each other for support.

ANDREW descended from the terrace to move through the crowd. All around him people were holding out hands to be shaken, babies to be kissed. They were eager for a word or a look, as if his touch and presence were the cure for the king's evil. He paused to answer reporters' questions, to talk crops to farmers, pasture to cowmen and oil to drillers. He asked after wives and children and smiled at pretty girls. Behind him, looking as theatrical as a painted backdrop, the great marble palace was a testament to his success. Above, the flags flew flat in the Oklahoma wind, and all around him there was the sound of martial music, raucous laughter and bursts of gunfire, the sure proof that every man in the West was a law unto himself.

In case the crowd pressed him too close, a little knot of bodyguards hovered nearby, ready to separate him from their overeager, unwanted attentions. Standing so close to Andrew that he could have reached out and touched him, Lovell might have been just anyone in the crowd—an ordinary young man in a ten-gallon hat, chaps, a holster and a six-shooter. He watched Andrew and listened to him uttering pleasantries.

"Glad you could come. Have a real good time now, you hear? How you all doin'? You're looking good."

Lovell knew that Andrew's concern and friendly manner were as phony and all for show as the marble palace set out on an alien prairie. Why couldn't any of the rest of them see that? What made them stand in awe of him, as if to be in his presence were to be standing before God Almighty?

Suddenly there was a fanfare. A guard of honor appeared to escort Andrew to the speakers' stand set at the end of the terrace in front of a long colonnade of marble pillars. Andrew allowed himself to be led through a parting sea of people, like Moses heading for the promised land. On the stand, decorated in patriotic red, white and blue, there were businessmen of state and national importance, the mayor of MacClaren City, one senator, several congressmen and a minister of the gospel, ready to lend his blessing to the occasion.

Once the mob heard that Andrew was about to speak, they began to push forward toward the platform, shouting his name, firing off their guns, as if this were the beginning of a barrage. Lovell was swept forward by the tide of people till he stood in front of the stand, staring up at Andrew. Still they roared and whistled, until Andrew rose to silence them.

"Listen," Andrew shouted. "Give the preacher here a chance to say a prayer and the mayor to introduce me. Then I can say a few words and you can go put your noses in the feedbag." They laughed, stamped and whistled again, and then, because he had asked them to, they grew silent enough for an invocation.

The minister thanked God for the glorious day, for the opportunity for them all to be together and for a friend and neighbor like Andrew MacClaren. He said, "Amen," and the mayor rose, perspiring, eager to please, sensible of the fact that he must be brief and yet appear to do Andrew every honor. He cleared his throat.

"Ladies and gentlemen, I'm here to introduce a man who needs no introduction."

"Then why do it?" someone shouted from the back. As the crowd laughed and churned and shifted, Doc and Jack edged their way forward so they could get a better view of Andrew in all his glory.

"He's our friend, our neighbor, our host today." The mayor had a style of delivery best suited to calling in the cows. "He's a man who has brought good times to MacClaren City and will bring good times to the great state of Oklahoma."

The crowd roared and shouted its approval of Andrew and the state in which they lived.

"He's the kind of man we need in this state to keep the Eastern bankers, the Standard Oil crowd and all those Yankee rascals out of our business. He's a businessman whose business is the good of the people. And we're proud to call him neighbor and friend. Who do you want?" the mayor shouted.

"MacClaren," the people cried.

"When do you want him?"

"Now, now, now!" They roared and stamped their feet, whistled, clapped and cheered. The gunshots ran in a fusillade. They were for Andrew all the way, and they let him know it.

Andrew stood accepting the people's homage. He waited as the roar grew. A dozen photographers' cameras caught his likeness. He'd expected a good turnout today. He'd made sure of it by giving every MacClaren employee the day off with pay to attend, but this crowd was bigger than he'd hoped for. Maybe they'd come to gawk and for the free eats, but they'd also come because he'd asked them to. As the roar began to diminish, he raised his arms in a gesture of total authority, willing them, commanding them to be silent. His eyes—cold, clouded aquamarine like the sea in winter—encompassed them all. When at last they were still, he began to speak, to tell the crowd what they wanted to hear.

"My friends, I know you want to get at the grub, so I won't keep you long. I just want to thank you all for coming here today. I thank you for being my friends. No matter how good things get, I'll always need friends like you."

Lovell watched, stunned and sickened by the brute stupidity of the crowd. How could they believe that Andrew was their friend? He'd conned them, as he had all his friends. He'd taken their birthright; they'd sold it to him for less than a mess of potage. They were blind to his faults, mesmerized by his words, oblivious to his deeds. He'd lied to them in the past, he was lying to them now and they were prepared to bow down and worship him for it. The more he lied, the more they believed him.

He'd taken the land and laid it to waste. He'd robbed it of its treasure without any plan to renew or redeem it. Why couldn't they see that for themselves? Why could they see nothing, when Lovell saw Andrew so clearly that the vision was bright as a burning light. He held up his hand to shade his eyes.

If they were blind, then he must make them see what manner of man Andrew really was. He must open their eyes for them, and the only way to do that was to force Andrew to confess before them that he had no regard, only contempt for them. That he was not now, nor had he ever been, their friend. The only way they'd ever believe that Andrew wasn't what he pretended to be was to hear it from his own lips. Lovell had asked Reanna for help and then he'd asked Pride. They had both refused him. Now, if he wanted Andrew exposed, it would be up to him.

Suddenly he felt possessed by the idea that he must seize this moment. With a great surge of strength, he leapt out of the crowd and onto the platform. As he landed square before Andrew, he drew his gun from its holster.

The two men stood facing each other, Lovell's gun pointing toward Andrew's heart. It seemed to Lovell that the shouting had died away. He heard a gasp, muffled cries of surprise and then silence. In the distance there was the faint, echoed laughter of children by the Ferris wheel and from above the slapping whip of the flags in the wind and the tapping of ropes against the flagpoles. In this brief moment he and Andrew were caught, held in time. Andrew stared at him, his eyes wide, but without any recognition. Lovell could see the throbbing of a vein in Andrew's forehead. He saw his father's eyes widen as they gauged the angle of the pointed gun. Then at last Andrew found his voice.

"Well, son, and what can I do for you?" From the tone of Andrew's voice and by his manner, Lovell could see that calling him *son* meant nothing. Andrew didn't know him from Adam. "Speak up, boy. What do you want?"

Anger seared Lovell's mind. Andrew was making a joke of him. "I want . . ." he said. He was ashamed to see that his hand was unsteady. "I want you to tell them the truth."

"And what truth is that?" Andrew seemed unable to understand the question.

"I want you to tell them you're a cheat, a liar and a swindler."

"That's a tall order." Andrew's smile mocked him.

Lovell felt sick at heart. Andrew was laughing at him. He was no match for Andrew; suddenly the fear of failure cut at him. He felt helpless and there were tears of rage in his eyes. "You cheated your family, your friends, and now you're cheating the people. Tell them that." His hand continued to tremble.

Andrew's gaze flickered for a moment. A little smile caught at the corner of his mouth. He gave an almost imperceptible nod of his head to the waiting bodyguards, and at his signal they sprang forward toward Lovell. One grabbed his gun arm and jerked it upward. As his arm was forced into the air above his head, Lovell heard a shot ring out. His other arm was wrenched behind his back, held in a hammerlock—turned, twisted in its socket until the pain made him sick and he was afraid he might throw up. It was almost a relief to hear Andrew whisper, "Get him out of here before he causes any more trouble."

Lovell looked at Andrew. He saw that his face was white as if from pain. As their eyes caught, for one jagged moment Lovell thought Andrew knew who he was and why he'd come, but then he saw a little spill of blood from above Andrew's elbow. Then he felt himself being dragged over the rear edge of the platform back into the cool colonnades, toward the great marble palace, a palace so large it must have a dungeon.

And then, when they were out of sight of the crowd, there was a rain of blows aimed at his head and back and stomach. Just as Lovell was about to beg for mercy, he felt himself sliding into a dark oblivion.

Andrew turned to the waiting crowd. He held his arm at the elbow to hide the blood and to keep the pain from being unbearable. He swallowed and forced a smile. "Well, that's one way of getting me to cut my speech short."

They roared their approval and relief. Everything was all right. Andrew was safe and the incident was over.

"I'd say that boy just had a little too much party spirit." Again they laughed and clapped. "But I can take a hint. I don't need a building to fall on me. I'll cut the speech extra short."

There were cries of "Speech!" and "Good old Andrew!"

"Seriously," Andrew went on, "I want to say I'm glad you came. And now, friends and neighbors, it's time to dig into the feed trough and eat hearty."

There was some more applause as he let himself be led from the stand. When it was clear he wouldn't return, the crowd turned and began a stampede toward the field outside the garden and all the free food they could eat.

Left behind in the rush, riveted to the spot where they stood, were Doc and Jack Levy. "My God, Doc," Jack said, "I think that boy was Lovell."

"Are you sure?" Doc was suddenly sober.

"So sure I'm going into town to get Reanna. She's at your house, isn't she?"

"Yes, she's there with Amoretta and Lillian. I'll go with you, Jack."

"No, Doc, you stay. Andrew's shot, and no telling what his bruisers are doing to the boy."

SLUMPED in the corner of a basement storeroom was the crumpled figure of Lovell MacClaren. The boy's face had been beaten out of shape; his eyes were swollen and already closing. His nose was bloody and crooked. He held his sides where sharp-toed boots had dug into his ribs. His lip was split so deep that blood oozed from the corner of his mouth. Andrew stood, holding his bleeding arm, glaring at Lovell's inert body. "Who is he?" he demanded of his bodyguards. "Who is he and why did he want to kill me?"

"He hasn't told us diddly squat," one of the men said. "We worked him over good."

Lovell groaned.

"Try again." Andrew spat out the words.

Two of the men hauled Lovell up so that he hung limp between them. Another hit him on the kidneys. Lovell made a sound like air escaping from a cushion. His head sagged and bobbed against his chest.

"Hasn't he got any identification?" Andrew demanded.

A fourth man began rifling Lovell's pockets and in a moment, with a sheepish look, handed Lovell's wallet to Andrew. Andrew opened it and began to read a receipt for a cow Lovell had bought, as Doc Hersey appeared in the doorway. Doc said, "You don't have to beat the boy anymore. I can tell you who he is."

"Who the hell let you in here?" Andrew spoke as he glanced again at the receipt and saw the name. He slammed the wallet shut. "Jesus H. Christ."

(542)

"I came because I thought you might need a doctor. Now I see I have two patients."

Andrew sighed. He looked at the boy; the face was no longer recognizable, but he should have guessed something from Lovell's red hair.

"Somebody will have to tell his mother," Andrew said. "It might as well be you."

"Jack's already on his way to town. Reanna's at my house, visiting Amoretta."

Andrew's jaw set hard; his eyes flashed with sudden rage. "She knew he was coming here gunning for me? Is that what you're saying? You all knew he was coming here and you did nothing to stop him."

"I didn't know any such thing." Doc stared back at Andrew. "But if I had, I don't know as I'd have stopped him. Now, let's get him cleaned up before his mother sees him. After that I'll have a look at that arm."

REANNA drove fast down the back road to Andrew's marble palace. She was grim-faced and pale. Jack, sitting beside her, knew better than to break the silence. He'd already told her all he knew—Lovell was at Andrew's powwow, there'd been a ruckus, a shot had been fired and Doc had gone to look after the boy.

They came onto the property by the north gate, the dust rising up behind them like a red wall. They drove up to the service entrance and walked in without anyone stopping or questioning them. Jack had been sure they'd brought the boy down this way. They wouldn't take him upstairs where he might be seen.

"I don't like coming in the back like a sneak," Reanna said, as they walked down the basement hall, opening first one door and then another.

"I understand," Jack said, "but if you'd come in the front, you'd have been recognized. You don't want the papers all over this."

"Are there lots of reporters here?"

"Yes, Andrew invited every newspaper in the state and most of them came. You know what they'd make of this if they knew it was Lovell."

At the end of the hallway she saw a man guarding a door. "He's in there," she said. "Wait for me at the car." She walked straight to the door and motioned the man to move. "I'm Mrs. Mac-Claren," she said. He stood aside.

She opened the door into a small laundry sorting room. Andrew didn't seem surprised to see her there. "Where's Lovell?"

"Hello, Reanna." He had one arm in a sling, but he looked all right otherwise.

"I want to see Lovell." She looked past Andrew to a door behind him. She started toward it but Andrew stopped her.

"Not so fast, Reanna. Doc's in there with him."

"I'm going to see him." She went around Andrew and opened the door to the laundry room. Lovell was lying on top of a long table. Doc was just rolling down his sleeves. He looked up, shrugged and stepped aside.

She looked down at Lovell and wanted to scream, to cry out, to protest that they'd played some cruel trick on her. This couldn't be her beautiful boy. This couldn't be Lovell. "Oh, dear God. Oh, God." She put her hand on his forehead and let it rest there lightly. He was hot to her touch.

He felt her cool hand. She'd come to him, as she'd used to do when he was a little boy with a fever, only then he'd never hurt so or known such pain. He tried to see her, but the shape he saw through swollen eyes was blurred.

"Don't be angry, please. I'm sorry." What a stupid thing to say. He'd mumbled the words without thinking.

"I'm not angry. Don't worry about anything. You're going to be all right. Doc's looking after you, and in just a little while I'll take you home to Lochleven. It's all over and there's nothing to worry about."

He closed his eyes. It could have been a dream or it could have been real, but he hoped she'd really come to take him home.

"I've given him something to kill the pain," Doc said.

"Thank you." She stood, looking at Lovell. She felt as if the heart had been torn out of her. The sudden shock of seeing him like this had been a sort of anesthetic for her, too. She felt disembodied, a part of her looking at Lovell, another part lost, wandering in a long tunnel. He'd asked that she not be angry with him, when all the while it was she who should have asked his forgiveness for not keeping him safe.

"I'd like to kill Andrew," she said quietly.

"It wouldn't help Lovell, and they'd only send you to jail." Doc turned her away from Lovell and toward the door. "I'll stay with him while you talk to Andrew."

"Yes," she said mechanically. "I'll have to talk to Andrew now."

She opened the door and went back into the other room. She knew that whatever it cost her, she must remain calm. No matter how she felt, she mustn't show Andrew. She must go one step at a time, as carefully as if she were on a tightwire, walking over a deep chasm. What she wanted was to get Lovell out of here. To do that, she had to have Andrew's permission.

SHE stood in the doorway staring at Andrew, hating him. Her heart was beating very fast. She had to clench her fists to keep from striking out at him.

"Why have you done this to him?"

Andrew gave a short, dry, unpleasant laugh. "It's not what I've done to him, Reanna, it's what he's done to me." He held up his arm in the sling. "He shot me."

"Why?"

"You'll have to ask him that."

"He must have said something, given some reason." She was fighting for calm, for control of her emotions. She felt as if she were in a nightmare and everywhere she looked there were specters and goblins.

"He was acting crazy," Andrew protested. "He jumped up on the speakers' stand. Everything he said sounded like gibberish to me. I didn't know who he was. He just jumped up there, pulled a gun and shot me."

She didn't believe him, but she wouldn't argue the point now. "I want to take him home."

Andrew shifted from one foot to the other. "There may be a few difficulties about that. The police will want him too."

"What for?"

"There'll be charges. Assault with a deadly weapon—intent to kill."

Her eyes blazed and she lost hold of her temper. "Don't give me that! Don't threaten me. You won't give him to the police because you don't want a public scandal."

"I didn't cause the trouble, he did." Andrew smiled.

She'd forgotten how that smile of his could bring her to rage. She wanted to strike out at him, to see him dead.

"I don't see," Andrew drawled, "how we can help but have a scandal with all the newspapers here."

She must control herself. She bit at the inside of her lip until she felt the blood, warm and salty in her mouth. "Did you tell the reporters who he was?"

Andrew hesitated. "They'll guess soon enough."

"But if you don't identify him, then what can they report? Just that a young man caused a disturbance and that your speech was interrupted by 'an incident.' They'll have to put it down to high spirits."

"Trying to shoot your father is more than high spirits. There's bound to be talk."

"Then let them talk. They can't prove anything. You don't want a scandal or the police here asking embarrassing questions. If you don't press charges, they'll have to believe any story you tell them."

He shrugged. What she said made sense. She'd won a point, but the game was far from over. There was a silence while each considered what was won and what was lost and where next to attack the other.

"Why do you think he did it?" Andrew blurted out. He wanted the answer. "Did you put him up to it?"

"No!" She looked at him with loathing, her gaze as cold and steady as his. "He doesn't like you, Andrew, or what you stand for. He doesn't want to be like you."

"Then you can tell him there's no fear of that. He's not like me and we both know why."

She ignored the barbed thrust. "The world thinks he's yours, Andrew. You claimed him. If you let him go you're a hero and if not, if you tell everyone your son hates you enough to shoot you, you'll look like a fool. Or worse, you'll look like a villain."

Andrew thought carefully. "You always were a smart one, Reanna. I'll give you that."

"I'm right. You know I am. So turn him over to me. Let me take him home. I'll be responsible for him."

"Whoa! Not so fast." The smile had gone. He was angry now, provoked as she had always provoked him. "You always liked to work me, jerk me, manipulate me first to last. This time you're out of luck. I've got the boy and I mean to keep him."

"You always liked to pretend I'd backed you into a corner, made

(546)

you marry me against your will. Well, believe me, if I did I'm heartily sorry for it. I've lived to regret it. But this is a little different, isn't it? How can I manipulate you? You hold all the cards. You have what I want, Andrew. I want Lovell, I want my son. I want to take him home." She kept her eyes on his face, but for the first time her voice was unsteady. It betrayed her. He must see her calm was all a bluff.

Despite the pain of his arm, Andrew felt a sudden elation. He had her cornered. She was up a tree with no hope of escape unless he called off the dogs. "I can't let the boy go scot-free, Reanna," he said slowly, relishing each word.

"Why not?"

"How do I know he won't try this sort of stunt again? Next time he took a shot at me his aim might be better."

They stood, toe to toe, eye to eye. The time of hard bargaining had come. Each waited for the other to blink and back off.

"He won't come after you again."

"How can you guarantee that?"

"You have my word on it."

He hesitated. "That's not quite good enough. I'll need more than that. I think I deserve something more."

"What do you want?"

"Your production's way up, I hear." Andrew was smiling again. She knew now what he was after and what he meant to have. "I always need crude," he said. "You could guarantee me all of your product. Then I wouldn't have to go scurrying around looking for leases, begging for crude from independents when I go short."

"I'd have thought you'd have enough crude, now you've got the leases on tribal surplus land. I'd have thought you'd have enough crude with the Indian land to last you from now to kingdom come."

He considered what she'd said gravely, as if it might make a difference and change his mind. Then he shook his head. "That surplus land might take a while to develop and prove out. I'll need more than that."

"And so you want what's mine? You want my product?"

"What's yours was once mine, don't forget." He smiled again, but there was winter in his eyes.

"You want my crude at market price."

From outside she could hear the faint, muffled sound of people cheering. They all thought Andrew was a hero. Suddenly she felt sick at heart. She knew she was beaten. He'd won. The stakes were too high. Lovell was the prize, and Andrew knew she'd pay any price for him.

"Well, do I get it? Do I get your production?"

She nodded. She found it too difficult to speak.

"Every barrel, every drop of oil that comes into the *Reanna* or any other field under lease to you will be sold at market price and piped to me? Understood?"

"Yes." She whispered the word and then spoke clearly. "Yes, you give me Lovell and I'll give you my product, at market price."

"You give me your word on it?"

"Yes! I've said that." She was sharp now, anger returning to her numbed mind.

He'd pressed his advantage too far and he saw it. "Then take him home. Take him back to Lochleven and keep him there. See he stays out of my oil patch."

She wanted to laugh. It was a kind of supreme, cosmic joke. As if God were playing a prank on them all. At last Lovell was going to get what he'd always wanted—to stay at home. She'd spent years trying to keep him away so that he would be safe and he'd bucked her all the way, trying to get home again. Now she must promise Andrew to keep him there. "I agree," she said.

Andrew began to expand, to relish his victory. "You're damn right, you agree. See he keeps his guns locked up. He's too young to be playing with firearms."

"You've beaten Lovell and now you've beaten me. I'll pay the ransom as you knew I would. But let's get this over with. I want to take him home."

"I'll get the lawyers on it today. I'll send you the agreement."

"When you're ready, I'll sign the papers."

"You don't want to dicker over terms?" He goaded her, tearing at her like a Choctaw bone picker.

"No. May we go now?"

She was too quiet, too passive; it was too easy. He wanted more. "Then go, but don't come crying to me, begging me to forget this."

"I'm too old to cry, Andrew, and if I come to you again, I won't come begging. But there's one more thing."

He frowned. "What's that?"

"If I promise to keep Lovell at Lochleven, you must promise you'll leave him alone."

(548)

"I never wanted to have anything to do with him in the first place. He came after me."

"And now I want you to promise that you won't come after him."

"A standoff?" he asked.

"A standoff."

Suddenly Andrew grinned. His eyes flashed with joy at his cunning victory. "With your crude I'll be able to expand coast to coast. With your crude and the new refinery I'm dickering to buy up in Ohio, I'm going to give Standard a run for their money. So you see, I don't have time to think anymore about you or your . . ." He paused. ". . . your bastard of a son. Now get him out of here. Take him out the back way. I want to forget this ever happened."

"But you'll always remember it," she said evenly. "Just as I will, whenever you ship, refine or sell a barrel of my oil."

Doc had given Lovell enough painkiller that the trip home was not too agonizing. Both Doc and Jack had helped her get Lovell into the car and offered to come to Lochleven with her, but she'd thanked them and said no. This was something she had to do alone. She wanted to get Lovell home and hide him out, like a lioness taking a wounded cub to her cave.

Lovell lay in the front seat, his head cradled in her lap. She drove slowly so as not to jar him. As she glanced down at his battered face, she swore that if it took from now until the day she was laid in her grave, she'd pay Andrew back for what he'd done to Lovell. She'd see Andrew stripped bare, flayed alive, driven out in disgrace. But now was not the time to lay her plans. First, she'd bring Lovell back where he belonged, back to Lochleven.

Jack had phoned ahead to say they were coming. Taffy was on the porch waiting, Cima and Snow beside him. When Taffy saw the car, he sprang down the steps and opened the car door. When he saw Lovell, he went white beneath his weathered tan.

"Oh, God damn Andrew. Damn him to hell. Here, boy, let me help you."

Lovell rose up and groaned, "I can walk."

"I know, but you lean on me." Taffy hoisted one of Lovell's arms around his neck and half carried, half held him as they got up the steps. Cima put her apron over her face. Snow began to cry, great tears of pity streaming down her face.

"Get out of the way," Taffy barked. "We don't need crying women hovering over us. I'll take care of this boy now."

He got Lovell up to his room and onto his bed. The women followed after, ignoring Taffy's protests. They crowded in the doorway. Taffy turned. "I'll tell you when we need company. Now git." He bent over Lovell, crooning soft encouragement. "You're going to be fine, boy. Just fine. Tell me, how did the other fellow look?"

"Better than me," Lovell murmured through swollen lips.

"I'm sorry to hear that."

"I shot him. I shot Andrew."

Taffy nodded. He'd already heard as much. "The son of a bitch deserved it and worse. Now lie still. I've got to get a poultice on them eyes and liniment on them bruises."

"Doc said it would take a week at least for the swelling to go down." It was hard for Lovell to talk, his lips were so swollen, and he could barely see Taffy's face close to his.

"What does Doc know?" Taffy snorted. "The only thing he knows to do with liniment is to drink it." He pressed a poultice on Lovell's eyes and began rubbing liniment on his side and shoulders.

Lovell winced. "That stuff stinks."

"Stinks? That's the best liniment there is. Taffy Owen's elixir, good for man or beast."

"I wasn't much of a man today."

"That's your opinion. Don't get all down in the mouth. You'll live to fight another day, and it won't take any week before you're better. Why, I've seen many a cowboy right after a tangle with a bunch of stampeding steers—I've seen grown men with ribs stove in, tromped on, pounded to a pulp—recover overnight after only one application of this here elixir. Tomorrow you'll be up and runnin', ready, rarin' to fight again. You just leave the doctorin' to me."

REANNA sat in the cupola room, staring out the window at the *Reanna* and *MacClaren* fields. From down the hall she heard the sound of Taffy's voice, talking, crooning over Lovell.

The oil had made her rich and the oil had cost her dear, but she'd even the score. For what Andrew had done to Lovell, she meant to have her revenge. She remembered the first day she'd come to the Nation. She'd seen a boy hanged from a gallows tree in Maitland. Andrew had said it was for revenge, that revenge was the Indian way. He'd said that a Chickasaw would walk a thousand miles to even a score. Today, to even the score with Andrew, she'd gladly walk ten thousand miles. She'd have an eye for an eye, a tooth for a tooth. She wanted him dead—buried. But there were ways of killing Andrew that would be worse for him than death, more terrible than hell.

If it was the last thing she ever did, she'd see that his house would fall down about his head. She'd see him run from the state in humiliation and disgrace. She'd live to go to his hanging. She'd walk a thousand times ten thousand miles, but she'd have her revenge.

She began to think of a plan—a way to bring him down. It would take time. It would take money. It would take patience, but it could be done. And she would do it.

LOVELL slept until dark. She sat beside him, holding his hand while Taffy paced the hall. When Lovell woke, Cima brought him soup and Reanna fed it to him from a spoon. It was slow and painful going and she soon gave it up. Then he slept again and she sent them all away. The night watch was hers to keep alone.

Sometime toward dawn he stirred and moaned. With effort he opened one eye and saw her and turned his face away toward the wall.

"I'm sorry," he whispered. "I'm so sorry and so ashamed."

She'd seen men worse off than Lovell. Andrew had been beaten nearly dead by Pride; his blood had stained the snow. She'd seen men burned beyond recognition in oil field fires, men scalded alive in steam. She'd seen them broken beyond repair in falls from derricks. But the worst accidents, the worst injuries, were not to the body but to the spirit. Pain could be forgotten. One could live as a cripple, but to live in shame was a violation of the soul. She must make Lovell proud and whole again.

She said, "You've been asleep a long time."

"What time is it?"

"Nearly dawn. How do you feel?"

"Stiff, sore—better." He turned back to her. "I really messed things up this time, didn't I?"

"It's all right."

"How can you say that?"

"Because what happened yesterday was my fault."

"I shot Andrew," he said, "you didn't."

"Did you mean to shoot him?"

"No, but I'm not sorry I did."

"Why did you do it?"

"I wanted everyone to see him for what he is. I asked you to help me, and Pride Beauvaise. When neither of you would, it was up to me."

"You went to see Pride?" Her heart stopped, and then after what seemed to be an eternity, began to beat again.

"Yes, I wanted him to take the land back, but he wouldn't. He doesn't want it or need it. He has something better. If he were a United States attorney, he'd prosecute Andrew for the tribal land deal but he'd do nothing for himself."

A long time passed. Then she was able to ask. "What did you think of him?"

"He's wonderful. He knows everything I want to know. You should see his cattle and the grass."

She felt tears on her cheeks and hoped he couldn't see them. "I've been very stupid about you."

"How do you figure that?" He was interested, intrigued by what she'd said. He'd always thought she was the smartest woman in seventeen counties. He propped himself up on one elbow. She saw him grimace with pain.

"I've tried to make you go against your nature, to be somebody, something you weren't. It can't be done, and I was wrong to try. I've spent years sending you off to school with you wanting to come home."

"I'm a bad penny," he said, but he didn't sound as depressed as he had before.

"No, Lovell." She wouldn't allow him to turn it away lightly. "You know what you want, you always have. You want to grow grass and breed cattle. You don't want to be a scholar or an oilman. You want to be the best damn rancher in the state of Oklahoma, and if I'll let you alone that's what you will be."

"You can't be sure." He was trying to smile at her.

"I'd bet on it. I'll tell you something else; you'd even be a good oilman if you put your mind to it."

"No." He drew back from her, thinking this might be the thin end of the wedge, but he did her an injustice.

"You might not go looking for it, but if the oil was yours to manage, you'd have the sense to prorate production." He waited, thinking she'd ask him to work with her once more, but she surprised him. "So . . ." She took a deep breath. "So, as soon as you're up and around, you'd better be getting on with what you want to do with your life. Buy some cattle. Start cleaning up the field. See if anything will grow again out there."

He was stunned. It took him a little while to think. "What are you going to be doing?"

"I'm going away."

"Where?"

"I'm going to travel. You don't want me to stay here, do you, and always be looking over your shoulder?"

"You wouldn't do that."

"Well, you don't have to worry. I'm going East."

"Why?"

"It's time I took a holiday. I want to go to Virginia for a spell and then on to Washington and New York. I've worked hard. I think I deserve a little rest."

"But who's going to tend the oil business for you while you're gone?" He was suspicious again.

"There'll be nothing to do," she said. "I'm getting out of oil play for a while."

"Getting out?" He'd never known a time when oil wasn't her life.

"Yes, I've contracted to sell my production."

"Who to?"

"To Andrew."

"Because of me?" He sat up straight and groaned.

"No," she said, "not altogether. I told you oil is no longer a woman's game. It's all different. It's time I had a change."

Lovell didn't believe her. Yet he had never known her to lie. "You made a deal with Andrew so he'd let me go, didn't you?"

"I made him a promise. Now I want one from you. I promised him you'd keep out of his oil patch. That you'd keep out of his way. Do you agree to that?"

He nodded.

"Do you promise?"

"Yes." It was easy to promise. He never wanted to see Andrew again.

"And in exchange, Andrew has promised not to do you any more harm."

"And for his promise you gave him your oil?"

"I contracted him my production. I didn't give it to him."

"You've shaken hands with the devil."

She smiled. "I'll get better than I gave. That's my promise to you."

"When are you going?"

"When you're up and around."

"Taffy says I'll be up tomorrow."

"Please!" she said in mock dismay. "Don't rush me. I have lawyers to see, plans to make and cables to send. I have a lot of talking to do on the telephone. I'll need at least a week."

WHILE Lovell recovered from the beating Andrew's men had given him, Reanna made her plans for Andrew's downfall. The cupola room was her command post. Cables were sent to and from England. Telephone calls were made to Ohio, Washington and New York. She studied confidential reports on men she meant to see in the East. She conferred for hours with Doc and Jack Levy behind closed doors, and at night, after the household was asleep and she had looked in on Lovell, she paced up and down thinking out her strategy, step by step.

She had three main objectives. She wanted Andrew's public disgrace, his financial ruin and her oil back.

It would be a sweet revenge if, after all Andrew had stolen from Snow and Pride, she could arrange for Pride to prosecute Andrew in federal court. She knew in her bones that Andrew had paid a bribe to get his lease on tribal surplus land. It was time Andrew was branded a thief.

It would be an even sweeter revenge if she could maneuver Andrew out of the oil business. He had taken advantage of her love for Lovell to get control of her oil. Like a giant tick, he meant to bleed her fields dry to make himself big and fat. If MacClaren Oil went under, and she meant to do everything in her power to see that it did, then her contract with Andrew would be broken.

The third part of her plan depended on Simon's friends in England. When she managed to get control of her oil again, she wanted to sell it to men who were interested in keeping world oil prices stable and who knew the advantage of conserving proven reserves.

To make these three objectives a reality would take time and money. It would mean that she must leave Lochleven. She must work slowly and carefully behind the scenes, so that Andrew would not suspect what she was up to. It would be worth any price or personal sacrifice, for if she won, when she came back Andrew would no longer have any power to hurt her or hers ever again.

SHE put off her going until Lovell was well. Then she began to pack. Cima stood watching her cram shirtwaists into a worn gladstone bag.

"What are you up to?" Cima demanded. "You been in here a-ginnin' and a-goin'. What are you fixing to do now?"

"I'm going home for a visit," Reanna said coolly.

"Why?"

"Why not? It's time I took a vacation."

"How long will you be gone?"

"I don't know."

"When will you be back?"

"When I get here."

"What does that mean?"

"It means I'm going to Virginia, to Washington and New York. I may even go to England to visit Frampton."

Cima shook her head. "Gettin' anything out of you is like tryin' to pull hen's teeth. I say you're goin' off because of what happened between Lovell and Andrew."

"I don't know what you're talking about."

"Don't try an' pull the wool over my eyes. Everyone's saying Lovell shot Andrew. There was a lot of people saw it. It ain't like Lovell shot him in private."

Reanna snapped her bulging suitcase shut and turned on Cima. "No one can prove anything against Lovell. No charges were filed. And since when did you listen to gossip?"

"Is that why you just give Andrew all your oil—to keep it quiet?"

"I didn't give Andrew my oil. I contracted to sell it to him at market price. It won't be forever, I guarantee you that. I'll find a way to get it back."

"And how do you aim to do that?"

"I have a few ideas." Reanna avoided Cima's eyes.

"You cross Andrew on this deal, and you could get hurt bad."

Reanna's mouth set in a hard line. "That's my business."

"Fair enough," Cima admitted grudgingly. "But you set a fire, you can get burned. You lay a trap, and you can get caught."

"Have you any more words of wisdom?"

"No." Cima shook her head. "I've had my say."

"If you need anything extra while I'm gone, you can get in touch with Jack Levy. He's handling my finances."

"We'll get along fine." Cima smoothed out her skirt, trying not to show how near to tears she was.

There was a moment of silence and then Reanna held out her arms. "I'll miss you, Cima."

"I'll miss you too, lady." Cima hesitated a moment and then the two women embraced, held to each other before Cima pushed Reanna away. "You act nice now, you hear?"

Reanna smiled. "I'll try."

"And get some new clothes so you won't look like a ragbag come to town."

"I will."

"And don't shame us before Yankees."

"I promise."

REANNA made her goodbyes at Lochleven. She refused to let Cima or Snow or Lovell come to the station. She knew word would get back to Andrew that she'd gone. If she knew him, he'd take credit for driving her away. Only Taffy rode with her in the Rolls, sitting beside her as straight as if he had a poker up his back.

"I've told Lovell he's to be in charge at Lochleven," she said.

"That don't mean I can't make a suggestion now and again, does it?"

"No, but let Lovell do anything he wants to. He can grow grass or graze cattle or put beans in his ears."

"But you still want me to ride herd on him. Right?"

"I want him safe," she said fiercely. "I want backup men with him wherever he goes. Hire good men, men you can trust. Be discreet, but keep your eye on him."

"And who's going to look out for you while you're off up East?"

Her chin went up. "I can take care of myself."

"You buck heads once more with Andrew, and he'll turn as mean as a yellow dog."

"Thank you for your advice."

"I know you. You don't mean to let Andrew call the tune."

"When I finish with Andrew," Reanna said slowly, "he won't call a tune, let alone dance ever again."

When she was safe inside the compartment and the train had begun to move, she pulled down the shade and hung out a Do Not Disturb sign on the door. She was bone-tired. As she looked at herself in the washbasin mirror, she was shocked by her reflection. "Reanna," she said aloud, "you've got as mean and tough as old boots."

She'd let her looks go and that was a fact. If she was going to succeed in the East, she'd have to mend her looks and her manners. What passed in the oil patch would never get by in a drawing room. To whip herself into shape to charm city men, she'd need all her mother's Southern skill.

"I hope you're planning to stay more than a week this trip." Mrs. Lovell was helping Reanna to settle into her old room. It had been newly done up in fresh paper; there were new curtains and a floral bedspread, but it still looked like a little girl's room.

"Yes, Mama, I'm going to make you a nice, long visit."

"To what do we owe the honor?"

"I need you."

Mrs. Lovell gasped. "Even when you were little, you never said you needed me."

"I do now."

"What's happened? What's wrong?"

"Nothing's wrong, Mama." Reanna smiled indulgently. "I need your special talent to get me fit to appear in polite society."

Mrs. Lovell's eyes narrowed and she frowned. "Is this some kind of joke? I never know when you're serious."

"I'm serious. You've always wanted to teach me to act like a fine lady. Now's your chance."

"You've left it a little late," Mrs. Lovell grumbled. "I mean, look at you. Hair like a rat's nest. Skin speckled as a guinea hen egg. You never used a night cream the way I told you. And a pauper wouldn't wear those clothes."

"I know what's wrong, Mama. What I want is for you to make it right."

Mrs. Lovell sighed. "I'll try, but it won't be easy."

It took a month of cucumber lotion, red elm cream, lemons on her elbows, rainwater shampoos and a hundred strokes with a stiff brush every night before her mother allowed dressmakers near the house. Even then she wasn't really pleased with the result.

"If you were ever going to buy yourself some decent clothes, why did you wait till the twenties when the styles are the ugliest things ever seen in God's creation. No waists, flat chests, skirts up to your knees and those awful silk stockings gleaming like a gold tooth. Honestly, even if you get the best fabrics, they don't improve the cut." She stood back from Reanna, as she'd once done at Cousin Lucy Marr's, and surveyed her handiwork. "Are you doing this because Andrew has taken a fancy to another woman?"

"No, Mama."

"Because you have a lover?"

"Mama!" For once her mother had managed to shock her.

"Or because you're nearly forty?"

"My age has nothing to do with it," Reanna said tartly. "I'm in my prime."

"Is that what you call it?" Mrs. Lovell shook her head. "Well, if you're going to try to be the fine lady, lower your voice. You don't have to shout as if you were in a high wind. And keep your ankles crossed, your hands folded in your lap, and at least try to keep your opinions to yourself."

"I'll never learn the rules."

"That's because you don't want to."

"I can't spend much longer at this nonsense. Tell me, will I pass muster or not?"

"I've done what I can; the rest is up to you."

"Do you want to come to Washington with me?"

For a moment Mrs. Lovell's eyes lighted up. Then she shook her head. "No, Ree, I can't leave your Papa. He's not been well, you know. He's getting old. For that matter, we both are."

Reanna found her father in the garden. Mr. Lovell spent his afternoons dozing beneath an apple tree. There was a blanket over his knees and his chin rested on his chest. He would have denied that he ever took a nap. But between lunch and dinner he was seldom wide awake.

The old apple tree was Reanna's favorite. When she was little she used to climb it to hide away from the world.

She leaned down and kissed her father on his dry cheek. His eyes remained closed, but he reached out for her hand and she knelt down beside him.

"That my girl?"

"Yes, Papa."

"You went west and made good. No one thought you'd do it but me. I always backed you for a winner."

"What odds would you give on me now?"

"I'd bet the farm."

"I hope you're right, Papa. I hope you're right, because this time I'm playing for mighty high stakes."

REANNA chose to make her formal entrance into Washington society at a reception at the British embassy. As she moved down the receiving line, she could tell by the stares and the whispered comments that she was looking exceedingly well. She had refused to bob her red-gold hair; instead, she wore it in a coronet of braids. Her complexion was creamy ivory, and her brown eyes were set off by her nile green, chiffon dress. She wore a single rope of perfect pearls caught with a diamond clip that even her mother had not been able to fault.

She had come into town and taken a suite at the Willard. She'd been photographed at the Smithsonian for the Sunday *Ladies' Supplement*—"Oklahoma Woman Visits Washington." She had been interviewed at the National Press Club—"Oklahoma Oil Pioneer Gives Woman's View." She had chosen to appear at a British embassy reception after she'd made sure that Senator Curtain from Oklahoma would be present.

The British ambassador, primed by a request from Frampton, had invited the senator and was paying Reanna special attention. The ambassador had had many duties far less pleasant than guiding Reanna through a mob of self-interested politicians and diplomats toward Senator Clyde Wilcox Curtain.

"Mrs. MacClaren," the ambassador rumbled, "may I present Senator Curtain from your home state of Oklahoma. It's hard to believe that you two, who have so much in common, have never met."

"How do you do, ma'am." Senator Curtain gave a courtly little bow. "Alas, I've never had the honor of meeting Mrs. MacClaren."

The reason they'd never met was simple. The senator was Andrew's. Andrew owned him lock, stock and gold watch fob.

Reanna gave the senator her most dazzling smile. "Senator Curtain is a great friend of my husband's." And, as if that were explanation enough for anyone, the ambassador suavely, expertly excused himself and left them alone. "I believe you know Andrew very well, Senator?" The question was completely innocent or full of meaning, whichever way the senator chose to interpret it.

"Yes, indeed. A fine man, Mr. MacClaren. A mighty fine man—and a good friend to me." It was an understatement, considering that Andrew augmented the senator's income threefold.

"And you have been a good friend to Andrew." There was nothing Andrew wanted that he could not have if it was in Senator Curtain's power. At a price, of course.

"I do my best."

"I know he depends on you for favorable legislation for the oil industry."

"Many of my constituents are interested in oil, Mrs. MacClaren. I try to keep all my constituents happy. That's my job; that's why they elected me."

"I am one of your constituents."

"And anything I can do for you while you are in Washington I would be happy to do. I know Andrew would want me to look after you."

"Thank you, that's very kind of you."

"Andrew is coming to Washington later this week. But then, I am sure you knew that."

She smiled. She had hoped Andrew would arrive just as she left town; the timing was perfect. "Senator, I find it a little warm in here. I wonder if we could talk on the terrace. It's so close and crowded in here."

They went out onto the terrace; he gallantly stepped aside so that she could precede him. On the terrace it was not much cooler than inside, but there were fewer people. They could talk without being observed or overheard.

"Senator, there is something I would like you to do for me, if you will."

"What is that?"

"I understand there's a position open for a United States attorney in the state of Oklahoma. Is that true?"

(561)

"There may well be," he hedged.

"And I also understand that although the president makes the appointment, you, Senator, must recommend the candidate."

"That is so," he said stiffly. "It's a matter of senatorial courtesy for the president to accept the man I recommend."

"And have you decided on a man to fill the position?"

"No, not yet. There are several qualified men. I'm considering them all."

"Have you considered Pride Beauvaise?"

"No, I have not considered Pride Beauvaise."

"He is highly qualified, is he not?"

"I really couldn't say."

Reanna looked at the senator carefully. "I hope, Senator, that you will consider Pride Beauvaise very seriously indeed."

"And why should I do that?"

"Because it would be worth a great deal to me if you did." There. It was out on the table. She waited to see if he would pick it up.

"I'm not sure I understand you."

"I think you do."

"Then let us say, I am not sure Andrew would understand if Pride Beauvaise were appointed to the position you mentioned."

"Whatever the appointment would be worth to Andrew, it would be worth more to me."

He held his hand up like a policeman stopping oncoming traffic. "One thing Andrew and I have never done is to discuss money. Not ever in all the years I have known him."

"Then how," she asked incredulously, "do you ever reach any kind of understanding?"

"I write down a figure for him on an envelope, like this." He took an envelope from his inside jacket and a nub of a pencil. He thought carefully for a moment and then wrote down six digits. "What I do is to write down a figure and show it to him. If he agrees, then we have no further need to discuss the matter."

"And the figure is?" she asked and waited for him to show her the envelope.

He turned it up to her like a trump card.

She reached for it, but he kept it in his own hand. "It seems a very reasonable figure to me."

"And so we have agreed," he said, and put the envelope and pencil back in his pocket.

"And then what does Andrew do?" she asked.

"Why, Andrew comes around to my office with the figure we agreed on in cash. He gives his envelope with the cash in it to my personal, executive secretary."

"I see. Will your secretary be in your office tomorrow?"

"Yes, ma'am. I tell that man that he works too hard, but he's there seven days a week." She nodded. "Any more questions, Mrs. MacClaren?"

"One. I have always understood, Senator Curtain, that you were an honest politician. I wonder if you would give me your definition of an honest politician."

"An honest politician is a man who, when he has been bought, stays bought."

"Then we have a deal."

"Yes, ma'am, and may I say what a pleasure it is to serve all my constituents."

The next morning Reanna went to the Senate Office Building to Senator Curtain's office. Good to the senator's word, his secretary was there working even on Sunday. There was no explanation necessary. She would have paid twice the amount the senator had asked. It was, after all, Andrew who long ago had taught her to buy only the best.

Reanna left Washington the next morning early on the train for New York. It had been childishly simple to make a deal with the senator. If the situation hadn't been so shabby, so pathetically venal, she would have felt a sense of victory.

THE man she was going to see in New York was another matter entirely. He was no bumbling, grass-roots politician. Max Anselm was different, an unknown, a man she didn't know how to manipulate. He would be a challenge. Max Anselm, of the merchant banking house of Burgess-Anselm, was a man upon whose favor both companies and countries alike depended for their lines of credit.

Reanna had studied the report on him carefully. She knew his background, his habits and his assets. She knew that it was not easy to see a man of his caliber in New York in summer. Most bankers retreated to the cool comfort of their Long Island estates, their camps in Maine, or the woods of Nova Scotia. The very fact that Max Anselm stayed in town during the summer, living at the Brevoort Hotel, was in itself enough to make him an oddity.

She took a suite at the Brevoort on the floor above his. She unpacked with the help of a hotel maid. Her mother had said she needed a maid of her own to travel with her, but Reanna rebelled at the idea of having someone wait up until she came in at night, or wake her in the morning. She would run her own bath and keep her privacy.

The next morning she was up early, in the dining room, sitting at a table facing his when Max Anselm came down for breakfast. Max Anselm was neither young nor old—a short, powerfully built man whose head was overlarge for his body. He had heavy-lidded eyes that she felt saw everything and betrayed nothing. Reanna watched, fascinated, as he consumed steak, eggs, toast, fresh fruit and honey and a large pot of black coffee. Once he looked up and caught her staring at him. She thought he nodded to her, but she couldn't be sure; she took care not to let the incident repeat itself.

After his breakfast she waited in the lobby until he came through, paused to take a small paper sack from the bell captain and proceeded out the revolving door to the street. Reanna followed him at a distance as he strolled into Washington Square Park, found his usual bench and sat down to feed the pigeons. It took the better part of half an hour. Then he stood, brushed the stray crumbs from his linen suit, folded the sack neatly and put it in his pocket and walked to the edge of the square where his limousine was waiting for him.

He was driven to his office in Wall Street. He always worked a full morning, seldom ate lunch out and just past one o'clock, wet or fine, he took a turn in Trinity churchyard. Then, precisely at three, he left the bank for the day.

That afternoon when Anselm left the bank, Reanna followed him uptown into Madison Avenue booksellers and into art galleries. At last she was stopped from following him further when he turned into the Union League Club. In all that time, the banker never once gave any indication that he knew he was being watched or followed. She congratulated herself on keeping up with him in the steaming gorges of tall, stone buildings. She'd suffered and endured all kinds of terrible summers in western droughts. She'd survived days in the broiling, glaring sun by a balky, stubborn rig, but a day of summer in New York left her limp from fatigue. She was sure that she was stalking a most unusual breed of man.

The next morning she again sat at a table opposite his at breakfast. Again she followed him into Washington Square, but this morning she had made up her mind to attack head-on. She walked boldly up to the park bench where he was sitting and stood waiting for him to speak. When he neither looked up nor spoke, she said, "Mr. Anselm?" At the sound of her voice the birds took flight, scattering up into the sky.

"Won't you sit down, Mrs. MacClaren." He still didn't look at her. He only threw more crumbs, hoping to coax the pigeons back to him.

"You know who I am?"

"You followed me yesterday. In the ordinary way, I might have called the police." There was a slight quiver at the corner of his mouth, which passed for a smile. "But I had had a cable from Simon Frampton telling me that you would be in New York and asking me to help you in any way I could. The Frampton family has always banked with Burgess-Anselm. Lord Carding, Simon's nephew, is well known to us. We handle all their affairs." He set the sack of crumbs on the bench beside him and turned to her. The force of his eyes was unexpected. "I take it you are a close personal friend of Frampton's?"

His meaning was unmistakable. She was angry and flattered all at once to be mistaken for any man's mistress. "Simon Frampton is a business associate of mine."

"Ah!" It was almost a sigh. "There was really no need for you to have followed me. It would have saved a good deal of time and effort on your part if you had simply made an appointment to see me at my office."

"Mr. Anselm, what I have to say to you is highly confidential. I wouldn't want anyone, not even your secretary, to know that we've met."

"And what is it you want to say? What can I do for you?"

She hesitated for a moment, then her chin went up. "Not what you can do for me, Mr. Anselm, but what I can do for you."

He looked at her curiously. "And what exactly is it that you can do for me?"

"I can show you a way to control MacClaren Oil."

At first she thought he hadn't heard her correctly. He shook his head and appraised her like a piece of real estate that had been offered to him at a suspect price. "My dear Mrs. MacClaren, why should I or Burgess-Anselm want MacClaren Oil?" It was a curt, cold dismissal. He'd meant to put her in her place, relegate her to some stratum beneath his notice or contempt.

"It is to your advantage."

His eyebrows arched like a question mark. "How so? If it is money you want, Frampton should have told you that Burgess-Anselm is not a commercial bank. We are merchant bankers. We deal in private interests."

"And one of your private interests is Standard Oil."

"We've done some business with Standard. So have many other banks."

She'd had enough of his condescension. "Don't patronize me," she snapped. "You advise Standard, and I think if you weren't too pigheaded to listen, both you and Standard would benefit by acquiring MacClaren Oil."

He considered what she said. She was either a beautiful annoyance or a madwoman come to vex him and disturb the birds. But she was right; he was often too opinionated, not a desirable trait in a banker. He had formed one impression of her and now he must revise and form another.

"I hardly see how a small, western oil company like MacClaren could be competition for Standard Oil. Besides, since the antitrust breakup of Standard, competition, within limits, is encouraged."

"It might interest you to know that Andrew MacClaren means to do just that—compete with Standard. He's no longer content to be just a small, independent oilman in the West. He's crossed the Rubicon into your great, sacred East. He's in Washington now, staying at the Carlton, he and his entourage. He's negotiating to buy a refinery in Tarbert, Ohio."

Anselm stopped feeding the pigeons and gave her his full and undivided attention. "Go on, I'm listening."

"I don't have to tell you that if Andrew gets a refinery in the East, he'll have considerable leverage. Up to now, you and your unofficial friends have managed to keep refining east of the Mississippi in your control. Andrew means to change all that. When he's got his refinery, he can begin to expand his retail outlets. He means to go coast to coast."

"He may want to go coast to coast. Many have tried and many have failed. I had already heard he was dickering for the Tarbert refinery. Well, let him. He doesn't have enough product to keep it running or to supply retail stations."

"He has a new lease on tribal surplus land."

"A lease that's not proven."

"And now he's contracted to buy my entire output—every barrel from my *Reanna* field and all my leases. That will double his production. Believe me, my oil will keep the Tarbert refinery busy for years to come."

"You have given him a contract for all your output?" At last she had taken him by surprise. "That I didn't know. That is another matter entirely."

"Now can we talk business, Mr. Anselm?"

He shifted uncomfortably. "I'm not used to talking business with a woman."

"And I'm not used to doing business with a Yankee."

"Are Yankees so different from other men?"

"I can't speak for them all, but you are different. The men I know are rough; you are smooth. You've never been out in the weather unless it suited you. You've never worked with your hands. You've never settled an argument with your fists. You beat men with your brains."

Suddenly he smiled. It changed his look completely. "You, too, have a head on your shoulders, Mrs. MacClaren. May I suggest that this is too nice a summer day to be indoors? How would you like to spend it with a Yankee? We can walk in Greenwich Village, see the artists' studios, have lunch at an Italian restaurant I know. And while we get to know each other, we can talk about our mutual interests."

They walked to the edge of the square. He excused himself for a few minutes to speak to his driver, then dismissed the car. They walked through charming, winding, narrow side streets as if they had all the time in the world. They had lunch in a vine-covered backyard of an Italian restaurant. They ate pasta, drank Chianti and ended the meal with delicious rich pastries and bitter coffee. Reanna found that she was enjoying herself in his company. After the coffee, Max Anselm lit a cigar and leaned back in the creaking, cane-bottomed chair. He looked at her with admiration mixed with curiosity.

"May I ask you a question?"

"Yes."

"If you know a way to control MacClaren Oil, why tell me? Why not take control yourself?"

She returned his admiring gaze. "I need a hired gun."

He coughed as if smoke had caught in his throat. "I beg your pardon?"

"It's a Western custom. If you want a man killed and for some reason you can't do the job yourself, you hire a gunslinger from another part of the country to do the job for you."

He laughed, his head thrown back. He looked younger and more vulnerable when he laughed. "I've been called a lot of things, but never a hired gun. Believe me, Mrs. MacClaren, I have never killed anyone."

"No?" She was suddenly angry. "You manipulate the market; you cause panics and depressions. Lititle men go under while you make a profit. You ruin men every day. You don't have to kill with a gun; money and power are your weapons."

His smile was gone; his eyes were dark and serious. "If I'm so wicked, why would you want to do business with me?"

"Because you're the best at what you do. You're efficient and ruthless, and I need you. I can tell you how to set the trap and what bait to use, but I can't do the job myself. I can't let Andrew know I had anything to do with any of this. If you have scruples, I promise you'll never have to fire a shot or draw blood to kill Andrew. Give him half a chance and Andrew will destroy himself. He has a flaw within him, more deadly than any gun or bullet—his conceit. Just ask him to lunch with you at your bank; call it a favor to you. Just open the door to him, flatter him, point him in the direction you want him to go, and he'll run toward his own destruction."

"And if I agree to open the door? If I show him the way?"

"I'll have to leave the rest up to you. I'll have to stay out of it. I can't have him suspect I've had any part in this."

He was silent and thoughtful, then he said, "Go on."

"Andrew is in need of cash for expansion. Until recently he had an open line of credit. It's been severed. He's in Washington now, trying to negotiate for the Tarbert refinery. He'll need new financing, a new line of credit, and you can give it to him."

Anselm's jaw dropped in wonder. "My dear, you beat the Dutch. You came here to tell me you'll give me control of MacClaren Oil, a gift I never sought, and now you have the colossal effrontery to ask me to lend your husband the money to buy the Tarbert refinery so that he can compete in Standard's market. Whatever do you take me for? I've been set up in my day, but nothing like this."

She let him simmer until his anger fizzled out and then continued. "If Andrew doesn't get the money from you, he'll get it somewhere else. If you give it to him, you'll control him. If you can't see that, then I'm just wasting your time and mine. You know all the ways to do it. You're a master at the game. You ask him in, you flatter him, you offer him money. In exchange you put a man on his board of directors and take some of his stock for security. Every time you extend credit for his expansion, one of your men will sit down and one of his will get up. It will take time, but in the end you'll own MacClaren Oil."

"And what will I do with it? Standard can't be seen to have a hand in this."

She drew a deep breath and played her high card. "You'll have enough crude at your disposal to make even Colorado Minerals respectable."

He gasped audibly. He was a sharp man, but she was sharper and this thrust cut deep. "What do you know about Colorado Minerals?" he demanded. There was no point in denying its existence.

"I had a report made, a dossier on you and your holdings."

"You've done your homework."

"I've tried."

"What do you know about Colorado Minerals?" he repeated.

"Colorado Minerals is a small company that was owned by Standard Oil. When the division came during the antitrust suit, Colorado Minerals went out on its own, though actually it was still run by Standard's hand-picked men. Unfortunately those men got caught up in the Teapot Dome scandal. Your bank took receivership of Colorado Minerals, and it's been hanging around your neck like a tainted millstone ever since. If you have Andrew MacClaren's assets and oil, you can merge the two companies. In one stroke you can make Colorado Minerals respectable and Standard will have one less competitor." She paused. "That's all unofficially, of course."

"And what will you get out of this? You've sold your crude to Andrew and MacClaren Oil."

"If Andrew goes under, there is no contract. The contract was with him personally, exclusively. No Andrew, no contract. My price will be to get my crude back."

He leaned toward her. He put his hand on hers and she felt his fingers tighten. "What did Andrew MacClaren ever do to you that would make you want this kind of revenge?"

"He hurt someone I loved."

"And you want to hurt him in return. Oh, my dear, revenge isn't always sweet."

"To me it will be as sweet as clover honey."

"I hope so." He fell silent. She watched him relight his cigar and inhale deeply. He sat wrapped in smoke, deep in thought. At last he said, "Very well, if you're sure that's what you want."

Her heart began to beat like a hammer. "You'll do it? You'll ask Andrew to meet you at your bank?"

He nodded.

"When?"

"In a day or two. I need to do a little homework of my own first." He looked at her inquiringly. "When this plan of yours is in motion, what will you do?"

"When I see Andrew safe in your hands, I'll leave for England. The *Mauretania* sails this week."

"When will you come back?"

"Not until this business is settled. Andrew mustn't suspect I've had a hand in this. Out of sight, out of mind."

"It will take a year, maybe more," he said.

"I understand."

"Then we have a deal?" He held out his hand.

"Yes, a deal. You get MacClaren Oil and I get my crude back."

"On one condition."

"What is that?"

"Dine with me tonight." She hesitated. "Dine with me tonight, and I'll send Andrew MacClaren a personal invitation to lunch with me at Burgess-Anselm."

On the day Andrew was to have lunch with Anselm, Reanna had hired a car to take her to the Cunard docks. On her way, she ordered the driver to wait across the street from the bank until she saw Andrew and his entourage arrive. She watched as Max Anselm came down personally to greet Andrew at the door, as if Andrew were a visiting head of state.

Then she gave the order to drive on. She wished she could have been there for that meeting between Andrew and Anselm. She felt cheated that she must remain silent and invisible, but she had no other choice. From now on she'd have to depend on Max Anselm to follow the plan she had given him. She'd have to trust him to carry it out. And trust in anyone but herself came hard to her. To-day she'd set a chain of events in motion that couldn't be stopped.

ANDREW walked toward Max Anselm with his hand outstretched and a big grin on his face. At first, when the invitation had come to the Washington Carlton inviting him and his associates to lunch at Burgess-Anselm, he had thought it was some kind of prank. He didn't know much about banks in the East, but he knew who Burgess-Anselm was the way he knew who Mellon and the Roth-schilds and J. P. Morgan were. What he didn't know was what they would want with him. The invitation turned out to be the genuine article; he'd had one of his boys check it out. Max Anselm had really asked Andrew MacClaren and his associates to lunch with him and his partners at one o'clock at the bank.

The word *associates* already put Andrew one up on Anselm. The men Andrew had with him weren't associates, they were his hired hands.

There was his fancy Harvard lawyer, Tom Porter. Tom Porter was one of Andrew's favorite acquisitions. He had gone shopping for a lawyer who could outtalk and outsmart the Eastern crowd. Porter just fit the bill. A Yankee—Massachusetts born and bred— and Harvard. He belonged to something called Porcellian, which Andrew had never heard of, but no matter, and he had made the law review. Tom Porter was a comer and no mistake. He'd been chosen as law clerk by Supreme Court Justice Hannamer. The pay was not much, but the prestige would be worth gold.

Andrew had invited the young man to meet him for lunch in the Senate dining room. Senator Curtain had made the arrangements. "I hear," Andrew had said, "that you're from an old Back Bay family."

"Poor relation." Tom Porter had been polite but a little wary. Andrew knew all about being wary himself. He had liked that in the young man.

"Then this job with Justice Hannamer is not for you. If you work for him, you're going to keep on being poor. Now I'm not as impressive as a Supreme Court justice, but what I'm offering as a starting salary is . . ." He had written down a figure on a piece of paper and shoved it over for Tom Porter to take a look at it. It was a trick Andrew had learned from Senator Curtain. Never dis-cuss money.

Tom Porter had looked at the figure on the paper and then looked again to be sure he had seen right.

He was indeed a poor relation, in a family that never discussed money but worshipped it none the less. His lineage was the best. The Porters had not come over on the *Mayflower*, but they had arrived not long afterward, when the situation in the colonies was a little more settled and a little less dangerous. They were still early enough to get credit for being founding fathers. Each generation of Porters had made themselves better off than the one before. There had been enough spirited members of the family for them to have been thought public-spirited. They had been known as high-minded and plain-living, but perhaps miserly would have been more accurate.

It was in Tom's father's generation that the family tree had begun to suffer from rot. His father had married beneath him, a mistake that might have been overlooked if his father had not also lost his capital. That lapse the family could not forgive. When Tom's parents had proved too irresponsible to look after him—one a bolter and the other a drunkard—a great-aunt Edith had taken him in. She was, to be kind about it, a most eccentric maiden lady who liked Tom best when he was sitting still on a high-backed chair.

Tom had been sent to boarding school and college on her money, and he had distinguished himself for the highest marks and the lowest spending money in his class. The family had taken him in on sufferance at Thanksgiving and Christmas and allowed him to summer with them in Maine. They had grudgingly written him letters of introduction, while they had despised him for needing to ask for their assistance. A job in the West would take Tom well out of the range of their disapproval for his father's sins. Tom knew that, do what he might, he would never be a real, fully accepted member of the clan, merely the black sheep's unfortunate son.

Tom considered all that and consented to take Andrew MacClaren's salary and his salt. "I've always wanted to go West," Tom said, "and the salary is very generous."

"Don't worry that I'm paying you too much, Tom. Can I call you Tom?" Andrew grinned. "You'll more than earn your keep."

Among Andrew's other favorite acquisitions were his bright young engineers and his geologists. He paid them plenty and he treated them right, but they were still hired hands, traveling with him because he didn't like to travel alone.

Andrew took care of his men. He had built them fine houses in MacClaren City, a country club, schools for their children, a hospital and a civic center. He had met their every need, and in return he expected them to be on call twenty-four hours a day. They must be free to meet with him day or night, to travel with him on a moment's notice. And since Mrs. MacClaren never traveled with him, they must be willing to leave their wives and families behind.

The trips he and his men took were strictly stag affairs. They took whole floors of hotels; they played cards till all hours and football in the halls. There were always willing party girls with bobbed hair and rouged knees available, and he never failed to put hundred-dollar bills in their garters. This trip East to dicker for the Ohio refinery was no different. The Carlton was like any other hotel, only a little fancier and the party girls a little prettier.

WHEN the invitation from Anselm's had been confirmed, Andrew had gotten rid of the party girls, sobered up his boys and got on the limited for New York. Now here they were, all duded out in city clothes standing in Wall Street, which in Andrew's opinion was the genuine tall cotton.

Andrew was mighty impressed that Anselm had actually come down to meet him in person. The ol' boy had manners, Andrew would say that for him. And style. Think of it, a dining room in a bank, and he had a right good cook too. When they'd gone through cold soup and salmon and roast duck and were lighting up a lot of big cigars, Anselm finally got to it, the reason for the invitation. If Anselm had tried to pretend it was a purely social occasion, Andrew would have been on his guard. But Anselm was better than that. He laid his cards on the table face up.

"Mr. MacClaren." Anselm leaned toward him. "My partners and I are thinking of going more widely into petroleum issues. We've been asked to underwrite some stock offerings in that line in the past. The trouble is that we know little or nothing about how the day-to-day oil business operates. It's one thing to read up on a subject and look at the balance sheets, and another to know how a business operates in the field. We've asked you here because we need your help."

Andrew nodded. "I knew if you asked me to come to eat with you that you wanted something."

(573)

Anselm coughed. "We always try to get the best advice."

"You can't beat field experience," Andrew said.

"Mr. MacClaren, since you know the business from every angle, I was hoping that while you're here in New York you'd be willing to take some of your valuable time to meet and talk with us and answer some of our questions."

Andrew hesitated. He didn't want to make it too easy on the banker.

"I know this is short notice"—Anselm was deferring to him in word and manner—"and that you're a very busy man. But I assure you, if you could possibly see your way clear to help, my partners and I would be most grateful."

"Yes." Andrew nodded. "I'd be glad to help you fellows out."

There was a fraction of a second's pause, and then Anselm sighed and smiled. Andrew was tickled to see that Anselm hadn't been sure of him after all.

"That's very generous of you," Anselm said. "Very generous indeed." He smiled again and offered Andrew some of the fine vintage port from a crystal decanter. "You see, Mr. MacClaren, I feel—we feel—and I hope you'll agree, that the world need for oil is going to expand at a remarkable rate. And we want to be in on the financial side of that market."

"I can't blame you for that." Andrew gave Anselm a roguish grin. "But why come to me? Why not go ask Rockefeller's advice? He's richer than I am."

They all took it as a joke and laughed politely.

Then Anselm pulled a sober face. "I'm afraid I must contradict you there. John D. may know more than anyone else about transportation and rebates, but you, Mr. MacClaren, have a wider overall view of the real oil business."

Andrew felt a wave of warmth wash over him. Anselm was flattering him, of course—laying it on with a trowel—but beyond flattery, Anselm was being smart. He saw Andrew as a coming winner and he wanted to climb on the bandwagon.

Suddenly Andrew grinned. He was happier than he could ever remember being in his whole life. It had happened. He was going to be king of the hill, top of the world. The big boys had come to him. A dream had come true for him. These boys were afraid of him and how big he might become. When he got his Ohio refinery, with Reanna's product, he would be a threat to all of the Eastern crowd. Anselm wanted to get on the good side of him before he got too big to talk to. "I'll be glad to tell you and your partners whatever you want to know."

He talked all that afternoon. He talked and the men around the table listened. He came back the next day and the next, and he told them how to find oil, how to lease it, how to drill for it, how to pipe it, how to refine it and how to market it. From time to time, as Anselm and his partners listened to him, they asked a brief question. He answered at length. For three days he spun them a tale of what he saw for his future.

"One day soon," he said, "I mean to have retail outlets coast to coast. I want to get overseas leases now, before the Anglo-Dutch or the Russians have a chance to put their fingers in every pie. I want to go into Mexico and South America and explore, because I believe they have rich, untapped deposits. Now is the time to expand." As he spoke he was flushed with his dream and the telling of it. "To reach an even wider world market, I need ships and a pipeline to the Gulf."

"All that could cost millions," Anselm said quietly when he had finished.

"Yes, but don't you see, it could make millions more."

Anselm sat silently tracing and retracing a figure with his finger on the tabletop. Then he looked up. "To make that large a capital investment feasible, one would have to be sure of a large supply of crude."

"I've already started." Andrew was impatient with such small-minded caution. "I have leases on tribal surplus land that will prove out to be one of the richest fields in America."

Anselm glanced up at Andrew. "To get a lease like that, you must have friends in high places."

Andrew nodded. "I have a friend in Washington."

"A friend you can depend on?" Anselm queried softly.

"Yes, a senator. He made the connection—the introduction, I should say—with this fellow at the Department of the Interior. Both men have been very obliging."

Anselm nodded, knowingly. He knew how these things worked.

"And"—Andrew puffed up with pride—"I've just gotten the guarantee of doubling my present production this year by contracting for the entire production of the *Reanna* field at market price."

"Well then"—Anselm shrugged—"it would seem to me, and I believe I can speak for my partners, that you are a man we'd want to back. That is, if you ever need financing."

"Every oilman needs that." Andrew felt his heart pound.

"And finance is our business, Mr. MacClaren. I bring it to your attention because in order to take advantage of some of these special situations which you mean to develop, I believe that you've already been obliged to borrow from a number of different commercial banks."

"That's no secret," Andrew said, but he felt nettled at having it spelled out that way.

"We like to do our homework." Anselm smiled. "What I'm suggesting is this. The only flaw I can see in any of your projected plans is that there might come a time when you would have to let some opportunity slip away from want of ready cash. It might conceivably go to another bidder while you had to shop for credit."

"There's always that danger." Andrew clenched his jaw, wondering how Anselm had found out so much about him.

"The point I am trying to make is that it might be to your advantage to have a stipulated amount of money at your disposal—a permanent line of credit with one bank, so that you could spend all your valuable time exploring and expanding the MacClaren Oil Company. Then, if you needed cash to close a deal, you wouldn't have to go looking for it. The money would always be available to you when you wanted it."

It took a moment for the full implication of what Anselm had said to sink into Andrew's mind. His eyes met Anselm's and he looked away again quickly. Anselm wasn't just trying to get in on the ground floor. He wanted to deal himself in.

"What kind of capital could you see clear to risking in oil?" Andrew asked and held his breath as he waited for the answer.

"Five million—ten—whatever is a convenient figure for you, Mr. MacClaren. Secured by stock in MacClaren Oil."

Andrew made a sound; it came from deep within him. He tried to pretend he'd merely coughed or gotten something lodged in his throat.

"I don't need your answer now," Anselm said. "I know you'll want to consult with your board of directors. But if you agree, I wonder if it wouldn't be a good idea for one of our men to sit on your board, just as an observer, a liaison with us. You'll want to work that out with your lawyers, of course, along with the amount of stock to be pledged as security for loans."

There was silence in the room. Andrew didn't know how to answer or if his voice would betray him if he did.

"That is," Anselm said, "if you want to consider our proposal."

"Of course," Andrew said, and he began to laugh. "I'll be happy to consider your proposal. I'd have to be a fool not to." He laughed, laughed so long and so hard that he had to wipe away tears from his eyes. "And as for my board, you can put anybody on my board that you want to."

He had to laugh, because he had no board and no stock. He owned MacClaren Oil outright. But what Anselm didn't know wouldn't hurt him. He'd get a board and quick; for that kind of money, he'd get a dozen boards.

"And of course it's understood," Anselm said, "that you'll still be president of MacClaren Oil."

"Sure." Andrew felt elated. "I'll take the title. But we have a saying out home. 'Leave the glory to God and take the money home to Oklahoma!' And gentlemen, that's just what I mean to do. And listen here, to clinch this deal, I want you all to come out real soon and visit me. Come just as soon as the August weather breaks. August in Oklahoma might be a tad too much for you Yankees' thin blood. But you come in September, and we'll show you one hell of a good time." And Andrew gave Anselm a big, wide, satisfied Western grin.

Midway across the Atlantic on the *Mauretania*, Reanna received a cablegram from Anselm. It read, "Fish has taken the bait. Traveling to Oklahoma to get him on the hook." And she cabled back, "Play him in slowly," and knew that it would be a long, long time indeed before she could hope to go home again.

FRAMPTON was at Southampton to meet Reanna.

"Just look at you." He embraced her. "You're younger and more beautiful than ever."

"And you're more outrageous."

He held her close. "I'm so happy to see you," he whispered, "so happy you're here."

He held her hand like a boy with a prize, as he walked her through customs and immigration with a minimum of fuss. He arranged for her luggage to be sent on after them, and then he bundled her into a waiting Daimler limousine.

He pulled a lap robe up around her and smiled. "Summer in England can be a trifle chilly." Then he hesitated for a moment before he leaned close to her and kissed her warmly and sweetly on the lips. "I'm so glad you came. I've asked you to come for years, and now that you're here I hope you'll stay forever." He kissed her again—this time a longer, deeper kiss.

She felt herself respond to him and was caught off guard. She'd always known Simon cared for her, as she did for him, but this kiss was different, more insistent and demanding. He was asking for a deeper response than she could freely give him.

"How long before we get to London?" she asked hurriedly.

"We're not going to London." Frampton was exuberant. "We're going down to Carding. My nephew is looking forward to meeting you."

She glanced out at the passing green countryside. "But I'm booked at the Savoy."

He shook his head and smiled like a delighted child. "I've canceled that. Can't have you staying in hotels. I wouldn't hear of it. You're staying at Carding. Tonight is the tenants' summer fete and you're the guest of honor. The whole county is waiting to have a look at you."

"I don't want to impose on Lord Carding. Wouldn't it be easier if I stayed at an inn nearby?"

"No, there's plenty of room for you at Carding." He dismissed her protests. "Now tell me about everyone at Lochleven. How are they all?"

She told him everything she could think of. First, that Molly May was still going. She was older, but then who wasn't? She talked and talked about Taffy, Cima and Snow, and Lovell. She was so wrapped up in what she was saying that it was nearly an hour before she looked up and saw that they were passing through a little village of thatched cottages and small shops.

"This is Ewemarket, our village."

"Your village. It sounds so quaint to own a village."

"Andrew owns MacClaren City."

She nodded but said nothing. She didn't want to talk about Andrew, not just yet. Instead she said, "I thank you for getting in touch with Max Anselm for me."

"You've seen him, then?"

"Yes."

"Everything worked out all right?"

"Time will tell."

Again she watched the passing landscape. They had come out of the village and begun to climb to the top of a ring of small, soft, green hills which surrounded the valley below. From the crest of the hill she could see a small river winding lazily through the valley. Then they passed through ornate, high gates marked with the letter C, down through a woods and out onto a wide formal park. It was then that she saw the house for the first time, and she heard herself gasp.

"That's Carding?"

"Yes, we've been on the grounds since we passed through Paradise Gate. The estate's called Carding because all this used to be sheep country."

She looked at the imposing west front, three stories of creamy yellow stone, and was nearly blinded by a blaze of windows gleaming in the setting sun. "Great glory," she said, "it's breathtaking."

"The house was started in the sixteenth century, but it's all bits and pieces. Every generation had a different notion of how it ought to look. One added a wing here, another a wing there. The stables don't match, or the orangery."

As he spoke, she could see how much the place meant to him. She could only imagine how much it must have cost him to be away from it all those long years. He must have missed Carding as much as she already missed Lochleven.

"You should have warned me. You should have given me some idea." She laughed. "Well, one thing is sure."

"What's that?"

"I won't put Lord Carding out. There's plenty of room."

COMING to Carding was like stepping into a fairy tale. Reanna was swept past a line of servants through the great hall, up the wide stairs, past drawing rooms, a state dining room, to a luxurious bedroom and a bathroom big enough to stable horses.

"This is fit for a queen," she said to Simon.

"Two queens have slept here. Anne and Victoria. I'll come just at eight and take you down to dinner."

She was grateful for that. She didn't think she'd be able to find her way back without him.

There were fifty invited for dinner, with two hundred coming in afterward. As guest of honor she sat on Lord Carding's right. He was a civil, pleasant young man—a little pale and bowed down, she thought, under the weight of the responsibilities of his title and this house.

She looked down the long table. Somewhere, there at the other end, almost hidden by silver candelabra and epergnes full of hothouse fruit, was Simon Frampton. She couldn't help considering how far they were from his ranch on the prairie and the relaxed, carefree days they'd spent there together. That place seemed so far away, she might never find her way back home again.

The dancing began in the great hall. The strains of the music floated down from a little gallery above the hall. Lord Carding bowed to her and led her out to open the ball, but he did not dance. He still had to walk with a cane because of his war wounds.

Then Simon claimed her. "We danced like this once before,

remember? The night I met you. That night changed my life. Now you're here, my life has changed again. I mean to make you want to stay." She didn't know how to answer him. She was grateful when she was cut in on by another partner and then another. It seemed they were all eager to dance a fox-trot with the American woman, as if she had some patent on the new steps.

At last, when she couldn't bear the small talk or the dancing one second longer, she wandered out onto the terrace and stood half-hidden in the shadows, looking up at the summer moon.

"You must be tired." The voice startled her. She turned to see young Lord Carding looking at her. "We rushed you into this evening. I'm sorry, it couldn't be helped. The tenants' ball is an annual affair. It's always held on this day. Tradition. I'm afraid we're keen on tradition at Carding."

As he spoke, she knew he had followed her out on the terrace not to make an unnecessary apology but to say something quite different. And now that he was here, he was finding it difficult to begin. "It is a wonderful party," she said.

"There wouldn't be a party if it weren't for my uncle Simon. He saved this house and the honor of this family."

"Oh." She had not expected this.

"He must have told you the story of why he went to America."

"I know it had something to do with gambling. That's all he told me." She did not want to betray Simon's confidence.

Carding sighed. "Yes. It's like him not to have told you more than that." He pointed up at a pair of casement windows above them. "It happened up there in the room just to the right of that balcony. In Queen Victoria's day, gentlemen at house parties used to play cards there. They liked to sit late, playing for high stakes.

"One night the Marquis of Wrentham and his friends lost twenty thousand pounds—about a hundred thousand American dollars. My uncle Simon was the winner. Being gentlemen, the Marquis and his friends paid up. When they'd settled their debts and were having a last brandy, my father idly turned up a handful of cards. It was then that the Marquis and the rest of them discovered the extra ace. An ace of hearts.

"It was my father's house, and it was already awkward enough that his brother should have won such a large sum. Now it was painfully clear that someone at the table had cheated. My father had dealt the last hand, but it was unthinkable that he was the cheat. He didn't need the money. My father as the eldest son had inherited everything, my uncle nothing. My uncle had only the allowance my father made him. My uncle Simon was as poor as his brother was rich. So it was to my uncle Simon that the Marquis turned for an explanation. My father too looked to my uncle Simon, waiting to hear what he would say.

"After a terrible silence, when my uncle said nothing in his defense, my father spoke up in a cold, clear voice and said, 'Lord Wrentham, I believe the ace of hearts that you hold in your hand is my brother's.'

"It was an unthinkable disgrace. For my father's sake it was kept quiet. The money was repaid. It was settled by the men involved out of court and out of the newspapers, but my uncle Simon might as well have been put in the dock and branded a thief and a cheat. In those days, there was only one circle of acceptable people. They all knew each other, and they all abided by the same code of honor. To be out of that circle was to be in exile. My father arranged for my uncle Simon to leave the country, to go abroad. Instead of India or South Africa or Canada or Australia, where he might be known, Uncle Simon chose the Indian Territory. I suppose it seemed the end of the earth, a place where no one he might know would ever find him and disclose his shame.

"Simon left England. His name was never mentioned again in this house or in polite society. When I was a child and I heard the story whispered by the servants, I used to have nightmares about his ruin. I'd wake up sobbing, unable to tell anyone why I was crying."

Reanna felt as if she too were in a nightmare, a nightmare that belonged to someone else. She said, "No matter how it looked, I'll never believe that Simon cheated at cards. I know him. There must have been a misunderstanding. There must be an explanation, otherwise how could he be here now, in this house, with these people who are clearly his friends?"

"Yes," Lord Carding said bitterly, "a misunderstanding. When my father lay dying, he made a confession to the Marquis of Wrentham and the other men who had been in the room that night. He told them that it was he, not Uncle Simon, who had cheated them. It was he who had dealt the winning cards and planted the extra ace."

Reanna was incredulous. "But why? Why did your father do such a thing? If it wasn't for money, I don't understand."

(582)

"He did it to discredit my uncle. My father knew that my uncle would never let my father's name be tarnished. My father was the head of the family. To Simon, honor, tradition, family meant everything."

"And your father put the blame on Simon?"

"Yes."

"Let him be ostracized—banished?"

"That's right."

"And Simon never said a word in his own defense?" She couldn't believe it. "You must think me stupid and American, but I don't understand. It doesn't make sense to me. I can't understand why Simon would keep silent, or why his brother would want to discredit him."

"My father knew Simon would say nothing, because he wouldn't let my mother suffer the disgrace of being married to a cheat."

"Oh." Suddenly she understood Simon and his motives.

"Now do you see?"

She nodded. "Simon was in love with your mother."

"She was as gentle and good as my father was cruel and vindictive. Her family had made the match, and she had obeyed them. It wasn't long before she found out what kind of man her husband was. It wasn't hard for my mother to learn to despise my father and to love my uncle Simon. I think I can speak for both of them when I tell you that they were both incapable of doing anything dishonorable or wrong. But my father was an insanely jealous man. So he had his revenge. Now you see why I owe Uncle Simon everything."

"What happened to your mother?"

"She died when I was very small. It is romantic and old-fashioned perhaps, but I believe she died of a broken heart."

"And your father waited all those years to reveal what he'd done to Simon? That's wicked and cruel."

"That's what I say too, but Simon sees it differently."

"And how is that?"

"He says he is proud that my father finally found the courage to make his confession." Lord Carding looked pale and drawn; telling his story had been an ordeal for him. "I think," he said, "that my uncle is the finest man in the world. I want him to be happy." He paused. "I know he cares for you very much, and I wanted you to know his story."

"I'm glad you told me."

"I wouldn't want you to pity him."

"I don't. I could never pity Simon. I care for him too, as a dear friend."

Lord Carding looked at her imploringly. "Then I can hope the best for both of you?" He reached out to touch her arm and then stopped as they saw Simon coming toward them, beaming his approval.

"There you are, you two. Reanna, I've been looking everywhere for you. I wanted to make sure you were enjoying yourself."

"Oh, yes. I am." Her voice sounded high and hollow.

Lord Carding coughed discreetly. "I've been trying to persuade Mrs. MacClaren to stay at Carding. I wanted her to know how welcome she is, how much we both want her to stay."

"And what do you say to that?" Frampton demanded.

"I say it's time you danced with me again."

As they spun around the dance floor, her brain went into a whirl, her thoughts tripping over themselves. She was here. She meant to stay until her plans came right. The events she'd set in motion now had a life and a momentum of their own. There could be no turning back. And far away across the ocean and half a continent was Pride, a man whose love she had forfeited.

"What are you thinking?" Simon asked.

"I was thinking about you, Simon." She lied, but it was a lie kindly meant. "I was thinking about you and how much I care for you."

His arm tightened around her waist. "I want you to be happy here. I mean to take you everywhere and show you off to all of England."

She must be careful what she said next. She did not want to give him any false hopes. "You know I'll never be free." He nodded. "Andrew will never give me a divorce." She looked up at Simon, at his good, kind face, his adoring eyes. "I want to be honest with you. It's time I met those oilmen you've been telling me about. I came to England on business."

"And I hope to see me?" Suddenly his smile had disappeared and his expression had crumpled in dismay.

"Of course to see you, Simon. I've missed you. You're my friend and always have been."

"Your friend . . ." His tone was an echo of hers. "Yes, I'm your friend and I love you, but then you know that."

"When my business is finished here, I must go home again."

"You can't blame me if I do everything in my power to make you want to stay."

"No, I can't blame you for that, but I wanted you to know from the start why I have come and that I will go. I hope you can accept the time we'll have together and not ask for anything more."

"If that's what you want, then I must agree." He held her close. "I'll do my best to make you happy. I so want you to be happy."

She had tried to give him fair warning, to be completely honest. Yet she did not have the heart to tell him that all her happiness now and forever was half a world away.

LOVELL was happier than he'd ever been in his whole life. He missed Reanna, as they all did, but he was busy from dawn till dusk. He rode and walked over every acre of Beauvaise Ridge. He couldn't make the wells vanish or the pipelines disappear, but he took the measure of its boundaries and made lists of what could be done. In the pasture to the south of the Ridge, he began to plant fenced sections with different mixtures of grass, hoping to find one that would hold despite wind, weather and the change in the water table. It wasn't all he intended to do, but it was a beginning.

Taffy had sweet-talked some of the old hands into coming back for a while until they got started up again. When Lovell was sitting with them in the evenings out in the bunkhouse, it was almost like the old days. He never went into MacClaren City, but he often went over to Maitland and the little surrounding towns with one of the boys for company. He met people he'd known as a child. He renewed friendships, heard the gossip and the news. And on a day in early September, he came roaring home with the best news of the summer.

He ran from the barn into the backyard, calling out for Cima and Snow. Snow was by the well with Daisy. Snow had made a pet of the calf, who followed her everywhere, begging corn bread from her apron pocket and eating from her hand. "What is it?" Snow asked in alarm.

Cima burst out onto the back porch. "What's going on here? Where's the fire?"

"Drop everything, you two. Get a big basket full of food, pots, blankets—anything we'll need. We'll be staying out one night, maybe more."

"What are you talking about?" Cima demanded.

"There's a big dance and powwow over at the stomp ground and we're all going. Taffy's getting the truck and a tent."

"I can't just drop everything and scat," Cima said, but she was already taking a mental inventory of the larder.

"Who'll take care of Daisy while we're gone?" Snow looked uncertain and put her hand protectively on Daisy's head.

"One of the hands will tend to Daisy," Taffy bellowed as he came striding up from the barn. "Aren't you ladies ready yet? What's keeping you?"

"We can't go off on short notice like that," Cima said.

"Course you can," Taffy jollied her. "You might as well start packing. Lovell's hell-bent to go. He's got his heart set on it."

In an hour the supplies were packed and loaded onto the truck. Cima and Snow, Taffy and Lovell crowded into the front seat, and they set off down the road, suddenly carefree, cracking jokes, singing and laughing as if they'd never had any other plans for the day. It was perfect weather for an outing. The sky was clear blue with little white powder puffs of clouds skimming along above them.

"A day like this," Cima said, "you forget how mean Oklahoma weather can be."

In another hour they came to the end of the county line road, found an open fence and took off across a new-mown field, bumping along in deep tracks cut in the red earth.

"Lots of folks been this way. Who all's coming, Chickasaw and Choctaw?" Cima asked.

"Mostly," Lovell replied, "but they said any tribe was welcome that wanted to come to feast and play Indian ball and dance."

At the end of the field, they forded a running stream. Lovell changed gears for the run up the far steep bank onto the wide plateau above. At the top, stretched out before them, was a large assembly of people, a good hundred and more. In the center of the plateau was the ceremonial dance fire, bounded, in tribal tradition, by a rectangle of logs. Around the great fire, in a semicircle, families had made little camps for themselves of brush arbor tents and little cooking fires of their own.

As Lovell drove around them looking for a place to make camp, people looked in the truck, saw who had come and began to spread the word. By the time they'd settled on a spot, the cry had gone up that the Beauvaises had arrived. No sooner had Taffy and Lovell begun to set up their tent and Cima to get out her cooking pots than there was a rush of women bringing children and grandchildren to see them, many to meet the *picaunli* for the first time. Rose Dawn and Annoyi were among the first. They embraced Snow and Cima, and their babies were made a fuss over as Snow held each in turn.

Lovell was pleased to see Snow taking her rightful place and thankful that she seemed to be doing it all with such ease and dignity. When he'd done what he could to help them settle, he started toward the creek.

"Where are you going?" Taffy asked.

"I thought I'd drink *hahtok*, the red drink, and play a little stick ball. You want to come?"

"Not me. I'm too old for that foolishness. Too old and too smart. You be careful. You can get hurt playing that game."

"I played lacrosse at school."

"Well, ain't we hoity-toity? This ain't for schoolboys. You can get hurt bad playing Indian ball. Don't say I didn't warn you. That red drink, *hahtok*, is made from red willow root. It's supposed to purify the soul and make you feel strong and healthy, but once was enough for me. I was sick for a week."

"I still think I'll play."

Lovell joined up with the boys on the playing field. It was a stretch of cleared, hard-packed, clean-swept earth, in the center of which was a tall pole topped with a steer skull and feathers. He sat in a circle of boys of all shades of white and tan and brown. When the cup was passed to him, he drank and then ran with the others to the creek to vomit. He stripped and bathed in the creek until he was purged and purified and ready for battle. When the boys returned to the field, sides were chosen. The hard, deerskin ball was tossed in and the play began.

At first the long stick with its webbed end felt unwieldy in Lovell's hand. Then he got the balance of it and joined in the rough play. The only rules were to take the ball, hold it, throw it over the goal and score. It was every man for himself. In the melee, sticks hit arms and shins and backs; they cracked against cheeks and noses. There was the crunching, sickening sound of wood against flesh. There were yelps of pain, and the blood ran as the fierce play continued. When the dust rose so that neither side could see, a little pump engine from a local fire company was called in to damp down the ground. And the play began again.

Lovell was hit. He was hurt and bloodied, but still quick and sharp, using all the moves he'd learned in New England. In the end, just as time was about to be called, he made a run, smashing right and left, caught the ball in the web and sent it flying over the goal so that his side won by a narrow margin. He was hoisted up on his fellow players' shoulders and carried back to the creek for a good dunking.

As he came limping up to the Beauvaise tent, he was so happy and so hungry that he would have eaten bark. As he sat by their little fire eating *pishofa* and fatback and Cima's greens and corn bread, he knew without a doubt that this was the best day of his life. And it was not over yet.

At dusk, when it was time for the ceremonial dance fire to be lit and the tribes to gather at their traditional places around it, Cima and Snow came out of the tent. Snow shyly looked at Lovell, waiting for his approval. She was dressed in a long, cotton print dress. The yoke and the bottom of the skirt were edged with ruffles. From her shoulders there hung a cascade of many colored ribbons. On her head was a diadem worked with bright beads.

"You look beautiful," Lovell said, "every inch a *picaunli*, a true princess. May I have the honor of being your escort?" He held out his hand and she took it. He felt her fingers cool and trembling against his warm, protective clasp. She looked at him, drew a deep breath and smiled tremulously. Together they walked toward the fire. Every eye was upon them. No one made a sound.

The rectangle of logs that bounded the fire was separated into the two great tribal divisions of *koi* and *ishpanee*, the *koi* the warriors and the *ishpanee* the chiefs. Snow took her place as the *picaunli* at the head of the *ishpanee*. Cima, a member of the tribe, sat beside her. Taffy and Lovell, as Snow's guests and part of her household, sat behind her.

Then each clan division of the tribe—the fox and raccoon, the bear and the cougar—and their guests from other tribes took their appointed places. The fire was lit and the dancing began.

A lone man in a Sioux warbonnet began a buffalo dance, weaving in and out around the fire. He was joined by a second dancer and a third. They were skilled performers in the dance, from the plains to the north.

The women would dance alone tomorrow—the old steps of the bean and corn dances. But tonight all would join together in a serpentine. One of the elders and leaders of the dance came to Snow to ask her permission for a snake dance. She gave it, smiling with pleasure that she'd been recognized and honored. The snake dance wound in and out, growing longer and longer as dancer after dancer joined in. The rhythmical beat of the drum and the stomp of feet against the ground was compelling and hypnotizing.

"Are you glad you came?" Lovell asked.

Snow turned to him. "Yes. Oh, yes. Thank you for bringing us. You've made me very happy."

Taffy cleared his throat. "And here's another reason for the Beauvaises to celebrate."

Lovell looked up to see Pride Beauvaise coming toward them out of the dark night into the light of the dance fire. As Pride stood looking down at them, the shadow of the flames played across his face. Lovell started to rise, but Pride motioned him to stay seated, and Taffy and Pride knelt down by Snow.

"You remember your uncle Pride Beauvaise?" Taffy said.

Snow stared at Pride.

"Of course you remember him, honey," Cima said. "You saw him last before he went to war. You remember how you missed him when he went away."

"Snow." Pride spoke her name in English and then in Chickasaw: "*Oktosha.*"

"*Umi imoshe,*" she answered him. "My uncle."

He smiled. "You are beautiful, like your mother. I've missed you, Snow."

"I've missed you." Their hands reached out to each other and met and clasped.

Taffy broke the silence. "You'll all have to congratulate Pride. He's got a letter from the president himself. Pride's been made a United States attorney."

"I'm only one of many," Pride said modestly, looking at Lovell for his reaction.

"It's happened!" Lovell shouted out a war whoop. "Congratulations. Now you can bring a suit to get back the tribal surplus land." He didn't say Andrew's name, but it was between them as surely as if he had shouted it aloud.

"It will take time," Pride said cautiously.

"But it will happen."

Pride nodded. "It will happen. And you, what about you? Are you planting grass?"

"Yes," Lovell said, "but it will take time for the pasture to come back."

"It's the same with the law. It will be a year or two, perhaps more, but in time the law will make wrong right."

"Yes." Lovell's eyes shone with happiness. "Well then, let's dance together and celebrate this good night."

They all joined hands and linked themselves with the others in an ancient ritual of thanksgiving.

ANDREW MacClaren stood in the broiling September sun on the platform of the MacClaren City railroad station, waiting for Max Anselm and his crew of Eastern bankers to arrive. Beside him stood his lawyer, Tom Porter, and behind him an array of young Mac-Claren executives.

Andrew gave a big grin when he saw Max Anselm step from the train onto the MacClaren City platform. Nothing made him happier than seeing a perspiring Eastern banker come west to him, hat in hand. Anselm had treated him right up in New York, and now Andrew meant to show Anselm and his folks a little Oklahoma hospitality. He escorted Anselm to a waiting open car. As they drove down MacClaren Avenue, Andrew pointed out the Mac-Claren Building and the MacClaren Hotel. He showed him the MacClaren Library and the MacClaren Memorial Park. Then he drove him out to the Marble Palace, where he put Anselm and his coterie up in fine style.

After dinner, which was lunch to them, he drove them to the MacClaren refinery and up and down the oil fields, his and Reanna's, past tank farms and earthen holding pools full to overflowing with crude. Then he brought them all home to a big barbecue. He had hired two bands and the prettiest girls. He had laid in the finest whiskey and invited a sampling of the oil crowd to come in to play a little poker. He saw to it that the house picked up all the dudes' losses.

The next day he had airplanes land on the lawn to collect Anselm and his gang so they could have an overflight view of his domain. When they set down again, he said to Max Anselm, "To-day you've just seen the home patch. I own all that and a good deal more besides."

He hired a steamboat to take them all up and down the Arkansas River where he had some leases on Indian land. He took them camping up on Miller's old 101 *Ranch*, where he gave them an Indian powwow. Then he treated them to a Wild West show. He saw to it they could hunt or fish or, if they wanted other sport, they could sample the Indian girls in the squaw tent he provided.

At the end of their visit, he took them back to the Marble Palace for one last big feed. After supper, dinner to them, he showed them a map of the world he meant to conquer. "I'll run my pipeline from here at MacClaren City up to my new refinery in Ohio, and I'll start pumping up the crude. My production is doubled over last year. Even with the Indian surplus leases still undeveloped, I can keep that oil coming from now to kingdom come. Then I'll run another line down to the Gulf, and I'll build me another refinery there at Port MacClaren. Then, when the Mexican fields prove up, I'll be able to refine that crude, ship it by boat up the West Coast and to the East. I mean to cover the country with MacClaren oil. Hell, there's nothing to stop me from shipping around the whole damn world." When he'd finished, Andrew stood waiting for Anselm's response.

Anselm sat with his fingertips together, a faraway, detached look in his eyes. Then he cleared his throat and said, "You've made some very big plans, Mr. MacClaren. I can see you've thought it all out carefully. Just how long do you expect this dream of yours will take to become a reality?"

"This dream, as you call it, will take a year or two—three at the most. And, as you've been generous and smart enough to offer me unlimited financing, maybe I can do it in less."

"Yes." Mr. Anselm sighed, and then he smiled. "The credit you need is available, but this plan is so complex, so far-reaching and intricate, I wonder if you'd accept a second man from our bank—just to observe and to oversee your management. And, of course, to help us agree on the stock we'll hold as collateral."

"Why not?" Andrew grinned back. "You give me the money for expansion, and I'll gladly give another of your men a place on my board. With a seven-man board—I believe that's what Tom Porter's set up—I still have the majority vote, don't I?"

"Indeed you do, Mr. MacClaren, indeed you do."

THE men from the East left the next day. At the first station stop out of the state, Max Anselm left the train and sent a cable to Reanna in England. It wasn't in code, but the telegrapher found it a strange message to send from hot, dry Kansas, with not a lake or a river within miles. The message read, "Have hooked big fish. Am playing him out slowly as instructed. In a year or two, three at the outside, I'll have him stuffed and mounted."

*I*N the second year the grass began to come green at Lochleven. By the third year Lovell could see enough improvement so that he began running cattle in the south pasture.
By the fourth year he was twenty-one and this was a man's estate
to be proud of. He never failed to feel a jump of his heart when he
looked at the grass bending and blowing in the wind.

But even in this perfect setup there was trouble to be had. Wind
erosion had scarred and loosened the topsoil. A sandstorm sometimes roared in from the plowed Great Plains, shrouding the pasture in a rain of grit like a messenger of worse things to come. And
of late he found that no matter how he kept tabs on the herd, he
was losing one or two head a month. "They could have strayed
onto the oil patch," Lovell said to Taffy. "Or else the coyotes could
be getting them."

"Maybe."

"Well something's getting them, that's for sure."

"Yeah," Taffy growled. "That's for dang sure." Sometimes
Taffy was less company than no company at all.

One fine summer morning Lovell and Taffy rode west, heading
along under the south rim of the Ridge, looking for strays. There
in a little cut they found a butchered steer and the remains of a
campfire.

"Nothing left but hide and horn," Taffy muttered.

"Who's getting them?" Lovell demanded. "Coyotes don't build campfires."

"Two-legged coyotes." Taffy hit at his thigh with his hat. "The Starretts are back."

"How do you know it's them?"

"I know their tracks. Damn them, camping all over, helping themselves. They always felt this place was theirs."

"Why?"

Taffy told Lovell the bare bones of the old feud. He spoke briefly of the attack on Reanna. The Starretts had told it on themselves and were proud of it, damn them! Lovell knew some of the story. The old bitter hatred was a part of the legend of the Beauvaises, but it was the first time he'd heard about the Starretts threatening Reanna. It sickened him to think of one of them laying a hand on her. "I'll put a stop to them coming in on us. Get the sheriff on the phone; tell him to get out here. I'll find the Starretts and see them put in jail."

"I'll call him, but I'll bet he's already had complaints from the foreman up at the *Reanna* pump station. Those Starretts go any old where on Beauvaise land, helping themselves and setting up camp. Up there in the oil patch, they could start a fire you couldn't put out."

Lovell's chin shot up. "I'll find them, the bastards! You round up a man or two and head back along the top of the Ridge. We'll flush them out. You better come back armed, all of you. If they are as bad as you say, we don't want to take chances."

"The real bad uns are dead and gone. Junior is left, but he's been too drunk for the last twenty years to give anyone trouble. No sir, this here's the tag end of a played-out lot. Just a passel of women and children and old men. Drifters and squatters. Trash, with no land to call their own."

"I want them off the place." Lovell was resolute. "I can't afford to be host to a bunch of drifters. Especially the Starretts. I want them off the place and in jail where they belong."

Knowing better than to argue, Taffy rode off at a gallop. Lovell urged his horse up the craggy side of the steep cliff. The ground below still turned up bones of the cattle that had gone over the edge in the great blizzard. It was a place Lovell always tried to avoid, as if there were evil spirits still in the earth and the air.

He spurred his way to the cliff face and onto the plateau above. As he came onto level ground, there, to his astonishment, he saw a girl sitting beneath a bois d'arc tree. She was calmly eating a sandwich. She was a small-boned, dainty girl with fair hair escaping in bright tendrils from beneath a sun visor. She had smoke blue eyes, and when she looked up at him, her gaze was direct and calm. She did not seem surprised to see him. She was completely self-possessed. He doubted that she was ever afraid of anything.

"What are you doing here?" Lovell demanded.

"Eating my lunch."

"You're trespassing." It sounded more harsh than he had meant it to.

"Am I?"

Her self-possession unsettled him. He felt he was being put on the defensive. "Beauvaise Ridge is private property."

"Are you a Beauvaise?"

He flushed. "No."

She eyed him thoughtfully. "They say that the Beauvaises stole this land from the Starretts and that the MacClarens stole it from the Beauvaises."

"Where did you hear that?"

"In town. In Maitland."

The flush spread up his neck to his cheeks. "I'm Lovell Mac-Claren. This is my property."

"Oh." Her eyes widened. "They told me about you too."

"And what did they say about me?"

"They say you shot your father." She flushed. "I shouldn't have said that."

He should have been used to that story being spread by now, but somehow he still felt a raw hurt, a sense of shame. "Whoever they are, they talk too much," he said angrily.

"Yes, telling tales about people can cause a lot of unnecessary harm." She held out a paper sack toward him. "Do you want a sandwich?"

"No." He was hungry, but he'd be damned if he'd say so. The girl was maddening. He was no skirt-chaser, but he'd had a certain success with the town belles. This girl was something else entirely. She looked like a rose, but she was all thorns.

"You still haven't told me why you're on my land."

"I'm looking for the Starretts," she said.

It was the last answer he'd expected. "What do you want with them?"

"I'm with the Presbyterian Church Mission in Maitland. I'm here to investigate the Starretts' case."

He gave a short, dry laugh. "You're a missionary?"

"No, not a missionary," she corrected him. "I'm a student in sociology at William Woods College. I'm on a summer field-study program."

"A do-gooder and a schoolgirl. That's even worse. What makes you think you can come down here for a summer and suddenly know all about the people and the land just by listening to a lot of old gossip?"

"What is there to know?" She stood up and faced him. "The Starretts are in need of help. They need food, housing, medical services and a school for their children. I want to help them."

"They're a bunch of thieving, no-good squatters."

"They're human beings." Her eyes blazed in indignation.

"If you want to help the needy, why not pick on someone else? There are lots of people who deserve help."

She looked at him with disdain. "The concept of the deserving poor went out with Queen Victoria. I hope Americans are beyond that."

He dismounted, tied his horse to a persimmon tree and walked toward her. "Listen, this is my land. The Starretts are on it, stealing my cattle, and I want them off. When I find them, I mean to turn them over to the sheriff."

"And I mean to see that they get help."

If he was stubborn and stiff-necked, so was she. He felt like a boy in a schoolyard who had just drawn a battle line in the dirt with the toe of his shoe.

"How did you get up here?"

"I drove to the foot of the Ridge along the oil field road, and then I walked the rest of the way hoping to find them."

"You came alone?"

"No, several others from the mission have gone on around further to the west."

"Well then, you can go down the same way you came up."

"But not until I've looked for them." She made a neat parcel of her lunch and closed the sack. "I want to get them to the mission, and then you and your sheriff won't have any claim against them."

"They've stolen my cattle."

"Your cattle will be paid for."

"My God!" He felt like he was fighting a tiger with a twig. "You don't know anything about the Starretts; they're a bad lot."

"I happen to know a good deal about them." Her eyes flashed up to meet his. "I'm one of them."

He felt like she'd knocked the wind out of him. "I don't believe it."

"It's true." She was enjoying his discomfort. "My great-grandfather was Jasper Starrett. My mother, his granddaughter, was taken to California by do-gooders, as you call them. She went to school there, married my father, had me, and now I'm back."

"You're making it up."

"No." She turned and started clambering over the rocks toward the edge of the Ridge. She was wearing a print cotton dress and had on two-toned, flat shoes with white ankle socks. She looked as out of place as her clothes.

"It's too far to walk down in this heat," Lovell said gruffly.

"I walked up." She kept on going.

"And you can ride down." He untied his horse, mounted and walked the animal to where she was standing above him on a flat rock. "Do you think you can hold on to me and that paper sack at the same time?" he asked.

She considered his question carefully. "I think so."

"Then you can ride down with me." He swung her up behind him. She put one arm around his waist and then the other. He heard the rustle of the paper sack as she held it like a sack of gold. Her body rested against his back. He felt the outline of her breasts and had the uneasy feeling that she held him a prisoner in her arms. They set off at a walk, slowly swaying together in the saddle.

"Will we look for the Starretts on the way down?" Her breath teased against his ear.

"If you want to." He took the long way down and made sure they went nowhere near any possible Starrett hiding place.

At the car he held the door for her. "Where will you pick up the others?"

"At the end of the road." She looked at her Elgin watch. "My goodness, it's getting late."

When he still didn't close the door, she glanced up at him. "I must go."

"There's a new Harold Lloyd movie in Maitland." He couldn't believe he was saying this. "It's supposed to be funny. I'll come by for you about seven."

She stared at him. "A movie?"

He had developed a sort of line to use with girls. A take-charge attack. It usually worked to his advantage. But now he felt stupidly out of control. "I'll pick you up at the mission."

She eyed him thoughtfully. "Tomorrow will you help me look for the Starretts?"

"We'll talk about that after the movie."

"If we find them, will you let the mission take them instead of the sheriff?"

"We'll talk about that too."

"OK," she said, "seven o'clock." She pulled at the door, but he still held fast.

"What's your name?"

"Edna Earle Spencer." She firmly closed the door and drove away. He was left holding air as the dust rose behind the car and enveloped him.

He rode home to bathe and change. He ran up the stairs feeling out of breath and recklessly carefree. He put on his best boots and pony jacket. For the third time, he made sure his hair was slicked down, and then, carrying his new Stetson, he ran down the stairs and across the hall toward the front door, hurrying past the dining room where Taffy, Cima and Snow were at the dinner table.

"Where are you going?" Cima called to him.

"Out."

"When will you be back?"

"Late."

"Who you going with?"

Cima heard the slam of the screen door. If Lovell had answered her, she had not heard him. "Where's he going?" she demanded, looking accusingly at Taffy as if he had had a hand in Lovell's sudden departure.

"From the look of that hair, I'd say there's a boy that's goin' courtin'."

"Who's the girl?"

"Don't know."

"Have you seen her?"

He shook his head.

"Where did they meet?"

"You got me."

"Well, do you know anything?" Cima was exasperated and frustrated.

Snow smiled shyly and spoke almost to herself. "I say Lovell's in love."

Both Taffy and Cima turned to stare at her. Cima put one palm to her cheek. "Who's going to write that to Reanna?"

"Nobody at this table," Taffy growled, "I'd lay hard cash money on that. We already got all the trouble we need."

LOVELL picked Edna Earle up at the mission residence. She was one of five students on the work-study program. The other four watched them go, as silent and sullen as if he'd come to carry her off to Hades.

"What's the matter with them? What's happened to Christian cheerfulness and joy?"

"They know who you are."

"So?"

"So, a Starrett and a MacClaren. They think you're a dangerous, unsuitable date. Montague and Capulet." She smiled. "That's Shakespeare."

"You're a Spencer, not a Starrett, and I've read *Romeo and Juliet*. I went to school." He flushed; he was being belligerent and rude. But there was something about this girl that pulled him two ways at once. He wanted to be with her, and he wanted to run away from her.

He could not concentrate on the movie. Harold Lloyd kept falling out of windows and hanging on to roof ledges. The audience roared, while Lovell felt he was being swept over Niagara Falls into a river of churning rapids. He glanced at her. She was the prettiest girl he'd ever seen. Her features were irregular, but taken together they were perfect. She smelled delicious, better than new hay or summer mornings or tobacco smoke on a dry day. Better even than campfire coffee. He felt like he wanted to laugh and cry all at the same time. He felt displaced and homesick, as if he were at school again.

After the movie, he took Edna Earle to Jerome's Candy Kitchen, where they had chocolate sodas and chicken salad sandwiches. As she sipped the soda through a straw, she looked up at him from beneath a fringe of dark lashes. "Lovell."

He felt startled, bewildered, as if he'd never heard his own name before.

"You want the Starretts off your property, right?"

He nodded dumbly.

"And I want them to be taken care of at the mission until they can care for themselves. Believe me, I'd want that even if they weren't Starretts and my blood kin."

"I know you would." It was the best he could manage to say. Someone, some thief, had gotten into his mind and stolen all the words he used to know.

"There's one thing about them I still don't understand." She frowned, perplexed.

"What?"

"Why don't they have any land of their own? Why didn't they get allotments like the other Indians?"

"They wouldn't sign up for them."

"Why not?"

"Too stubborn, too stupid, too proud. It happened to other Indians besides the Starretts."

"But the Starretts had a double reason for not signing." She took another sip of her soda. "They believed the Beauvaise land was already theirs. Is that it?"

"I guess so." She made him uncomfortable. She seemed so cool and so unaffected by him, while he was bound up and trussed like a calf to be branded.

"Maybe," she said thoughtfully, "if you were to rent them a little piece of your land—"

He was furious that she would ask such a thing. "No! Get that right out of your mind. I'm not going to give them land. Not the Starretts."

"I didn't say give. I said rent. The mission tried keeping them once before, but they wandered off. They need a place where they will stay."

"Not mine!" He exploded. "You think you know them? Well, you don't. They are scum, trash, thieves and worse. In Jasper's generation, they murdered one of their own best leaders, Pride Beauvaise. And in the next, three of them tried to rape my mother."

She bit at her lip. "I didn't know that."

"Well it's true." It gave him some satisfaction to see her admit that she didn't know it all.

"So then it's really your mother who won't let them stay on the land?"

"No!" He was shouting. Heads turned to stare at them, but he didn't care. "It's my decision. My mother isn't even here, she's in England."

"Oh."

"What about your mother and the Starretts?" he demanded. "Did she send you out here to find them?"

"My mother?" Edna laughed. Her eyes crinkled up at the edges. "My mother thinks even worse of the Starretts than your mother does. My mother doesn't want to admit she's kin to them, let alone part Indian. She acts like she doesn't know where Oklahoma is. She much prefers her nice California bridge and garden club ladies." She shook her head. "No, it's my father who understands what I'm doing, and he's behind me one hundred percent."

"He sounds nice."

"He is. What about your father?"

Lovell felt himself tense and a knot tighten in his gut. "I don't talk about him."

"They say you shot him." She waited for an explanation. "Did you?"

"It was an accident," he said softly.

"Oh." She looked relieved.

"But I'm not sorry it happened. I hate him. He's a spoiler of the earth."

"And is that why you're so determined to spend your life hiding out in the country with your pasture and cattle?"

"I'm not hiding. I'm a rancher. Ranchers live out in the country; they don't do their work in town."

"And that's what you really want to do with your life? Grow grass and fatten cattle?"

"Yes. I want to grow fine grass and improve the breed. What do you want to do with your life that's so much better?"

"Not better, but different. You want to improve the land, and I want to improve the people."

"You won't be able to improve the Starretts; they were always a bad bunch. Bad blood. They're lazy, dirty, stupid and shiftless."

"I'm Starrett blood. I'm not dirty or lazy or stupid, and I hope I'm not shiftless." She was still smiling, but her blue eyes were dark as smoke.

"No," he protested quickly, "you're different."

"Only because I had different opportunities. You think you can improve dumb animals with outbreeding and better pasture. Well I think you can improve people if you give them better housing, education and nutrition."

"Is that something you studied in school?"

"Didn't you have to study to learn about grass? Surely even Lovell MacClaren didn't come into this world knowing everything."

"No. I'm not a know-it-all. I had a lot of help from Taffy Owen and an extension course from Stillwater. And I learned most from Pride Beauvaise."

"It's getting late." She'd finished her soda, but he was unwilling to let her go just yet.

"What about when you've finished school?"

"I'll get a job." She spoke with confidence.

"Don't you want to get married and have a home, a husband and children?"

"Maybe, but I'll still want to work to use what I've learned. When you get married, have a wife and a home and children, you'll still want to be a rancher, won't you?"

"Sure." He didn't see how the two things were equal, but he let it go.

"I don't intend to sit home all day watching grass grow." She flushed. It was the second time he'd seen her do that, both times because of something she'd said about him. Maybe she was more interested in him that he'd thought. Suddenly his spirits brightened.

"You want to come looking for the Starretts tomorrow?" he asked.

"Yes."

"I can't let you come out to the Ridge alone. The Starretts, whether you believe it or not, are capable of violence. They are our old enemies. When you're on my property, I'll have to be responsible for you."

"I'll come with the others from the mission."

"If the Starretts see a bunch of strangers, they'll light out for sure. I think," he said carefully, "we'd do better on our own."

She looked at him, weighing all he'd said, sifting out the true and the false. "I'll come with you alone if you call off the sheriff." She looked at her watch. "I have to go. I have to be in by ten o'clock."

He drove her down the main street and turned the few blocks to the mission. He walked her politely to the door. He did not try to kiss her goodnight. It was a first date, and as much as he wanted to hold her and kiss her, he could not run the risk of her rebuffing him. He could not take the chance of not seeing her again. He must make sure of her feelings before he made his next move.

For the next hot, dry weeks, Lovell and Edna Earle spent their days looking for the Starretts. He'd gotten her a horse to ride and loaned her a pair of jodhpurs to wear so they could head into rough country. But when they found a campfire, the ashes were dead. When they followed a trail to a cave high in the rock face of the Ridge, they found it had been abandoned and left strewn with squalid litter.

There were rumors the Starretts had been seen in the oil patch, on the road to MacClaren City and as far away as the river, but they were nowhere to be found. The Starretts, being wise in the ways of the hunted, had simply disappeared, vanished like the will-o'-the-wisp.

In the evenings, after Lovell and Edna had ridden over the place, they went out to a band concert in the Maitland town park, to a dance at the Lakeview casino, to a chautauqua lecture at Maitland College on travel in the Himalayas, and to the quarter horse races at the fairgrounds. Lovell never asked her in advance if she'd like to go out or what she might like to do. He always pretended it was a spur-of-the-moment decision, not like a real date at all. Since by the third date he had not kissed her goodnight, she stood on tiptoe and kissed him. "There now," she said and smiled up at him. Then she ran for the safe shelter of the mission.

By the end of the summer, Lovell was still shy of Edna and the Starretts' trail was still cold. Edna was very discouraged on both counts. She sat on a rock ledge overlooking the south pasture. She was hot and disheveled; the wind had blown her hair into a tangle. And she was more mystified and bewildered by Lovell's behavior than ever. Other boys had pursued her. She thought Lovell liked her as much as she liked him, otherwise he would not keep spending time with her. But if he really liked her, why did he hang back? If given half a chance she could fall in love with him. She wanted to ask him a dozen questions, but instead she said, "You wouldn't think one little band of people could just disappear into thin air."

"You don't know the Starretts!" He fanned himself with his hat. "That's what they're good at—being nomads, wanderers and gatherers. They come and go like thieves in the night."

"Do you think we still have a chance of finding them?"

"A chance."

She sighed. "I know if I can find them and keep them at the mission, they can change. They only need the experience of another way of life."

"You're a dreamer."

She wanted to make some quick, sharp retort, but she saw Taffy riding toward them, spurring his horse hard.

At the beginning of the search Taffy had wondered why he and the boys were always sent in one direction and Lovell went off in the other stringing a pony, but it didn't take him long to put one and one together and get two. He liked the girl, what he'd seen of her. He didn't wonder Lovell would want to keep her to himself. He'd watched them at a distance and liked the way she sat a horse, but he'd kept clear of them till now. He didn't want to horn in where he wasn't asked or wanted.

Now he could see close up that she was even prettier than he'd first thought. Cima and Snow had deviled him for particulars, but all he'd been able to say was that she looked nice enough. He'd been dead wrong. She was a beauty and she was trouble, real trouble, because Lovell was crazy in love with her.

"We found the Starretts," Taffy said when he reined up in front of them.

"Where are they?" Lovell demanded. "Where did you find them?"

"Down by the seep springs."

"What are they doing there?"

"We won't know till we ask them."

They rode, the three of them together, down the sloping Ridge. They joined up with the boys, the sheriff's men and a car full of students from the mission. To Lovell's mind they were a ridiculous cavalcade, like a silly circus coming to town. If the Starretts had half a brain, they'd be long gone by the time this Keystone posse got to them.

But they were still there, clustered around the springs, not far from the *Reanna One*, which was still pumping oil like it was a new well. As Lovell came closer, he had to admit to himself that they were without a doubt the sorriest-looking bunch of people he'd ever seen.

There were maybe twenty—old women, young women who looked older than they were, children with twisted bones and babies wailing in their mothers' arms. They were the ill-fed, ill-housed, ill-clothed and ill-educated. At the center of this mess of humanity was the slumped figure of Junior Starrett. Possibly he was drunk, but certainly he was a sick man.

The women had been dosing him with muck from the spring, giving him oil poisoned by chemicals and dirt. And then, for good measure, they had been smearing it on the children. He watched with sickening horror as the flies buzzed about the most pitiful of the babies. If there had ever been young men or boys with this band, they'd long since fled for the hills, deserting the wretched and the starving.

Out of the silence, while the do-gooders and the law looked on, Lovell heard Edna Earle say, "Are these your dangerous enemies?"

"They can't stay here." That came from the foreman of the pump station. "They can't stay on the lease."

"We'll take them in, then." The sheriff spoke with authority. After all, it was his job.

"Aren't you going to do something?" Edna kept staring at Lovell.

"Yes." He turned to Taffy. "Get the truck—some blankets, whatever—and then take them all into Maitland to the mission."

There were protests from the sheriff, but he didn't listen or pay them any attention. All he heard was Edna Earle's "Thank you."

NOTHING had been settled between them about meeting in the evening, but he knew she wouldn't leave the mission until she'd got the Starretts settled. Just as she must know that when she was finished for the night, he would be waiting for her.

He parked in front of the mission, turned off the lights and sat trying to sort out the way he felt about Edna Earle. He had to make a decision. He knew he loved her. He wanted her to stay here with him and forget about going back to school. He wanted her to marry him and never leave the Beauvaise Ridge. That's what he wanted, but on the other side of the ledger that he was keeping in his mind he saw the glaring debit column. He couldn't balance the two and make them come out even. Sometimes he considered that the worst thing that had happened to him in the last few weeks was the need to weigh up costs, to be a practical man, when he would rather have been a carefree lover.

At nine he saw the light in the dormitory dim. The mission door opened and Edna Earle walked toward him. She got into the car and sat limp and pale with fatigue.

"Where do you want to go?" he asked. His voice sounded rough, as if he had a cold.

"Somewhere, anywhere. Why don't we just drive?"

He drove for a while through the town and then into the country toward Lakeview. There was no dance tonight and the pavilion was dark. He drove behind the building, up a secluded lovers lane, and parked. The silence between them amplified the sounds of the night creatures. A fish splashed in the lake; a frog croaked and made him start. The wind stirred softly at the trees, but it grated against his ears.

At last, when he could bear the silence no longer, he said, "Are the Starretts all right?"

"Yes." She hadn't spoken all the way. "We gave them baths and supper—soup and custard, simple things. They were starving, but we had to coax them to eat. We sent Junior to the hospital." She stopped, her emotions close to the surface.

"And?"

"And at least he'll die in a clean bed. As for the others, when I left, one of the little ones was lying there in bed wearing pajamas for the first time in his life. He had the sheet pulled up over his nose with just those big eyes staring out. He was terrified. It seemed almost as if comfort and civilization had taken his identity and given him nothing in return but fear."

Lovell thought she might cry. He had never seen her cry. "They'll be all right in a day or two. It will take time. They're not used to living inside four walls."

"I'm not so sure it will be that quick or that easy. I can't be so positive now that, given the choice, they will want to be useful citizens or clean, cheerful scholars." She sighed. "Did you ever read *Mill on the Floss?*"

"No."

"I feel like Maggie Tolliver gone to the gypsies. I have all this wealth and treasure of good feeling and knowledge to give, and as far as I can see, nobody wants it."

He wanted her and everything she had to offer. He put an arm around her shoulder. He felt his mouth dry; his heart was pounding. He'd been here to park before in this lane. Then it had seemed that there was nothing easier than sparking in the moonlight. Why was it so hard now? Other times, buttons had flown open, arms had spread wide to receive him and warm lips had parted. Then it had meant nothing to him. He had been curious, wanting to explore and to experiment, but now when it meant everything to him, he was clumsy and inept.

He was torn apart, wanting her with all his heart, yet knowing that the barrier between them was too high for him ever to leap over, too strong for him to break down. Then, while he was still in turmoil, she turned to him and kissed him. Passion flamed up like a great fire and made him forget what was right.

They were touching, caressing; instead of resisting, she returned his ardor with equal feeling, helping him, guiding him to her. His mouth on hers discovered the milk and honey that lay under her tongue. With the world shut outside, they were the only two people in the universe. He was on the brink, the edge, of having all he wanted and more, and then he knew it could not be. He stopped and thrust her away. He sat breathing as if he had run a long race.

She sat frozen, staring at him. "What's wrong? Why did you stop?"

"I can't. It wouldn't be fair or right."

She drew up her blouse to cover her naked shoulder.

"Why?"

"It's wrong." It wasn't what he meant to say. It explained none of his reasons.

"Wrong? How can it be wrong, if it is what we both want?"

He couldn't speak, it hurt too much. He thought he might die of this kind of hurt, but he knew she deserved something more than he could ever offer her.

"I thought you cared for me." Her voice was trembling. He had hurt her, and yet he could do nothing else.

"I do care for you," he whispered. "I do care, that's why." He ached with caring and wanting. He was in torment in mind and soul and body.

"Then why is this wrong? I love you, Lovell. You know that, you must. I loved you from the first day. I'm going to love you always. I'm going to marry you."

He said nothing. The hurt and bewilderment in her eyes deepened as if he had struck her.

"You do love me too, don't you?"

He was still silent. He could not lie to her, not about that.

"Don't you want to marry me?" When he didn't answer, she went on trying to evoke some response from him. "Oh, I don't mean now this minute or this year. I have school to finish first, but sometime, sometime when . . ." She stopped and waited. The space inside the car was so still.

"No," he said, "I'm not going to marry you."

"I see." She turned away from him. "All this was a summer romance, a fling, something to amuse you. And now that summer is over, you want it finished. I'm an easy conquest for you, so I'm not worth the taking. It was all a game to you, wasn't it? A game, like hunting down Starretts."

"No, it wasn't a game, but I'm not going to marry you."

She turned back to him, her eyes blazing. "It's because I'm a Starrett, someone tainted—is that what repels and revolts you? You think nobody in his right mind would want to marry into such a slatternly clan?"

"No!" he shouted, letting go at last of his pent-up emotions. "No, it's not because of the Starretts. I won't marry you because I'm a MacClaren."

She stared at him. "I don't understand."

"I hate my father and everything he stands for. I hated him enough to want him dead. I nearly killed him."

"But you didn't. You said it was an accident."

"I wished him dead just as I wished there was none of his blood in me. I'm the one with the bad blood, not you. I'm tainted, poisoned by him and everything he's ever done. He ruins everything he ever touches. He's evil, and I won't pass that evil on to another generation."

She stared at him, her mouth open in amazement. "That's nonsense! That's the silliest excuse for getting rid of a girl I ever heard."

"It's not an excuse. It's what I think and feel and believe with all my heart. There's something flawed in me, something that must never be passed on. I'd never want a child of mine to suffer for what he's done."

(608)

"That doesn't make sense. You say you don't think I'm responsible for what the Starretts have done. That I'm not guilty for their murder and thievery and rape and drunkenness."

"No, of course you aren't."

"If you honestly don't think I'm responsible for the sins of my family, why do you think you're responsible for what your father has done?"

"It's different." His chin went up. "I'm trying to protect you, to keep you from harm."

"I think you're crazy. You believe land and cattle can change but not people. You believe Starretts can change but not MacClarens."

"I'm not going to marry you or anyone."

"All because of Andrew MacClaren?"

"Yes."

She stared at him, shaking her head as if she could make him deny his words. At last she said, "Then there's nothing more to say. Take me back."

They drove back in silence as they had driven out in silence, only now there was nothing to hope for, nothing to be said or done. He hurt so he felt his bones had been broken along with his heart, but he had to believe he was doing the right thing for her. At the mission they stopped.

"Will I see you tomorrow?" He couldn't bear to let her go.

"I won't be here tomorrow."

"What?"

"I'm going tomorrow. I think it would be best for me if I went back to school early."

"What about the Starretts?"

"They're safe now. There are a lot of people at the mission, trained, qualified to take care of them."

"Will I see you again?"

"What for? There's no point in seeing me." She opened the door, but he held her back.

"I've made you late."

"It won't matter." She walked toward the darkened building.

He got out of the car and followed her like a lost dog. "I can't bear to let you go. Not to see you again."

She turned on him, angry, puzzled. "You can't bear to let me go? It's your idea, Lovell, not mine. You rejected me. You said no to me. I didn't say no to you. You know the trouble with you, Lovell MacClaren? You don't have the sense to know a good thing when you see it. I think we would have made a fine match. I think we would have been really happy together. You want me, I know you do, and I want you. But for your own crazy, wrongheaded reasons you'd rather kick happiness to death than give it a chance. You know something, you'd have to be crazy to let me go." She went in and closed the door behind her.

He telephoned the mission the next day, but they said she'd gone. He knew it would be so, but he had to hear it to believe it. He felt empty and bereft, but he knew what he had done was right. It didn't make it any easier to bear. He felt friendless and alone. He could not talk to Taffy or to anyone at Lochleven. The only person in the world who might understand what it meant to be so totally alone was Pride Beauvaise. He had lived his life with nothing to fill the emptiness but his work. How had he managed to survive the loneliness? Lovell would have liked to have asked Pride if there was somewhere a law that could put his life right.

In Pride Beauvaise's office, in the federal courthouse in Muskogee, the lights often showed until well past midnight. As the workday came to an official end, Pride's secretary, Miss Bunner, hovered in the doorway. "Are you staying late again this evening?"

"I'm afraid so."

"Then I'll stay too."

Pride frowned. "I don't want you to stay overtime if it's going to mean trouble at home."

Miss Bunner was the sole support of a widowed, invalid mother. She had arranged adequate help to stay with her mother during the day, but the old woman was alone in the evenings.

"No," Miss Bunner said hastily, "I've left her a cold supper in the icebox and a neighbor will look in on her. Besides, she's gotten used to me coming in at all hours. We haven't kept regular hours since you began working on the *United States* versus *Andrew Mac-Claren.*"

Pride leaned back and looked up at Miss Bunner's wispy snips of gray hair. Why on earth would she have believed that cutting off all her hair and having a marcel that looked like corrugated iron would make an improvement in her appearance? Perhaps it was an expiation, an atonement for a life lost in service to others. He understood her totally in that regard. Sometimes he felt he was a monument to duty, a man of stone. His own hair was grayer with every passing year.

"The case of the *United States* versus *Andrew MacClaren* is on the fall court calendar."

"Oh, Mr. Beauvaise," Miss Bunner said, beaming, "that is good news." One hand fluttered toward Miss Bunner's heart. "You've worked so hard for nearly four years. All those months to return a true bill against him and then the struggle for the indictment. The delays, the postponements. Oh, I'm so happy for you." She was near tears. "The whole tribe has always had faith in you."

He shrugged and tried to turn the compliment away gracefully. "Well, once the case does go to court, at least you'll have all your evenings free again."

"Yes," she said sadly. "I'm happy about the case, of course, but I have enjoyed working with you both day and night." She flushed, thinking that perhaps she'd said too much and that he might have guessed her secret feelings for him. "You'll win, I know it."

"You can never tell how a judge will find."

"I know you'll win. I'm so proud to have been even a small part of it."

"You were a great help." He hesitated. "I tell you what." He rose and snapped off the desk light. "Let's celebrate. Let's go out to dinner."

"Dinner?" She blinked.

"Yes, unless you have other plans."

"No." She was shocked, surprised and full of joy unforeseen. "Are you sure?"

"Quite sure. I want to go out to dinner with you very much. Unless you have other plans." Once, not so long ago, he would have had a willing widow waiting for him, but she had gotten tired of waiting. This last year she had married someone else.

Miss Bunner could not believe her good fortune. "Of course I want to go, if it's not too much trouble for you."

"No." Pride smiled sadly. "No trouble. I've saved up all the trouble I can manage for Andrew MacClaren. I'd say Andrew Mac-Claren deserves to have a lot of trouble coming to him, wouldn't you?"

* * *

Tom Porter followed Andrew down the steamy greenhouse aisles, trying to get and hold his attention. "Andrew, listen to me, for God's sake. You've got trouble, big trouble."

"The only trouble I've got," Andrew growled as he stopped to inspect some wild daisy, "is lawyers. I'd rather dig a dry hole than talk to lawyers."

Tom wiped his brow. "You're going to have to talk to me."

"And pay you for the privilege."

"Listen to me, Andrew, they're coming at you from all sides."

"Now what?" Andrew shot him a glance. "Not a week goes by that you don't hound me with some new tale of gloom and doom."

"Andrew, for the last time, I'm going to try and get through to you. The United States Government is prosecuting you for bribing an employee of the Department of the Interior to obtain a lease on tribal lands. That's a criminal charge."

"You don't see me in court yet, do you? I've been cited, indicted and I've already been tried in the newspapers, especially that damn *Daily Oklahoman*." He gave Tom a bitter, scathing look. "And I'm still not in court."

"You will be this October. You're on the calendar. They've arranged to squeeze you in. They mean to have you tried, Andrew."

Andrew suddenly grinned at Tom's harried, sweating face. "Don't worry about it."

"Andrew, they've got a case against you, and a damn good one."

"What have they got? Tell me. You're going to anyway."

Tom sighed. He'd been over all this a dozen times. Wearily and with the feeling that he was talking into the wind, he began. "You obtained a lease for tribal surplus land from the Department of the Interior. Right?"

"We've been over all this before." Andrew was impatient.

"We're going over it again. You know a man up there in Washington by the name of Wilnave. He works for the Department of the Interior."

"That's right." Andrew grimaced. "Where is it written that I can't know a man in the Department of the Interior? Senator Curtain introduced us. We all three had lunch together."

"Andrew, this is serious." Tom was exasperated. "Trying to talk to you is like trying to sing with my head in a bucket of sorghum molasses."

Andrew glared at Tom. "Speaking of Senator Curtain, that senator isn't much of a friend to me. He appointed Pride Beauvaise

United States attorney." Andrew held up a pot of gaillardia to the light. "I've told that bastard I'm not going to give him one red cent more. Next time elect me another senator. One that's smarter and friendlier."

"If you told him that, no wonder he's threatening to testify for the prosecution."

"He doesn't dare do that. He's in too deep."

"You've got bigger worries than an election. This 'friend' of yours at the Department of the Interior gave you the lease on tribal surplus land without any competitive bidding. He gave you the lease on sweetheart terms."

"Stop saying he gave me anything. I paid him for that lease and I paid him damn well."

Tom went pale as a white petal. "Don't say that, Andrew, don't say it even when we're alone. Don't ever say you gave Wilnave anything. That's why the government is suing you. That's what they're trying to prove."

"Sorry." Andrew grinned. "Go on." He liked to get Tom Porter's goat, but of late it was so easy to do it was becoming boring child's play.

"Let's start this again," Tom said. "Senator Curtain introduced you to this Mr. Wilnave in the Department of the Interior. Wilnave granted you the lease, and the same week he bought a new house."

Andrew stared, seemingly uncomprehending. "Yes. So?"

"The house cost forty thousand dollars. Wilnave makes seven thousand a year. He has no private income, nor does his wife. He paid cash for the house. What the government is asking is, where did he get the money?"

"He was thrifty."

"What they intend to prove is that Wilnave got the money from you."

"So what if he did? It was a loan. Call it a loan."

"Don't joke, Andrew. You can't joke this away."

"I gave him the money in cash, didn't I?"

Tom shook his head. The perspiration ran in rivulets down his neck and under his shirt. "You gave him thirty-five thousand in cash, and you gave him a check for five thousand dollars drawn on MacClaren Oil."

"Well, that's not so much."

"That's evidence—hard, cold evidence—and they'll use it."

Andrew felt he was being put upon. "You want to hear the joker?" Andrew grimaced. "You want to hear something really funny?"

Tom nodded warily. He didn't need any more surprises from Andrew.

"That tribal lease, the one the government is so hot and bothered about, is a dud. That field hasn't proved out. I haven't made any money to speak of on it, nothing like what I paid to get the lease. In fact, it's cost me money, so I don't see what they're all screamin' and yellin' and yappin' about."

There was a warm silence filled with the sound of Tom Porter's labored breathing. "There's more, Andrew." The topic of the government's suit against Andrew had been comparatively easy to discuss; this next item was going to be hard.

"What?"

"About money." Andrew started to interrupt, but Tom held up his hand. "You've got money problems that have to be faced."

"How can I have money problems? You know what the company grossed last year."

"And I know you spent three times that."

"We're growing, expanding. We have to spend to make."

"Andrew, you went flat-out into the Ohio refinery deal. You bought up and built new retail outlets from here to there. You're drilling in five new fields, and none of them has proved out."

"They will." Andrew seemed supremely confident.

"You're building a pipeline that's not completed. Three years and it's nowhere near completion."

"Give it time," Andrew said reasonably. "There've been a few hitches."

"You've got a refinery under construction in Texas." Tom's voice rose sharply. "There've been a few hitches there too."

"Listen, all this is part of a big, overall plan to integrate the growth of this company. When the oil comes up from the field in Mexico, we'll need the pipeline to ship it. We'll need that plant in Texas to refine it. And then we'll need more pipe to ship it up the West Coast. As for that Ohio refinery, it's going night and day. Don't worry about it, the future looks rosy."

"It's not the future I'm worrying about, Andrew, I've got plenty to worry me right now. You're in the red. If you don't believe me, look at the books. Talk to your accountant."

(614)

"I'd rather talk to lawyers than bookkeepers. They take the joy right out of the day."

"He's tried to talk to you, Andrew, but you wouldn't listen. You write checks anywhere, for any amount. You don't bother to find out what the cash position is. Then he has to raise the money the best way he can to cover you. You charge personal items to the company."

"Like what?"

"Paintings. You've bought enough works of art to fill a museum."

Andrew was indignant. "And they're worth every nickel. They're going to appreciate in value. I got them cheap, a lot of new French artists and some fine paintings of the West."

"But you didn't pay for them with your own money. It was company money."

"What do you mean it wasn't my money? It's my company, it's my money. I found the oil! I drilled the wells! I earned it and I can spend it."

"Once maybe, but you're a corporation now, with stock and a board of directors. Every penny spent has to be accounted for. When you spend, you have to have authorization; you have to get receipts."

"That's damn foolishness."

"Let me bring to your attention the little matter of a check for ten thousand dollars. A check, to cash, that no one can account for. Your signature is on it. What was it for, Andrew? The bookkeeper has asked you. He says you don't give him an answer."

Andrew was irate. "I don't deny I wrote the check. I just don't remember what it was for."

"My God, Andrew, you're hopeless."

Andrew looked brighter, as if a light had just gone on in his head. "I think I know what the check was for. I think I gave it as a donation to the MacClaren Hospital. They said they needed it. I couldn't turn them down. That hospital's named for me. They need more space." He seemed exonerated, vindicated in his own eyes.

"The point is," Tom said wearily, rubbing at his forehead, "the company didn't have the cash in the bank to cover the check."

"Not enough money to cover the check?" Andrew was incredulous. "That's not possible!"

"You don't understand zero funding. We only syphon into the business enough to keep it operating. You see?"

Andrew shook his head.

"What that check and dozens like it meant was that the company had to borrow more money from Anselm."

"The bank could have waited for its money."

"They didn't wait, Andrew. Banks don't make a habit of waiting. From the beginning you borrowed too much from Anselm."

"Only because he asked me to."

"You've kept on borrowing."

"He made it easy."

"You now have two board members and they have four. You now own only forty-five percent of your own stock. They own fifty percent and five percent more they can call in at any time. Burgess-Anselm controls MacClaren Oil. They can take you over anytime it pleases them."

"Why would they want to do that? What would they do with MacClaren Oil? They don't know anything about running an oil company. Anselm said so."

"Maybe they don't know oil, Andrew, but they sure as hell know how to run a bank. They've got you out on a limb. They own you."

"And who got me into banks and stocks and members of boards? You did!"

"No, Andrew, you got yourself in. You saw a way to get a quick dollar and you took it."

"Anselm insisted on it. You know that. You were there. You should have protected me. You should have talked me out of it." There was a long silence as Tom Porter stood mopping his streaming brow. Then Andrew said, "What do you think they mean to do?"

"They've got you by the balls and they mean to squeeze hard. Anselm will watch how this trial goes, but even if you win, you've been tarred with publicity. I think they want to dump you. Get clear of you and wipe the mud off their shoes."

"And will I win in court?" Tom was silent, his head bowed. "I'm paying for your opinion. Let me hear it."

"Pride Beauvaise means to hang you high. If Senator Curtain testifies against you, Pride and the United States Government has got you dead to rights. They'll string you up, and Anselm will leave you there swinging in the wind as a horrible example to the next independent who thinks he can get as big as Standard."

Andrew stroked at the leaf of a plant. His touch was tender and caressing. At last he said, "Don't worry about it, Tom. Everything's going to be all right. Pride Beauvaise will never prosecute me."

"I wish you'd tell me why."

"I will. When the time comes, I will. I promise you. Now why don't you get out of here. Go get a bath and some dry clothes. You've soaked right through that jacket."

"Tell me now, Andrew," Tom Porter pleaded.

"You don't need to know right now. Right now what you got to do is keep those Eastern wolves off my ass. You know the ins and outs of corporation law. Go play pussy with them. Find a way to get me my five percent of that stock back, or you'll be out of a job."

"Why won't Pride Beauvaise prosecute you?"

"I said I'll tell you when you need to know."

"And when will that be?"

"The day we go to court. Boy howdy!" Andrew's face broke into a big grin. "Is that courtroom ever going to be some big show."

*I*N London, Reanna and Simon had been to the theater, then to supper afterward at the Savoy. They had driven back by way of the Embankment and Buckingham Palace to Reanna's house in Eaton Square. Simon had been unable to take his eyes off of her the entire evening. In the car he leaned toward her and said, "You look absolutely lovely, my dear."

"Thank you." She knew her look was expensive—silver lamé and sable. To do Simon credit, while she was in England she had put herself out to dress with care.

Simon had gone to a great deal of trouble to make her a part of his world. He had taken her fishing in Scotland, sailing at Cowes and hunting in the west country. He had taken her to London in the social season and always to Carding at Christmas.

He had introduced her to a circle of men who were powers in the City—lords of finance like Sir Marcus Samuel and Lord Deterding, who had control of a world oil market. She had found them fascinating as they spoke of places where they held oil interests, places like Roumania, the Dutch Indies and South America, but it shocked her to find that not one of them had ever spent a night by a well or taken a sampling of sand. They none of them had ever waded knee-deep in mud to find a break in a pipeline.

In their turn, they found her fascinating because she had. They were kind and generous. They advised her on what shares to buy and what to sell. She gave them small dinner parties, served them chili and corn bread and made them like the novelty of the experience, as well as the novelty of relaxing in a businesswoman's company.

She listened as they talked of the American stock market, where one might make a fortune on nothing but luck and a wide margin. As stock prices climbed, she gambled along with the rest of them, on Anselm's advice. She trusted Anselm. She had reason to. He had executed, move for move, the plan she'd worked out to defeat and discredit Andrew. Every year Anselm owned more and more MacClaren stock. She knew it was all going as fast as Anselm thought prudent, but she was wild with impatience. She had said to play Andrew out slowly, but this waiting was agony.

Simon had tried to divert her and to make her happy here in this soft, green, gentle climate. No man could have been a more kind or considerate lover, but she missed the flat prairie, the cruel, unremitting wind and the place where no two days were the same. She was rooted there at Lochleven on the Beauvaise Ridge, and she'd never feel easy or at home anywhere else.

She knew she didn't always manage to conceal her feelings from Simon. Tonight had been one of those times. Sometimes, after an evening out, Simon stayed the night, but they had arranged to motor down to Carding in the morning, and tonight Simon had intended to drop her off and then go back to the Albany, where he kept a flat. She knew she had been silent and withdrawn all evening; to make up for her behavior, she said, "Come in for a nightcap?" She half expected him to decline, but he said yes at once.

She let herself in with a latchkey. She'd made concessions to London and society. She had a butler, several maids, a cook and a housekeeper, but she made it a rule that none of them was to wait up for her. Gossiping among themselves, they put it down, she was sure, to her unfathomable American ways and her desire to be discreet about Simon. In truth, she wanted to be on her own. She still found it hard to be waited on hand and foot.

As the door swung open, she was surprised and annoyed to see Grey, the butler, coming toward her down the passage. "Good evening, Grey. I didn't expect you to still be up." It was a soft but definite rebuke.

He coughed, a nervous mannerism of his that often took the place of words, and he held out a silver salver. "This came after you had left, m'lady. I thought it might be important."

He always called her *m'lady*, as if to serve anyone of lesser rank might demean him. Reanna looked at the familiar envelope of a cablegram. She took it in her hand slowly. "Thank you, Grey."

"There are sandwiches and a fire in the study. I thought perhaps you might be wanting a fire."

"Thank you, Grey. That will be all."

She and Simon went into the study. He warmed himself at the fire for a moment and then headed for the drink table while she opened the envelope. She read the message and stared blindly into the fire, mesmerized, hypnotized by the flames. The cable fluttered from her hand and fell at her feet.

Simon returned and held out a whiskey toward her. "Here, drink this."

She took the glass and stood like a statue.

"Is it bad news? Is it trouble?" Simon asked, his kind face mirroring his concern for her.

"No. No trouble, at least not for me."

"What is it?"

She looked up at him, her eyes bright, glistening with sudden tears of happiness. "It's from Anselm. I'm going home. At last everything's come right and I'm going home."

He sat in the wing chair, stunned by her news.

"Andrew's trial begins in two weeks. That won't give me much time. I have to leave at the weekend."

"How do you know there's a ship sailing?"

"I always keep track of the sailings. It's the first thing I look for in the *Times*." She glanced at Simon and saw his face crumple. She was sorry and ashamed of having been so blunt.

"I can't believe it. I can't believe you're going." He shook his head to try to clear his brain.

"I'm sorry. I know it must seem sudden, but I've always told you that one day I must go." She had never wanted to hurt him. She knelt down beside him. "I must go. It's what I've worked for and waited for. I told you that from the first."

He put his hand over hers. "I know you told me. You've always been completely honest and straight with me. Still . . ." He hesitated. "I hoped—I let myself believe you might stay."

"I'm sorry, Simon. So sorry."

"You have nothing to reproach yourself with." He stroked her hair, staring intently into her face as if he meant to capture her in his memory.

"Even if I sail at the weekend, it will be cutting it fine. I'll have to ask you to tidy up loose ends."

"I'll see to everything."

"The staff will have to be let go and the furniture put in storage. I don't know what to do about the lease."

"Don't worry. I'll see to it all."

"I don't like to ask you."

"Don't worry." He smiled ruefully. "It will give me something to do to fill in the time." He spoke without self-pity.

His resignation tore her up. "I've been nothing but trouble to you. From the first you've been the giver and I the taker."

"Oh, my dear." He drew her into his arms. "Never say that, never think that. Loving you has been my blessing and my joy. It doesn't happen very often in life that you love someone completely. I wanted the moon, but I'll always be grateful for what I've had."

She let him hold her. After a time she said, "The fire is getting low. It's time to go up now. I'll pack in the morning."

REANNA's ship, the *Aquitania*, docked in New York three days before Andrew's trial was to begin. There seemed no possible way she could get to Muskogee on time. Anselm, who met her at the dock, suggested that she charter a plane and fly by day and travel by train at night. It seemed a daring, dangerous thing to do, but she agreed.

As for MacClaren Oil, Anselm assured her that now when he wished he would take control and that Andrew would be out. Her oil would be hers again.

She telegraphed Taffy and Lovell to meet her at a ranch near Muskogee, where the pilot said there was a field flat enough for him to land. Then she took off and was on her way home.

As Reanna climbed out of the rear cockpit of the plane onto the wing, she took off her flight jacket and helmet and goggles and felt like shouting for joy. If she had been alone and unobserved, she would have kissed the red earth of Oklahoma. The wind whipped and shook the small craft like a warning and a welcome. She squinted up at the sky—clearer and bluer than anywhere else in the world—and then gazed out in pure rapture onto the rolling prairie. Today had been worth all the waiting and the sacrifice, for today

(621)

she would see her plans come right. Today she would see Lovell once again.

She shaded her eyes and looked at an approaching car. She watched as the door opened and Taffy bounded out. He came running toward her, his face a map of anxiety. As he lifted her down from the wing, he said, "What in tarnation possessed you to come home in that contraption? We've all been worried sick."

"I had to get here today," she said, looking behind him for Lovell. "Where's Lovell, isn't he with you?"

"He's coming later." Taffy walked her toward the car.

"Why later? What's wrong?" Her disappointment was sharp and bitter. All during the long journey, she'd thought of this moment and seeing Lovell's face.

"Nothing's wrong." Taffy was brusque. "He went to cattle market yesterday in the City, that's all."

"He went to market rather than meet me?" She couldn't believe it possible.

"He'd planned on getting his cattle to market today. You didn't give us much warning." He wasn't going to say that Lovell hadn't been himself since that girl had left. He didn't know the straight of all of it, but not even the news that Reanna was coming home had lifted Lovell out of the dumps.

"You're sure Lovell's all right?"

Taffy nodded and pointed at her overnight case. "Is that all you brought with you?"

"It's all I had room for. The rest of my luggage will be coming by train."

"You look pretty good, considerin'." He looked her up and down. She did look different from when she'd left.

"Thanks." She was pleased Taffy had noticed the change. She was wearing a dusty rose Chanel suit she had bought in Paris, and she had a small Breton straw hat in her case. She had put herself out to look her best despite her travel difficulties.

"You came in the Rolls," she said.

"That's what you ordered," Taffy growled. "We got a new driver. The old one quit on us, said he had nothing to do." He held the door open for her and looked askance at her two-toned high-heeled pumps. She didn't look like herself at all.

"Tell me the news," she said, as she settled into the back seat and began to arrange her hair and powder her nose.

(622)

"No news we haven't already wrote you."

As they pulled away down the field, she saw a cloud of dry dust rise up behind them. "The ground looks parched. Is it this dry at Lochleven?"

"Nope. Up here they're callin' it a drought. Wind and sand-storms mostly is what's doin' it. The big news is this here trial. That's what's in all the papers. There's goin' to be a mob."

THERE was a throng of people already around the courthouse. There were reporters from all over the country, as well as the curious, a sample of the Oklahoma oil crowd and a little knot of Anselm's men here to observe, analyze and report to New York.

There was a traffic jam in front of the foursquare federal court building. The big Rolls nosed out the smaller cars and drew up close to the curb in front of the steps. Taffy started to get out of the car first, but Reanna held him back.

"Let the driver do that," she said. "I want them to know we've arrived." After all the years of waiting, she meant to savor every moment of this day.

"If you ask me, this here is like walking into a bag of snakes," Taffy muttered, as he tried to hold back the rush of photographers and reporters who had caught sight of Reanna.

They had to fight their way up the steps. When they were almost at the top, she saw Andrew standing on the porch, head and shoulders above a ring of reporters, lawyers and well-wishers. He looked as at home as if he were at one of his own barbecues. He was shaking hands, joking, calling people by their first names, slapping them on the back.

Then he caught sight of her. He separated himself from the mob and walked down to meet her. It was the first time she had seen Andrew since they had shaken hands over Lovell and she had made her pact to sell Andrew her oil. You would have thought from his expression that they had parted only yesterday and on friendly terms. The sight of the two of them together drove the photographers to a new frenzy. Cameras clicked and questions came at them like a rain of arrows. Andrew ignored them all and said jovially, "Hello, Reanna. Have you come to see me hang?"

"I've come to see you have your day in court." She was calm and full of confidence. This was her day to triumph over him.

He began to smile as if she'd just told him a joke. It made her suddenly uneasy to see that wide-open smile. She'd never seen him smile like that unless he was sure of causing someone else grief.

"You know something, Reanna?" he drawled. "Lately I've had a feeling that somehow you might be behind all my misfortunes." He held up a cautioning hand. "I know that's what I've thought. I hope I'm wrong about that." His eyes were as cold as his smile was warm. She had reason to remember the color of those eyes, as cold as cemetery stones. "It would be a pure pity," he went on, "to think a wife would be her husband's enemy."

"I only want to see you get what's coming to you, Andrew," she said quietly.

Andrew's smile vanished. "Let me give you a word of advice, Reanna. Don't measure me for my coffin just yet."

His lawyer, trying to catch Andrew's attention, tugged at his sleeve. Andrew shrugged Tom Porter away. "You've had some surprises for me, Reanna, and now I may have some for you." He turned to Taffy. "Taffy, take Mrs. MacClaren inside. I've saved her a front-row seat."

Taffy ground his dentures together. Andrew acted like Taffy was still his hand to order here or there as it pleased him, but he got Reanna by the elbow and herded her into the courthouse.

"What was all that about surprises?" he asked.

"Nothing," she said, convincing herself it was so. "That was just Andrew having his fun."

THE courtroom was already full to overflowing. The hum of voices like angry bees in a swarm was still for a moment when Reanna walked in. The crowd stared at her, gaping, pointing, and then the hiss of whispers ran wild and the babble started again.

True to his word, Andrew had saved space for Reanna and Taffy in the front row behind the defense. She would have preferred to sit elsewhere, but there was no choice. There was not another seat to be had. They would have to squeeze in tight when Lovell came.

Taffy groaned at the hardness of the bench. "This is worse than church," he grumbled. He'd never liked church, and he sure as hell didn't like court. In his view, this was going to take longer than a protracted camp meeting. From all around he could hear people discussing Andrew and Reanna. She must have heard them too.

She smiled. The gossip was just the same. "That's her, she's one good-looking woman. Nobody knows why, but she's out on the place and he's in town. They say she's been to Europe and back. Paris, France, too! Poor old Andrew, he ain't done nothing the rest of them don't do, only he got caught. But he'll get hisself out of it, you'll see. That Andrew, he's a slick article!"

She listened, more sure than ever that Andrew must be discredited once and for all. She glanced at the bank of lawyers at the defense table. It gave her a sense of enormous satisfaction to know that all the lawyers in the world couldn't save Andrew today.

The hands on the clock above the judge's bench came closer to the hour. From a door behind the judge's bench, the prosecution lawyers, with Pride in the lead, came toward their table opposite the defense lawyers. Pride was deep in conversation with one of his staff. He did not look up or glance in Reanna's direction. He sat with his back to her.

She had tried to anticipate what her reaction would be at seeing Pride again after all these years. She had expected the sight of him to have an impact on her, but she had in no way gauged just how great that effect would be. She was astonished by the rush of sharp pain. She felt magnetized, pulled toward him as if by some great force of gravity. She wanted to go to him, to have him take her in his arms and embrace her. Her desire was so overwhelming that she had to will herself to stay in her place.

Her glimpse of his face had been brief, but she had seen the new lines around his eyes, the gray in his hair, the silver wings at his temples. And she had seen that there was a slope to his shoulders, as if he had carried too many heavy burdens. But in her eyes he was the boy she had loved and loved still with all her being. It was a torment to be so near him and not be able to touch him. She could almost feel the remembered touch of his hands on her body. She could hear the sound of a deer-bone flute and the thread of a song only Pride knew.

She sat, racked by memories, and was astonished to think that Pride had not seen her. How could he be so near her and yet not be aware of her presence? She bit at her lip to keep back his name and closed her eyes to stop seeing him. Even so, his face was imprinted behind her eyelids, as bright and clear as the noonday sun.

"Are you all right?" Taffy asked.

"Yes," she answered. "It's just a little warm in here with all this crowd."

"Are you sure?" he asked.

"I'm tired; it was a long journey home."

"You're pale as a ghostie. You want some water?"

"I'm fine," she snapped at him.

"I was only askin'." He shuffled his boots and wished he was anywhere but here.

As the clock hand crept slowly toward the hour, the waiting became almost intolerable. Reanna saw Andrew talking rapidly and intently into his attorney's ear. She saw Tom Porter turn abruptly and stare at Andrew. His jaw went slack and then Porter turned slowly, as if his head were on a stick, to look first at her and then across the courtroom at Pride. Then he turned back to Andrew, and Andrew nodded his head and smiled again, that cold smile of complete satisfaction.

Precisely on the hour, the federal marshal acting as clerk of the court stood calling out, "Hear ye, hear ye, hear ye! All rise. The United States District Court for the Eastern Division of Oklahoma is now in session, the Honorable Vernon R. Le Matt presiding." The judge in his robes took his place, and after banging his gavel like a hammer of heaven, he ordered the charges and particulars of the case to be read out.

Reanna looked closely at the judge. He seemed dispassionate. He was neither young nor old, short nor tall; he was as evenly balanced as the scale of justice. She knew Andrew had bought many men in positions of power, but by the look of him, this man—like Pride—was not for sale.

As the long litany of Andrew's misdeeds was recited for the world to hear, Reanna began considering her own true bill of charges against him. Andrew was the killer and exploiter of love. He was a man who had robbed his foster mother, his first wife, his brother and his child, to make himself richer. He had taken all and given nothing in return. It would be a sweet, sweet revenge to see Pride prosecute Andrew and to have the end of Andrew's tyranny.

Suddenly, as the list of wrongdoing was being spelled out in legal jargon, Andrew's attorney Tom Porter was on his feet interrupting, demanding attention.

"Your Honor, may I approach the bench?" Without waiting for an answer, he advanced toward the center of the court and half turned, like an actor preparing to give a practiced speech to an audience.

Judge Le Matt frowned, unsure of what had provoked such behavior.

"Your Honor." Tom Porter was ostensibly addressing the judge alone, but his voice could be heard clearly in every corner of the room. "Your Honor, I ask for a mistrial."

There was a shocked silence in the courtroom, then a babble of voices as the judge pounded his gavel for silence. Judge Le Matt was visibly angry at the outburst and at Porter for having provoked it.

"Your Honor," Porter proceeded, apparently impervious to the chaos he had caused, "my client is innocent. This case has been trumped up, the charges springing solely from the personal motives of the prosecuting attorney. First to last, this is a hell-inspired conspiracy, spawned in the fevered, warped mind of Pride Beauvaise."

There was a gasp, then a persistent murmuring. Pride rose abruptly and stared in disbelief at Porter as Judge Le Matt again called for silence.

"Pride Beauvaise," Tom Porter thundered, "is not qualified to conduct this or any case against my client."

"Silence, Mr. Porter." Judge Le Matt's voice rose above all others. "You come close to contempt. You do not instruct me on whom I may or may not hear in my court. If you had any reason to object to the prosecution of this case, you should have done so before now in my chambers."

"Your Honor, I beg the court's indulgence. This information has just come to me. It is of such a damning nature that as an officer of the court I must present it to you before any more harm can be done to my client and before there is a grave miscarriage of justice. Your Honor, the prosecution has personal reasons for wanting to see my client found guilty. I suggest to you that it is not my client who should be on trial here, it is Pride Beauvaise, for it is Pride Beauvaise who has broken the law."

Pride rose to his feet to voice his objections. The judge's gavel rose and fell, but Tom Porter, in peril of being cited for contempt, ignored the danger. Andrew had paid well for Porter's performance, and Porter was delivering it with all the dramatic and emotional skill he possessed. He raised his fist above his head in a gesture of defiance.

"It is Pride Beauvaise who is the thief. It is Pride Beauvaise who has stolen from my client. He has taken from Andrew MacClaren that which is most sacred—his good name—and like a thief in the night he has made foul the sanctity of Andrew MacClaren's home."

For the first time since Tom Porter had begun his harangue, Reanna saw with terrible clarity what line he was taking. She knew now with sickening certainty that he meant to lead them all into the flames of the fire she had set. It was with a sort of shocked, numbed detachment that she listened as Tom Porter continued. He shouted as an evangelist might on Judgment Day, when all must be known and all revealed.

"Pride Beauvaise is the criminal here. He has committed a crime against God and man. He has broken one of the Bible's ten great commandments. He has been guilty of taking Andrew MacClaren's wife in adultery."

The roar of voices was like the sound of the sea raging over her. She saw Pride take a step backward. The impact on him was like a mortal blow. She could almost feel the sharp knife cut deep within him.

And then she looked at Andrew. She knew now why Andrew had been smiling and what great mischief that smile signified. She remembered his intense conversation with Tom Porter and knew that that had been the instant of Pride's betrayal.

When his back was to the wall, Andrew had used the one weapon she had been sure he would never use, a weapon he had had in his possession all these years. A weapon she had given him. She had been so sure that Andrew, with his vaulting conceit, would never accuse Pride or her that she had dismissed the possibility. For when he struck at them, he shamed and diminished himself. He must have been truly desperate to use such a way out for himself. No matter what Tom Porter might charge in an effort to turn popular sentiment in his favor, Andrew might still face conviction. And certainly he faced the taint of scandal. He must have been sure of going down in defeat to have so coldly and cruelly decided to take Pride and her with him. It had been Andrew doing his worst to hurt them.

"And the most terrible crime of all committed by Pride Beauvaise against my client," Tom Porter's voice thundered above the roar of the crowd, "was to father the child Andrew MacClaren was to call his own. He gave that boy his name, his fatherly affection, when all along that boy was the misbegotten bastard of Pride Beauvaise and his dearly beloved wife, Reanna MacClaren."

It was a bombshell; it exploded all around them. She heard herself say, "Oh God, oh God no." But the plea and the prayer were lost in the tumult.

"There they are!" Tom Porter pointed first at Pride and then at Reanna. "Sinners free to go among you, to hold their heads high, while my client sits falsely accused before the bar of justice."

As Tom Porter's accusing finger pointed at her, Pride's eyes followed the gesture and he saw Reanna for the first time. She was there, sitting behind Andrew. He must have believed that she was a part of this hellish attack on him. In his face she read shock, disbelief and bewilderment. He shook his head like an animal caught in a trap. His eyes dulled with the pain as he realized that there was no way out of the predicament, no way to escape. There was no turning back now for any of them.

Pandemonium swept the courtroom. Over and above the tumult, she heard the sound of Judge Le Matt calling for silence. He might as well have asked for the sun to rise in the west. He roared out his condemnation of Tom Porter. He ordered him held for contempt and removed from the court. She heard the pounding of the gavel, but it was not as loud as the pounding of her heart.

She saw Pride's stricken face as he shook his head back and forth in agonized shock. She saw, from the corner of her eye, Andrew's face, which had broken into an obscene grin. Beside her, Taffy cursed beneath his breath, "Damn Andrew. Damn his eyes!" while all the time he held fast to her arm, his grip like an iron claw.

A ring of reporters crowded about her. Cameras were pointed at her, questions were hurled at her as the room began to spin. She felt the floor grow unsteady beneath her feet, as if there had been an earthquake and the world were falling down around her head.

She could find no way to forgive or free herself from this awful debacle. Her only shred of comfort was that Lovell had not been there to see or hear. It was the only mercy that the gods had left her. She looked back again at Pride, who was still staring at her in pain, bewilderment and despair. And then, as she turned to look away from Pride's hurt and Andrew's pleasure, she saw Lovell standing at the back of the courtroom, his outline unmistakably framed in the doorway.

At first she tried to pretend to herself that Lovell was an illusion, a trick of her eyes. Then she perceived he was real and she wanted to cry out to him to turn and run, as if from some great disaster.

But she couldn't make her voice heard over the roaring crowd. She lifted her free arm to signal to him only to have it roughly grasped by a stranger. Even if Lovell could hear her, where would he run, where was there a place now for him to hide or be safe?

The tumult grew even higher, growing louder with the shrill sound of scandal. She was obsessed with the idea that she must get to Lovell to try to explain what she had done and why. She tried to push through the crowd toward him. She must make him understand. But she was caught up in the cruel crush. Hands reached out and clutched at her. She was mobbed, penned in by the curious, the questioning, as the angry called her ugly names. It seemed she was in a thicket of brambles, their hands holding her like thorns.

Then, just as she might have got free, something held her back, rooted to the spot. It was the expression on Lovell's face. At first he smiled at her, a boy's wide-open smile, and then he began to laugh, his head thrown back, laughing as if this were a sovereign joke.

She couldn't hear the laughter for the noise, but it didn't signify. She knew that Lovell was laughing at her, mocking her for all the lies she had told him, for the awful, terrible charade she had made of their lives. Tears filled her eyes. The image of Lovell laughing was blurred. Suddenly, instead of Lovell's face, she saw the death-warped face of a young boy hanging, twisting in the wind—the face and figure of the boy she'd seen hanged the day she came to the Territory as a bride, a boy who had been the awful, tragic victim of a Chickasaw revenge.

All around her there were mouths open, pressing close to her ear, asking her questions she couldn't answer for herself or for Lovell. Fists shook at her. She tried to beat them off, but to no avail. A flash exploded in her face; someone had taken a close-up portrait of her despair. And then with a kind of mercy, the room began to turn around her, swirling into a bottomless pit. She felt herself descending into darkness as her knees gave way and she began to crumple. For the second time in her life, Reanna fainted.

Taffy caught and held her. The mob, half-shamed, drew back and made a path for him to carry her from the courtroom. When Taffy, with Reanna in his arms, came even with Lovell, Lovell took her from him. He carried her gently and tenderly the rest of the way to the waiting limousine, while Taffy pushed aside anyone foolish enough to get in their way. Together they laid her against the cushions of the back seat. As Taffy climbed in beside her, Lovell said, "Get Reanna out of here. Get her home to Lochleven." He started to close the door when Taffy reached out to him.

"Ain't you coming with us?"

"No. There's somewhere I must go. Something I must do before I can come home again."

"What are you saying? Your ma needs you. Can't you see that?"

"Tell her I'll come back just as soon as ever I can, but this is something that can't wait."

Lovell slammed the door and motioned the driver to go on, and as Taffy looked back, he saw Lovell disappear into the crowd.

As soon as Lovell saw that Taffy would take Reanna safely home, he headed north toward the border, driving as fast as he could toward Fulton, Missouri, William Woods College and Edna Earle. He drove all night, singing nonsense songs and shouting out her name to keep himself awake. He arrived at dawn, only to find the college gates closed and locked.

But nothing would keep him out, not now, when he had such good news to tell her. He shinnied over the fence, dropped down on a pile of autumn leaves and walked briskly toward the nearest building that looked like a dormitory. At the front door he rang the bell, and when no one answered, he began to pound with his fist.

At last the door opened a crack. An irate housemother in a brown flannel wrapper and a pink hairnet glared at him. "What do you want?"

"I'm sorry to disturb you, ma'am. I know it's early, but I must see Edna Earle Spencer."

"Young man, you've no business here. This is a residence for young ladies."

"Please, I have to see her. It's very important. Where is her room?"

Befuddled by surprise, she replied without thinking. "On the second floor front."

Lovell, determined to seize his chance, started past her toward the stairs, but the dragoness was suddenly alert, prepared to defend the young ladies in her charge from any possible male contact. She swiftly, resolutely, barred his way. "You can't come in here," she screeched. "Go away at once or I'll call the police." She pushed him outside and slammed the door shut. He heard the bolt being shot into place.

Lovell backed away from the door and stood in the courtyard looking up at the expanse of brick and gleaming windows. No trellis or ivy vine marred the bare front. There was no way to climb up to the second floor, but he would not be stopped from seeing Edna Earle. He had come from the depths of hopeless despair to the pinnacle of joy, and he would, he must, see her. He bent down, picked up a handful of pebbles, and threw them at the center windows. Then he threw a second handful and a third, all the while calling out her name.

Suddenly, a center, second-story window opened and Edna Earle appeared like a vision in polka dot pajamas. She blinked down at him, rosy from sleep. She looked to him as radiant as Juliet on her balcony. He stood for a moment mute with wonder at her beauty, and then he shouted, "Edna Earle, it's me."

"I see that. What are you doing here, Lovell?"

"I have something to tell you."

"You could have written me a letter."

"It was too important to write. It's something wonderful." He waited for her to ask him what his wonderful news was, but she only looked down uncertainly at him, as if he might be a part of a dream.

"What I have to tell you changes everything." He took a deep breath. "Andrew MacClaren is not my father. I'm Pride Beauvaise's son." She remained silent, as unresponsive as if she hadn't heard him. "Did you hear me, Edna Earle? I'm a Beauvaise." He stretched out his arms ready to embrace the world and whirled around and around, letting out a wild Chickasaw yell. "I'm a Beauvaise."

Windows went up all along the the dormitory front. Heads appeared in curl papers and plaits. He'd attracted an audience. He felt like a fool, but there was no point in trying to keep it quiet now. "I'm a Beauvaise." He stood looking adoringly up at Edna Earle.

"And is that what you came to tell me?" she asked.

"Yes." She didn't seem to grasp the enormity of what he had said.

"Don't you see? This changes everything. Now I can marry you." He tried to ignore all the eyes staring down at him from along the dormitory front and keep only Edna Earle's face in his view.

"What did you say?" She leaned out onto the window ledge, one hand cupping her chin.

"I said now I can marry you."

"What?"

"I can marry you." He repeated the words, but they seemed to blow away in the wind.

"Oh, now you want to marry me? Is that it?" There was an outbreak of giggling, like birds twittering. "Is that why you're here, Lovell?"

"Yes." He felt his face go scarlet. She was teasing him. Making him pay for having been such a fool before. Damn her. She always knew how to get at him, and he never saw it coming.

"You're a Beauvaise, and you want to marry a thieving, landless Starrett? Whatever will people say to that?"

"I don't care what anyone says. I'm going to marry you, Edna." He was angry now, determined to get her down here on his level where he could kiss some sense into her.

"Starrett and Beauvaise!" She shook her head sadly. "Montague and Capulet." She sighed. "No, Lovell, it would never work in real life any better than it did in the play."

"OK, Edna Earle. OK. I know I was a fool before. I hurt you, but that's all in the past. Marry me, and I'll spend my life making it up to you."

"What about the children?" She leaned further out, as if to hear his answer better. "What about all that Starrett blood?"

"Damn it, Edna Earle. If you'll marry me, I'll ask the Starretts to dinner every Sunday. I'll give them forty acres and a cow apiece. Only say you'll marry me."

She considered his request, as if there could be more than one answer. "When?"

His heart picked up a beat. "Now! Today! We'll elope. We'll find a justice of the peace."

"I have an eight o'clock class."

"Skip it."

"I want to graduate."

"Do it later."

"I'm not cut out for a rancher's wife."

"You can be anything you want to, only please marry me."

Her smile disappeared. "You'll have to make me a better offer than that, Lovell." She waited, her head held high.

"What do you want? Name it. You know I love you."

"You what?"

"I love you." He closed his eyes and shouted it at the top of his lungs. "I love you." When he opened his eyes she was smiling, looking like her old, familiar self and not some distant vision high above.

"That's more like it," she said, as pleased as if he'd given her diamonds.

She never failed to astonish him. She hadn't said yes, but she hadn't said no. "Does that mean you'll marry me?"

"Yes, Lovell, of course I'll marry you."

A cheer and a round of applause went up from the spectators as more windows flew open and more heads appeared. Their audience was getting too big to suit him.

"And that's it?" He was staggered by her. "That's what you wanted me to say?"

"That's right. I wanted to hear you say it just once. You never have."

"I love you," he shouted, throwing all caution and sense away with his heart. He would never understand her. "I love you now and forever. Now will you come down?"

Edna Earle didn't reply. As he looked up, he saw her turn. She was disappearing from his view. He knew a moment of sudden panic. She could not be so cruel. It wasn't in her nature. She would not turn her back on him as he had once on her. "Where are you going?" he shouted.

He dashed forward. If he could, he would have scaled the smooth brick as surely as a knight climbing up a glass mountain to claim a princess. She turned back again and said brightly, "If I'm going to marry you today, Lovell, I'm not going to do it in my pajamas."

This time the cheer that went up was loud enough to rattle windowpanes.

They were married at ten o'clock that morning by a justice of the peace. Edna Earle wore a trim little traveling suit and a felt hat with a feather in it. He did not notice the color of either.

They drove to the nearest lodge in the Ozarks for their honeymoon. For the next three days they did not leave their room. They spoke to no one but the hall porter who brought them food, which they ate, and newspapers, which they did not read. The world outside was of no interest to them. They had all they wanted—a wide, soft double bed and each other.

REANNA sat alone in the cupola room in the dark, reliving the nightmare of the courtroom. She had been at Lochleven three days now, or was it four? She had lost track of time. All she was sure of was that she had lost Lovell forever.

Taffy had tried to tell her otherwise, but she hadn't believed him. She had asked him over and over exactly what Lovell had said until Taffy was sick of repeating it. "He said to take you home. I asked him wasn't he comin' and he said no, there was somewhere he had to go, somethin' he had to do, and then he'd come."

"Did he say where he was going?"

"No."

"Or when he'd be back?"

"No."

"Then how can you be sure that he's coming back?"

Taffy sighed wearily. "I'm only tellin' you what the boy told me."

She felt like an invalid—weak, hollow-eyed, sitting huddled in the big leather chair sick at heart and soul. Hour after hour she'd sat there, staring at nothing, while all around her there were trays left untouched and newspapers left unread. In the beginning, the telephone had rung constantly. She had been besieged by reporters, Jack and friends, Lillian, Doc, Amoretta and a host of the curious. Everyone had called her but Lovell, and now the phone was as silent and cold as her hopes.

Beyond her window the night was dark and unfathomable. There were no stars, not even a ghost of a moon. The low-hanging clouds held the threat of rain and made the air oppressively heavy. The closeness of the night weighed in on her like her conscience.

She knew this misery was of her doing, that the harm was all her own fault. When Andrew had exploded his bombshell in court, her house of cards had come tumbling down. She had been made to witness the terrible consequence of her deeds.

She had destroyed Pride's work and tarnished his reputation. She had robbed the tribe of their champion and tainted their trust in him. And in that last awful moment of consciousness, she had seen

Lovell disgraced, branded a bastard before the world. She had seen his laughing face, his eyes mocking, condemning her for all the monstrous lies she had told him.

She had meant to have her day of triumph, but it was she who had been defeated and Andrew who had had the final victory. He had blown away all her hopes and plans. He had whipped her into the dirt. For Andrew, not her, all the old scores were now canceled and the slate wiped clean.

How Pride and Lovell both must hate her, and they had every reason, every right. She couldn't expect either Lovell or Pride to forgive her when she couldn't forgive herself. She could only hide away, ashamed to show herself. She couldn't eat or sleep. Not even Cima had been able to talk her guilt away.

Her head ached with the unremitting ticking of the clock. Then, out of exhaustion, she must have dozed, for she woke to hear it strike the hour and to see Snow standing, a tray in her hands, staring down at her. Reanna sat upright. "Have you come to gloat over me, Snow, to say I told you so?"

"No." Snow shook her head. "Perhaps once that would have given me satisfaction, but not now. I promised Cima I'd try and get you to eat."

"I'm not hungry."

"Cima made some broth especially for you. Drink it, and while you do I'll read you the papers."

"I don't care what's in the papers."

"You can't hide here forever," Snow said quietly. "I know, I've tried." She put the tray on Reanna's lap and handed her a cup of steaming broth. Reanna saw that Snow meant to stay there until she had drunk it. To oblige her, she took the first sip. The broth was hot, salty and delicious. She was surprised to find out just how hungry she was.

Snow pulled up a footstool and sat beside her. "I'll read you the headlines." She cleared her throat and began. "Prosecutor Withdraws From Case." Snow glanced at Reanna. "I'm sorry about my uncle," Snow said, "but he did the right, the only thing." She waited for Reanna to say something in return. When she saw she would not, she laid aside the first paper and picked up the second.

"MacClaren Wins Suit, Loses Company," she began to read quickly. "Senator Curtain, witness for the defense, swears the money MacClaren gave to an employee of the Department of the

(637)

Interior was a donation for charity." Snow made a grimace of disbelief. "It also says that there will be an investigation into all tribal leases. The leases from the Chickasaw to the MacClaren Oil Company are suspended pending the outcome of that investigation."

Again Snow waited for Reanna to comment before she picked up the third paper. On it there was a bold two-word headline, "MacClaren Out." Snow began to read. "Andrew MacClaren, founder of MacClaren Oil, is replaced as head of the company by majority stockholders. Mr. MacClaren, in an exclusive statement to this paper, blames Eastern banking interests for his ouster and vows to leave Oklahoma. A source high up in the company is quoted as saying there is no reason for MacClaren employees to worry about their jobs. The MacClaren Oil Company will merge with Colorado Minerals to become a new company, Lorado Oil."

Snow looked up and was gratified to see that Reanna had drunk the broth and that there was some color in her cheeks. Then she stared down at the newspaper and said, "It's hard to believe Andrew MacClaren is going away. But then he's got nothing to stay here for, has he?" She might have been speaking of a stranger and not her father.

"He won in court," Reanna said bitterly.

"He has no company and no friends or family." Snow's tone was dry and dispassionate. She quickly scanned the other papers. "There's nothing else about Andrew MacClaren." Snow hesitated, then said, "What about you, Reanna? What about your crude oil?"

"It will be mine again."

"So it's really you who won in court." Snow eyed Reanna with an open, bold gaze.

Reanna stared at Snow. She had grown into a woman who was calm and serene, a woman Reanna could envy for her tranquillity. "I got my oil back," she said, "but Pride and Lovell paid dearly for what I won."

"I benefited," Snow said, her head high. "I'm going to file for my certificate of competency. I'm going to manage my own affairs."

"I'm glad."

"I should have done it a long time ago, but I was afraid of my father and what he would do or say. Most of all I was afraid of myself."

"And you're not afraid now?" Reanna asked.

Snow nodded. "Oh, yes. I'm still afraid of being stupid, of being called names and being hurt, but Lovell gave me confidence. He made me see that I could do something on my own. It started with one calf, Daisy, and then he showed me that I had a place in the tribe. Lovell has been a good brother to me, and he's even more dear now because he is a Beauvaise, a man of the blood."

Reanna felt tears in her eyes. "You are very kind to come to me and to tell me all this."

"I would have come before, but I was too stubborn to admit what a good, decent woman you were. I could never see that you cared for me or for this place."

"Oh, I cared." The words caught in Reanna's throat. "I cared too much perhaps, and now I've cost you all dear. I've cost you a brother. Lovell will never come back."

Snow held out her hand to Reanna. "He'll come back."

"I don't think so." Reanna could not allow herself comfort or false hopes.

Snow was adamant. "He'll come back. This is Lovell's place, his home, and he loves you."

Reanna turned away and looked out into the night. She was a gambler and she knew the odds. "If Lovell were coming back, he would have been here by now."

Snow stood firm. "If he's not here, he has a good reason for staying away." She picked up the tray and set it on the desk. "Now you must get some rest." She covered Reanna's knees with a quilt, bundling her up as if she were a child.

"And Pride?" Reanna asked. "Will he ever forgive me and come back home again?"

Snow thought for a long moment and then said, "I can't tell you the answer to that. I only know that Pride Beauvaise will do what is right and best for all of us."

PRIDE, in his office in Muskogee, was packing up a pile of law books into a carton. Beside him on the desk were a few personal mementos of the past—a deer-bone flute, a bird carved in ash wood and a brightly colored stone he had kept to remind him of a special day with Reanna. He could see his past in those talismans, but the future was as dark and unreadable as the night outside his window.

There was a discreet knock at the door, and Miss Bunner entered with a newly typed letter for his signature. She had obviously been crying. Her eyes were red-rimmed; she held the letter in one hand and a balled-up, damp handkerchief in the other. She thrust the letter awkwardly toward him.

"Here," she sniffed, "it's finished."

He took the letter, put it on the desk and picked up a pen.

"There's no reason for you to resign, Mr. Beauvaise." Miss Bunner blurted out the words and then dabbed at her flowing eyes. "You're too valuable a man. Your work means everything to you and to the tribe." She stepped back, a blush flooding her cheeks.

"Thank you, Miss Bunner," Pride said, "for the vote of confidence, but I'm no longer of any value to the tribe. I've been discredited in my professional and personal life. I stepped down as prosecutor and, worse, I failed to get a judgment on the tribe's behalf. The man who appointed me, Senator Curtain, was a witness for the defense. I have no choice. I have to resign."

"The tribe still needs you," Miss Bunner protested with feeling. "The lease will be canceled. They'll get their land back, you'll see, and in the end they will all know that you won, not lost." She sniffed again. "As for your honesty, no one could doubt that."

"Thank you again. I appreciate it, but I must resign as United States attorney. It's the right thing to do." He signed his name with a brave flourish.

Miss Bunner's face was a mask of tragedy. "Where will you go? What will you do now?"

Pride paused for a moment before he answered. Then he shrugged, uncertain of what to say. "First I'll go down to my ranch for a while. I need a little time to think things through. Then I may go back into private practice." He handed Miss Bunner the letter. "I'll want you to stay on, on full salary, of course. Though I can't expect you to wait forever if you get a better offer."

Miss Bunner bristled at the idea. "Oh, I'll wait," she said breathlessly, drying her eyes. "I wouldn't want to work for anyone but you." She flushed again. "I mean I've gotten used to working all hours." She turned to leave, then at the door she hesitated and faced him tremulously. "I want you to know that I don't believe any of the terrible things Mr. Porter said about you and Mrs. Mac-Claren." She hesitated, waiting for him to deny the charges. When he was silent she hurried on. "Even if it was true, I understand and so will the tribe. You're a good man, Mr. Beauvaise, and a fine human being. No one expects you to be God."

Then she hurried out, closing the door behind her on the past and all his mistakes, both of omission and commission. Pride stood staring at the brightly colored stone. He picked it up and held it, turning it slowly in his hand as if it had some magical power to change the past or foretell the future.

IN the ornate, formal dining room of the Marble Palace, Andrew was playing host at a farewell dinner for his old cronies and top employees. It had been a bang-up, gala affair. To see him at the head of the table, smiling and cracking jokes, one would not know he was a man without a place or a company. Only the telltale vacant spaces on the walls told the story of his art collection already packed up and sent into MacClaren City to the private train that was waiting to take him out of Oklahoma.

It was a bitter irony that he had won his case in court only to have Anselm take control of MacClaren Oil. This dinner tonight, which might have been a victory celebration, was instead his last supper. He had been roasted and toasted, and now it was his turn. He stood, tapping his wineglass for silence. Then he said, "There have been a lot of speeches made here tonight. The last, and I trust the best, I've left for me. We've been through a lot together. We've seen good times and bad. Tomorrow it will be business as usual for you, but not for me."

He gave a wry and rueful grin. "I hear they're already painting out my name and putting up Lorado Oil in its place." He hesitated for a moment and then stood tall. "So, for the last time I'm going to give you some orders. I'm going to ask you to forget the bad, remember the good and don't—for God's sake—make any long goodbyes. Just get your hats and go." He looked for the last time at the grave, familiar faces around the table. "What the hell are you waiting for? You all know the way out."

They sat dumbstruck, staring at Andrew as he walked abruptly out of the dining room onto the terrace. As he went, he signaled Tom Porter to accompany him.

On the terrace, Andrew stood with his back to the dining room, looking out past the greenhouses toward the refinery, the tank farm and the *MacClaren* field. The dark clouds hung heavy in the sky. The night was moist and unusually warm for the end of October. The clouds and wind mixed in such a turbulent stirring that it might have been spring.

"That was a fine speech," Tom said, uncertain if Andrew heard him. "They'll be sorry to see you go."

Andrew grunted. "Tomorrow they'll already be kissing new ass. I'm finished and they know it. I'm down and out."

From another man, it would have sounded like self-pity. From Andrew, Tom couldn't be sure it was not a sign of high arrogance. "You won in court," Tom said.

"I lost MacClaren Oil."

"You got a good price for your stock. You got the top dollar before the market fell. You're a rich man."

"Yeah." Andrew turned on him. "I've got money in my jeans, but I've got nothing to do and no one to do it with."

"You can travel."

"I don't like to travel. I'm too old and too rich to start over."

"You'll be fine, Andrew," Tom said, wondering what he'd do if he were a millionaire and free to go and do as he pleased.

"What about you, Tom?" Andrew asked. His face was twisted and grim. "Why don't you come with me?"

Tom had been expecting and dreading the question and his answer. "Sorry, I can't. My family want to stay here. I've been too busy to be much of a husband or a father. I owe it to them."

"The pay is good." Andrew was baiting Tom, sweetening the tip of the dagger that he used to goad him with. "In these times lawyers are going to be a dime a dozen. Lorado Oil may keep on the others, but not you, Tom."

"I'm not coming." Tom faced Andrew straight on. "When you won in court, that was the end of the road for me. I used to be a pretty good lawyer. I had a future in jurisprudence. Then you hired me and I learned to bend the law. I was your dog and I barked for you.

"I'm ashamed of what I did in that courtroom. I hurt a fine and honorable man. I knowingly conspired with a witness to commit perjury. I've been cited for contempt for disrupting the judge's courtroom, and I expect to be hauled up before the ethical committee. If I'm lucky, I'll only be suspended; if not, I'll be disbarred. Thanks again for your generous offer, Andrew, but it's time I stayed and faced the music."

Andrew applauded Tom Porter with mock solemnity. "That's right noble of you, Tom, but if you get hard up, remember the offer's still open."

"I'll remember." Tom felt a sense of relief. He had made up his mind and he had spoken out; still it was an awkward moment. The silence now lay between them as heavy and threatening as the night air. In the distance there was a flickering of lightning that played across the sky, followed by the long, low roll of thunder.

"Sounds like rain," Tom said, to break the silence.

As he spoke, the first jagged bolt of lightning flashed out of the clouds—bright, terrible as a polished sword. Both men watched, mesmerized, as the tip hit an oil storage tank in the center of the tank farm near the MacClaren refinery. For a second both men held their breath, blinded by the fierce light. A peal of deafening thunder rolled like a great drum. Then there was an explosion of flames, as the fire reached up toward the sky.

They were awed and transfixed; they might have been statues immobilized by the sight of such destruction. At last, it was Tom who spoke first. "Andrew, we can't just stand here. We've got to do something."

Andrew turned on him, his eyes glittering, shining bright, reflecting the fire. "I don't have to do one damn thing. It's their oil field now, not mine. Let them save it, if they can."

AFTER Snow had left her, Reanna had been no easier in her heart about Pride or Lovell, but at last she slept fitfully, sitting slumped in the great chair. She had no notion of how long it was before she woke again to find she was drenched in perspiration, her heart pounding. The air was so close that she felt she was suffocating. She flung the quilt from her knees and stumbled toward the windows. As she reached out to open them, she saw a flash of angry lightning. It flickered across the sky and was followed by a long roll of distant thunder. Then there was a second flash of lightning. This time it was blindingly bright, and as she watched in fascinated horror, she saw it strike in the cluster of oil storage tanks near the MacClaren refinery.

She held her breath, waiting for the thunder that must come, but she was unprepared for the deafening peal or the sight of flames leaping up from the tank back to the sky through a dark column of smoke. The flames, orange-red, rose a hundred feet and were reflected in an angry, eerie stain against the clouds.

Then the lightning struck again and again in rapid, deadly succession. Each strike hit a tank or a well nearer and nearer to the *Reanna* field. She heard herself crying out above the thunder and the explosions, screaming out her protest against the waste and the senseless destruction.

She didn't know if it was the sound of her voice or the fury of the storm that brought Taffy, Cima and Snow running down the hall. They stood behind her, watching the prologue to holocaust as if it were a raree-show.

"Has it got the refinery?" Taffy asked.

"No, it's in the tank farm and I think it's hit two or three wells." As Reanna spoke the rain came in a torrent. It lashed savagely against the windows, the wind blowing in a howling gale out of the north. "We can't stand here doing nothing." Reanna spoke with quiet intensity. "We must stop that hell from coming in on us."

Reanna was in action now, grabbing up jodhpurs, boots and an old flannel shirt. She disappeared behind a screen, calling back to Taffy, "Taffy, get on the phone to Will Bassett at the *Reanna* pump station. Tell him I want him to start back-pumping every barrel of crude out of the tank farms along the border between the *Reanna* and the *MacClaren* fields. I don't want any crude left in our tanks that could catch fire."

Her head appeared around the side of the screen. "It's been three years. I don't even know if Will Bassett is still at the pump station."

"He's there." Taffy was clicking the receiver up and down, trying to get the operator.

"When you get him, tell him I'll need a map of all the gathering and pipelines, the storage tanks and oil wells." She was hastily pulling on a boot as she came out from behind the screen. "Then get onto the section bosses. Tell them to get all the families out of company housing and every man off the rigs. They are to pack up the generators and every piece of dirt-moving equipment and meet us at the main pump station on the line between the *Reanna* and *MacClaren* fields."

Taffy, feeling pressed and exasperated, finally had the operator on hold. He would rather tangle with a diamondback rattler than talk on the telephone. "Anything else?" he growled.

"Yes, tell them we need extra men, teams, wagons, mules and not to forget picks and shovels. We'll need every man we can get to dig a fire ditch between the Ridge and the *MacClaren* field." She was dressed, looking like her old self in an outlandish outfit of mismatched clothes. "And we'll want to call in every fire-fighting unit in the surrounding counties."

Taffy nodded, trying to keep in his mind all Reanna wanted done. He began barking orders into the mouthpiece as Cima tried to talk sense to Reanna. "You can't put out an oil fire with no pump and hose. If oil and water mixed, this rain would have had the fires out by now."

"I know that." Reanna was impatient. "But I'll need every man I can get to dig the ditch and run generators."

"And what about us?" Cima cocked a thumb at herself and at Snow. "What are we supposed to do while you dig this big ditch?"

"Get the stove going and that old wood range out in the summer kitchen. Make coffee and sandwiches, get a soup kettle on to simmer. We'll have the men and their families to feed." She hesitated a moment. "We'll need medical supplies, salve and bandages. Pray there are no burns, but we'll have to be prepared." She went on quickly, trying to think of everything that must be done. "Snow, look for blankets and quilts and put up beds and cots in the halls and out on the verandah."

"We'll get right to it," Cima said. She and Snow turned toward the door, but Reanna stopped them.

"Listen to me. Before you get started, you know as well as I do that in case of fire the Ridge is the most dangerous place you could possibly be. There are fissures of gas running all through it. If they ignite, the Ridge and everything on it could blow sky-high. So, if you want to come out with me now, I'll understand."

Cima's face twisted in a grimace of displeasure. "We're staying," both Cima and Snow said almost at once. Then Cima added, "We've stayed here through wind and weather. No little fire is going to drive us off."

"This fire isn't little," Reanna said. "If this fire gets to the Ridge, it won't be something you can put out with a damp burlap bag."

Cima bridled. "I wish you'd stop treating me and Snow like we was a couple of simples. You go and do whatever you have to in the oil patch, and Snow and me'll see to the house. You hear me?"

"I hear you." As Reanna spoke, the lights in the room began to flicker and dim.

"The power line's hit," Cima said flatly.

"And the telephone's gone dead," Taffy reported.

"We've got to go." Reanna spoke in the half-light. "I hate to leave you here like this. As soon as I can, I'll get a phone hookup to the Ridge. I'll want to know what's happening up here." She was edging out the door and toward the stairs.

"Take this with you," Cima said, lighting a kerosene lamp kept for emergencies.

"What about you?" Reanna asked as Cima handed it to her.

"We'll be fine. Now, you and Taffy go, and God help you."

REANNA, with Taffy beside her, drove along the Ridge, going east toward the pump station at the boundary between the two fields. The rain lashed down, wave after savage wave, blurring the windshield as the lightning and thunder crashed and rolled overhead and the wind buffeted the car like a plaything.

Reanna looked north toward the *Reanna* field. Dimly, through a water-misted window, she could just make out the work lights going out on the rigs. One by one, the gas flares dimmed and disappeared like yellow-gauze ghosts. As the field went dark, it seemed to her as if the end of the world were at hand. And before her was the specter of hell and damnation. The fires around the refinery had already multiplied and spread. Those closer were blazing bright and terrible in the frenzied, swirling, lurid smoke.

She clenched the steering wheel as the car was shaken in the fury of the storm. It was one thing to rush out to fight this disaster and another to get there to fight it. But she must fight and she must win. The alternative was too terrible to consider.

At the pump station at the end of the Ridge, off the MacClaren City road, there was already a gathering of men, reporters and photographers, many of whom she'd seen at the trial. They were clustered around the small, square building. They were sheltering in trucks and wagons. The teams, made restless by the storm, were straining against their harnesses, their hooves churning mud into mire.

"Taffy," Reanna said, "get those reporters out of there. Keep them back from the fire. Then get the men divided into work parties. Assign them to their regular field section bosses. Then get a phone line. I don't care how, just do it. We can't fight a fire if we don't know where it is."

"Anything else?" Taffy growled.

"Not till I talk to Will."

Inside the pump station, Will Bassett was peering down at a map of the two fields. He glanced up as Reanna came in. He was clearly a man under a great strain.

"Good to see you again, Will," Reanna said, forcing the door shut against the wind and rain.

"Good to see you again, Mrs. MacClaren. Sorry you had to come home to this."

She shook water from her slicker and crossed to the desk. "Is this map up-to-date?"

"Yes, ma'am. Everything's on it. The location of every well, every tank farm and pump feeder and pipeline, plus the railroad tracks where they circle and cross both fields."

Reanna leaned down to study the map like a general taking stock of a battlefield. Rain dripped from her wide-brimmed felt hat. "Have you back-pumped all the oil out of the tanks bordering the *MacClaren* field?" she asked as a matter of course.

"I did the best I could." Will Bassett was uncomfortable and on the defensive.

"What does that mean?" She looked up at him sharply.

"It means the pipeline we've got now hasn't the capacity to carry that kind of load. The new lines aren't completed. We've got the ditch dug. It runs from here at the pump station back to the gathering lines by the *Reanna One*, but the pipe's not in place yet."

"So how much oil is still in the tanks?"

"They're over half, more like three-quarters full."

"And what's in the line?"

"That's full, too. We don't have the capacity to handle what's being drilled, and that's a fact."

"What about the excess oil? The oil you haven't got in the line or the tanks?"

"It's in earthen holding pools. See the circles here by the tank farm? They're all open pools."

She counted them and the other pools all along the pipeline. They were at close intervals all the way from the *Reanna One* to the edge of the *MacClaren* field. "How much oil is in the tank farm here at the pump station?"

"They've got different tank loads," Bassett muttered. "Some sixteen hundred barrels and some twenty-five hundred."

She tried to keep her voice even, not to show her rising fear. "How many barrels in all?"

"In the tanks?" he asked, as if it were an outlandish question.

"Give me a rough estimate."

"A quarter of a million barrels," he mumbled.

"A quarter of a million!" She felt her lips go stiff and dry. "And the pipeline's full?" She traced it with her finger on the map, a dark line all along the northern edge of the Ridge, and parallel to it, a dotted line for a ditch that was dug but not laid with pipe.

"That's right," he said, barely audible. "The pipe's full up."

"And how many barrels of crude in the open pools?" She dreaded the answer to the question.

"That's harder to say."

"How many?"

"Another quarter of a million, maybe more."

"So, all told, there's better than a half a million barrels of oil sitting out there in tanks and pipe and pools strung out along the north edge of the Ridge from here to the *Reanna One*. Half of it in open pools—exposed, vulnerable, waiting for a spark to set it on fire. A half a million barrels of oil and no place for it to go. How could you let this happen?"

"It wasn't my doing." He was hurt and angry at being so falsely accused. "I begged 'em at MacClaren to off-load on tank cars and take the crude out by rail, or wait until we had the new pipeline in place. I tried." He was near a whimper now.

"I'm sorry." She was ashamed to have jumped all over Bassett. "I know it wasn't your fault. It's Andrew's doing. He was so greedy to get every barrel out of my field at the lowest market price that he was willing to take any risk just to pump me dry. Every sensible oilman knows the only safe place to store oil is underground." She shook her head sadly. "What's done is done. And tonight we'll all have to pay the piper."

It was too late to argue, too late for recriminations. All she could do now was to fight to preserve what was hers. At bottom it was a fight for mere survival.

"We'll get some tank cars in here by rail and off-load as much as we can." She spoke with confidence.

Bassett looked whipped and near tears. "We've got no cars on the track."

"Where is the nearest tank train now?"

"MacClaren City, at the loading dock, but they won't send anything through a field that's on fire." He was plaintive, near the breaking point.

(648)

"There must be a string of tank cars somewhere, Will."

"In Maitland, but they're already leased."

She felt her jaw tense, and her chin shot up. "I want those tank cars, Will. Just as soon as Taffy has the phone working, get Maitland. I want the tank cars. I want them all and I want more men. Promise them any price and a bonus, but get them here." She turned toward the door. "Right now I've got to get what men we do have to work."

Reanna stood on the back of an open, flatbed truck. The rain, running down her cheeks in rivulets, looked like grimy tears. There were not as many men or as much equipment as she had hoped for, but she must make do with what she had. They were a tense, uneasy bunch who kept looking over their shoulders at the fires behind them.

"You all know the situation," she said, not meaning to tell them any fairy tales. "We've got to stop that fire from getting to these tanks and this field. If it was just wells on fire we'd know how to handle it, but there are fires all over the *MacClaren* field and the wind's blowing them in our direction. So there are two ways for us to fight what's coming." She had to shout to be heard over the rain and the wind. "Contain or divert. We haven't got enough men or equipment to shore up around every tank and open earthen pool. So what we're going to do is to dig a wide fire ditch along this end of the Ridge and run it north to south between the end of the Ridge and those tanks and pools.

"When we've got this ditch finished, we'll join it with the smaller one that's already been dug along the north edge of the Ridge to hold the new pipeline." She paused, waiting for a response to her plan.

"What if this big ditch don't hold?" The rough voice came out of the dark, like a soul asking an oracle its fate.

"Fair question," she said. "If we can't contain and the tanks or pools are in danger, then we'll divert the oil. We'll run it off out of the tanks and pools through the ditches, just like sending it down creeks to a river."

"We ain't got no river." Another voice, this time high and whining. "Where you goin' to send this oil?"

She took a deep breath. "South into the open pasture."

"Onto the pasture!" Taffy bellowed in outrage. "You let that hell onto the grass and, God Almighty, the whole place will be ruined."

"It's the only way, Taffy. You know it and so do I. I can't allow

(649)

half a million barrels of flaming oil to reach the Ridge. But there's no need to borrow trouble. If we luck out, the fire won't get this far." Her words were meant to assure and appease Taffy, but they did nothing of the kind.

"What if we don't have time to finish this here ditch?" The question came from the huddle of men as lightning flashed and cracked overhead. It voiced her worst fear, worse than the ruin of her field or the sack of the south pasture.

"We won't have time if you don't start digging. We'll use this pump station as headquarters for hot food, coffee and, hopefully, a telephone so you can check on your families and friends. Now let's get going and good luck to you all."

They split up into their work parties. She saw them disappear into the dark. Then, as the generators began to flare, she could see the long line of lights, laying out the distance they must dig. The task seemed endless in the beating rain and drifting smoke as they raced the storm and the fire.

She turned to Taffy to ask him if he thought they had a chance of success, but he was walking away from her, his shoulders hunched up under his hat. "Where are you going?"

He wheeled around, his face contorted with fury. "I wisht I could tell you I was goin' to get blind, pie-eyed, fallin'-down drunk. Instead of which, I'm goin' to see to some damn telephone so you can talk to railroads." He spit. "Anythin' else?"

"No, Taffy, nothing else."

She stood alone in the dark, the cold, driving rain beating at her. She stared ahead at the fire, which was like a judgment on them for all their sins. She felt lost, adrift in the fury of the storm. She had been alone before, but never had she felt so abandoned or bereft as now.

THROUGH what was left of the long night, she rode and walked the line, coaxing and bullying the men on. The wind howled in protest as the lightning struck again and new fires flared up in the distance, one after another. She couldn't be sure of a count. It was impossible to tell in the dark and the smoke. She watched through field glasses as a wooden derrick twisted like matchwood and fell into eternal darkness. The fires were so bright and deadly she could almost feel the heat.

(650)

As she watched the men digging, straining every muscle to make the ditch wider and deeper, she was dismayed to see the mud slide from the top of the trench back down into the bottom of the pit. They had to dig every foot twice over.

They were good men and they were trying, but the odds were against them. She bent her head, discouraged and bone-weary. Then someone called out, "Don't give up, missus, it's always darkest before the dawn." She hadn't the heart to say that by her watch it was already morning. In this smoke-filled hell it was no longer possible to tell day from night.

Exhausted, the men rested in shifts at the pump station. They had worked like brute animals and now they sat huddled in sodden blankets, beneath tarpaulins, in the cabs of trucks and under wagons, sitting mute and uncaring in the mud. Their faces were streaked with dirt and soot and dotted with oil spray blown from miles away by the force of the wind.

Taffy appeared, looking sheepish and ashamed. He dug the heel of his boot in the mud. "I'm sorry about jawin' at you last night. It was just the idea of the grass goin'."

"That's all right," she said. "I understand."

"The phone's workin'," he reported happily. "We've been on to Maitland, both me and Will."

"And?"

"And they've got an engine and tank cars and plenty of men willin' to work, but the stationmaster won't let the train leave the station."

"Why not?"

"He says it's too dangerous."

"Tell him the railroad can name its own price."

"Will's done that."

"Say I'll be responsible for any damage."

"I told them so, but he won't let the train come."

"He has to." She couldn't keep the desperation out of her voice. If she couldn't get the tanks off-loaded and the rest of the ditch dug, they were still in jeopardy.

"Listen," Taffy said, trying to reassure her. "Don't worry. Even if the train won't come, the worst is over. The storm is settlin' down."

"You think so?" She would have liked to believe him.

Taffy nodded. "It's been ten hours since this fire broke out. No lightnin' strikes in a while, and the wind and rain are dyin' down. All you have to do now is hang on."

"How many wells are on fire in the *MacClaren* field?" she asked.

"I talked to Doc and Jack Levy. They say forty or fifty. They don't have a true head count."

"I would have said more like fifty fires, not counting the storage tanks."

"Jack says this fire is front-page news. We've made all the papers from California to Maine."

She turned away, trying not to show what she was feeling. She was tired, worn out and sick at heart. If the storm was really over, it was good news for the men and for the field. But if the news had been in all the papers, then Pride and Lovell must both know what was happening here. If they hadn't cared enough to come home last night, then she was sure now they never would.

*I*N an Ozark lodge bedroom, Lovell lay propped up on one elbow, looking down at the sleeping face of Edna Earle. He had been lying there for the better part of half an hour, trying to decide whether she was more beautiful awake or asleep. It was a question that, happily, he would have the rest of his life to answer.

There was a knock at the door. As she stirred, a tendril of wondrous, fair hair fell across her cheek. "What's that?" she murmured.

"Breakfast," Lovell said.

She groaned. "Tell them to go away, we don't want any."

"We have to eat, Edna Earle, if only to keep up our strength."

She smiled, her eyes closed tight, crinkled up at the corners. She looked as pleased as if she had explored all the mysteries of the world and found them to her liking.

Lovell took the tray from the hall porter and set it down on the bed. There was bacon and eggs, toast, fruit and coffee. As Lovell reached for the coffeepot, his eye caught the headlines of the newspaper he had let fall carelessly to the floor. Two words jumped up at him. *Oil* and *Fire*. He picked up the paper, read and then hastily began to pull on his trousers.

Edna Earle stirred again and reached out for Lovell. He wasn't beside her. She sat up, pulling the sheet around her. "What is it, Lovell? What's wrong?"

"There's a fire in the *MacClaren* field. They don't say if it's spread to the *Reanna* field or not. But the story was written hours ago; anything could be happening." He stopped short and shook his head, as if trying to order his thoughts. "I have to go home."

Edna Earle was awake now, her eyes open very wide. "A fire?" she gasped. "Not the Starretts, pray God the Starretts didn't start it!"

"No, no," he reassured her. "It was lightning. A storm hit the tank farm near the refinery. I have to go home. I have to be there."

"Of course."

He leaned down and kissed her. "You don't have to come. You can stay at school."

"No, Lovell." She had already made up her mind. "I'm coming with you. I didn't promise to obey you, but I did promise for better or for worse." She flung back the covers. "Besides, I want to be with you."

They dressed, packed, drank a quick cup of coffee and were on their way. As they drove, Lovell reached out for Edna Earle's hand. "Thank you for marrying me."

"Thank you for asking me."

"It was a wonderful honeymoon," he said.

"We'll have a wonderful life." She rested her head on his shoulder. "Don't worry, Lovell. Everything will be all right."

"Will it?" He wasn't so sure. "I hope so. With any luck we'll be at Lochleven in a few hours." His foot pressed hard on the gas pedal, and his eyes fixed on the road ahead.

In his office, Pride switched off the desk lamp. He stood and stretched; he was stiff from having worked the night through. He made a neat stack of his files; each had a note attached for Miss Bunner. There was nothing left for him to do. His business in Muskogee was finished. He picked up his briefcase and looked uncertainly around the office where he had hoped to do so much and felt he had done so little. Then he walked quickly to the door.

By the doorsill in the hallway lay the morning paper. He picked it up. He'd forgotten to cancel the paper. He glanced at the headline, then stopped still and read. He had finished only the first paragraph before he began to run down the stairs and out to his car. If he drove straight through, he could be at Lochleven by evening.

* * *

Reanna stood on a heap of muddy slag. She looked east through field glasses toward the *MacClaren* field. She was still unable, because of the ever-shifting smoke, to make an accurate count of the fires. Those nearest to her were burning bright, but they seemed no closer than before. Still, she felt a sense of unease, as if she were on the edge of a sea of mud and fire that threatened to engulf and overwhelm her. She was so swept up in this thought that she was not aware of Taffy talking to her.

"Listen to me." Taffy raised his voice. "You have to let up on the men. They're whipped, beat out, and so are you. Look at you. If you don't sit down, you'll fall down." He might as well have been talking to the air. At last, out of patience, he took her arm and turned her toward the pump station. She pulled back and planted her boots in the mud. "What in tarnation are you standin' out here for?" he pleaded. "It's all over, I tell you. What are you waitin' for?"

And suddenly there came a violent, earth-shaking answer, as the first of the oil storage tanks in the *MacClaren* field exploded.

The long night had been merely the prologue; now the real drama began to unfold. For twelve hours, the oil in the storage tanks had been boiling inside the iron cylinders. At last, the gas at the top of one of the tanks was hot enough to explode, shooting flaming oil upward with all the force of a volcano. The fiery oil poured over the side of the tank, filled the moat around it, then breached the earthen bank and spilled over, running out in a stream of black fire.

As the flames billowed up to the clouds, some as high as five hundred feet, the clouds responded as if attacked. They opened once more to deluge the land with rain. Six inches had fallen in the night. Now the sea of mud became a shifting, treacherous river of mud and fire. The lightning struck again and again, but this new electrical storm hit out in a wider, more random pattern. The lightning was followed by such loud, reverberating peals of thunder that Reanna and Taffy had to hold their hands over their ears so as not to be deafened.

Cold, exhausted men, who only a moment before had been too tired to move, were on their feet, running in confusion, holding rearing horses, beating at braying mules and digging with desperate futility against an avalanche of sweeping, sliding mud.

First one storage tank and then another exploded. They went off in a sequence. It might have been the planned finale to a great celebration. As the flames showered out in terrible beauty and hit the refinery, it burst apart in an extravaganza of color and stifling, corrosive chemicals, adding a deadly undercurrent to the already smoke-filled air.

This was hell on earth, a plague of fire, bent on destroying them all. Stunned, held in place, motionless as the world blew skyward around her, Reanna watched in horror as the lightning at last struck at the *Reanna* field. It was what she had feared, and it had come upon her. The first hit a gas well to the north of the pump station. She saw it hit and then heard the roar as the gas spewed out in a raging rush, as if Cronos had a fire in his entrails.

She stood watching as first one *Reanna* well and then another was hit and fired. She saw the arrows of lightning strike them ruthlessly, one by one, as if loosed from some Olympian bow. The wind lashed the flames from one side to another like so many candles sputtering and flickering but never going out. She felt Taffy shaking her and heard him shouting, "It's got in on us. We're hit bad!" He turned her toward him. "Now what do we do?"

She wasn't calm, but she made herself answer slowly and without a show of emotion. "First we get a steam generator up to the gas well."

"And then?"

"And then we let the rest of the wells burn themselves out. We can't fight them all. We haven't enough men or equipment."

"You'd let the oil wells go?" He seemed incredulous.

"I have to! If I'm to save the Ridge, I have to keep the ditch open. I need every man to keep digging to make it longer and wider. Talk to Maitland again. Tell them we must have those tank cars and more men."

"I've tried." He shook his head wearily. "This time you talk to them."

She struggled through the brutal wind and the blinding rain, toward the pump station. The mud gave beneath her feet and the oil spray from the wells made her look as if she were being anointed for some pagan ritual. Inside, she lifted the receiver. She must convince the stationmaster in Maitland to send the tank cars and the men. They must come, no matter what the price or what the danger, for she knew that if she didn't get help, she couldn't contain or channel the deluge of oil that would soon break through from the earthen holding pools.

She listened, waiting for a connection; then she realized that the line was silent, as dead as her hopes. She clicked the receiver up and down, more out of habit than expectation. Then, without blinking, she looked from Taffy to Will Bassett. "The line's gone dead." She knew it was redundant, but she felt better for saying it aloud, as if words could give her some control of chaos. "Will, Taffy and I have to get back to the line. You keep trying to reach Maitland." He stared at her, mouth open. "Keep trying. When you get them, call me. Can you do that for me, Will?"

Will Bassett nodded, thinking that she had more grit than any man among them.

"We must get through to Maitland," she said. "It's a matter of life or death."

She pulled down her hat, turned up her slicker collar and went out again into the storm. There were sparks flying everywhere, as bright and beautiful as deadly fireflies. They skipped from well to well and pond to pond, blown in all directions by the wind. As she watched, they were wafted south toward the pasture. She stood transfixed, dumb with shock as she heard Taffy moaning, "Oh sweet Mary and Jesus, look'ee down there. Do you see that? All Lovell's work gone up in smoke." It was a cry of despair for the pasture.

First, the grass caught fire in patches and burned until the rain damped the flames into smouldering ash. She watched without feeling any emotion. She had gone past exhaustion, past desperation to a kind of numbed acceptance. Then she saw Taffy wipe at his face with the back of his hand, as if to wipe away the rain and oil, and she knew that he was crying for the grass and for Lovell. It broke her heart in two.

"What about the cattle?" she asked him.

"They'll drift west." His voice was rough. "You'd best get out now, too. The fire's on three sides of us and no help coming."

"I can't go, Taffy," she said gently. "I have to stay."

"Cattle have more sense than people," he growled, but he knew better than to argue; she'd made up her mind.

In the pasture, as the cattle drifted west toward safety, the wild animals—fox, rabbit and possum—sprang from their burrows. Does were separated from fawns, quail broke upward out of cover, birds abandoned their nests. A coyote jumped a circle of flames and was suddenly on fire, running circles on himself until he dropped, howling in agony.

All around Reanna, the ring of fire was pulling in tighter and tighter, more deadly than a noose. This, then, was to be a siege of fire and wind and water, with no way to win and little hope of survival.

LOVELL drove with grim determination. They had stopped only for gas. While Lovell had seen to the car, Edna Earle had bought cheese and crackers and bottles of pop to eat and drink on the way. Now that they were coming into MacClaren City, they were both tense with fatigue and apprehension.

As they drove over a rise about a mile out of town, they saw the angry, orange glow beneath the clouds. At first they thought it was the setting sun; then they realized it was the fire that lit up the horizon. They were awed by the sight.

"My God," Lovell said, "I've never seen anything like it."

"It's like a nightmare." Edna Earle spoke softly, almost in a whisper. "Something you dream about, but something that can never really happen."

Lovell was impelled to hurry to find Doc and Jack Levy, who could tell him what the situation was. But he was brought up short at a roadblock by a state trooper. The officer was polite but firm. "Sorry folks, we're turning back all traffic. There's a big fire up ahead, and the roads are closed."

"I must get through," Lovell said. "I must get home. I live on Beauvaise Ridge."

The officer leaned down and looked into the car, studying Lovell and Edna Earle. "Sorry, Mr. MacClaren. I didn't recognize you at first. Sure, you can go on into MacClaren City, but I doubt you can get out of town. Those roads are all closed."

"Thanks." Lovell felt his mouth dry. His heart was pounding. "Is the fire in the *Reanna* field too?" he asked.

The trooper shook his head. "Not the last I heard, but you can't tell what's going on inside all that smoke." The trooper motioned him ahead, and Lovell waved his thanks.

Driving into MacClaren City and down Main Street, Lovell felt he was in a town he had never seen before. The neat, white clapboard houses were tarred with oil and feathered with ash that blew out of swirling, foul-smelling smoke. People who dared to venture out covered their faces with handkerchiefs, kept their heads down and hurried to the next place of safety. The carefully planted and tended lawns were all withered and brown.

Lovell and Edna Earle found Doc Hersey and Jack Levy on the roof of the bank building. Doc was looking west through a telescope. As Lovell approached, Jack Levy turned and stared uncertainly, as if Lovell were an apparition.

"Lovell," Jack asked cautiously, "is that you?"

"Yes," Lovell said, "I just got into town. I didn't know about the fire until this morning. I've been off in Missouri getting married." He nodded toward Edna Earle. "Doc Hersey, Jack Levy, I'd like you to meet my wife, Edna Earle. Doc and Jack," he explained to Edna Earle, "are my mother's best and oldest friends." They all shook hands with such solemnity that, had the circumstances been normal, they would have laughed at themselves.

"Now tell me, what's the situation?" Lovell braced himself for the news.

Jack looked to Doc for support and began. "The storm struck last night a little after midnight. The MacClaren tank farm is gone, and the refinery and a hundred wells." Jack stopped, shifting from one foot to the other.

"Go on," Lovell said. "What about the *Reanna* field?"

Jack looked down at the tip of his shoe. "It was hit today about noon. We thought the storm was over, then all hell broke loose. Sorry," he said to Edna Earle, "but I'd use worse language than that if it would do any good."

"My mother," Lovell broke in, "is she all right?"

"She's fine," Doc said.

Jack Levy seemed less sure. "She's holding her own. She's got a crew digging a ditch between the fire and the Ridge, but she needs more men."

"We all need more men," Doc said. "It would take an army to fight this fire."

"And what about Andrew?" Lovell asked. "What's he doing?" He clenched his fist, still wanting to hit out at Andrew in any way he could.

"Andrew's leaving town," Doc said contemptuously. "He's got a private train waiting at the station."

"Leaving?" Lovell couldn't believe what he had heard. "Andrew's going?"

"Let him go and good riddance. No one will weep for him." Doc had passed judgment and sentence.

"Then my mother's fighting on her own?"

"She's got Taffy and Will Bassett and a lot of good men doing their damndest," Jack burst out.

"I have to get home."

Jack was skeptical. "You can't get there through the *MacClaren* field. The tanks and wells are still going off like firecrackers. You can't tell where the fire'll spread next."

"Then I won't go through the *MacClaren* field. I'll go west to the county line road, down the section line south, and up from the south across the pasture to the Ridge."

"The fire's got into the south pasture too." Jack tried to break it gently, but there was no way.

Lovell took a deep breath, then shrugged at the irreversible facts. "That's only a grass fire. Not oil. The rain will have put most of that out."

"It's still too dangerous."

"I'm going," Lovell said. "I have to. You understand?"

Jack nodded. "Yes, I understand."

Lovell turned to Doc. "Doc, do you mind if I leave Edna Earle with you two?"

"No, no," Doc said hastily. "Amoretta will be tickled to have her."

"Thank you," Edna Earle said quickly, "I'm grateful to you both for being so generous, but I'm going with Lovell."

"You heard them," Lovell said, trying to look stern. "It's too dangerous."

"What's safe for you is safe for me. I didn't marry you, Lovell, so you could leave me behind. Not even with two such charming men as Doc Hersey and Mr. Levy. I'm going with you and that's that."

Lovell was silent, trying to think of an argument that would convince Edna Earle to stay. Doc grinned at his discomfort and clapped Lovell on the back. "You've done all right for yourself, Lovell."

Jack nodded, beaming. "Congratulations, you've got yourself a winner."

"I've got myself a stubborn wife," Lovell admitted ruefully. Then he smiled. "And I've got myself a wonderful father, too."

There was a moment's silence while Jack and Doc took in the meaning of his words, and then they both nodded.

"The best!" Doc said.

"The best!" Jack agreed. "There's no finer man than Pride Beauvaise."

"Have you heard from him?" Lovell asked.

"No," Jack said, and then tried to qualify, "but even if he has tried to phone, the lines are out more than in."

Lovell nodded. "If you do hear from him, would you give my father a message for me?"

"Of course," Jack said.

"Tell him his son says that he's needed at home."

AT first, when Pride arrived at Maitland, he thought dusk had fallen early. Then he discovered it was a haze of smoke drifting east from the fire. He had decided it was best to stop in Maitland to find out what roads were open and if he could avoid MacClaren City and the *MacClaren* field.

As he came toward the railroad tracks at the edge of town, he saw the road was blocked by a mob of angry men. They were shouting words he couldn't make out and shaking their fists in the air. Some of them broke away from the mob, surrounded his car and began to rock it back and forth like a cradle.

He rolled down the window and called out to the man nearest to him, a big, burly, meaty-faced fellow. "What's all this? What's going on?"

The man was stopped short by the sight of Pride's face. His mouth opened and he blinked uncertainly. He had obviously expected someone else. He held up his hands and shouted, "Stop it, you damn fools. This ain't no railroad man, it's Pride Beauvaise." The men reluctantly backed away from the car, scowling and cursing beneath their breath. Pride was not sure if they would attack again or not.

"Bobby Dean Six. You remember me, Mr. Beauvaise, you took a case for my uncle one time over an allotment."

Pride did not remember Bobby Dean Six or his uncle, but he thought it was as well not to say so. "Well, Bobby, what's going on here?"

"There's a fire down in the oil fields. A big one."

"Yes?"

"We signed up, all of us, to go down there and fight it. They're paying top wages and we need the money, but now the railroad won't let the train out of the station."

"Why not?"

"They say it's too dangerous, but we don't see that. If we're willing to take the risk, why ain't they? Answer me that."

"Who's in charge of the train?"

"The stationmaster's a son of a bitch named Crowder. He's got a job, so why should he care that we don't?"

"I'll talk to him." Pride pulled over to the side of the road. The men offered no resistance. Then, with Bobby Dean Six to run interference, he shouldered his way through the crowd to the station. Beyond, in the switchyard, standing on the top of the loading platform, was Mr. Crowder. His arms were akimbo and he was glaring down at the unruly mob. At either end of the ramp were armed guards, their shotguns ready to keep the men from coming near the string of tank cars or the engine. Crowder looked pale and harassed, as if he were about at the end of his tether.

Pride made his way to the front of the platform and shouted up, "Mr. Crowder, I'm Pride Beauvaise and I'd like to talk to you." Without waiting for permission, Pride started up the ramp. At first he was held off at gunpoint, then Crowder signaled the guards to let him pass. Bobby Dean Six and the others were forced to stay behind.

Pride confronted Crowder. "What's holding up this train?"

Crowder was nervous, that was plain. He kept reaching for his watch and then replacing it in his watch pocket without looking at the time. "I'm in charge here," Crowder said. "I'm holding up the train."

"You must have some good reason," Pride said. "These men say they're ready to go fight the fire."

"They're a mob." Crowder's eyes narrowed. His face looked pinched. "They must be brought under control." He took out his watch again.

Pride decided that Crowder must be expecting reinforcements; he must act quickly. "If the men are willing to fight the fire, why not let the train go? You don't want to keep them here where they can make trouble."

"They don't care about the fire." Crowder dismissed the men with a wave of his hand. "They're only in it for the pay. Why should that concern you? Have you taken the mob on as your client?"

The innuendo angered Pride, but he kept his temper in check. "No, I'm asking for myself."

Crowder looked uncomfortably afraid he'd gone too far. "Mr.

Beauvaise, you have a reputation for being a fair man. You must understand my position. I can't take the responsibility of letting valuable rolling stock and that engine go into any kind of risky situation. When I was first asked about sending the tank cars, I was considering it, but then only the *MacClaren* field was on fire and I knew I could route the train in from the north straight down to the Ridge. That's changed now. The fire has spread everywhere."

"It's in the *Reanna* field, too?" Pride asked. He felt his heart lurch. He had hoped against hope that it would not happen.

"Yes." Mr. Crowder was impatient. "And Mrs. MacClaren can't seem to understand that I don't have the authority to make that kind of decision."

"It was Mrs. MacClaren who asked you for the train?" Pride asked.

Crowder nodded. "She said she'd make good the risk, but I can't let the train go on just a verbal agreement. What if"—his eyes shifted again—"what if something happened and no one paid the bill?"

"Mrs. MacClaren would pay you. She's not a woman to break her word. She must need the train badly, or she wouldn't have asked for it."

"Oh yes," Crowder agreed readily, "she needs the train to off-load the storage tanks between the two fields, and she needs the men to dig a fire ditch. She explained all that several times."

"Then if she needs the train, you must send it." There was an edge to Pride's voice that made Mr. Crowder uneasy.

"I've told you I can't. I can't take the chance of railroad property being destroyed or damaged without someone higher up giving the OK."

Pride shook his head. This was getting them nowhere and taking valuable time, when all the while Reanna needed help and needed it now. "I'll be responsible," Pride said. "I'll be liable for any damage. I'll make out a contract and sign it."

Mr. Crowder blinked. "I'd still need collateral."

For one moment Pride came close to striking Crowder, but instead of instigating a case of aggravated assault, he took out his pen and wrote a short agreement, legally binding, and handed it to Mr. Crowder. "Call Jack Levy or Doc Hersey in MacClaren City. They're my bankers. They'll tell you I'm good for it."

"Well . . ." Mr. Crowder hesitated, looking uncertainly at the piece of paper. "If that's what you want."

"And now," Pride said, "I'm taking the train."

"You'll have to wait while I can get a line through to MacClaren City. I'll have to verify this with the bank."

"You can do what you please," Pride said, "but I'm taking the train and I'm taking it now." He walked to the edge of the loading platform and shouted out to the men.

"Listen to me. Listen well, because I'm only going to say this once. I'm going to take this train out of this station and into the *Reanna* field." A great shout went up from the men, who saw the prospect of money in their pockets.

"You'll get top wages, but don't think this is going to be a picnic. The fire has spread into both fields and is still going. You'll have to work hard and with no guarantees. But if you go, I promise I'll do my best to see you get there and back again safe. So now you know the risks. If you still want the work, get on board."

They surged forward. The guards hesitated, then lowered their guns and stepped aside as the tide broke. Pride was going and the men were going with him; there was no way to stop them now.

Pride made his way to the engine. The driver stood before the cab like a sentinel. "Have you got steam up?" Pride asked.

"Yes, I've got steam up and the engines ready to go, but if you're hell-bent on being a damn fool and blowing up this train and getting yourselves killed, you're going to have to do it without me." He took off his cap and flung it to the ground.

"Is there another engineer in the yard?" Pride called up to the fireman in the cab, who shook his head.

"Nope, he was it."

Pride bent down and picked up the engineer's hat. He put it firmly on his head and jumped aboard. "We're going." He turned to the fireman. "Are you ready?" The fireman nodded, grinning as Pride blew the whistle and opened the throttle to full. The wheels turned, and the train was on its way toward the *Reanna* field and the unknown.

Pride looked ahead at the onrushing track, hoping he would be in time. That hope warmed him and made him feel alive for the first time since he had left Reanna and Lochleven. He felt he had been frozen in some arctic waste. Now the sun was rising once more in the golden kingdom of the heart.

* * *

ANDREW stood watching the sunset from the terrace of the Marble Palace. The last light was almost obscured by the smoke, but Andrew seemed unaware of it. Tom Porter was not sure if Andrew was even aware of his presence. He had spent the night listening to Andrew's tirade against those Andrew believed had wronged him, ruined him and then deserted him. Today, while Andrew had continued to rave against his fate, the fires had raged out of control. Andrew had ignored them, as if they did not exist. He had spent hours in the greenhouse; only moments ago Tom had got him back to the terrace.

Tom knew he must get Andrew away from here soon, but he didn't know how. He felt it would be easier to lure Achilles out of his tent. Each time he had tactfully tried to mention the time or that the train was waiting, he had only set Andrew off again on some new imagined grievance.

The heat from the fires magnified and reached out toward them. Tom could feel the heat on his face like a blast of summer wind. The force of that heat at last reached the greenhouses, and the glass began to shatter, the shards blowing up and showering down in sharp fragments on the terrace.

Andrew turned; he looked bewildered by the ruin that lay all about him. He bent down and picked up the broken stem of a gaillardia. The fire storm had returned the wildflower to nature. It seemed to him some kind of terrible joke played by the fire and the wind and the rain, a joke at his expense; all the world was laughing at him.

"Come on, Andrew," Tom said gently. "It's time to go." He held Andrew's arm and led him away to the waiting car, as if he were an old man and an invalid.

As the car drew away from the house that he had built, Andrew looked back and saw the first tongues of flame licking beneath the eaves. They skipped greedily over marble and slate to find what they could feed on. It was the end of his palace. It was lost to him forever. But what he regretted losing most of all was not the house but the one flower he had let fall from his hand.

LOVELL drove west, away from MacClaren City. The smoke was all around him. He felt as if he could reach out and catch it in his hand. It was in his lungs and eyes. It seemed the world was made of rain and smoke—acid, corrosive, searing smoke—and ahead lay a wilderness of flame. He couldn't say for certain how far they had come since they had left MacClaren City, but they must be near the Marble Palace.

Suddenly, a car appeared out of the billowing, murky smoke. It came at such a pace and was so unexpected that it startled Lovell. He swerved to miss it and ended up on the side of the road, braking hard, stopping just at the edge of a culvert. He sat, his heart pounding, reaching out for Edna Earle. "Are you all right?"

"Yes." Her voice sounded as unsteady as his own.

"You're sure?"

"Yes." She caught her breath. "Lovell, who was that man?"

"What man?"

"In the limousine."

"I didn't see him."

"He saw you. He stared right at you."

Lovell didn't answer.

"It was Andrew MacClaren, wasn't it?"

"I told you I didn't see him."

"He passed you by without even stopping to see if you were safe. Why didn't he stop? Was he too ashamed?"

Lovell shook his head. "Andrew MacClaren wasn't ashamed. He just didn't care. All Andrew MacClaren ever cared about was himself."

Lovell edged the car back onto the road. It had been a near miss; now he went even slower than before, trying to see a landmark to gauge how far they had come. In a mile he came level with the gates to the Marble Palace. They were open, and one hung loose at an awkward angle. Lovell turned in at the gates and stopped. He knew he shouldn't take the time, but it was an awesome, sobering sight. Beyond the gates at the end of the wide drive they could see the house, a flaming shell of marble pillars and thick walls. The interior was already gutted by the fire, and the tile roof smouldered under a driving, pelting rain.

Being here brought back memories of a day when he would have given anything to see Andrew MacClaren in disgrace and ruin. Now that day had come, but he found it less pleasing and satisfying than he had imagined.

Edna Earle leaned forward, staring in wonder, and then said, " 'My name is Ozymandias, king of kings. Look on my works, ye mighty, and despair.' That's a poem by Keats."

"It's a poem," Lovell said, "but it's Shelley."

Edna Earle looked at Lovell, astonished. "You're right. I think it is Shelley. I hadn't thought you'd know the romantic poets."

"There's a lot about me you don't know." Lovell grinned. "Being a rancher's wife is going to be full of surprises for you." Then the grin faded. "And," he said, "danger. I'm sorry I got you into this."

"I came of my own free will."

"This is going to get worse before it gets better," Lovell predicted. He backed out of the driveway and went slowly on toward the county road that ran south along the section line.

The whole pasture was smoking, the barbed wire bent and snapped apart by the fire. Even the sturdy bois d'arc posts were charred. Lovell had expected to find a clear section and go in on it, but there was none. He had anticipated that he might have to run on the rims if the tires didn't hold up, but he hadn't envisioned the extent of the fire's devastation or the hazard the mud would present. Even if he drove twisting and turning along hard-packed cow paths, it would be rough going.

Lovell handed Edna Earle a bandana handkerchief. "Put this over your face. It may keep out some of the smoke." She did as she was told. The two of them looked like rustlers on a raid, except there were no cattle, and the once rich pasture that he had tended so carefully was a scorched, oil-slicked, scalded bog of mud.

They slipped and slid northward toward the west end of the Ridge and the pump station. They skidded in and out of mud holes and took turns getting out to push. The wheels spun up mud, coating them both with mud and ash and oil. Then at last they were mired in up to the hubcaps, held fast. As a new fire blazed up beside them, they were forced to abandon the car and struggle the rest of the way to the pump station on foot.

They appeared at the pump station out of the smoke and rain, looking as though they'd drowned and been dragged up from the bottom of a muddy river. Taffy saw the bedraggled pair first and cried out, "Oh, glory be, it's your boy. It's Lovell. He's come home. I told you he would, didn't I? Didn't I tell you?" He was pounding Lovell on the back. Then he stopped short, looked at Edna Earle and grinned. "Well, look'ee here."

Reanna felt paralyzed with joy. Lovell had come home after all. She was afraid to speak his name or touch him, afraid he might disappear into the smoke like a mirage.

"I would have come sooner," Lovell said, embracing her, "but I didn't know about the fire." He stepped back. "I was on my honey-moon. That's why I went away, you see, to get married." He reached out and took Edna Earle's hand and pulled her forward like a rich prize he'd won and brought home to be admired. "I want you to meet my wife, Edna Earle." He waited for a response from Reanna; when none came, he said, "Edna Earle, this is my mother."

Reanna looked from Lovell to Edna Earle and back again. It was impossible to form any opinion of what she really looked like, this girl Lovell had run off to marry. She was rain-soaked and spattered with mud and oil. But whatever she looked like or whatever she might be, Lovell was home. That was what mattered.

The four of them stood in an uneasy silence; the only sound was the wind and the roar of the flames. The rain had let up and the wind had risen, drawing the ring of fire ever closer. This was no time for hesitation. Reanna held out her hand to Edna Earle. "This is not much of a homecoming for you, I'm afraid, but when this is over and done with, we'll give you a real bride's welcome."

Edna Earle looked with undisguised curiosity at this woman everyone had told her was formidable, a size bigger than life. Given time, she considered, they might come to like each other very much. For they had in common one person they both loved, Lovell.

"Thank you," Edna Earle said. "Lovell and I are glad to be here. How can we help?"

As she spoke, from somewhere nearby they heard the unexpected roar of another gas well exploding. The sound of the erupting gas was like a giant's scream magnified in the wind. This fire was too close for comfort. Each well fired brought the danger that much nearer to the Ridge.

"It's bad everywhere," Taffy said, "and gettin' worse. I've been tryin' to get your mother out of this while the way's still clear, but she's got other ideas." He appealed to Lovell to add his weight to the argument.

"Why not go now, while you can?" Lovell asked.

"I must save the Ridge," Reanna said.

"And do you honestly think you've got a chance of doing it?" Lovell demanded, looking all around him at the tanks and pools of oil sitting like an invitation to a holocaust.

"Yes." She meant to be straight with Lovell and tell him the best and the worst. "I've got a chance, but the price will be high."

Reanna drew a sketchy map on the back of an envelope as Edna

Earle and Lovell looked on. "I hope to join the pipeline ditches that run west to east from the *Reanna One* to the ditch we've just dug that runs north to south here at the pump station. If I can make the join, I can open the pipeline. The crude that's now in the tanks and open holding pools at the *Reanna One* will flow out like water down a creek."

"That sounds easy," Lovell said skeptically, "almost too easy. What's the catch?"

"The catch is that as yet those two ditches don't meet. The men are digging as fast as they can, but they're tired, and for every foot they dig they have to dig another because of the mud." She stopped, the pencil poised over the rough drawing.

"And?" Lovell asked. He felt uneasy. Whatever she was counting on, it was risky and she knew it.

"And," she sighed, "if and when the ditches do join, unless I get the train of tank cars in here from Maitland to drain out the storage tanks here, the oil will flood and overflow. The ditches don't have the capacity to carry it all. The fire will spread to the Ridge, and we'll be worse off than if I'd done nothing." She looked at him from beneath her dripping hat brim to make sure he understood.

"What else?" Lovell asked. "There's something more you aren't telling me."

"Yes. The worst place of all will be the south pasture. If the tanks are drained and the ditches joined in time, and if I drain out the open pools around the *Reanna One* and here at the pump station, the oil will have only one place to go—into the south pasture."

He looked grim. The idea took some getting used to.

"Do you follow me?" she asked. "Do you understand what I'm saying?"

"I understand," he said roughly. "There's no place else for the oil to go. It's either save the Ridge or the pasture, and you've chosen the Ridge."

"It may not work," she said, "things can go wrong."

"It will work," he assured her. "Have faith."

"There are a lot of ifs." She counted them up for him. "If the ditches are joined, if the tanks are emptied and—" She hesitated and then said, "And if the wind is with us."

"The wind?" Lovell looked blank.

"The wind is running out of the north. One breach or break in the ditch and it could carry the fire straight onto the Ridge. For us to have any hope of success, the wind must change direction. The wind must turn and run from the south."

Lovell started to laugh. It was a wild, gallows kind of laughter. Edna Earle looked uncertainly at Taffy and then at Reanna.

"Why are you laughing, Lovell?" she asked. "What's so funny?"

Lovell wiped the tears from his eyes. "I'm laughing because my mother is one of the great gamblers of all time. The fact is, she doesn't have a chance in hell."

"So now do you see why I want you to talk some sense into her?" Taffy growled. "She ought to get out now while the gettin's good."

"We have to have the train and more men." Reanna ignored Taffy as she continued. "Then we might have a very good chance."

"A chance to what?" Taffy demanded. "It's too dangerous to stay here any longer, and that's the straight of it."

And, as if to prove his point, a truck came skidding and sliding toward them from above the pump station. There were men crowded in the cab of the truck and more on the running boards. One jumped clear and ran ahead to Reanna.

"We've got a man hurt bad here," he gasped. "He got hisself burned when the gas well exploded." He waited for Reanna to decide what to do. She could hear the injured man scream in agony. The sound was harrowing. It was what she had dreaded all along— that there would be accidents, casualties.

"Get the medicine kit from the pump station." She turned to Taffy, but he had already gone to fetch it. She went at once to try to comfort the injured man.

He was a horrible sight to behold. His face, hands and body were discolored by oil and mud imbedded in the burned flesh. He was moaning piteously, trying to mumble something through the puffed, swollen flesh of his hideously marred face. There was no sense to what he said; his words were a jumble lost in the wind. No matter how fast they worked to give him relief from pain, it would not come quickly enough.

Taffy ran back from the pump station, the medicine kit in his hand. He was winded from the run and from fear. This was all going against them.

"There's some morphia in the kit," Reanna said to Taffy. "Give him a shot of that."

Taffy thrust the box at Reanna. "I never gave a needle," he said, his voice trembling. "I don't know how."

"I do." Edna Earle took the medicine kit from Taffy.

"Are you a nurse?" Reanna looked at Edna Earle, who was deftly and efficiently making the necessary preparations.

"No," Edna Earle said, "but I had some hospital training when I worked at the mission." She filled the syringe and with a sure touch gave the merciful injection.

"How badly off is he?" Reanna asked Edna Earle, noting that there was far more to this girl than met the eye.

"I can't say for certain. I know he needs a doctor."

Reanna nodded. "I want you to get him up to the house. You can try to telephone from there for a doctor and an ambulance. If there's any delay getting a line through, he'll be more comfortable at Lochleven." She turned to Taffy. "Taffy, you go with Edna Earle. I want to be sure she has everything she needs."

"I'm not leavin' here," Taffy blurted out.

"Nor am I," Edna Earle added, her eyes flashing.

"I'm afraid you'll have to go," Reanna said to Edna Earle. "You have more nursing experience than anyone else, and I need Taffy to make the arrangements for the hospital. Taffy will take you up to the house." Reanna had given the orders, and neither Edna Earle nor Taffy could find a way to change her mind. The burned man must come first. This was no time to argue; he was already beginning to shiver with shock.

Taffy drew Reanna sharply to one side and whispered in a low voice, "What are you up to now? Will you tell me that? Why send me off with the girl?" He flushed. "Not that I don't like her and think Lovell's got a fine wife."

"I want you and Edna Earle out of it and up on the Ridge."

"I got that, sharp as a pointed stick. But if anyone goes with her, it should be you."

Reanna put her hand gently on Taffy's arm. "Taffy, I'll need you there. If the train and men don't get here soon, there's going to come a time when I can't contain or divert this fire. Then it will be imperative to get everyone off the Ridge, and fast." He started to interrupt, but she silenced him. "You know as well as I do what a near-run thing this is. If I find I can't hold out here, I'll send up a signal."

"What kind of signal?"

"A flare—one when I let the oil go and two if the plan fails. One for success and two for failure. You understand?"

He nodded. She saw him fighting off his emotions.

"When you see the second flare, then you must get everyone away from Lochleven and off the Ridge. I couldn't trust anyone but you to take care of Cima and Snow and Edna Earle." She paused, waiting for him to give her some back talk. "Will you do this for me, Taffy, please?"

His eyes glistened and his mouth was tight. Then he got control of himself and said, "I never could say no to you, and I guess it's too late to start now."

She took her hand from his arm. "Thank you, I'll always be grateful." She looked over at Lovell and Edna Earle. They were standing close together in a tender embrace. Looking over his wife's shoulder, Lovell's eyes met Reanna. She gave him a nod that it was time to go and looked on as he helped Edna Earle into the waiting truck. Then Lovell came to stand beside Reanna. They both waved good-bye as the truck disappeared into the swirling smoke.

They stood in silence for a moment, as if they half hoped to see the truck just once more. Then Reanna said, "I'm glad you found yourself a wife, Lovell. And," she added, "I'm glad that you came home again."

"You knew I hadn't gone for good." He seemed surprised. "I told Taffy I'd come back as soon as I could."

"So he said." She spoke in a dry tone that told him nothing of her days of worry.

"Thanks for getting Edna Earle out of this. Things are going to get rough around here." He turned to her. "Well, Ma, what next?"

"We have to hope for the best and prepare for the worst. I think that—" Before she could finish the sentence, Will Bassett came running from the pump station. He looked stricken, as if he had had some sort of seizure that kept him from forming the words he wanted to say.

"What is it, Will?"

His mouth opened crazily but still no sound came out.

"Tell me."

"It's the *Reanna One*." His voice was barely audible.

"What about the *Reanna One*?"

"She's on fire." He backed away, as if she might blame him for bringing the bad news.

She felt as though he'd struck her down. This blow was the straw that could break her. The fire had come into the heart of the field, and from there it could now easily spread to the seep springs and the open, unprotected pools of oil. From them it was only two small ditches away from the gas fissures of the Ridge. She heard herself saying, "I can't let the *Reanna One* burn itself out."

"What will you do?" Lovell asked.

"Put it out if I can."

"How?"

"Dynamite the well. Blow out the fire."

"Won't that destroy the well?"

"I'll have to take that chance." She felt the fear of what her failure would mean twisting at her heart. It was all happening too fast. She wanted to scream, to cry out against the monstrous wind that had brought her this misfortune. She felt she was in a vise that was tightening all around her. She was in such anguish that for a moment she thought she heard herself screaming out as the injured man had done against the pain—a shrill, sharp scream, first one and then another. Then she realized with a flood of hope that it was not her voice she heard but the shrill sound of a train's whistle. The train was coming from the north, coming on the track that lay between the two fields. She turned to look at Lovell. Had he heard it too?

"The train," she said. "Thank God, the train is coming. You know what this means," she shouted above the wind. "It means we've got a real chance after all. I have to get down to *Reanna One*. I'll leave Will Bassett to oversee the off-loading, and you can come with me."

"No." Lovell shook his head. "I can't come with you. I'm staying here."

"Why?" Her heart began to pound again. "I want you with me. I need you."

"You don't need me. You only want to make sure I'm safe. I can't go with you. I must stay here."

"Why, for heaven's sake, why?"

"You began with the *Reanna One* and you must try to save it. That's your place to stand, but this is mine. The flood, when—if— it comes, will destroy the pasture. The grass was mine, and if it must go, I want to be the one to flood it." He waited for her to say something. "Do you understand?"

"Yes. I understand that you're a grown man and not a boy. And you're a fine man like your father." She started to say more, but there was no need. She embraced him quickly. "I must go. When the train gets here, you and Will start off-loading crude into the tank cars. What men you can spare must start digging to join the two ditches." She hesitated another last precious second. "You'll be careful?"

Lovell nodded. "Yes, and you? You be careful too. You're the brave and reckless one, not me."

"Yes, I'll be careful. I'll hold on at the *Reanna One* as long as I can. I'll wait for the wind to turn. Then, when I know it's time and I can't wait any longer, I'll signal you."

"Signal?"

"One red flare and you must get the men on the train here at once, and then open all the feeder lines whether the tank cars are full or not. Ten minutes, no more, for you to get the train out. Then I'll open the master pipeline at the *Reanna One.*"

Lovell eyed her steadily. "And if the wind doesn't change?"

She held herself straight. "And if the wind doesn't turn and the Ridge is lost, I'll send up two flares, and Taffy will get everyone away from Lochleven by the west way."

"Do you really think the wind will turn?" As Lovell looked up uneasily at the sky, the north wind struck against his face like a slap.

"Yes."

"Why?"

"Because it must. The Ridge, our fortunes and our lives depend upon the wind, as they always have."

And before he could think of a reply, she'd gone, and out of the north he saw the train slowly pulling up to the loading platform. He looked at the engine, wiped the rain from his eyes, and then ran toward the train to make sure that the man in the engineer's cap was really Pride Beauvaise. As the engine came to a squealing, grinding halt, he was certain.

"You came," Lovell shouted, looking up at Pride and grinning. "You got my message."

"No." Pride looked glad to see him but puzzled. "I got no message."

"But you came." Lovell didn't understand what was happening.

"I came because I heard your mother needed help."

"And she does," Lovell assured him. "She needs all the help we can give her."

"I came for your mother," Pride said, climbing down from the cab of the engine, "but I'm mighty glad you're here too." He started to embrace Lovell and then held himself back. "What was the message?"

Lovell grinned. "The message was, your son says you're needed at home." He saw the tears start into Pride's eyes. "Now you're here"—Lovell felt the lump in his own throat—"we must get started off-loading. We haven't time now for a family reunion, but we will. I promise you. We've got a lot to catch up on. A lot to say."

"And we'll say it all," Pride agreed.

Pride and Lovell began to work in a frantic race against the clock. Pride siphoned off oil from the tank farm into the tank cars. Car after car was coupled to the funnels, filled and uncoupled as Pride backed the train up the tracks, ready to pull out quickly when it was time.

Lovell, with the fresh crew he had mustered, began to dig, struggling against the rain and the unrelenting, cold north wind. The men worked—grunting, straining every muscle, digging as if the salvation of the whole world depended on uniting the two ditches. As they dug, Lovell saw the faces of the men glowing darkly in the red, angry illumination of the ever-nearing fires and looked beyond them toward the west, waiting for a signal from Reanna.

The light of a different fire cast its glow over Reanna's face as she watched the column of flames bursting from the wellhead of the *Reanna One*. The derrick lay to one side where it had fallen, like a crumpled, discarded toy.

This was where the field had begun and where it would end. She had blown it in with nitro when she had been as green as springtime, and she would blow it out with dynamite. The charge was already carefully loaded and set, attached to a long boom pole. The amount, like the equipment, was prescribed by hard-won experience. With luck, the explosion of dynamite over the well would cut off enough oxygen to snuff out the fire like a candle.

She gazed at the fire, her hand on the handle of the plunger, waiting until the charge was swung into place before she pushed down and detonated it. All around her the men were hanging back, edging away, afraid of getting too close. She couldn't blame them. The inferno was coming closer to the tank farm, the open pools and to them. When she set off this charge, the fire could shift and the flames come even nearer.

She saw the sweat, mingled with the rain, running down their faces. In ordinary circumstances these were all brave men, but now they held their ground only because they were ashamed to turn tail and run before a woman. She understood that they were all exhausted and afraid; they knew all too well what would happen to them if they were caught trapped here between the *Reanna One* and the open pools of oil. They wanted to go now, while there was still time and the way to the west was clear. She couldn't blame them. She too would like to be home, safe and dry. She looked up toward the crest of the Ridge at the dim lights of Lochleven, where they were waiting for her signal as the men here waited for her to lower the plunger.

For a moment she heard the exquisite whispering of her own fear. It would be so easy for her to go now, to cut and run. It would be seen not as a loss of honor but as an act of prudence and common sense. Only she would know that she had been a coward not to stand her ground, not to make, quite literally, her last-ditch stand. Looking at that ditch, which disappeared into the smoke, she didn't know whether the join had been made or, if it had, whether the ditch was wide and deep enough to carry the torrent of oil she must soon release. But it didn't matter. She could never leave without putting it and herself to the test.

With one brief motion she pushed down the plunger, and the dynamite exploded above the wellhead. For an instant the giant flame flickered, then sputtered. The fire at the *Reanna One* was out. A moment of relief, and then she could feel the tension in the men rise, for now that this fire was out, the real business must begin. She must make her move to open the controls, valve by valve, and let the oil, the lifeblood of the field, flow out down the pipeline and ditch toward the open pasture.

She was unwilling to take that last, final action until the wind changed. She faced north, testing the wind. She felt sure it had dropped a little. But to save the Ridge, the wind must shift completely around and run hard from the south.

She looked with compassion at the pale and shaken men. The strain of waiting was breaking them. It would be only fair to let them go. If the wind changed, if that hoped-for miracle really came to pass, she alone could release the oil. It was only a matter of turning a master wheel at the *Reanna* pump station. She could do that without them.

"Time to get out of the oil patch. Time to go." She gave the order to the men nearest her. It took only a few seconds for the news to circulate. She heard the men give a great cheer, and without waiting for a second invitation, they began to make a hurried getaway. No one looked back for Reanna; only a madwoman would stay behind. She went along with the crowd just as far as the *Reanna* pump station and stopped, unnoticed under the cover of billowing smoke.

As she watched the last band of men heading up the Ridge, she realized that she was truly alone. She experienced a moment's panic, knowing the position she had put herself in. Then she pulled all her courage together and faced west.

There, beneath the sky, Breathholder waited for them all. He had already taken Miss Jane and her beloved Pride, Father Soule, John's Dead and many a brave cowboy who had been lost in the great storm. In time he would take her too, but now, while she was still on this earth, she must make some accounting to all of them who had gone before her. She had promised Miss Jane that she would keep the place together, that both brothers would have their equal share. In that she had failed. Because of her it had all gone wrong, and she must take the blame.

She closed her eyes, waiting for some blessing, some release, but none came. All around her this place that had been a demi-Eden when she had first seen it was now in flames, a hell on earth. She had not been wise enough to keep her paradise. She had done more than her share to lead them into this terrible jeopardy. She wished she could say a prayer that would atone for all her sins and redeem all her faults, but she had none to say, just as she wished she knew some ancient ritual, some magic words that would give her the power to turn the wind at her will, but again she had none.

She stood waiting, knowing that it was almost over. Soon she must send up a flare—one for success and two for failure. She must turn the master wheel and open the floodlines. Time was running out, and still she stood waiting just a little longer for the wind. And as she waited, she closed her eyes and heard herself saying, "Turn wind, turn, I beg you, turn. If only you will turn, I promise you that I . . . " She stopped. Her eyes opened wide and her chin rose high in a gesture of defiance. She would not be a suppliant to the wind. She would not put her courage or her honor on the altar as a sacrifice. She would not beg. In that moment, she made her bargain with the wind.

"I will bend and bow down before you, but I will never break. And I will never be a beggar. If you turn now, I will make only one promise—to fight you until the day I die. I will learn to be more cunning. I will stay here in this place and fight. I will stay here and defy you with the last breath in my body."

It was foolhardy, perhaps even mad, to talk to the wind. But as she spoke, she felt a stillness all around her like a great circle, and then slowly, quietly, so quietly that she thought it was her imagination, she felt a gentle breeze rising from the south—a soft, warm, loverlike caress. It touched her, bringing a hint of moisture from the Gulf. She held up her hand and laughed aloud. It wasn't her imagination. A south wind had begun to run strong and true, a south wind running hard. And in a display of the wind's caprice, mixed in with the south wind there were sudden, violent gusts from the west.

She felt a rush of elation, as if she had already won a great victory. She fired off the first flare high into the sky, where it burst above her in a great, red glow, like a badge of glory. She waited, counting out the minutes. Then, in the distance, she heard the whistle of the train as it began to move, and her hands touched, held fast and turned the great master wheel to open the pipeline and the feeder valves. All were opened full. The oil began to flow out of the tanks and pools, flowing through the pipe and the open ditch, swept away, borne along by the wind, and at the end all the streams ran together to cover the pasture in a lake of flaming oil.

It was done, and the soft, gentle south wind that had kept the fire from the Ridge blew even harder, bringing in more moist air, so moist that as it struck the wall of cold northern air, a fog fell like a damp, smothering blanket over the field. Reanna watched with wonder as the fires began to go out, one by one. And when the fog lay thick and white and even as winter snow, she pulled herself away. At last it was safe to head toward the Ridge and home.

IT was dawn when Reanna got to Lochleven. The yard and verandah were full of people taking shelter from the storm and the fire. She was too tired to make conversation. To avoid people, she went in the back way.

In the kitchen she found Cima and Snow and Edna Earle all at the stove, laughing and talking as they cooked up huge pans of sausage and gravy and biscuits and a griddle of eggs and ham. They seemed as easy together as if they had known each other a lifetime. It occurred to Reanna that she had never been made as welcome as Edna Earle was in Cima's domain. The girl had passed muster and come out with flying colors.

At the end of the long kitchen table, Taffy sat watching as Lovell demolished a stack of hotcakes, washing them down with a mug of steaming coffee. They all looked up when she came in and stared at her as if she were a stranger. Wearily she took off her hat. Even that effort exhausted her. She had not realized how bone-tired she was. Suddenly, the warmth of the room, the smell of food made her weak. Then they all crowded in around her and began asking questions, all of them at once. Where had she been, what had taken her so long, was she all right?

"We were about to send out a search party for you," Taffy declared.

The barrage of questions continued until Cima called out, "Stop that. You all quit pickin' on her. Can't you see she's dead on her feet?"

Cima took Reanna by her arm and turned her toward the hall. "Go on up, take a hot bath and get into bed. I'll bring you up something on a tray."

Reanna passed her hand across her grimy forehead. "I am tired," she admitted wryly, "and I could use a bath and some clean clothes." She looked at Edna Earle. "I'm sorry you arrived when we're in such a state of confusion. When we get all this sorted out, we'll give you a proper bride's dancing."

Edna Earle glanced hurriedly at Lovell, as if she was unsure of what to say.

"Oh yes." Snow clapped her hands. "It's the Indian custom. It's one of our traditions."

Lovell put his arm protectively around Edna Earle. "Edna Earle knows what a bride's dancing is, Snow, she just isn't sure if her whole family will be welcome."

"Of course," Reanna said with feeling, "we're all one family now." She saw Edna Earle blush and didn't know why.

"What we haven't had a chance to tell you is . . ." Lovell hesitated and then went on. "What we were going to tell you later is that Edna Earle is related to the Starretts. Her mother was a Starrett." He stopped and waited for Reanna's reaction. Reanna could hear Cima gasp and Taffy mutter to himself. Snow was silent, round-eyed, looking at her. "I know it's a surprise," Lovell said.

Reanna hadn't seen him look so contrite since he was a little boy.

It was a surprise, but in the rush of memories of that old feud and of days past came the memories of the sweet times. It seemed to Reanna that the past had come full circle. The old feud must end sometime. She knew what bitter herbs revenge could be; they needed none at a new bride's feast. "All the tribe is welcome at Lochleven," she said evenly, "as long as they come as friends." She turned to Snow. "Is that not right, Snow?"

Snow nodded. "Yes, as long as they come as friends," she said, and held out a hand to Edna Earle.

Reanna started toward the door to the passageway, but Lovell stopped her. "There is something else I have to tell you." Lovell stole a glance around the circle. He looked like a conspirator and the others like part of a cabal. "There's someone waiting to see you. He's in the hall."

Reanna saw Snow turn back to the stove to hide her face. Cima suppressed a smile, and Taffy had a fit of coughing. Edna Earle looked as if she were made of marble, betraying nothing.

"I don't think I'm up to seeing anyone now." This was not a time for strangers.

"You'll want to see this man."

"Why?"

"He's the man who brought the train in from Maitland. I know you'll want to thank him yourself."

"Yes, yes of course, I'll see him. Where did you say he was?"

"Waiting for you in the hall."

SHE walked alone down the passageway toward the front hall. Last night it had been a dormitory, but now the furniture was pushed back against the walls and the cots and pallets folded away. The room was empty save for the figure of the one man standing by the fireplace, his back to her. He was looking up at the portrait of Pride Beauvaise which, like the house, was a faithful copy of the original. When the man heard her footsteps he turned, and she saw that he was holding the Beauvaise cup in his hands. In the early light she saw his face, and her vision blurred. It seemed her eyes were playing her tricks. Her knees went weak. The double illusion of portrait and man must be a hallucination.

He broke the silence between them. "*Alali-o*. I am come," he said.

(680)

"*Icla tco*," she replied, as if it were an ordinary greeting and an ordinary homecoming. "It was you who brought the train?" Her lips felt stiff and her voice came, it seemed, from a long way off.

"Yes." He put down the cup on the mantel and turned back to her, his eyes steady, probing, questioning.

"Why?"

"You needed help."

She shook her head, uncertain still that this was real and not something imagined out of her own longing. "I thought," she said slowly and distinctly, "that you would never want to see me or to speak to me again."

"How could you think that?"

"I cost you everything. Because of me you lost Lochleven, your case against Andrew and your reputation. I thought that was why you wouldn't come home again."

"I didn't know if I would be welcome." He continued to look at her. Their eyes met, held and drew them closer together. "I regret losing the life we might have had together," he said gently, "but because of you I have my son."

It all seemed so unreal and impossible. She wanted to reach out and touch him, to make sure he was flesh and blood. Her longing for him had not diminished in all the long years.

"He is a fine son," Pride said, "a son to be proud of."

Another flood of memories rushed over her. It was here in this place, the day she had come to Lochleven as a bride, that she had seen him for the first time. She could not imagine that she had ever been that young or that full of hope for the life she had thought she would find out here, where no two days were the same.

"I have changed," she said. "I am grown old."

"Not you. You are the same."

"You are a liar then, my dear, or you are blind." She reached out then and touched his cheek and let her fingertips trace the gray at his temples. "To me you are still the boy I loved then, now and forever."

"Then we still have time," he said, "all the time in the world."

"You will stay?"

"I will stay for as long as you need me."

She smiled. "Then you will stay for as long as the sun shines, the grass grows and the rivers run. You will stay for as long as the wind blows." And at last she felt his arms around her.

REANNA drove through the *Reanna* field up onto the Ridge. Spring had come, and it was, as ever, a time of hope and renewal. But it was also a time to take stock and accept her losses. Since the storm, Lochleven had suffered a two-year drought. The land was parched and barren. The red cloud that the dust formed around the car was a portent of more dry weather to come.

Behind her the field was still a scene of devastation, but it gave her enormous satisfaction to know that out of her one hundred and twenty-three wells that had been on fire, ninety-nine were in operation again. New methods of reentry and secondary recovery meant that with prudent voluntary reduction, the field would produce for her lifetime and far beyond. She pulled her battered felt hat down to shade her eyes from the glare of the sun and to keep the grainy dust from blowing into her eyes. The total losses had been staggering. Over half a million barrels of oil were gone forever, and the tally of storage tanks, rigs and equipment that had been lost was enormous.

It had been a senseless, shameful waste, but more than the storm was to blame. The stupidity and greed of men had taken the oil from the ground with no thought for the future. Now new laws must be made by men to ensure that never again would so much crude be lying out in the open—vulnerable, waiting for possible destruction. There must be new, strong laws regulating the storing of oil, the spacing of wells and storage tanks. Now that she was again in a position to control the output of her fields and leases, she must be a more responsible steward and stand as advocate for change and reform.

She had begun to fight for new laws, but it was easier said than done. Times were bad. In October the stock market had toppled and crashed. Reanna had not been hurt; Anselm had seen to that. He had made her sell out in time, and her fortune was safe. But the price of oil was at an all-time low. The true test of prudence and regulation would come when prices rose again. Depression and drought could not last forever. At least they never had. She knew she was in an unusually comfortable position. She had enough cash in hand to wait out a dozen depressions, but others were not so fortunate. She was in luck, not only in her bank balance, but in the security of her family. It was as if all she had ever lost had been returned to her a hundredfold.

On the Ridge, as she circled past Lochleven, she felt her spirits rise with satisfaction. The house and outbuildings had been repainted and the marks of the storm repaired. It was the Indian New Year, and Snow and Cima had cleaned the house from attic to foundation. The fire had been taken from the hearth and stove and a new one laid and kindled in the clean-swept yard. Cima was there now, presiding over a kettle full of *pishofa* and a beef turning on a spit. The weather was so dry, there were dust devils whirling around Cima in a circle. Tonight there would be a celebration for the new year, the rebirth of spring.

Snow, the rightful princess of her people, was in another clearing surrounded by a clump of giggling girls. She was trying to teach them the steps of the New Year's dance. Reanna heard the sound of terrapin rattles, saw the ribbons flying in the air and felt the ancient beat of the drum. While they danced, they were also learning the words for the new song the whole tribe would sing in Pride's honor. They had made him the song for his return, because they held him in affection and esteem and because they wished to thank him for all he had done for them. In the song they gave Pride his new name, the name he had earned for himself.

It seemed with Pride's return that they had all come full circle. Now each must make a new beginning. Edna Earle was a part of that new way. She was sitting beneath the gnarled and broken catalpa tree, holding school for the children, their mothers and grandmothers. She was teaching them to read and write and do sums. The babies cried and the children wandered at will but, all told, the experiment in a farm school was a great success. Part of the group were Starretts. For them, too, the world had come round full circle, and the lost had been regained. Reanna only hoped that Miss Jane would have approved of the reconciliation and that she would not have too much to answer for in the way she had arranged the new Lochleven.

There could only be joy at the sight Reanna saw beyond the Ridge. In the south pasture there were three figures on horseback— Pride, Taffy and Lovell. They were trying to bring back the grassland that had been swept away in one night. There the signs of devastation were the worst and would be the hardest to erase. It would take more than these two years for the stain of the oil spill to be blotted out and for the grass to come again. Pride and Lovell had begun a new program of planting, but this time was more difficult than before. They had to find a new mixture of grasses to combat the oil and the drought and to accommodate the lowered water table.

And no matter what mix they had tried, it was wiped away by the plague of wind and dust that was now sweeping down on them from the Great Plains. There the farmers had plowed the prairie grass in straight, deadly, unbroken furrows, and now the wind was blowing the topsoil away. Each day more and more of it swept over Lochleven. This wind and dust were more devastating than fire or oil or water. Some days it seemed the wind would blow and there would be nothing left on earth to sustain or hold them. They would all vanish, blow away forever, dust into dust.

But in time, when the drought broke and the rains came and the oil was still pumping, then she would be richer than ever before. And more than gold, she would have Pride. She saw him catch sight of her and wave, then break away from the others and ride toward her, the man of his people, the man of the blood who had earned himself the name He Who Came Home in the Evening.

ABOUT THE AUTHOR

MARGARET RITTER was born in Oklahoma and has lived in New York, Madrid, and London. She has worked at the MacDowell Colony and the Bread Loaf Writer's Conference. She is at present living in Europe doing research for a new novel.